PENGUIN BOOKS

BEFORE THE MAYFLOWER

Lerone Bennett Jr. is a social historian and the author of nine books on the life and history of black Americans. A graduate of Morehouse College, he was visiting professor of history at Northwestern University in 1968–69 and Senior Fellow of the Institute of the Black World in 1969. He was named senior editor of *Ebony* in 1958 and executive editor in 1987. His articles have earned him an enviable reputation as one of the most eloquent, scholarly, and readable of American writers. In 1978 he received the Literature Award of the American Academy of Arts and Letters. Mr. Bennett has served as advisor and consultant to several national organizations and commissions, including the National Advisory Commission on Civil Disorders. His poems, short stories, and articles have been translated into French, German, Japanese, Swedish, and Arabic. Mr. Bennett is the author of *The Shaping of Black America*, also available in Penguin Books.

Before the
MAYFLOWER

A HISTORY
OF
BLACK
AMERICA

SIXTH EDITION

Lerone Bennett Jr.

PENGUIN BOOKS

PENGUIN BOOKS
Published by the Penguin Group
Penguin Books USA Inc., 375 Hudson Street,
New York, New York 10014, U.S.A.
Penguin Books Ltd, 27 Wrights Lane,
London W8 5TZ, England
Penguin Books Australia Ltd, Ringwood,
Victoria, Australia
Penguin Books Canada Ltd, 10 Alcorn Avenue, Toronto,
Ontario, Canada M4V 3B2
Penguin Books (N.Z.) Ltd, 182–190 Wairau Road,
Auckland 10, New Zealand

Penguin Books Ltd, Registered Offices:
Harmondsworth, Middlesex, England

First published in the United States of America by
Johnson Publishing Co., Inc., 1962
Second revised printing published 1963
Revised edition published 1964
Published in Pelican Books 1966
Third revised edition published by
Johnson Publishing Co., Inc., 1966
Fourth revised edition published 1969
Fifth revised edition published 1982
Published in Penguin Books 1984
Sixth revised edition published by
Johnson Publishing Co., Inc., 1987
This volume with an updated "Landmarks and Milestones"
section published in Penguin Books 1993

1 2 3 4 5 6 7 8 9 10

Copyright © Johnson Publishing Co., 1961, 1969, 1988
All rights reserved

THE LIBRARY OF CONGRESS HAS GIVEN THE FOLLOWING CATALOG CARD NO. TO THE HARDCOVER: 82-082391

ISBN 0-87485-029-0 (hc.)
ISBN 0 14 01.7822 8 (pbk.)

Printed in the United States of America
Set in Bodoni Book

The lines from "Heritage" are reprinted from Countee Cullen's *Color*, copyright 1925 by Harper & Row, by permission of the publishers, Harper & Row; the lines from "Fifty Years" are reprinted from James Weldon Johnson's *Saint Peter Relates an Incident*, copyright 1917, 1935 by James Weldon Johnson, by permission of the Viking Press, Inc.; the lines from "If We Must Die" are reprinted from Claude McKay's *Harlem Shadows*, copyright 1922 by Harcourt, Brace and Company, by permission of Twayne Publishers, Incorporated. Appreciation is also due the following persons, institutions, and corporations for permission to reproduce photographs: Metropolitan Museum of Art, page 9; Chicago Historical Society, pages 63, 73; Schoenfeld Collection, Three Lions, Inc., pages 92–93, 100, 118, 132, 151, 159, 220–221, 238–239; Carl Van Vechten, photograph of Bessie Smith, page 288; Magnum Photos, Inc., page 289; Wide World Photos, Inc., pages 373 and 427; United Press International, pages 221, 351, 372, 380, 427; Associated Press, Watts photo, page 396; Volunteers of America, page 414; McAdams Photo, page 414.

For the Black Woman
For my Grandmother, Mother and
  Wife
Lucy Reed, Alma Love and Gloria S. Bennett

Preface
To The Sixth Edition

HISTORIANS and history books are historical. They are products of history. They are born at a certain time, and they bind time and express time and their times. More to the point, they participate in the "callings and responses" of succeeding generations which Maurice Merleau-Ponty considered the very essence of history.

In this limited sense, *Before the Mayflower*, which was born twenty-five years ago at a historic turning of worlds, has participated in a historical dialogue that was started by the "Black and unknown bards of slavery" and carried to new heights by George Washington Williams, Carter G. Woodson, W. E. B. Du Bois, Charles Wesley, John Hope Franklin, Benjamin Quarles and Vincent Harding, among others.

I said twenty-five years ago that I hoped this book would make the seminal insights of scholars available to a larger audience and restore the human and dramatic dimensions of our history. In subsequent editions, I have tried to participate in contemporary efforts to redefine the time-line of the African-American odyssey.

I am indebted to Publisher John H. Johnson and Norman L. Hunter, Basil Phillips, Carmel Tinkchell, Beverly Coppage and Pamela Cash Menzies of the Johnson Publishing Company family. I am also indebted to the tens of thousands of readers who have been generous enough to say that they have found in these pages some echo of their own history and hope.

LERONE BENNETT JR.

Chicago, 1987.

PREFACE
To The Fifth Edition

THIS is the first major revision of *Before the Mayflower* since its publication twenty years ago. Instead of following the traditional method of adding a new chapter to cover developments since 1962, I have revised the entire book, taking great pains to retain the flavor and style of the original. I have also incorporated some of the insights of *Confrontation: Black and White*, which was originally published as a companion volume to *Before the Mayflower.* Since that volume, which detailed the black struggle for freedom, is now out of print, I have adapted here some of its basic concepts and analyses. I have also incorporated the latest insights of modern scholarship.

In a number of books published since 1962, I argued, along with others, for a complete rethinking of the concept of black time. I have followed my own advice here, detaching epochal black events—the Founding of Black America, for example—from the white shell and reinserting them into a black time-line extending from the African past to the transformation of Black America in the twentieth century.

In preparing the fifth revised edition, I have been assisted and supported by the Johnson Publishing Company staff. I am especially indebted to Publisher John H. Johnson, Basil Phillips, Carmel Tinkchell, Beverly J. Coppage and my wife, Gloria S. Bennett. The new book was redesigned by Norman L. Hunter, who created the original book jacket. Pamela Cash of the Johnson Publishing Company Special Library was very helpful in checking elusive dates. I am also indebted to Sharon Scott of the Harsh Collection of the Carter G. Woodson Regional Library and the staff of the Newberry Library.

I am convinced today, more than ever, that the story outlined on the following pages is central to an understanding of American reality. Since the publication of the first edition of *Mayflower*, there has been a new appreciation of the centrality of this adventure. But despite the gains, there is still a regrettable tendency in some circles to regard black history as an intellectual ghetto. Worse yet, some people regard it as a minor-league pastime involving the recitation of dates and the names of black greats. But black history, read right, is a much more fateful encounter than that. Read right, within the context of social forces struggling for dominance, the history detailed on these pages raises total question about the destiny of America and the orientation of our lives. It is on this deep level, and within this context, that we are invited to understand an extremely perceptive remark by Ralph Ellison, who said once, in another connection, that "the end is in the beginning, and lies far ahead."

LERONE BENNETT JR.

Chicago, 1982.

PREFACE
To Second Impression

SINCE publication of the first edition of *Before the Mayflower*, there has been a small revolution in the role of the Afro-American and in the perception of the Afro-American's role. In this, the fourth edition of the book, I have revised the terminology and added new material on the new developments. I have not found it necessary, however, to change the central concepts and conclusions of the first edition. In addition to the persons named in the preface to the first edition, I am indebted to Beverly Adams, Carmel Tinkchell, and Brenda Biram.

Today, as in 1962, there is a critical need for a deeper understanding of the role of the Afro-American in American history and culture. For it is becoming increasingly evident that Santayana was right when he said that men who cannot remember the past are condemned to repeat it.

LERONE BENNETT JR.

Chicago, 1968.

Preface

To First Edition

THIS BOOK grew out of a series of articles which were published originally in *Ebony* magazine. The book, like the series, deals with the trials and triumphs of a group of Americans whose roots in the American soil are deeper than the roots of the Puritans who arrived on the celebrated *Mayflower* a year after a "Dutch man of war" deposited twenty Negroes at Jamestown.

This is a history of "the other Americans" and how they came to North America and what happened to them when they got here. The story begins in Africa with the great empires of the Sudan and Nile Valley and ends with the Second Reconstruction which Martin Luther King, Jr., and the "sit-in" generation are fashioning in the North and South. The story deals with the rise and growth of slavery and segregation and the continuing efforts of Negro Americans to answer the question of the Jewish poet of captivity: "How shall we sing the Lord's song in a strange land?"

This history is founded on the work of scholars and specialists and is designed for the average reader. It is not, strictly speaking, a book for scholars; but it is as scholarly as fourteen months of research could make it. Readers who would like to follow the story in greater detail are urged to read each chapter in connection with the outline of Negro history in the appendix.

Without the help and encouragement of many people, this book would not have been possible. John H. Johnson, president of Johnson Publishing Company, conceived the idea for the series and made it possible for me to spend fourteen months researching and writing it. The editors of Johnson Publishing Company were also helpful with suggestions and criticisms. I am especially indebted to the managing editors of *Ebony*, Herbert Nipson and Era Bell Thompson, and Doris Saunders, Lucille Phinnie, Basil Phillips, Norman L. Hunter, Ariel Strong, Herbert Temple, Lacey Crawford and Robert E. Johnson. I should like to express my appreciation to the personnel of the University of Chicago Library, the Johnson Publishing Company Library, the Hall Branch of the Chicago Public Library, and the Chicago Historical Society. My wife, Gloria, also has my thanks for her suggestions and understanding. Whatever virtues this book has are due to the help and encouragement of other people. The errors are my own.

When this material appeared in *Ebony* magazine in an abridged form, a great many readers—Negroes and whites—were surprised by the depth of involvement of Negroes in the American experience. They were surprised, for example, to discover that Negroes were at Lexington and Concord and that they stood with Andrew Jackson at the Battle of New Orleans and with William Lloyd Garrison in the battle against slavery. The reader, I believe, will be astonished by the richness of the Negro's heritage. He will also perceive, I hope, that this story is relevant to the struggle of all people and that it is a moving chapter in the human drama.

LERONE BENNETT JR.

Chicago, 1962.

Contents

Illustrations

Before the
MAYFLOWER

A HISTORY
OF
BLACK
AMERICA

*In stripes, in imprisonments, in tumults, in labors, in watchings,
in fastings;*

*By pureness, by knowledge, by long-suffering, by kindness, by the
Holy Ghost, by love unfeigned,*

*By the word of truth, by the power of God, by the armor of
righteousness on the right hand and on the left,*

*By honour and dishonour, by evil report and good report; as
deceivers, and yet true;*

*As unknown, and yet well known; as dying, and, behold, we live;
as chastened, and not killed;*

*As sorrowful, yet always rejoicing; as poor, yet making many
rich; as having nothing, and yet possessing all things.*

II CORINTHIANS 6:5-10

1

The African Past

What is Africa to me:
Copper sun or scarlet sea,
Jungle star or jungle track,
Strong bronzed men, or regal black
Women from whose loins I sprang
When the birds of Eden sang?
                    COUNTEE CULLEN

SPEAK of Africa and golden joys."
     We know now that Shakespeare spoke truth.
     For an academic breakthrough, which is as challenging on its own level as the political renaissance of colored peoples, has yielded a new perspective on African and world history. Africa, long considered the "Dark Continent," is now regarded as the place where mankind first received light. Ancient Africans, long considered "primitive," are now revealed as creative contributors to Egyptian civilization and builders of powerful states in the Sudan.

From Olduvai Gorge in East Africa, from caves in the Sahara and excavations in the Nile Valley come bits of bone and husks of grain which speak more eloquently than words of the trials and triumphs of the African ancestors of American blacks. The evidence from these and other areas can be summarized briefly under four headings:

Olduvai Gorge: A series of astonishing discoveries in this Tanzanian canyon suggest that the most important and fascinating developments in human history occurred in Africa. Discoveries by Dr. L. S. B. Leakey and other archeologists indicate that the human race was born in Africa. A growing body of research from this and other African sites indicates further that toolmaking began in Africa and that this seminal invention spread to Europe and Asia.

The Nile Valley: Important finds in the Sudan and the Nile Valley prove that people of a Negroid type were influential contributors to that cradle of civilization—ancient Egypt. Discoveries at excavations near Khartoum in the Sudan and at El Badari on the Nile indicate that Stone Age Negroes laid the foundation for much of the civilization of the Nile Valley and manufactured pottery before pottery was made in the world's earliest known city.

Central and South America: American and African-American scholars, working primarily in the United States and Mexico, unearth new archeological evidence, including carbon 14-dated sculpture, which suggests that African mariners explored the New World before Columbus. This evidence and corroborative data from the diaries and letters of explorers, Arabic charts and maps and the recorded tales of African griots indicate that there was extensive pre-Columbian contact between ancient Africa and the Americas.

"An overwhelming body of new evidence," says Professor Ivan Van Sertima (*They Came Before Columbus*), "is now emerging from several disciplines, evidence that could not be verified and interpreted before, in the light of the infancy of archaeology and the great age of racial and intellectual prejudice. The most remarkable examples of this evidence are the realistic portraitures of Negro-Africans in clay, gold and stone unearthed in pre-Columbian strata in Central and South America."

The Sahara: French explorer Henri Lhote discovers rock paintings which suggest to author Basil Davidson that "peoples of a Negro type were painting men and women with a beautiful and sensitive realism before 3000 B.C. and were, perhaps, the originators of naturalistic human portraiture."

The implications of all this are extensive, as W. M. Whitelaw pointed out in a general summary of the evidence. "Later discoveries," he wrote, "all the way from Kenya to Transvaal not only of early human remains but also of advanced anthropoid types have brought the historical anthropologists to a state of confused expectancy. Considerably more evidence will have to be brought to light, however, before even the main outlines of man's early history in Africa can be drawn. It is already reasonable, however, to believe that such evidence may be forthcoming as will require a radical change of perspective on African history, if not on history itself."

It is already reasonable, in fact, to believe that the African ancestors of American blacks were among the major benefactors of the human race. Such evidence as survives clearly shows that Africans were on the scene and acting when the human drama opened.

For a long time, in fact, the only people on the scene were Africans. For some 600,000 years Africa and Africans led the world. Were these people who gave the world fire and tools and cultivated grain—were they Negroes? The ancient bones are silent. It is possible, indeed probable, that they were dark-skinned. More than that cannot be said at this time.

Civilization started in the great river valleys of Africa and Asia, in the Fertile Crescent in the Near East and along the narrow ribbon of the Nile in Africa. In the Nile Valley that beginning was an African as well as an Asian achievement. Blacks, or people who would be considered blacks today, were among the first people to use tools, paint pictures, plant seeds and worship gods.

In the beginning, then, and for a long time afterwards, black people marched in the front ranks of the emerging human procession. They founded empires and states. They extended the boundaries of the possible. They made some of the critical discoveries and contributions that led to the modern world.

Looking back on that age from our own, one is struck by what seems to be an absence of color consciousness. Back there, in the beginning, blackness did not seem to be an occasion for obloquy. In fact, the reverse seems to have been true, for whites were sometimes ridiculed for "the unnatural whiteness of their skin."

During this critical period in the evolution of man, blacks were known and honored throughout the ancient world. Ancient

Ethiopia, a vaguely defined territory somewhere to the south of Egypt, was hailed as a place fit for the vacation of the gods. Homer praised Memnon, king of Ethiopia, and black Eurybates:

> *Of visage solemn, sad, but sable hue,*
> *Short, wooly curls, o'erfleeced his bending head....*
> *Eurybates, in whose large soul alone,*
> *Ulysses viewed an image of his own.*

Homer, Herodotus, Pliny, Diodorus and other classical writers repeatedly praised the Ethiopians. "The annals of all the great early nations of Asia Minor are full of them," Flora Louisa Lugard wrote. "The Mosaic records allude to them frequently; but while they are described as the most powerful, the most just, and the most beautiful of the human race, they are constantly spoken of as black, and there seems to be no other conclusion to be drawn, than that at that remote period of history the leading race of the Western world was a black race." The Ethiopians claimed to be the spiritual fathers of Egyptian civilization. Diodorus Siculus, the Greek historian who wrote in the first century B.C., said that "the Ethiopians conceived themselves to be of greater antiquity than any other nation; and it is probable that, born under the sun's path, its warmth may have ripened them earlier than other men. They supposed themselves to be the inventors of worship, of festivals, of solemn assemblies, of sacrifices, and every religious practice."

Whatever may have been the spiritual influence of the ancient Ethiopians, it is established beyond doubt that blacks *from somewhere* were an important element among the peoples who fathered Egyptian civilization. Badarian culture proves that blacks camped on the banks of the Nile thousands of years before the Egypt of the Pharaohs. Bodies were excavated at El Badari amid artifacts suggesting a date of about eight thousand B.C. In the intestines of these bodies were husks of barley which indicated that the dark-skinned Badarians had learned to cultivate cereals. The beautifully fashioned Badarian pottery was never surpassed, not even in Egypt's days of greatest glory.

Still more evidence comes from the testimony of bones. Scholars who examined some eight hundred skulls of the predynastic Egyptians found that at least one-third were definitely Negroid. "The more we learn of Nubia and the Sudan," Dr. David

Randall-MacIver said, "the more evident does it appear that what was most characteristic in the predynastic culture of Egypt is due to intercourse with the interior of Africa and the immediate influence of that permanent Negro element which has been present in the population of Southern Egypt from the remotest times to our own day."

If black people were a major element among the peoples who fathered Egyptian civilization, who were the Egyptians? The question bristles with thorns. The only thing that can be said with assurance is that they probably were not Caucasians. The evidence suggests that they were a black-, brown-, and yellow-skinned people who sprang from a mixture of Negro, Semitic and Caucasian stocks.

How did the Egyptians see themselves?

They painted themselves in three colors: black, reddish-brown, yellow. The color *white* was available to them, but they used it to portray blue-eyed, white-skinned foreigners. One of the clearest examples of this is the great mural of a procession from a tomb of Thebes in the time of Thotmes III. The Egyptians and Ethiopians in the procession are painted in the usual brown and black colors, but thirty-seven whites in the procession are rendered in white tones. Who were they? G. A. Hoskins said they were probably "white slaves of the king of Ethiopia sent to the Egyptian king as the most acceptable present."

Great black scholars, such as W. E. B. Du Bois, Carter G. Woodson and William Leo Hansberry, have insisted that the ancient Egyptians, from Menes to Cleopatra, were a mixed race which presented the same physical types and color ranges as American blacks—a people, in short, who would have been forced in the forties to sit on the back seats of the buses in Mississippi. "If the Egyptians and the majority of the tribes of Northern Africa were not Negroes," Carter Woodson said, "then, there are no Negroes in the United States." There is supporting testimony on this point from Africanist William Leo Hansberry, who said that the evidence seems to indicate that "the Egyptians were a mixed group consisting of Negroids, non-Negroids and an Intermediate Group which represented, for the most part, mixed bloods." Summarizing the evidence of scientists who made a systematic examination of the skeletal remains of the ancient Egyptians, he said that "Negroids were particularly well represented

Mural from an Egyptian tomb illustrates the color ranges of the Ethiopians and Egyptians. Whites in the procession, G. A. Hoskins said, were probably slaves the Ethiopian king sent to the Egyptian king as a present.

Black Egyptian queen, Nefertari, "one of the most venerated figures" of Egyptian history, is pictured in this painting from an ancient tomb with her husband, Aahmes I.

in the pre-dynastic period. At one phase of the pre-dynastic period . . . the Negroid element amounted to 42 per cent. In the Old Kingdom, however, the Negroid percentage shows a substantial decline, although the mixed bloods totaled approximately 30 per cent. During the Middle Kingdom period, the Negroid element is again exceptionally strong, rising to 40 per cent in the 11th, 12th, and 13th dynasties. It again declines during the period of the 18th Dynasty of the New Empire but rises again toward the end of the period, particularly in the 20th Dynasty when Negroids and mixed bloods composed 40 per cent of the total population."

It is scarcely surprising, given the biases of Western scholarship, that this point is hotly disputed by various white scholars. But the dissenting scholars are contradicted by an eyewitness. Herodotus, the Greek historian, visited the country some five hundred years before Bethlehem. The Egyptians, he said, were "black and curly-haired."

Racial identity and racial origins apart, there is overwhelming evidence that Negroes or Negro types played a major role in the development of Egyptian civilization. Many, perhaps most, of the soldiers were black. Blacks toiled on the pyramids, offered prayers to the sun-god and served with distinction in the state bureaucracy. "Ancient Egypt knew him [the Negro]," Alexander Chamberlain said, "both bond and free, and his blood flowed in the veins of not a few of the mighty Pharaohs."

Ra Nehesi and several other Pharaohs have been identified as blacks by eminent scholars. So has Queen Nefertari, "the most venerated figure," Sir Flinders Petrie said, "of Egyptian history." Nefertari, the wife of Aahmes I, Egypt's great imperial leader, was cofounder of the famous Eighteenth Dynasty. She has been described as a "Negress [sic] of great beauty, strong personality, and remarkable administrative ability."

There was long and intimate contact between the dark-skinned Egyptians and the dark-skinned Ethiopians. For fifty centuries or more they fought, traded and intermarried. During the Middle Empire Ethiopia was a tribute-paying dependency of Egypt. Then, in the middle of the eighth century B.C., the Ethiopians turned the tables and conquered Egypt. Kashta, a bold Ethiopian monarch, began the conquest which was completed by his son, Piankhy. When Piankhy returned to his capital at Napata, he had subdued sixteen princes and was master of both Egypt and

Ethiopia. The legs of his enemies, he said, trembled "like those of women." Piankhy was keenly aware of the value of good public relations. The celebrated stela in which he recounted his deeds of valor is one of the gems of Egyptology. A modern scholar, Sir Alan Gardiner, said it is "one of the most illuminating documents that Egyptian history has to show, and displays a vivacity of mind, feeling, and expression such as the homeland could no longer produce."

For more than a century Ethiopian kings occupied the divine office of the Pharaohs. Shabaka, who succeeded Piankhy, attempted to restore the dwindling fortunes of Egypt. He sponsored a cultural revival, built a chapel at Karnak and restored a temple at Thebes. Diodorus Siculus said he "went beyond all his predecessors in his worship of the gods and his kindness to his subjects." Herodotus said he abolished capital punishment in Egypt.

Taharka, the greatest of the Ethiopian Pharaohs, ascended the throne about 690 B.C. at the age of forty-two. He was, by all accounts, a remarkable leader who improved the economic and cultural life of his realm. Sir E. A. Wallis Budge said Taharka (the Tirhakah of the Bible) was "a capable and energetic king, and under his able rule the country, notwithstanding his wars with the Assyrians, enjoyed a period of prosperity for about twenty-five years." This resourceful leader left inscriptions which indicate that he conquered the Hittites and the Assyrians—claims most Egyptologists discount. So complete was his sway and so absolute was his power that he dubbed himself "Emperor of the World." A famous Egyptologist called his reign that "astonishing epoch of nigger [sic] domination." Dr. Randall-MacIver said, "It seems amazing that an African Negro should have been able with any sort of justification to style himself Emperor of the World."

When, in 667 B.C., Taharka was defeated by the Assyrians, he retired to Napata, where Ethiopians continued to rule for several centuries. The capital was later moved farther south to Meroë, where strong-willed queens called Candaces ruled. One of these queens, a one-eyed woman "with masculine characteristics," led the Ethiopians in unsuccessful forays against the Romans.

The connection between this civilization and modern Ethiopia is far from clear. Some scholars call ancient Ethiopia "Kush" and begin the history of modern Ethiopia with the rise of the Axumite

kingdom in what is now Eritrea and northern Abyssinia. Whatever the true origins of modern Ethiopia, there is no exaggeration
in saying that it is one of the oldest countries in the world. The
African kingdom, which traces its lineage back to the famous
visit the legendary Queen of Sheba ("black but comely") paid
Solomon some one thousand years before Christ, reached the
height of its power in the fifth century, when Christianity became
the official religion. With the rise of Islam, the Ethiopians of
Axum were isolated and slept, historian Edward Gibbon wrote,
"for nearly a thousand years, forgetful of the world by whom they
were forgotten."

During the early Christian era, blacks were scattered to the four
corners of the world. For many centuries black merchants traded
with India, China and Europe. Other blacks were sold as slaves in
Europe and Asia. By the beginning of the Islamic era, blacks—as
merchants and merchandise—had integrated Europe, Asia and
the Far East. By that time blacks were well known in Venice in
Europe and in the deserts of Arabia. Perhaps the best known of
the Arabic blacks was Antar, the impassioned lover-warrior-poet.
The son of an attractive slave woman and an Arab nobleman,
Antar became a famous poet and was immortalized after his
death as the "Achilles of the Arabian Iliad." Fearless, impetuous,
ready to fight, sing a lyric or drink wine, Antar won fame in the
poetic contests which were common in pre-Islamic days. His
fame spread and he was hailed as the greatest poet of his time.
Like most poets, Antar had an eye for ladies and love.

> 'Twas then her beauties first enslaved my heart—
> Those glittering pearls and ruby lips, whose kiss
> Was sweeter far than honey to the taste.

Antar died about A.D. 615 and his deeds were recorded in literary form as *The Romance of Antar*. This book, Edward E. Holden
wrote, "has been the delight of all Arabians for many centuries. . . . The unanimous opinion of the East has always placed
The Romance of Antar at the summit of such literature. As one of
their authors well says: '*The Thousand and One Nights* is for the
amusement of women and children; *Antar* is a book for men.' "

As a religious ethic, Islam seems to have been unusually effective in cutting across racial lines. All Moslems, whatever their

color, were brothers in the faith. "If a Negro slave is appointed to rule you," Mohammed said, "hear and obey him, though his head be like a dried grape."

In this climate a man could be a slave today and a prime minister tomorrow. It is not at all surprising, therefore, that many blacks played heroic roles in the rise and spread of Islam—men like Mohammed Ahmad, the Sudanese black who claimed to be the Messiah; Abu'l Hasan Ali, the black sultan of Morocco, and Bilal, the friend of Mohammed. There were also numerous black generals, administrators and poets. When, in the eighth century, the Arabs exploded and carried Islam across North Africa and into Spain, blacks went with them. Among the black personalities at the court of Almansur in Seville, for example, was a "learned and celebrated poet, a black of the Sudan, Abu Ishak Ibrahamin Al Kenemi."

In the same period three powerful states—Ghana, Mali, and Songhay—emerged in the western Sudan, a broad belt of open country, sandwiched between the Sahara in the north and the rain forests of the Guinea Coast on the south. At one time the peoples and rulers of these countries were classified out of the Negro race. It is now known that they were blacks, some of whom were converted to Islam in the eleventh century. The extent of Moslem influence is debatable, but it seems probable that the upper classes and leaders, especially in the large cities, were black Moslems.

As political entities, Ghana, Mali and Songhay do not suffer in comparison with their European contemporaries. In several areas, in fact, the Sudanese empires were clearly superior. "It would be interesting to know," Basil Davidson wrote, "what the Normans might have thought of Ghana. Anglo-Saxon England could easily have seemed a poor and lowly place beside it."

The economic life of these states revolved around agriculture, manufacturing and international trade. Rulers wielded power through provincial governors and viceroys and maintained large standing armies. Chain-mailed cavalry, armed with shields, swords and lances, formed the shock troops of the armies. Ibn-Batuta, an Arab traveler who visited Mali in the fourteenth century, was impressed by the flow of life in these states. "Of all people," he said, "the blacks are those who most detest injustice. Their Sultan never forgives anyone who has been guilty of it."

Ancient Sudan empires reached the peak of their power in the Middle Ages. Ghana dominated the Sudan for almost three centuries. Mali rose in the thirteenth century. Songhay was a Sudan power in the fifteenth and sixteenth centuries.

West African warriors fought for the medieval African empire of Kanem-Bornu. Chain-mailed cavalry were shock troops of the powerful black states of the western Sudan.

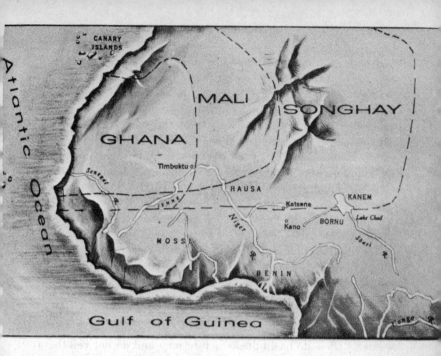

Timbuktu was one of the world's greatest cities in the fifteenth and sixteenth centuries. The intellectual center of the black empire of Songhay, Timbuktu was famed for its scholars and its social life.

Proud, a little haughty perhaps, the Sudanese were a formidable people. When the monarch of one state was overthrown, the women committed suicide because "they were too proud to allow themselves to fall into the hands of white men." Ibn-Batuta was astonished by the servile behavior of the whites in Mali. The black viceroy who received the merchants of the caravan with which Batuta was traveling remained seated while the whites stood before him. He spoke to the whites through an interpreter, although he understood their language. He did this, Ibn-Batuta said, "solely to indicate his disdain for them."

Trade and commerce flourished in the great cities that sprang up in the Sudanese savannah, and the intellectual life was brisk and stimulating. Jenné and Timbuktu were known throughout the Moslem world as centers of culture and learning. Ibn-Batuta said the black woman of these cities were "of surpassing beauty." They were neither downtrodden nor meek, these women. Ibn-Batuta said they were "shown more respect than the men," adding: "Their men show no signs of jealousy whatever" and the women "show no bashfulness before men and do not veil themselves."

The power and wealth of Ghana, Mali and Songhay stemmed from the trans-Saharan trade, which exerted a profound influence on Sudanese civilization. The basis of this trade was gold. From the north came caravans of twelve thousand or more camels, laden with wheat, sugar, fruit, salt and textiles, which were exchanged in the Sudan for gold and other products. In the power politics of that day, the country that controlled this trade controlled the Sudan.

Ghana, which was old when the Arabs first mentioned it in A.D. 800, dominated the Sudan for amost three hundred years, flourishing in the ninth and tenth centuries and reaching the peak of its power in the early part of the eleventh century. The rulers of Ghana, which was one of the main suppliers of gold for North Africa and Europe, were fabulously wealthy. Al-Bakri, an Arab geographer who wrote in 1067, said the king owned a nugget of gold so large that he could tether his horse to it.

Tenkamenin, who ruled Ghana in the middle of the eleventh century, had an army of two hundred thousand men and lived in a castle decorated with sculpture and painted windows. "When he gives audience to his people," Al-Bakri said, "to listen to their complaints ... he sits in a pavilion around which stand his horses caparisoned in cloth of gold; behind him stand ten pages holding shields and gold-mounted swords; and on his right hand are the sons of the princes of his empire, splendidly clad and with gold plaited into their hair. The governor of the city is seated on the ground in front of the king, and all around him are his vizirs in the same position. The gate of the chamber is guarded by dogs of an excellent breed, who never leave the king's seat, they wear collars of gold and silver."

In the eleventh century Ghana fell to a band of Moslem zealots, and the torch of Sudanese civilization passed to Mali, which began as a small Mandingo state on the left bank of the upper Niger River. Although the history of this country goes back to the seventh century, it owes its fame to two men—Sundiata Keita and Mansa Musa. Keita transformed the small state into a great empire. Musa, the most celebrated ruler of the ancient Sudan, came to power in 1307 and put together one of the greatest countries of the medieval world. Musa is best known for a pilgrimage he made to Mecca in 1324. He went in regal splendor with an entourage of sixty thousand persons, including twelve thousand servants. Five hundred servants, each of whom carried a staff of pure gold weighing some six pounds, marched on before him. Eighty camels bore twenty-four thousand pounds of gold, which the black monarch distributed as alms and gifts. Musa returned to his kingdom with an architect who designed imposing buildings in Timbuktu and other cities of the Sudan.

Mali declined in importance in the fifteenth century and its place was taken by Songhay, whose greatest king was Askia Mohammed. Askia, a general who had served as prime minister, seized power in 1493, a year after the European discovery of America. He reigned for nineteen years and built the largest and most powerful of the Sudan states. His realm was larger than all Europe and included most of West Africa. "He was obeyed," a Sudanese writer said, "with as much docility on the farther limits of the empire as he was in his own palace, and there reigned everywhere great plenty and absolute peace."

A brilliant administrator and an enlightened legislator, Askia reorganized the army, improved the banking and credit systems and made Gao, Walata, Timbuktu and Jenné intellectual centers. Certain scholars, Alexander Chamberlain in particular, believe he was one of the greatest monarchs of this period. "In personal character, in administrative ability, in devotion to the welfare of his subjects, in open mindedness towards foreign influences, and in wisdom in the adoption of non-Negro ideas and institutions," Chamberlain said, "King Askia . . . was certainly the equal of the average European monarch of the time and superior to many of them."

Timbuktu, during Askia's reign, was a city of some one hundred thousand people, filled with gold and dazzling women. One of the most fabled and exotic cities in the medieval world, the Sudanese metropolis was celebrated for its luxury and gaiety. The towering minarets of two great mosques dominated the face of the city. From the Great Mosque, flat-roofed houses (of wood and plaster) radiated in all directions. The older Sankore Mosque, to which was attached the University of Sankore, was the center of intellectual life. The mosque and the university were of cut stone and lime. Other buildings fronted the narrow streets: factories and shops where one could buy exotic goods from North Africa and faraway Europe. Leo Africanus, a Christianized Moor who visited the city in the sixteenth century, said it "is a wonder to see what plentie of Merchandize is daily brought hither and how costly and sumptious all things be. . . . Here are many shops of . . . merchants and especially of such as weave linnen."

In the narrow streets of this Sudanese metropolis, scholars mingled with rich black merchants and young boys sat in the shade, reciting the Koran. Visiting Arab businessmen wandered the streets, looking, no doubt, for the excitement for which the city was famed. Youths from all over the Moslem world came to Timbuktu to study law and surgery at the University of Sankore; scholars came from North Africa and Europe to confer with the learned historians and writers of the black empire. Es Sadi, a Timbuktu intellectual who wrote a history of the Sudan, said his brother came from Jenné for a successful cataract operation at the hands of a distinguished surgeon. Es Sadi, incidentally, had a private library of sixteen hundred volumes.

If we can credit contemporary reports, Timbuktu, during the reign of Askia the Great, was an intellectual's paradise. A Sudanese literature developed and Es-Sadi, Ahmed Baba and other intellectuals wrote books.

"In Timbuktu," Leo Africanus said, "there are numerous judges, doctors, and clerics, all receiving good salaries from the king. He pays great respect to men of learning. There is a big demand for books in manuscript, imported from Barbary. More profit is made from the book trade than from any other line of business." Since man first learned to write, few cities have been able to make such a claim.

The University of Sankore and other intellectual centers in Timbuktu had large and valuable collections of manuscripts in several languages, and scholars came from faraway places to check their Greek and Latin manuscripts. The seeds scattered here put down deep roots. Hundreds of years later Heinrich Barth met an old blind man in the Sudan. "This," he reported, "was the first conversation I had with this man. . . . I could scarcely have expected to find in this out of the way place a man not only versed in all the branches of Arabic literature, but who had even read, nay, possessed a manuscript of those portions of Aristotle and Plato which had been translated into Arabic."

How did the people of Timbuktu amuse themselves? If the writers of Songhay can be believed, Timbuktu was Paris, Chicago and New York blended into an African setting. Shocked Songhay historians said most of the people amused themselves with parties, love and the pleasures of the cup. Music was the rage (orchestras with both male and female singers were preferred) and midnight revels were common. The dress of the women was extravagantly luxurious. Men and women were fond of jewels, and the women dressed their hair with bands of gold.

Dramatic displays, including dancing, fencing, gymnastics and poetic recitations, were popular. So was chess. The story is told of a Songhay general who bungled a military campaign and explained that he became so engrossed in a chess game that he paid no attention to the reports of his scouts. Askia—a liberal man who had several wives and one hundred sons, the last of whom was born when he was ninety—was disturbed by the free and easy life of Timbuktu and attempted, apparently without too much success, to curb the social excesses.

Timbuktu and the civilization of which it was a flower declined in the seventeenth century and the reign of the great West African states came to an end. Why did Sudanese civilization collapse? W. E. B. Du Bois says it fell before the triphammer blows of two of the world's great religions, Islam and Christianity. Other students cite the difficulties of defense in the open Sudanese

Sandstone column is part of the ruins of an Ethiopian temple. There are monuments in Ancient Ethiopia which rival the ancient treasures of Egypt in grandeur and beauty.

Naturalistic bronze head from
Ife, West Coast art center,
and abstract rendering of
human face in mask (below)
show the great variety and
strength of African sculpture.

savannah and the corrupting influence of the slave trade. Es-Sadi, who wrote the *Tarikh al-Sudan* in the dying days of the Songhay empire, advanced another reason—social dissolution. The people, he said, had grown fat and soft on luxury and good living. "At this moment," he said, "faith was exchanged for infidelity; there was nothing forbidden by God which was not openly done. . . . Because of these abominations, the Almighty in his vengeance drew upon the Songhai the victorious army of the Moors."

The age of the great Sudan empires ended, but several states to the east and south, notably Mossi, Hausa, Kanem-Bornu and Ashanti, retained political identities down to the eighteenth and nineteenth centuries. Great Zimbabwe and other stone cities in Southern Africa suggest that strong states flourished inland. Vigorous centers of culture also existed on the East Coast, where black and Arab merchants traded with India and China.

European penetration and the slave trade debased much that was vital in African culture. The popular myth depicts the conquering European carrying the blessing of civilization to naked "savages" who sat under trees, filed their teeth and waited for fruit to drop into their hands. The truth is less flattering to the European ego. On the West Coast of Africa, from whence came most of the ancestors of American blacks, there were complex institutions ranging from extended family groupings to village states and territorial empires. Most of these units had all the appurtenances of the modern state—armies, courts, and internal revenue departments. Indeed, more than one scholar has paid tribute to "the legal genius of the African." Anthropologist Melville J. Herskovits said that "of the areas inhabited by non-literate peoples, Africa exhibits the greatest incidence of complex governmental structures. Not even the kingdoms of Peru and Mexico could mobilize resources and concentrate power more effectively than could some of these African monarchies, which are more to be compared with Europe of the Middle Ages than referred to the common conception of the 'primitive' state."

Agriculture was the basis of the economic life of these states, although herding and artisanship were important. Specialization was advanced, with one nation, for example, concentrating on metallurgy and bartering with another nation which specialized in weaving or farming. A money system based on the cowrie shell was in use before European penetration. Contemptuous of the concept of private property, West Africans believed that the land belonged to the community and could not be alienated.

Iron was known and used from the Atlantic Ocean to Ethiopia. With simple bellows and charcoal fires, the Africans smelted iron and manufactured beautiful implements. "It seems likely," Franz Boas said, "that at a time when the European was still satisfied with rude stone tools, the African had invented or adopted the art of smelting iron. . . . It seems not unlikely that the people who made the marvelous discovery of reducing iron ores by smelting were the African Negroes. Neither ancient Europe, nor ancient western Asia, nor ancient China knew iron, and everything points to its introduction from Africa."

The core of West African society was the family which was organized in some tribes on a matrilineal basis—that is, descent was traced through the mother. Polygamy was common, although, in practice, the poor, like poor people everywhere, contented themselves with monogamy. Social life was well organized. The old, the sick, the infirm were cared for. Spinsters were rare; prostitution was unknown. Some nations, incidentally, were acquainted with the allegedly modern practice of birth control. Bantu people said it was not good for a woman to give birth to more than one child in a three-year period. Some nations vaccinated for smallpox and said there was a cause and effect relationship between the mosquito and malaria. A European traveler in Abyssinia reported that "the Natives hereabouts say that Malaria is caused by the bite of the mosquito, but, of course, we know better—it is caused by the miasmas of the swamps!"

The West Africans were a bewildering mixture of various stocks. Centuries of contact and interbreeding had already produced different types. Some of the West Africans were short and broad-nosed. Some were tall with straight hair and aquiline noses. They were of all colors: chocolate, asphalt, café au lait, persimmon, cream.

Although West Africans spoke many tongues, there was a common substratum. Only four African languages were reduced to writing before the coming of the white man: Egyptian, Ethiopian, a variety of Berber and an invention of the Vai people of Liberia. Though not reduced to writing, African languages were far from simple. There is no better summary of the flavor of these languages than Mario Pei's analysis of Swahili, which, he said, "is a complete refutation of the rather general belief that languages of 'primitive' peoples are necessarily primitive, and consist largely of grunts, groans and mixed-up ideas. Swahili has a euphony that is comparable to Italian, with clear, distinct sounds, vowel endings, and a most pleasing arrangement of syllables that consist for the most part of consonant-plus-vowel. It is capable of such absolute precision that the Swahili version of the Pentateuch contains fewer words than the Hebrew original, without the slightest loss or distortion of meaning. Its grammatical and syntactical structure is logical, almost to the point of being philosophical."

Of whatever tongue, of whatever color, Africans were a deeply religious people. For a long time their religion was written off as a form of animism. We know now that it was a great deal more complicated than that. Like advanced peoples everywhere, the Africans wrestled with the big questions. What is man? What happens to him after death? Is life a gigantic hoax or has it purpose and meaning?

The answers Africans gave to these questions determined the form of their religion. There was, to begin with, a supreme God who created the earth. There was also a pantheon of lesser gods, identified sometimes with terrestrial objects. Intertwined with these concepts were the cults of fate and ancestor worship. Undergirding all was the basic concept of "life forces." The life force of the Creator was thought to be present in all things, animate and inanimate. This force, "a kind of individualized fragment of the Supreme Being itself," continued to exist, even after the death of the individual. It continued, the African said, in a pure and perfect state which could influence the lives of living things.

This sophisticated concept bears a striking resemblance to Henri Bergson's *élan vital* and other modern philosophies and theories. Bernard Fagg, an expert on these matters, found some parallels between African philosophy and modern subatomic physics. "African thought," he said, "is conditioned by their ontology, that is, their theory of the nature of being; for them being is a process and not a mere state, and the nature of things is thought of in terms of force or energy rather than matter; the forces of the spirit, human, animal, vegetable and mineral worlds are all constantly influencing each other, and by a proper knowledge and use of them a man may influence his own life and that of others."

Religion, to the African, was life. Every event was charged with religious significance, and the climax of life was death. The African's attitude toward death, anthropologists say, survived the Atlantic crossing and took root in the soil of black American life. Another religious root, spirit possession, thrives, they say, in the shouting and ecstasy complex of some black American churches.

Art, like religion, was a life expression. There were no art museums or opera houses in pre-white man Africa. Art and aesthetic expression were collective experiences in which all the people participated. Art, in short, was not for art's sake, but for life's sake.

The different faces of beauty—line, color, sound, rhythm—fascinated the African ancestors of American blacks. And their plastic art—embodied in cubistic masks, terra-cotta pieces, gold figurines, three-dimensional objects and naturalistic representations of the human body—is one of the great flights of the human spirit. Fascinated by the abstract geometry of African art, Picasso and other modernists turned their backs on the Greco-Roman and Renaissance visions and adopted the vocabulary of Benin, Ife and other West African art centers. In 1907 Picasso altered the faces of his huge canvas, *Les Demoiselles d'Avignon*, to resemble African masks. This was the beginning of a cubism, a turning point in Western art.

Before the coming of the European, music and rhythm were everyday things in Africa. Music was everywhere and it was grounded in two techniques which survived in the New World: polyrhythmic percussive technique and the call-and-response pattern (leader and chorus alternating). The poetry of tom-toms, the symphonies of synchronized bodies: these ebbed and flowed with the rhythm of life. Men and women danced because dancing had a social and religious meaning and because dancing *was* meaning, was life itself. This attitude came to America, too. The Afro-American dances from Afro-Cuba and the Afro-American dances from Afro-Harlem are rooted in an African *mystique*. It is of more than casual significance that films made in an African village contained a perfect example of the Charleston.

There was much, to be sure, that was mean and base in African life: slavery, for example, although it was a thousand times more moderate than American slavery and, of course, the use of humans by humans. Humans used other humans in Africa, as they did in Greece and Rome. The only thing that can be said for human exploitation in Africa is that it was as well organized as it was in "more advanced" cultures.

The individuals who emerged from this African chrysalis were courageous and creative. They were not soft; they were hard. They had fought the tsetse fly and hundreds of nameless insects, and they had survived. They had wrested from the hungry jungle gaps of land and they had found time to think beautiful thoughts and to make beautiful things. They were used to hard work and they were accustomed to an elaborate social code. If they were aristocrats or rich merchants or priests — if, in short, they belonged to the upper classes, as did some who came to America in chains, they were used to political responsibility, to giving orders and taking them, to making and altering rules, to governing. In fine, as Stanley M. Elkins said, in an otherwise questionable essay, they were "the product of ... cultural traditions essentially heroic in nature."

Was this rich cultural heritage transplanted and preserved in the American environment?

Some scholars find little in African-American life that can be traced to the African past. Others, like Melville J. Herskovits, find Africanisms (survivals of African cultural patterns) in the family life, motor habits, religious practices and music of black Americans. Lorenzo Turner found a large number of survivals in the syntax, word-formations and intonations of black Americans. Among the words he found "in fairly general use... especially in the South" were goober (peanut), gumbo (okra), ninny (female breast), tote (to carry), yam (sweet potato). Turner also found "several hundred" African names among Americans on the South Side of Chicago, including the following:

> *Bobo*, one who cannot talk (Vai)
> *Geeji*, a language and tribe in Liberia
> *Agona*, a country in Ghana (Twi)
> *Ola*, that which saves (Yoruba)
> *Zola*, to love (Congo)

It is obvious from this — from the evidence of the names and habits, religious practices and music of African-Americans—

that Africa's golden past is crucial to an understanding of black America. What is equally true and equally important is that Africa's past is critical to an understanding of white America. For it is impossible to understand white America, it is impossible to understand Thomas Jefferson or George Washington or the U.S. Constitution, without some understanding of Africa's gift to the New World. And what that means, on the level of history and on the level of reality, is that America, contrary to the generally accepted view, is an African as well as a European invention.

> *One three centuries removed*
> *From the scenes his fathers loved,*
> *Spicy grove, cinnamon tree,*
> *What is Africa to me?*

2

Before the Mayflower

*Your country? How came it yours? Before the Pil-
grims landed we were here. Here we have brought
our three gifts and mingled them with yours: a gift
of story and song — soft, stirring melody in an
ill-harmonized and unmelodious land; the gift of
sweat and brawn to beat back the wilderness, conquer the soil, and lay the foundations of this vast
economic empire two hundred years earlier than
your weak hands could have done it; the third, a
gift of the Spirit.*

W.E.B. DU BOIS

SHE CAME out of a violent storm with a story no
one believed, a name no one recorded and a
past no one investigated. She was manned by
pirates and thieves. Her captain was a mystery man named Jope,
her pilot an Englishman named Marmaduke, her cargo an assort-
ment of Africans with sonorous Spanish names — Antoney,
Isabella, Pedro.

A year before the arrival of the celebrated *Mayflower*, 113
years before the birth of George Washington, 244 years before the
signing of the Emancipation Proclamation, this ship sailed into
the harbor at Jamestown, Virginia, and dropped anchor into the
muddy waters of history. It was clear to the men who received

this "Dutch man of War" that she was no ordinary vessel. What seems unusual today is that no one sensed how extraordinary she really was. For few ships, before or since, have unloaded a more momentous cargo.

From whence did this ship come?

From somewhere on the high seas where she robbed a Spanish vessel of a cargo of Africans bound for the West Indies.

Why did she stop at Jamestown, the first permanent English settlement in America?

No one knows for sure. The captain "ptended," John Rolfe noted, that he was in great need of food and offered to exchange his human cargo for "victualle." The deal was arranged. Antoney, Isabella, Pedro and seventeen other Africans stepped ashore in August, 1619. The history of Black America began.

It began, in a way, with Antoney. And it began with a love story. Antoney, who had no surname, fell in love with Isabella and married her. In 1623 or 1624 Isabella gave birth to the first black child born in English America. The child, a boy named William, was baptized in the Church of England.

There were other ships, other Williams, other Antoneys and other Isabellas—millions after millions. This is a story about those millions and the way they came to the Americas. This is a story about the merchandising and marketing of human beings. This is a story about the "greatest migration in recorded history."

The story of Antoney and Isabella is only one act in a larger drama—the European slave trade—which began in 1444 and continued for more than four hundred years. During this period Africa lost an estimated forty million people. Some twenty million of these men and women came to the New World. Millions more died in Africa during and after their capture or on the ships and plantations.

These figures, though instructive, do not say anything meaningful about the people involved. The slave trade was not a statistic, however astronomical. The slave trade was people living, lying, stealing, murdering, dying. The slave trade was a black man who stepped out of his house for a breath of fresh air and ended up, ten months later, in Georgia with bruises on his back and a brand on his chest.

The slave trade was a black mother suffocating her newborn baby because she didn't want him to grow up a slave.

The slave trade was a "kind" captain forcing his suicide-minded passengers to eat by breaking their teeth, though, as he said, he was "naturally compassionate."

The slave trade was a bishop sitting on an ivory chair on a wharf in the Congo and extending his fat hand in wholesale baptism of slaves who were rowed beneath him, going in chains to the slave ships.

The slave trade was a greedy king raiding his own villages to get slaves to buy brandy.

The slave trade was a pious captain holding prayer services twice a day on his slave ship and writing later the famous hymn, "How Sweet the Name of Jesus Sounds."

The slave trade was deserted villages, bleached bones on slave trails and people with no last names. It was Caesar negro, Angelo negro and Negro Mary. Above all, it was Captain Tomba, who came to America, and Nealee, who didn't.

Nealee started out but she couldn't or wouldn't make it. She was being driven to the West African coast for sale when she became ill and refused to walk another step. Mungo Park, who was one of the last persons to see Nealee, said she was put on an ass "but the ass was so very unruly, that no sort of treatment could induce him to proceed with his load; and as Nealee made no exertion to prevent herself from falling, she was quickly thrown off, and had one of her legs much bruised. Every attempt to carry her forward being thus found ineffectual, the general cry of the coffle [slave caravan] was, *kang-tegi, kang-tegi*, 'cut her throat, cut her throat'; an operation I did not wish to see performed, and therefore marched onwards with the foremost of the coffle. I had not walked above a mile when one of Karfa's [the leader] domestic slaves came up to me, with poor Nealee's garment upon the end of his bow and exclaimed, 'Nealee *affeeleeta*.' (Nealee is lost.) I asked him whether the Slattees had given him the garment as a reward for cutting her throat; he replied that Karfa and the schoolmaster would not consent to that measure, but had left her on the road; where undoubtedly she soon perished, and was probably devoured by wild beasts."

Captain Tomba, who came to America, was first seen in a slave pen in Sierra Leone. John Atkins, a surgeon who saw him there, said he was a handsome man "who scorned looking at us, refusing to rise or stretch out his Limbs, as the Master Commanded."

A few days later Captain Tomba and a companion led a revolt on a slave ship and killed three sailors before they were subdued.

What happened to Captain Tomba?

"Why," John Atkins wrote, "Captain Harding weighing the Stoutness and Worth of the two slaves [Captain Tomba and a companion] did, as in other Countries they do by Rogues of Dignity, whip and scarify them only; while three others, Abettors, but not Actors, nor of Strength for it, he sentenced to cruel Deaths; making them first eat the Heart and Liver of one of them killed. The Woman he hoisted up by the Thumbs, whipp'd, and slashed her with Knives, before the other Slaves till she died."

Captain Tomba living, Nealee dying, John Newton praying, the King of Barsally stealing, the fat bishop baptizing, Captain Harding torturing—these people and millions like them made the slave trade one of the cruellest chapters in the history of man.

This chapter started in the fifteenth century, but it cannot be understood if it is not placed in the flow of history from which vantage point it will appear that slavery is not a disgrace peculiar to blacks but a universal phenomenon that has been practiced in almost all countries. Slavery was old when Moses was young. In Plato's Athens and Caesar's Rome, humans—white, black and brown—were bought and sold. Slavery existed in the Middle Ages in Christian Europe and in Africa. In the ancient world almost anyone might become a slave. Slavery was so prevalent, in fact, that Plato said every person has slaves among his ancestors.

There was a crucial difference, however, between ancient slavery and modern slavery. Ancient slavery, which had little or nothing to do with race, was justified primarily by the rules of war. Christians and Moslems added a new dimension to this ancient institution, capturing and enslaving one another for religious reasons. The same rationale served both groups when economic interests and improved technology focused world attention on Africa.

The Moslems got there first. For several decades before the opening of the European trade, Moslem merchants dragged dark captives across the hot Sahara sands. Then, in the fifteenth century, Portugal diverted this trade to the Atlantic. The prime mover in this development was a devout and covetous prince named Henry the Navigator. Excited by stories of the great wealth of Africa and Asia, he ordered his ships to explore the coast of Africa. There, on a fateful day in 1444, Henry's men came upon the first large group of Africans. They tiptoed through the high grass and crept to the edge of the village and then, said a contemporary, "they looked towards the settlement and saw that the Moors, with their women and children, were already coming as quickly as they could out of their dwellings, because they had caught sight of their enemies. But they, shouting out 'St. James,' 'St. George,' 'Portugal,' attacked them, killing and taking all they could."

The pious Portuguese captured seventy more Africans, including a girl they found sleeping in a deserted village, and sailed home, where they baptized the captives and enslaved them. Within ten years Portugal was importing one thousand Africans a year. A century later blacks outnumbered whites in some sections of Portugal, where there was a big demand for black domestics, stevedores and agricultural laborers, especially in the southern section. "By the middle of the sixteenth century," Mary Wilhelmina Williams commented, "the inhabitants of the Algarve were largely Ethiopians, and even as far north as Lisbon blacks outnumbered whites. There was no marked color line, and the blood of the two races mingled freely, resulting eventually in Negroid physical characteristics in the Portuguese nation."

This phase of the slave trade was relatively unimportant. There was no widespread demand for slaves in Europe, and the number of Africans captured was relatively small. As a consequence, the European monologue quickly became an African-European dialogue based on a trade in humans *and* goods and ideas.

Africa just then was in a state of highly unstable equilibrium. The continent had emerged from the Golden Age of the Great Empires with a number of critical problems, including climatic changes which pushed the Sahara south, triggering massive migrations and isolating large sections from the dominant currents of the age. No less obvious and ominous was the absence of modern firepower, a fact that would prove decisive in the coming confrontation with Europe. Despite these problems, life in some African states compared favorably with life in some European states. (Europe's eminence, one must remember, came in large part *after* the fall of Africa and as a direct result of that fall.) In fact, in some areas, Africans were a step or two ahead. The Sudanese empire, with its showplace of Timbuktu, had passed its peak, but the ancient continent could still show Europe a thing or two. There were large empires and populous cities—some as large as all but the largest European cities—along the coasts, and Benin and other African centers were thriving inland. In the six- teenth century, when the whole of America was a howling wild er- ness and large sections of the European peasantry had been re- duced to beggary, Benin City was a dazzling place, twenty-five miles wide, with imposing boulevards and intersecting streets, flanked by substantial houses with balustrades and verandas.

Impressed by these and other evidences of African power, the first European emissaries greeted Africans as allies and partners in trade. The letters and diaries of traders show that down to the eighteenth century they had no conception of Africans as racial pariahs. On the contrary, many of these traders said Africans were their equals and superior to many of their countrymen back home.

Africans were of substantially the same mind. They did not consider themselves inferior to Europeans. If anything, they con- sidered themselves superior to the odd-looking men with pale skins. We are told that the king of Dahomey seldom shook hands with white men and that when he did it was a "very uncommon mark of royal condescension." A French trader complained in 1660 that the Fanti were "so proud and haughty that a European trader there must stand bare to them."

Standing up to one another, as equals and partners in trade and commerce, both Africans and Europeans profited. Plenipoten- tiaries were exchanged, and bright young men of the ruling stratum went to Lisbon and Rome to study and observe. Black and white kings exchanged letters filled with terms of royal endear- ment ("my fellow brother and my fellow queen"). They also exchanged gifts and mistresses of various hues and dispositions. On May 15, 1518, one hundred years before the Jamestown landing, Henry of the Congo led a mission to the Vatican, formal- ly addressed the Pope in Latin and was appointed bishop of the Congo. In Rome, Lisbon and other European centers, Africans rose to high positions in church and state.

In the fervor of worldwide exploration and the commingling of peoples from different lands and cultures, new vistas opened up for both Africans and Europeans. It seemed for a spell that Chris- tianity would have the same fertilizing influence in Africa in the

sixteenth century that Islam had had in the eleventh and twelfth
centuries. But it was not to be. While the bright young black men
were feasting in the courts of Lisbon, while the eager black
priests were genuflecting in the courts of the Vatican, events
were happening in the outer world that would destroy the dream
and change Europe and Africa forever.

The most important of these events was the European discovery
of America and the opening of the New World. It is a point of
paradoxical interest that descendants of the first black captives—black Christians born in Spain and Portugal—were with
the first European explorers and settlers. Black explorers —
servants, slaves, and free men—accompanied Spanish and Portuguese explorers in their expeditions in North and South
America. They were with Pizarro in Peru, Cortes in Mexico
and Menendez in Florida. Thirty blacks were with Balboa when
he discovered the Pacific Ocean. Typical of the early black explorers in America was Estevanico, who opened up New Mexico
and Arizona for the Spaniards. Other blacks, W. E. B. Du Bois
said, "accompanied DeSoto and one of them stayed among the
Indians in Alabama and became the first settler from the Old
World."

Spaniards, who took the lead in the exploration, attempted at
first to enslave Indians. But they died so fast that Bishop Bar-
tolomé Las Casas, a famous missionary, recommended in 1517
the importation of Africans, a recommendation he lived to regret. The development of large-scale sugar planting created a
demand for men that casual kidnapping couldn't supply. In the
wake of that development, the vision of European monarchs
shifted, and the African-European dialogue became a monologue
focused almost exclusively on a trade in men. Within a few years
hundreds of thousands of blacks were crossing the Atlantic each
year, and the soil of Africa and America was drenched with their
blood. "Strange," said Eric Williams, "that an article like sugar,
so sweet and necessary to human existence, should have oc-
casioned such crimes and bloodshed!"

An estimated million of these slaves found their way to the land
that became the United States of America. But the first black
immigrants (Antoney, Isabella, and the Jamestown group) were
not slaves. This is a fact of critical importance in the history of

Black America. They came, these first blacks, the same way that most of the first white immigrants came — under duress and pressure. They found a system (indentured servitude) which enabled poor whites to come to America and sell their services for a stipulated number of years to planters. Under this system thousands of whites—paupers, ne'er-do-wells, religious dissenters, waifs, prisoners and prostitutes—were shipped to the colonies and sold to the highest bidder. Many were sold, as the first blacks were sold, by the captains of ships. Some were kidnapped on the streets of London and Bristol, as the first blacks were kidnapped in the villages of Africa.

In Virginia, then, as in other colonies, the first black settlers fell into a well-established socioeconomic groove which carried with it no implications of racial inferiority. That came later. But in the interim, a period of forty years or more, the first black settlers accumulated land, voted, testified in court and mingled with whites on a basis of equality. They owned other black servants, and certain blacks imported and paid for white servants whom they apparently held in servitude.

During these fateful forty years, the black population of the Virginia colony grew by natural additions and importations. In 1621 the *James* arrived from England with a number of immigrants, including a black man named Antonio. In 1623 the *Swan* arrived with still another black from England, a man named John Pedro. In 1623 or 1624, as we have seen, Isabella, the wife of Antoney, gave birth to what was probably the first black child born in America. The new American, the first of a long black line that would swell to millions, was christened William in the Church of England, and a new account was opened in the ledger book of history. At that juncture, according to the first detailed census of 1624–25, blacks constituted about 2 per cent of the total population of 1,227. The twenty-three black pioneers—eleven males, ten females, and two children—lived in six of the twenty-three settlements in Virginia.

We can only imagine the feelings of these seminal African-Americans. The record burns with their presence but is strangely silent on their reactions. The black founding fathers and mothers enter history thus: faceless men and women uprooted from Africa and flung into a maelstrom of history. Nothing in the record indicates that the cultural shock was great for either the blacks or whites. There were skilled farmers and artisans among the first group of African-Americans, and there are indications in the record that they were responsible for various innovations later credited to English immigrants. An early example of this was reported in Virginia, where the governor ordered rice planted in 1648 on the advice of "our Negroes," who told the whites that conditions in Virginia were as favorable to the production of the crop as "in their Country."

There is furthermore the testimony of Washington Irving, who made the following observation in a contemporary satirical skit: "These Negroes, like the monks of the Dark Ages, engross all the Knowledge of the place, and being infinitely more adventurous and more knowing than their masters, carry on all the foreign trade; making frequent voyages in canoes, loaded with oysters, buttermilk and cabbages. They are great astrologers predicting the different changes of weather almost as accurately as an almanac."

A large proportion of the first generation of African-Americans entered America with Spanish names. For reasons that are not readily apparent, many black males were called Antonio, a name that quickly became Antoney or Anthony. Other popular names of the period included Michaela, Couchaxello, Mingo, Pedro, Francisco, Jibina, Maria, Wortello, Tomora, Angola, and Tony Kongo. Shortly after their arrival in America, many blacks discarded African and Spanish names and adopted English titles. Thus within the span of a generation the black soul moved from Africa to England to Spain to America — from the X of the severed African family tree to Antonio and the William X or the William? of the first native American black, who apparently had no surname at the time of his christening.

During the next forty-odd years, hundreds of Africans made that extraordinary cultural leap. In 1625 Brase, another victim of piracy, was brought into the colony. Four years later, in 1629, there was a substantial increase in the black population when the first ship from Africa arrived at Port Comfort, bringing blacks captured from a Portuguese ship off the coast of Africa. In the 1630s and 1640s approximately 160 blacks were imported. By 1649 colonial officials were able to report that "there are in *Virginia* about fifteene thousand English, and of *Negroes* brought thither, three hundred good servants."

The "good servants" came from different backgrounds with different experiences. Quite a few, as we have noted, came from England, where blacks had lived since the middle of the sixteenth century. Many came from Spain, Portugal and the West Indies. Significantly, many were Christians, baptized either in Spain or Portugal or on the high seas. In 1624 John Phillip testified in a Jamestown court and his testimony against a white man was admitted because he had been "christened in England twelve years since. . . ."

In a limited but nonetheless significant sense, then, the Jamestown experience was an open experience which provided unusual opportunities for individual blacks. This comes out most clearly in the life and times of Anthony Johnson, who came to America in 1621 or thereabouts from England. Like many other blacks of the period, Johnson quickly worked out his term of indenture and started accumulating property. In 1651, according to official records, he imported and paid for five servants, some of whom were white, and was granted 250 acres of land on the basis of the headright system, which permitted planters to claim fifty acres of land for each individual brought to the colony.

The abstract of the deed reads as follows:

> ANTHONY JOHNSON, 250 acs. Northampton Co., 24 July 1651, ... At great Naswattock Cr., being a neck of land bounded on the S.W. by the maine Cr. & on S.E. & N.W. by two small branches issueing out of the mayne Cr. Trans. of 5 pers: Tho. Bemrose, Peter Bughby, Antho. Cripps, Jno, Gesorroro, Richard Johnson.

In the years that followed, Johnson and his relatives established one of America's first black communities on the banks of the Pungoteague River. In 1652 John Johnson, who was probably Anthony Johnson's son, imported eleven persons, most of them white males and females, and received headrights for 550 acres adjacent to Anthony Johnson. Two years later Richard Johnson imported two white indentured servants and received one hundred acres. Here are the records of the deeds:

> JOHN JOHNSON, 550 acs. Northampton Co., 10 May 1652 . . . At great Naswattocks Cr., adj. 200 acs. granted to Anthony Johnson. Trans. of 11 pers: John Edward, Wm. Routh, Tho. Yowell, Fra. Maland, William Price, John

Owen, Dorothy Rily, Richard Hemstead, Law. Barnes, Row. Rith, Mary Johnson.

RICH. Jnoson (Johnson—also given as John), Negro, 100 acs. Northampton Co., 21 Nov. 1654, . . . On S. Side of Pongoteague Riv., Ely. upon Pocomock Nly. upon land of John Jnoson., Negro, Wly. upon Anto. Jnoson., Negro, & Sly. upon Nich. Waddilow. Trans. of 2 pers: Wm. Ames, Wm. Vincent.

The Johnson settlement at its height included only a handful of blacks with large holdings. Other blacks lived in integrated communities in other areas of the colony. In 1656, for instance, Benjamin Doyle received a patent for three hundred acres in Surry County. In 1668 John Harris bought fifty acres in New Kent County; and Phillip Morgan, reflecting the optimism of the age, leased two hundred acres in York County for ninety-nine years.

One can hardly doubt, in the face of this clear evidence, that the first generation of blacks had, as J. H. Russell noted, "about the same industrial or economic opportunities as the free white servant." Additional evidence of the relatively high status of the first American blacks is to be found in colonial documents which indicate that they voted and participated in public life. It was not until 1723, in fact, that blacks were denied the right to vote in Virginia. According to Albert E. McKinley, blacks voted in South Carolina until 1701, in North Carolina until 1715, and in Georgia until 1754. Not only did pioneer blacks vote, but they also held public office. There was a black surety in York County, Virginia, in the first decades of the seventeenth century, and a black beadle in Lancaster County, Virginia.

Nor was this sort of thing confined to Virginia. The first blacks in Massachusetts—they arrived in 1638 on the *Desire*, America's first slave ship — were apparently assigned the status of indentured servants. In his classic work, *The Negro in Colonial New England*, Lorenzo J. Greene said that "until almost the end of the seventeenth century the records refer to the Negroes as 'servants' not as 'slaves.' For some time no definite status could be assigned to incoming Negroes. Some were sold for a period of time only, and like the white indentured servants became free after their indenture."

The available evidence suggests that most of the first generation of African-Americans worked out their terms of servitude
and were freed. A very interesting and instructive case in point is
that of Richard Johnson, a black carpenter who came to Virginia
in 1651 as a free man and signed a contract of indenture. Within
two years Johnson was a free man. Within three years he was
acquiring pounds and property and servants.

In addition to Johnson and other blacks who were freed as a
matter of course, the record lists other cases in which colonial
courts freed black servants. Such a case was that of Andrew
Moore, who migrated to Virginia and bound himself out for a term
of five years. In October, 1673, the General Court "ordered that
the Said Moore bee free from his said master, and that the Said
Mr. Light pay him Corne and Clothes according to the Custome of
the Country and four hundred pounds tobac and Caske for his
service done him Since he was free, and pay costs."

Looking back on that age from our own, one is struck by what
can only be called equality of oppression. Not the least among the
things that startle us in this period is that the colony's power
structure made little or no distinction between black and white
servants, who were assigned the same tasks and were held in
equal contempt. This has caused no end of trouble for latter-day
white historians, who have tried to explain away a record that is
understandably astonishing in view of the later practices of some
whites. It is interesting, for example, to observe that many white
historians deny that white women worked in the fields. But
contemporary witnesses tell us in no uncertain terms that white
women not only worked in the fields but were also flogged at
colonial whipping posts. There are also court records in which
white women asked the courts to relieve them of this burden.
Historian Philip A. Bruce conceded this point and commented
with disapproval: "The class of white women who were required
to work in the fields belonged to the lowest rank in point of
character; not having been born in Virginia and not having thus
acquired from birth a repugnance to associations with Africans
upon a footing of social equality, they yielded to the temptations
of the situations in which they were placed."

There is contradictory testimony which indicates that character, Bruce to the contrary notwithstanding, had little or nothing to

do with the status of white servants. "They became in the eyes of the law," J. B. McMaster said, "a slave and in both the civil and criminal codes were classed with the Negro and the Indian. They were worked hard, were dressed in the cast off clothes of their owners, and might be flogged as often as the master and mistress thought necessary." There is also the testimony of T. J. Wertenbaker, who said that "the indentured servants. . . were practically slaves, being bound to the soil and forced to obey implicitly those whom they served."

Working together in the same fields, sharing the same huts, the same situation, and the same grievances, the first black and white Americans, aristocrats excepted, developed strong bonds of sympathy and mutuality. They ran away together, played together and revolted together. They mated and married, siring a sizeable mixed population. In the process the black and white servants—the majority of the colonial population—created a racial wonderland that seems somehow un-American in its lack of obsession about race and color. There was, to be sure, prejudice then, but it was largely English class prejudice which was distributed without regard to race, creed or color. There were also, needless to say, prejudiced *individuals* in the colony, but—and this is the fundamental difference between prejudice and racism—their personal quirks and obsessions were not focused and directed by the organized will of a community. The basic division at that juncture was between servants and free people, and there were whites and blacks on both sides of the line.

Of all the improbable aspects of this situation, the oddest—to modern blacks and whites—is that white people did not seem to know that they were white. It appears from surviving evidence that the first white colonists had no concept of themselves as *white* people. The legal documents identified whites as Englishmen and/or Christians. The word *white*, with its burden of arrogance and biological pride, developed late in the century, as a direct result of slavery and the organized debasement of blacks. The same point can be made from the other side of the line. For a long time in colonial America, there was no legal name to focus white anxiety. The first blacks were called Blackamoors, Moors, Negers and Negars. The word *Negro*, a Spanish and Portuguese term for black, did not come into general use in Virginia until the latter part of the century.

A similar course of development was roughly characteristic of New York, where the black settlement preceded the English and the name *New York*. There are records from 1626 identifying eleven blacks—about 5 per cent of the non-Indian population—who were servants of the Dutch West Indian Company. The eleven black pioneers were males. Responding to the pleas of these males, the Dutch imported three women, identified as "Angolans," in 1628.

In 1644, some eighteen years after their arrival, the "Dutch Negroes," as they were called, filed a petition for freedom, the first black legal protest in America. The petition was granted by the Council of New Netherlands, which freed the blacks because they had "served the Company seventeen or eighteen years" and had been "long since promised their freedom on the same footing as other free people in New Netherlands." The eleven blacks cited in the petition were Paul d'Angola, Big Manuel, Little Manuel, Manuel de Gerrit de Rens, Simon Congo, Anthony Portuguese, Gracia, Peter Santome, John Francisco, Little Anthony and John Fort Orange. All received parcels of land in what is now Greenwich Village.

What is essential to grasp about the first blacks in New York is that they stood on the same footing as white indentured servants from the very beginning. "They had almost full freedom of motion and assembly," James Weldon Johnson wrote in *Black Manhattan*. "They were allowed to marry; wives and daughters had legal protection against the lechery of masters, and they had the right to acquire and hold property."

What has been outlined above with reference to New York and Virginia holds good also—though with minor variations—for other colonies, including Pennsylvania, where the system of black indentured servitude was so deeply rooted that black servants outnumbered black slaves at the time of the Revolution.

There are no accurate figures on the number of blacks who came to America in this period. In 1715, according to one estimate, there were 2,000 blacks and 96,000 whites in Massachusetts, 4,000 blacks and 27,000 whites in New York, 2,500 blacks and 45,800 whites in Pennsylvania, 9,500 blacks and 40,700 whites in Maryland, 23,000 blacks and 72,000 whites in Virginia, and 10,500 blacks and 6,250 whites in South Carolina.

Who were these blacks?

The answer is simple. They were Africans. This fact, as I said in *The Shaping of Black America*, is so big and obvious that it is easily overlooked or assumed without question. And yet it is the key to an understanding of the first *and* the tenth generation of African-Americans. *They were Africans*: that's the first fact. They were former citizens of states and principalities on the West Coast of Africa.

It is scarcely possible to understand the history of African-America unless we make at the least an effort to understand that fact and the further fact that the Africans brought their mind and ethos to America with them. The important point here is that the first generation of African-Americans were carriers of an African world view. They had ideas about social organization and the nature of the forces that controlled the universe. They also had technical skills, especially in the area of agriculture, which was well developed in Africa.

Although the black immigrants came from the same historical space and shared certain cultural and philosophical presuppositions, they were far from homogenous. Some came by way of Europe or the West Indies, and others came from different sections of Africa. Not only did they come from different countries and different kinship groups but they also spoke different languages. Most apparently were ordinary citizens, but some were warriors and some were from the highest ranks of African society. This fact was noted by a number of contemporary witnesses, including Hugh Jones, who said that Africans "that have been kings and great men [in their countries] are generally lazy, haughty, and obstinate." Discounting the obvious bias in that statement, it appears from this and other testimony that not a few "great men" were among the founding fathers of Black America. There is corroborative evidence on this point from John Josselyn, an English traveler who visited Samuel Maverick of Massachusetts in 1639 and made this observation:

> The second of October, about 9 of the clock in the morning, Mr. Mavericks Negro woman came to my chamber window, and in her own Countrey language and tune sang her very loud and shrill, going out to her, she used a great deal of respect towards me, and willingly would have expressed her grief in English; but I apprehended it by her countenance

and deportment, whereupon I repaired to my host, to learn of
him the cause, and intreat him in her behalf, for that I understood before, that she had been a Queen in her own Countrey, and observed a very humble and dutiful garb used
towards her by another Negro who was her maid. Mr.
Maverick was desirous to have a breed of Negroes, and
therefore seeing she would not yield by persuasions to company with a Negro young man he had in his use, he commanded him, wil'd she nill'd she, to go to bed with her, which
was no sooner done, but she kicked him out again, this she
took in high disdain beyond her slavery and this was the
cause of her grief.

In this anonymous queen from an unnamed country, we catch a
glimpse of the many people of differing ranks who were forced by
history to sing their "own Countrey language and tune" in a
strange land.

The dominant note in that tune from the seventeenth century to
the end of slavery was resistance to white oppression. An English
traveler named Edward Kimber said it was extremely difficult to
break the will and spirit of new black immigrants. "To be sure,"
he said, "a *new Negro*, if he must be broke, either from Obsti-
nacy, or, which I am more apt to suppose, from Greatness of
Soul, will require more hard Discipline than a young Spaniel; You
would really be surpriz'd at their Perseverance; let an hundred
Men shew him how to hoe, or drive a Wheelbarrow, he'll still take
the one by the Bottom, and the other by the Wheel; and they often
die before they can be conquer'd."

It was no less difficult to destroy the cultural heritage of Africans. This was manifested most notably in the widely reported
"feasts and burials" of colonial blacks. In 1680 the Virginia Assembly said that "the frequent meetings of considerable numbers
of Negroe slaves under pretence of feasts and burials is judged of
dangerous consequence." One of these funerals was witnessed
by Henry Knight, who said it was customary in that day for black
Virginians to "sing and dance and drink the dead to his new
home, which some believe to be in old Guinea."

Though the evidence is not as firm as one could wish, there are
indications that Africans hoped for more than a century that a
miracle would enable them to return to Africa. As the years went
by, with no sign of the intervention of African gods, many aban-

doned hope and began the long process of adapting themselves to a new situation.

The adaptation was made with a facility that gives point to Kenneth Stampp's observation that the first generation of blacks were as prepared for freedom as the tenth generation. In addition to the Virginia cases already cited, we might add the case of the black woman who became a member of a Dorchester, Massachusetts, church three years after her arrival on the *Desire*. By that time, 1641, there were at least forty black members of Bouweire Chapel in New Amsterdam. In the same year two Africans—Antony van Angola and Lucie d'Angola—were married in the Dutch church in New Amsterdam. These cases are instructive—as are several others—for the light they shed on the activities of the first generation of blacks, who were slowly and painfully shaping the foundations of the black family.

Not all blacks welcomed the newfangled rites. Large numbers, especially in the South, wooed and wed in feasts and weddings which synthesized African and European forms. An early instance of an improvised African-American wedding in North Carolina was reported by Thomas Brickell, who said, with some bias, that "their marriages are generally performed among themselves, there being very little ceremony used upon that Head; for the Man makes the Woman a Present, such as a Brass Ring or some other Toy, which she accepts of, becomes his wife. . . ."

Such was the system called into life by the establishment of European and African fragments on the American mainland. For at least forty years—until the 1660s—this system contained the seeds of at least four alternatives. Indentured servitude could have been continued for black and white servants or both groups could have been reduced to slavery. Other options were Indian slavery and a free labor system for blacks and whites, Indians and immigrants. Socioeconomic forces—a worldwide demand for sugar and tobacco and the development of capitalist planting techniques based on the use of gang labor—tilted the structure in the direction of black slavery.

To understand this fact in its fullness, we have to notice first that the rulers of the colonies were not overly scrupulous about the color or national origin of the work force. They tried Indian slavery, and they also tried to enslave white men and women.

When these attempts failed, the spotlight fell on Africans, who were tried and found not wanting. How explain this? The explanation is to be found in the situations that defined Africans and Europeans and Indians. Whites, to begin with, were under the protection of recognized governments: they could appeal to a monarch or to white public opinion. Whites, moreover, were white: they could escape and blend into the crowd. Indians, too, could escape: they knew the country and their brothers were only a hill or a forest away. The white rulers of the colonies also said and apparently believed that Indians tended to sicken and die under conditions of slavery.

Africans—from the standpoint of the colonial ruling class—did not have these disadvantages. They were strong: one African, the Spanish said, was worth four Indians. They were inexpensive: the same money that would buy an Irish or English servant for seven years would buy an African for life. They were visible: they could run, but they could not blend into the white crowd. Above all else, they were unprotected. And the supply, unlike the supply of Irishmen and Englishmen, seemed to be inexhaustible. The rulers of the colonies fell to thinking. Why not?

In the fateful sixties of the seventeenth century, the men who ran the colonies, egged on by the slave-trading royalists of London, made a decision that would lead, step by step, to the fateful sixties of the nineteenth century and the fateful sixties of the twentieth. Heedless of the consequences, these men decided to base the American economic system on human slavery organized around the distribution of melanin in human skin. Virginia and Maryland led the way, enacting laws in the 1660s that forbade intermarriage and made blacks slaves for life. Under the new dispensation, which was adopted with minor modifications by other colonies, children born of African women were ruled bond or free, according to the status of the mother.

Thus, white America and black America crossed a great divide. And white America, finding itself on the other side of that divide, found it necessary almost immediately to take two additional steps. The first was the creation of an ideology of racism that justified the subordination of blacks. The second, flowing with and out of the first, was the destruction of the bonds of community between black and white servants, who constituted the majority of the population.

Who was responsible for this policy?

The planters, the aristocrats, the parsons, the lawyers, the founding fathers—*the good people*: they sowed the seeds of the bitter harvest in a painful and protracted separation movement which continued for more than a century.

Astonishingly enough, the first rationalization for this policy was religion. Africans, it was said, were good material for slavery because they were "heathens." The limitations of this ideology were obvious to almost everyone. It was not permanent: people could become Christians. Since many black immigrants were already Christians, and since many more became Christians in the colonies, planters and planter ideologists set about to find a more enduring mark, something that could not be changed. But before this step could be taken, it was necessary to clear up certain theological difficulties. Was it not a sin to baptize slaves? This question was debated with passion, and the Scriptures were searched for supporting and dissenting opinions. Finally, to the surprise of almost no one, it was decided that it was a Christian duty to bring heathens into the fold of Christian civilization so their souls could be cleansed and whitened. Thus, in the end, God and profits were reconciled, as Virginia noted in its law of 1667: "The conferring of baptisme doth not alter the condition of the person as to his bondage or freedom." After that it was easy. A series of laws stripped black slaves of all rights of personality and made color a badge of servitude. The black population, which had grown slowly during the twilight interim of freedom, now lunged forward. In 1710 the number was fifty thousand. When the Declaration of Independence was signed, there were a half-million. When the Civil War opened, the twenty black seeds of Jamestown had become four million.

Where did these people come from?

How did they come?

Why did they come?

Most of the slaves came from an area bordering a 3,000-mile stretch on the West Coast of Africa. They came, chained two by two, left leg to right leg, from a thousand villages and towns. They came from many racial stocks and many tribes, from the spirited Hausas, the gentle Mandingos, the creative Yorubas, from the Ibos, Efiks and Krus, from the proud Fantins, the courageous Ashantis, the shrewd Dahomeans, the Binis and Sengalese. Some of these slaves were captured in African wars and sold to slave merchants, who sold them to Europeans. Many were kidnapped by Europeans and Africans. Some were sold into slavery for infractions of African laws.

Certain captives made forced marches of five hundred miles to the coast, where they were examined like cattle and packed into the holds of ships. They came, on these forced marches, across rivers and over mountains, barefooted and naked to their enemies, with chains on their ankles, burdens on their heads and fear in their hearts.

Were they — these people who gave to the world the black American—were they the dregs of society? No. The strong came and the weak, too. Priests, princes, warriors, merchants and nobles came. Slave traders said that it was not at all unusual for an African to sell an African today and to be captured and sold tomorrow. The story is told of a major slave merchant who sold a parcel of slaves and unwisely accepted a social drink to seal the transaction. One drink led to another—and to America. The slave merchant woke up the next morning with a hangover and a brand on his chest. He was in the hold of a slave ship with his victims and over him stood the captain, laughing to beat the band.

This story underlines a rather obvious fact: Africans as well as Europeans were involved in the slave trade. There has been a systematic attempt, however, to overemphasize the degree of African involvement. The picture of a whole continent of Africans kidnapping and selling one another for rum, guns and gewgaws is wide of the mark. It is true that some Africans, corrupted by Europe's insatiable desire for human flesh, sold their countrymen. But many Africans, like King Almmammy and Captain Tomba, loathed the whole business and forbade their subjects to take part in it. Thus, to cite only one example, Mani-Congo, the ruler of a Congo state, tried to end the trade in 1526. In a strong letter to John III of Portugal, he said "we need from [your] kingdoms no other than priests and people to teach in schools, and no other goods but wine and flour for the holy sacrament: that is why we beg of Your Highness to help and assist us in this matter, commanding the factors that they should send here neither merchants nor wares, because it is our will that in these kingdoms [of the Congo] there should not be any trade in slaves or markets for slaves." This would be a different world if Mani-Congo's plea for

"Point IV aid" had been heeded in the sixteenth century. But Europe was impervious to such pleas. She was only interested in the gold of black bodies, and she forced that obsession on Africa—to the undoing of both Europe and Africa.

European nations fought each other for the privilege of managing this trade. Portugal, which ran the first leg, was ousted by Holland which in turn surrendered supremacy on the African coast to France and England. Portugal, one trader said, "served for setting dogs to spring the game." Once the game was sprung, all Europe rushed to the playing field. Spain, barred from Africa by a papal bull which gave her most of the New World, made money by giving other powers a contract to supply her colonies with slaves. This contract, the infamous asiento, was the national status symbol of the day, indicating commercial and political supremacy. In the eighteenth century, when England held the asiento, the slave trade was the basis of European commerce, the cause of most of her wars and the prize politicians competed for.

An intricate set of trading arrangements existed on the Guinea Coast (the West Coast of Africa) for processing Africans bought and stolen. Europeans—French, Swedish, Danish, Portuguese, Dutch, English and Prussian traders—dotted the coast with a series of forts and factories. Each fort and factory had a dungeon or "Negroe House," where the slaves were confined until shipment. Into these factories Europeans poured a steady stream of goods—colorful cloth, trinkets, rum and "other strong water," blankets, old sheets—which were converted into human beings. Europeans, operating as representatives of powerful companies or as private entrepreneurs, bartered these goods for men and women. A woman might change hands for a gallon of brandy and six beads. A man might bring eight guns, a wicker bottle, two cases of whiskey and twenty-eight old sheets.

Slaves were purchased from brokers at the forts and factories or in open markets. An appalling report on conditions in these open markets has come down to us. "As the slaves come down to Fida from the inland country," trader John Barbot said, "they are put into a booth, or prison, built for that purpose, near the beach, all of them together; and when the Europeans are to receive them, they are brought out into a large plain, where the surgeons examine every part of every one of them, to the smallest member, men and women being all stark naked. Such as are allowed good and sound are set on one side, and the others by themselves; which slaves so rejected are there called Mackrons, being above thirty-five years of age, or defective in their limbs, eyes or teeth; or grown grey, or that have the venereal disease, or any other imperfection. These being so set aside, each of the others, which have passed as good, is marked on the breast, with a red-hot iron, imprinting the mark of the French, English or Dutch companies. . . . In this particular, care is taken that the women, as tenderest, be not burnt too hard."

The newly purchased slaves, properly branded and chained, were then rowed out to the slave ships for the dreaded Middle Passage across the Atlantic. They were packed like books on shelves into holds, which in some instances were no higher than eighteen inches. "They had not so much room," one captain said, "as a man in his coffin, either in length of breadth. It was impossible for them to turn or shift with any degree of ease." Here, for the six to ten weeks of the voyage, the slaves lived like animals. Under the best conditions, the trip was intolerable. When epidemics of dysentery or smallpox swept the ships, the trip was beyond endurance.

"On many of these ships," a contemporary said, "the sense of misery and suffocation was so terrible in the 'tween-decks— where the height sometimes was only eighteen inches, so that the unfortunate slaves could not turn round, were wedged immovably, in fact, and chained to the deck by the neck and legs—that the slaves not infrequently would go mad before dying or suffocating. In their frenzy some killed others in the hope of procuring more room to breathe. Men strangled those next to them, and women drove nails into each other's brains." It was common, John Newton said, to find a dead slave and a living slave chained together. So many dead people were thrown overboard on slavers that it was said that sharks picked up ships off the coast of Africa and followed them to America.

Not all blacks came this way. There was a trickle of free immigrants from the West Indies, and some blacks got on boats in Africa and paid their way to America. In 1772, for instance, the governor of Georgia issued a certificate to Fenda Lawrence, "a free black woman and heretofore a considerable trader in the river Gambia on the coast of Africa [who] hath voluntarily come to be and remain for some time in this province." The certificate gave Miss Lawrence permission to "pass and repass unmolested within the said province on her lawful and necessary occasions." Fenda Lawrence, of course, was an exception. Most blacks came in chains, followed by wise and greedy sharks.

The survivors of this gruelling ordeal were sold either on the ships or in slave markets in American ports. In New England, where there was a large "retail" demand, slaves were sold in taverns, stores and warehouses. They were also "shown," as the ads put in, in the homes of merchants. It was common for merchants to sell blacks and whites, liquor and clothing. A typical advertisement of the times indicates the general tendency: "Several Irish Maid Servants time/most of them for Five Years one/Irish Man Servant—one who is a good/Barber and Wiggmaker/also Four or Five Likely Negro Boys."

The price of men, like the price of butter, fluctuated. In 1754 George Washington bought a male slave for $260. But when he went to the market ten years later, he had to pay $285. Slaves were sold for small downpayments and "on reasonable terms." An advertisement of 1726 noted that "the Buyer shall have 3, 6, 9 or 12 months Credit." There was also a mail-order business. One New Englander made the following entry in his diary: "I wrote Mr. Salmon of Barbadoes to send me a negro."

The human factories in Africa struggled to keep up with the demand. In the eighteenth century between fifty thousand and one hundred thousand slaves crossed the Atlantic each year. The greatest number, by far, went to the West Indies and Brazil. At least two million were shipped to the West Indies. João Pandiá Calogeras, the Brazilian historian, said at least eighteen million were shipped to Brazil. Arthur Ramos, another Brazilian, thinks this figure is too high. Five million, he says, is a more accurate figure.

Large blocks of slaves were dropped off in Spanish colonies in the Caribbean and in Central and South America. As early as 1553 there were twenty thousand blacks in Mexico. Some two hundred thousand slaves were imported before slavery was abolished in Mexico in the first quarter of the nineteenth century.

Hundreds of thousands of slaves were scattered over the areas of present-day Panama, Colombia, Ecuador, Chile, Peru, and Venezuela. In 1810 Venezuela had some 500,000 blacks in a total population of 900,000. In 1847 there were 496,000 blacks and only 418,000 whites in Cuba. In the same year there were 4,400,000 blacks in Brazil's population of 7,360,000. More than 1,000,000 of the Brazilian blacks were free.

Because of widespread amalgamation and unreliable census data, it is difficult to assess the impact of these millions on South American life. But in some South American countries people with "Negro blood" still comprise a considerable proportion of the population. What Gilberto Freyre, the Brazilian sociologist and philosopher, said of Brazil is true for large areas of the New World: "Every Brazilian, even if he is light skinned and has fair hair, bears in his soul . . . the shadow or the mark of the native or the Negro. . . . The influence of the African is direct or vague and remote. In our way of expressing tenderness, in our excessive mimicry, in our Catholicism which is a delight of the senses, in our way of walking and talking, in the songs which cradled our childhood, in short in all the sincere expressions of our life, the Negro influence is patent."

For the human beings involved, the slave trade was a stupendous roulette wheel. The boats fanned out from Africa and scattered human freight over the Western Hemisphere. Around and around the wheel went, stopping here and there, sealing, wherever it stopped, the fate of mothers and fathers and their children to the nth generation.

It made a great deal of difference to the slaves where the dice of fate fell—whether they landed, for example, in a country where *the* word was the Spanish *yo* or the French *je* or the English *I*. Slavery, to be sure, was a form of hell wherever it existed. But there were gradations of hell, Dantesque circles, as it were, within circles. By all accounts, the British-Protestant colonies were the deepest pit. The French and Spanish could be cruel, and often were. But they did not seem to be driven by the same demons that pursued the Puritans. For this reason, among others, African religious practices and other elements of African culture were not as vigorously opposed in Roman Catholic colonies as they were in the Protestant colonies. The Protestant colonies, with an instinct for the jugular vein, rode herd on tom-toms and joyful noises unto the Lord. The difference this made in social cohesion is roughly the difference between the successful Haitian

Revolution and the abortive Nat Turner insurrection. The final meeting of the Haitian Revolution was held at a voodoo ceremony and the signal went out by tom-toms. Another difference, minor perhaps, but important to the people involved, was the texture of the different societies. The Catholic colonies were gay and colorful; the Protestant colonies, by comparison, were a dull shade of gray.

One of the dominant characteristics of the Roman Catholic colonies was the relative absence of color prejudice. One result was that the life of a slave in these colonies was less hopeless and unhappy than the life of a slave in, say, South Carolina. There were other differences—differences of style and structure—to add to this underlying difference of racial orientation. In Brazil, for example, there was a state officer, a protector of slaves, who looked after the welfare of the disadvantaged.

Manumission was easier in Brazil and Spanish America, and a manumitted slave inherited the rights and privileges of citizens. There were several ways in which a slave could win freedom in these colonies. If he earned his purchase price, he could walk up to his master and hand him the money—and the master had to accept it. Another means of salvation was childbearing. If slave parents had ten children in Hispanic America, the whole family was freed.

The difference between Hispanic America and Protestant America reduces itself, as so many racial problems do, to the problem of sex. The Spanish and Portuguese were willing to marry blacks. In America, white men drew the line—at marriage, that is.

Surface differences apart, slavery was a dirty business in both Hispanic and Protestant America. In both areas slaves were given a new conception of themselves—according to the different lights of their captors. This process, whether it took place in liberal Brazil or harsh South Carolina, was a painful, mind-reversing operation in which two or three out of every ten died. In one form or another, every slave from Africa went through this "breaking-in" period. During this period, which varied from one to three years, the slave was taught pidgin English or French or Spanish. He got a new name and began to look at himself and others in a different manner. Yahweh took the place of Olorum; Legba became St. Peter; the Mass or hymnal replaced African rituals* The strain was too much for tens of thousands, who died of old and new diseases and the shock of psychic mutilation. But millions of others, testifying to physical and spiritual strength that transcended the heroic, survived. And, surviving, they insured the survival—and prosperity—of America, which fashioned out of their misery the takeoff capital that made American capitalism possible. Many of the first great American fortunes, in fact, were founded on the slave trade and its allied industries. By the American Revolution, as Dr. Lorenzo J. Greene has shown, the slave trade "formed the very basis of the economic life of New England; about it revolved, and on it depended, most of her other industries."

The same situation obtained in England, France, Holland, Spain and Portugal. In these countries, as in New England, the slave trade provided direct returns to financiers and investors and stimulated the growth of ancillary industries, such as shipbuilding and distilleries.

"This contribution of the Negro," Eric Williams wrote, "has failed to receive adequate recognition. . . . England and France, Holland, Spain and Denmark, not to mention the United States, Brazil and other parts of South America are all indebted to Negro labor."

Africans helped build Liverpool, Nantes and Newport. They helped finance the Industrial Revolution. They helped clear the forest in America. They made these enormous contributions, but the price—to them and to American and European whites—was frightfully high, and it was not paid without protest. Protests began in Africa, where mutinies on ships were common, and continued in America, where revolts were common. "The Negroes," Captain Thomas Phillips said, "are so willful and loth to leave their own country, that they have often leap'd out of the canoes, boat and ship, into the sea, and kept under water till they were drowned, to avoid being taken up and saved by our boats,

---

*Melville J. Herskovits and other students have analyzed the process by which African slaves blended African and Western religious figures. In some cases Western saints and rituals were identified with African gods and rituals. Legba, the African trickster-god, was sometimes identified with St. Peter. Damballah, the snake god, was sometimes identified with St. Patrick. In some cases an African deity was given the name of a Roman Catholic saint as well as an African name.

which pursued them; they having a more dreadful apprehension of Barbadoes than we can have of hell, tho' in reality they live much better there than in their own country; but home is home, etc."

Home being home, etc., many slaves revolted, brained the captain and crew and escaped to the shore. Rebellions on ships were so common that a new form of insurance, insurrection insurance, was introduced.

Many slaves refused to eat when well and refused to take medicine when ill. One man, for instance, attempted to cut his throat. After the wound was sewed up, he ripped out the sutures with his fingernails. He was patched up again but refused to eat and died ten days later of starvation.

This resistance—desperate, doomed, definitive—continued throughout the slaving period. A long series of conspiracies and revolts culminated in the great Haitian Revolution, which played an important part in the abolition of the trade. Pushed by fear of the unmanageable slaves and pulled by humanitarian motives stemming from the American and French revolutions, politicians abolished the trade in the first decades of the nineteenth century. It continued surreptitiously, however, until the abolition of slavery in the United States.

The slave trade left a bloodstained legacy. During the four centuries the trade was pursued, it wrecked the social and economic life of Africa, set nation against nation and village against village. The trade was no less disastrous in Europe and America where it left a legacy of ill will and guilt and a potentially explosive racial problem.

"Raphael painted," W. E. B. Du Bois said, "Luther preached, Corneille wrote, and Milton sang; and through it all, for four hundred years, the dark captives wound to the sea amid the bleaching bones of the dead; for four hundred years the sharks followed the scurrying ships; for four hundred years America was strewn with the living and dying millions of a transplanted race; for four hundred years Ethiopia stretched forth her hands unto God."

3

The Founding of Black America

*The petition of A Great Number of Blackes detained
in a State of slavery in the Bowels of a free &
Christian Country Humbly sheweth that your
Petitioners apprehend that they have in Common
with all other men a Natural and Unaliable Right
to that freedom which the Great Parent of the
[Universe] hath Bestowed equalley on all menkind
and which they have Never forfeited by any Compact or agreement whatever. . . . They cannot but
express their Astonishment that It has [Never Been
Considered] that Every Principle from which
Amarica has Acted in the Cours of their unhappy
Dificulties with Great Briton Pleads Stronger than A
thousand arguments in favours of your petitioners.*

MASSACHUSETTS SLAVE PETITION, 1777

THE DAY was Thursday, April 12, 1787.
On that day — one month before the first
session of the U.S. Constitutional Convention
and two years before the election of George Washington — eight
men sat down in a room in Philadelphia and created a black social
compact. The compact, called the Free African Society, was a

prophetic step that marked a turning in the road that is critical to the history of Black America.

"How great a step this was," W. E. B. Du Bois wrote later, "we of to-day scarcely realize; we must remind ourselves that it was the first wavering step of a people toward organized social life."

The founding of this seminal organization was only one wave in a tide of institution-building that rolled over the North in the 1780s and 1790s. At the crest of that tide similar societies were formed in Boston, New York and Newport, Rhode Island. The flowing waves of these efforts were followed by an independent church movement, an independent lodge movement and the founding of black schools and cultural organizations.

The organizing energies of this effort flowed in concurrent waves, propelled by two powerful currents—one negative, the other positive. The positive current was a new sense of identity and peoplehood that rejected black subordination and exclusion. The negative current, flowing with and out of the white founding, was a campaign to exclude black Americans from the national social contract.

Outraged by this campaign and spurred on by a new image of black being, the founding fathers of Black America organized a movement of self-creation and self-definition that continued for more than forty years. There were no precedents and no models for what they were trying to do, and the pressure from all sides was almost overwhelming. Despite or perhaps because of these pressures, the movement continued; and by the turn of the century a new black polity was rooting in and expanding in the midst of the emerging white polity.

The founding of the black polity, which was a new thing, never before seen in the world, grew out of and reflected the ambiguities of the white founding. More than that, it was a direct result of the failures of the white founding fathers. To grasp its true significance, we must draw back for a moment and view it against the background of the American Revolution, which simultaneously and paradoxically produced a new nation and black and white fragments wedded to each other and to conflict by the terms of their common birth—terms that involved a contradiction between affirmation (equality) and reality (inequality). It was in the struggle surrounding the Revolution that the founders of Black America defined themselves and re-positioned themselves.

It was the failure of that Revolution—it was the realization that the makers of the Revolution didn't believe what they said—that forced Black America to create itself. In assessing that momentous event, it is important to keep in mind that the black creation accompanied the white creation but was not contained by it or defined by it. Like the countermelody in a great symphony, the black founding effort moved in the same time frame as the white melody, which it oftentimes contradicted and always challenged. This effort unfolded in roughly four stages.

The first stage began with the first act of the Revolution. When the white colonists, with incredible audacity, on July 4, 1776, issued a Declaration of Independence, blandly observing that all men were entitled to liberty, the slaves poured out their feelings in vehement protestation. Seemingly oblivious to the fact that the Declaration condemned them first of all and most of all, the colonists—slaveowner Thomas Jefferson foremost among them —scattered four revolutionary seeds to the four corners of the earth, saying:

1. That all men are created equal and are endowed by their Creator with natural and inalienable rights no man or government can bestow or take away.

2. That to secure these rights men create civil communities and civil authorities, who derive their just power from the consent of the governed.

3. That members of the community are colleagues and not subjects and that legitimate government consists in the dominion of equal laws applied equally—in the dominion, in short, of people over themselves and not in the dominion of communities over communities or groups over groups.

4. That when governments are destructive of these ends as evidenced by bad faith ("a long train of abuses and usurpations pursuing invariably the same object") it is the duty of citizens to alter or abolish these governments.

The crystallization of these ideas in the Declaration of Independence enclosed the white colonists in a net of their own making and made black freedom an inevitable corollary of white freedom. This became clear almost immediately to colonists like Thomas Paine and James Otis, who denounced both English tyranny and slaveowner tyranny. Paine said slavery was no less immoral than "murder, robbery, lewdness and barbarity" and urged Americans to "discontinue and renounce it, with grief and abhorrence." Rhetoric apart, this was substantially the same position of Abigail Adams, who told her husband, John, that "it always appeared a most iniquitous scheme to me to fight ourselves for what we are daily robbing and plundering from those who have as good a right to freedom as we have."

So it appeared also to blacks, who sprang into action, organizing the first phase of the black struggle for freedom. This phase began in the pre-Revolutionary War period and was pressed by slaves who brilliantly exploited the contradictions between colonial practice and colonial pretensions, calling for a declaration of independence *in* America. In the course of this struggle, which raged in Northern cities and on Southern plantations, the black soul expanded and made its first major probes into white territory. During this period of struggle and hope, blacks developed a concept of themselves as deprived citizens and dishonored native sons. Proceeding from this new self-concept, they invented techniques for demanding their rights within the bounds of the state, using the state, in fact, as a point of leverage. Their first technique, one that would reach full flower 188 years later, was legal contention. As early as 1766, Boston blacks filed a test case against slavery. The legal movement spread later to Connecticut and other colonies. Under the leadership of men whose names were not recorded, blacks collected money, hired lawyers and filed suits, asking for freedom and damages for unlawful detention in America.

Black patriots also experimented with mass pressure, holding meetings, circulating petitions and bombarding legislatures with pleas. Ingenious blacks found other ways to turn the revolutionary turmoil to their advantage. Certain blacks appropriated American slogans and assumed leadership roles in the agitation that forced an open break with England. Black patriots, for instance, were prominent in the tumultuous Stamp Act riots. One encounter—in 1765—was noted by author John Miller who said "the tension continued to increase, until, on the night of August 28, boys and Negroes began to build bonfires in King Street and blow the dreaded whistle and horn that sent the Boston mob swarming out of taverns, houses and garrets. A large crowd immediately gathered around the bonfires, bawling for 'Liberty and Property.'"

When, in 1768, British troops were dispatched to Boston to awe the population, they were repulsed by black and white patriots. Shortly after their arrival in September, 1768, the red-coated British troops fought a pitched battle with a largely black group on the Commons. The Boston *Journal of the Times* reported the incident, saying that the soldiers were "severely whipped," and adding: "To behold Britons scourged by Negro drummers was a new and very disagreeable spectacle."

The struggle between the British troops and black and white patriots continued almost uninterruptedly for the next year and reached a peak in Boston in the winter of 1770. During this struggle there were provocations on both sides and innumerable tavern fights and street brawls. One such incident involved three soldiers who got into a scrape with the ropemakers on Friday, March 2, 1770. The soldiers were driven off and returned with reinforcements, including a tall black man who apparently sided with the Redcoats. This infuriated a white Bostonian, who shouted: "You black rascal, what have you to do with white people's quarrels?" The black man replied, "I suppose I may look on." He looked on—and threw a few punches. Despite his help, the soldiers were forced to give ground. Battered and bruised, they stalked away, shouting curses and threats.

In the hours that followed, rumors and predictions of disaster swept the town. By Sunday night, March 4, Boston was boiling.

Monday morning dawned cold and grey. There was a film of ice on the ground. Toward evening the sky cleared and a young moon bobbled up over Beacon Hill. Lights and eerie shadows played over the streets, which were filled now with boys and men spoiling for a fight.

A little after eight, soldiers, armed with cudgels and tongs, emerged from Murray's Barracks near the center of town. To the surprise of almost no one, a crowd—composed largely, a hostile witness said, "of saucy boys, Negroes and mulattoes, Irish Teagues and outlandish Jack Tars"—gathered and traded insults with the soldiers. In the center of this crowd stood an imposing man who was no stranger to "white people's quarrels." His name was Crispus Attucks, and he was a Massachusetts native who had escaped from slavery and sailed the seas. Tall, brawny, with a look that "was enough to terrify any person," Attucks was well known around the docks in lower Boston. Needless to say, he was not a proper Bostonian, a fact that has pained innumerable historians. He was instead a proper rebel, a drifter, a man who loved freedom and knew what it was worth. He was about forty-seven on this memorable night, and he had that undefinable quality called presence. When he spoke, men listened. Where he commanded, men acted.

By a paradoxical act of poetic justice, it was this American—an oppressed American, born in slavery with, it is said, African and Indian genes—who carried the American standard in the prologue that laid the foundation of American freedom. It was Attucks, according to eyewitnesses, who shaped and dominated the action on the night of the event known to history as the Boston Massacre. When the Bostonians faltered, it was Attucks, according to almost all contemporary reports, who rallied them and urged them to stand their ground. The people, responding to his leadership, stood firm; so did the soldiers. The two sides exchanged insults, and a fight flared. Attucks, who seems to have been everywhere on this night, led a group of citizens who drove the soldiers back to the gate of the barracks. The soldiers rallied and drove the Boston crowd back. In the middle of this row, someone ran to the Old Brick Meeting House and rang the fire bell, filling the streets with frightened and excited people.

At this precise moment an incident occurred that probably changed the course of events. A barber's apprentice ran through the crowd holding his head and screaming, "Murder! Murder!" He told the people that the sentry in front of the customhouse had struck him across the head with a musket. The report angered the crowd, which moved now, in three groups, to the customhouse. The largest group, holding clubs over their heads, huzzaing and whistling, followed the lead of Crispus Attucks. John Adams, who later served as defense counsel for the British soldiers, told the court that a witness "saw the mulatto [Attucks] seven or eight minutes before the firing, at the head of twenty or thirty sailors in Cornhill, and he had a large cord-wood stick." Adams added:

"So that this Attucks, by this testimony of Bailey compared with that of Andrew and some others, appears to have undertaken to be the hero of the night; and to lead the army with banners, to form them in the first place in Dock Square, and march them up King Street with their clubs."

Regardless of what conservatives said about Attucks, it is a fact that the crowd followed him up King Street and gathered before the sentry in the square facing the customhouse. The barber's apprentice came up and said, "This is the soldier who knocked me down."

Someone said, "Kill him! Knock his head off!"

Another voice said, "Burn the sentry box. Tear it up."

Backing off, the frightened sentry climbed the steps of the customhouse and called for help. Down King (now State) Street came seven soldiers, clearing the way before them with bayonet thrusts. The soldiers made a half-circle around the sentry box and were joined by Captain Thomas Preston.

"Don't be afraid," Attucks and his group cried. "They dare not fire."

The people took up the cry.

"Fire! Fire and be damned!"

Attucks and the men following him gave three cheers and moved to the front of the crowd. A stick sailed over their heads and struck Pvt. Hugh Montgomery who fell back, lifted his musket and fired. The bullet hit Attucks, who pitched forward in the gutter. Samuel Gray made a step toward Attucks and another soldier fired, mortally wounding Gray. When the smoke cleared, several persons lay bleeding in the snow.

The die was cast.

"From that moment," Daniel Webster said later, "we may date the severance of the British Empire."

"On that night," John Adams said, "the foundation of American independence was laid."

One hundred and eighteen years later, in 1888, a handsome monument was erected to the five victims. Poet John Boyle O'Reilly contributed a spirited poem to the occasion:

> And honor to Crispus Attucks, who was leader and voice
>   that day:
> The first to defy, and the first to die, with Maverick, Carr
>   and Gray.
> Call it riot or revolution, or mob or crowd as you may,
> Such deaths have been seeds of nations, such lives shall be
>   honored for ay.

Author Samuel A. Green saw the hand of fate in this. "Attucks

Black patriots were conspicuous in the fighting at the Battle of Bunker Hill. Two blacks, Peter Salem and Salem Poor, were outstanding soldiers in the battle. Poor was later commended for his valor.

The Boston Massacre was one of the events which led to Revolutionary War. Several blacks were in the group which fought British soldiers on the night of March 5, 1770. Crispus Attucks (below, right) was the first martyr of the Revolution.

little thought," he wrote, "that in future generations a monument of granite and bronze on a public site would be erected in honor of himself and his comrades for the part they took in the State Street fight; and that his own name, cut in stone, would lead the list of those who fell on that eventful evening." Green added:

" 'Thus the whirligig of Time brings in his revenges,' and verifies the Gospel saying: 'But many that are first shall be last; and the last shall be first.' "

Having played a major role in precipitating the conflict, black patriots pushed to the front lines of the armed struggle, creating the second great wedge of the black offensive. In the forefront of this offensive were men with different perceptions and motivations. Some volunteered for service because they believed the Declaration meant what it said. Others, more cynical perhaps, certainly more realistic, entered American lines with the limited hope that the conflict would change their status and the status of their brothers and sisters. Individual motives apart, the immediate result of the second phase of the struggle was an intensification of the contradictions in the American effort and an enormous extension of the white debt to Black America.

This phase began with the shot heard around the world. When Paul Revere galloped through the Massachusetts countryside, he alerted black and white patriots. Black Minutemen, most notably Lemuel Haynes, Peter Salem and Pomp Blackman, were at Lexington and the bridge at Concord. Lemuel Haynes was also at Ticonderoga when Ethan Allen invoked Jehovah and the Continental Congress. So were Primas Black and Epheram Blackman, two members of the famous Green Mountain Boys.

When British troops stormed up Breed's Hill in the battle mistakenly called Bunker Hill, they were repulsed by black and white patriots. One of the heroes of that hot June afternoon was Peter Salem, who shot Major Pitcairn when he popped up and announced, a trifle prematurely, "The days is ours." Among the black soldiers who fought at the Battle of Bunker Hill were Pomp Fisk, Cuff Hayes, Caesar Dickerson, Caesar Weatherbee and Salem Poor. The two Salems—Peter Salem and Salem Poor—were among the great heroes of the war. Poor was later commended by fourteen officers who said he "behaved like an experienced officer, as well as an excellent soldier. To set forth particulars of his conduct would be tedious. . . . In the person of this said Negro centres a brave and gallant soldier."

The Battle of Bunker Hill was fought in June. In July George Washington took command of the American troops, and an order went out from his headquarters forbidding the enlistment of black patriots. Back of this order were two moving causes, one growing out of the air men breathed, the other flowing with the paradox that defined the white American position. The first, of course, was the racism that made high-ranking American officers doubt the fighting ability of slaves. The second, which contradicted the first, was a deep-seated fear of black involvement. One dimension of this all-pervading fear was the idea that it was dangerous to use black troops. If America used blacks, some officers reasoned, so would England.

The argument over this issue continued throughout the fall of 1775. The question was debated in Congress and in coffeehouses and manors. In October General Washington convened a high-level conference on the subject. It was decided finally to bar all blacks, slave and free. Washington issued an order to that effect on November 12, 1775.

By that time one important fact had changed the situation. Seven days before the Washington order, Lord Dunmore, the deposed royal governor of Virginia, had issued a proclamation offering freedom to all slaves who were willing and able to bear arms for England. The slave response was swift and instructive. To the consternation of American patriots, thousands of slaves, including some bondsmen of General Washington, left the plantations to fight for their freedom. What this meant militarily was spelled out at an encounter at Kemp's Landing in Virginia, where a band of former slaves proved their mettle by defeating a group of white Virginians. When the whites broke ranks and retreated into the swamps, the former slaves gave chase. There then occurred one of those little vignettes that illuminate a whole era. One Colonel Hutchings, a proper Virginian, was cornered by a black man he recognized as one of his escaped slaves. The indignant colonel fired at the former slave, but the bullet missed. The black rebel closed in and whacked his former master across the face with a saber. Then, in the greatest humiliation of all, Colonel Hutchings was led into the British lines by his own former slave.

Alarmed by the impact of the Dunmore proclamation, Virginians attempted to pacify their slaves. One newspaper ran a long editorial under the heading: "CAUTION TO NEGROES." Another newspaper, the *Virginia Gazette*, said: "Be not then, ye Negroes, tempted by this proclamation to ruin yourselves. . . . Whether we suffer or not, if you desert us, you most certainly will."

It quickly became apparent that this rhetoric was worse than useless, and General Washington reversed himself and permitted the enlistment of free blacks who had fought in the early battles. Congress approved this order but again refused to countenance the enlistment of slaves. Circumstances, however, made this a moot point. For one thing, it was very difficult to coax white men into the Continental Line. Although there were some one million men of fighting age in the colonies, the Continental Line never exceeded fifty thousand soldiers. Bounties of land and money were offered to volunteers. Some states even offered bounties of slaves. Nothing, however, flushed the colonial backsliders. "Such a dearth of public spirit," Washington said, "and want of virtue, such stock-jobbing and fertility in all the low arts to obtain advantage of one kind or another . . . I never saw before, and I pray God I may never be a witness to again. Such a dirty mercenary Spirit pervades the whole that I should not be at all surprised at any disaster that may happen." Washington went into the ordeal of Valley Forge in December, 1777, with some nine thousand men. By March of 1778 more than three thousand American soldiers had deserted.

After Valley Forge every able-bodied man, black or white, slave or free, was welcome in the Continental Army. Washington sent an officer from Valley Forge in 1778 to ask the Rhode Island Assembly to authorize the enlistment of slaves. In February the Assembly took this precedent-shattering step. Two months later Massachusetts followed suit. By the end of the war some five thousand blacks, slaves and free men, had shouldered arms in defense of American liberty. There were black soldiers from all of the original thirteen states, including South Carolina and Georgia. Most of these soldiers served in integrated units, although there were some all-black units. A black soldier named Colonel Middleton commanded a company of black volunteers from Massachusetts.

Several witnesses remarked on the integrated character of the

American army. In the first months of the war, British writers
taunted Americans with this jingle:

> The rebel clowns, oh! what a sight
> Too awkward was their figure
> 'Twas yonder stood a pious wight
> And here and there a nigger.

A Southern soldier serving in the army around Boston wrote in
a letter of September, 1775: "Such Sermons, such Negroes, such
Colonels, such Boys and such Great Great Grandfathers." Two
years later a Hessian officer noted that "the Negro can take the
field instead of the master; and therefore, no regiment is to be
seen in which there are not Negroes in abundance, and among
them there are able bodied, strong and brave fellows." Black
soldiers also served as drummers and fifers in several Revolutionary War units, although this fact is ignored in the widely
disseminated pictures of the Spirit of '76.

Black soldiers fought in practically all of the big battles of the
war. They were at Monmouth, Red Bank, Saratoga, Savannah,
Princeton and Yorktown. Two blacks, Prince Whipple and Oliver
Cromwell, made the famous Delaware Crossing. Another black
participated in the capture of General Prescott in Rhode Island.

By almost all accounts, black soldiers were among the most
valiant defenders of the Revolution. One of the most memorable
tableaux of the war came from the bloody battlefield at Eutaw,
South Carolina, where a black soldier and a British soldier were
found dead, each impaled on the bayonet of the other. At the
Battle of Rhode Island, a regiment of black soldiers repulsed the
vaunted Hessians three times.

"Had they been unfaithful," one soldier said, "or even given
away before the enemy all would have been lost."

The story was very much the same at Fort Griswold in Connecticut. When the British officer, Maj. William Montgomery,
was lifted over the walls, Jordan Freeman ran him through with a
pike. When Col. William Ledyard was killed with his own sword,
Lambert Latham immediately avenged his death by slaying the
British officer. The Redcoats pounced on Latham, who fell dead,
pierced by thirty-three bayonet wounds.

Black patriots also distinguished themselves in the American
navy. Caesar Terront piloted the Virginia vessel, the *Patriot*,

and was cited for his gallantry in action. Captain Mark Starlin, the first black naval captain in Virginia's history, made daring night raids on British vessels in Hampton Roads. After the war Starlin was reclaimed by his master and died in slavery.

American forces also used black spies and undercover agents. A slave named Pompey was largely responsible for Anthony Wayne's capture of the Stony Point, New York, fort in 1779. Feigning ignorance, he obtained the British password and helped a detachment of Americans overpower the British lookout. Pompey was one individualist; a very different one was James Armistead, who helped trap Gen. Charles Cornwallis. Gen. Marcus de Lafayette told Armistead to infiltrate Cornwallis's camp and learn his strength and battle plans. Armistead was so successful that Gen. Cornwallis asked him to spy on Lafayette. The black spy shuttled between the British and American camps, carrying false information to the Cornwallis camp and bona fide information to Lafayette.

Every schoolboy knows that Lafayette and Kosciusko answered America's call for help. Not so well known is the fact that blacks from Haiti came to America to fight. The Haitians, called the Fontages Legion, were in the front ranks at the siege of Savannah and helped prevent a rout of the American forces.

While thousands of Haitian and American blacks were pressing the American cause, other blacks, no less courageous, were pursuing the same objective—black freedom—in the ranks of the British army. Lord Dunmore and other British commanders issued open-ended invitations, and thousands of American slaves, including certain slaves of the white founding fathers, abandoned the plantations and picked up guns and picks in defense of the British cause. Some of these soldiers participated in major battles, but most were confined to labor details and many, if we can credit contemporary reports, were abused and betrayed by their British colleagues. Even with these drawbacks, the British army offered many blacks, especially Southern slaves, opportunities denied them by American patriots. It is well worth noting that some twenty thousand blacks, four times as many as served in the American army, embarked with the British troops when they left American ports in 1782 and 1783. The descendants of some of these soldiers later played key roles in the founding of the African country of Sierra Leone.

There was still another front in this war, and it was perhaps the largest front of all for black Americans. Fighting on this front, which constituted the fourth phase of the black war, tens of thousands of slaves maneuvered between the contending forces in generally successful attempts to achieve their own freedom. By the end of the war, more than one hundred thousand slaves, according to some authorities, had freed themselves by escaping to Canada, Spanish Florida and the Indian camps.

Not all fugitive slaves left the country. Sizeable numbers hid in the swamps and staged guerilla raids on slavemasters. In 1781 a Virginia slaveholder told a correspondent that "we have had most alarming times this summer, all along the shore, from a set of Barges manned mostly by our own Negroes who have run off— These fellows are really dangerous to an individual singled out for their vengeance whose Property lay exposed.—They burnt several houses." As late as 1786 a group of former slaves who called themselves the King of England's Soldiers were fighting guerilla actions against slaveowners along the Savannah River in Georgia and South Carolina.

To all this lastly must be added the thousands who were manumitted by slaveholders infected by the germinal ideas of the Declaration. In one characteristic transaction, Philip Graham of Maryland freed his slaves and said the holding of his "fellow men in bondage and slavery is repugnant to the golden law of God and the unalienable right of mankind as well as to every principle of the late glorious revolution which has taken place in America." Similar words came from Richard Randolph, brother of John Randolph, who wrote the following letter to his guardian: "With regard to the division of the estate, I have only to say that I want not a single Negro for any other purpose than his immediate liberation. I consider every individual thus unshackled as the source of future generations, not to say nations, of freedmen; and I shudder when I think that so insignificant an animal as I am is invested with this monstrous, this horrid power." Randolph, of course, was an exception, but his act and the words undergirding his act pointed to one of the powerful currents of the time.

Slavery in the North died as a direct result of these currents. The Northern emancipation process, prodded and shaped by black and white patriots, began in 1777, at the height of the revolutionary struggle, when Vermont, responding to the Rights

of Man ideology, became the first American state to abolish
slavery. Moved by like sentiments, and pressure from black and
white rebels, Northern states, one after another, followed Vermont's lead. In some of these states, notably New York and
Pennsylvania, legislative emancipation was a gradual process
that extended over several years. The preamble of the Pennsylvania act of 1780 accurately reflected the spirit of the age, saying
it was the duty of Pennsylvanians to give proof of their gratitude
for deliverance from the oppression of Great Britain "by extending freedom to those of a different color by the work of the same
Almighty hand."

With the founding of the American commonwealth and the emancipation of Northern slaves, Black America entered that phase of
its history that I have called elsewhere the Black Pioneer period.
There was no consensus at that point on the place of blacks in a
commonwealth founded on the inalienable rights of all men. It
was apparent to most people that the Declaration had created a
new situation, but few believed that the new social compact included blacks or Indians or even white women. For all that, there
was a provocative fluidity to the first years of the American venture. There was, to be sure, an undercurrent of racism, but
people seemed to be uncertain about its meaning and use in a new
climate governed by the egalitarian ideals of the Declaration of
Independence.

During this interesting interim period, blacks like Josiah
Bishop of Virginia and Lemuel Haynes of New England pastored
white churches, and the Baptist and Methodist denominations
strongly condemned slavery. In the same period Phillis Wheatley
became an internationally known poet, and Benjamin Banneker
became a celebrated mathematician. Banneker and Wheatley, in
different ways and in different places, dramatized the possibilities and limitations of the age. In an age in which few
women—or men for that matter—read books, Phillis Wheatley
wrote one. Her book, *Poems on Various Subjects, Religious and
Moral*, was the first volume by a black woman and the second
book by an American woman.*

---

*Jupiter Hammon, a New York slave, was probably the first black author. His
poem, *An Evening Thought: Salvation by Christ, with Penetential Cries*, was
printed as a broadside in 1760.

The pioneer American poet did not write as a *black* American; she wrote as an eighteenth-century Bostonian, a *proper* eighteenth-century Bostonian. When Washington was appointed commander in chief of the American army, she celebrated the event in herioc couplets. Washington was delighted and acknowledged receipt of the poems in a February 28, 1776, letter addressed to "Miss Phillis":

> I thank you most sincerely for your polite notice of me, in the elegant lines you enclosed; and however undeserving I may be of such encomium and panegyric, the style and manner exhibited a striking proof of your poetical talents; in honor of which, and as a tribute justly due to you, I would have published the poem, had I not been apprehensive that, while I only meant to give the world this new instance of your genius, I might have incurred the imputation of vanity.

According to Benson Lossing, the poet visited Washington at Cambridge and was entertained by the general and his staff.

Above everything else, the Boston poet sang songs of thanksgiving. She was grateful for the gift of Christianity, grateful even that a slave ship brought her to it:

> *'Twas mercy brought me from my* Pagan *land,*
> *Taught my benighted soul to understand*
> *That there's a God, that there's a* Saviour *too:*
> *Once I redemption neither sought nor knew.*

A delicate wisp of a woman, black, slight of build, with great glimmering eyes, Phillis Wheatley was born in Africa in an unknown place. She came to America in 1761, remembering nothing save that her mother poured out water each morning "before the sun at its rising." She was seven or eight when the slave ship deposited her in Boston. John Wheatley, a rich merchant and tailor, saw her shivering on a Boston slave block, stark naked except for a dirty piece of carpet around her loins. Wheatley bought the young girl and took her home to his wife, Susannah. Within sixteen months the slave girl was reading and writing fluent English. She read every book she could lay hands on: the Bible, Milton and Alexander Pope's translation of Homer. Pope, the neoclassic Englishman, was her special favorite. Timidly at first and then with increasing confidence, she put down words in

With Washington when he crossed the Delaware were at least two blacks, Prince Whipple and Oliver Cromwell. Whipple was a bodyguard to Washington's aide, General William Whipple of New Hampshire.

Richard Allen, Phillis Wheatley, and Prince Hall were outstanding blacks in the Black Pioneer period. Allen organized the AME Church. Wheatley became an internationally known poet. Hall (right) organized the first black Masonic lodge.

the Pope manner. Within six years after her arrival in America, she was writing poetry. Her first poem, written at the age of fourteen, was a blank verse eulogy of Harvard University. In 1773 she visited England and was hailed as a prodigy. An English publisher brought out her slim volume.

Her poems do not excite modern critics. The verdict is practically unanimous: too much Pope and not enough Wheatley. But her ease with words, her genius for sound and color and rhythm: these still excite awe and wonder.

Phillis Wheatley lived in the State Street house with the white Wheatleys and moved in a white world, apparently as an equal. When her patron, Susannah Wheatley, died, the poet came face to face with racial reality. She married John Peters, a handsome grocer who "wore a wig, carried a cane, and quite acted out '*the gentleman*.'" The marriage didn't work. Proud and, some say, irresponsible, Peters alienated his wife's white friends. The couple drifted from place to place, carrying with them the first child and then the second child. Poverty and disease dogged them; the first child died and then the second. After the birth of a third child, the poet was reduced to earning her bread in a mean boarding house. She had never been physically strong and the exertion and the cold and the wretchedness were too much for her. On a cold day in December, 1784, mother and child died within a few hours of each other.

Phillis Wheatley said nothing of her personal griefs in her poems that survive; nor did she say much about the trials and tribulations of blacks. But on at least one occasion she abandoned Pope and Homer and said words from a woman's heart.

The poem was to the Earl of Dartmouth:

> *Should you, my lord, while you peruse my song,*
> *Wonder from whence my love of* Freedom *sprung,*
> *Whence flow these wishes for the common good,*
> *By feeling hearts alone best understood,*
> *I, young in life, by seeming cruel fate*
> *Was snatch'd from* Afric's *fancy'd happy seat:*
> *What pangs excruciating must molest,*
> *What sorrows labour in my parent's breast?*
> *Steel'd was that soul and by no misery mov'd*
> *That from a father seiz'd his babe belov'd:*
> *Such, such my case. And can I then but pray*
> *Others may never feel tyrannic sway?*

Benjamin Banneker, like Phillis Wheatley, was a child of an age of birth pains. He was born in Maryland, the grandson of an Englishwoman and an African native. His grandmother, Molly Welsh, came to America as an indentured servant, worked her time out and bought a farm and two slaves. She later freed the slaves and married one of them. Banneker's mother, Mary, was one of four children born to this union and she, too, married an African native.

Banneker attended a local school with black and white children. Like Phillis Wheatley, he hungered and thirsted after books. His forte, however, was mathematics and astronomy. He became so proficient in these subjects that he was named to the commission which made the original survey of Washington, D.C. The Georgetown *Weekly Ledger* of March 12, 1791, noted the arrival of the commission. Banneker, the paper said, was "an Ethiopian whose abilities as surveyor and astronomer already prove that Mr. [Thomas] Jefferson's concluding that that race of men were void of mental endowment was without foundation." Beginning in 1792, Banneker issued an annual almanac which has been compared with Benjamin Franklin's *Poor Richard's Almanac*. He also continued the study of astronomy, mathematics and other scientific subjects.

Banneker lived on a farm about ten miles outside Baltimore. A confirmed bachelor, he studied all night, slept in the morning and worked in the afternoon. He washed his own clothes, cooked his own meals and cultivated gardens around his log cabin. He had an early fondness for "strong drink" but later became a teetotaler. His habits of study were odd, to say the least. Local annalists said he wrapped himself in a great cloak at night and lay under a pear tree and meditated on the revolutions of the heavenly bodies. According to these reports, he remained there throughout the night and went to bed at dawn.

A contemporary left a portrait of the stargazer. "His head was covered with a thick suit of white hair, which gave him a very dignified and venerable appearance. . . . His dress was uniformly of superfine broadcloth, made in the old style of a plain coat, with straight collar and long waistcoat, and a broad-brimmed hat. His color was not jet-black, but decidedly Negro. In size and personal appearance, the statue of Franklin at the Library of Philadelphia, as seen from the street, is a perfect likeness. Go to his house when you would, either by day or night, there was constantly standing in the middle of the floor a large table covered with books and papers. As he was an eminent mathematician, he was constantly in correspondence with other mathematicians in this country, with whom there was an interchange of questions of difficult solution."

Banneker, unlike Wheatley, lashed out at the injustices of the age. In a famous letter of 1791 he told Thomas Jefferson that words were one thing and slavery was another: "Suffer me to recall to your mind that time, in which the arms of the British crown were exerted, with every powerful effort, in order to reduce you to a state of servitude; look back, I entreat you . . . You were then impressed with proper ideas of the great violation of liberty, and the free possession of those blessings, to which you were entitled by nature; but, sir, how pitiable is it to reflect, that although you were so fully convinced of the benevolence of the Father of Mankind, and of his equal and impartial distribution of these rights and privileges which he hath conferred upon them, that you should at the same time counteract his mercies, in detaining by fraud and violence, so numerous a part of my brethren under groaning captivity and cruel oppression, that you should at the same time be found guilty of that most criminal act, which you professedly detested in others."

Banneker, like Wheatley, was a metaphor of the limitations and possibilities of the burgeoning American Dream. To be sure, as Banneker's letter indicates, things were far from rosy in this period. But some blacks, a very few blacks, had room to dream and dare and hope. Then the roof caved in. When did this happen? No one can say. It happened at different times in different ways at different places. In Boston and New York City free blacks were insulted and assaulted on the streets. In the South slaveowners elaborated new laws and rules which were designed to deny blacks every right of personality.

There were many reasons for this. One of the triggering mechanisms was a machine, the cotton gin, which cooled the ardor of patriots and made slave-grown cotton a national mania. A second factor was the wave of reaction that rolled over America after Shays's Rebellion and the French and Haitian revolutions. A further contributing cause was the sharp rise in the number of free blacks and the failure of various plans to get rid of them.

The Haitian Revolution, the invention of the cotton gin, slave conspiracies in America, the increase in the number of free blacks, and a rising tide of mercantilist greed—this combination of facts and circumstances created the conservative reaction which forced blacks North and South to look around them and ask the question of the Hebrew poet of captivity: "How shall we sing the Lord's song in a strange land?"

How indeed? And which Lord?

These questions gave rise to thought and to Black America or, to be more precise, African-America, for all of the first black institutions bore the interesting prefix—African. Rebuffed, insulted, incessantly villified, postwar blacks turned inward and formed their own social institutions and, in the process, created themselves.

This act of self-generation created a community out of a collectivity of isolated individuals. When the process started, in the late 1780s, there were 757,000 black individuals in America—697,000 slaves and 59,000 free blacks. Almost all of the slaves—92 per cent—lived in the South. The free population, in sharp contrast, was concentrated in the Northeast and revolved around two competing centers of black power and creativity—New York and Philadelphia. Although free blacks in these Northern centers gave institutional form to Black America, they worked from a matrix created by the mass of maintaining slaves. More to the point, most of the free black leaders were former slaves.

In this period, as in the nineteenth century, most free blacks were confined by racism to low-paying jobs; and most of them lived, for the same reason, in cellars and shanties on narrow streets. But even at that early date there were black artisans and merchants who lived in comfortable surroundings. It is to be observed, too, that certain of these merchants and artisans operated in the mainstream of money. One could see examples of this all over the North in the Black Pioneer period. Specifically, there was the case of Emanuel and Mary Bernoon who opened the first oyster and ale house in Providence, Rhode Island, in 1736 and reportedly had one of the largest businesses in that city. Bernoon, according to Dr. Lorenzo J. Greene, was the model for the band of black caterers who dominated the catering industry in several cities for more than a century. But Bernoon is only one case in point. In New York City, in the same period, Samuel Fraunces

operated Fraunces's Tavern, one of the major social centers of
the East. It was in his restaurant in 1768 that the New York
Chamber of Commerce was organized. Significantly and ironically, George Washington said farewell to his officers at the end
of the Revolutionary War in rooms provided by this pioneer black
businessman. Fraunces and Bernoon were only the most dramatic examples of the emerging artisan-merchant class. Throughout these early years black artisans and merchants held commanding positions in Eastern cities. Between 1790 and 1820,
according to Du Bois (*The Philadelphia Negro*), "a very large
portion, and perhaps most" of the artisans of Philadelphia were
black.

In that day, as in this one, there were systematic attempts to
undermine black artisans and merchants. This disturbed a
number of witnesses, including a French traveler named Brissot
de Warville. "Those Negroes who keep shops," he said, "live
moderately, and never augment their business beyond a certain
point. The reason is obvious; the whites . . . like not to give them
credit to enable them to undertake any extensive commerce nor
even to give them the means of a common education by receiving
them into their counting houses."

Despite these pressures, certain blacks managed to reach the
top ranks in their fields. One such entrepreneur was James Forten, who invented and patented a device for handling sails and
became one of the major sailmakers in Philadelphia. Another
major entrepreneur was Paul Cuffe, the ship captain and ship
builder. In 1797 Cuffe built a wharf and warehouse on the
Westport River in Massachusetts. By 1806 he owned one ship,
two brigs and several smaller vessels. For many years he commanded black crews, making voyages to Europe, Russia, Africa
and the West Indies.

Concurrently with the elaboration of businessmen like Paul
Cuffe there was a parallel development in the cultural field.
Slowly before the war but with remarkable acceleration thereafter, black intellectuals emerged from the masses; and by 1780
there were at least four recognizable types in the black community. The first type, symbolized most notably by Jupiter Hammon,
defected and went over to the enemy, astounding and delighting
them by producing intellectual products that objectively buttressed their world view. The second type—Phillis Wheatley was

an example—offered no direct challenge to the system but subtly challenged its premises by the authority of their work which was, like all works of art, an appeal to freedom. The third category found its voice in the anonymous Othello,* who directly and militantly challenged the intellectual and cultural premises of the white dispensation. Less militant but no less direct was the fourth category of intellectuals, composed of men like Richard Allen and Absalom Jones, who spoke in muted tones but created big sticks of organization.

From these different strata, from the artisans and merchants and intellectuals, and from the great mass of maintaining laborers and slaves, came the founding fathers and mothers of African-America.

This group included Richard Allen and Absalom Jones and thousands of laborers and former slaves who have disappeared from a record that still vibrates with their presence.

Of these men and women—that is to say, of the known men and women—at least twenty-one should be starred for the record: Richard Allen, cofounder of the Free African Society, pioneer bishop of the African Methodist Episcopal (AME) Church, and first president of a national black convention; Absalom Jones, cofounder of the Free African Society, protest leader, and founder of one of the first black churches in the North; Prince Hall, founder of the first black Masonic lodge and protest leader; George Liele, founder-pastor of a pioneer black Baptist church; Andrew Bryan, founder-pastor of a pioneer black Baptist church; Phillis Wheatley, poet; James Forten, industrialist and protest leader; Benjamin Banneker, astronomer, mathematician, protest leader; Jean Baptiste Pointe DuSable, leader in the Westward movement and founder of Chicago; Peter Williams Sr., cofounder of the African Methodist Episcopal Zion Church; James Varick, first bishop of the African Methodist Episcopal Zion Church; Paul Cuffe, ship captain and African colonizationist; William Whipper, protest leader and magazine editor; Austin Steward, merchant and protest leader; Abraham Shadd, protest leader;

---

*In 1788, an anonymous writer who called himself "Othello" published a slashing antislavery essay which denounced white Americans for betraying the principles of the Revolution. "So flagitious a violation," he wrote, "can never escape the notice of a just Creator, whose vengeance may be now on the wing, to disseminate and hurl the arrows of destruction."

Dr. James Derham, pioneer black physician; Samuel E. Cornish, Presbyterian minister and cofounder of the black press; John B. Russwurm, cofounder of the black press; Daniel Coker, cofounder of the AME church; David Ruggles, protest leader, and founder of the first black magazine; and Nathaniel Paul, pioneer black Baptist minister.

It was these men and women, working with thousands of unsung laborers and protestants, who laid the cornerstones and created the first tiers of the emerging structure of Black America.

The first step in that process, as we have seen, was the founding of the Free African Society by eight black pioneers: Absalom Jones, Richard Allen, Samuel Boston, Joseph Johnson, Cato Freeman, Caesar Cranchell, James Potter, and William White. The organization founded by these men was a church, a mutual aid society and an embryonic political cell. It also contained the germinal concept of the black insurance company.

The same archetypal figures and the same issues dominated the racial dialogue in other cities; and within a short time similar organizations were established in other Northern centers with large black populations. The leaders of these societies quickly established a correspondence network that linked—and identified and shaped—Black America for the first time. The creation of this network was a formative experience for pioneer black leaders. Through the medium of these organizations, blacks exchanged information, ideas and programs. More importantly, they began to see their lives in a time-line extending from Africa to the Day of Judgement they believed would vindicate them.*

The second step on the road to Black America—and the second tier of the structure of Black America—was the independent black church movement, which started in the late 1770s with the founding of the first African Baptist churches in South Carolina, Virginia and Georgia by pioneer black ministers like Andrew Bryan and George Liele. This movement continued unabatedly throughout the war and reached a peak in postwar Philadelphia with the first public demonstration against Jim Crow. The demonstration occurred at St. George's Methodist Episcopal Church at Fourth and Vine in the year of the founding of the Free African

*The Shaping of Black America

Society. When, in November of that year, a group of black wor-
shippers, composed largely of members of the Free African Society, were pulled from their knees during prayer, they stood up,
without a word, and filed out of the church in a body. Looking
back on that pivotal moment many years later, Richard Allen
said:

"A number of us usually attended St. George's church in
Fourth street; and when the colored people began to get numerous in attending the church, they moved us from the seats we
usually sat on, and placed us around the wall, and on Sabbath
morning we went to church and the sexton stood at the door, and
told us to go in the gallery. . . . We expected to take the seats
over the ones we formerly occupied below, not knowing any better. . . . Meeting had begun and they were nearly done singing
and just as we got to the seats, the leader said, 'Let us pray.' We
had not been long upon our knees before I heard considerable
scuffling and low talking. I raised my head up and saw one of the
trustees . . . having hold of the Rev. Absalom Jones, pulling him
up off his knees, and saying, 'You must get up—you must not
kneel here.' Mr. Jones replied, 'Wait until the prayer is over.'
[The trustee] said, 'No, you must get up now, or I will call for aid
and force you away.' Mr. Jones said, 'Wait until prayer is over,
and I will get up and trouble you no more.' With that [the trustee]
beckoned to one of the other trustees . . . to come to his assis-
tance. He came, and went to William White to pull him up. By
this time prayer was over, and we all went out of the church in a
body, and they were no more plagued with us in the church."

By withdrawing from the white Methodist church, the band of
protestants affirmed the new forces moving within them. But the
withdrawal raised large questions of identity, which were discussed at several heated meetings of the Free African Society.
Certain members of the society suggested affiliation with the
Quakers, while others held out for an entente with the Episcopa-
lians or Methodists. Behind this debate was another question:
What relation, if any, should blacks have with white institutions?

After a protracted and somewhat acrimonious debate, the Free
African Society split into two groups. The larger group followed
Absalom Jones, an affable, easy-going former slave, into the
Episcopal church. In 1794 the African Church of St. Thomas was

erected in Philadelphia and eleven words were engraved in the vestibule: "The People Who Walked in Darkness Have Seen a Great Light."

But had they—really?

Richard Allen didn't think so. The new black communicants were denied full status in the Episcopal church and were barred from annual conferences and governing boards. This, to Allen, was rank discrimination. He demanded full rights in a white church, if possible, and in a black church, if necessary. In his mind, in an unmanifested seed state, was an image of *Negritude*, of Negro being and becoming.

Who was Allen?

He was a former slave who started his career with an act of extraordinary symbolic significance: the conversion of his master. Shrewd and hardworking, Allen accumulated enough money to buy his freedom and migrated to Philadelphia. After the split in the Free African Society, he formed an independent black Methodist church. In 1816 he became the first bishop of the African Methodist Episcopal Church, the first national organization created by blacks. During the whole of this period, according to contemporary witnesses, his house was never shut "against the friendless, homeless, penniless fugitive from the house of bondage." So persuasive was Allen's image, so dynamic was his example, that author Vernon Loggin nominated him for the title of "Father of the Negro." A second and independent nomination came from historian John W. Cromwell, who said Allen had "greater influence upon the colored people of the North than any other man of his times."

Men and women made in Allen's image dominated the second phase of the Black Pioneer period, creating a tier of independent black churches that spanned the North. In 1821 leading black Methodists, James Varick in particular, organized another national organization, the African Methodist Episcopal Zion Church. By 1830 there were black churches of almost every conceivable description, including an Ethiopian Church of Jesus Christ in Savannah, Georgia, and a black Dutch Reformed Church in New York City.

On the foundation of these churches rose a third tier of social and fraternal organizations. The leading spirit in this movement was Prince Hall, a leather-dresser and Revolutionary War veteran who organized the first black Masonic lodge. Like Richard Allen, like Absalom Jones, like all leaders of the period, Prince Hall tried first to enter white American institutions. Rebuffed on this front, he turned to England and was granted a charter by the Grand Lodge of England. On May 6, 1787, African Lodge No. 459 was formally organized in Boston with Hall as Master. In 1797 Hall helped organize lodges in Philadelphia and Providence, Rhode Island, thereby becoming a pioneer in the development of black interstate organizations.

While Hall and other leaders were pressing forward on this level, they were at the same time creating the fourth tier of the Black American structure, the perennial movement for equal rights. From the beginning that movement was based on internal development and external protest. In succeeding years different protest leaders would emphasize different dimensions of this concept. Booker T. Washington, for example, would make an artificial distinction between external protest and internal development. But in the beginning black leaders articulated a total concept, involving a double and reciprocal struggle *for* black development and *against* white restrictions on that development.

True to their rhetoric, these leaders founded black schools and organized the social capital of the community. A major leader in this effort, as in so many others, was Richard Allen, who opened a day school for children and a night school for adults in Bethel AME Church in Philadelphia. In Boston, in the same decade, Prince Hall opened a school for black children in his home. This movement was supported by Quakers like Anthony Benezet, who organized a black school in Philadelphia, and the New York Manumission Society, which organized the famous Free African Schools of New York City. According to some authorities, the opening of the first African Free School in November, 1787, marked the beginning of free secular education in New York.

All the while, on another level of existence, black leaders were pressing an increasingly sophisticated campaign against discrimination and segregation. In a 1794 pamphlet Richard Allen and Absalom Jones attacked slavery and its Northern twin, bigotry. Six years later Jones and other Philadelphians sent an antislavery petition to Congress. Allied with Jones and Allen in the Philadelphia protest movement was industrialist James Forten, who attracted national attention with a series of letters that demolished the arguments of whites who wanted to limit the number of free blacks entering Pennsylvania.

Along with equal rights, blacks pressed the equal education movement. On October 17, 1787, Prince Hall and other Boston blacks filed one of the first public petitions in this field, telling the Massachusetts legislature that "we. . . must fear for our rising offspring to see them in ignorance in a land of gospel light, when there is provision made for them as well as others and [they] can't enjoy them, and [no other reason] can be given [than that] they are black. . . ." In a different but allied development, Paul Cuffe raised the issue of black suffrage. When, in 1780, he was barred from the ballot box in Dartmouth, Massachusetts, he refused to pay taxes and filed a defiant petition of protest. After a long controversy, it was decided that taxation without representation was tyranny in America. The case was widely regarded as establishing a precedent for black suffrage.

Buttressed by the four tiers of these ascending levels of expressiveness, the horizons of black pioneers expanded in widening circles that, in some cases, overlapped the efforts of white pioneers. Not only in the South but also in the North black pioneers contributed to the common effort, building schools and roads and extending the social capital of America. In one characteristic transaction, Paul Cuffe donated a school to his town and built a meeting house for the Quakers.

There were also black pioneers who extended the boundaries of America, founding new communities and towns. The most celebrated of these pioneers was Jean Baptiste Pointe DuSable, who founded Chicago, Illinois. There is abundant evidence—a deed in the Wayne County courthouse, the contemporary reports of British officers and the journals and records of travelers and traders—that DuSable settled in the area in the 1770s and created the foundations of Chicago, building the first home there and opening the first business.

The contributions of DuSable and other black founding fathers had no appreciable effect on the level of racism in America. There are even indications that DuSable the founder was isolated and pushed to the sidelines of Chicago life in the 1790s when large numbers of white Americans settled in the area, bringing with them traditional American perceptions. If, as seems probable, DuSable was indeed the victim of his own creation, he shares that mournful distinction with thousands of other black pioneers who found themselves under increasing attack in the last decade of the eighteenth century.

What did it mean to be black in the America of that period?

Prince Hall, the activist and Revolutionary War veteran who organized the first black Masonic lodge, provided one answer in his charge to Boston's African Lodge.

"Patience, I say; for were we not possessed of a great measure of it, we could not bear up under the daily insults we meet with in the streets of Boston, much more on public days of recreation. How, at such times, are we shamefully abused, and that to such a degree, that we may truly be said to carry our lives in our hands, and the arrows of death are flying about our heads."

A similar answer came from Colonel Middleton, another Revolutionary War veteran. During a Boston riot, a group of whites attacked blacks in front of his home. The old soldier stuck a musket out of his door and threatened to kill any white man who approached. One of his neighbors, a white man, asked the whites to leave. Then he approached Colonel Middleton and begged him to put away his gun. Colonel Middleton stood silent for a moment. Then he turned and tottered off, dropping his gun and weeping as he went.

Colonel Middleton's America, Prince Hall's America and Thomas Jefferson's America tottered into the nineteenth century, divided and afraid.

4

Behind the Cotton Curtain

The [slave] consciousness is, for the master, the object which embodies the truth of his certainty of himself. But it is evident that this object does not correspond to its notion; for, just where the master has effectively achieved lordship, he really finds that something has come about quite different from an independent consciousness. It is not an independent, but rather a dependent consciousness that he has achieved.... The truth of the [master] consciousness is accordingly the consciousness of the bondsman.

G. W. F. HEGEL

FOR TWO HUNDRED YEARS black, brown and yellow men and women were held in bondage in America. During these years "a social system as coercive as any yet known" was erected on the framework of "the most implacable race consciousness yet observed in virtually any society."

A curtain of cotton rang down on some four million human beings.* It became a crime to teach these men and women to read and write; it became a crime to give them a Bible.

Behind this cotton curtain four million human beings were systematically deprived of every right of personality. Vice, immorality and brutality were institutionalized. The sanctity of the family was violated; children were sold from mothers and fatherhood, in effect, was outlawed. The rape of a slave woman, a Mississippi court ruled, is an offense unknown to common or civil law. The "father of a slave," a Kentucky court ruled, "is unknown to our law."

Out of this system came the black American and, though some would like to forget it, the white American; for everyone—black and white, free and slave, slaveholder and nonslaveholder—was stained by it. In this system, in this back alley of American history, the American Dream was temporarily derailed for millions. It is not possible to know much about blacks or whites unless one knows a little about those terrible two hundred years through which they came together.

"The pro-slavery theory of the *ante-bellum* South," Gunnar Myrdal said, "is basic to certain ideas, attitudes, and policies prevalent in all fields of human relations even at the present time."

It was fashionable, for many years, to view this era through the astigmatic lenses of *Gone with the Wind*. A radical reevaluation in scholarly circles has largely destroyed that myth. Although a number of white scholars have tried to pump new life into the old and discredited myth with computer printouts and other scholarly sleight of hand, it is established by irrefutable evidence that American slavery was a moving and instructive chapter in the history of mankind. Historian Kenneth M. Stampp, whose book *(The Peculiar Institution)* helped shape the new interpretation, said: "The record of slave resistance forms a chapter in the story of the endless struggle to give dignity to human life. Though the history of southern bondage reveals that men *can* be enslaved under certain conditions, it also demonstrates that their love of

*The U.S. Census report of 1860 listed 3,953,700 slaves and 488,070 free men and women.

freedom is hard to crush. The subtle expressions of this spirit, no less than the daring thrusts for liberty, comprise one of the richest gifts the slaves have left to posterity."

Let us go back in time to the peculiar institution which stamped these people.

Let us feel the lash which broke their skins and sing the spirituals that soothed their hearts: "O Lord, O my Lord! O my good Lord, keep me from sinking down."

Let us visit the houses and fields where the trouble started.

The big white house stands in colonnaded splendor on a hill which overlooks fields fleeced with cotton or lined with tobacco or sugar cane or rice. Near this house, which oftentimes was neither big nor very white, huddle two rows of "log-and-daub" cabins. Other houses and buildings dot the landscape: the overseer's quarters, the stables, the corn cribs, the gin and press. The center of this agricultural factory is the "big house." From it radiate like spokes the fields and gardens: the sweet potato field, the watermelon patch, the cornfield, the pews of cotton or sugar cane or tobacco or rice.

This is a plantation. This is where the trouble started.

Not all blacks were slaves: there was a substantial free population, even in the South. Nor did all slaves work on plantations: some five hundred thousand worked in cities as domestics, skilled artisans and factory hands. But they were exceptions to the general rule. Most blacks were slaves on plantation-sized units in seven states of the Deep South.

Plantations and planters varied. There were small farmers with two or three slaves, planters with ten to thirty slaves and big planters who owned a thousand or more slaves. Scholars generally agree that slaves received better treatment on the small farms and plantations which did not employ overseers or general managers. Almost half of the bondsmen, however, lived, worked and died on plantations where the owners delegated much of their authority to overseers. Of much more pointed social relevance is the fact that the plantation and its fleecy flower, King Cotton, gave tone and direction to the whole society.

The plantation was a combination factory, village and police precinct. Its most conspicuous external characteristic was totalitarian regimentation. One manifestation of this—to begin with slave children—was a communal nursery which prepared

slave children for slavery and made it possible for their mothers
to work in the fields. The woman who cared for black children was
commonly designated "aunty" to distinguish her from the "mammy," the nurse of white children. Sometimes one women cared for
both white and black children. Children — boys and girls —
flopped around in a state of near-nudity until they reached the
age of toil. On some plantations they were issued tow-linen shirts;
on others they wore guano bags with holes punched in them for
the head and arms. Children were never issued shoes until they
were sent to the fields, usually at the age of six or seven. Young
workers were broken in as water boys or in the "trash gang." At
the age of ten or twelve, children—boys and girls—were given a
regular field routine.

"Children had to go to the fiel' at six on our place," a former
slave recalled. "Maybe they don't do nothin' but pick up stones or
tote water, but they got to get used to bein' there. Uncle Zack had
fought the injuns an' had a twisted leg. Used to set in the shade
lookin' at the children goin' to the field and mutter, 'Slave young,
slave long.' "

Cooking, in many instances, was also a collective project. On
most plantations food was prepared in a common kitchen and
sent to the workers in the field. In most cases, however, slaves
were expected to cook the evening meal in their cabins. The food,
which was issued once a week, was generally coarse and lacking
in variety. The usual allocation was a peck of corn and three or
four pounds of bacon or salt pork. Fractional amounts, usually
one-half, were allotted to each child in the family. Most slaves
supplemented this meager fare by trapping coons and opossums
in the fields or by "stealing" corn from the master's corn cribs
and chickens from his chicken coops. Slaves, it should be noted,
made a distinction between "taking" and "stealing." It was considered right and proper to "take" anything that belonged to
white folk. It was considered wrong to "steal" the property of
other slaves.

Twice a year the regimented slave was issued a clothes ration.
A South Carolina planter described a typical allowance in his
plantation manual: "Each man gets in the fall 2 shirts of cotton
drilling, a pair of woolen pants and a woolen jacket. In the spring
2 shirts of cotton shirting and 2 pr. of cotton pants. . . . Each
woman gets in the fall 6 yds. of woolen cloth, 6 yds. of cotton

drilling and a needle, skein of thread and ½ dozen buttons. In the
spring 6 yds. of cotton shirting and 6 yds. of cotton cloth similar to
that for men's pants, needle, thread and buttons. Each worker
gets a stout pr. of shoes every fall, and a heavy blanket every
third year."

Clothes came in two sizes, large and small, and women and
men were apparently issued the same kind of shoes. Former
slaves said "the Negro brogans" burned and blistered in the
summer and "got stiff as a board in cold weather." On some
plantations the same man shod slaves and horses. West Turner,
who was a slave in Virginia, remembered Old Black Jack Fly, a
blacksmith, who would "trace yo' foot in the dirt with a stick, but
it didn't do no good, 'cause he ain't never made the shoes like the
dirt say."

Most slaves lived in family-type cabins, but some lived in large
barracks "literally alive with slaves of all ages, conditions and
size." Some of the family cabins were two- and three-room brick
or frame structures with windows and brick fireplaces. The vast
majority, however, were rickety structures, built flat on the
ground. It was a common procedure to put five or six slaves into
one room. "Everything," a former slave said, "happened in that
one room—birth, sickness, death—everything."

There was considerable specialization on larger plantations. The
basic division in the work force was between field slaves, who, as
the name implies, worked in the fields, and house slaves, who
worked in and around the house (maids, cooks, butlers) or performed services as specialists (nurses, gardeners). Although work
in and around the house was generally lighter, it brought disadvantages, including constant surveillance by whites and the
psychic tension of wearing a public mask. For this reason, and
others as well, many slaves preferred field work to house work, a
fact noted by Frederick Law Olmsted, who said: "Slaves brought
up to house work dread to be employed at field-labour; and those
accustomed to the comparatively unconstrained life of the
Negro-settlement detest the close control and careful movements
required of the house-servants. It is a punishment for a lazy
field-hand to employ him in menial duties at the house . . . and it
is equally a punishment to a neglectful house-servant, to banish
him to the field-gangs."

In addition to house slaves and field slaves, there was another and different layer composed for the most part of highly skilled technicians, such as engineers, millwrights and master carpenters. From this layer came the men who were largely responsible for the construction and maintenance of antebellum mansions and plantation mills and machinery. "Such slaves," according to the Atlanta University study, *The Negro Artisan*, "were especially valuable and formed usually a privileged class, with a larger degree of freedom. . . . Many if not most of the noted leaders of the Negro in earlier times belonged to this slave mechanic class, such as [Denmark] Vesey, Nat Turner, Richard Allen and Absalom Jones. They were exposed neither to the corrupting privileges of the house servants nor to the blighting tyranny of field work and had large opportunity for self development." There is furthermore the testimony of J. D. Smith, an engineer who learned his trade from a slave engineer: "One only needs to go down South and examine hundreds of old Southern mansions, and splendid old church edifices, still intact, to be convinced of . . . the cleverness of the Negro artisans, who constructed nine-tenths of them."

At the apex of the white-imposed slave structure was an ambiguous figure called the driver, an unambiguous title which pointed to the function, driving slaves in the fields and maintaining order in the quarters. Feared and detested by most slaves, the driver was an integral part of the plantation command structure, holding a position roughly comparable to a master sergeant under a lieutenant (overseer), under a captain (slaveholder). When there were two or more drivers, one was named head driver. "The head driver," one planter said, "is the most important Negro on the plantation, and is not required to work like other hands. He is to be treated with more respect than any other Negro by both master and overseer. . . . He is to be required to maintain proper discipline at all times; to see that no Negro idles or does bad work in the field, and to punish it with discretion. . . ."

The operative words here are "with discretion." Real, that is to say, instructive punishment was administered and/or supervised by the slavemaster or overseer. The usual punishment was thirty-nine lashes with a cowskin whip. It was not unusual, however, for slaves to receive one hundred or more lashes. And few slaves, no matter how obedient or humble, reached old age with-

Slave coffles, driven by "soul-drivers," marched in Washington, D.C., in the shadow of the Capitol. Washington was a famous American slave market until 1850.

Men, women and children worked in the fields during the slave regime. The large plantation was a combination factory, village and police precinct. For some two hundred years, blacks were held in bondage in America.

An invoice of ten negroes sent this day to John B Williamson by Geo Kremer named & cost as follows

To wit. Betsey Kackley	. . . . .	$410. 00
Nancy Aulick	. . . .	515. 00
Harry & Helen Miller	. .	1200. 00
Mary Kostz	. . . .	600. 00
Betsey Ott?	. . . .	560. 00
Isaac & Fanny Breul	.	992. 00
Lucinda Luckett	. . . . .	467.50
George Smith	. . .	510. 00

Amount of my traveling expences & boarding	5 254.50
of lot No 9 not included in the other bill	39. 50
Kremers expences Transporting lot No 9 to chicha	51. 00
Carryall hire . .	6. 00
	$ 5351. 00

I have this day delivered the above named negroes costing including my expences and other expences five thousand three hundred & fifty dollars this May 26th 1835—

John. W. Pittman

I did intend to leave Nancy child but she made such a damned fuss I had to let her take it I could of got fifty Dollars for so you must add forty Dollars to the above

Plantation invoice lists prices paid for slaves. The seller noted: "I did intend to leave Nancy child [*sic*] but she made such a damned fuss I had to let her take it."

out receiving at least one lashing. As one would expect, psychotic and sadistic masters added embellishments. But even "kind" slavemasters whipped the skin off the backs of slaves and washed them down with brine.

The most common "offense" was impudence. And what was impudence? "Impudence," Frederick Douglass said, "might mean almost anything, or nothing at all, just according to the caprice of the master or overseer at the moment. But, whatever it is, or is not, if it gets the name of 'impudence,' the party charged with it is sure of a flogging. This offense may be committed in various ways; in the tone of an answer; in answering at all; in not answering; in the expression of the countenance; in the motion of the head; in the gait, manner and bearing of the slave."

There was method in this seeming madness, which was designed, at least in part, to keep slaves off balance. And the method was reinforced by the bells, horns and military formations of plantation life. One need only read Charley Williams's classic description to pick up the tempo of that life:

"When the day begin to crack, the whole plantation break out with all kinds of noises, and you could tell what was going on by the kind of noise you hear.

"Come the daybreak you hear the guinea fowls start potracking down at the edge of the woods lot, and then the roosters all start up round the barn, and the ducks finally wake up and join in. You can smell the sowbelly frying down at the cabins in the Row, to go with the hoecake and the buttermilk.

"Then pretty soon the wind rise a little, and you can hear a old bell donging way on some plantation a mile or two off, and then more bells at other places and maybe a horn, and pretty soon yonder go Old Master's old ram horn with a long toot and then some short toots, and here come the overseer down the row of cabins, hollering right and left, and picking the ham outen his teeth with a long shiny goose-quill pick.

"Bells and horns! Bells for this and horns for that! All we knowed was go and come by the bells and horns!"

Generally speaking, the horn ("that old fo' day horn") or bell sounded about four in the morning. Thirty minutes later the field hands were expected to be out of their cabins and on the way to the fields. Stragglers and late-sleepers were lashed with the whip. An eyewitness recalled seeing women scurrying to the field "with their shoes and stockings in their hands, and a petticoat wrapped over their shoulders, to dress in the fields the best way they could." Overseers and drivers, armed with whips, drove the work force. The overseer sometimes carried a bowie knife and a pistol. He often rode a horse, accompanied by a vicious dog.

Solomon Northup, a free black who was kidnapped and sold into slavery, said the hands worked steadily and "with the exception of ten or fifteen minutes, which is given them at noon to swallow their allowance of cold bacon, they are not permitted to be a moment idle till it is too dark to see, and when the moon is full, they often labor till the middle of the night." Another former slave said that it seemed that the fields stretched "from one end of the earth to the other." Men, women and children worked in these fields. Women cut down trees, dug ditches and plowed. The old and the ailing worked, oftentimes in the yards, feeding poultry, cleaning up, mending clothes and caring for the infants and the sick. Male and female, the quick and the halt worked the traditional hours of slavery—from can (see) to can't (see).

What happened at the end of the day?

Former slaves said the day never really ended. After work, to quote Northup again, "each must then attend to his respective chores. One feeds the mules, another the swine—another cuts the wood, and so forth. . . . Finally, at a late hour, they reach the quarters, sleepy and overcome with the long day's toil. Then a fire must be kindled in the cabin, the corn ground in the small hand-mill, and a supper, and dinner for the next day in the field prepared. . . . By this time, it is usually midnight. The same fear of punishment . . . possesses them again on lying down to get a snatch of rest. It is the fear of oversleeping in the morning. Such an offense would certainly be attended with not less than twenty lashes. With a prayer that he might be on his feet and wide awake at the first sound of the horn, he sinks to his slumbers nightly."

Fear, toil, the lash, hard words, a little ash cake and bacon, and fields stretching "from one end of the earth to the other"—such was life, for most slaves, day in and day out, season after season, with a half-day off on Saturday perhaps and a whole day off on Sunday. Small wonder that the burdened bondsmen eased his weary frame down and addressed God in stark eloquence:

> *Come day,*
> *Go day,*
> *God send Sunday.*

If all this was designed to crush the spirit of the slaves, it had precisely the opposite effect. For the slaves, in the most astonishingly creative act in our history, transcended their environment, creating a new structure of meaning and putting their oppressors and the world in their debt. No one can read the record of that transcendence without a sense of awe at the audacity of the slaves' hope. This hope was clearly visible in the concentric circles of community that started in the family and radiated in larger and larger circles that enveloped the whole of Slave Row. From that community came the rhythmic, spiritual and psychic piles that bottomed the new synthesis called Black America. The results—the spirituals, the blues, the rhythmic tonality of Black America — point to and guarantee the medium, which was a community of passion and creativity.

This community was a product of the plantation, but it was neither defined nor contained by the plantation. On the contrary, it was defined by difference, by the fact that it contradicted and called into question the values and institutions of the plantation. The fundamental difference was orientation. The community of slaves was a communal entity characterized by a collective orientation stemming partly from the African past and partly from the exigencies of the situation. Unlike the slaveholder community, it was oriented toward freedom, toward freedom of the body and soul, which were not defined as two different things but as two aspects of the same thing.

Although the slave community was located in Slave Row, the prototype of the Harlems and South Sides of today, it was not defined by the geography of any one Slave Row. Like the invisible church of slavery, the community was everywhere and nowhere—which is to say that it was a being which inhabited the slave and moved with him through time and space. Unwittingly and with the worst of motives, slaveowners furthered and deepened this reality by selling and shipping slaves from one Slave Row to another, from one state or region to another.

Because the bridges of the slave community were stronger than the chasms of plantation society, all slaves—house and field, artisan and laborer—participated in this reality. These bridges were based on the strongest of all human needs, the imperative need for a home place for the heart. No matter how many airs the house slaves might put on, they knew, and their slavemasters knew, that the only real home slaves had on the plantation was in the quarters, where they could drop their masks and stretch out their legs and souls. "House servant and field hand might meet there," the authors of the *Negro in Virginia* wrote, "and the testimony of the living ex-slave does not support the tradition of animosity between the two. House servants would regale other members of the 'row,' some of whom had never set foot in the 'big house,' with tales of 'master' and 'missus,' would 'take them off' in speech and gesture so faithful that the less privileged would shake with laughter." The words *less privileged* are questionable in view of the fact, already noted, that many slaves did not consider it a privilege to work in the house. And it would seem from this quotation and from the contemporary views of slaves and slaveowners that many house slaves realized the limitations of their alleged privileges. The evidence for this is chiefly in the fact that house slaves ran away and attacked slavemasters directly with blows and indirectly with poison and fire.

Subject to the same oppression and sharing the same interests, slaves of all ranks were bonded together by a common commitment to a common cause. This was clear to both black and white contemporaries. In 1842, for instance, a hostile white witness named Charles C. Jones noted:

"The Negroes are scrupulous on one point: they make common cause, as servants, on concealing their faults from their owners. Inquiry elicits no information; no one feels at liberty to disclose the transgressor; all are profoundly ignorant; *the matter assumes the sacredness of a 'professional secret'*; for they remember that they may hereafter require the same concealment of their own transgressions from their fellow servants, and if they tell upon them now, they may have the like favor returned them: besides, in the meantime, having their names cast out as evil from among their brethren; and being subjected to scorn, and perhaps personal violence or pecuniary injury (my emphasis)."

There is corroboration on this point in a Tennessee court case of a slave named Jim, who killed a slave named Isaac for betraying him after his escape. At the trial the judge noted that "Isaac seems to have lost caste. . . . He had combined with the white folks . . . no slight offense in their eyes: that one of their own color, subject to a like servitude, should abandon the interests of his caste, and betray black folks to the white people, rendered him an object of general aversion."

In this case, as well as in the acts and words of both slaves and slaveholders, we find most conclusive proof of the dominating influence of the countercommunity of the slaves.

The status hierarchy of this community was composed of ascending levels that paralleled and challenged the plantation-imposed hierarchy. Although slavemasters tried to make drivers the leading figures of Slave Row, the influence of these functionaries seldom exceeded the circles of white power they reflected. The slaves instead looked to natural leaders who received their credentials from age, wisdom, strength, and the powers of the world of the spirits. One slaveholder said it was "a notorious fact" that "on almost every large plantation of Negroes, there is one among them who holds a kind of magical sway over the minds and opinions of the rest; to him they look as their oracle. . . . The influence of such a Negro, often a preacher, on a quarter is incalculable." Such a person was "Old Abram," a plantation patriarch who was said to be "deeply versed in such philosophy as is taught in the cabin of the slave."

The slaves also had their own specialists in matters of decorum, dress, worship, and marriage. Significantly, the slave community was totally democratic in the sense that the highest roles were open to female talent. A Louisiana planter noted that a slave woman called Big Lucy was an indigenous leader who "corrupts every young Negro in her power." On a South Carolina plantation, a leader named Sinda prophesied the end of the world and for a long time no slave on the plantation would work.

There was also an interesting and significant circle of elders, who occupied a position in slave society roughly equivalent to the position of the elders in West African society. The influence of this institution was most clearly visible in the status of older slaves, commonly called uncle or aunt, who were revered and respected on almost all plantations. The best description of the institution is in the narrative of Frederick Douglass:

"These mechanics were called 'Uncles' by all the younger slaves, not because they really sustained that relationship to any, but according to plantation etiquette, as a mark of respect, due from the younger to the older slaves. Strange, and even ridiculous as it may seem among a people so uncultivated, and with so many stern trials to look in the face, there is not to be found, among any people, a more rigid enforcement of the law of respect to elders. . . . A young slave must approach the company of the elder with hat in hand, and woe betide him if he fails to acknowledge a favor, of any sort, with the accustomed 'tankee' etc."

The roles in the slave community were organized into institutions or proto-institutions. There were institutions, i.e., organized patterns of behavior, for maintaining community standards, for dealing with the slavemaster, for inducting new members into the group, and for expressing the soul and style of the people. Some of these institutions were more or less direct translations of African institutions. Others were creative blendings of African and European forms. Still others were free improvisations on European themes.

The energies flowing through these forms organized themselves around three axial forces. The first, of course, was the axis of the spirit. In this realm, as in others, the slaves reinterpreted white patterns, weaving a whole new universe around biblical images and giving a new dimension and new meaning to Christianity. This enormous achievement, which astonished Arnold J. Toynbee and other historians, contradicted the religion taught the slaves. That religion was a censored pablum which dwelt almost always on the duties of patience and obedience. J. W. Fowler of Coahoma County, Mississippi, told his overseer that he had no objection to his slaves hearing the gospel if they heard it in its "original purity and simplicity." What did this mean? Ephesians, 6:5, usually: "Servants, be obedient to them that are *your* masters. . . ."

American slaves, with few exceptions, rejected this version of Christianity. Their God was the God who delivered the Israelites.

> *Didn't my Lord deliver Daniel,*
> *And why not every man.*

In a total and passionate quest for *this* God, the slaves, tempered and toughened by the annealing heat of adversity, turned American Christianity inside out, like a glove, infusing it with African-oriented melodies and rhythms and adding new patterns, such as the ring shout, ecstatic seizure and communal, call-and-

Fugitive slaves are shown arriving at the home of Levi Coffin, who was a leading "conductor" on the Underground Railroad. Many slaves escaped from plantations and rode the Underground Railroad to freedom in Canada.

Religion was a source of solace for many slaves.
One writer said slaves poured all their emotion
into religious services "with an intensity . . .
almost terrible to witness."

response patterns. The seeds sown here produced a new synthesis, which colored and changed the white original. The new creation surfaced first in the invisible church of slavery, which centered in the portable "hush-harbors." We get a glimpse of these "hush-harbors" in a description in Peter Randolph's book, *From Slave Cabin To Pulpit:*

"Not being allowed to hold meetings on the plantations, the slaves assembled in the swamps, out of reach of the patrols. They have an understanding among themselves as to the time and place of getting together. This is often done by the first one arriving breaking boughs from the trees and bending them in the direction of the selected spot. Arrangements are then made for conducting the exercises. They first ask each other how they feel, the state of their minds, etc. The male members then select a certain space, in separate groups, for their division of the meeting. Preaching in order, by the brethren; then praying and singing all around, until they generally feel quite happy. The speaker usually commences by calling himself unworthy, and talks very slowly, until, feeling the spirit, he grows excited, and in a short time, there fall to the ground twenty or thirty men and women under its influence."

Important as this institution was, it is necessary to perceive it in proper perspective. For it was only one element in a complex world view that included spirits that were not visible to white Christians. And so, to mention only the most obvious fact, many American slaves believed in Jesus *and* an overlapping world of spirits who could be manipulated and persuaded to serve the living. Hence, the widespread belief in "hants," charms and taboos.

Undergirding all this, undergirding everything, in fact, was the second great axis of music and rhythm. This axis, which informed every element of slave life, was characterized by the so-called "blues" tonality and a rhythmic, collective and emotional orientation. The same elements are evident in slave folklore and philosophy, especially the Brer Rabbit, Brer Fox and Old John cycles. The expressions of this orientation were as varied as the people and included cries, hollers, work songs, devil songs, spirituals and blues. There have been repeated attempts by latter-day students to separate these expressions,

and the people who created them, into blues archetypes and
spiritual archetypes. But the slave world view was antidichoto-
mies and recognized no such distinction, and it is almost certain
that both the spirituals and the blues were products of a common
blues-spiritual matrix. This totality — America's only original
contribution to the world of music—was a collective product, but
it was shaped by creative geniuses, by men and women of large
vision and even larger voices, men and women immortalized by
James Weldon Johnson in the poem, "O Black and Unknown
Bards." The mood and meaning of the products they created
varied, as we can see if we look for a moment at the spirituals.
There were coded spirituals of protest and defiance, based on the
passion and eventual triumphs of the Hebrew slaves of Egypt.

> *Oh, Mary, don't you weep, don't you moan;*
> *Pharaoh's Army got drowned.*

There were joyful sounds unto the Lord:

> *I went down in the valley to pray.*
> *My soul got happy and I stayed all day.*

And regrets:

> *Don't know what my mother wants to stay here for,*
> *This old world ain't been no friend to her.*

And tears:

> *I know moon-rise, I know star-rise,*
> *Lay this body down.*
> *I walk in the moonlight, I walk in the starlight,*
> *To lay this body down.*
> *I'll walk in the graveyard, I'll walk through the*
> *graveyard*
> *To lay this body down.*
> *I'll lie in the grave and stretch out my arms;*
> *Lay this body down.*
> *I go to the judgement in the evenin' of the day,*
> *When I lay this body down;*
> *And my soul and your soul will meet in the day*
> *When I lay this body down.*

I'll lie in the grave and stretch out my arms. The words made shivers run down Thomas Wentworth Higginson's back.

"Never," he said, "it seems to me, since man first lived and suffered, was his infinite longing for peace uttered more plaintively than in that line."

This longing was also expressed—though in different language—in the jubilations of the slaves. These temporary releases from toil—on Saturday nights and holidays, notably Christmas —were rare, and slaves made the most of them, holding dances and parties in barns, open fields and Slave Row shacks. On these festive occasions the slaves did jigs, shuffles and "set de flo." They danced to the fiddle or the banjo and beat out rhythms with sticks and bones or by clapping their hands and stomping their feet. The slaves had a word for it, even then. A "cool cat" in those days was a "ring-clipper." If the slave was aware, or, in the jazz idiom, if he was hip, he was no "bug-eater." On most plantations there were comely lasses like Miss Lively, a Louisiana belle who had a "well-earned reputation," Solomon Northup said, "of being the 'fastest gal' on the bayou."

The third great axis was the extended family. In interpersonal relationships, as in the fields of music and religion, the slaves triumphed by transcending and transforming the institutions of their oppressors. We can see this in its purest form in the field of family relations, for the slave family had no standing in law and was the focus of some of the strongest pressures of the slave regime. In all slave states, the wife or husband or children could be separated and sold to other slaveholders in other counties and regions. Worse yet, certain slaveholders sanctioned polygamy and polyandry and bred slaves for the market.

Apologists for the slave regime deny that slave breeding— sustained efforts to produce the maximum number of slave children—occurred, but there is abundant evidence to the contrary. The subject was bruited about by men and women, black and white. Travelers in the South—Harriet Martineau, Frederick Law Olmsted and others—frequently mentioned the subject. Olmsted, a perceptive observer, believed that slave breeding was common. "Most gentlemen of character," he wrote, "seem to have a special disinclination to converse on the subject. . . . It appears to me evident, however, from the manner in which I hear the traffic spoken of incidentally, that the cash value of a slave for sale, above the cost of raising it from infancy to the age at which it commands the highest price, is generally considered among the surest elements of a planter's wealth. . . . That a slave woman is commonly esteemed least for her laboring qualities, most for those qualities which give value to a brood-mare, is, also, constantly made apparent."

Southerners admitted as much. In a letter to Olmsted a slaveholder said that "in the states of Md., Va., N.C., Ky., Tenn. and Mo., as much attention is paid to the breeding and growth of Negroes as to that of horses and mules. Further South, we raise them both for use and for market. Planters command their girls and women (married or unmarried) to have children; and I have known a great many Negro girls to be sold off, because they did not have children. A breeding woman is worth from one-sixth to one-fourth more than one that does not breed."

Advertisements listing slave women for sale were brutally frank. A South Carolina advertisement of 1796 offered fifty "prime" Negroes for sale. "They were purchased," the advertisement said, "for stock and breeding Negroes, and to any Planter who particularly wanted them for that purpose, they are a very choice and desirable gang." Another advertisement of May 16, 1838, offered a slave "girl of about 20 years of age [who] is very prolific in her generating qualities and affords a rare opportunity for any person who wishes to raise a family of strong and healthy servants. . . ." Other advertisement relied on suggestive terminology: "She is a No. 1 girl," "This is truly a No. 1 woman." "Breeding slaves," "child-bearing women," and "breeding period" were also stock advertising terms.

The black family in America was shaped by this system and by a breathtakingly creative response to the system. For in the violence and humiliation of one of the vilest systems created by man, American slaves—males and females—created unique mating and marriage patterns that made it possible for the black spirit to survive and grow.

By far the most ingenious of these patterns was the slave marriage, which was generally organized around the proverbial broomstick. We don't know, we may never know, the symbolic

importance of this ceremony, but former slaves said couples usually celebrated their marriage by jumping over a broomstick.
Georgianna Gibbs, who was a slave in Virginia, said the slaves
jumped "a broom three times," but the procedure in Kentucky,
another former slave said, was for the man to jump the broom
while the woman stood still. At any rate, it was necessary,
according to almost all observers, to jump high, for, according to
Jeff Calhoun, who was a slave in Alabama, "to stump your toe on
the broom meant you got trouble comin' 'tween you."

A revealing portrait of one of these marriages was drawn by
Carolina Johnson Harrison, who was a slave in Virginia, and who
was married by "Ant Sue," one of the leaders of Slave Row.

"Didn't have to ask Marsa or nothin'," she said. "Just go to Ant
Sue an' tell her you want to get mated. She tell us to think 'bout it
hard for two days, 'cause marryin' was sacred in the eyes of
Jesus. After two days Mose an' I went back an' say we done
thought 'bout it an' still want to get married. Then she called all
the slaves after tasks to pray fo' the union that God was gonna
make. Pray we stay together an' have lots of children an' none of
'em gets sold way from the parents. Then she lays a broomstick
'cross the sill of the house we gonna live in an' join our hands
together. Fo' we step over it she ask us once mo' if we was sho' we
wanted to get married. 'Course we say yes. Then she say, 'In the
eyes of Jesus step into the holy land of matrimony.' When we step
'cross the broomstick, we was married. Was bad luck to touch the
broomstick. Folks always stepped high 'cause they didn't want no
spell cast on 'em—Ant Sue used to say whichever one touched
the stick was gonna die first."

Everything indeed suggests that slave marriages were resilient
institutions, unencumbered by traditional considerations of
property and paternalism. In almost all cases the bride was a
worker who toiled in the fields with her husband and other males.
She thus entered marriage as a free spirit (within the confines of a
system of equality of oppression) and she was free to opt out when
she wanted to. The marriage she and her mate consummated was
thus a love match in the true sense of the word.

It was customary until recently to suggest that slave men and
women lived a life of riotous debauchery. But a pathfinding study
by Professor Herbert G. Gutman (*The Black Family in Slavery
and Freedom*) destroyed that myth and established four points

that are central to an understanding of the slave community and the black family:

1. Most slaves lived in family units headed by a father and mother, and "large numbers of slaves lived in long marriages," some of thirty or more years.

2. Fathers were strong and respected members of the family circle, and male children were often named for their fathers.

3. Premarital sex was fairly common, although the slave community expected a premarital pregnancy to be followed by marriage. The slave community was more open—and more honest—about sex, but it did not approve or condone indiscriminate mating and begetting. More than that, the slave community expected males and females to remain faithful after marriage. Robert Smalls, who later served in the U.S. Congress, told the American Freedmen's Inquiry Commission in 1863 that "if a woman loses her husband, she mourns for him and will not marry for a year and a half unless she is driven to it by want and must have somebody to help her."

4. In slavery—and afterwards—black marriage was buttressed by extended family groupings that included a wide range of personal relationships.

This was the general situation in the veil within the veil that American slaves created behind the cotton curtain. Within this internal veil, the slaves created a community with its own values and orientation. It was this community that sustained them as they struggled, day in and day out, to maintain a sense of humanity and expectancy in a white-dominated world bounded by fields and fences and the seasons of the year.

Largely because of the existence of the slave community, the struggle continued behind the lines of slavery until the end of slavery. Men and women nourished and sustained by the slave community pressed that struggle on several levels. Militants, as we shall see, organized and led revolts and conspiracies. Activists, aided by members of the community, who provided food and medicine and kept their mouths shut, ran away to Canada or to Indian reservations on the Underground Railroad. It has been estimated that at least 100,000 slaves escaped from the South during the antebellum period.

Besides these more or less organized forces, there was resistance and pressure from runaways who remained in the South and raided nearby plantations from their bases in the swamps. Frederick Law Olmsted was told that escaped slaves lived, bred and died in the swamps. "What a life it must be!" he wrote, "born outlaws; educated self-stealers, trained from infancy to be constantly in dread of the approach of a white man as a thing more dreaded than wildcats or serpents, or even starvation." A typical instance of this was reported in Virginia. A deputy, sent out to capture a runaway slave, saw his man standing neck deep in a dangerous recess of the swamp. The deputy went back to the courthouse and scratched the slave's name off the book. He wrote across the warrant: "Seeable but not Comeatable."

Another runaway, cornered by his pursuers, chose death. A contemporary newspaper account says that when pursuers found him he was standing "at bay upon the outer edge of a large raft of driftwood, armed with a club and a pistol. In this position he bade defiance to men and dogs—knocking the latter into the water with his club, and resolutely threatening death to any man who approached him. Finding him obstinately determined not to surrender, one of his pursuers shot him. He fell at the third fire, and so determined was he not to be captured, that when an effort was made to rescue him from drowning he made battle with his club, and sunk waving his weapon in angry defiance at his pursuers."

A further complication was added by black rebels who attacked the system from within, using poison and the torch. As early as 1723, fifty-three years before the Declaration of Independence, Boston was terrorized by a series of fires. On April 18, 1723, the Rev. Joseph Sewell of Boston preached a sermon on "The Fires that have Broken out in Boston, supposed to be set purposely by ye Negroes."

Fires and rumors of slave-set fires convulsed Southern cities until the end of slavery. Beyond any question the antebellum South was a high-risk area. An official of the American Fire Insurance Company of Philadelphia sent the following letter to a Savannah, Georgia, man on February 17, 1820:

"I have received your letter of the 7th instant respecting the insurance of your house and furniture in Savannah. In answer thereto, I am to inform you, that this company, for the present, decline making insurance in any of the slave states."

Arrayed against rebellious slaves was a police apparatus of

unparelleled severity. Each slave state had a slave code which was designed to keep slaves ignorant and in awe of white power. Under the provisions of these codes, slaves were forbidden to assemble in groups of more than five or seven away from their home plantation. They were forbidden to leave plantations without passes and they could not blow horns, beat drums or read books. Slave preachers were proscribed and hemmed in by additional restrictions; and slaves were forbidden to hold religious meetings without white witnesses. Other provisions forbade slaves to raise their hands against whites and gave every white person police power over every black, free or slave. A free black, when challenged by a white person, was obliged to produce papers proving that he was free. The presumption in most slave states was that a colored person was a slave. Slave patrols or "paderollers," as the slaves called them, were authorized to make periodic searches of slave cabins and to chastise bondsmen found off plantations without passes.

The police power of the state, the state militia and the U.S. Army stood behind these totalitarian laws. But power alone could not uphold them. More was needed: the slave, if slavery was to be successful, had to *believe* he was a slave. Anticipating the devious tactics of the modern police state, masters laid hands on the minds of their human chattel. Each slave was taught, by various methods and with varying success, that he was totally helpless and that his master was absolutely powerful. Each slave was taught that he was inferior to the meanest white man and that he had to obey every white man without thinking, without questioning. Finally, if these lessons were learned, the slave looked at himself through the eyes of his master and accepted the values of the master.

Masters, with few exceptions, recognized the necessity of mind control. A Louisiana planter told Olmsted that he wanted to buy the land of poor whites who lived near his plantation. "It was better," he said, "that they [slaves] never saw anybody off their own plantation; they should, if possible, have no intercourse with any other white man than their owner or overseer; especially, it was desirable that *they should not see white men who did not command their respect, and whom they did not always feel to be superior to themselves, and able to command them* (my emphasis)."

That some slaves succumbed to this assault on the mind is not unusual. Faced with absolute power in a closed system, American white men and Europeans succumbed in concentration camps in Korea and Germany. What was surprising was certainly not that some blacks succumbed to the pressure of slavery. It was rather that so many with so few resources never stopped fighting back. Many rebels who could not and would not be whipped by one man were overpowered by groups and killed. Some were sent to "professional Negro breakers" and broken. Several "persisted in their folly." They poisoned masters and mistresses with arsenic, ground glass and "spiders beaten up in buttermilk." They chopped whites to pieces with axes and burned their houses and barns to the ground. Not a few "bad Negroes" were women.

Court records speak for the "bad Negroes" some historians would like to forget.

One slave said:

"He would be damned if he did not kill his master, if he ever struck him again."

Another was ecstatic as he dug his master's grave.

"I have killed him at last."

Patrick vowed revenge.

"Their master had attempted to whip Patrick . . . and it took five persons to hold him. That Patrick said that he was not done yet, that he was a good Negro when he was let alone, but if he was raised he was the devil."

A woman slave prodded a timid male.

"If she, the witness, were a man, she would murder her master."

Another woman was frank.

"If old mistress did not leave her alone and quit calling her a bitch and a strumpet, she would take an iron and split her brains out."

The court records of this period yield ample evidence that a large number of slaves refused to play the game of slavery: they would neither smile nor bow. Other slaves bowed but would not smile. Still others, perhaps the majority, went through the ritual of obeisance. What about them? What did they think of slavery? What they thought can be inferred from what they did. Black and white historians have uncovered a mass of material on their passive "day-to-day resistance" to slavery. These slaves, who smiled sometimes and bowed sometimes, used a variety of techniques to indicate their dissatisfaction with the system. They staged deliberate slowdowns and sit-down strikes. They broke implements and trampled the crops. In a now visible, now invisible underground struggle which continued until the end of slavery, they quietly and subtly and deliberately sabotaged the system from within. By resisting, maintaining, enduring and abiding, by holding on and holding fast and holding out, they provided one of the greatest examples in history of the strength of the human spirit in adversity.

5

Blood on the Leaves: Revolts and Conspiracies

Brethren, arise, arise! Strike for your lives and liberties. Now is the day and the hour....Rather die free men than live to be slaves....Let your motto be resistance! *resistance!* RESISTANCE!

HENRY HIGHLAND GARNET

I T WAS a long hot summer.

On colonnaded verandas in the French possession of Haiti, planters sipped tall cold drinks and looked into the apocalyptic sun. Black men—slaves—served the drinks, bowing, scraping, listening. The planters sipped the cool liquid, fondled the tall glasses and chewed over the revolution then raging in the mother country.

Liberté, Egalité, Fraternité.

What precisely did these words mean?

The planters speculated. The black men bowed, scraped and listened.

The planters were going to die, but they didn't talk about death in the red summer of 1791. Lush summers and cold drinks do not lend themselves to reflections on blood and doom; nor do men situated as these men were situated look gift horses in the mouth. They ruled a half-million slaves. God, they reasoned, made the sugar cane to grow and sent black men from Africa to cultivate it and white men from Europe to divide the profits. It had always been so, they reasoned; it would always be so. But weren't they playing with fire? To prattle about liberty, equality and fraternity in the presence of slaves—wasn't this suicidal? No, of course not. Slaves were not men; they didn't have the same desires as Europeans. They were primitives. Like children, really.

The planters speculated. The blacks sharpened their knives. *Liberté, Egalité, Fraternité.*

What precisely did these words mean?

All summer long the tom-toms talked in the hills. If a visitor remarked on the rumbling, the planters had a ready answer. The servants were worshipping their tribal gods. They were a superstitious people. Like children, really.

The boom-boom-boom continued, summoning slave leaders to secret meetings in the hills. On August 14 men moved noiselessly through the night, responding to the insistent telegraphy of the tom-toms. They came from many plantations, slave foremen and black men of distinction. Noiselessly, they assembled in a glade in a forest called Bois Cäiman.

They sat in a great half circle, facing a fire, behind which, magnified by the flames, stood a tall man who leaned on an improvised altar. The man answered to the name Boukman. He was a *houngan*, a celebrated voodoo priest who had come to Haiti via Jamaica. Boukman seemed pleased, as well he might. Overhead, lightning zigzagged through the sky and the heavens rolled with thunder. It was a good sign: *Bon Dieu*, the good God, was angry. Moreover, as Boukman pointed out to the delegates, *Bon Dieu* demanded action, a slave revolt—now. Boukman, speaking for *Bon Dieu*, vowed vengeance for the wrongs of his people. Speaking in a deep, hollow voice, playing on the strings of his listeners' emotions, Boukman raised the assembly to a pitch of religious frenzy. The only problem, it turned out, was the time of D-Day. Some of the black leaders wanted to start the revolt that night, but cooler heads prevailed. Eight days were set aside for deliberation and planning.

Boukman gave a sign and acolytes brought a black pig. A

gleaming knife flashed through the air. Every man present moved forward, dipped his hands in the blood of the animal and, holding them up, swore *liberté ou mort*. A streak of lightning seared the sky; the heavens thundered and rolled. Boukman, observing this, was pleased; it was a good sign: *Bon Dieu* was giving his approval.

Meanwhile, the ceremony continued with a religious dance by a young woman. As she danced, swaying from side to side, moving her hands, her arms, her entire body, she chanted a strange song of prophecy, of a land laid waste, of a people finding themselves and rising to greatness through inspired leadership. She finished at last and Boukman, a master of crowd psychology, fell to his knees and improvised—or did the wily old Jamaican have it all written out—the famous Creole prayer—*Bon Dieu*.

"Good God, who makest the sun to light us from on high, who raisest up the sea and makest the storm to thunder—good God who watches over all, hidden in a cloud, protect and save us from what the white men do to us.

"Good God, the white men do crimes, but we do not.

"Good God, give us vengeance, guide our arms, give us help. Negroes show the image of the good God to the white men, that we thirst not.

"Good God, grant us that freedom which speaks to all men!"

Down below in the valley, all was quiet. Here and there, planters sat on the wide porches and watched the play of the lightning in the heavens.

Liberté, Egalité, Fraternité.

What precisely did these words mean?

Eight days later—at midnight on August 22, 1791—one hundred thousand slaves answered with a revolution that changed the meaning of the question.

"In an instant," a writer said, "twelve hundred coffee and two hundred sugar plantations were in flames; the buildings, the machinery, the farmhouses, were reduced to ashes; and the unfortunate proprietors were hunted down, murdered or thrown into the flames, by the infuriated Negroes." Day after day, week after week, for three weeks, the Haitian revolutionaries pressed their advantage, burning, hacking, destroying. A French planter named Carteau was there. "Picture to yourself," he said, "the whole horizon a wall of fire, from which continually rose thick vortices of smoke, whose huge black volumes could be likened only to those frightful storm-clouds which roll onward charged with thunder and lightning. The rift in these clouds disclosed flames as great in volume, which rose darting and flashing to the very sky. Such was their voracity that for nearly three weeks we could barely distinguish between day and night, for so long as the rebels found anything to feed the flames, they never ceased to burn."

Thus began a revolution which had profound repercussions in America where planters began sleeping with pistols under their pillows. Fear, a deep, miasmic fear, seeped into the consciousness of planters everywhere. There had been earlier revolts, scores of them, in the Caribbean, in South America, in North America; but these revolts had been suppressed and the details expunged from memory. The Haitian revolt reopened old wounds and magnified old phobias.

Historians, armed with hindsight, have written a great deal of romantic nonsense about the docility of the slaves. The planter who lived with the slaves knew them better. He knew from bitter experience that the slaves were dangerous humans because they were wronged humans. Slaves smiled, yes. But they also cut throats, burned down houses and conceived plots to kill every white person within reach. This happened so often that many whites weakened under the strain. Some died of heart failure. Some went insane.

"These insurrections," a Virginian wrote during a period of panic, "have alarmed my wife so as really to endanger her health, and I have not slept without anxiety in three months. Our nights are sometimes spent in listening to noises. A corn song, or a hog call, has often been the subject of nervous terror, and a cat, in the dining room, will banish sleep for the night."

Continuing, he said:

"There has been and there still is a *panic* in all this country. I am beginning to lose my courage about the melioration of the South. Our revivals produce no preachers; churches are like the buildings in which they worship, gone in a few years. There is no principle of life. Death is autocrat of slave regions."

Fear fed by guilt made men do strange things. Two poor whites told Frederick Law Olmsted how it was in the South's palmiest days. "Where I used to live [Alabama]," the husband said, "I remember when I was a boy—mus' ha' been about twenty years ago—folks was dreadful frightened about the niggers [*sic*]. I remember they built pens in the woods where they could hide, and Christmas time they went and got into the pens 'fraid the niggers [*sic*] was rising." This man's wife had seen similar scenes. "I remember," she said, "the same time where we was in South Carolina, we had all our things put in a bag so we could tote 'em, if we heard they was coming our way."

The fears of this couple were not entirely groundless, for there were, according to Herbert Aptheker and other students of slave resistance, some 250 revolts and conspiracies in America during the slave era. In fact, according to Aptheker, "the first settlement within the present borders of the United States to contain slaves was the locale of the first slave revolt." The revolt occurred in a settlement of some five hundred Spaniards and one hundred slaves, located in all probability on the Pedee River in contemporary South Carolina. When, around November, 1526, the slaves rebelled and settled in nearby Indian camps, the Spaniards returned to Haiti, "leaving," Aptheker said, "the rebel Negroes with their Indian friends—as the first permanent inhabitants, other than the Indians, in what was to be the United States."

With the arrival of the first permanent English settlers— eighty-one years later—Africans and Indians, fighting separately sometimes and sometimes together, mounted a campaign of resistance which grew in force and depth. An early instance of this was the African-Indian uprising in Hartford, Connecticut, in 1657. Thirty-three years later, in 1690, there was a panic in Newbury, Massachusetts, after Isaac Morrill was arrested on a charge of inciting insurrection among Africans and Indians. In Queen's County, New York, in 1708, an Indian slave and a black woman killed their master, his wife and five children. In 1712, in New York City, a band of black warriors, with marginal Indian support, revolted and killed nine whites. This spreading wave of resistance crested in South Carolina in 1739 when a group of slaves, under the leadership of a brilliant black rebel named Jemmy, fired a number of buildings and set out for Spanish Florida. They "called out Liberty," a contemporary report said, "marched on with Colours displayed, and two drums beating."

Approximately twenty-five whites were killed before Jemmy and his band were subdued.

The flood of ideas released by the American and French revolutions stirred slaves greatly. The rhetoric of Thomas Jefferson and Patrick Henry, both slaveholders, also impressed slave conspirators. But the biggest influence in the slave cabins was a short black man who once made a four-word speech on liberty. Holding up his musket, he told Haitians slaves, "There is your liberty!" In Brazil, in the Caribbean, in Charleston, wherever slaves chafed under chains, this man's name was whispered. The name was François Dominique Toussaint L'Ouverture.

"You think me a fanatic," Wendell Phillips said, "for you read history, not with your eyes, but with your prejudices. But fifty years hence, when Truth gets a hearing, the Muse of history will put Phocion for the Greek, Brutus for the Roman, Hampden for the English, Layfayette for France; choose Washington as the bright, consummate flower of our earliest civilization; and then, dipping her pen in the sunlight, will write in the clear blue, above them all, the name of the soldier, the statesman, the martyr, Toussaint L'Ouverture."

When the Haitian Revolution began, Toussaint was an obscure carriage driver on the Bréda plantation in the northern province of Haiti. He had lived the life of a slave, had married, sired sons and gained some local fame from his skill in mixing herb potions. A devout Roman Catholic, he was literate in French and knew some Latin phrases. He was, it seems, a model slave. His master trusted him implicitly and had given him a succession of important jobs. Now, in the autumn of his life, Toussaint drove his master's carriage, sitting barefooted on the box, smiling and bowing at the proper times. He was almost fifty and it seemed that life had passed him by. But the fire of the Haitian Revolution transformed Toussaint, burning away the dross. Within two years this grey-haired carriage driver electrified the world and sent shivers down the backs of American slaveholders. He defeated the English and Spanish armies, unified Haiti and held his own in slippery maneuvering with the wily Napoleon.

The Haitian Revolution began, as we have seen, with the firing of the plantations. Toussaint, who did not participate in this phase of the Revolution, saw that more was needed if the slaves

A condemned slave is burned at the stake after "Negro Plot of 1741." Citizens believed black and white conspirators intended to burn New York City and kill the white citizens. Thirteen slaves were burned and eighteen were hanged.

Toussaint L'Ouverture was the leader of the Haitian Revolution. The black general defeated Napoleon's troops and freed Haitian slaves.

After passage of the Fugitive Slave Act of 1850, black Americans became increasingly militant. In Christiana, Pennsylvania, blacks defeated a group of slave hunters.

were to gain and keep their freedom. There were dangers on all sides. The whites, driven from the fertile plains, were plotting in the seacoast towns. Spain and England, having declared war on France, were demanding a division of the Haitian spoils. All this was observed by the ever-watchful Toussaint, who realized almost immediately that the only hope for the Haitians was to drive a wedge between the contending forces. Moreover, as Ralph Korngold points out, Toussaint seemed determined "not to permit a white man to claim the honor of having freed the slaves."

Joining the tattered rebel army, Toussaint trained and hardened a crack corps of black troops. Then he took to the field, first as an ally of Spain against France then as an ally of France against England and Spain. Playing off the Spanish against the French and the French against the English, he outmaneuvered the best diplomats of his day and gained freedom for the slaves.

Contemporary observers called Toussaint a military genius, He had complete control over his men and he maneuvered them with a rapidity that seemed miraculous. "He disappears—he has flown—as if by magic," Antoine Metral said. "Now he reappears again where he is least expected. He seems to be ubiquitous. One never knows where his army is, what it subsists on, how he manages to recruit it, in what mountain fastness he has hidden his supplies and his treasury. He, on the other hand, seems perfectly informed concerning everything that goes on in the enemy camp." Using these tactics, Toussaint outmaneuvered General Maitland and forced the withdrawal of the English army. Historians say England lost forty thousand soldiers in a vain attempt to take the island from the black general.

After the English withdrawal, Toussaint annexed the eastern two-thirds of the island (now the Dominican Republic) and squashed a dissident force of mulattoes. By 1801 he was at the height of his power. He was then in his middle fifties, a lean, wiry man, small of stature, black, with large eyes, a broad uptilted nose and prominent lips. He was not, by any standard, handsome; yet there was something about the man. The face was strong, magnetic, noble even; and he had that without which actors and generals are mere puppets: personal presence. A French general said, "Nobody can approach Toussaint without fear or leave him without emotion." Always alert to the drama of his cause, Toussaint usually wore a yellow madras handkerchief, carelessly knotted about his head. When he entered Santo Domingo at the head of a triumphant army, he was dressed in a blue uniform with gold-embroidered cuffs and epaulettes.

Vision, daring, energy: Toussaint had all these qualities in abundance. He despised flattery and was contemptuous of titles and empty show. He was also, it seems, something of a Puritan; he forbade divorce and kept a stern eye on the moral tone of the country. When an attractive young French girl appeared at a social function in a low-cut dress, Toussaint modestly covered the exposed flesh with his handkerchief and asked the girl's mother to take her home. He was puritanical, cynical historians say, "at least as far as other people's morals were concerned." This is a veiled reference to reports that Toussaint had a number of mistresses of varying hues and ages. However that may be, it is well worth noting that the Haitian leader remained devoted to Suzanne, the wife of his captivity, and their two sons.

After the Revolution, Toussaint embarked on an extraordinary career as an administrator. Roads were built; buildings were repaired; the administrative machinery was overhauled. With enemies all around him, with the major powers waiting for him to make a mistake, Toussaint decreed total mobilization, making every citizen a soldier and imposing a heavy tax schedule to finance an ambitious program of arms procurement. Colonel Poyen, the French military historian, said Toussaint "was responsible for the most extraordinary activity in all departments of the administration. He busied himself with the building of the fortifications, the stocking of the arsenals, the acquisition of supplies, the instruction and discipline of the army. He spurred the agricultural inspectors to intense activity. He restored and embellished the cities and built bridges. He administered justice, kept an eye on the exercise of religion, visited schools and distributed prizes to the best scholars. He frequently visited hospitals and barracks. It is difficult to sum up the amazing activity of this extraordinary Negro, who slept only two hours out of twenty-four. His body, accustomed to privations, was entirely under the control of his will."

Perhaps the most outstanding accomplishment of Toussaint's reign was the integration of the white minority. As to one thing, almost all observers are agreed: he had a way with whites. "Races," General Vincent said, "melt beneath his hand." Convinced that the country needed the technical know-how of whites, Toussaint went out of his way to quiet their fears. The whites, out of fear *and* love, reciprocated. When the black general made a triumphant entrance into Port-au-Prince, the whole populace turned out. Little white girls, carrying baskets of flowers, lined the parade route and pelted Toussaint and his staff. Priests, planters and city officials walked up the road to greet him. Behind these functionaries were white women in elegant carriages and an honor guard composed of the planters' sons. The next day a delegation of planters, headed by the mayor, gave Toussaint a gold medal bearing his likeness and the words: "AFTER GOD—HE." Later, during a similar welcome to Le Cap, white men chose the most beautiful white woman in the city to place a laurel on Toussaint's head. The woman eulogized Toussaint in verses in which he was compared to Hercules and Alexander the Great.

Though Toussaint ruled nominally in the name of France, he was in reality the military and political dictator of Haiti. This fact pained Napoleon, another small-statured man of great military ability. Napoleon did not have a high opinion of men with dark skins. "I will not leave an epaulette," he said, "upon the shoulders of a single black."

There were other considerations. The French empire was not big enough for two Napoleons. It irritated the First Consul when men compared him with the Black Consul and found parallels in their careers. Beyond all that, Toussaint was in Napoleon's way. Napoleon had dreams of a vast empire in the Western Hemisphere; he needed Haiti and slave labor to complete the plans he had for the Louisiana Territory. Toussaint was thwarting these plans; Toussaint, therefore, had to go. Napoleon sent his brother-in-law, Victor Emanuel Leclerc, and some twenty-five thousand soldiers to do the job. Toussaint fell back into the mountains and harried Leclerc with a scorched-earth campaign. "Raid the roads," Toussaint instructed his subordinates, "throw the bodies of dead horses in all the springs; destroy and burn everything. May they find an image of the hell they deserve!"

The scorched-earth campaign continued until Henri Christophe, one of Toussaint's top generals, defaulted and went over to the French. Always a realist, Toussaint sued for a temporary peace and retired to his plantation. The French believed and many modern historians say that the cagey general was waiting for yellow fever to decimate the ranks of his enemies. Toussaint was a devout Roman Catholic, but there are reports that his faith weakened near the end. His nephew is authority for the story that the deposed general walked up to an altar in a village church and denounced it. "You! You are the God of the white man, not the God of the Negroes! You have betrayed men, and deserted me! You have no pity for my race!" He then, according to this report, hurled a marble crucifix to the floor.

Like most conquerors, Toussaint was vain. There came to his plantation one day a letter calculated to appeal to his vanity. The letter, couched in deferential, respectful terms, was from General Brunet, one of Leclerc's aides. Could Toussaint come to Brunet's headquarters for an important conference? He would not find all the comforts Brunet would like to put at his disposal, but he would find, the letter said, a "frank and honest man, whose only ambition is to promote the welfare of the colony and your happiness."

Toussaint, normally a cautious man, took the bait. When he reached Brunet's headquarters, he was arrested, hurried on a ship and dispatched to France. Napoleon, taking no chances, locked him up in a cell in a medieval fortress high in the Jura Alps on the French-Swiss borders. There, sometime between April 3 and April 7, 1803, death came to one of the greatest men produced in the Western Hemisphere. He was alone when he died, sitting in a straight-backed chair, in a dank, dark cell far from the Haitian sun. William Wordsworth, the English poet, saw him as "the most unhappy of men."

> O miserable Chieftain! where and when
> Wilt thou find patience! Yet die not; do thou
> Wear rather in thy bonds a cheerful brow:
> Though fallen thyself, never to rise again,
> Live, and take comfort. Thou hast left behind
> Powers that will work for thee: air, earth, and skies:
> There's not a breathing of the common wind
> That will forget thee; thou hast great allies;
> Thy friends are exultations, agonies,
> And love, and man's unconquerable mind.

Noble words, these; but Toussaint had a horror of mere words; and his friends, in the first instance, were the friends he always relied on—muskets. After his capture the mass militia he had organized sprang into revolt. Harried by the heat, yellow fever, and black soldiers who materialized from nowhere and disappeared into nowhere. Leclerc resorted to wholesale slaughter and terror.

If Leclerc and his successor, General Jean-Baptiste Rochambeau, wanted to play with fire, Jean-Jacques Dessalines was their man. A slim, handsome general with a fondness for elegant uniforms, Dessalines was mercurial and relentless. He had suffered in slavery and he had scars to prove it. In him was a loathing for all Frenchmen. As Toussaint's aide, he had demonstrated a military genius second only to the master. Now, as Toussaint's successor, he hurled a defiant challenge: "War for war, crime for crime, atrocity for atrocity." Dessalines was not talking for literary effect. He later organized a systematic extermination of white opponents of the new regime. One day, so the story goes, he stood watching a group of whites who were marching to their death. Suddenly, a man darted from the line, "Governor!" the man shouted. "They are going to kill your bootmaker. Save me!" Dessalines saved the man—vengeance was one thing and ill-fitting boots another.

The war continued—blow for blow, crime for crime. Leclerc bombarded Napoleon with appeals for help. "The [black] men," Leclerc wrote, "die with a fanaticism that is unbelievable. They laugh at death." One Haitian soldier, unfortunately nameless, immolated and immortalized himself by walking into a fire. "He was greater," a French officer wrote, "than Mucius Scaevola. The Roman hero burned his own hand. The Negro thrust his whole body into the fire to show his enemies that he knew how to die. And those were the men we had to fight!"

Time—it was only a matter of time. The hours ran out on Napoleon's men on November 28, 1803, at Vertieres outside Le Cap. After Rochambeau surrendered, Dessalines ripped the white from the French tricolor, joined the red and blue and proclaimed the second republic in the Western Hemisphere. The venture was doubly disastrous for Napoleon. The French lost some sixty thousand men and a rich colony, and Napoleon soured on the Western Hemisphere and sold the Louisiana Territory to

America for four cents an acre—the biggest real estate bargain in history. "Thus," said De Witt Talmadge, "all of Indian Territory, all of Kansas and Nebraska, Iowa and Wyoming, Montana and the Dakotas, and most of Colorado and Minnesota, and all of Washington and Oregon states, came to us as the indirect work of a despised Negro. Praise, if you will, the work of a Robert Livingstone or a Jefferson, but today let us not forget our debt to Toussaint L'Ouverture, who was indirectly the means of America's expansion by the Louisiana Purchase of 1803."

No monument was needed to remind nineteenth-century Americans of Haiti and Toussaint L'Ouverture. Every hint, every rumor of slave disaffection called back his memory. And the names of Gabriel Prosser, Denmark Vesey and Nat Turner turned memory into a nightmare.

The first of this triumvirate was a young man, only twenty-four, when he burst upon the guilty consciousness of the slave power. He stood six-feet-two and wore his hair long in imitation of his biblical idol, Samson. Like most leaders of American slave revolts, Gabriel was a deeply religious man. The Old Testament, particularly the blood and doom passages, fascinated him. In the dying days of the eighteenth century, Gabriel meditated on the Bible and dreamed dreams of a black state—not in the Caribbean, but in Virginia, the land of Thomas Jefferson and George Washington.

Gabriel laid plans for his uprising in the spring and summer of 1800. For four or five months he held meetings at fish fries and barbecues. Every Sunday he slipped into Richmond and studied the town, making a mental note of strategic points and the locations of arms and ammunition. Among Gabriel's associates were his brothers, Martin and Solomon, and his wife, Nanny. Martin was a religious exhorter and a firebrand. When a cautious slave advised delay, Martin exploded: "Before he would any longer bear what he had borne, he would turn out and fight with a stick."

Gabriel's plan was simple. Three columns would attack Richmond. The right wing would grab the arsenal and seize the guns; the left wing would take the powder house; the key central wing would enter the town at both ends simultaneously and would cut down every white person, except Frenchmen, Methodists and Quakers. After Richmond was secured Gabriel planned

lightning-like attacks on other cities in the state. If the plan succeeded, he was to be named king of Virginia. If it failed, the
insurgents were to flee to the mountains and fight a guerrilla war.

By August, 1800, several thousand (estimates range from two
thousand to fifty thousand) slaves had been enlisted. A date—
midnight, August 30—had been selected. Weapons—scythe
swords, pikes, guns—had been assembled. On the Saturday
selected Gabriel and his aides reviewed their plans and sweated
out the hours. At that juncture disaster struck. Two slaves informed their master, who, in turn, communicated the intelligence
to the authorities. The governor was so impressed with the magni-
tude of the danger that he shifted to a war footing, shoring up the
guard at vital installations and calling out the militia.

Unaware of the betrayal, Gabriel pressed forward, assembling
some one thousand slaves that night at the rendezvous point, six
miles outside Richmond. Certain historians believe they would
have carried the day if nature had not interceded with a tumultuous thunderstorm, which washed out bridges and roads and made
it impossible to get into Richmond. White Virginians said later
that an act of God saved them. We can only imagine what Gabriel
called the deluge that forced him to postpone the invasion. The
postponement was fatal. Before he could reassemble his forces,
the state attacked. Gabriel and some thirty-four of his men were
arrested, convicted and hanged. At the trial one of the defendants, perhaps Gabriel, made a stirring speech.

"I have nothing more to offer than what General Washington
would have had to offer, had he been taken by the British and put
to trial by them. I have adventured my life in endeavouring to
obtain the liberty of my countrymen, and am a willing sacrifice to
their cause; and I beg, as a favour, that I may be immediately led
to execution. I know that you have pre-determined to shed my
blood, why then all this mockery of a trial?"

When details of the plot leaked out, a chilling fear spread
through Virginia. "They could scarcely have failed of success,"
wrote the Richmond correspondent of the Boston *Chronicle*, "for,
after all, we could only muster four or five hundred men, of whom
not more than thirty had muskets." Another correspondent told
the Philadelphia *United States Gazette*: "Let but a single armed
Negro be seen or suspected, and, at once, on many a lonely
plantation, there were trembling hands at work to bar doors and

windows that seldom had been even closed before, and there was shuddering when a grey squirrel scrambled over the roof, or a shower of walnuts came down clattering from the overhanging boughs."

Denmark Vesey and Gabriel were cast in the same mold. In the year of Gabriel's defeat, Vesey won a lottery and purchased his freedom. From that date until 1822 he worked as a carpenter in Charleston, South Carolina, accumulating money and property. He was, by his own admission, satisfied with his own condition; yet he risked everything in a bold effort to free other men. Offered a chance to emigrate to Africa, Vesey balked, saying, a witness reported, "that he did not go . . . to Africa, because he had not a will, he wanted to stay and see what he could do for his fellow creatures."

There burned in Vesey's breast a deep and unquenchable hatred of slavery and slaveholders. A brilliant, hot-tempered man, he had served for some twenty years as the slave of a slave trader. In this work he traveled widely and learned several languages; he learned also that slavery was evil and that man was not meant to slave for man. Vesey reached a point, it is said, where he could not bear to have a white person in his presence.

The conspiracy this firebrand conceived is one of the most elaborate on record. For four or five years he patiently and persistently played the role of an agitator, telling slaves their lives were so miserable that even death would be an improvement. Vesey buttressed his arguments with quotations from abolitionists, Toussaint L'Ouverture and the Bible. He would read to the slaves "from the Bible *how the children of Israel were delivered out of Egypt from bondage*." But he warned that God helped those who helped themselves. Always, everywhere, the words of Joshua were on his lips:

> And they utterly destroyed all that was in the city, both man and woman, young and old, and ox, and sheep, and ass, with the edge of the sword.

Vesey threw himself into the task, holding nothing back. When slaves bowed to whites in the street, he would rebuke them. When the slaves replied, "But we are slaves," Vesey would comment with biting sarcasm, "You deserve to be slaves." Asked what slaves could do, he would tell the story of Hercules and the man whose wagon stuck at the bottom of the hill. The wagoner began to cry and pray; Hercules told him, Vesey would say, "to put the whip to the team and his shoulder to the wheel."

Never for a moment did Vesey himself slacken, or permit others to slacken, in the conspiracy which he stepped up from month to month. "I know Denmark Vesey," a slave said; "on one occasion he asked me, what news? I told him, none. He replied, 'We are free, but the white people here won't let us be so; and the only way is to raise up and fight the whites.' " Another witness said that "if it had not been for the cunning of the old villain Vesey, I should not now be in my present situation. He employed every strategem to induce me to join him. He was in the habit of reading to me all the passages in the newspapers that related to St. Domingo [Haiti], and apparently every pamphlet he could lay his hands on, that had any connection with slavery."

Ridiculing, taunting, threatening, Vesey gained a viselike hold on the minds of blacks in Charleston and surrounding areas. Many slaves feared him more than they feared their masters. One man said he feared Vesey more than he feared God.

Now, at the peak of his power, Vesey switched from the role of agitator to the role of organizer. Around Christmas in 1821, he chose lieutenants and created an organization. He was then in his early fifties, a vigorous, big-bodied man with a keen insight into human nature. "In the selection of his leaders," said the judges, "Vesey showed great penetration and sound judgment." In this effort he relied heavily on slave artisans and class leaders in the Methodist church. But he did not disdain the magical arts. A valuable functionary in his organization was Gullah Jack, an African-born sorcerer who was considered invulnerable. If Gullah Jack could not convince a potential recruit, the talents of Blind Phillip were available. Phillip reportedly could see ghosts and other invisible phenomena. Timid recruits were carried to his house, and Phillip would run his unseeing eyes over them and inquire: "Why do you look so timorous?" The recruits, thunderstruck that a blind man knew how they looked, would remain silent. Blind Phillip would quote Holy Scripture, "Let not your heart be troubled."

The chief lieutenant of this remarkable organization was Peter Poyas, a "first-rate ship carpenter" who displayed an organizing ability bordering on genius. Ice water ran in the veins of Poyas, who was undoubtedly the coolest gambler in the history of American slave revolts. Like a good poker player, he was a blend of caution and recklessness. Characteristically, he volunteered for the most dangerous assignment: the surprise and capture of the main guardhouse. The plan called for Poyas to advance alone, surprise the sentinel and quietly slit his throat.

Vesey recognized the unique gifts of Poyas, who coordinated organizing activities and decided who should and shouldn't be approached. It was Poyas who pinpointed the greatest danger to a slave revolt: house servants. He told one of his recruiting agents to "take care and don't mention it to those waiting men who receive presents of old coats, etc., from their masters, or they'll betray us: *I will speak to them.*"

As a tactical means of realizing their objectives, Vesey and Poyas created a cell-like organization. Each leader had a list of recruits and an assignment. Only the leaders knew the details of the plot; the average recruit knew nothing except the name of his leader and vague outlines of the plan. This meant that the arrest or betrayal of a single recruit would not endanger the whole plot.

For four or five months the Vesey organization recruited slaves in Charleston and surrounding areas. Whole plantations were signed up. Weapons were constructed. A barber was hired to make Caucasian disguises. It has been estimated that some nine thousand slaves were recruited.

Final plans for the insurrection were discussed at a series of meetings at Vesey's house. One conspirator left an interesting account of these discussions in his testimony at the trial. "I was invited to Denmark Vesey's house and when I went, I found several men met together, among whom was Ned Bennett, Peter Poyas, and others, whom I did not know. Denmark opened the meeting by saying he had an important secret to communicate to us, which we must not disclose to anyone, and if we did, we should be put to instant death. . . . He said, we were deprived of our rights and privileges by the white people . . . and that it was high time for us to seek for our rights, and that we were fully able to conquer the whites, if we were only unanimous and courageous, as the St. Domingo people were."

This witness said Vesey then proceeded to explain his plan, saying "that they intended to make the attack by setting the governor's mills on fire, and also some houses near the water, and as soon as the bells began to ring for fire, that they should kill every man, as he came out of his door, and that the servants in the yard should do it, and that it should be done with axes and clubs, and afterwards they should murder the women and children, for he said, God had commanded it in the Scriptures. At another meeting at Denmark's, Ned Bennett and Peter Poyas and several others were present in conversation, some said, they thought it was cruel to kill the ministers and the women and children, but Denmark Vesey said he thought it was for our safety, not to spare one white skin alive, for this was the plan they pursued in St. Domingo."

The plan of attack was simple and serviceable. It was based on the element of surprise and called for the slave army to strike at six points simultaneously on Sunday, July 16, 1822, taking possession of arsenals, guardhouses, powder magazines and naval stores in Charleston.

It could have worked and probably would have worked, but fate again intervened in the person of a slave named William Paul, who violated Poyas's order and tried to recruit a house slave. This happened on a Saturday in the last week of May. Within five days the authorities were in possession of the bare outlines of the plot.

There then followed one of the most extraordinary poker games in the history of slave conspiracies. At one end of town the mayor and other city officials worked feverishly to crack the plot. In another room, at the other end of town, Vesey and his aides worked feverishly to spring their trap. The city officials and Vesey were working under certain difficulties; neither side knew what cards the other side held. The city officials did not know the names of the leaders or the details of the plot, but Vesey did not know this. With incredible boldness, he continued to hold meetings and walked the streets as though nothing had happened.

The maneuvering continued for two weeks. Then word came through the grapevine that city officials were getting close; two of the top leaders—Peter Poyas and Mingo Harth—were under suspicion. A weak organization would have crumbled at this point, and men and leaders would have scurried to the hills. But the Vesey organization didn't work that way. Poyas and Harth ran not to the hills but to the mayor's office. They were indignant; their honor had been questioned and justice demanded that they be questioned and cleared. The authorities were confounded:

guilty slaves didn't act that way. Poyas and Harth were released and the cops-and-robbers game continued. Vesey, in his rooms on Bull Street, read the signs and moved D-Day up. Then, on the Friday before D-Day, another slave went over to the enemy. This slave, unlike the others, knew the plans and the names of some of the leaders. With mingled emotions of terror and relief, city and state officials alerted the militia and arrested Vesey and most of the leaders. Vesey and five of his aides were tried and hanged at Blake's Landing in Charleston on July 2, 1822. They behaved nobly, eyewitnesses say. Only one leader confessed; the rest remained silent in the face of abuse, threats, promises and torture. Peter Poyas, the official report said, was splendid in defeat. His only anxiety, the report said, was "to know how far the discoveries had extended; and the same emotions were exhibited in his conduct. He did not appear to fear personal consequences, for his whole behaviour indicated the reverse. . . . His countenance and behaviour were the same when he was sentenced; and his only words were, on retiring, 'I suppose you'll let me see my wife ‚and family before I die?' and that not in a supplicating tone. When he was asked, a day or two after, if it was possible he could wish to see his master and family murdered, who had treated him so kindly, he only replied to the question with a smile."

So cool, so carefree was Poyas that he spurned last-minute pleas for additional information. "Do not open your lips," he said to the other rebel leaders. "Die silent as you shall see me do." Archibald Grimké said such "words, considering the circumstances under which they were spoken, were worthy of a son of Sparta or of Rome, when Sparta and Rome were at their highest levels as breeders of iron men."

Gabriel Prosser plotted and was betrayed. Denmark Vesey plotted and was betrayed. Nat Turner plotted and executed.

The man called the Prophet was born in the year Gabriel died—1800. His mother, an African-born slave, could not bear the idea of bringing a slave into the world and was "so wild . . . that she had to be tied to prevent her from murdering him." The son survived and demonstrated his hatred of slavery in his own way.

A mystic with blood on his mind, a preacher with vengeance on his lips, a dreamer, a visionary, a revolutionary, Nat Turner was a

Planning the 1831 slave uprising, Nat Turner (above, center) outlines plans at a secret meeting in the woods. Turner's capture (left) ended the Southampton insurrection. He was hanged on November 11, 1831.

The trail of terror traveled by Nat Turner and his
men is indicated by a gray line. Some sixty whites
were killed in the insurrection.

fantastic mixture of gentleness, ruthlessness and piety. Of middling stature, black in color, in demeanor commanding and bold, he was five feet, six inches tall, a little dumpy perhaps, running to fat around the middle, with a mustache and a little tuft of hair on his chin.

Early in life Turner came to the view that God had set him aside for some great purpose. To accomplish this purpose, he avoided crowds and close companionships and wrapped himself in mystery. Systematically ascetic, he renounced tobacco, liquor and money. There was method in this maneuver, as Turner himself admitted:

"Having soon discovered [that] to be great, I must appear so, [I] studiously avoided mixing in society and wrapped myself in mystery, devoting my time to fasting and prayer."

In a lesser man this would have been bombast. But Turner was clearly no ordinary man. There was something, even at an early age, that set him apart. As a child he was inventive with his hands. Using pieces of wood and metal, he cast different things in molds made of earth and attempted "to make paper, gunpowder, and many other experiments."

By the time the black rebel reached maturity, he was a person of some importance in Southampton County. Slaves in the neighborhood, we are told, looked to him for advice and direction. Even whites were affected. An overseer fell under Turner's influence and so far overstepped the bounds of propriety that he let the slave preacher baptize him. The conversion took, and the overseer gave up his bad habits. The whites were so scandalized that they hounded the overseer out of the state.

With maturity and increasing recognition came a feeling that he was destined to lead his people out of bondage. Like Gabriel, like Denmark Vesey, Turner found food for insurrection in the Bible. He immersed himself in religion; he even prayed at the plow. He saw visions and heard voices. One day he had an unusual vision: he saw black and white spirits wrestling in the sky; the sun grew dark and blood gushed forth in streams.

Ordinary things appeared to the mystical slave in a strange light. While plowing the field, he saw drops of blood on the corn. While walking in the woods, he found hieroglyphic characters and blood on the leaves. He concluded from all this that the day of judgment for slaveholders was nigh. Another vision confirmed this conclusion. The "spirit," he said, told him that on the appearance of a sign "I should arise and prepare myself and slay my enemies with their own weapons." The sign appeared in the form of a solar eclipse in February, 1831.

Turner immediately chose four disciples, Henry Porter, Hark Travis, Nelson Williams and Samuel Francis, and set his face towards Jerusalem. Some historians believe he found warrant in the famous passage:

> From that time began Jesus to show unto his disciples, that he must go unto Jerusalem, and suffer many things of the elders and chief priests, and scribes, and be killed.

There was a Jerusalem in Virginia in that year: it was the county seat of Southampton. Turner decided to attack it on July 4, but he became ill and the day passed. There then came another sign—the peculiar color of the sun on August 13. Turner set another date, Sunday, August 21, and told his disciples to meet him at a wooded retreat near his slavemaster's farm.

On the appointed day the disciples gathered on the banks of Cabin Pond, where they ate barbecue, drank brandy and discussed death. Nat, a nondrinking man who appreciated the value of a dramatic entrance, did not join them until late in the afternoon. Then he appeared suddenly and ran his eyes over the group, noting that two additional slaves were present at the invitation of his disciples. Turner asked one of them, Will, "how came he there." Will replied that "his life was worth no more than others, and his liberty as dear to him." Six feet tall, or nearly so, well-developed, with a back covered with whip scars and a face disfigured by a scar extending from his right eye to his chin, Will was the slave of a cruel master. He was said to be the strongest man in the county and he bore a special grudge: his master had sold his wife to a Negro trader. Will later handled the broadax with such passion that Nat dubbed him, "Will, the executioner."

The defiant spirit of the disciples pleased Turner, and he outlined his plans. They would strike that night, beginning at the home of his master, and proceed from house to house, killing every man, woman and child. In this way, he explained, they would terrorize the whites and stampede them. Then, he said, women and children would be spared and "men too who ceased to resist."

About 10 P.M., the conspirators left their retreat and moved to the home of Joseph Travis. They were seven men, armed with one hatchet and a broadax. Twenty-four hours later, they would be seventy and at least fifty-seven whites would be dead.

At the Travis home Turner climbed through the window and led his men to the bedroom of the couple who had the great misfortune to own papers certifying their ownership of a slave named Nat Turner. Without preamble or warning the said Nat Turner aimed a death blow at the head of Joseph Travis. But his aim was faulty, and Will finished the job, killing both Travis and his wife. Two teenagers in an upstairs bedroom were also killed. An infant, sleeping in a cradle, was overlooked. As they left the house, Turner remembered and invoked the terrible rule that neither sex nor age was to be spared. Two men returned and slew the infant.

Moving swiftly and quietly through the night, the little band cut a swath of red, chopping down old, young, male, female. At almost every stop, additional slaves joined them.

"I took my station in the rear," Turner said later, "and, as it was my object to carry terror and devastation wherever we went, I placed fifteen or twenty of the best armed and most to be relied on in front, who generally approached the houses as fast as their horses could run. This was for two purposes—to prevent their escape, and strike terror to the inhabitants."

All through that terrible night, men, women and children died. No one with a white skin was spared except a family of poor whites who owned no slaves.

In reading the grisly accounts of this affair, it is impossible not to extend to the victims that human sympathy the victims were unable to extend to their victims—and their executioners. It is to be observed, too, that the victims were victims, more than anything else, of history and of the boomerang effect of a violent system they supported and/or derived benefits from. It is not true, as so many commentators have said, that Nat Turner initiated a wave of violence in Southampton. The violence was already there. Slavery was violence, and Nat Turner's acts, however regrettable they may be on a personal level, were responses to that violence and must be appraised historically, systemically, and politically.

None of this was apparent or perhaps even relevant to the white citizens of Southampton, who were seized with a nameless dread when the first bodies were discovered on Monday morning. Not knowing who or what was behind the killings, the citizens panicked, fleeing to the swamps or barricading themselves in public buildings. Some left the county; several left the state.

Meanwhile, Nat Turner rode on, picking up slave recruits at each stop, moving closer and closer to Jerusalem. On Monday afternoon, he reached the Parker farm, only three miles from Jerusalem. Turner wanted to bypass the farm and push on to the town, but his men, some of whom were groggy from periodic raids on cider stills, wanted to stop. Turner gave in—a fatal mistake. While waiting, he was attacked by a group of eighteen or twenty whites, who advanced with guns drawn. Turner, undaunted, counterattacked. The whites held their ground for a moment and then turned and fled. The slaves gave chase, crossed a hill and discovered that the whites had been reinforced by a larger group from Jerusalem. Forced to give ground, the rebel leader decided to retrace his steps and recruit additional slaves. But by now the tide was running strongly in favor of the slaveholders, who defeated the rebels at a second skirmish on Tuesday. After this encounter Turner retired to Cabin Pond and waited for his disciples to regroup. After waiting for a day or so, he dug a cave and went into hiding.

By this time soldiers were flocking to the county from all points. Three companies of artillery from Fort Monroe and detachments of men from the warships *Warren* and *Natchez* arrived. Hundreds of soldiers and militiamen from North Carolina and other Virginia counties thronged into the area. All in all, some three thousand armed men came to Southampton to put down the insurrection.

A massacre followed. The editor of the *Richmond Whig* said that "men were tortured to death, burned, maimed and subjected to nameless atrocities. The overseers were called upon to point out any slaves whom they distrusted; and if any tried to escape they were shot down." Another eyewitness, the Reverend G. W. Powell, told a correspondent that there were "thousands of troops searching in every direction, and many Negroes killed every day;

the exact number will never be ascertained." The purpose of all this was not to find or punish members of Nat Turner's army; the purpose, frankly acknowledged by many of the participants, was to terrorize and condition potential Nat Turners. Writing in the Richmond *Constitutional Whig* on September 3, 1831, John Hampdlen Pleasants put it bluntly:

"Let the fact not be doubted by those whom it most concerns, that another such insurrection will be the signal for the extermination of the whole black population in the quarter of the state where it occurs."

Among those most immediately concerned was a slave who later told Thomas Wentworth Higginson that "at the time of the old Prophet Nat the colored folks was afraid to pray loud; for the whites threatened to punish 'em dreadfully, if the least noise was heard. . . . The brightest and best was killed in Nat's time."

The object of all this attention eluded capture for almost two months. While he was at large, a panic seized large parts of Virginia, North Carolina and Maryland. Gen. W. H. Broadnax told the governor that "the consternation unfortunately was not confined to the county where the danger existed, but extended over all immediately about it. Not a white family in many neighborhoods remained at home, and many went to other counties, and the rest assembled at different points in considerable numbers for mutual protection. Numerous females, with their children, fled in the night with but one imperfect dress and no provisions. I found every hovel at Hicks' Ford literally filled with women and children, with no way to lodge but in heaps on the floors, without any article of food or the means of procuring or cooking provisions."

In North Carolina, too, people feared Nat Turner more than starvation. The situation in Murfreesboro was desperate, according to an eyewitness, who said: "It was court week, and most of our men were twelve miles away, in Winton. Fear was seen in every face; women pale and terror-stricken, children crying for protection, men fearful and full of foreboding, but determined to be ready for the worst." When a boy rode into the town and reported falsely that a hostile force was within eight miles, Murfreesboro went up in hysteria. An old man keeled over and died. Two other white men died of heart failure in the state.

The panic rolled over a large part of the South. A niece of George Washington said the hysteria was "like a smothered volcano—we know not when, or where, the flame will burst forth but we know that death in the most horrid form threatens us. Some have died, others have become deranged from apprehension since the Southampton affair."

When Turner was finally captured, guns were fired all over Southampton County. The women, thinking he had assembled another force, fled to the swamps, misinterpreting the cry, "Nat is caught!" for "Nat is coming!"

Nat Turner was taken to Jerusalem in chains. At his trial he pleaded not guilty, saying that he did not *feel* guilty. Judge Jeremiah Cobb pronounced sentence. "The judgement of the court, is that you be taken hence to the jail from whence you came, thence to the place of execution, and on Friday next, between the hours of 10 A.M. and 2 P.M. be hung by the neck until you are dead! dead! dead! and may the Lord have mercy upon your soul."

On November 11 the bold black man called the Prophet dangled from the end of a rope in a town called Jerusalem. Author W. S. Drewry said that Turner prophesied that it would grow dark and rain after his execution. "It did actually rain," Drewry wrote, "and there was for some time a dry spell. This alarmed many whites as well as Negroes." But this was a misunderstanding of Turner and his prophesy. For the storm he saw, came. It came in a generation of crisis in which the issue of slavery almost severed the nation. Nat Turner's "dark arm of vengeance" did much to bring that crisis to a head. In this, Drewry is correct. For, as he observed, Nat Turner's insurrection "was a landmark in the history of slavery. . . . It was the forerunner of the great slavery debates, which resulted in the abolition of slavery in the United States and was, indirectly, most instrumental in bringing about this result. Its importance is truly conceived by the old Negroes of Southampton and vicinity, who reckon all time from 'Nat's Fray' or 'Old Nat's War.' "

6

The Generation of Crisis

Let our posterity know that we their ancestors, uncultured and unlearned, amid all trials and temptations, were men of integrity; recognized with gratefulness their truest friends dishonoured and in peril; were enabled to resist the seductions of ease and the intimidations of power; were true to themselves, the age in which they lived, their abject race, and the cause of man; shrunk not from trial, nor from sufferings — but conscious of Responsibility and impelled by Duty, gave themselves up to the vindication of the high hopes, and the lofty aims of true Humanity!

ALEXANDER CRUMMELL

THE WHOLE STORY is in three boys and an old man.

In the years of hope and promise before the big war, before the blood and the rats and the bleached bones, the old man and the three boys dreamed dreams and made prophecies.

The old man heard fire bells ringing in the night.

Before old age downed him he had spoken the language of desperation and death, saying, this is "a reprieve only, not a final sentence." He added:

"This momentous question, like a fire bell ringing in the night, awakened me and filled me with terror."

The old man was talking about the Missouri Compromise, a thing of lines and words, and slavery, a thing of words and compromises. The old man knew whereof he spoke: for he was involved in the compromise that he, more than anyone else, had made impossible. He had, when his blood was hot, put words on paper.

> We hold these Truths to be self-evident, that all Men are created equal, that they are endowed by their Creator with certain unalienable Rights, that among these are Life, Liberty, and the pursuit of Happiness.

He had written these words in a room in Philadelphia when he was thirty-three. Now, in another room, in another age, fifty years to the date after the signing of the Declaration of Independence, Thomas Jefferson, the sage of Monticello, the architect, the philosopher, the slaveholder, lay dying in a house filled with rare books and old slaves. All his life he had wrestled with the awful presence of *his* slaves and the noble sound of *his* words and he had gone down in defeat. He was not a small man and his defeat gives no man joy. In him was the strength and the weakness of America. He died on July 4, 1826, and went to his grave, borne by slaves.

In that same year, over in Little Pigeon Creek, Indiana, a big awkward boy of seventeen, all arms and legs, was reading books and chopping down trees. He was dirt poor, a descendent of poor people who left Europe running and came to America looking for something better than the life they had. Some of his kin signed their names with an X, but he was dreaming bigger things. He read books in an area where few people read books. People said, "There's somethin' peculiarsome about Abe."

"Peculiarsome," too, was Frederick Augustus Washington Bailey, a nine-year-old slave in Baltimore, Maryland. Frederick and Abe were two of a kind. Both would climb out of their narrow prisons on ladders of words; both would climb steep mountains and walk lonely paths; and both would grapple with the revolutionary implications of Thomas Jefferson's words. Fate had sent their forefathers across the same ocean. Abe's folks had been pushed out of Europe by need and want, and Frederick's folks had been pulled out of Africa by greed and gold. Fate had implanted in both of their bosoms a hunger for letters. Frederick's mistress wanted to teach him the alphabet, but his master forbade it. "Give a nigger an inch," he said, "and he will take an ell. . . . Learning would spoil the best nigger in the world." Listening, thinking, dreaming, Frederick came to the conclusion that words were power. He hid dirty pages in his pockets and when no one was looking he extracted the pages and spelled out the magic words. Like Abe, Frederick was a comer.

Up the country a bit, another comer was deep in the happy world of books and dreams. Jefferson Davis, eighteen, the grandson of an illiterate Welsh immigrant, a namesake of the great Thomas Jefferson, was studying war at West Point. Like Abraham Lincoln, like the slave who would take the name Frederick Douglass, Jefferson Davis was ambitious. It would be said of him later that he was "ambitious as Lucifer and cold as a lizard."

In these three boys, in their hopes, in their dreams, in their fears, is the whole story of the drama that reached a climax in a Civil War and the emancipation of four million slaves with a book value of four billion dollars. The crisis was a compound of many things, of machines and turnpikes and railroad tracks; of sin, sex and salvation; of the restless yearnings of poor whites and the volcanic stirrings of poor blacks; of the fear, guilt and anxiety which lay like a slave chain across the American soul. Abraham Lincoln, Frederick Douglass and Jefferson Davis did not make the crisis, but they would stand in the eye of the storm and each, in his own way, would symbolize the latent possibilities in the American Dream.

How did the crisis come about?

It came about because millions of men made choices, acted and were called upon finally to back up their acts. It came about because men said words, wrote them and were called upon finally to back up their words.

The crisis had been a long time coming. It went back to the founding fathers who gave in to Southern threats, compromised and wrote slavery into the Constitution. They were not little men, the founding fathers, and they were ashamed of what they were doing. They could not bring themselves to write the ugly word *slave*; they used instead weasel words like "persons held to serve or labor" (Art. IV, Sec. 2) and they contented themselves with the idle hope that slavery would wither and die. But slavery did not die. A machine, a thing of brushes and cylinders and wire teeth, made black men and white fibers big business. Year by year the evil spread until it ate into the tendons of American life.

The Missouri Compromise made people look at the monster they had created. A line was scratched on a map and slavery was forbidden to the north of that line; but, as it turned out, nothing had been settled. Far off on the horizon, a storm was rising; but people were walking in the streets without umbrellas. Leaders with eyes to see, saw it. Thomas Jefferson saw it and cried out in despair. John Quincy Adams saw it and told his diary that the bargain between slavery and freedom in the U.S. Constitution was "morally and politically vicious." Other Americans saw it and moved with a vague sense of disquiet to contain the monster. Step by step, act by act, compromise by compromise, America moved toward the great antislavery crusade which brought the issue to a head.

This crusade, which was one of the great social movement of modern history, unfolded in two phases and was shaped by black action and perception at every point. The first phase, a phase marked by muted rhetoric and reformist demands for limited improvements in the slave system, grew out of and reflected the antislavery impulses of the Rights of Man movement, which was based on Thomas Jefferson's massive and ambiguous ALL. Black pioneer leaders, as we have seen, were in the front ranks of this struggle, which led to the manumision of thousands of slaves and the death of slavery in the North. When, after the Treaty of Paris, it became clear that the war had neither killed nor wounded slavery, black leaders leaped into action on new fronts, organizing antislavery groups and vigilance committees which not only agitated against slavery but also pressed the dangerous—and illegal work—of aiding and transporting fugitive slaves.

One outstanding fact about this early period, well understood in earlier times, but afterwards forgotten, is that pioneer black abolitionists educated themselves and their white colleagues, most of whom were stuck in reformist-gradualist holes and had unrealistic perceptions about slaveowners and slaves. The Black abolotionists, most notably Samuel E. Cornish and James Forten, were primarily responsible for turning pioneer white abolitionists, such as William Lloyd Garrison and Gerrit Smith, against the deportation fantasies of the American Colonization Society. Still another contribution was the creation of the first level of antislavery organization. According to author John Daniels, blacks initiated the antislavery struggle in Massachusetts around 1826 with the organization of the General Coloured Association, which was formed to promote the welfare of the race, principally by working for the destruction of slavery. In the years that followed, pioneer black leaders created scores of antislavery cells, including the African Abolition Freehold Society, the African Female Anti-Slavery Society, and the New York Committee of Vigilance, headed by David Ruggles, who has been called the "Father of the Underground Railroad." By 1830 there were more than fifty such groups in Northern centers.

Beginning in the first year of the nineteenth century, pioneer abolitionists started to move in a new and different directions. Two events signalled the new departure. The first was a simple petition, filed in the House of Representatives on January 2, 1800. The petition came from a group of Pennsylvania blacks, including Absalom Jones and James Forten, who sought legislative relief from the slave trade, the Fugitive Slave Law and the institution of slavery. Congressional reaction to this gambit was instantaneous and explosive. John Rutledge Jr. of South Carolina said the petition was a product of "this new-fangled French philosophy of liberty and equality." Harrison Gray Otis of Massachusetts thought the matter was more serious. "To encourage a measure of this kind," he said, "would have an irritating tendency, and must be mischievous to America very soon. It would teach them [blacks] the art of assembling together, debating, and the like, and would so soon, if encouraged, extend from one end of the Union to the other." The petition died in committee after the House expressed the opinion that it had a "tendency to create disquiet and jealousy."

By singular circumstance, this petition coincided with a great upswelling of indignation in the slave South, an upswelling that peaked with the second disquieting event of that year, the Gabriel Prosser uprising in the state of Virginia.

These developments and others of similar tone and texture

made a profound impression on whites, who responded on two levels. The first was a tightening of the screws of slavery. The second was the creation of a colonization movement which called for the resettlement of free blacks ("a dangerous and useless element") in Liberia. Various white abolitionists were faked out of position by this development, but it was clear to most blacks that the colonizationists were generally anti-black and proslavery. One black put the case against the colonizationists with militant bluntness. "The colonizationists," he said, "want us to go to Liberia, if we will. If we won't go there, we may go to hell."

Most free blacks didn't intend to emigrate to either place. To emphasize this determination, they organized an extremely effective anticolonization campaign, which marked a new and decisive moment in the antislavery struggle. In examining that campaign, we must bear in mind that forced deportation—an idea repeatedly advanced by prominent whites — was perhaps the greatest fear of pioneer black leaders. This fear, which came from the greatest depths and which engaged explosive emotions that transcended logic, clashed with a competing desire to advance the cause of Africa, a name that was emblazoned across the front of most black institutions. The solution adopted by most free blacks was support for individual emigration and resistance to mass emigration. This solution—contradictory, ambivalent and deeply worrisome—was the expression, on one level, of a will to peoplehood. It was the expression of the idea, dimly grasped at first but always waxing clearer, that African-America was a whole irrevocably wedded to the historical coordinates that defined it.

This idea was expressed haltingly and in imprecise language in a tentative and illuminating dialogue in the fateful and momentous year of 1787. Responding to a communication from the Negro Union of Newport, which had suggested a mass exodus to Africa, the powerful Philadelphia Free African Society said:

"With regard to the emigration to Africa you mention we have at present little to communicate on that head, apprehending every . . . man is a good citizen of the . . . world."

This was not, by any means, the end of the discussion, which continued in the following years and became a permanent obbligato to the black American dialogue. In 1815 Captain Paul Cuffe moved the discussion to a new level, carrying thirty-eight blacks to Sierra Leone in his own ship. Although Captain Cuffe re-

mained in America—he died in Massachusetts in 1817—other
blacks, believing and saying that white America would never
change, decided to emigrate to Africa. The leading exponents of
this view were Daniel Coker, the pioneer AME leader, and John B.
Russwurm, the coeditor of the first black newspaper. Russwurm,
who said it was "a waste of words to talk of ever enjoying
citizenship in this country," was denounced as a traitor by various
Northern leaders and found it necessary to relinquish his position
on *Freedom's Journal*.

Russwurm's critics said it was an objective betrayal of the
slaves to call for a mass exodus of free blacks. They contended
that a mass exodus would objectively strengthen the bonds of
slavery and deprive slaves of cells of support and sustenance.
They also said that Russwurm's white colleagues were deliberately fanning the fires of racism in a devilish plot to drive
free blacks out of America.

To forestall this threat and to counter a rising tide of repression, activists launched a major counteroffensive. For perhaps
the first time, they utilized mass pressure techniques. The largest
and perhaps most significant of a series of mass meetings was
held by three thousand blacks who met at Philadelphia's Bethel
AME Church in January, 1817. James Forten presided over the
deliberations of this pivotal meeting, which denounced the
American Colonization Society and published the following declaration:

> Whereas our ancestors (not of choice) were the first suc-
> cessful cultivators of the wilds of America, we their descend-
> ants feel ourselves entitled to participate in the blessings of
> her luxuriant soil, which their blood and sweat manured; and
> that any measure or system of measures, having a tendency
> to banish us from her bosom, would not only be cruel, but in
> direct violation of those principles, which have been the
> boast of this republic.
>
> Resolved, That we view with deep abhorrence the unmer-
> ited stigma attempted to be cast upon the reputation of the
> free people of color, by the promoters of this measure, "that
> they are a dangerous and useless part of the community,"
> when in the state of disfranchisement in which they live, in
> the hour of danger they ceased to remember their wrongs,
> and rallied around the standard of their country.

> Resolved, That we never will separate ourselves voluntar-
> ily from the slave population in this country; they are our
> brethren by the ties of consanguinity, of suffering, and of
> wrong; and we feel that there is more virtue in suffering
> privations with them, than fancied advantage for a season.

In this resolution, and in similar resolutions adopted by mass meetings in Richmond, Virginia, New York City and other urban areas, the avant-garde of the free blacks of America committed themselves to the view that they were Americans or, to be more precise, African-Americans. So resolving, they closed one of the mighty doors of history. For it was still possible at that point to "solve" some racial issues by emigration. As a matter of fact, this was perhaps the last chance for a solution by mass flight. The delegates rejected that solution in a decision that would echo and re-echo down the corridors of American time. It seems from available evidence that they accurately reflected the views of most free blacks.

All this was of vast importance in the political education of the free blacks of the North. Out of the ferment of the anticolonization movement came the first militant abolitionists, the first black newspaper, *Freedom's Journal*, and the first national black convention. Richard Allen was elected president of this convention, which opened on Wednesday, September 20, 1830, and was attended by about forty delegates from eight states. This was the first of a series of national conventions which completed the national structure started by blacks in the Black Pioneer period. Periodically, after 1830, blacks met in national conventions and debated strategy and tactics. In succeeding years, as in 1830, they issued addresses to the nation, deploring the plight of black Americans and urgently calling for national and local action. By these means, leaders established channels of communication and concrete links between blacks in different cities. With this development, the basic structure of Black America was essentially complete. The only major task remaining—institutionally—was the creation of an effective national protest organization, a task that eluded Black America for more than seventy years.

If the national black convention did not complete that task, it did set the stage for the second and more militant phase of the antislavery campaign, a phase that began with the words of a free black and the acts of a slave. The free black, David Walker, was a product of the evolving group consciousness of black Americans. Born free in Wilmington, North Carolina, in 1785, he decided that the very air of a slaveholding community was noxious. "If I remain in this bloody land," he said, "I will not live long. As true as God reigns, I will be avenged for the sorrows which my people have suffered. This is not the place for me—no, no. I must leave this part of the country. . . . Go, I must." Walker left, going to Boston where he opened a secondhand clothing store. In 1828 he branched out as a radical agitator; a year later, on September 28, 1829, he published *Walker's Appeal*, one of the great abolitionist documents. The full title of this pamphlet of some eighty pages was *Walker's Appeal, in Four Articles: Together with a Preamble, to the Coloured Citizens of the World, but in particular, and very expressly, to those of the United States of America*. Walker's appeal, as the title indicates, was an appeal for universal emancipation. He believed the blacks of the world were linked by chains of blood and destiny and that there could be no emancipation of American blacks without a simultaneous emancipation of the blacks of Africa and the West Indies. Speaking specifically and "very expressly" to American blacks, he said:

"Your full glory and happiness . . . shall never be fully consummated, but with the entire emancipation of your universal brethren all over the world. . . . For I believe it is the will of the Lord that our greatest happiness shall consist in working for the salvation of our whole body. When this is accomplished a burst of glory will shine upon you, which will indeed astonish you and the world."

What, then, was to be done?

Walker proposed a sustained and total struggle using all available means, including violence. In this pamphlet, and in other utterances, he was scornful of the slaveholding Christians of "this Republican Land of Liberty!!!!!" and he urged slaves to cut their tormentors' throats from ear to ear. "Kill or be killed," he said, adding: "If you commence, make sure work—do not trifle, for they will not trifle with you. . . . Now, I ask you, had you not rather be killed than to be a slave to a tyrant, who takes the life of your mother, wife, and dear little children? Look upon your mother, wife, and children, and answer God Almighty; and believe this, that it is no more harm for you to kill a man, who is trying to kill you, than it is for you to take a drink of water when thirsty."

Like a cry of fire in a crowded theater, like the sound of screeching tires on a crowded thoroughfare, these words constricted hearts and made sweat run down backs. The governors of Virginia, Georgia and North Carolina called special sessions of their legislatures to discuss Walker's words, and a number of Southern mayors asked the mayor of Boston to lock Walker up and burn his book. The uproar over this event had hardly subsided when the slave power was struck by a far more devastating blow, the midnight ride of Nat Turner. With these two events, the Abolitionist movement entered a decisively new phase. It is quite clear in retrospect that Walker and Turner midwifed that phase and prepared the way for the militant abolitionists.

There had never been a group of Americans like the men and women who emerged in the 1830s and assumed new postures under a new banner demanding immediate emancipation of the slaves without compensation to slaveholders. Like David Walker, like Malcolm X, like Martin Luther King and Nat Turner and W.E.B. DuBois, the militant abolitionists were distant echoes of Thomas Jefferson's Declaration. But they, unlike Jefferson, seemed to believe the words. Not only did they believe the words but they also acted them, going out into the streets and highways and goading and provoking a slumbering people into facing the greatest moral issue of the day.

The abolitionists accomplished this feat by creating a mass movement remarkably similar to the Freedom movement of the 1960s. Like the demonstrators of the sixties, the militant abolitionists pioneered in nonviolent direct action, holding mass meetings, singing freedom songs, staging sit-ins and freedom rides. They, like their modern counterparts, marched, demonstrated and picketed. In the end the militant abolitionists discovered that the issue of black freedom is a total issue that raises total questions about the meaning of America. The end result was that the militant abolitionist crusade, like the Freedom movement of the sixties, branched out into the issues of women's rights, sexual freedom and economic democracy.

There were other parallels, including the missionary tone of the movement. The abolitionists said slavery existed because it was sanctioned by "the good people." Proceeding on this assumption, they tried to alter public opinion and isolate slaveholders. To accomplish this, they attacked the U.S. government, the

John B. Russwurm was one of the founders of the black press. Russwurm and Samuel E. Cornish founded the first black newspaper, *Freedom's Journal*, in 1827.

Henry Highland Garnet, minister and editor, was an abolitionist and diplomat. In a famous speech of 1843, he called for a slave revolt.

Fugitive slaves played a major role in the events which led to the Civil War. Some cities refused to return fugitive slaves. Some two thousand soldiers were required to escort Anthony Burns, a captured slave, to the Boston ship which returned him to the South.

church, the business establishment—everyone, in fact, who supported the status quo. This strategy led William Lloyd Garrison to attack the U.S. Constitution—which contained clauses protecting and legitimizing slavery—as "a covenant with death and an agreement with hell." When, in 1850, the U.S. Congress passed the Fugitive Slave Law, Garrison tore up a copy of the Constitution, put a match to the fragments and shouted: "And let the people say, Amen." The people said: "Amen."

With missionary fervor, and with slashing impartiality, the abolitionists, black and white, pressed a revolutionary war against slaveholders and supporters of slaveholders. Wendell Phillips and several other abolitionists refused to vote, practice law, or exercise any function under the Constitution until slavery was abolished. Various preachers gave up large churches and committed themselves to a full-time ministry of agitation.

The white wing of this movement was composed largely of middle-income people, ministers, lawyers, teachers. But there was substantial and surprising support from individuals in the upper strata of Northern society. The Tappan brothers were New York merchant princes; Gerrit Smith was the largest landowner in New York state; the Grimké sisters, Sarah and Angelina, were South Carolina bluebloods who were hounded out of Charleston because of their advanced racial views.

William Lloyd Garrison, who shared movement leadership with whites like Wendell Phillips and blacks like Frederick Douglass, came from the poor white class. A former indentured servant, born dirt poor in Newburyport, Massachusetts, Garrison educated himself and became a provocatively brilliant propagandist. Like so many other white abolitionists, he began his career as a gradualist but soon switched to a more radical posture. Although Garrison was white, he threw himself into the struggle with so much fervor that some people assumed he was black. "I never rise before a colored audience," Garrison said, "without feeling ashamed of my race."

Heavily influenced and subsidized by blacks, Garrison opened his famous paper, the *Liberator*, in Boston on January 1, 1831. The first editorial sounded a new note:

> I will be as harsh as truth, and as uncompromising as justice. On this subject [slavery], I do not wish to think, to

> speak, or write, with moderation. No! No! Tell a man whose
> house is on fire to give a moderate alarm; tell him to moder-
> ately rescue his wife from the hands of the ravisher; tell the
> mother to gradually extricate her babe from the fire into
> which it has fallen; but urge me not to use moderation in a
> cause like the present! I am in earnest—I will not equiv-
> ocate—I will not excuse—I will not retreat a single inch—
> AND I WILL BE HEARD!

This was clear enough and—to slaveholders—ominous
enough. And Garrison, to his credit, lived up to it—at least until
the Civil War when he, along with a number of other white
abolitionists, retreated and equivocated. But all that was far in
the future on the day he climbed the heights and looked far into
the future, inspiring men and women and summoning them to the
same height by the breadth of his vision.

The appearance of Garrison marked a profound change of pace
in the Abolitionist movement, which became a force to be reckoned with after the founding, in 1833, of a national umbrella
group, the American Anti-Slavery Society. The first board of
managers of this seminal society included five black abolitionists:
Peter Williams, Robert Purvis, George B. Vashon, Abraham
Shadd and James McCrummell.

From the founding of the American Anti-Slavery Society until the
end of slavery, thirty-two years later, a seemingly endless procession of remarkable men and women held the center stage of
American life. Of these men and women the most interesting and
courageous by far were the fugitive slaves who traveled the Underground Railroad. Far from being passive, as they are usually
portrayed, they were major antagonists in the sectional drama. As
much as William Lloyd Garrison, as much as John Brown, they
made men and women confront the evils of the slave system. In
an age when most people wanted to forget, "running abolitionists" made them remember.

Fugitive slaves scaled mountains, forded creeks and threaded
the forests. They came across the Ohio River and the Chesa-
peake Bay. They came with ailing women and sick children.
Softly sometimes and sometimes imperiously they rapped on
windows and begged help: a piece of bread, a spoon of medicine,
directions to the next town. Wherever they rapped, wherever

they stopped, men and women had to make a decision—either for or against slavery. Fugitive slaves reached people who were cool or hostile to the "speaking abolitionists." Whigs helped them and Democrats, too; Quakers helped them, and Southern Baptists. Frederick Douglass said, "We seldom called in vain upon Whig or Democrat for help. Men were better than their theology, and truer to humanity than to their politics, or their offices."

The implications of all this were shrewdly weighed in a *Boston Commonwealth* article: "It was said long ago that the true romance of America was not in the fortunes of the Indian, where Cooper sought it; nor in New England character, where Judd found it; nor in the social contrasts of Virginia planters, as Thackeray imagined, but in the story of the fugitive slaves."

Thousands of fugitive slaves—estimates range from forty thousand to one hundred thousand—escaped from the South in the years of crisis. In the background of each succeeding crisis—the fight over the Wilmot Proviso, the Kansas-Nebraska Bill, the Compromise of 1850—was the constant irritant of intrepid slaves who lectured with their feet. The road these slaves traveled ran from the sunny South to the distant shores of Canada. One great route ran through Ohio and Indiana; the other went through Maryland, Delaware and Pennsylvania. Following the North Star, fugitives made their way along these routes to Canada. Along the way they were aided by "a company of godly men"—some of them white, some of them black, many of them women. White abolitionists like Levi Coffin and Thomas Garrett and thousands of gentle Quakers were among the undercover agents who hid slaves and slipped them through to the next Underground Railroad station. More potent still was the counsel and example of scores of black agents who did the same thing at far greater risks. Two black men, David Ruggles and William Still, were in charge of the key Underground Railroad stations in New York City and Philadelphia, respectively. White abolitionist James G. Birney said the Underground Railroad in his area was "almost uniformly managed by the colored people. I know nothing of them generally till they are past." Levi Coffin, who was a major white leader of the Underground Railroad, said that fugitive slaves generally stopped at the homes of black sympathizers and agents.

Was it true what they said about Dixie?

This question was the core of the slavery dialogue; and no one could answer it better than fugitive slaves, who quickly moved into the front lines of the antislavery battle. In the 1840s no abolitionist meeting was complete without a black speaker or a black exhibit (a fugitive slave). Audiences would accept a white speaker, if necessary; but they preferred the real thing, a speaker like Henry Highland Garnet who could say: "I was born in slavery, and have escaped, to tell you, and others, what the monster has done, and is still doing."

"Oh," Sarah Grimké cried out, "that the slaves could write a book!"

In the two decades preceding the Civil War, many slaveholders asked slaves to stop writing books. In these decades scores of slaves escaped and told, increasing the abolitionist audience and creating a new branch of literature. An English clergyman, Ephraim Peabody, observed that "America had the mournful honor of adding a new department to the literature of civilization—the autobiography of escaped slaves."

The pioneer black abolitionists gave way in the forties to the giants of the movement: Charles Lenox Remond, the first black to take the platform as a professional antislavery lecturer; Samuel Ringgold Ward, the eloquent black man who pastored a white church; Henry Highland Garnet, the brilliant activist of the movement; Martin R. Delany, the Harvard man who was the first major black nationalist; William Wells Brown, the grandson (he said) of Daniel Boone and the first black to write a novel and a play. There were others: the big-souled, God-intoxicated women, Sojourner Truth and Harriet Tubman; and scholars like J. W. C. Pennington, the minister who received a degree from the University of Heidelberg; Alexander Crummell, the erudite Episcopal priest; and James McCune Smith, the New York physician who graduated from the University of Glasgow.

Frederick Augustus Washington Bailey, the giant of the giants, graduated from the school of slavery. He escaped from Baltimore in 1838 by borrowing a sailor suit and an official-looking paper with a big American eagle on it. Catching a train, young Bailey traveled to New York, flashing his eagle-stamped paper as he

went. Three years later he stood on a platform with a new name,
Douglass, and an old story. The story was old, but no one had
ever told it that way before. By turns humorous, dolorous and
indignant, Douglass transported his audiences to Slave Row. A
master mimic, he could make people *laugh* at a slaveowner
preaching the duties of Christian obedience; could make them
see the humiliation of a black maiden ravished by a brutal
slaveowner; could make them *hear* the sobs of a mother separated from her child. Through him, people could cry and curse
and *feel*; through him, people could *live* slavery. "White men and
black men," William Wells Brown said, "had talked against slavery, but none had ever spoken like Frederick Douglass."

As Douglass's reputation as a speaker grew, he came to the
attention of the Garrisonians, who added him to their stable of
traveling agitators. This was something of a mixed blessing, for
abolitionist agitators traveled from town to town preaching to the
unconverted, who often responded with verbal abuse and violence. It was not at all uncommon in this age for white abolitionists to be thrown from platforms, but a special venom was reserved for black abolitionists like Frederick Douglass. There
were riots and other disorders during and after his speeches, and
swaggering whites repeatedly charged the platform, yelling, "Kill
the nigger!" Although Douglass was pelted with eggs and thrown
down steps, he held tenaciously to his course and his audiences
grew. Intrigued, people came, listened and went away convinced.
More importantly, for Douglass anyway, they left singing his
praises.

Douglass grew in the job; so did his ambition; so did his problems. To some abolitionists, the slave was an exhibit, not an
advocate. Douglass disturbed these people. He did not fit into the
usual pattern; he not only recited evils but he also denounced
them. "People won't believe that you were a slave, Frederick,"
one abolitionist said, "if you keep on in this way." Another
abolitionist told Douglass, "Better have a little of the plantation
speech than not; it is not best that you seem too learned." More
blunt were the repeated exhortations: "Give us the facts, we will
take care of the philosophy." More and more sure of himself, and
conscious of his growing powers, Douglass refused to be
stereotyped. "I could not always follow the injunction," he wrote

later, "for I was now reading, and thinking. New views of the subject were being presented to my mind. It did not entirely satisfy me to narrate wrongs; I felt like denouncing them. . . . Besides, I was growing and needed room."

Douglass found room and a practical finishing school in England, which had emancipated its slaves in 1834 and was now preaching against the sin of slavery with the missionary fervor of a reformed sinner. When, in 1845, Douglass arrived in England, he found that black abolitionists were in vogue. Lords, Ladies and earls welcomed them to suburban estates; ambassadors feted them in Regent's Park; ordinary people flocked to their lectures in Exeter Hall and Finsbury Chapel. "It is good," the *New York Herald* said indignantly, "to be dyed black if you come up to London, for Negro love is filling all ranks, from Prince Albert and the Queen, down to the poorest subjects." Douglass, who left America hurriedly after publication of his autobiography alerted his former master to his whereabouts, found this environment stimulating. After nineteen months in England, he said, "I seem to have undergone a transformation. I live a new life."

Tall, well-made, with an impressive mane of hair, a throbbing baritone voice, and a vast forehead over deep-set smoldering eyes, Douglass created something of a sensation in England. One Englishman found him "touchy, huffish, haughty" with "many of the characteristics of the man of genius." Another abolitionist wrote, "You can hardly conjure how he is noticed." Douglass's female admirers, he added, "exceed the bounds of propriety or delicacy as far as appearances are concerned."

The celebrated abolitionist crisscrossed England and Ireland, winning friends and influencing people for the antislavery cause. His reception was so warm that he was tempted to remain abroad. But in an eloquent farewell speech at London Tavern on March 30, 1847, he said:

"I choose rather to go home; to return to America. I glory in the conflict, that I may hereafter exult in the victory. I know that victory is certain. [Cheers.] I go, turning my back upon the ease, comfort, and respectability which I might maintain even here, ignorant as I am. Still, I will go back, for the sake of my brethren. I go to suffer with them; to toil with them; to endure insult with them; to undergo outrage with them; to lift up my voice in their

William Lloyd Garrison, a major figure in the Abolitionist movement, worked closely with black abolitionists like James Forten and Charles Lenox Remond.

Frederick Douglass, one of the great men of the nineteenth century, was a leading abolitionist, politician and editor.
Born a slave in Maryland in 1817, Douglass escaped in 1838.

Pennsylvania Hall, erected by abolitionists in Philadelphia, was burned on May 17, 1838, by Northerners who opposed the antislavery crusade. There were five major anti-black riots in Philadelphia between 1832 and 1849.

behalf; to speak and write in their vindication; and struggle in their ranks for that emancipation which shall yet be achieved by the power of truth and of principle for that oppressed people."

So, turning his back on ease, comfort and respectability, Douglass returned to America. For almost six years he had labored in the Garrison vineyard. Now he stepped out on his own. In 1847, the year that Abraham Lincoln entered the House of Representatives, the year that Jefferson Davis, the Mexican War hero, entered the Senate, Frederick Douglass started publishing the *North Star* in Rochester, New York. From that year until the abolition of slavery, he was in the forefront of the abolitionist ranks. Fredrika Bremer, the Swedish traveler, saw Douglass in Rochester when he was about thirty. "I found him," she wrote, "to be a light mulatto . . . with an unusually handsome exterior, such as I imagine should belong to an Arab chief. Those beautiful eyes were full of dark fire." Douglass, at the time, employed a white governess. The Swedish traveler wondered why a white woman would expose herself to the scorn of the community. "But," said she, "possibly has that former slave, now the apostle-militant of freedom that greatness of character which makes such a sacrifice easy to an ardent soul."

For fifty years, from 1845 to 1895, the apostle-militant stood on the watchtower of American freedom, championing the cause of all oppressed men and women. In these years, which spanned the Abolitionist movement, the Civil War, Reconstruction, and the post-Reconstruction period, Douglass helped define the roads and boundaries of black protest, earning the title of "Father of the Protest movement." Like W. E. B. DuBois, he ranged all over the landscape, changing his tactics as the terrain changed. But from first to last, he held to the philosophy of reform that informed the great speech he made at the West India Emancipation Celebration at Canandaigua, New York, on August 4, 1857. The burden of the speech is in one word: struggle. "The whole history of the progress of human liberty," he said, "shows that all concessions yet made to her august claims, have been born of earnest struggle. . . . If there is no struggle there is no progress. Those who profess to favor freedom and yet deprecate agitation, are men who want crops without plowing up the ground, they want rain without thunder and lightning. They want the ocean without the awful roar of its many waters."

What kind of struggle was Douglass talking about?

Was this a moral struggle or a physical struggle?

"This struggle," he said, coming to close grips with the subject, "may be a moral one, or it may be a physical one, and it may be both moral and physical, but it must be a struggle. Power concedes nothing without a demand. It never did and it never will. Find out just what any people will quietly submit to and you have found out the exact measure of injustice and wrong which will be imposed upon them, and these will continue till they are resisted with either words or blows, or with both. The limits of tyrants are prescribed by the endurance of those whom they oppress."

As for the concrete grievances of blacks, he said:

"Negroes will be hunted at the North, and held and flogged at the South so long as they submit to those devilish outrages, and make no resistance, either moral or physical. Men may not get all they pay for in this world, but they must certainly pay for all they get. If we ever get free from the oppressions and wrongs heaped upon us, we must pay for their removal. We must do this by labor, by suffering, by sacrifice, and if needs be, by our lives and the lives of others."

Such, then, was the gospel of struggle preached by the black edge of the varicolored and variegated abolitionist procession. Douglass was unquestionably the major black actor in that procession, but he shared the spotlight with a number of men and women, who covered the spectrum from pre-Martin Luther King Jr. passive resisters to prototypical Malcom X's.

Charles Lenox Remond, the first major black abolitionist, leaned toward the Garrison tenets of nonviolence and nonvoting. Born in Salem, Massachusetts, the son of a free West Indian hairdresser who got on a boat and paid his way to America, Remond was an elegant little man in elegant clothes—a lover of fine horses and the New England air, fastidious, spare, with a long, deeply furrowed face and an aquiline nose. He began his career as a professional abolitionist in 1838 and shot to fame after a triumphant tour of England. Although Remond was a devoted Garrisonian, he later abandoned nonviolence and championed slave revolts.

One of the seventeen members of the first antislavery society in America, Remond later served as vice-president of the New England Anti-Slavery Society and president of his county unit. A bitter foe of intolerance, he lectured against slavery until its abolition. In the forties and fifties, however, he was overshadowed by the rising star of Frederick Douglass—and he was human enough to resent it. Remond was not a lucky man; and history, largely the story of lucky people, has passed him by. He did not have the firsthand knowledge of slavery that Douglass had and his speeches lacked Douglass's concreteness and fire. In Remond's later years illness, bad luck and frustration made him somewhat peevish. When Douglass broke with Garrison, Remond supported Garrison and publicly thanked God that he was not a slave or the son of a slave. Douglass, stung to the quick, retorted; "I thank God that I am neither a barber nor the son of a barber."

Samuel Ringgold Ward, one of the most eloquent men of an age of eloquence, was a fugitive slave and the son of a fugitive slave. Unlike Remond, who was a major supporter of the Massachusetts Garrisonians, Ward was a New Yorker who advocated a militant, political brand of abolitionism. Born in 1817 in Maryland, he was carried to New York at an early age by his fugitive slave parents. He was educated there, became a Presbyterian minister and pastored a white church in South Butler, New York. He became a professional antislavery agent in 1839 and was one of the first blacks to join the Liberty party. Big-framed, eloquent, "so black that when he closed his eyes you could not see him," Ward was an imposing presence on abolitionist platforms. He was advertised as "The Black Daniel Webster," but some experts thought he was a better speaker than either Webster or Frederick Douglass. In 1851, after passage of the Fugitive Slave Law, Ward fled America, going first to England and then to Jamaica, where he died in poverty.

No less audible in this period were black female abolitionists, who organized female antislavery societies and staged protests and boycotts in support of immediate emancipation. There was also independent protest action on the West Coast under the leadership of Mary Ellen Pleasant and Biddy Mason, two wealthy California businesswomen. The pioneer women leaders supported the fledgling women's liberation struggle. There was a certain tension, however, between black female abolitionists and white suffragettes. The leaders of the white suffrage movement, women like Elizabeth Cady Stanton and Susan B. Anthony, were not at all sure of their priorities and tended, in moments of pressure, to confuse the black struggle for basic human rights with the women's struggle for an extension of human rights. There was no such confusion in the ranks of black female abolitionists, who believed the abolition of slavery was the first and indeed only priority.

One of the first women to smash the taboo against female public speakers was Maria W. Stewart, a free black woman who lectured in New England in the 1830s. In the following decades Sarah Parker Remond, Frances Ellen Harper, Mary Shadd and Mary Bibb followed her example. The swirling currents of the age reached full tide in Sojourner Truth and Harriet Tubman, who created the twin mountain peaks of the heroic tradition of black women. Both women were deeply religious, but they expressed their religion in different ways. John Brown liked to make a rough distinction between "talking" abolitionists and "acting" abolitionists. Sojourner Truth was a "talking" abolitionist—a preacher, seer and teacher. Born Isabella in upstate New York in 1797 or thereabouts, she had an interesting succession of slavemasters, including one who was coarse and profane and another who was coarse and profligate. By 1827, when she became free under New York's gradual emancipation act, Isabella had been through an emotional wringer. With hardly a breath, she headed straight for another one, joining a group of eccentrics who preached a "religious" doctrine of "match spirits." Isabella followed this group to Sing Sing, New York, where it disintegrated amid wild headlines of murder and loose sexual goings-on. Isabella was not involved in the shady sexual experiments— not, however, because of strength of character. Isabella was frank: it was impossible, she said, to match her spirit.

At this juncture, at perhaps the low point of her life, she went through a powerful spiritual experience that changed her life. And on June 1, 1843, she walked out of New York City with a bag of clothes, twenty-five cents and a new name: Sojourner Truth. "The Lord," she said, "gave me [the name] Sojourner because I was to travel up and down the land showing the people their sins and being a sign to them. Afterwards I told the Lord I wanted another name 'cause everybody else had two names; and the Lord gave me Truth, because I was to declare the truth unto people."

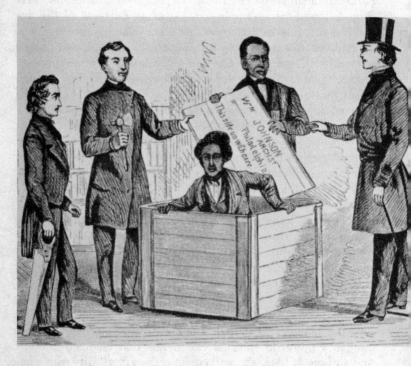

Henry ("Box") Brown escaped from slavery in a box lined with
baize. A friend locked him in the box and shipped it from
Richmond to Philadelphia. Brown stepped from the box
and sang: "I waited patiently for the Lord, and he heard
my prayer."

Among the outstanding women in the antislavery ranks were Harriet Tubman (left), who helped three hundred slaves escape from the South, and Sojourner Truth, who was an abolitionist lecturer.

True to both names, she walked the land for more than forty years, preaching, teaching, testifying. The great and near-great sang her praises and quoted her strong and striking utterances. Harriet Beecher Stowe could never forget the sight of her—a gaunt, misty-eyed woman in a gray dress, a white turban and a sunbonnet, calm and erect, like "one of her native palm trees waving alone in the desert." Novelist Stowe said she had never met anyone who had more personal presence. "She seemed perfectly self-possessed and at her ease; in fact, there was almost an unconscious superiority in the odd, composed manner in which she looked down on me."

On a platform, Truth was unforgettable. Though illiterate, she had power and an incisive mind that reduced things to their essentials. On one occasion, a proslavery heckler told her: "Old woman, do you think your talk about slavery does any good? Do you suppose that people care what you way? . . . Why I don't care any more for your talk than I do for the bite of a flea." Sojourner Truth smiled and replied: "Perhaps not, but the good Lord willing, I'll keep you scratching."

If the talking campaign of Sojourner Truth illustrated one approach to the abolitionist dilemma, the walking campaign of Harriet Tubman illustrated another. Tubman, like Truth, was born in slavery. One of the eleven children of Harriet and Benjamin Ross, she was born in 1820 or 1821 in Bucktown near Cambridge on the Eastern Shore of Maryland. Short, tough, black and luminous as the night, she opposed the slave system almost from birth and ran away when she was twenty-five, going by way of the Underground Railroad to the North. Characteristically, she went with a threat in her heart:

"I had reasoned this out in my mind; there was one or two things I had a *right* to, liberty or death; if I could not have one, I would have the other; for no man should take me alive; I should fight for my liberty as long as my strength lasted, and when the time come for me to go, the Lord would let them take me."

And how did freedom feel?

"I looked at my hands to see if I was the same person now I was free. There was such a glory over everything, the sun comes like gold through the trees."

Freedom felt so good that Harriet Tubman returned to the

South nineteen times and brought out more than three hundred slaves. Rewards for her capture mounted to $40,000. No matter. The short black woman continued her dangerous work, bringing out her brothers and sisters, her aging parents and anyone else who wanted to go. By 1852 she was a legend in antislavery circles. "A more heroic soul," the Rev. Samuel M. Hopkins said, "did not breathe in the bosom of Judith or of Jeanne D'Arc." Abolitionist Samuel J. May said, "She deserves to be placed first on the list of American heroines."

Like Harriet Tubman, like Samuel Ringgold Ward, like Benjamin Banneker and Frederick Douglass, Henry Highland Garnet was born in Maryland, that early nursery of black greats. He was the grandson, tradition said, of an African chief. This was said of almost everyone in those days, but in Garnet's case it could have been true. When he was ten his family escaped and carried him to New York, where he received an education and became a Presbyterian minister. Even then, the "Thomas Paine of the abolitionist movement" was a striking figure, tall, commanding, black, broad-nosed, with "eyes that look through you." Garnet was a sufferer; he suffered more than any other figure in abolitionist circles. Like John Brown, he could not stand to hear the word *slavery*. In 1840, at the age of twenty-four, he attracted attention with a slashing attack on slavery at the American Anti-Slavery Convention. Three years later he made one of the great speeches of American history. Speaking to a national convention of colored men in Buffalo, New York, in August, 1843, he called for a national slave strike.

"Brethren," he said, speaking directly to the slaves, "the time has come when you must act for yourselves. . . . Look around you, and behold the bosoms of your loving wives heaving with untold agonies! Hear the cries of your poor children! Remember the stripes your fathers bore. Think of the torture and disgrace of your noble mothers. Think of your wretched sisters, loving virtue and purity, as they are driven into concubinage and are exposed to the unbridled lusts of incarnate devils. Think of the undying glory that hangs around the . . . name of Africa—and forget not that you are native born American citizens, and as such, you are justly entitled to all the rights that are granted to the freest. Think how many tears you have poured out upon the soil which you have cultivated with unrequited toil and enriched with your blood; and then go to your lordly enslavers and tell them plainly, that you *are determined to be free*. . . . Do this, and for ever after cease to toil for the heartless tyrants, who give you no other reward but stripes and abuse."

Was Garnet suggesting violence?

What were the slaves to do if the slavemasters attacked them?

"If they then commence the work of death, they, and not you, will be responsible for the consequences. You had better all die—*die immediately*, then live slaves and entail your wretchedness upon your posterity. If you would be free in this generation, here is your only hope . . . there is not much hope of redemption without the shedding of blood. If you must bleed, let it all come at once—rather *die freemen, than live to be slaves*."

This passionate and eloquent appeal triggered a sharp internal debate that grew in scope and depth as the struggle continued. In the course of this debate, black abolitionists, Garnet and Douglass foremost among them, advanced the furrows of black assertion, asking and answering questions that are still live issues in Black America. Like the black pioneers before him, and the black rebels who followed, Frederick Douglass asked the old and insistent question: "How shall we sing the Lord's song in a strange land?" The answers revolved around the traditional trilogy: ballots, bullets or Bibles, and Iago's injunction: "Go, make money." The Garrisonians, led by the Philadelphians and Charles Lenox Remond, condemned "complexional institutions" (black churchs, lodges, schools, newspapers, and conventions).

The Garrisonians also abandoned political action and advocated a campaign based on passive resistance and moral force. William S. Whipper, a leading Garrisonian, was one of the first Americans to deal at a depth level with the nonviolent philosophy, publishing in 1837 an "Address on Non-Resistance to Offensive Aggression." In this essay, which preceded Thoreau's celebrated essay by twelve years, Whipper said "the practice of nonresistance to physical aggression is not only consistent with reason, but the surest method of obtaining a speedy triumph of the principles of universal peace." Samuel E. Cornish opposed Whipper's agruments, saying, "We honestly confess that we have yet to learn what virtue there would be in using moral weapons in defense against kidnappers or a midnight incendiary with a torch in his hand."

Cornish and the leading members of the New York wing (Ward, Garnet and, after 1851, Douglass) favored ballots, if possible, and bullets, if necessary. The New Yorkers were opportunists on the issue of "complexional institutions." They were in favor of complete integration, but if circumstances made this impossible they unhesitatingly recommended special institutions. Douglass, for example, anticipated Booker T. Washington with his plan for a manual training college. The New Yorkers also favored black conventions and black newspapers. At stake here was a bitter issue of power. Douglass, Ward and Garnet felt uncomfortable in subsidiary roles; they demanded a share in the "generalship" of the movement. Douglass broke with Garrison on this issue. In a statement reminiscent of Toussaint L'Ouverture, he said, "No people that has solely depended on foreign aid, or rather, upon the efforts of those, in any way identified with the oppressor, to undo the heavy burdens, ever stood forth in the attitude of Freedom." He also lashed out at the "colored mail-wrappers" in the Garrisonian camp, saying, "Our oppressed people are wholly ignored, in one sense, in the generalship of the movement."

Douglass believed black abolitionists could make a positive contribution by proving that blacks were active rather than passive cogs in the antislavery machinery. He said, "The man who has *suffered the wrong* is the man to *demand redress*,—that the man STRUCK is the man to CRY OUT—and that he who has *endured the cruel pangs of Slavery* is the man to *advocate Liberty*. It is evident that we must be our own representatives and advocates, not exclusively, but peculiarly—not distinct from, but in connection with our white friends."

Black abolitionists were also divided over words. When Daniel Payne, the AME leader, uttered the plaintive cry, "Who am I, God? And what?" there was no dearth of possible answers. Early black leaders ("Sons of Africa") identified themselves in African terms (African Lodge, Free African Society, African Baptist Church). When the campaign to send blacks back to Africa moved into high gear, a black convention, dominated by Philadelphians, urged blacks to "abandon use of the word 'colored,' " and "especially to remove the title of African from their institutions." Philadelphia leaders later recommended the use of

the term "Oppressed Americans." This brought an indignant
retort from New Yorkers. "Oppressed Americans!" snorted
Samuel Cornish, *"who are they?* Nonsense brethren!! You are
COLORED AMERICANS. The Indians are RED AMERICANS and the
white people are WHITE AMERICANS and *you are as good as they,
and they are no better than you.*"

A complicating factor in this internal dialogue was the presence
of black nationalists like Martin R. Delany of whom Douglass
said: "I thank God for making me a man simply; but Delany
always thanks him for making him a black man." Delany said
no people could gain respect unless they retained their identity.
He urged blacks to identify as Africans, blacks, mulattoes and
coloreds. A short, brilliant man of a "most defiant blackness,"
Delany was one of the backers of a black convention which made
the surprisingly modern prediction that the "question of black
and white" would one day decide the future of the world. In his
1852 book, *The Condition, Elevation, Emigration, and Destiny of
the Colored People of the United States Politically Considered*,
Delany gave one of the earliest and still one of the best definitions
of the concept of Negro nationality:

"Every people should be the originators of their own designs,
the projectors of their own schemes, and creators of the events
that lead to their destiny—the consummation of their desires. . . . We have native hearts and virtues, just as other nations; which in their pristine purity are noble, potent and worthy
of example. We are a nation within a nation;—as the Poles in
Russia, the Hungarians in Austria, the Welsh, Irish, and Scotch
in the British dominions. . . . The claims of no people, according
to established policy and usage, are respected by any nation, until
they are presented in a national capacity."

Delany pressed "the national issue" until the Civil War when
he entered the Union army and rose to the rank of major. He later
had a turbulent and somewhat erratic career as a politician in
reconstructed South Carolina, endorsing and supporting various
conservative white Democrats. His major work, however, was
done in the antebellum period when he almost singlehandedly
made black nationalism a national black force.

The tide of black nationalism, and the tide of Delany's career,
ebbed and flowed, inversely, with the ebb and flow of the black
cause. When that cause was going well, and when there seemed
to be a reasonable chance of a breakthrough, black nationalism

receded. When the cause suffered massive shocks, and when there seemed to be no chance of peace and safety on American shores, black nationalism crested. It is scarcely surprising therefore that the black nationalist tide reached such a high level in the difficult days of the fifties that no black leaders could ignore it. Seizing on a moment which seemed to confirm their predictions, Delany and H. Ford Douglass repudiated "American hypocrisy" and called for the establishment of a black state in Central American, Africa or the Wild West.

Working the same side of the street, but with a different emphasis, was Alexander Crummell, a pioneer advocate of the concept of Negro identity. A thin, intense Episcopalian priest who preached in Liberia before returning to America as rector of a Washington church, Crummell explored some of the territory covered by modern advocates of *Negritude*. Blacks, he said, were a race God had preserved "to do something with." In an eloquent sermon, "The Destined Superiority of the Negro," Crummell said that the black American was destined to emerge as a superior human being with the best qualities of other races.

To that end, Crummell and other abolitionists used the traditional weapons of agitation, the platform, the pulpit and the press. But a surprisingly large number of black leaders championed direct action—violent and nonviolent. Nor were traditional political techniques ignored. Garnet and Ward were pioneer leaders of the Liberty and Free Soil parties, which prepared the ground for the Republican party.

Litigation, the perennial black tactic, was also used. In 1849 Benjamin F. Roberts filed a suit in Boston on behalf of his daughter, Sarah, who had been barred from white schools near her home. Boston abolitionists, led by historian William C. Nell, collected money and employed Charles Sumner as attorney. The Boston court ignored Sumner's eloquent plea and delivered the first "separate but equal" legal decision. Astonished by the implications of this new doctrine, Nell and his group organized a propaganda campaign, which included, interestingly, sit-ins and stand-ins. The issue was resolved finally by the state legislature, which passed a law banning school segregation.

The Abolitionist movement was only one front in a total struggle that engaged every level of black society. Not only black protesters but also black students, artists and businessmen were pressed into service in that struggle. "Any Negro living well," Samuel Ringgold Ward said, "is an anti-slavery fighter." This was not, strictly speaking, true, but it was close enough to the truth to make the second front—building the strength and resources of the black community—a matter of absorbing interest to every black leader. In the nineteenth century, as in the eighteenth century, most of the action on this front was a re-action to the continuing attempt to deny blacks equal education. The case of Prudence Crandall, the celebrated Quaker teacher, illustrated the problem perfectly. When, in 1833, she opened a school in Canterbury, Connecticut, the villagers tried to burn it down. The state later passed a law banning black schools, and Prudence Crandall was convicted. She successfully appealed the conviction, but whites again attacked the school, which was closed, it was said, "for the protection of the students." There was a similar uproar in Canaan, New Hampshire, where villagers used one hundred oxens to pull a black school to a swamp a half-mile away.

Neither hooliganism nor discriminatory laws checked the black education movement. In 1807 the first black school in Washington was opened by three former slaves. In 1840 the *Ecole des Orphelins Indigents* (School for Needy Orphans) was founded in New Orleans by well-to-do free blacks, notably Thomy Lafon, Madame Couvent and Aristide Mary. By 1850 there were more than one thousand free blacks in New Orleans schools and fourteen hundred in Baltimore. When the Civil War opened, there were 32,692 blacks in educational institutions in the United States and its territories.

No less important, but far less successful, were the first tentative forays in the field of higher education. In 1823 Alexander L. Twilight received a degree from Middlebury College and became the first known black to graduate from an American institution of higher learning. In 1826 Edward A. Jones received a B.A. degree from Amherst College and John B. Russwurm received an A.B. degree from Bowdoin College. In the following years a handful of blacks graduated from other white colleges, including Oberlin and Rutland. Three black scholars, William G. Allen, Charles L. Reason and George B. Vashon, also taught at Central College in McGrawville, New York

More important in its final effect was the founding of the first black colleges. In 1842 the Institute for Colored Youth was incorporated in Philadelphia under the leadership of Charles L. Reason, In 1849 Avery College was organized in Allegheny City, Pennsylvania. Two years later Myrtilla Miner established an institution in the District of Columbia which later became a college bearing her name. Lincoln University, which began as Ashmun Institute under Presbyterian sponsorship, was incorporated in 1854 and admitted students two years later. In 1855 the Cincinnati conference of the Methodist Episcopal Church began to raise money for a black college which was incorporated in 1856 as Wilberforce University. The school was later reorganized under the direction of the African Methodist Episcopal Church.

In the meantime, powerful voices, almost all of them identified with the Abolitionist movement, emerged in the cultural arena. This development was largely a product of the study circles and literary societies founded by pioneer black leaders. By the 1840s there was a network of these institutions in major free black centers. In 1841 the anonymous author of *Sketches of the Higher Classes of Colored Society in Philadelphia* noted that "colored Philadelphians . . . have established numerous literary associations." The most prominent, the report said, was the "Philadelphia Library Company of Colored Persons," organized on January 1, 1833. The library, according to this report, contained "nearly six hundred volumes of valuable historical, scientific and miscellaneous works, among which are several encyclopedias. . . ." The library company, the author said, also sponsored a debating department which "has of late greatly improved in regard to the intelligence and ability of those who usually participate therein."

Another major cultural institution was the Free African Theater of New York City. This theater, at the African Grove, corner of Bleecker and Mercer streets, presented performances of *Othello, Richard III* and other European fare. Ira Aldridge, the celebrated Shakespearean interpreter, began his career there and later became one of the greatest actors of the age, receiving medals from the kings of Prussia and Austria. Other black artists who received national or international recognition in the antebellum period were singer Elizabeth Taylor, poet Frances E. W. Harper, sculptor Edmonia Lewis and Patrick Reason, the painter and engraver.

The most important cultural development of the period was the founding of the first black newspaper, *Freedom's Journal*, published for the first time in New York City on Friday, March 16, 1827. The coeditors of this journal were Samuel E. Cornish, a prominent minister and abolitionist, and John B. Russwurm, who later withdrew from the editorship and settled in Liberia, where he published a pioneer African newspaper, *the Liberia Herald*.

"It is our earnest wish," Cornish and Russwurm said in the first issue of *Freedom's Journal*, "to make our Journal a medium of intercourse between our brethren in the different states of this great confederacy: that through its columns an expression of our sentiments, on many interesting subjects which concern us, may be offered to the publick: that plans which apparently are beneficial may be candidly discussed and properly weighted; if worth, receive our cordial approbation; if not, our marked disapprobation."

The editors went on to add words that remain uncomfortably pertinent:

"We wish to plead our own cause. Too long have others spoken for us. Too long has the publick been deceived by misrepresentations, in things which concern us dearly, though in the estimation of some mere trifles; for though there are many in society who exercise towards us benevolent feelings; still (with sorrow we confess it) there are others who make it their business to enlarge upon the least trifle, which tends to the discredit of any person of colour; and pronounce anathemas and denounce our whole body for the misconduct of this guilty one. . . .

"Our vices and our degradation are ever arrayed against us, but our virtues are passed by unnoticed. And what is still more lamentable, our friends, to whom we concede all the principles of humanity and religion, from these very causes seem to have fallen into the current of popular feeling and are imperceptibly floating on the stream—actually living in the practice of prejudice, while they abjure it in theory, and feel it not in their hearts. Is it not very desirable that such should know more of our actual condition; and of our efforts and feelings, that in forming or advocating plans for our amelioration, they may do it more understandingly?"

This theme was taken up and expanded by the forty additional newspapers founded before the Civil War. Among the best known of these journals were Frederick Douglass's *North Star* (later named *Frederick Douglass' Paper*), the *Mystery* and the *Colored American*. David Ruggles, another major black abolitionist, was editor of the first black magazine, *Mirror of Liberty*, which appeared in August, 1938.

The abolitionist struggle also stimulated black scholarship, creating an audience for slave narratives and literary and historical works. Frederick Douglass wrote two autobiographies, *Narrative of the Life of Frederick Douglass* (1845) and *My Bondage and My Freedom* (1855). (He returned to this form twenty-six years later with *The Life and Times of Frederick Douglass*.) There were other slave narratives of enduring value, including the works of Solomon Northup (*Narrative of Solomon Northup*), Samuel Ringgold Ward (*Autobiography of a Fugitive Negro*), Austin Steward (Twenty-Two Years a Slave), Henry Bibb (*Narrative of the Life and Adventures of Henry Bibb*), and William Wells Brown (*Narrative of William Wells Brown*). Brown was also the first American black to write a play, *The Escape; or, A Leap for Freedom* (1858) and a novel, *Clotel, or, The President's Daughter* (1853). The leading black poet was abolitionist Frances E. W. Harper, who published her first book, *Poems on Various Subjects*, in 1854.

The first substantial works on black history appeared in this period and were responses to struggle. In 1841 James W. C. Pennington published *Textbook of the Origin and History of the Colored People*. William C. Nell's valuable volume, *Services of Colored Americans in the Wars of 1776 and 1812*, was published in 1852 and appeared in a revised edition with a new title, *The Colored Patriots of the American Revolution*, in 1855. Martin R. Delany's *The Condition, Elevation, Emigration, and Destiny of the Colored People of the United States* appeared in 1852.

In the wholly different sphere of economic development, as Delany's book recounted in some detail, there was measurable forward movement. Nowhere was this more clearly visible than in the enormous expansion of black mutual aid societies. By 1821 there were thirty to forty such societies in Baltimore. By 1838 Philadelphia had one hundred mutual aid societies with 7,448 members.

These societies, like the germinal Free African Society from which they sprang, were collective business enterprises with ethical, fraternal, welfare and insurance dimensions. The

Petersburg (Virginia) Beneficial Society of Free Men of Color, for instance, was organized "to care for the sick, to pay death claims, and to promote the social group spirit."

The social group spirit was also evident in the continued development of the artisan-merchant class. According to the New York census of 1850, the black business community of that state included two hatters, three jewelers, two confectioners, eleven inkmakers, twenty-one boardinghouse keepers, eight cigarmakers, twenty-three tailors, twenty-three hosemakers and more than one hundred barbers.

The story was very much the same in Southern cities like Charleston and New Orleans, where a disproportionately large number of the leading artisans were black. One of Charleston's leading hotels in this period was owned by Jehu Jones, a free black. Another Charleston free black, Anthony Western, was one of the most celebrated millwrights in the South. Of similar tone and texture, though more pointed, was the business activity in New Orleans, where, according to Delany's book, there was "nothing more common . . . than Colored Clerks, Salesmen, and Business Men." At the time of his survey, one Mr. Cordovell, a mercer and tailor, reportedly dominated the New Orleans fashion world. "The reported fashions of Cordovell," Delany reported, "are said to have frequently become the leading fashions of Paris; and the writer was informed by . . . a leading merchant tailer . . . that many of the eastern American reports were nothing more than a copy, in some cases modified, of those of Cordovell." Nor was Cordovell unique. John Jones was a major force in the tailoring trade in Chicago, where he accumulated a small fortune and constructed one of the city's first office buildings. Other leading tailors and clothing merchants were Henry Topp of Albany, New York, and Thomas Dalton of Boston.

The spirit of commerce and self-determination surfaced in men like Samuel T. Wilcox of Cincinnati and Edward Hamlin of Petersburg, Virginia, who were leading operators in the wholesale and retail grocery trade. It is to be observed, too, that black caterers—most notably Thomas J. Dorsey and Henry Minton—dominated the catering trade in Philadelphia and other Eastern and Midwestern cities.

Despite the confusion and bias of the period, black businessmen held prominent and in some cases preeminent positions in the coal and lumber industry. Among their number was Robert Gordon, a former Virginia slave, who owned a major coal yard and a private dock in Cincinnati. Similarly gifted with the Midas touch was Stephen Smith, a lumber merchant and moneylender who was perhaps the wealthiest black in America. The size and range of his business can be gauged from an 1849 inventory which showed that he owned or controlled 2,250,000 feet of lumber, 22 cars on the Philadelphia to Baltimore railroad, $9,000 in Columbia (Pa.) Bridge stock, and $18,000 in Columbia bank stock. Black businessmen also operated foundries, made rope, and manufactured hair oil. They were to be found, according to contemporary reports, in practically every industry and occupation. We also learn from contemporary accounts that the spirit of trade and commerce ran deep in the black community. Much of the trading near railroad stations and boat terminals in both the North and South was controlled by black hucksters, male and female.

There were also gains in the fields of science and technology. In 1834 Henry Blair of Maryland, who was probably the first black to receive a patent, invented a corn harvester. In 1846 Norbert Rillieux, a New Orleans machinist and engineer, received a patent for a vacuum evaporating pan that revolutionized the sugar-refining industry.

These developments, small but promising, were expressions of the tenacity of spirit of a people who never stopped testing the wall, sending line after line into the breach, losing many and paying a frightfully high price for the handful who managed to slip through. Over and beyond this, the gains in commerce and culture tell us what nineteenth-century blacks could have contributed to America if they had been given a tenth of a chance. The gains tell us all this and more, but they do not tell us anything meaningful about the nature of the system of oppression that absorbed these challenging facts and went right on producing and reproducing itself, crushing slaves, pushing the mass of free blacks down to the subsistence level, and turning poor white resentment against blacks instead of their common oppressors.

Because Black America was confronted with a system, because the foundation of that system was the use and abuse of blacks, and because there were men in America who believed their power and identity depended on the continuation of the system, individual breakthroughs did not—and could not—change the nature of the system. And so, in spite of the genius of Douglass, in spite of the sensational successes of black caterers and artisans, in spite of the eloquence of Ira Aldridge, the ingenuity of Rillieux and the rugged individualism of Stephen Smith, the system went right on piling burdens on the backs of blacks. To make matters worse, the system, responding to its own feedback, readjusted itself and began the long process of undermining and eliminating the burgeoning artist-merchant class.

This process unfolded against the background of three ominous developments. The first was a national political decision called the Compromise of 1850. This compromise, introduced in Congress by Henry Clay, provided for "the final settlement" of the slavery controversy on the basis of a trade-off between free and slave states and the enactment of a national Fugitive Slave Law, which threatened the lives and liberties of almost all free blacks. There then followed a second "final" settlement, the Kansas-Nebraska Act, which opened Northern territory to settlement by slaveholders. The third development, no less ominous, was a U.S. Supreme Court decision which said, in the case of Dred Scott (1857), that no black could be a U.S. citizen and that black people had no rights in America that white people were bound to respect. The net effect of all this was the *de facto* nationalization of the slave system.

These developments created a no-exit situation which almost destroyed Black America. There had been difficult moments before, and there would be difficult moments in the future, but this decade—the white and whitening fifties—was one of the deepest pits of the black ordeal. It seemed then that the spirit of slavery would live forever and that there would never be hope or a place of safety for blacks in American society.

The signs were clear for all to see.

There was, to begin with, the increasing confidence of slaveholders, who moved to the offensive with demands for the permanent enslavement of all blacks. Flowing with and out of this offensive, which was based on the idea that slavery was the natural and God-ordained state for blacks, was an economic offensive which made it increasingly difficult for blacks to earn a living outside the slave system.

Fate itself seemed to conspire with the slaveholders, for at that juncture a political famine in Ireland and political complications on the European continent sent millions of poor white immigrants to America. Between 1830 and 1860 more than five million of these immigrants—poor, confused, and willing to accept almost any job at almost any price—settled in American cities, depressing wages and driving blacks from traditional black preserves. In some cities this contest approached the dimensions of an open war, the worst kind of war, a war for bread and milk and potatoes. It was a dreadful contest, but it was a contest which, in the nature of things, could only go one way—after all, the white immigrants *were* white.

The struggle between the Irish immigrants and black workers was particularly acrimonious. At that point and for several decades thereafter, the Irish were considered "white niggers" and were subjected to the same indignities as blacks. "To be called an 'Irishman,' " an English traveler noted, "is almost as great an insult as to be stigmatized as a 'nigger feller,' and in a street row, both appellations are flung off among the combatants with great zest and vigour."

The results of all this were curious and tragic.* Instead of linking up with black workers, the white immigrants joined the oppressors of both groups. The grand outcome was not only the disappearance of traditional black jobs but the strengthening of white workers at the expense of black workers. Year by year, decade by decade, black workers were forced out of occupation after occupation. The traditional image of wave after wave of white immigrants rolling to relative security over the backs of blacks is rooted in fact and history. Writing in the *Colored American* in 1838, a black analyst said "these impoverished and destitute beings—transported from the trans-Atlantic shores are crowding themselves into every place of business and of labor, and driving the poor colored American citizen out. Along the wharves, where the colored man once [commanded] the whole business of shipping and unshipping—in stores where his services were once rendered, and in families where the chief places were filled by him, in all these situations there are substituted foreigners or white Americans."

The Shaping of Black America.

As the years passed, the situation of free blacks became worse, and a tone of desperation crept into the black dialogue. Frederick Douglass, who witnessed all this and was horrified, sounded a general alarm with an editorial in the March 4, 1853, edition of *Frederick Douglass' Paper*. The editorial, entitled LEARN TRADES OR STARVE, began with a masterful analysis of the white displacement of black labor:

"White men are becoming house-servants, cooks and stewards on vessels—at hotels.—They are becoming porters, stevedores, wood-sawyers, hod-carriers, brick-makers, white-washers and barbers, so that the blacks can scarcely find the means of subsistence—a few years ago, and a *white* barber would have been a curiosity—now their poles stand on every street. Formerly blacks were almost the exclusive coachmen in wealthy families: this is so no longer; white men are now employed, and for aught we see, they fill their servile station with an obsequiousness as profound as that of blacks. The readiness and ease with which they adapt themselves to these conditions ought not be lost sight of by the colored people."

What was the meaning of this?

"The meaning," Douglass continued, "is very important, and we should learn from it. We are taught our insecurity by it. Without the means of living, life is a curse, and leaves us at the mercy of the oppressor to become his debased slaves. Now, colored men, what do you mean to do, for you must do something. The American Colonization Society tells you to go to Liberia. Mr. [Henry] Bibbs tells you to go to Canada. Others tell you to go to school. We tell you to go to work; and to work you must go or die."

This was easier said than done. For the essence of the situation, as the editorial pointed out, was that blacks were no longer permitted to do work they had done for centuries. At the same time blacks were barred from certain trades by Jim Crow unions, which also controlled apprenticeship programs. In this same period the president of a Cincinnati mechanics association—to cite one representative case—was tried for the "crime" of helping a black youth learn a trade.

The economic restrictions were parts of an orchestrated attack that limited the movement and aspirations of blacks. Some states, Illinois and Ohio in particular, would not admit free blacks if they could not post large bonds. Outside New England, free blacks were generally denied the ballot and could not testify against whites in court cases.

Most free blacks at this juncture lived along the docks and wharves and in alleys. Wherever they lived, people wanted them to go away. Time and time again, whites herded blacks into groups and pointed to the city limits. Time and time again, immigrants, fresh from the boats, cracked their skulls and burned their homes and churches. Some whites said openly that the only solution to the "Negro problem" was the "Indian solution." An Indianian said, "It would be better to kill them off at once, for there is no other way to get rid of them." He added: "We know how the Puritans did with the Indians, who were infinitely more magnanimous and less impudent than the colored race."

Such then was the increasingly desperate situation of blacks as the walls of the white fifties closed in on them. Standing outside the pale of justice, enslaved in the South, despised in the North, nineteenth-century blacks tasted the dregs of bitterness.

"What stone," New York blacks asked in 1860, "has been left unturned to degrade us? What hand has refused to fan the flame of popular prejudice against us? What American artist has not caricatured us? What wit has not laughed at our wretchedness? What songster has not made merry over our depressed spirits? What press has not ridiculed and condemned us? Few, few, very few."

Why did they take it?

Why didn't they give up the struggle and go elsewhere?

The answer is stunning in its simplicity: they believed in the *real* America, the one that was dreamed and betrayed. Their forefathers, they said, had settled the land and "manured it" with blood. The land was theirs, the country was theirs—they were willing to fight for it.

Listen to Henry Highland Garnet.

He stands now on the platform of a National Negro convention in Buffalo, New York. Tall, black, erect, famous at twenty-seven, Garnet is silent for a moment, thinking perhaps of his father, who escaped from slavery, and his sister, who was kidnapped and returned to slavery. He stands now, looking out into the audience, and the fury rolls out of him. "Brethren," he says, speaking directly to the slaves of the South, "arise, arise! . . . The diabolical injustice by which your liberties are cloven down, NEITHER GOD, NOR ANGELS, OR JUST MEN, COMMAND YOU TO SUFFER FOR A SINGLE MOMENT. THEREFORE IT IS YOUR SOLEMN AND IMPERATIVE DUTY TO USE EVERY MEANS, BOTH MORAL, INTELLECTUAL, AND PHYSICAL THAT PROMISES SUCCESS."

They came out of the darkness, across swamps, across rivers, across mountains. They came in twos, threes, twelves. One came all the way from Alabama, traveling, the report said, "only by night, feeding on roots and berries," swimming every river between Tuscaloosa and Pennsylvania. Ellen and William Craft came from Macon, Georgia, stopping at first-class hotels on the way, the light-skinned Ellen posing as a Southern planter, the dark-skinned William acting the part of a devoted manservant. Henry Box Brown came from Richmond, Virginia, locked in a box marked THIS SIDE UP. He came via Adams' Express and when the box was opened he stepped out and sang the song he had promised to sing: "I waited patiently for the Lord, and He heard my prayer."

Listen to Sojourner Truth.

She rises at a meeting in an area suffering from a boll weevil blight to answer a speaker who praised the U.S. Constitution. "Children," she says, "I talk to God and God talks to me. I go out and talks to God in the fields and woods. This morning I was walking out, and I got over the fence. I saw the wheat a-holding up its head, looking very big. I go up and take holt of it. You b'lieve it, there was *no* wheat there. I say, 'God, what is the matter with this wheat?' And He says to me, 'Sojourner, there is a little weasel [weevil] in it!' Now I hear talkin' about the Constitution and the rights of man. I come up and I take hold of this Constitution. It looks mighty big, and I feel for my rights, but there ain't any there. Then I say, 'God what ails this Constitution?' He says to me, 'Sojourner, there is a little weasel in it.' "

They came across a river, armed with bowie knives and guns, refugees from words and compromises. "Nearly all the waiters in the hotels," a Pittsburgh paper said, "have fled to Canada. Sunday, thirty fled; on Monday, forty; on Tuesday, fifty; on Wednes-

day, thirty. . . . They went in large bodies armed with pistols and bowie knives, determined to die rather than be captured." They came from all over, some three thousand of them, in the first three months after passage of the Fugitive Slave Law of 1850. But some remained at home. In Boston blacks crashed into a courtroom and rescued a slave who was being returned to slavery. In Syracuse, New York, blacks rammed the door of the courtroom with a log and spirited away another fugitive. Down in Christiana, Pennsylvania, slave catchers, led by a man named Gorsuch, surrounded the home of a free black named William Parker. The blacks asked the slave catchers to go away, but Gorsuch said he would "go to hell, or have his slaves." When the smoke cleared, Gorsuch lay dead, and his supporters were hiding in the tall corn. In Washington Daniel Webster cried, "Treason!" Henry Clay wondered "whether government of white men is to be yielded to a government of blacks."

Listen to Samuel Ringgold Ward.

He sits on a platform in New York City, listening to William Lloyd Garrison. A proslavery Northerner interrupts Garrison. What does Garrison know about slavery? He is a white man; he has been free all his life. Frederick Douglass leaps up and presents himself for inspection. Is he not a Negro and a man? The heckler laughs: Douglass is light brown; he is only half-Negro. Samuel Ringgold Ward rises and moves to the front of the platform "like a dark cloud." "Well," the scoffer exclaims, "this is the original nigger." Ward raises big, eloquent hands and stills the crowd. "My friends," he says, "hear me for my cause and be silent that you may hear me. . . . I have often been called a nigger, and some have tried to make me believe it; and the only consolation that has been offered me for being called nigger was that when I die and go to heaven, I shall be white. But, if I cannot go to heaven as black as God made me, let me go down to hell and dwell with the Devil forever."

They came across a river, a woman, a man and three children, tiptoeing on the ice. The slave hunters caught them the next morning, but Margaret Garner was too quick. Out came the gleaming butcher knife and slash—across the throat of her beloved daughter. The daughter died and Margaret Garner rejoiced. Slavery, she said, was hell for a black woman; and she was glad her daughter would never know. The slave catchers carried Margaret Garner to court and she begged the judge to kill her; she said she would "go singing to the gallows rather than be returned to slavery."

Listen to Frederick Douglass, who is the featured speaker at a Fourth of July celebration in Rochester, New York. Douglass begins in a low key. "Fellow-citizens, pardon me, and allow me to ask, why am I called upon to speak here today?" Perhaps, he says, you mean to mock me. For what have I to do with your celebration? "What, to the American slave, is your fourth of July? I answer; a day that reveals to him, more than all other days in the year, the gross injustice and cruelty to which he is the constant victim. To him, your celebration is a sham; your boasted liberty, an unholy license; your national greatness, swelling vanity; your sounds of rejoicing are empty and heartless; your denunciation of tyrants, brass-fronted impudence; your shouts of liberty and equality, hollow mockery; your prayers and hymns, your sermons and thanksgivings, with all your religious parades and solemnity, are to him, mere bombast, fraud, deception, impiety, and hypocisy—a thin veil to cover up crimes which would disgrace a nation of savages."

They came out of swamps, woods, rivers—men, women and babies led by a bold woman. A baby whimpered; the woman poured opium down its throat. A man said he was tired, sick; he couldn't make another step. The woman cocked her pistol. "Dead niggers," she said, "tell no tales. You go on or die." The man went on. They came to a road. Something told the woman there was danger ahead. The woman talked to God: "You been with me in six troubles, Lord, be with me in the seventh." Somebody—was it the Lord?—spoke to Harriet Tubman, telling her to turn right. Turner turned right and carried her passengers to the Promised Land— Canada.

Frederick Douglass speaks again. He stands on a stage, saying he no longer believes in words. He calls for a slave revolt. He recites the wrongs inflicted on his people, the whips, the chains, the taunts, the cracked skulls, the—"

"Frederick!" The big, booming voice comes from out of nowhere. *"Is God dead?"*

Sojourner Truth's question electrifies the audience and no one hears Douglass's answer. "No, God is not dead and therefore slavery must end in blood."

They came out of the darkness, thirteen white men, five blacks and an old man. Talk. Talk. Talk. John Brown was tired of talk; he was on his way to the gallows. With him was Dangerfield Newby, forty-four. Newby was a free black who had a wife and seven children in slavery about thirty miles from Harpers Ferry. His wife had written him a letter: she had begged him to buy her and the baby who had just "commenced to crawl" for "if you do not get me somebody else will." The letter ended with a passionate plea: "Oh, Dear Dangerfield, come this fall without fail, money or no money, I want to see you so much." Dangerfield made it as far as Harpers Ferry where he was the first of John Brown's men to die.

Frederick Douglass protests again. A brilliant, self-made aristocrat named Jefferson Davis has been elected president of a Confederacy founded on the "great corner-stone" of human slavery. An eloquent commoner named Abraham Lincoln has been named President of the not-so-United States. Lincoln says slavery is wrong, but he also says he is opposed to giving blacks social and political equality. Who is this Lincoln? What does he stand for? Douglass writes an editorial. "With the single exception of the question of slavery extension, Mr. Lincoln proposes no measure which can bring him into antagonistic collision with the traffickers in human flesh."

Men were marching, flags were flying, banks were closing, stocks were falling. Death was in the air and few wanted to die for the Negro. The South turned in on itself in an agony of fear and guilt. Some Southerners denounced the Declaration of Independence and demanded that free blacks and poor whites be enslaved. Some Southerners went so far as to deny that blacks and whites belonged to the same species, The North tied itself up in an orgy of appeasement, The Negro, "the cause" of it all, bore the brunt of the emotional frenzy. Already stripped of citizenship by the Dred Scott decision, he stood naked before his enemies. South Carolina, anticipating Nazi Germany, required free blacks to wear diamond-shaped badges. In Boston, in New York, in Washington, men scurried to and fro with the word compromise on their lips. Northern governors promised to repeal the personal liberty laws which made slave-catching difficult. The U. S. Congress passed a constitutional amendment which guaranteed slavery forever.

Frederick Douglass grows weary. Disappointed by Lincoln's inaugural address, alarmed by public persecution, he fears for his people. For the first time in twenty years, he loses faith in the American Dream. Maybe, a still voice whispers, maybe blacks would be better off somewhere else. Douglass decides to investigate Haiti as a possible haven. A boat is chartered, and he writes an editorial announcing his proposed trip. Then comes a shattering announcement. Douglass yanks out a fistful of type and inserts an announcement below his editorial.

> Since this article upon Haiti was put into type, we find ourselves in circumstances which induce us to forego our much desired trip to Haiti, for the present. The last ten days have made a tremendous revolution in all things pertaining to the possible future of the colored people in the United States. We shall stay here and watch the current of events. . . .

What gave Douglass heart, what made him shout, "God be praised!" was the firing on Fort Sumter and the beginning of the Civil War.

7

The Jubilee War:
Witnesses and Warriors

> *Ride in, kind Saviour!*
> *No man can hinder me.*
> *O, Jesus is a mighty man!*
> *No man can hinder me.*
> *We're marchin' through Virginny fields.*
> *No man can hinder me.*
>
> SPIRITUAL

FAR OFF to the east, far out over the Atlantic Ocean, the first faint glow of the sun tinged the blue-black sky. In a ravine near Richmond, Virginia, black men in blue hugged the ground and watched the blotch of red widen and glow. Shells howled and burst over their heads, bullets whined and whacked into the trees.

The men waited, watched, listened.

A general came and said it was necessary to capture the Confederate redoubt over the hill and that they—the Third Division of the Eighteenth Corps of the Army of the James—had to do it. The men checked their muskets, fixed their bayonets and listened to the words and the heavy beating of their hearts. They waited a few more minutes for the coming of the sun and then moved out, winding their way through a forest of pines to the crest of the hill. It was 4:30 A.M., Thursday, September 29, 1864.

Benjamin Franklin Butler, the Union general, watched the soldiers climb the hill. He had a big stake riding on the throw. A political general with a genius for agitating the explosive "Negro issue," Butler was despised by many of his aides. It was said that he couldn't command a Sunday school class. Ben Butler intended to show them. He had drawn up an elaborate plan for a two-pronged attack on Richmond, which was cordoned by a meandering maze of slave-built fortifications. As the black division moved to the attack on New Market Road, a column of white troops was advancing on the Varina Road, a mile or so to the west. Behind Butler, another column (which included a brigade of black troops) was waiting for the black division to take the strong redoubt on New Market Heights. This redoubt commanded the New Market Road down which Butler wanted his second column to march. If all went well, Butler would establish a toehold in the suburb of Richmond. If he got a little luck, he would go all the way. In either case he would have a laugh on people who said he couldn't command and blacks wouldn't fight.

A great deal depended on the action of the black division which was moving now over the brow of the hill. The land before the troops sloped down to a swamp and a shallow brook, then rose sharply to the crest of a hill commanded by a Confederate redoubt and some one thousand troops. The Confederates, noticing the black troops on the opposite hill, gave a wild whoop and opened fire. They were understandably confident, for their artillery swept the narrow neck of land over which the Union soldiers had to charge. Fifty yards down the hill from their entrenchments was an abatis (a barricade of felled trees with sharpened branches pointing toward the attackers); one hundred yards below this was another abatis. The storming party would have to cross the brook, come uphill under artillery and musketry fire and wait at the first and second lines of abatis until axmen could cut a way through. While waiting, they would be sitting ducks. The rebels, anticipating a rout, gave another wild whoop and urged the soldiers on. On they came, getting mired in the muck of the swamp, splashing across the brook with their guns held over their heads, faltering, reforming and moving up the hill, one man falling and another man replacing him in line, the whole column swept by grape shot and canister, the ground wet with the blood, the entrails and the brains of the dead.

After what seemed like an eternity of minute-hours, the troops reached the first barricade, and axmen rushed forward and hacked away. As they hacked, rebel sharpshooters leisurely picked them off. Other men, undeterred, stepped over their bodies, seized the axes and cut a hole, through which the first rank of soldiers streamed. Only 150 yards to go. Could they make it? By now most of the white officers were wounded or dead, and black sergeants and corporals were commanding companies and platoons. Cursing, pleading, threatening, they drove the men on. On they went, stepping over the wounded, to the second abatis. Axmen sprang forward, steel ate into wood, men dashed through the opening. One of the first soldiers through the opening was Cpl. Miles James, who spun around suddenly, stunned by a bullet that turned his arm into a dripping mass of blood and pulpy tissue. Brushing off the pain, as though it were a matter of no importance, Corporal James dropped to his knees, loading and firing his gun with one hand and cheering his men on. A rebel officer was equally gallant, leaping upon the parapet, waving his sword and shouting, "Hurrah, my brave men." Pvt. James Gardiner rushed forward, shot the officer and ran him through with his bayonet. The Confederate soldiers then abandoned their posts and ran up the road to Richmond. With a resounding cheer, the black men in blue clambered over the parapet of the dearly purchased real estate on New Market Heights. Behind them on the hill running down to the swamp lay 543 of their comrades.

It had been a bloody thirty minutes' work. But on this day and largely in these thirty minutes, twelve blacks (Corporal James, Private Gardiner and ten others) won Congressional Medals of Honor.

With the New Market Road secured, the Union troops pressed on towards Richmond. A white division seized Fort Harrison, but the advance ground to a halt at Fort Gilmer, where Gen. William Birney's black brigade made a daring but unsuccessful assault. Despite this repulse Union soldiers were too close to Richmond for comfort. Gen. Robert E. Lee, President Jefferson

Davis and other Confederate dignitaries came out to the battle-field and peered through field glasses. The next day Lee sent ten of the South's finest brigades against the Union soldiers in Fort Harrison. The first charge and the second charge were neatly repulsed. And then someone—was it Lee?—had a bright idea. The rebel soldiers came back again, but this time the charge was against Brig. Gen. Charles J. Paine's New Market veterans. The long gray lines swept forward, came to the very edge of the earthwork, and black and rebel soldiers fought hand to hand.

For an agonizing moment the issue hung in dispute. White soldiers stood with their mouths agape, oblivious to shot and shell. So great was "their realization of the danger," wrote R. B. Prescott, a white Union officer, "so keen the anxiety, so doubtful the issue, that every eye was riveted upon [the scene], unmindful of the storm of lead and iron that the Confederate sharpshooters and artillery poured upon us from every available point. It seemed impossible in such a storm for any to escape, but happily in a few moments, the Confederates broke in disorder and sought safety under the protecting guns of Fort Gilmer, while the Union troops shouted themselves hoarse with delight."

It was a bitter moment for the South. Robert E. Lee had failed to retake an important position within sight of the steeples of the Confederate capital. Lieutenant Prescott stood cheering on the parapet of Fort Harrison and he believed he could see "the beginning of the end."

That black soldiers should play an important role in this action seems somehow poetic. For in the beginning, in the middle and in the ending of the Civil War, the black American—as soldier and civilian—was central.

In the beginning, people tried hard to get around this fact. In the first blast of emotion which followed the fall of Fort Sumter, even Abraham Lincoln tried to get around it. Nothing shows this more clearly than his response to the black volunteers who thronged the recruiting stations, eager for a chance to fight for black freedom. Other blacks, responding to Lincoln's appeal for volunteers, hired halls, drilled and formed military units, such as the Hannibal Guards of Pittsburgh and the Crispus Attucks

Guards of Albany, Ohio. In Philadelphia, in New York, in Boston, blacks came forward. The Lincoln administration thanked the black volunteers and sent them home with an understanding that the war was a "white man's war."

Dr. G. P. Miller, a black physician in Battle Creek, Michigan, asked the War Department for authority to raise "5,000 to 10,000 free men to report in sixty days to take any position that may be assigned to us (sharpshooters preferred)." He received, in reply, a wonderfully comic bureaucratic masterpiece. "The War Department," the letter said, "fully appreciates the patriotic spirit and intelligence which your letter displays, and has no doubt upon reflection you will perceive that there are sufficient reasons for continuing the course thus far pursued in regard to the important question upon which your letter is based."

What Dr. Miller perceived upon reflection is not recorded, but it is a matter of record that the Lincoln administration continued "the course thus far pursued," barring blacks from the army and returning fugitive slaves to rebel masters. Some generals went further, saying that if slaves rose behind enemy lines they would stop fighting the enemy and start fighting the slaves. They would, in the words of Gen. George McClellan, put down slave insurrections with "an iron hand." It occurred to some people that this was a novel way to fight a war. Congressional liberals, abolitionists, black leaders, and "hard-war" Unionists asked Lincoln to stop the "military slave hunt" and hit the South where it would hurt the most: free the slaves and give them guns. What kind of war was the president fighting anyway? What was he trying to do? Lincoln said he was trying to save the Union. What then was to be done with slaves who abandoned their masters in droves and flocked to the Union lines? Lincoln said his policy was to have no policy. When Gen. John C. Frémont issued a proclamation freeing the slaves of Missouri rebels, Lincoln revoked the proclamation and kicked up a storm of abuse. Congressional liberals, abolitionists, black leaders and "hard-war" Unionists said he was weak-kneed, vacillating, spineless, dumb.

Morning, noon and night, Lincoln was pressed by the one problem he was determined to ignore. A White House visitor reported that the mere mention of the word *slave* made Lincoln nervous. For almost two years Lincoln held to this course, appeasing the slaveholding Border States and maintaining the official fiction that the war was a polite misunderstanding between white gentlemen, a war in no way related to blacks and slavery. "The soul of old John Brown may have been marching," Dudley Taylor Cornish wrote, "but it marched in exclusively white company."

Insofar as it can be said that Lincoln had a policy it was to rid America of both slaves and blacks. To this end, he launched a powerful propaganda campaign in support of his pet project of colonizing blacks in Central America. On August 14, 1862, he called a hand-picked group of five blacks to the White House for the first major conference of black Americans with an American president. In "a curious mixture of condescension and kindness," to use James M. McPherson's phrase, Lincoln told the men that it was their duty to leave America. "You and we are different races," he said. "We have between us a broader difference than exists between almost any other two races. Whether it is right or wrong I need not discuss, but this physical difference is a great disadvantage to us both, as I think your race suffer very greatly, many of them by living among us, while ours suffer from your presence."

Lincoln did not seek the opinion of his visitors. He did not propose, he said, to discuss racism or to debate whether it was founded on reality or justice. He was simply, he said, presenting a fact: white people didn't want black people in America and therefore black people would have to go. "There is," he said, "an unwillingness on the part of our people, harsh as it may be, for you free colored people to remain with us." What then was the solution? The only solution, he said, was a black exodus. "It is better for us both . . . to be separated." He proposed a black settlement on Central American land, "rich in coal," and he asked his visitors to help him find black settlers "capable of thinking as white men."

The response in Black America was swift and angry. Outraged by Lincoln's insensitivity, free blacks organized protest meetings and bombarded the White House with letters and petitions. Although there was minority support for the plan in colonization and nationalist circles, most free blacks denounced the overture, expressing particular dissatisfaction with Lincoln's suggestion that black people were the cause of racism and the war.

"A horse thief," Frederick Douglass said, "pleading that the
existence of the horse is the apology for his theft or a highway
man contending that the money in the traveler's pocket is the sole
first cause of his robbery are about as much entitled to respect as
is the President's reasoning at this point. No, Mr. President, it is
not the innocent horse that makes the horse thief, nor the
traveler's purse that makes the highway robber, and it is not the
presence of the Negro that causes this foul and unnatural war,
but the cruel and brutal cupidity of those who wish to possess
horses, money and Negroes by means of theft, robbery and
rebellion."

That Lincoln's policy was changed at all is due not to
humanitarianism but to rebel battlefield brilliance—the South
knew what it was fighting for—and the daring and hope of fugitive slaves. By digging in and fighting, the South brought the
North to a realization that it was in a real brawl and that it needed
all the weapons it could lay hands on. It came to some soon and to
others late that all men, at the very least, are buried equal. By
flocking to the Union lines, by leaving bed and cabin and rallying
to the flag, fugitive slaves made the North define its terms. It
came to some in 1861 and to others in 1863 that blacks were
inextricably involved in the struggle and that the war could not be
fought without taking them into consideration; nor, and this was
most frightening, could the war be ended without coming to grips
with the meaning of blackness and the meaning of America.

It came fairly soon to Ben Butler, an odd character who seemed
to be everywhere in this war. Ben Butler was a Massachusetts
politician who wangled a general's commission and went down to
Virginia to fight. He got there at a good time. The Union was in a
dither over fugitive slaves who persisted in leaving their masters
and seeking refuge under the American flag. Nobody knew what
to do with these people. Ben Butler acted, welcoming slaves into
his line, putting them to work and grandly dubbing them "contraband of war." The word *contraband* caught on; the word—and
a great many people had been waiting for a word—permitted the
North to strike at slavery without using that dangerous word
slavery.

Thus, the first step was taken. Congress and Robert E. Lee
did the rest. Congress, pushed by liberals like Charles Sumner,

William H. Carney of the Fifty-fourth Massachusetts Volunteers received the Congressional Medal of Honor for bravery in the Union assault on Fort Wagner, South Carolina, on July 18, 1863.

John H. Lawson won the Congressional Medal of Honor for his heroism in the Battle of Mobile Bay. At least three other black sailors received Medals of Honor for bravery in naval battles.

Making the famous charge on Fort Wagner in Charleston, South Carolina, harbor, soldiers of the Fifty-fourth Massachusetts Volunteers are repulsed by Confederate defenders. The charge won plaudits in the North.

Ben Wade, Henry Wilson and Thaddeus Stevens, forbade Union officers to return fugitive slaves to rebels, emancipated District of Columbia slaves, declared free the slaves of all rebels and gave Lincoln discretionary power to use black troops. Robert E. Lee and other rebel generals taught the Union that war, in Sherman's pithy phrase, was hell.

It came to Lincoln in the summer of 1862 that the Union, in his phrase, could not escape history. "Things," he explained later, "had gone from bad to worse, until I felt that we had reached the end of our rope on the plan of operations we had been pursuing; that we had about played our last card." On Tuesday, July 22, Lincoln called his cabinet together and put his "last card" on the table. It was a good one, a draft of a preliminary Emancipation Proclamation. The document was discussed pro and con until Secretary of State William H. Seward came to the heart of the matter. The timing, he said, was bad. "The depression of the public mind," Seward said, "consequent upon our repeated reverses, is so great that I fear the effect of so important a step. It may be viewed as the last measure of an exhausted government, a cry for help; the government stretching forth its hand to Ethiopia, instead of Ethiopia stretching forth her hands to the government." There was some truth in this. Lincoln put the document into his desk drawer and waited, he said later, for the Union to win a battle.

While Lincoln waited three generals stretched out their hands to Ethiopia. Without waiting for official approval, David ("Black David") Hunter and Jim Lane started organizing black regiments. Hunter organized the First South Carolina Volunteers, the first black regiment, and Jim Lane organized the First Kansas "Colored" Volunteers. The government did not get around to extending official recognition to the South Carolina and Kansas volunteers until January, 1863.

Down in New Orleans, in this long hot summer, Ben Butler was thinking. He needed men, and there were thousands of black men in his military district. Why not use them? Butler turned the problem over in his fertile mind. There was a prejudice against the use of black troops. This prejudice, however, was crumbling. The sons of thousands of white mothers were dying, and people were beginning to say that blacks could stop bullets as well as white men. Humorist Miles O'Reilly marked the shift in a poem:

"Sambo's Right to be Kilt."

> *Some say it is a burnin' shame*
> *To make the naygurs fight,*
> *An' that the thrade of bein' kilt*
> *Belongs but to the white;*
>
> *But as for me upon my sowl'*
> *So liberal are we here,*
> *I'll let Sambo be murthered in place o'meself*
> *On every day in the year.*

The wind was changing, and Ben Butler was an excellent weather vane. In New Orleans at that very moment were fourteen hundred free blacks who had organized a regiment of free black Confederate soldiers. Butler sent for the leaders of the regiment and asked them if blacks would fight.

"General," the spokesman said, "we come of a fighting race. Our fathers were brought here because they were captured in war, and in hand to hand fights, too. We are willing to fight. Pardon me, General, but the only cowardly blood we have got in our veins is the white blood."

Butler issued the necessary papers and the First Louisiana Native Guards became the first black regiment to receive official recognition in the Union army.

While Butler was organizing his black regiment, Lincoln was polishing the phrases of the preliminary Emancipation Proclamation. On September 22, 1862, five days after the Battle of Antietam, he notified the South that he would free all slaves in states in rebellion on January 1, 1863. The one hundred days between the preliminary proclamation and the signing of the real thing were anxious ones for black Americans. Would Lincoln go through with his threat? No one knew. On the issue of black rights, Lincoln was an unknown and unpredictable quantity. In Illinois he had opposed granting blacks social and political equality. In Washington he had campaigned for gradual emancipation and abrupt (voluntary) emigration of free Negroes. To most liberals and militant black leaders, the president was something of an enigma; a good man, to be sure, honest, decent and kind, but slow, timid, vacillating even, in his approach to the supreme moral issue of the age. As the moment of truth approached, many people said Lincoln would never go through with it. Nor was this all speculation. The Reverend Byron Sunderland told Lincoln one day that people were saying he would never sign the proclamation. "Well, Doctor," Lincoln replied obliquely, "you know Peter was going to do it, but when the time came, he did not." It was an ominous sign in the dying days of 1862 that Abraham Lincoln was meditating on the example of Peter and the cock that crowed thrice.

Wednesday, December 31, 1862, was a day of anticipation and rumor. People gathered in little knots and tried to read the signs of the time. That night, blacks gathered in churches and prayed the Old Age out and the New Age in. There was no doubt about what Lincoln would do at the "watch meeting" held in the Washington, D.C., "Contraband Camp." An eloquent old "contraband" got up and told the gathering what time it was. "Once, the time was," he said, "that I cried all night. What's the matter? What's the matter? Matter enough. The next morning my child was to be sold, and she was sold; and I never 'pected to see her no more till the day of judgement. Now, no more that! No more that! No more that! With my hands against my breast I was going to my work, when the overseer used to whip me along. Now, no more that! No more that! No more that! . . . We'se free now, bless the Lord! [Amen! Amen! said the audience.] They can't sell my wife an' child no more, bless the Lord! [Glory! Glory!] No more that! No more that! No more that, now!" A few minutes before midnight, the people went to their knees and greeted the New Age in prayerful silence.

Down South, on the Sea Islands off South Carolina, blacks and whites celebrated at the camp of the First South Carolina Volunteers. Boats brought the celebrants from the mainland and a makeshift platform was erected in a grove on the edge of the camp. There, under the giant oaks, the celebrants listened to the reading of Lincoln's preliminary proclamation. There were additional words, too many words, and when Col. T. W. Higginson got up to speak, unfolding a new flag as he collected his thoughts, an old dry voice came from the audience. The old man carried it by himself for a little while. Then two women joined in and another man and another until the words swelled out:

> My country, 'tis of thee,
> Sweet land of liberty,
> Of thee I sing.

A few whites chimed in, but Colonel Higginson waved them silent. "I never," he said later, "saw anything so electric; it made all other words cheap. It seemed the choked voice of a race at last unloosed."

On the night of the first day of January in "the Year of Jubilee," blacks and whites gathered at Boston's Tremont Temple. Newspaper reports on the signing of the Proclamation had not reached Boston and the group waited impatiently as speaker after speaker mounted the platform. Frederick Douglass spoke and others, but the words lacked fire; all minds were locked on Lincoln. Eight o'clock came and nine and nine-thirty and ten, and still there was no word from Washington. People who were given to saying, "I told you so," said it; even Frederick Douglass began to doubt. Finally, when the most sanguine began to droop, a man ran screaming into the room, "It's coming! It's on the wires!" Suddenly, everyone was on his feet, shouting, laughing, weeping. The meeting went on all night and it seemed, Frederick Douglass recalled later, "that almost everything seemed to be witty and appropriate to the occasion."

The morning after was a little more prosaic. Examining the proclamation in the hard glare of daylight, Douglass and others were disappointed.

The gist of its message was in one paragraph:

> And by virtue of the power [invested in me] I do order and declare that all persons held as slaves within said designated States, and parts of States, are, and henceforward shall be free; and that the Executive government of the United States. . . will recognize and maintain the freedom of said persons.

The document was as dry as a brief in a real estate case. There was in it none of the King James nobility that Lincoln carried to Gettysburg; nor, it seemed, did the proclamation do much emancipating. It did not apply to slaves in loyal Border States and in sections under federal control in the South. Still, there was something about the piece of paper. In spite of its matter-of-fact dryness, in spite of its repeated pleas of "military necessity," in spite of its many exceptions, the document became one of the great state papers of the century. More concretely, it converted a vague war for Union into something men would get their teeth into: a war for freedom.

The black response to the proclamation was immediate and electric. Cryptic messages sped along the invisible telegraph wires that ran into every slave cabin, and men, women and children went looking for President Lincoln's soldiers. Planters, in desperation, attempted to "run the Negroes," i.e., move them further into the interior away from the advancing Union army. This had little or no effect on the mass migration which reached mammoth proportions. There had never been anything quite like it, John Eaton said, a slave population "rising up and leaving its ancient bondage, forsaking its local traditions and all the associations and attractions of the old plantation life, coming garbed in rags or in silks, with feet shod or bleeding, individually or in families and larger groups." Eaton said it was like "the oncoming of cities."

The slaves said it in a song:

> No more peck of corn for me,
>   No more, no more.
> No more peck of corn for me,
>   Many thousand gone.
>
> No more driver's lash for me,
>   No more, no more.
> No more driver's lash for me,
>   Many thousand gone.

Many thousands found employment in the Union army. By the end of 1863 there were some fifty thousand black soldiers in Union ranks. Although black soldiers were not accepted as brothers in arms by everyone, they courageously defended the Union and black freedom at Port Hudson, Milliken's Bend, Fort Wagner, Poison Spring, Olustee, Nashville, Tupelo, Petersburg, Richmond and 440 other places. But this, as Col. N.P. Hallowell said, is not the most that can be said for them. Black soldiers in the Civil War, Colonel Hallowell said, demonstrated that "highest order" of courage which America demands of men with dark skins. He added:

"They were promised the same pay, and, in general, the same treatment as white soldiers. No one expected the same treatment in the sense of courtesy, but everyone believed a great nation would keep faith with its soldiers in the beggarly matter of pay.

They were promised thirteen dollars per month [the pay of white privates]. They were insulted with an offer of seven dollars."

Many regiments refused to accept the seven dollars. When the Massachusetts legislature passed a bill providing the six dollars difference, the state's black regiments refused to accept the money. They were fighting, they said, for a principle, not money. Many blacks fought for fourteen, sixteen and eighteen months (until the inequity was corrected) without accepting a penny from the government. There is a kind of bittersweet poetry in the fact that the Fifty-fourth Massachusetts Volunteers went into the Battle of Olustee with the cry, "Hurrah for Massachusetts and seven dollars a month."

Black soldiers were paid less money, but they faced grimmer hazards. Some black POWs were accorded the rights of civilized warfare, but others were murdered or sold into slavery. "I hope," Jerome Yates of Mississippi wrote his mother, "I may never see a Negro soldier or I cannot be . . . a Christian soldier." Not a few white Southerners found it impossible to reconcile the conflicting claims of Christianity and white supremacy. In the ugliest incident of the war, a rebel force, commanded by Maj. Gen. Nathan Bedford Forrest, massacred a predominantly black group at Fort Pillow, Tennessee. The rebels entered the fort, shouting, "Kill the god-damned niggers! Kill all the niggers!" A congressional investigating committee said Forrest's men murdered three hundred soldiers and civilians after the fort surrendered. According to official reports, black soldiers were shot in cold blood, nailed to logs and buried alive. Black women and children were also murdered. General Forrest rode among the dead and the wounded, stopping here and there to say that he recognized some of the black men. "They've been in my nigger-yard in Memphis," the former slave trader said.

At Memphis, a few days after the Fort Pillow Massacre, black soldiers dropped to their knees and swore remembrance. After April 12, 1864, black soldiers entered battle with the cry, "Remember Fort Pillow."

Long before Fort Pillow, and long before Sherman's dagger thrusts in Georgia, black soldiers and sailors became indispensable elements in a war that could not have been won without their

Black sailors served on the famous Union ironclad, the
Monitor. Large numbers of blacks served on Union
vessels. Black sailors held all ranks below petty officer,
were stewards, cooks, seamen and pilots.

Soldiers of the Second U.S.C.T. artillery participated in the Battle of Nashville. There were twelve black heavy artillery units in the Union army, which recruited some 90,000 black soldiers in the South.

help. They handled themselves brilliantly in the fall of 1862 in minor actions at Island Mounds, Missouri, and in skirmishes in Georgia and Florida. But their first major battles came in the summer of 1863. The first of these battles was the Union assault on Port Hudson, Louisiana, the last Confederate obstacle to the capture of Vicksburg. This heavily fortified position, thirty miles north of Baton Rouge, on the banks of the Mississippi, was attacked on May 27, 1863, by a determined Union force, which included five black regiments. Leading the attack were the First and Third Louisiana Native Guards, who made six suicidal charges, dashing across a treacherous sweep of land into the very mouth of artillery mounted on the parapet.

The black assault was led by Captain André Cailloux, a prominent Catholic layman from New Orleans. A well-to-do man who liked to boast of his blackness, Cailloux was all over the field. Speaking now in French and now in English, he urged his men on, leading the way himself. When his left arm was shattered by a bullet, he remained on the field and rallied his men for a final charge. Cailloux dashed to his death like a brave and reckless matador. As he sprinted across the field, with his broken arm flopping crazily, he shouted in English and French, "Follow me! *Suivez-moi!*" He fell mortally wounded some fifty yards from the fort. Although the Native Guards failed to capture the fort they earned widespread praise. The *New York Times* expressed the general view, saying on June 13, 1863, that "no body of troops —Western, Eastern or rebel—has fought better in the war."

The same thing can be said of the gallant charge of the Fifty-fourth Massachusetts Volunteers at Fort Wagner in the Charleston, South Carolina, harbor. In this celebrated encounter Col. Robert Gould Shaw and his Massachusetts volunteers sprinted across a half-mile of sand, mounted the parapet and struggled with the defenders. Colonel Shaw and a brave color sergeant were mortally wounded. They fell from the parapet and lay close together, integrated in death.

Milliken's bend was not a classic charge. A hand-to-hand, cutting, gouging brawl, it occurred ten days after the Port Hudson assault when two thousand Texans attacked the Union fort at Milliken's Bend, about twenty miles up the river from Vicksburg. The fort was held by 840 blacks and 160 whites. The Texans drove the Union soldiers back to the banks of the river, murdering

captured blacks as they advanced. Enraged by atrocities committed before their eyes, and helped at the last moment by a Union
gunboat, the troops counterattacked. The black and white soldiers stood toe to toe, clubbing each other, baseball fashion, with
the butts of muskets and gouging with bayonets. Finally, after a
ten- or fifteen-minute struggle, the Texans broke and fled.

Milliken's Bend was a sideshow. In 1864 black soldiers entered
the big tent. When Ulysses S. Grant crossed the Rapidan and
began his bloody duel with Robert E. Lee, a black division accompanied him. Moving at the same time, the omnipresent Ben
Butler advanced on Richmond from the Virginia peninsula, taking with him five thousand black foot soldiers and eighteen
hundred black cavalrymen. Grant wheeled around Lee's right
flank to Spotsylvania Court House and Cold Harbor and then sent
Gen. W. F. Smith down to Petersburg to make a sneak attack
with a mixed force. The black division spearheading the attack
knocked a mile-wide hole in the Petersburg defenses, captured
seven guns and two hundred prisoners. Petersburg lay open, but
Smith dallied and the Petersburg defenses were reinforced.
Grant then settled down for the ten-month siege which ended in
April, 1865, with the fall of Petersburg and Richmond. Thirty-
four black Union regiments played a part in this famous siege.
Black troops were especially prominent in the disastrous Battle
of the Crater and engagements at Darbytown Road, Fair Oaks,
Deep Bottom, Hatcher's Run, New Market Heights and Fort
Gilmer.

Black soldiers were in on the kill. The Second Division of the
all-black Twenty-fifth Corps was one of the Union divisions that
chased Lee's tattered army from Petersburg to Appomattox Courthouse. When the end came, the black and white troops were
moving forward at the double and Lee's men were retreating in
confusion.

The triumph of Union forces was due to a number of factors,
including Northern technology and the spirit of the age. But a
central, perhaps preeminent, factor was the contribution of black
Americans—slaves and freedmen—who provided the margin of
difference that turned the tide against the Confederate forces in
1864 and 1865. The enormity of the black contribution, a contribution generally ignored or overlooked, is underscored by the

calculus of the contending forces. There were, according to official records, 185,000 black soldiers in the Union army. These
soldiers, generally identified as United States Colored Troops,
were organized into 166 regiments (145 infantry, 12 heavy artillery, 7 cavalry, 1 light artillery, and 1 engineer).

Most of these soldiers—93,000—came from the South. Northern states contributed 52,000 black soldiers, and 40,000 soldiers
came from the Border States. The largest number of black soldiers came from Louisiana (24,052), followed by Kentucky
(23,703), and Tennessee (20,133). Since the War Department discouraged black applicants, there were few black officers. The
highest-ranking of the 70 to 100 black officers was Lt. Col. Alexander T. Augustana, a surgeon.

For various reasons, almost all of them linked to racism, the
black mortality rate was disproportionately high. Union records
list 37,638 black casualties, roughly 21 per cent of the total
number of black soldiers.

Black soldiers participated in 410 military engagements and 39
major battles, including Port Hudson, Fort Wagner, Olustee,
Petersburg Mine Assault, Chaffin's Farm, Nashville, Overton
Hill, Honey Hill, Yazoo City, Poison Springs, Tupelo, Bermuda
Hundred, Dutch Gap, Hatcher's Run, Fort Fisher, the fall of
Richmond, Deep Bottom and Appomattox. Sixteen black sol-
diers received Congressional Medals of Honor for gallantry in
action.

Equally visible — and heroic — were the sailors in the Union
navy, which accepted blacks from the beginning of the conflict.
Twenty-nine thousand blacks — one out of every four Union
sailors — served on Union ships as coal heavers, stewards,
boatswains, firemen and gunners. These sailors were quartered
and messed with whites and shared equally in the danger and
glory. Four black sailors received Medals of Honor.

In addition to these forces, the Union effort was forwarded by
the more than two hundred thousand civilians, mostly freed
slaves, who worked in Union camps as mechanics, cooks, barbers, teamsters, nurses and common laborers. Particularly important to the war effort were the black laborers who built fortifications and groundworks, freeing soldiers, black and white, for
combat duty.

Black civilians, in and out of the army, also served as spies and

scouts. By feigning ignorance and playing on the strings of Southern prejudice, various blacks managed to obtain invaluable information on Confederate plans and activities. A *New York Times*
article, written in the summer of 1862, said that "some of the
most valuable information that General McClellan has received in
regard to the position, movement, and plans of the enemy, the
topography of the country and the inclination of certain inhabitants has been obtained through contrabands. Even spies and
traitors have been detected and brought to the attention of the
authorities [by fugitives] slaves."

Of these spies, none was more successful than John Scobell, a
former slave of a Scotsman who could sing Scottish ballads with
impeccable diction and imitate Southern field hands. Disguising
himself as a laborer and as a cook and peddler, Scobell infiltrated
Southern lines at Fredericksburg, Leesburg and Manassas.

The most remarkable of all Union spies was a woman—the
celebrated abolitionist Harriet Tubman. Working in South Carolina and other states, she organized slave intelligence networks
behind enemy lines and led scouting raids. She also became the
first and possibly the last woman to lead U.S. Army troops in
battle. A graphic account of one of these battles appeared in the
Boston *Commonwealth* on July 10, 1863:

HARRIET TUBMAN

Col. Montgomery and his gallant band of 300 black soldiers, *under the guidance of a black woman*, dashed into the
enemy's country, struck a bold and effective blow, destroying
millions of dollars worth of commissary stores, cotton and
lordly dwellings, and striking terror into the heart of rebel-
dom, brought off near 800 slaves and thousands of dollars
worth of property, without losing a man or receiving a scratch.
It was a glorious consummation.

After they were all fairly well disposed of in the Beaufort
charge, they were addressed in strains of thrilling eloquence
by their gallant deliverer, to which they responded in a song

"There is a white robe for thee,"

a song so appropriate and so heartfelt and cordial as to bring
unbidden tears.

*The Colonel was followed by a speech from the black wom-
an who led the raid, and under whose inspiration it was
organized and conducted.* For sound sense and real native

Confederate troops, under the command of Gen. Nathan Bedford Forrest, killed some three hundred soldiers and civilians in the Fort Pillow Massacre. A predominantly black force held the Tennessee fort.

In a triumphant ride through Richmond, Virginia, on
April 4, 1865, Abraham Lincoln received wide acclaim
from the freed slaves. Lincoln issued the Emancipation
Proclamation on January 1, 1863. The Thirteenth
Amendment ended slavery in America.

eloquence, her address would do honor to any man, and it created a sensation. . . .

Since the rebellion she has devoted herself to her great work of delivering the bondsman, with an energy and sagacity that cannot be exceeded. *Many and many times she has penetrated the enemy's lines and discovered their situation and condition, and escaped without injury, but not without extreme hazard* (emphasis supplied).

This example is worth nothing, not only because of the light it sheds on the activities of a black spy and patriot but also because it points to the contribution of slaves, who sabotaged the Confederate war effort by slow-downs and sit-downs and unorganized malingering. The slaves were also creatively subversive in giving aid and comfort to the enemies of their enemies. We can cite here the testimony of both Confederate and Union sources. After a Union raid in South Carolina, a planter wrote that "the people about here would not have suffered near as much if it had not been for these Negroes; in every case they have told where things have been hidden and they did most of the stealing." There is similar testimony from Union sources. A Union soldier, foraging in Louisiana in 1863, said slaves stood at the gate with unerringly accurate information on the location of saddles, horses and valuables. He added that in most cases "it was the favorite servants who pointed out the hiding places and said, 'You give us free, and we helps you all we can.'" Slaves also assisted the Union war effort by hiding Union soldiers who escaped from Confederate prisons. Junius Henri Brown, who was held in prisons in North Carolina and Virginia, said that "during our entire captivity, and after our escape, they were our firm, brave, unflinching friends. We never made an appeal to them they did not answer."

By these different methods, by fighting and spying and weakening the Confederate war effort, black Americans helped turn the tide against their oppressors. There is no better authority on this point than Abraham Lincoln, who initially opposed use of black troops. But when it became apparent that "no human power" could subdue the rebellion "without the use of the emancipation policy," Lincoln changed his mind and told critics: "ABANDON ALL THE POSTS NOW GARRISONED BY BLACK MEN; TAKE TWO HUNDRED THOUSAND MEN FROM OUR SIDE AND PUT THEM IN THE BATTLEFIELD OR CORNFIELD AGAINST US, AND WE WOULD BE COMPELLED TO ABANDON THE WAR IN THREE WEEKS." One can hardly doubt, in the face of this testimony, that black Americans did as much as any other group to free themselves and American freedom.

With the defeat of Confederate forces, the freedom of words, the freedom of proclamations and political promises, became a live option involving concrete realities. As the news spread from plantation to plantation, in the spring and summer of 1865, the black South was convulsed by a chain of emotional bombs that exploded, one after another, shattering the silence of centuries and breaking the earth for a new growth. In celebrating that ending, and the hope of a new beginning, the former slaves of America staged a summer-long Jubilee of celebration, song and thanksgiving.

> *Free at last!*
> *Free at last!*
> *Thank God Almighty,*
> *We're free at last!*

Felix Haywood, who was a witness to this black apocalypse, said nothing quite like it had ever been seen before. "Hallelujah broke out," he said. "Soldiers, all of a sudden, was every-where — coming in bunches, crossing and walking and riding. Everyone was a-singing. We was all walking on golden clouds. Hallelujah!"

There were also golden clouds, according to Fannie Berry, over Pamplin, Virginia, near Appomattox. "Glory! Glory!" she said. "Yes, child, the Negroes are free, and when they knew that they were free they, oh! baby! began to sing . . . Such rejoicing and shouting you never heard in your life."

What did freedom mean to Fannie Berry and her generation?

The answer is that it meant different things to different freed-men and freedwomen. Freedom to some was getting married before a preacher and signing papers and knowing that it was for always and not until the next cotton crop. Freedom to others was the right to pick up and go. Freedom, in other words, was a many-layered thing. Freedom was Bibles, freedom was churches, freedom was gin. Freedom was two names. A man sat for a while and decided on a name and if he didn't like it he could change it again tomorrow. (Some former slaves chose the last names of their late masters, but many decided that they "had nuff o' old massa" and looked further for family identification.)

Freedom was all this and more. It was getting up when you wanted to and lying down when the spirit hit you. It was doing nothing, too. How was a person to know he was free if he couldn't sit still and watch the sun and pull on his pipe when he didn't want to do anything else? Over and above this, deeper than this, freedom was land and letters: an opportunity to learn and the right—and the means—to earn one's own bread. With a yearning born of centuries of denial, former slaves worshipped the sight and sound of the printed world. Old men and women on the edge of the grave could be seen in the dark of the night, poring over the Scripture by the light of a pine knot, painfully spelling out the sacred words.

According to contemporary reports, the freedmen demonstrated a passion for education that has never perhaps been equalled in world history. The whole race, eyewitnesses said, wanted to go to school, and it was reported that black "children love the school as white children love a holiday." Charlotte Forten, the granddaughter of James Forten, was teaching on the Sea Islands, off the coast of South Carolina, and she said she "never before saw children so eager to learn, although I had had several years' experience in New England schools. Coming to school is a constant delight and recreation to them. They come here as other children go to play."

The same fervor was reported in all Southern states. The Reverend Thomas Calahan, a missionary of the United Presbyterian Church, was teaching then in Louisiana, and he reported scenes of unprecedented enthusiasm.

"Go out in any direction," he said, "and you meet Negroes on horses, Negroes on mules, Negroes with oxen, Negroes by the wagon, cart and buggy load, Negroes on foot, men, women, and children . . . Negroes in rags, Negroes in frame houses, Negroes living in tents, Negroes living in rail pens covered with brush, and Negroes living under brush piles without any rails, Negroes living on the bare ground with the sky for their covering; all hopeful, almost all cheerful, everyone pleading to be taught, willing to do anything for learning. They are never out of our rooms, and their cry is for 'Books! Books!' and 'when will school begin?'"

Their cry was also for land. The freedmen had lived for decades in a primary relationship with the land, and it was inconceivable to them that the U.S. government would turn them loose without providing the economic wherewithal that would make freedom meaningful. For these reasons, among others, it was believed in the summer of 1865 that there would be a general distribution of the land on January 1, 1866. As the magic date approached, many freedmen abandoned the plantations and began to prepare for a real freedom based on a real foundation. But there was no land on January 1, 1866, or on January 1, 1867. Without the means to realize or validate their freedom, most freedmen were driven back to the plantations by hunger and violence.

It was in this setting, with enemies all around them and all the high ground in the hands of their adversaries, that the freedmen and freedwomen of America began their long march down a road called freedom.

8

Black Power in the Old South

[The Radical Republicans] instituted a public
school system in a realm where public schools had
been unknown. They opened the ballot box and the
jury box to thousands of white men who had been
barred from them by a lack of earthly possessions.
They introduced home rule in the South. They
abolished the whipping post, the branding iron, the
stock and other barbarous forms of punishment
which had up to that time prevailed. They reduced
capital felonies from about twenty to two or three.
In an age of extravagance they were extravagant in
the sums appropriated for public works. In all that
time no man's rights of person were invaded under
the forms of law.

ALBION W. TOURGEE

NEVER BEFORE had the sun shone so bright.
A former slave named Blanche Kelso
Bruce was representing Mississippi in the
United States Senate. Pinckney Benton Stewart Pinchback,
young, charming, daring, was sitting in the governor's office in
Louisiana.

In Mississippi, South Carolina and Louisiana, black lieutenant governors were sitting on the right hand of power. A black was secretary of state in Florida; a black was on the state supreme court in South Carolina. In these and other Southern states, blacks were superintendents of education, state treasurers, adjutant generals, solicitors, judges and major generals of militia. Robert H. Wood was mayor of Natchez, Mississippi, and Norris Wright Cuney was running for mayor of Galveston, Texas. Seven blacks were sitting in the House of Representatives.

Nor was this all. Blacks and whites were going to school together, riding on streetcars together and cohabiting, in and out of wedlock. An interracial board was running the University of South Carolina, where a black professor, Richard T. Greener, was teaching white and black youth metaphysics and logic.

These things were happening on the higher levels. What of the masses? How was it with them? They were struggling, as they had always struggled, with the stubborn and recalcitrant earth. But now there was hope. Never before—never since—had there been so much hope. A black mother knew that her boy could become governor. The evidence of things seen, the evidence of things heard fired millions of hearts. Black mothers walked ten, fifteen and twenty miles to put their children in school. They sacrificed and stinted. They bowed down and worshipped the miraculous ABCs from whom so many blessings flowed. The sky or at the very least the mountaintop was the limit. Had not Blanche Bruce been suggested as a possible vice-presidential candidate? Was it not clear that a black boy could go as far as nerve, energy and ability would carry him? Black mothers, bending over washtubs, could hope. Black boys, in cotton fields, could dream. The millennium hadn't come, of course, but there were some who believed it was around the next turning.

A man, in this age, went to mail a letter, and the postmaster was black. A man committed a crime, and, in some counties, was arrested by a black policeman, prosecuted by a black solicitor, weighed by a black and white jury and sentenced by a black judge. It was enough to drive some men mad; it was enough to warp some men's judgment. Come with James S. Pike, a hostile Northern reporter, into the South Carolina House of Representatives, the first Western assembly of its kind with a black majority. "The Speaker," Pike reports, "is black, the clerk is black, the doorkeepers are black, the little pages are black, the chairman of Ways and Means is black, and the chaplain is coal black."

There had never been an age like this one before, and there would never be one again—not in a hundred years anyway. Up in Maine, in these Democracy-in-Wonderland days, James Augustine Healy, the first black American Catholic bishop, was tending his flock and his Irish communicants were chanting a pagan ditty, "Glurry be to God, the Bishop is a Nee-gar!" Farther South, in Washington, D.C., the bishop's brother, Patrick Francis Healy, was sitting in the presidential chair at Georgetown, America's oldest Catholic university. Down in New Orleans Bourbons were doing what they would do again ninety years later. Policemen were escorting Governor Pinchback's children to a high school where organized gangs were making their lives miserable. "They were good enough niggers," one of the ringleaders would say, "but still they were niggers."

On the East Coast, in Columbia, South Carolina, people were sampling democracy and finding it to their liking. The fabulous Rollins sisters were operating a Paris-type salon for movers and shakers, and hostile critics were saying that more legislation was passed there than in the legislature. On hot nights blacks and whites walked the wide streets arm in arm and went perhaps to Fine's Saloon for a cold drink. The social life was gay, glittering and interracial. A dashing young militia captain gave a ball, and blacks and whites—some of them native South Carolinians— glided across the polished floor. At official balls, receptions and dinners, blacks and whites sat down together and got up in peace. Years later a renegade Republican would poke fun at these affairs. "The colored band," he would write, "was playing 'Rally 'Round the Flag.' . . . There was a mixture of white and black, male and female. Supper was announced, and you ought to have seen the scramble for the table. Social equality was at its highest pitch."

These things, improbable as they may seem now, happened in America during the ten improbable years (1867–77) of Black Reconstruction. W. E. B. Du Bois called them the "mystic years." Intoxicated perhaps by the emotional bang of the big war, taunted by the arrogance of the conquered South, and spurred on by economic and political forces, the North took in these years the

longest stride America has ever taken: it decided to try democracy. The decision was not a conscious one and it was not made
all at once. At war's end few politicians—Charles Sumner and
Thaddeus Stevens were exceptions—knew what to do with the
emancipated slaves. As late as April, 1865, Abraham Lincoln was
dallying with the idea of voluntary deportation. Ben Butler, the
former Union general and Massachusetts politician, said Lincoln
asked him to figure out the logistics of deporting the freedmen to
another land. Butler came back two days later with a sad story.
"Mr. President," he said, "I have gone carefully over my calcula-
tions as to the power of the country to export the Negroes of the
South and I assure you that, using all your naval vessels and all
the merchant marine fit to cross the seas with safety, it will be
impossible for you to transport to the nearest place . . . half as
fast as Negro children will be born here."

The black American, in short, was in America to stay. What
was to be done with him? Frederick Douglass, the leading black
voice leader, had an answer: "Do nothing with [him]. Your *doing*
with [Negroes] is their greatest misfortune. . . . The Negro
should have been let alone in Africa . . . let alone when the pirates and robbers offered him for sale in our Christian slave markets . . . let alone by the courts, judges, politicians, legislators
and slave drivers."

Having laid down this principle, Douglass at once deduced its
consequences:

"If you see [the Negro] plowing in the open field, leveling the
forest, at work with a spade, a rake, a hoe, a pick-axe, or a
bill—let him alone; he has a right to work. If you see him on his
way to school, with spelling book, geography and arithmetic in his
hands—let him alone. . . . If he has a ballot in his hand, and is on
his way to the ballot-box to deposit his vote for the man whom he
thinks will most justly and wisely administer the Government
which has the power of life and death over him, as well as
others—let him *alone*."

That was one answer. Thaddeus Stevens, the Pennsylvania
congressman, had another: Give him forty acres of land and a
mule.

On this issue, as on all others involving black rights, Stevens
and Douglass were far in advance of public opinion. And while
men were debating and public opinion was congealing, they

joined with others in supporting legislation which provided stop-gap relief to the millions of freedmen who had been hurled into the maelstrom of freedom without material supports. The freedmen, as Douglass and others pointed out, were free—free to the wind and to the rain, free to the wrath and hostility of their former slavemasters. They had no tools, they had no shelter, they had no cooking utensils; and they were surrounded by hostile men who were determined to prove that the whole thing was a monstrous mistake.

The temporary solution to this problem, approved by Congress on March 3, 1865, was the Freedmen's Bureau, the first federal welfare agency. During its lamentably short life (1865–72), the bureau was an Urban League, WPA, CIO and War on Poverty all wrapped up into a prototypical NAACP. It stood between the freedmen and the wrath of their former slavemasters. It gave direct medical aid to some one million freedmen, established hospitals and social agencies and distributed over twenty-one million rations, many of them to poverty-stricken whites. The agency also established day schools, night schools, industrial schools, institutes and colleges. Many of the major black colleges were founded or received substantial financial aid from the Freedmen's Bureau.*

All in all, the bureau, by almost all accounts, did the work of Hercules in building bridges from slavery to freedom. But it was handicapped by inadequate appropriations and the bitter hostility of white Southerners; and it did not and perhaps could not meet the massive needs of the freedmen. The inevitable result was that thousands died of disease and want. In some communities one out of every four blacks died. This, sad to say, delighted some Southerners who began to mourn, prematurely, for the black race. "The child is already born," crowed the *Natchez*

---

*The impoverished black community, as we shall see, also made large contributions to the first black schools. Major black colleges founded in the Reconstruction period include Atlanta University and Virginia Union, 1865; Fisk, Lincoln (Mo.), 1866; Talladega, Howard, Morgan, Morehouse, 1867; Hampton, 1868; Clark, Dillard, Tougaloo, Claflin, 1869; Allen, Benedict, LeMoyne, 1870; Alcorn, 1872; Bennett, 1873; Knoxville, 1875; Meharry, 1876. Black ministers and laymen, notably Frank Quarles, Alonzo Cardozo, James Lynch and William Jefferson White, organized several of the first black colleges, including Jackson College and Morehouse College.

Democrat, "who will behold the last Negro in the state of Missis-sippi." Dr. C. K. Marshall, a learned and wealthy minister, was more precise, saying: "In all probability, New Year's Day, on the morning of the 1st of January, 1920, the colored population in the South will scarcely be counted."

It was a vain hope. The freedmen tightened their belts and—to the consternation of the mourners—their tribe increased. Pain-fully, in fear and trembling, with almost every hand raised against them, they picked up the threads of a social life that had been shattered centuries before in Africa. Nothing attests more forcefully to the freedmen's priorities than the ingathering that characterized the first years of freedom. Witnesses said the roads of the South were clogged in 1865 with black men and women searching for long-lost wives, husbands, children, brothers and sisters. Some of the searchers were successful, but many families were never reunited. In some instances, if we are to believe stories told afterwards by the freedmen, certain blacks entered into marriages only to discover later that they had accidentally married a brother or sister or some other close relative.

The ingathering began in most communities with mass mar-riage ceremonies that legalized the slave vows. This was a volun-tary process, for husbands and wives were free to renounce slave vows and search for other mates. Significantly, most freedmen, some of them eighty and ninety years old, decided to remain with their old mates, thereby giving powerful testimony on the mean-ing they attached to marriage.

There was, of course, another side to this shining coin. Some slaves had married two or three women on different plantations, and some men and women had married new mates under the mistaken assumption that their old mates were dead. It required considerable legal and domestic genius to untangle these marital snarls. In most instances magistrates and civil officers urged freedmen to marry the oldest wife or the wife with the largest number of children. Some husbands and wives, however, devised original solutions and decided between competing mates on the basis of trial visits. Inevitably, there were men like Harry Quarls who had three wives and wanted to keep all of them. After a protracted argument and some legal prodding, Quarls decided—reluctantly—that one was enough. It should be noted here, at

Men, women and children attended primary schools
established for the freedmen. Reconstruction governments
created the first public school systems in the South.

Thaddeus Stevens was the architect of the Radical Reconstruction program. Stevens proposed a plan which would have given each adult freedman forty acres of land.

Freedmen voted for the first time in elections of 1867–68. Former slaves were passionate supporters of Reconstruction regimes. A South Carolina newspaper said "the polls were thronged with eager crowds of Negroes."

least in passing, that the problem of marital readjustment was complicated by the fact that there was then, as now, a large imbalance of black females.

While all this was going on, black men and women were creating new foundations for the black family. At the first stroke of freedom, almost all black women abandoned the fields and served notice that they would hereafter devote themselves to their homes and children. At the same time, and for the same reason, black men went into the public arena and demanded, oftentimes in the face of violence, traditional courtesies and titles for their women and children.

In the related sphere of social welfare, the freedmen played a major role in providing relief for black indigents. Most of the large number of black orphans were taken in by black families and black institutions, and black churches and organizations raised thousands of dollars for social welfare and education. John de Forest, a Freedmen's Bureau officer, said, with some bias, "However selfish, and even dishonest, they might be, they were extravagant in giving."

An understanding of this contribution—and of the financial sacrifice it implied—is crucial to an understanding of the spirit of the freedmen, who were among the major financial supporters of the first black institutions. Individual blacks contributed nickels and dimes and carpentry skills, and black communities organized suppers, excursions and entertainments to raise money for the first black schools and social agencies. Of the 236 schools in Georgia in 1867, 152 were entirely or partly supported by freedmen, who owned 39 of the buildings. By 1870 the freedmen of Virginia were supporting 215 schools and owned 111 school buildings. Between 1865 and 1870, according to an estimate by Du Bois, freedmen contributed $785,700 in cash to black schools.

It was against this background, and in this spirit, that African-Americans began their march down the hard road called freedom. That road branched off almost immediately into a swamp of racism and bad faith. We see this most clearly perhaps in the national reaction to the freedmen's petitions for land. Some farseeing politicians supported these petitions, saying that the freedmen were entitled, as a matter of justice, to retributive compensation for their 250 years of unrequited toil. Retributive was a big word to the freedmen; all they wanted was a little back pay. They saw what only the wisest saw: that freedom was not free without an economic foundation.

Charles Sumner and Frederick Douglass saw it.

So did Thaddeus Stevens. And it was to Stevens, more than to any other man, that the freedmen owed their undying faith in the vivid phrase, "Forty Acres and a Mule." In and out of Congress, the indomitable old Pennsylvanian demanded that large plantations be broken up and distributed to the freedmen in forty-acre lots. "We have turned, or are about to turn, loose four million slaves without a hut to shelter them or a cent in their pockets," he said. "The infernal laws of slavery have prevented them from acquiring an education, understanding the common laws of contract, or of managing the ordinary business of life. This Congress is bound to provide for them until they can take care of themselves. If we do not furnish them with homesteads, and hedge them around with protective laws; if we leave them to the legislation of their late masters, we had better have left them in bondage." Congress refused to budge and Stevens, always a realist, admitted that the dream was stillborn. The Great Commoner was seventy-four, old and gnarled like an oak tree, on the day he rose in the House and pronounced the eulogy:

"In my youth, in my manhood, in my old age, I had fondly dreamed that when any fortunate chance should have broken up for a while the foundation of our institutions [that we would have] so remodeled all our institutions as to have freed them from every vestige of human oppression, of inequality of rights, of the recognized degradation of the poor, and the superior caste of the rich. In short, that no distinction would be tolerated in this purified Republic but what arose from merit and conduct. This bright dream has vanished 'like the baseless fabric of a vision.' "

The bright dream, the brightest dream articulated in the American political arena, vanished also in the U.S. Senate. When that body refused to countenance homes and land for the former slaves, Charles Sumner, the elegant Harvard man, the scholar, the orator, the passionate advocate of human freedom, went home and wept.

There were tears, too, in South Carolina. When federal officials tried to reclaim land that had been distributed with temporary titles, blacks picked up stones and drove them away. Gen.

O. O. Howard, the head of the Freedmen's Bureau, went to South Carolina to explain the situation. The land had been given in good faith, but President Johnson had pardoned the owners and the land was to be returned to them. General Howard called a large assembly and stood on the platform looking out into the sea of black faces. He tried to say it, but the words wouldn't come. How do you tell a people that they have been taken *again?* To cover his confusion and shame, General Howard asked the people to sing a song. One old woman on the edge of the crowd was up to the occasion. She opened her mouth and out came words tinged with insufferable sadness: "Nobody Knows The Trouble I've Seen." Howard, a gentle, one-armed humanitarian, broke down and wept. There were tears, there were rivers of tears, but there were no mules and precious little land. Without land, without tools, without capital or access to credit facilities, the freedmen drifted into a form of peonage: the sharecropping system.

The land problem was linked to the larger problems of the South and the status of blacks. Nothing could be done with the conquered South until the status of blacks was settled. The reverse was also true. Nothing could be done for blacks until the status of the conquered South was settled. Lincoln's answer to this problem was liberal to the South. He wanted to readmit the Southern states as soon as 10 per cent of the prewar electorate had qualified by taking an oath of allegiance to America. Lincoln's successor, Andrew Johnson, was substantially of the same mind. Neither man came to grips with the status of blacks, although Lincoln suggested that "very intelligent" blacks and Union veterans be given the right to vote.

Stevens and Sumner were aghast at the presidential innocence. To turn the former slaves over to their former master without adequate safeguards, they contended, would be madness. It was soon apparent that their apprehensions were all too well founded. For the conservative provisional governors appointed by President Johnson organized lily-white governments with blatant proslavery biases. In 1865 and 1866 these governments enacted the Black Codes which indicated that the South intended to reestablish slavery under another name. The codes restricted the rights of freedmen under vagrancy and apprenticeship laws. South Carolina forbade freedmen to follow any occupation except farming and menial service and required a special license to do other work. The legislature also gave "masters" the right to whip "servants" under eighteen years of age. In other states blacks could be punished for "insulting gestures," "seditious speeches" and the "crime" of walking off a job. Blacks could not preach in one state without police permission. A Mississippi law enacted late in November required blacks to have jobs before the second Monday in January.

Even more serious was the vindictive attitude of Southerners, who vented their frustration on unarmed blacks. Gen. Carl Schurz, who made a special investigation for the president, was astonished by postwar conditions in the South. "Some planters," he said, "held back their former slaves on their plantations by brute force. Armed bands of white men patrolled the country roads to drive back the Negroes wandering about. Dead bodies of murdered Negroes were found on and near the highways and by-ways. Gruesome reports came from the hospitals—reports of colored men and women whose ears had been cut off, whose skulls had been broken by blows, whose bodies had been slashed by knives or lacerated with scourges. A number of such cases, I had occasion to examine myself. A . . . reign of terror prevailed in many parts of the South."

Throughout this period, and on into the 1870s, hundreds of freedmen were massacred in "riots" staged and directed by policemen and other government officials. In the Memphis, Tennessee, "riot" of May, 1866, forty-six blacks (Union veterans were a special target) were killed and seventy-five were wounded. Five black women were raped by whites, twelve schools and four churches were burned. Two months later, in New Orleans, policemen returned to the attack, killing some forty blacks and wounding one hundred.

"The emancipation of the slave," General Schurz concluded, "is submitted to only in so far as chattel slavery in the old form could not be kept up. But although the freedman is no longer considered the property of the individual master, he is considered the slave of society. . . . Wherever I go—the street, the shop, the house, the hotel, or the steamboat—I hear the people talk in such a way as to indicate that they are yet unable to conceive of the Negro as possessing any rights at all. Men who are honorable in their dealings with their white neighbors will cheat a Negro without feeling a single twinge of their honor. To kill a Negro, they do not deem murder; to debauch a Negro woman, they do not think fornication; to take property away from a Negro, they do not consider robbery. The people boast that when they get freedmen's affairs in their own hands, to use their own expression, 'the niggers will catch hell.' "

All of these factors—Southern intransigence and arrogance, the Black Codes, the Memphis and New Orleans "riots"—changed the national mood. Here and there, men fell into step with Sumner and Stevens. They did so for many reasons. Some believed it would be a major tragedy to hand the freedmen over to their former masters. Others saw a chance to insure the continued supremacy of the Republican party. Still others believed it would be dangerous to return ex-Confederates to national power. For various reasons, some of them contradictory, some of them noble, some of them base, people began to march by the sound of a different drummer.

Emboldened by the national mood, Stevens struck, wresting control of Reconstruction from President Johnson and vesting it in the Joint Congressional Committee of Fifteen. This committee reported legislation which put the South under military control and authorized new elections in which all males, irrespective of color, could participate. When the tallies were in, it was discovered that black voters outnumbered whites in five states—Mississippi, South Carolina, Louisiana, Alabama and Florida. In some counties black voters outnumbered whites by majorities of seven, eight and nine to one.

Not content with this political revolution, Radical Republicans, led again by Stevens and Sumner, pushed through Congress the Fourteenth and Fifteenth amendments and enabling legislation which sent troops into the South to protect the rights of blacks.

Day in and day out, all through the mystic years, Sumner and Stevens prodded, criticized, demanded. They made men squirm; even today they make men uncomfortable. No other white men in American public life have had a more profound understanding of the Declaration of Independence. Some there were who wanted to do it next week. Some there were who wanted to do it tomorrow. Sumner and Stevens wanted to do it NOW. They were men of different styles and temperaments. Sumner was an idealist, a lover of the classics, a declaimer of poetry. "I am in morals," he said, "not politics."

Stevens was in politics. A tart-tongued, tough-minded old Pennsylvanian with a clubfoot and a burning passion for the poor, the disadvantaged and the driven against the wall, Stevens dominated men not by quotations but by strength of will. Critics tried to dismiss him: they said he was a bitter, vindictive old fanatic. "There may be fanatics," Stevens replied, "in false religion, in superstition. But there can be no fanaticism, however high the enthusiasm, however warm the zeal, in true religion, or in the cause of national, universal liberty." Critics said Stevens not only preached social equality but that he also practiced it. This was a sly dig at Lydia Smith, who was Stevens's devoted housekeeper for twenty-two years. She kept his house in Lancaster, Pennsylvania, and when Stevens went to Washington, she went with him. Men said there was more to their relationship than met the eye. Stevens was a bachelor; Lydia Smith was a comely black widow. On this slim foundation and the fact that Stevens called his housekeeper "Mrs. Smith," the rumors grew. Indifferent to and contemptuous of public opinion, Stevens disdainfully ignored the gossips and went his lonely way.

To Stevens and Sumner, as much as to Lincoln, blacks owed their freedom. Long before Lincoln was ready, Sumner was demanding freedom for the slaves. Long before Lincoln was ready, Stevens was demanding that he arm them and let them fight.

What did Stevens want?

What was his real objective?

His real objective, he told the House, was a revolutionary restructuring of American institutions. "Governor [Benjamin] Perry of South Carolina and other provisional governors and orators proclaim that 'this is the white man's government.' . . . Demagogues of all parties, even some in high authority, gravely shout, 'This is the white man's government.' What is implied by this? That one race of men are to have the exclusive rights forever to rule this nation, and to exercise all acts of sovereignty, while all other races and nations and colors are to be their subjects, and have no voice in making the laws and choosing the rulers by whom they are to be governed."

Stevens rejected this argument, calling for the completion of the unfinished American Revolution:

"Our fathers repudiated the whole doctrine of the legal superiority of families or races, and proclaimed the equality of men before the law. Upon that they created a revolution and built

Ku Klux Klan and other secret
organizations undermined
Reconstruction with a revolutionary
campaign of terror and intimidation.
Klan was organized in 1866 in
Pulaski, Tennessee.

Among the leading
Reconstruction politicians were
Robert Brown Elliott (left),
the South Carolina congressman;
Blanche K. Bruce (center),
the first black to serve a full
term in the U.S.
Senate; and P. B. S. Pinchback, who
served briefly
as governor of Louisiana.

a Republic. They were prevented by slavery from perfecting the superstructure whose foundation they had thus broadly laid. . . .

"The time to which they looked forward with anxiety has come. It is our duty to complete their work. If this Republic is not now made to stand on their great principles, it has no honest foundation, and the Father of all men will still shake it to its center."

And so, in conclusion:

"This is not a white man's Government, in the exclusive sense in which it is used. To say so is political blasphemy, for it violates the fundamental principles of our gospel of liberty. This is Man's Government, the Government of all men alike; not that all men will have equal power and sway within it. Accidental circumstances, natural and acquired endowment and ability, will vary their fortunes. But equal rights to all the privileges of the Government is innate in every immortal being, no matter what the shape or the color of the tabernacle which it inhabits."

Two men—Stevens in the House, Sumner in the Senate—and when they died, the dream died with them. Sumner went to his death fighting for a national civil rights bill which would have banned discrimination and segregation in schools, churches, cemeteries, public conveyances, inns, hotels. On his death bed, surrounded by Frederick Douglass and other black friends, he whispered his last words: "Take care of my civil rights bill—take care of it—you must do it." Historian Benjamin Quarles very astutely observed: "Negroes whose sense of honoring their benefactors exceeded their knowledge of history might name their sons after Lincoln, but [Frederick] Douglass, with a truer appreciation, knew that if Negroes wished to honor the greatest friend they ever had in public life, they should place wreaths on the tomb of Charles Sumner."

Thaddeus Stevens had said that he intended to die "hurrahing." And he did, leaving instructions for burial in a black cemetery. The stone above the ground bears the words he wrote:

> I repose in this quiet and secluded spot,
> not from any natural preference for solitude,
> but finding other cemeteries
> limited by charter rules as to race,
> I have chosen this that I might illustrate in my death
> the principles which I advocated through a long life,
> Equality of Man before his Creator.

The principles Stevens and Sumner advocated turned the South upside down, leading freedmen to say that "the bottom rail is on top." The implications of this were clear enough, as the freedmen demonstrated in the political movement that swept the South. All through 1867, a critical year, freedmen flocked to open-air meetings, registered and organized political groups.

At the same time leaders emerged from the masses and demanded political and economic equality. The white South, stunned by these developments, disdainfully ignored the first political gathering, saying and apparently believing that blacks would make fools of themselves in the political arena. But the freedmen disappointed their late masters, demonstrating what one writer called a real genius for "the lower political arts."

Surprised apparently by the ease with which former slaves manipulated political symbols and structures, the white South fell back to a second line of defense, creating a paramilitary organization with an ominous name and an ominous purpose. The name: Ku Klux Klan. The first national meeting: April, 1867, Room 10, the Maxwell House, Nashville's big new hotel. The organizers: Confederate generals, colonels, substantial men of church and state, from Georgia, from Alabama, from all over. The leader: Nathan Bedford Forrest, the strong man of the Fort Pillow Massacre. The plan: reduce blacks to political impotence. How? By the boldest and most ruthless political operation in American history. By stealth and murder, by economic intimidation and political assassinations, by the political use of terror, by the braining of the baby in its mother's arms, the slaying of the husband at his wife's feet, the raping of the wife before her husband's eyes. By *fear*. Soon the South was honeycombed with secret organizations: the Knights of the White Camelia, the Red Shirts, the White League, Mother's Little Helpers and the Baseball Club of the First Baptist Church.

The secret organizations ran underground. Above ground there was a different strategy. In every Southern state Democrats tried to control the votes of their late slaves. There was irony in the situation: slaveholders and racists sitting on platforms with blacks, "reminding" them that Southern whites had always been their friends and that the North was "responsible" for slavery. A typical instance of this took place at Terry, Mississippi, with former governor A. G. Brown presiding and a black, Alfred Johnson, acting as vice-president. The group decided to have a

picnic and the committees named to arrange the affair were blatantly interracial: three blacks and three whites on each committee. The blacks came, ate, listened and went away and voted
Republican.

The upshot of all this, in Mississippi and all other Southern
states, was the election of Republican-dominated constitutional
conventions in which blacks constituted from 10 per cent (Texas)
to 61 per cent (South Carolina). The results were so unpalatable
to one Mississippian that he called for a day of prayer to God who,
he said, had permitted black men to attain political power because white folk had forgotten him.

When the constitutional conventions met, some Southerners
again put their heads into the sand, believing that blacks would
stumble and discredit themselves. After all, what did they know
about the whereases and therefores of Anglo-Saxon government?
Again the South was disappointed. The constitutions were excellent documents. They were so good, in fact, that some states
were content to live under them for several years after the white
Democrats regained power. The constitutions were not entirely
the work of black politicians. The much-maligned "carpetbaggers" (Northern-born white men) and "scalawags" (white Southerners) were major elements in all of the conventions. But blacks
played important roles, especially in South Carolina, Louisiana
and Mississippi.

South Carolina's Constitution, like most Reconstruction constitutions, created a positive state which assumed new and unprecedented (for the south) responsibilities in the fields of education and social welfare. It eradicated every form of slavery,
abolished imprisonment for debt, authorized universal male suffrage and gave the state its first divorce law. White women and
poor white Southerners, it should be remembered, were emancipated along with the slaves.

Black delegates were largely responsible for the most important innovation in Reconstruction governments—the establishment of a public school system for poor and rich, black and white.
In Mississippi, Louisiana and South Carolina the laws called for
interracial school systems. The Louisiana Constitution said:
"There shall be no separate schools or institutions of learning
established exclusively for any race by the state of Louisiana."

In all Southern states black leaders shared power with "carpetbaggers" and "scalawags." Only in Mississippi, Louisiana and South Carolina did blacks rise to the summit of power. Even in South Carolina, however, blacks were outnumbered in the state senate. It is a mistake, therefore, to speak of the Reconstruction era as one of "Negro domination." Blacks had power, blacks used power, but they showed no desire to "dominate whites." State by state the political situation was this:*

> SOUTH CAROLINA: 1860 population: 412,000 blacks, 291,000 whites. Voter registration, 1867 (males): 80,000 blacks, 46,000 whites. Black voters were in the majority in 21 of the 31 counties. Reconstruction constitutional convention: 76 black delegates, 48 whites. First Reconstruction legislature: 85 blacks, 70 whites. Blacks were in the majority in every legislative session. A. J. Ransier, R. H. Gleaves, lieutenant governors. F. L. Cardozo, secretary of state (1868–72), treasurer (1872–76). J. J. Wright, associate justice, state supreme court. R. B. Elliott, S. J. Lee, Speakers, lower house of the Assembly. South Carolina sent eight blacks to Congress during the Reconstruction and post-Reconstruction eras: R. B. Elliott, J. H. Rainey, Robert DeLarge, A. J. Ransier, R. H. Cain, Robert Smalls, T. E. Miller, G. W. Murray. Rainey, the first black in the House of Representatives, was sworn in on December 12, 1870.

> MISSISSIPPI: 1860 population: 437,000 blacks, 353,000 whites. Registration, 1867: 60,000 blacks, 46,000 whites. Blacks were in the majority in 30 counties. Constitutional convention, 17 blacks, 83 whites. First legislature: 36 blacks, 103 whites. A. K. Davis, lieutenant governor. James Hill, secretary of state. T. W. Cardozo, superintendent of education. Two senators, Hiram Revels (1870–71), B. K. Bruce (1875–81). One congressman: John Roy Lynch. Two speakers of the lower house: J. R. Lynch, I. D. Shadd.

*Texas, Tennessee and Arkansas did not send blacks to Congress. Although blacks did not wield much power in these states, they served in the legislatures and held state and municipal offices. J. C. Corbin was superintendent of education in Arkansas. Mifflin W. Gibbs was elected city judge in Little Rock, Arkansas, in 1873. Between 1869 and 1901 twenty-two blacks served in the U.S. Congress. South Carolina elected the largest number of black congressmen (eight), followed by North Carolina (four). In the same period 794 blacks served in Southern legislatures. South Carolina led with 210 state legislators, followed by Louisiana (121), Virginia (92) and North Carolina (78).

LOUISIANA: 1860 population: 350,000 blacks, 357,000 whites. Registration, 1867: 84,000 blacks, 45,000 whites. Constitutional convention: 49 blacks, 49 whites. First legislature: 42 blacks, 95 whites. P. B. S. Pinchback, governor, 36 days, on impeachment of former governor. Three lieutenant governors: O. J. Dunn, P. B. S. Pinchback, C. C. Antoine. P. G. Deslonde, secretary of state. Antoine Dubuclet, state treasurer. W. B. Brown, superintendent of education. One congressman: Charles E. Nash. Pinchback and James E. Lewis were elected to U.S. Senate, which refused to seat P. B. S. Pinchback on March 8, 1876. James Lewis did not press his case.

FLORIDA: 1860 population: 77,000 whites, 62,000 blacks. Registration, 1867: 16,000 blacks, 11,000 whites. Constitutional convention: 18 blacks, 28 whites. First legislature: 19 blacks, 57 whites. Jonathan C. Gibbs, secretary of state (1868-72) and superintendent of education (1872-74). One congressman: J. T. Walls.

NORTH CAROLINA: 1860 population: 629,000 whites, 361,000 blacks. Registration, 1867: 106,000 whites, 72,000 blacks. Constitutional convention: 15 blacks, 118 whites. First legislature: 21 blacks, 149 whites. Four congressmen: J. A. Hyman, J. E. O'Hara, H. P. Cheatham, George H. White.

ALABAMA: 1860 population: 526,000 whites, 437,000 blacks. Registration, 1867: 104,000 blacks, 61,000 whites. Constitutional convention: 18 blacks, 90 whites. First legislature: 26 blacks, 106 whites. Three congressmen: B. S. Turner, J. T. Rapier, J. Haralson.

GEORGIA: 1860 population: 591,000 whites, 465,000 blacks. Registration, 1867: 95,000 blacks, 96,000 whites. Constitutional convention: 33 blacks, 137 whites. First legislature: 34 blacks, 186 whites. One congressman: Jefferson Franklin Long.

VIRGINIA: 1860 population: 1,000,000 whites, 548,000 blacks. Registration, 1867: 105,000 blacks, 120,000 whites. Constitutional convention: 25 blacks, 80 whites. First legislature: 27 blacks, 150 whites. One congressman: J. M. Langston.

To justify the revolutionary methods by which these governments were overthrown, white Southerners manufactured and perpetuated the twin myths of corruption and ignorance. Black politicians, so the myths run, were corrupt or ignorant. So many blacks stole so much that it was necessary to cheat and kill in order to restore "honest" governments. Not only were the myths accepted by some historians but they were also believed by some blacks. Not a white but a black poet made the most withering comment on the black leaders of Reconstruction. "Some people," Paul Laurence Dunbar said, "are born great, some achieve greatness, others lived during the Reconstruction period." Concerning which, however, there is this further to be noted: political greatness is a complicated concept. A great leader in the Reconstruction period would have had the hardness of Nkrumah, the ascetic brilliance of Nehru, the Machiavellian adroitness of Franklin Delano Roosevelt, and the love-thy-neighbor vocabulary of Martin Luther King Jr. No such person emerged. No such person, in fact, has ever emerged in America. Judged by American standards, the major black leaders of the Reconstruction were leaders very much like the leaders of other eras: men who just missed greatness because they failed to solve the problem no American has solved—the fear and anxiety of whites and the presence and birthrate of blacks.

But, say the critics, black leaders were corrupt. The evidence on this subject is so confusing as to be almost worthless. Nine-tenths of the evidence is hearsay, innuendo, ex parte. Most of the rest would not be admissible in the meanest police court. The ex parte reports on which historians rely were produced by men who lied, stole, cheated and killed in order to take over the state governments—men, in short, who had to believe their enemies were barbarians in order to believe that they themselves were Christians. What evidence there is suggests that white men—Northern white men and Southern white men, South Carolinians, Georgians and Louisianians—got most of the money. Take Mississippi, for example. After an exhaustive study of reconstructed Mississippi, historian James Garner concluded that there were only two thefts on the state level: a black man was accused of stealing books from the state library, and a white man misappropriated $7,000. This was in marked contrast to Mississippi before and after Reconstruction. In 1866, for example, a Democratic treasurer stole $61,000. Years later, after white men had restored "honest" government, a treasurer misappropriated $315,000.

The conclusion is inescapable: the monstrous crime of Reconstruction was equality. A Southern historian said as much. "The worst crime of which they have been adjudged guilty," said F. B. Simkins of Reconstruction governments, "was the violation of the American caste system. The crime of crimes was to encourage Negroes in voting, office-holding, and other functions of social equality." It would be a mistake, however, to imply that all blacks were paragons of political virtue: that would be making the same mistake as some white historians who imply that all blacks were thiefs. In an era in which some men were bought and sold in New York (Boss Tweed), in an era in which some men were bought and sold in Washington (Crédit Mobilier scandal), it seems reasonable to conclude that some men were also bought and sold in South Carolina. Only the naïve or, what turns out to be the same thing, the cynical are horrified when some blacks do what some whites are doing. The key word here is *some*. There were black reformers, and there were black wheelers and dealers whose morals were no better—and no worse—than the morals of politicians in contemporary Chicago, New York or Washington.

Not corruption but honesty, not ignorance but brilliance horrified racists during the Reconstruction era. If there was anything Southern whites feared more than bad black government, it was good black government. If there was anything they feared more than an ignorant black politician, it was a brilliant one. There were many brilliant black politicians, Dunbar to the contrary notwithstanding: O. J. Dunn of Louisiana, Jonathan Gibbs of Florida, James T. Rapier of Alabama, J. J. Wright, Francis L. Cardozo, R. H. Cain and Robert Smalls of South Carolina, John R. Lynch and B. K. Bruce of Mississippi, and J. M. Langston of Virginia, to name only a few.

It has been said that the black leaders of Reconstruction were uneducated. But that is a false issue. For although a degree may be necessary for writing about politics or teaching it, a degree is not at all necessary for practicing the game. A politician needs drive, energy, the ability to deal with people, the skills of the conference table and the smoky room, nerve, cheek and an eloquent tongue. Many black leaders had these requisites. There were, to be sure, literate and cultured black politicians—but that's beside the point. Robert Brown Elliott was a brilliant politician, but his legal education does not seem to have helped him any more than the common school education of P. B. S. Pinchback who, if anything, was more brilliant on the political level. James T. Rapier of Alabama was more polished than most white men of his day, but S. D. Smith, an authority on blacks in Congress, believed that the uneducated Jeremiah ("Jere") Haralson was a better natural politician. Men admired Rapier's learning and literacy, but they cleared political matters with "Jere." It is enough to state the obvious: most of the major black leaders had more formal education than Abraham Lincoln. Ten of the twenty-two black men who served in Congress had attended college; five were lawyers. Both black senators had attended college, and both handled themselves well in the Senate. Revels, a minister, was a lucid speaker and a fair politician. After his Senate career, he spent so much time conciliating whites that he alienated blacks. When the Democrats drove the Republicans out of the statehouse, Revels, a timid, conservative man, supported them. As a reward he was returned to his old post as president of Alcorn College. Bruce was of different timber. A handsome, elegant man "with a magnificent physique," he made a good record in the Senate and later became register of the treasury.

Often in danger of death, and always in danger of betrayal, black leaders were forced by circumstances to moderate their demands in order to keep the Radical Republican coalition going. But there were definite limits to their willingness to placate the fears of Northern-born and Southern-born white Republicans. Against the advice of white party leaders, blacks enacted strong civil rights provisions in Mississippi, Louisiana and South Carolina. When the first South Carolina Republican convention met, whites told blacks that it would be diplomatic to elect a white chairman; R. H. Gleaves, a black, was elected. In Louisiana black leaders revolted against H. C. Warmoth, who was wooing Democrats and betraying the black cause. In Mississippi black leaders revolted against J. L. Alcorn, the aristocratic "scalawag" who opposed radical innovations in interracial living. In Louisiana, no politician, not even the governor, could operate without considering the wishes of Pinchback. The same thing was true in South Carolina, where the governor was under some pains

The first black elected to the House of Representatives,
John W. Menard, received premature
congratulations from congressmen on
December 21, 1868. Menard, who was elected
from Louisiana, received an ovation but was
denied a seat in the House.

L. A. Wiltz took possession of the Speaker's chair in the Louisiana statehouse on January 4, 1875. The last Southern states were "redeemed" by whites in 1876–77.

to determine the desires of Elliott. Even in Mississippi, where black leaders were conciliatory, the tide changed. By 1873 Mississippians were demanding an equal division of the loaves and the fish. A black newspaper, the *Vicksburg Plaindealer*, put it bluntly. Some white men, the newspaper said, believed blacks should do all the voting and white men should do all the directing. "This thing," the paper said, "has played out."

If blacks were so militant, why didn't they elect a governor? The answer is fairly simple. In the first phase of Reconstruction, black leaders attempted to assuage the fears of the whites. Many people, some of them sincere liberals, told blacks that it would not be politic to shock the sensibilities of whites. This gambit was accepted everywhere except Louisiana where Pinchback and Francis E. Dumas were nominated when the Republican convention met. Since nomination at that time was tantamount to election, there was considerable interest in the contest. Pinchback, believing it would not be wise to nominate a black the first time around, withdrew, a decision he would later regret. Dumas stood his ground. He was a free black, fair-skinned, wealthy, a Union veteran who had carried his slaves into the Union army and had been commissioned a major. On the first ballot no one had a majority. The real contest, it turned out, was between Dumas and H. C. Warmoth, who was a talented and unscrupulous Northern-born white. Black delegates were in the majority, but most of them were former slaves who had no love for former slaveholders, especially black former slaveholders. Between the first and second ballots, Warmoth made good use of the fact that his opponent, a black man, had owned slaves. On the second ballot Warmoth won—45 to 43. It seems, therefore, that the only man who had a good chance to be elected governor was defeated, ironically enough, because he had owned slaves. Later, when Pinchback and Elliott panted and thirsted after the governor's chair, whites controlled the election machinery and blacks were divided into several factions.

Some black politicians, perhaps many black politicians, were willing to sit on the right hand of power. The two most brilliant politicians in this era wanted to sit in the chair itself. Robert Brown Elliott and P. B. S. Pinchback were as unlike as two men could be. Elliott was a scholar, a linguist, and a brilliant lawyer, the owner of one of the largest private libraries in South Carolina.

Pinchback, on the other hand, was a former cabin boy, shrewd, capable, vain, a gambling type, a man who would put everything on an ace and, losing, walk away with a smile. Elliott was a dark-skinned free black with a somewhat mysterious background.* Pinchback was fair-skinned, the son of a Mississippi planter and a black woman who bore him ten children. To Pinchback and Elliott, racists would apply their most telling adjective, "dangerous." Both men understood the uses and, critics said, the "abuses" of power. There are conflicting reports on the political morality of both men, but there is unanimity on their ability in the political arena.

Elliott was elected to the South Carolina legislative assembly at twenty-six and to Congress at twenty-eight. But the House of Representatives bored him. He was elected twice and resigned both times to return to South Carolina where there was power to be used. An implacable foe of racism and intolerance, Elliott supported Sumner's civil rights bill and made one of the great speeches of the era. The situation was dramatic and Elliott, who had an eye for drama, made the most of it. On January 5, 1874, Alexander H. Stephens, former vice-president of the Confederacy, attacked the civil rights bill. When he finished Elliott seized the floor and held it until adjournment, thereby earning the right to continue the next day. The word went out: a black man would answer the former vice-president of the Confederacy. People came early the next morning to get seats; senators came over from the Senate chamber.

The stage was set when Stephens, elderly and ailing, was brought into the chamber in his chair.

All eyes turned to Elliott.

He was an impressive man, deep-chested, broad-shouldered, with abundant hair worn *au naturel* in the African style. "Face to face," a contemporary said, "stood the Anglo-Saxon and the undoubted African. The issue was between them; the contest began."

"I regret, sir," Elliott began, "that the dark hue of my skin may lend color to the imputation that I am controlled by motives per-

---

*There is no documentary support of Elliott's claim that he attended Eton and read law in the office of a London barrister. See Peggy Lamson, *The Glorious Failure*.

sonal to myself in my advocacy of this great measure of national justice. Sir, the motive that impels me is restricted to no such narrow boundary, but is as broad as your Constitution. I advocate it, sir, because it is right."

Elliott reviewed the history of blacks in America. They had shown their mettle in the Revolutionary War, had proved a decisive factor in the Civil War and had been praised by Andrew Jackson in the War of 1812. They had earned their civil rights in tears and blood. And what were civil rights? Like a teacher in a graduate seminar, Elliott explained civil rights, quoting Francis Lieber, Alexander Hamilton and the French Constitution. He scornfully dismissed Stephens. It ill behooved a man who tried to wreck the Constitution to read lectures to men who fought for it.

"I meet him only as an adversary; nor shall age or any other consideration restrain me from saying that he now offers his Government, which he has done his utmost to destroy, a very poor return for its magnanimous treatment, to come here and seek to continue . . . the burdens and oppressions which rest upon five million of his countrymen who never failed to lift their earnest prayers for the success of this government when the gentleman was seeking to break up the Union of these states and to blot the American Republic from the galaxy of nations. (Loud applause.)"

To another adversary, Elliott offered the back of his hand. "To the diatribe of the gentleman from Virginia, who spoke on yesterday, and who so far transcended the limits of decency and propriety as to announce upon this floor that his remarks were addressed to white men alone, I shall have no word of reply. Let him feel that a Negro was not only too magnanimous to smite him in his weakness, but was even charitable enough to grant him the mercy of his silence. (Laughter and applause on the floor and in the galleries.)"

Elliott pleaded for the bill. "The Constitution warrants it; the Supreme Court sanctions it; justice demands it." Black men, moreover, had earned it as soldiers in the Union army. He was mindful, however, that "valor, devotion, and loyalty are not always rewarded according to their just deserts, and that after the battle some who have borne the brunt of the fray may, through neglect or contempt, be assigned to a subordinate place, while the enemies in war may be preferred to the sufferers." Still, he was hopeful. Blacks were like the faithful Ruth who labored in the fields of Boaz. "The last vestiture only is needed—civil rights. Having gained this, we may, with hearts overflowing with gratitude, and thankful that our prayer has been granted, repeat the prayer of Ruth: 'Entreat me not to leave thee, or to return from following after thee; for whither thou goest, I will go; and where thou lodgest, I will lodge; thy people shall be my people, and thy God my God; where thou diest, will I die, and there will I be buried; the Lord do so to me, and more also, if aught but death part thee and me.' (Great applause.)"

The black South Carolinian sat down in triumph. For almost an hour he held court on the floor of the House. Even the Democrats were impressed. Ben Butler later compared Elliott to John Hancock, John Adams and that other South Carolinian, John C. Calhoun.

The applause was still ringing in Elliott's ears and he was at the height of his fame when he resigned from the House to return to South Carolina, where he became Speaker of the legislative assembly. Not content with applause and empty honors, Elliott intended, rumors said, to become governor. When he made an unsuccessful bid for the Senate, some racists hoped he would win. It was felt at the time that the Senate would satisfy his ambition and moderate his militancy. Elliott's motto, a reporter said, was: "I am what I am and I believe in my own nobility."

Pinchback was of like mind: he was what he was. A congressional investigating committee asked him if the governor acknowledged his strength. Pinchback was frank. "Oh, yes; he always acknowledged he couldn't get along without me. I have to tell you the truth." Bold, elegantly turned out, daring, Pinchback made his mark in reconstructed Louisiana. By turns a senator, lieutenant governor and governor, he held more major offices than any other black in American history. In the fall of 1872 he was elected to the U.S. House of Representatives. In January, 1873, he was elected to the Senate. He went to Washington, therefore, with the extraordinary distinction of being both a congressman-elect and a senator-elect. (There were also disquieting rumors that Pinchback intended to make himself vice-president elect.) Pinchback did not go as a beggar. "Sir," he told the Senate, "I demand simple justice. I am not here as a beggar. I do not care so far as I am personally concerned whether you give me my seat or not. I will go back to my people and come here again; but I tell you to preserve your own consistency. Do not make fish of me while you make flesh of everybody else."

For three years the Senate grappled with Pinchback's case. Almost the whole of an extra session of Congress was devoted to the senator-elect from Louisiana. Finally, after hours of debate, he was rejected. The real reason, some authorities insist, was that the senators' wives told them that they did not intend to associate with Mrs. Pinchback. During the controversy "Pinch," as he was called, became a national figure. Washington women, charmed by his "Brazilian" good looks, went out of their way to meet him and Pinchback stories made the rounds. The Washington correspondent of the *New York Commercial Advertiser* was impressed by the senator-elect.

"Aside from the political view of the question [two factions in Louisiana were competing for national recognition]," he wrote, "Pinchback's presence in the United States Senate is not open to the smallest objection, except the old Bourbon war-whoops of color. He is about thirty-seven years of age, not darker than an Arab. . . . His features are regular, just perceptibly African, his eyes intensely black and brilliant, with a keen, restless glance. His most repellent point is a sardonic smile which, hovering continuously over his lips, gives him an evil look, undeniably handsome as the man is. It seems as though the scorn which must rage within him, at sight of the dirty ignorant men from the South who affect to look down upon him on account of his color, finds play imperceptibly about his lips. . . . Mr. Pinchback is the best dressed Southern man we have had in Congress from the South since the days when gentlemen were Democrats."

Even more remarkable than the rise of Pinchback and Elliott and other major leaders was the mushroom growth of local leaders. "There is something fascinating," Vernon Wharton wrote, "about the suddenness with which, all over the state [Mississippi], they emerged form the anonymity of slavery to become directors and counselors of their race. In general, it can be said that they were not Negroes who had held positions of leadership under the old regime; the characteristics which made a man a slave driver or foreman were not those which would allow him to organize a Loyal League. Almost none of them came from the small group who had been free before the war. Such men, as barbers, artisans or small farmers, had depended too long on the favor of the whites for the maintenance of their existence. Servility had become a part of them." Wharton added: "A large proportion of the minor Negro leaders were preachers, lawyers, or teachers from the free states or from Canada. . . . There was a general tendency for them to combine preaching with their politics; as Sir George Campbell has said, they were rather preachers because they were leaders than leaders because they were preachers."

Local leaders bore the brunt of the sustained assault by which whites undermined Reconstruction. The word went out: "Forget the major leaders. Let them prance around in New Orleans, Columbia and Washington. Concentrate on the local leaders. Destroy the foundation and leave the major leaders dangling in mid-air."

One by one, the local leaders were killed, driven out of the state or compromised. In Mississippi, to cite only one case, Charles Caldwell, the courageous state senator, was killed in broad daylight and his body was "grotesquely turned completely over by the impact of innumerable shots fired at close range." Nobody knows how many Charles Caldwells died in this period. But conservative estimates run into the thousands. Albion Tourgee, a white Republican who lived through the counter-revolution, said: "Of the slain there was enough to furnish forth a battlefield, and all from those three classes, the Negro, the scalawag, and the carpetbagger,—all killed with deliberation, overwhelmed by numbers, roused from slumber at murk midnight, in the halls of public assembly, upon the river-bank, on the lonely woods-roads, in simulation of the public execution, tortured beyond conception."

And the wounded?

"Ah!" Tourgee wrote, "the wounded in this silent warfare were more thousands than those who groaned upon the slopes of Gettysburg."

What did this mean in personal terms?

John Childers of Alabama was on the witness stand:

> How long after the whipping did she die?
> In eight days.
> How old was she?
> She would have been ten years old on the 26th of next August.

What was she whipped for?

She was hired out as a nurse to see to the baby; she had taken the baby out to the front yard among a parcel of arbor vitae; and, being out there, the baby and she together, she was neglectful, so as to leave the baby's cap out where it was not in place when the mother of the child called for the cap. When I came home . . . I saw the rest of the children playing in the yard, and she was in the door sitting there, and I thought that was strange, because she was a mighty playful chap, and I asked, "What are you sitting here for?" And she says, "Pap, Mr. Jones has beat me nearly to death." (The witness weeping). . . .

Where a colored man is known as a Democrat, and votes the Democratic Party, is he ever whipped or interfered with?

Not at all, sir.

So it is only the radicals that are whipped, and their children killed?

Yes, sir; these men that contends for their equal rights for person and property with white men.

They are the men singled out and punished, are they?

Yes, sir.

How many of your people in this country do you think have been whipped or otherwise outraged because of their political sentiments?

O, hundreds. I could not number them to you, sir.

By 1874 only four states—South Carolina, Florida, Louisiana, and Mississippi—were still in the Republican column. In these states black voters were so deeply entrenched that nothing short of a revolution could dislodge them. Southern Democrats did not shrink from the task. "ORGANIZE! ORGANIZE! ORGANIZE!" said a bold headline in the *Charleston News and Observer*. "We must render this a white man's government," another newspaper said, "or convert the land into a Negro man's cemetery." Gen. John McEnery, the Louisiana terrorist said, "We shall carry the next election if we have to ride saddle-deep in blood to do it."

It was done.

Wavering Democrats were whipped into line. Newspapers which had been indifferent to or amused by the antics of black politicians turned mean. Now all black politicians were devils: "the shameless, heartless, vile, grasping, deceitful, creeping, crawling, wallowing, slimy, slippery, hideous, loathsome, political pirates." Now all black men were barbarians: "Does any sane man believe the Negro capable of comprehending the Ten Commandments? The miraculous conception and birth of our Savior. . . . Every effort to inculcate these great truths but tends to bestialize his nature, and by obfuscating his little brain unfits him for the duties assigned him as a hewer of wood and drawer of water. The effort makes him a demon of wild, fanatical destruction, and consigns him to the fatal shot of the while man."

While this propaganda campaign was going on, the white population organized for war and systematically disarmed the black population. By hook and crook, and on any and every pretext, the homes of blacks were searched and arms were systematically appropriated. Adroitly playing on the fears of white governors, who dreaded a race war, Democrats succeeded in disarming or emasculating the predominantly black state militia. The plan followed in almost all Southern states was drafted by Gen. M. W. Gary, the arrogant, hot-tempered leader of the South Carolina "straightouts."

"Every Democrat," the Gary plan said, "must feel honor bound to control the vote of at least one Negro, by intimidation, purchase, keeping him away or as each individual may determine how he may best accomplish it.

"Never threaten a man individually. If he deserves to be threatened, the necessities of the time require that he should die. A dead Radical is very harmless—a threatened Radical or one driven off by threats from the scene of his operations is often very troublesome, sometimes dangerous, always vindictive."

The Bourbon war intensified on election days when ballot box manipulation reached dizzy heights. To dissuade and discourage black voters, polling places were located on bayous and islands, in barns and fodder houses. Armed whites were stationed on roads leading to the polls "to prevent Negroes from seizing arms." In one Louisiana parish the polling place was located in an isolated wilderness. The whites gathered at the white church and were told, in whispers, how to reach the site. In another parish the polls opened in the dark of morning, and whites voted by the light of candles. When black voters showed up, the polls were closed for the day. In Mississippi white men from Alabama and

Louisiana streamed across state lines and voted early and often. In South Carolina "citizens" came from North Carolina and Georgia.

What made all this enormously effective was superior fire-power. Many Democratic clubs owned cannons, which were very useful, oftentimes turning the tide in the endless skirmishes and guerrilla wars fought by black and white voters. Some Democratic clubs went to the length of rolling out cannons on election days and training them on the polls. After the Mississippi election a U.S. Senate committee noted that "on the day of the election, at several voting-places, armed men assembled, sometimes not organized and in other cases organized; that they controlled the elections, intimidated Republican voters, and, in fine, deprived them of the opportunity to vote the Republican ticket. The most notable instance of this form of outrage occurred at Aberdeen, the shire town of the county of Monroe. At half past nine o'clock on the day of the election a cannon in charge of four or five cannoneers, and supported by ten or twelve men, a portion of the military company of the town, was trained upon the voting-place and kept in that position during the day, while the street was traversed by a body of mounted, armed men. . . ."

This was not politics: this was war, a war pressed by an armed and organized white population determined to use every means to achieve its end. The leaders of the white war conceded this point publicly. "The Republican journals of the North," the *Aberdeen Examiner* said, "make a great mistake in regarding the present campaign in Mississippi in the light of a political contest. . . . The present contest is rather a revolution than a political campaign." Since whites controlled the land and the capital, one of the major tactics of the revolution was economic intimidation. In the final phases of the struggle, black Republicans could not find work, their wives could not buy supplies, and their children could not get medical attention. Social artillery was also rolled out to intimidate the white allies of black Republicans. The children of these whites, many of them native Southerners, were hounded in school. Their wives were cut to the quick at church. Near the end there was an exodus—knowing Democrats called the party-switching "crossing Jordan"—from the Republican party. What

this meant in personal terms was spelled out by a native white
South Carolinian in a letter to the *New York Tribune:*

> The air is filled with reports of outrages and murders which
> never appear in print. No prominent Republican of either
> color can safely leave a town. Let a hint that he intends to ride
> out into the country get wind and he is sure to be ambus-
> caded. But more than this. The whites regard a Republican of
> their color with tenfold the vindictiveness with which they
> look upon the Negro. Scores of white Republicans are hurry-
> ing in alarm to the newspaper offices to insert cards in which
> they renounce their party and profess conversion to Democ-
> racy. If these men hang back and refuse or neglect to join the
> precinct club or the nearest military company, their conduct
> is reported to the township meeting. A committee is appointed
> to request an explanation. They call on the suspected man at
> their earliest convenience. If he is sensible, he will submit
> profuse apologies and regrets, and hurriedly take up his rifle
> and follow them to the drill room.

Vocal and visible blacks vigorously contested the new situation. Whenever possible, they organized defensive units and
counterattacked. They also appealed repeatedly and un-
successfully to the president of the United States, pointing out
with excellent but useless logic that it was his duty to enforce the
laws of the United States of America. Rejected by Washington,
abondoned by their local allies, and deprived of their leadership
by mass assassinations, blacks fell back on their own resources,
organizing an extremely effective campaign against conservatives and wavering black Republicans. Black women were in the
forefront of this campaign. Contemporary reports say women
refused to marry, date or cohabit with black men who weakened
and deserted the Republican party. Landladies evicted black
Democrats. Enraged maidens tore the clothes off "Uncle Toms"
who wore the distinctive red shirts of the Democrats, and outraged wives showed their apostate husbands to the door. A South
Carolina wife was frank. She did not, she said, intend to sleep
with "a Democratic nigger."

Outgunned though they were, black Republicans did not suc-
cumb without a fight. But their resources were meager, and there
was never any real doubt about the outcome. White Democrats

controlled the money, the land, and the credit facilities. More importantly, they had powerful and determined allies in the North. And to understand what happened next it is necessary to understand the fatal ambivalence of the Northern allies of Black Reconstruction. The greatest of these allies—Sumner and Stevens—recognized from the beginning that it was impossible for Reconstruction to succeed without a strong federal presence. They prevailed in the first years of Reconstruction because the interests of conservative white Republicans—national unity, supremacy of Northern fiscal policy, high tariffs—paralleled the interests of blacks—the supremacy of the Republican party and the consolidation of the party's Reconstruction program.

Confronted, in the beginning, with what seemed to be the implacable will of America, white Southerners accommodated themselves to black freedom. They remained relatively quiescent, in fact, until the early 1870s when the climate of Northern public opinion changed. As soon as the Northern victory was solidified beyond recall, beyond the power of the South to alter or disturb, voices of compromise and conciliation emerged, even among white abolitionists. There were also demands for a political settlement from Northern business interests, who said the political troubles in the South were impeding the establishment of a national domestic market. Northern sentiment crystallized in 1874-75, and white newspapers started hammering away at "Negroism" and "corruption." The Northern press said the South was "tumbling and rolling about in the Black sea of Negroism." A new slogan, reminiscent of the twentieth-century slogan "Reverse Discrimination," came into being: "Emancipate the whites."

Perceiving the drift of the age, which was made flesh in the increasing power of the Democratic party, white Southerners became increasingly bold. The whole thing came to a head in 1876, the centennial of the Declaration of Independence. Small wars were fought in that year by whites and blacks in South Carolina, Louisiana and Florida. Both Republicans and Democrats claimed victory in these states and established state governments.

As it happened, the presidential race between Republican Rutherford B. Hayes and Democrat Samuel J. Tilden hinged on the disputed electoral votes from these states. Hayes claimed the states and the presidency, and an electoral commission sustained him. But it was necessary for both houses of Congress to certify the results, and Democrats had a majority in the House of Representatives. As inauguration day approached, a group of Southerners in the House launched a filibuster that prevented the orderly counting of the electoral votes. If the Democrats could hold out until inauguration day, America would not have a president and disorder, perhaps war, would be inevitable.

From merchants and entrepreneurs, from molders of public opinion, from churches and universities, from the boards of trade and the chambers of commerce of Pittsburgh and Chicago and New York came one cry: "Peace! Peace at any price."

Translated into political language, this meant at the price of the U.S. Constitution and black freedom.

The center of decision shifted now to certain small rooms.

Men scurried to and fro in these rooms, speaking the word *compromise*. The South was willing to compromise, the South was willing to get on with the electoral count—if. Men scurried to and fro, exploring the possibilities of *if*. Representatives of Hayes and representatives of the South huddled together in smoky rooms. The price—that was the question. How much? The South wanted certain economic concessions, but most of all it wanted "home rule": a suspension of constitutional safeguards that protected blacks. *Quid pro quo*—something for something. "Home rule" for the South, withdrawal of troops, an end to agitation of the race question, a tacit agreement that the South would be allowed to deal with blacks in its own way. And for Hayes? The presidency.

The bargain was arranged in a series of conferences which reached a climax, ironically enough, in a fashionable hotel owned by James Wormley, a well-to-do black businessman. After the Wormley Hotel conference of February 26, 1877, Hayes's representatives handed Southern representatives a signed letter which represented the core of the bargain. The agreement, which shaped the future of American blacks as much as the Fourteenth and Fifteenth amendments, read:

> GENTLEMEN: Referring to the conversation had with you yesterday in which Governor Hayes's policy as to the status of

certain Southern States was discussed, we desire to say in reply that we can assure you in the strongest possible manner of our great desire to have adopted such a policy as will give to the people of the States of South Carolina and Louisiana the right to control their own affairs in their own way; and to say further that we feel authorized, from an acquaintance with and knowledge of Governor Hayes and his views on this question, to pledge ourselves to you that such will be his policy.

The bargain was signed, sealed and delivered. The Southerners called off the filibuster, Hayes was elected, the troops were withdrawn, and the South began the long process of whipping blacks into submission.

Must we conclude from this that Reconstruction was a failure? By no means. Reconstruction, as *Black Power U.S.A.* indicated, did not fail where it was expected to fail. It was Athanasius contra mundum, as DuBois said, but it was also Athanasius pro mundum. Long before the rise of Afro-Asia, long before the emergence of the United Nations, black Americans struck a blow—in the heart of the Western world—for all the peoples of the First World. For the first time anywhere, nonwhites appropriated "white" symbols and structures and managed whites in Western political environments. These efforts did not fail in the realm of the spirit; nor, for that matter, did they fail in the realm of the practical, for the Fourteenth and Fifteenth amendments were permanent and indispensable contributions to American democracy. If these amendments had not been ratified in this period, they never would have been ratified. There has never been a period in America, before or since, when the climate of public opinion was favorable to the passage of national legislation of the breadth and scope of the Fourteenth and Fifteenth amendments.

Future consequences apart, Black Reconstruction had an immediate impact on the lives of black Americans. Under the umbrella of black power, a small but significant number of blacks climbed a rung or two on the economic ladder. Some laborers managed to climb into the artisan class, and some artisans managed to withstand the strong challenge of white workers, who wanted to take their votes so they could take their jobs. Of equal or perhaps greater consequence was the economic growth manifested by the small but significant number of farmers who acquired relatively large plots of land and the black politicians who made small fortunes as cotton factors and directors of railroads, steamship companies, oil corporations and banks.

It was this growth, a growth made possible by black political power, that the black Methodists of Florida celebrated in a conference resolution:

> *Whereas* labor is the basis of all wealth, and wealth is an absolute necessity of civilized society, and a peaceful condition of society. . . .
>
> *Resolved* by the convention of ministers and laymen of the Methodist Episcopal Church of Florida, that we congratulate our people upon the rapid progress they have made in the past six years, and upon the increase of mixed industry, homesteads, and small farms in opposition to the ruinous plantation system, and [we consider] these together with the increase in school houses and churches, and also the deposit of nearly three million dollars in the savings-banks, as a greater pledge of our progress to the friends of freedom throughout the world than can be found in the house of any people who sprang from as lowly a condition as ourselves.

The Reconstructionists, black and white, left other legacies. Despite mistakes and blemishes, which were, in large part, inevitable under the circumstances, they extended the social capital of the South and created a base for industrialization by building roads, levees and dams. Over and above this, they created a public school system in a region hostile to public education and included poor whites and women in the social contract.

Thomas Miller, a former U.S. congressman, emphasized these and other legacies when he rose in the South Carolina Constitutional Convention of 1895 to answer the charges of Ben ("Pitchfork") Tillman of Edgefield County. "The gentleman from Edgefield," he said, "speaks of the piling up of the state debt; of jobbery and peculation during the period between 1869 and 1873 in South Carolina, but he has not found voice eloquent enough, nor pen exact enough to mention those imperishable gifts bestowed upon South Carolina between 1873 and 1876 by Negro legislators—the laws relative to finance, the building of penal and charitable institutions, and, greatest of all, the establishment of the public school system."

Summing up, Miller said:

"We were eight years in power. We had built schoolhouses, established charitable institutions, built and maintained the penitentiary system, provided for the education of the deaf and dumb, rebuilt the jails and courthouses, rebuilt the bridges and reestablished the ferries. In short, we had reconstructed the state and placed it upon the road to prosperity."

These, then, were the legacies, gargantuan on any showing, of the Reconstructionists, who made the first—and last—real attempt to bring the American Dream down from its parchment heaven to the hard and challenging earth of black hope.

9

The Life and Times of Jim Crow

> *Slavery has been fruitful in giving itself names. It has been called "the peculiar institution," "the social system," and the "impediment." ... It has been called by a great many names, and it will call itself by yet another name; and you and I and all of us had better wait and see what new form this old monster will assume, in what new skin. this old snake will come forth next.*
>
> FREDERICK DOUGLASS

THOMAS DARTMOUTH RICE, one of the white pioneers in comic representation of blacks, saw James Crow* somewhere in Kentucky or Ohio and immortalized him in dialect and song.

> *Weel a-bout and turn a-bout*
> *and do just so.*
> *Every time I weel a-bout*
> *I jump Jim Crow.*

*James Crow is an unknown soldier. Some writers say he was a Cincinnati, Ohio, slave; others say he was a Charleston, S.C., slave. Various writers say the Crow came from old man Crow, the slaveholder; others say the Crow came from the simile, black as a crow.

Wheeling about and turning about and jumping just so, "Daddy" Rice shuffled across the stage at New York's Bowery Theatre in 1832 and gave America its first international song hit.

By 1838 Jim Crow was wedged into the language as a synonym for Negro. A noun, a verb, an adjective, a "comic" way of life.

By 1839 there was an antislavery book: *The History of Jim Crow*.

By 1841 there was a Jim Crow railroad car—in Massachusetts, of all places.

By 1901 Jim Crow was a part of the marrow of America. But he was no longer singing. The song-and-dance man had turned mean: he had become a wall, a system, a way of separating people from people. Demagogue by demagogue, mania by mania, brick by brick, the wall was built; and by the 1890s America was two nations—one white, one black, separate and unequal.

The cornerstones of the great wall were two taboos: interracial eating and intermarriage. Anything approaching interracial eating was proscribed. Anything which might by any stretch of the imagination lead to intermarriage was interdicted. One law led to a hundred. One fear became a nightmare of ropes and chains and signs:

| WHITE | COLORED |

| NEGROES AND FREIGHT |

The root rationalization for all this was sex. South Carolina demagogue Cole L. Blease said it:

"Whenever the Constitution comes between me and the virtue of the white women of the South, I say to hell with the Constitution."

Fear.

Frenzy.

White womanhood.

Brick by brick, bill by bill, fear by fear, the wall grew taller and taller. The deaf, the dumb and the blind were separated by color. White nurses were forbidden to treat black males. White teachers were forbidden to teach black students. South Carolina made it a crime for black and white cotton mill workers to look out the same window. Florida required "Negro" textbooks and "white" textbooks. Oklahoma required "separate but equal" telephone booths. New Orleans segregated black and white prostitutes. Atlanta provided Jim Crow Bibles for black and white witnesses.

The laws and decrees were only the most dramatic examples of an overall system, a system that was designed to isolate, subordinate, degrade—push down. The thrust behind the system came from a variety of motives, including a desire to avoid assimilation and to limit or eliminate competition for scarce values. But there was also a desire to discipline, control, punish, humiliate. The legal system was buttressed by an etiquette of debasement which forbade whites to shake hands with blacks or to use courtesy titles in addressing them.

As in all oppressive regimes, as in Nazi Germany, as in South Africa, the system was made up of interarching systems that meshed and intermeshed. One of the major subsystems was educational discrimination, which prepared the way for and guaranteed discrimination in other areas. To accomplish their purposes in this field, Southern Bourbons manipulated tax monies and legal structure in a largely successful effort to destroy or limit the effectiveness of the school systems created by the Reconstruction regimes. It was clear to almost everyone that these maneuvers were designed to keep blacks ignorant for political and economic reasons. No state expressed this approach more clearly than South Carolina, which spent in 1915, $13.98 for every white student and $2.57 for every black student. Nor was South Carolina unique. In 1935 and 1936, ten Southern states spent $49.30 for every white student and $17.04 for every black student.

All this had the effect that white leaders intended it to have. Until well into the twentieth century, there were no public high schools for black students in most sections of the South. As late as 1933 there was not a single state-supported high school in Alabama or South Carolina offering a four-year program for blacks.

The cause and the consequence of all this was economic exploitation. From the end of slavery to the Great Migration, the great mass of blacks were confined to Black Belt plantations by the sharecropping system. Under this system, blacks worked the land of planters who supplied tools and advanced credit for food and clothing. In theory, the sharecropper and planter split the proceeds of the crop. But the books were kept by the planter, who also marketed the crop. The inevitable result was that tenants usually remained in a state of perpetual debt. The longer they worked, the more they owed. Year by year, they slipped deeper and deeper into debt, the victims of some horribly tangible nightmare.

The situation was equally bad in Southern towns, where jobs had a name and a color. "Negro" jobs were dirty, hot and heavy. White jobs were clean, light, and well-paid. But the line between these categories shifted with each business crisis. When whites were hungry, "Negro" jobs were reclassified. Crisis by crisis, recession by recession, job by job, blacks were displaced as waiters, porters, draymen, cooks, caterers and artisans. At the end of the Civil War, blacks virtually controlled the building trades industry in the South. It has been estimated that only 20,000 of the 120,000 artisans in the South at that time were white. By 1900 white artisans were well on the way to eliminating their black competitors.

The instruments of the state were freely used to minimize or eliminate black competition. A South Carolina law, for instance, put strict limits on the relations between black and white factory workers and had the general effect of barring blacks from the new textile industry.

The ultimate sanction, of course, was violence: random violence dispensed by men and boys who were authorized by the system to whip and discipline blacks; organized violence pursued by posses and police forces; communal violence executed by men, women and children who gathered in the tens of thousands to view and execute lynch law. Ida B. Wells-Barnett, who issued authoritative contemporary reports on the practice, said approximately ten thousand people were lynched in America between 1878 and 1898.

This, then, was the wall that fear and greed built. In the 1880s and 1890s that wall grew and grew until it seemed that it had always existed. But this was an illusion, magnified by lack of perspective. In fact, the system was an artificial creation of postwar origin. And in assessing that system, it is important to remember that there were no separate but equal privies in slavery. Nor, as C. Vann Woodward has shown in *The Strange Career of Jim Crow*, were there separate but equal restrooms for a considerable period thereafter. So long as blacks were slaves, so long as they posed no threat to the political and economic supremacy of whites, people were content to live with them on terms of relative intimacy. But when the slaves became citizens, when they got ballots in their hands and pencils and paper, there were demands for laws and arrangements that would humiliate them and keep them in their places.

What perhaps is most astonishing is that it took so long for this process to work itself out. For several years after whites undermined Black Reconstruction, blacks and whites were served in the same inns and buried in the same graveyards. There were even some communities where black and white children read letters out of the same spelling books in the same classrooms. As late as 1879, Vernon Wharton reports, most of the saloons in Mississippi "served whites and Negroes in the same bar. Many of the restaurants, using separate tables, served both races in the same room."

The story was very much the same in other Southern states. If we can believe the dispatches of lawyer-reporter T. McCants Stewart, who made the first Freedom Ride through the South, Jim Crow was a sometimes thing as late as April, 1885. "On leaving Washington, D.C.," he reported, "I put a chip on my shoulder, and inwardly dared any man to knock it off." Stewart was pleasantly surprised. He rode first class in a car in which several whites had to sit on their baggage for lack of seats. "Bold as a lion," he went into a station dining room in Virginia and was served at a table with whites. Encouraged by his reception, he sent a dispatch to his newspaper: "Along the Atlantic seaboard from Canada to the Gulf of Mexico—through Delaware, Maryland, Virginia, the Carolinas, Georgia and into Florida, all the old slave States with enormous Negro populations . . . a first-class ticket is good in a first-class coach."

Stewart's dispatch from Columbia, South Carolina, was lyrical. "I feel about as safe here as in Providence, R. I. I can ride in first-class cars on the railroads and in the streets. I can go into saloons and get refreshments even as in New York. I can stop in and drink a glass of soda and be more politely waited upon than in

some parts of New England." Stewart finally gave up: no news
was good news. "For the life of [me]," he wrote, "I can't 'raise a
row' in these letters. Things seem [remember I write *seem*) to
move along as smoothly as in New York or Boston. . . . If you
should ask me, 'Watchman, tell us of the night!' . . . I would say,
'The morning light is breaking!' "

It was a false illusion. The light Stewart saw was the coming of
the moon. There was still some daylight, but it would not last
long. Far off on the horizon a night storm was gathering, and that
storm would blow down the legal shelter Congress had prepared
for the freedmen. That shelter rested on three fragile legal props:

The Fourteenth Amendment:

> No State shall make or enforce any law which shall abridge
> the privileges or immunities of citizens of the United States,
> nor shall any State deprive any person of life, liberty or prop-
> erty without due process of law, nor deny to any person within
> its jurisdiction the equal protection of the laws.

The Fifteenth Amendment:

> The rights of the citizens of the United States to vote shall not
> be denied or abridged by the United States or by any State on
> account of race, color, or previous condition of servitude.

The Civil Rights Bill of 1875:

> All persons within the jurisdiction of the United States shall
> be entitled to the full and equal enjoyment of the accommoda-
> tions, advantages, facilities, and privileges of inns, public
> conveyances on land or water, theaters, and other places of
> public amusement; subject only to the conditions and limita-
> tions established by law and applicable alike to citizens of
> every race and color, regardless of any previous condition of
> servitude.

. These measures, supplemented by laws that sent federal
troops into the South to protect the constitutional rights of blacks,
seemed to settle the issue beyond all possibility of dispute or
recall. There were even some Americans, black and white, who
believed that the race problem had been solved forever. "Slavery," Wendell Phillips said, "is dead. We have not only abolished
slavery, but we have abolished the Negro. We have actually
washed color out of the Constitution." Another who saw things

this way said, "All distinctions founded upon race or color have been forever abolished in the United States."

The dreamers and prophets—and victims—were wrong, but it would take time and blood to undeceive them. The Fourteenth and Fifteenth amendments and the Civil Rights Bill were words on pieces of paper. The proof of the pudding would come literally in the eating and the riding and the balloting. When the lawyers got through with the words, these things became hedged about with prickly legal arrangements. A meal in a "white" restaurant, a ticket to a "white" opera house, a seat in a "white" railroad car: these became enormously complicated legal processes involving policemen, layers on layers of lawyers and judges and the expenditure of thousands of dollars on legal fees. It got so bad that almost everybody admitted that blacks had certain legal rights, but almost no one could tell them where to go for redress. "When we seek relief at the hands of Congress," a black editor in Richmond, Virginia, said, "we are informed that our plea involves a legal question, and we are referred to the Courts. When we appeal to the Courts, we are gravely told that the question is a political one, and that we must go to Congress. When Congress enacts remedial legislation, our enemies take it to the Supreme Court, which promptly declares it unconstitutional."

How did this situation come about? And why?

First, the why. The legal status of the black American depended, to a great extent, on world public opinion, white public opinion, and the opinions of the nine justices of the U.S. Supreme Court. In the fourth quarter of the nineteenth century, these supports collapsed, and the roof caved in. America, at that juncture, was reeling from the hangover of the Compromise of 1877; and the public mind, coarsened and corrupted by national scandals and the corrosive currents of the Gilded Age, was focused on the conquest of the Indians, the exclusion of the Chinese and the suppression of "little brown brothers" in the Philippines and the Caribbean. The situation was, if anything, worse in Europe, which was sharpening knives for the dismemberment of Africa. Everywhere the freedman turned in this age, he found people commanded by systems which gave them a terrible need to believe that nonwhites were biologically inferior.

Under these circumstances, with America committed to the

internal colonization of blacks and reds and the external colonization of the browns of South and Latin America, and with
Europe committed to the colonization and Balkanization of Africa
and Asia, there was little (white) public support for the shib-
boleths of justice and equal rights. The support, in fact, ran all
the other way. And since people can't do wrong without believing
that history or God is on their side, scientists, sociologists and
ministers were called on for the necessary rationalizations. The
great universities of Europe and America responded with theories and studies which proved at great length, and with abundant
documentation, that white oppression was either right or, what
came down to the same thing, inevitable. The tenor of the times—
and the bias of American scholarship—was expressed in sociologist William Graham Sumner's revealing epigram: "Stateways
cannot change folkways."

The Supreme Court was inclined to agree. In the Slaughterhouse cases of 1873, the Court said there were two categories of
citizenship, state and federal, and that the Fourteenth Amendment was designed to protect the rights of federal citizenship.
What were the rights of federal citizenship? The Court was
evasively vague. Most civil rights, it said, came from state
citizenship and could not be protected against state action under
the Fourteenth Amendment.

After that, it was easy, as the Civil Rights Cases of 1883 indicated. Ruling on several cases involving denial of equal rights to
blacks in hotels, railroads and places of public amusement, the
Court said the Fourteenth Amendment forbade *states*, not individuals, from discriminating. In an eloquent dissent Justice John
Marshall Harlan disagreed, saying that the Court had gutted the
Fourteenth Amendment "by a subtle and ingenious verbal criticism." Railroad corporations, inns, hotels and places of public
amusement, he said, are instrumentalities of the state. "It seems
to me that . . . a denial, by these instrumentalities of the States,
to the Citizen, because of his race, of that equality of civil rights
secured to him by law, is a denial by the State, within the meaning of the Fourteenth Amendment. If it be not, then that race is
left, in respect of the civil rights in question, practically at the
mercy of corporations and individuals wielding power under the
States."

As it turned out, Harlan was right. But this was no comfort to

blacks, who were pushed to the periphery of American life by a
majority decision that amputated the Fourteenth Amendment and
spawned an epidemic of Jim Crow laws. Tennessee had kicked off
the modern segregation movement in 1881, two years before the
Supreme Court decision, with a Jim Crow railroad law. Now every
Southern state, beginning with Florida in 1887, enacted Jim Crow
railroad legislation.

Blacks protested bitterly, holding mass meetings from Maine to
Florida. Timothy Thomas Fortune, the influential black editor,
said blacks felt as if they had been "baptized in ice water." The
polished John Mercer Langston told a full house at Washington's
Fifteenth Street Presbyterian Church that the decision was "a
stab in the back."

At that precise moment, almost as if it had been orchestrated, a
new and different voice joined the chorus. The voice belonged to
Booker Taliaferro Washington, a name that would soon be better
known. Behind the name and the voice lay an interesting and
revealing history. When Lee surrendered at Appomattox, the
man who would soon be hailed as a saviour of the South was a
nine-year-old slave on a farm near Hale's Ford, Virginia. Seven
years later, at the age of sixteen, he entered Hampton Institute.
Now, at twenty-eight, he was a comer, the president of Tuskegee
Institute, which he had built from the ground up. A year after the
civil rights decision, Washington traveled to Madison, Wisconsin,
to speak to the National Education Association. The white educators liked what he said:

"Brains, property, and character for the Negro will settle the
question of civil rights. The best course to pursue in regard to the
civil rights bill in the South is to let it alone; let it alone and it will
settle itself. Good schoolteachers and plenty of money to pay
them will be more potent in settling the race question than many
civil rights bills and investigating committees."

Eleven years later, on Wednesday, September 18, 1895,
Booker T. Washington turned up in Atlanta with the parable of
the open hand and the empty bucket. He came at the invitation of
the sponsors to give some color to the opening of the Cotton
States and International Exposition. The sponsors got their
money's worth. After pleasantries by the governor and other
white dignitaries, Washington was introduced perfunctorily, al-

most apologetically, as "Professor Booker T. Washington." The black educator, then only thirty-nine years old, moved to the front of the platform. James Creelman, the correspondent of the *New York World,* saw "a remarkable figure; tall, bony, straight as a Sioux chief, high forehead, straight nose, heavy jaws and strong, determined mouth, with big white teeth, piercing eyes, and a commanding manner. The sinews stood out on his bronzed neck, and his muscular right arm swung high in the air with a lead pencil grasped in the clenched brown fist. His big feet were planted squarely, with the heels together and the toes turned out. His voice rang out clear and true, and he paused impressively as he made each point. Within ten minutes, the multitude was in an uproar of enthusiasm—handkerchiefs were waved, canes were flourished, hats were tossed in the air. The fairest women of Georgia stood up and cheered."

What was all the shouting about? Metaphors, mostly—these and words millions were yearning to hear. Whether he is praised (as he was so often in the early years) or whether he is attacked (as he was so frequently in later years), it is incontestably true that Washington could make a figure of speech shimmer and dance. He was working this day with a metaphorical compound of ships and buckets and patient and "unresentful" blacks.

"A ship lost at sea for many days," he told the cheering crowd, "suddenly sighted a friendly vessel. From the mast of the unfortunate vessel was seen a signal, 'Water, water; we die of thirst!' The answer from the friendly vessel at once came back, 'Cast down your bucket where you are.' A second time the signal, 'Water, water; send us water!' ran up from the distressed vessel, and was answered, 'Cast down your bucket where you are.' A third and fourth signal for water was answered, 'Cast down your bucket where you are.' The captain of the distressed vessel, at last heeding the injunction, cast down his bucket, and it came up full of fresh, sparkling water from the mouth of the Amazon River. To those of my race who depend on bettering their condition in a foreign land or who underestimate the importance of cultivating friendly relations with the Southern white man, who is their next-door neighbor, I would say: 'Cast down your bucket where you are. . . .'"

To whites, Washington offered the same advice: "Cast down your bucket . . . among the eight millions of Negroes . . . who have, without strikes and labor wars, tilled your fields, cleared your forests, builded your railroads and cities . . . the most patient, faithful, law-abiding, and unresentful people that the world has seen. . . ."

Suddenly Washington flung his hand aloft with the fingers held wide apart.

"In all things that are purely social," he said, "we can be as separate as the fingers, yet [he balled the fingers into a fist] one as the hand in all things essential to mutual progress."

The crowd came to its feet, yelling.

A "great wave of sound dashed itself against the wall," Creelman wrote, "and the whole audience was on its feet in a delirium of applause."

Sure of his audience now, Washington mentioned the unmentionable—social equality.

"The wisest among my race understand that the agitation of questions of social equality is the extremest folly, and that progress in the enjoyment of all the privileges that will come to us must be the result of severe and constant struggle rather than of artificial forcing."

When Washington finished, waves and waves of applause dashed against the building. And the blacks in the audience—did they applaud, too? At the end of the speech, reporter Creelman wrote in a prophetically chilling sentence, "most of the Negroes in the audience were crying, perhaps without knowing just why."

The response in other black circles was more pointed. Five months after the Atlanta address, John Hope, a brilliant young educator, denounced Washington and his message, saying: "I regard it as cowardly and dishonest for any of our colored men to tell white people or colored people that we are not struggling for equality. If money, education, and honesty will not bring to me as much privilege, as much equality as they bring to any American citizen, then they are to me a curse, and not a blessing."

There was similar criticism from other blacks. Novelist Charles Chesnutt said "the time to philosophize about the good there is in evil is not while its correction is still possible, but, if at all, after all hope of correction is past. Until then it calls for nothing but rigorous condemnation. . . . Those who commit crime should bear the odium. It is not a pleasing spectacle to see the robbed applaud the robber. Silence were better." Another Washington critic was Henry McNeal Turner, the fiery AME bishop, who said that "the colored man who will stand up and in one breath say that the Negroid race does not want social equality and in the next predict a great future in the face of all the proscription of which the colored man is the victim, is either an ignoramus, or is an advocate of the perpetual servility and degradation of his race variety."

Hope, Chesnutt and Turner spoke from experience, and with wisdom, but to no avail. Washington had touched—and anesthetized—an exposed nerve in the white psyche, and whites, in grateful appreciation, showered him with honors and resources so other blacks would know that he was the way and the light. Twenty-one years later, one of Washington's disciples, William H. Lewis, memorialized him in the following words: "He knew the Southern white man better than the Southern white man knew himself, and knew the sure road to his head and heart." Unquestionably—and that knowledge made Washington the ringmaster of the Southern white man *and* the Northern white man, who joined forces and lifted him to an eminence attained by few blacks. Washington, not a man given to internal agonizing, made the most of his opportunities, using his power to silence doubters and to create a new line in Black America. In the process, he set the mold for conservative and accommodating black leadership in America.

Important as Washington's role was, it has been greatly misunderstood and exaggerated. For he was neither new nor revelatory. He was simply the most celebrated of a long line of accommodators, reaching into the present, who have articulated the view that it is better to buy peace by accommodating, working and studying than to disturb the peace by protesting, demanding and resisting. As a matter of fact, it is better to do both, to work and protest. And it is an interesting fact, worthy of long thought, that Frederick Douglass, who stressed both sides of the black assertion theme—internal development and external protest— was one of the pioneers of the industrial education idea that made Washington famous. A second point to bear in mind is that Booker T. Washington was a universal type, common to every oppressed people in every time. It is, in fact, inevitable that an oppressed people will produce a Booker T. Washington at some point in its history, as witness South Africa today. What distin-

guished Washington from his predecessors and the sizeable
number of men who said the same thing in the years before his
emergence, and since, was his undoubted oratorical flair and his
genius for political maneuvering.

In "the Atlanta Compromise," and in other speeches of the
day, Washington renounced, or seemed to renounce, social and
political equality, temporarily anyway. What did he expect in
return? Support for black education, Washingtonians say, an end
to lynching and a square deal in the economic field. It didn't turn
out that way. Down went the buckets and up they came, filled with
brine. Economic discrimination continued. Caste lines hardened.
Separate became more and more separate and less and less
equal, and lynchings reached new and staggering heights.
Washington was not responsible for these developments. But his
"submissive philosophy," C. Vann Woodward said, "must have
appeared to some whites as an invitation to further aggression."
Woodward, a white historian, went on to say that "it is quite
certain that Booker T. Washington did not intend his so-called
Atlanta Compromise to constitute such an invitation. But in pro-
posing virtual retirement of the mass of Negroes from the political
life of the South and in stressing the humble and menial role that
the race was to play, he would seem unwittingly to have smoothed
the path to proscription." Rayford Logan, a black historian,
hazarded "the guess" that Washington's philosophy "consoled
the consciences of the judges of the Supreme Court," who
crossed a legal Jordan in 1896, less than a year after the "Atlanta
Compromise." In the infamous case of *Plessy* v. *Ferguson*, the
Court said state laws requiring "separate but equal" accommodations for blacks were a "reasonable" use of state police powers,
adding: "The object of the [Fourteenth] Amendment was undoubtedly to enforce the absolute equality of the two races before
the law, but in the nature of things it could not have been intended to abolish distinctions based on color, or to enforce social,
as distinguished from political equality, or a commingling of the
two races upon terms unsatisfactory to either."

Justice John Marshall Harlan was prophetic in dissent. Laws
requiring segregation, he said, fostered ideas of caste and inferiority and would lead to additional aggression against blacks.
For "in view of the Constitution, in the eye of the law, there is in
this country no superior, dominant, ruling class of citizens. There

is no caste here. Our Constitution is color-blind, and neither knows nor tolerates classes among citizens. . . . It is, therefore, to be regretted that this high tribunal, the final expositor of the fundamental law of the land, has reached the conclusion that it is competent for a state to regulate the enjoyment by citizens of their civil rights solely upon the basis of race. In my opinion, the judgment this day rendered will, in time, prove to be quite as pernicious as the decision made by this tribunal in the Dred Scott case."

It took fifty-eight years for America and the Supreme Court to catch up with Justice Harlan, who was the son of a former Kentucky slaveowner. By that time the damage he predicted had been done. Only three states had required Jim Crow waiting rooms before 1899, but in the next decade other Southern states fell in line. Only Georgia before 1900 had required Jim Crow seating on streetcars, but in the first decade of the twentieth century the following states joined the procession: North Carolina and Virginia (1901); Louisiana (1902); Arkansas, South Carolina and Tennessee (1903); Mississippi and Maryland (1904), and Florida (1905).

Relentlessly, now, the white South increased the pressure, piling law on law. The laws came in spurts and waves, and every year brought some new twist or refinement. Blacks and whites were forcibly separated in public transportation, sports, hospitals, orphanages, prisons, asylums, funeral homes, morgues, cemeteries. Mobile, Alabama, required blacks to be off the streets by 10 P.M. Birmingham, Alabama, forbade blacks and whites to play checkers together.

Not content with these measures, the white South tried to give land a color by creating by law black and white residential areas. When the Supreme Court struck down these laws, the movement continued under the guise of restrictive covenants and "gentlemen's agreements." The immediate result was the creation of Jim Crow sections in almost every city and town—around Beale Street in Memphis and Cotton Row in Macon and Auburn Avenue in Atlanta.

As the Jim Crow movement continued, producing thousands of black casualties, fissures appeared in the ranks of the whites, who divided over the division of the spoils. The most significant

rift occurred between poor whites and remnants of the disinte-
grating planter class. This was a continuation of a centuries-long
struggle, which had been masked by slavery and the deliberate
use of racism to divert poor whites and blind them to their true
interests. One of the by-products of the emancipation of the
slaves was the unmasking of this struggle and the freeing, as
President Andrew Johnson so cogently noted, of the poor whites.
During the first phase of Reconstruction, sizeable numbers of
poor whites cooperated with the new regimes in the passage of
social legislation, including the free public education that the
planters had denied them. But the poor whites, lacking leadership and social and economic focus, were fair game for the
planters, who used the carrot of racism — "You oughta be
ashamed of yo'self for abandoning white women in their hour of
need" — and the whip of community pressure and economic
intimidation to bring them back in line.

After Reconstruction the aristocrats reverted to form, showing
by manner and act that they had almost as much contempt for
poor whites as they had for poor blacks. When the aristocrats
went further and enacted legislation that blatantly favored the
planters and their allies at the expense of poor whites (and poor
blacks), the long-suppressed poor whites exploded in a frenzy of
agrarian radicalism. Of much more pointed political significance,
they moved, under the pressure of events, into a close alliance
with poor blacks. In the first phase of this movement, white
Populist leaders championed the rights of all poor farmers and
tried to a form a union of poor whites and black farmers. Tom
Watson, the talented Populist leader who later became a fire-
eating racist, told both blacks and whites: "You are kept apart
that you may be separately fleeced of your earnings."

Heeding this and other appeals, blacks and whites, acting
sometimes as Readjusters, sometimes as Populists, sometimes as
Fusionists, attended integrated meetings and picnics and adopted
advanced political platforms that denounced lynching and supported black political rights. This unexpected development stimulated black and white agrarians and led to an informal alliance
between the major white group, the Southern Alliance, and the
Colored Farmers' Alliance. To measure the impact of this development, one must understand that both groups had deep roots in
the Southern population. In 1891, for instance, the Colored

Farmers' Alliance had more than 1,125,000 members, a figure that would be astonishing even today, and was organized in twenty states.

Spurred on by gains directly related to this expanding new front, blacks deepened their hold on traditional pockets of power and made new gains. The political climate in Danville, Virginia, was a striking example of the possibilities of the new age. In the 1880s blacks held a majority on the city council of that city. Four of the nine policemen were black and all of the justices of the peace were black. This situation disturbed white conservatives, who staged a coup on the Saturday before the municipal election of 1883, killing four blacks and systematically suppressing the black vote.

In spite of the terror tactics of white conservatives, the Fusion movement continued and reached a peak in 1894 when black Republicans and white Populists captured the North Carolina state government. The next year, in an act of interracial solidarity that would be unusual even today, the North Carolina legislature adjourned for a day to mark the death of Frederick Douglass.

Partly because of the Fusion currents and partly because of the survival of Republican structures, blacks continued to send representatives to Congress. Six blacks were elected in the 1880s: Robert Smalls, South Carolina, 1881–87; J. R. Lynch, Mississippi, 1881–83; John Mercer Langston, Virginia, 1889–91; James E. O'Hara, North Carolina, 1883–87; Henry P. Cheatham, North Carolina, 1889–91; Thomas E. Miller, South Carolina, 1889–91. Three Blacks were elected in the 1890s: Henry P. Cheatham, North Carolina, 1891–93; George W. Murray, South Carolina, 1893–97; George H. White, North Carolina, 1897–1901.

Terrified by the implications of these developments, the Southern white power structure ran up the white flag of racism and the Populist-Fusion movement collapsed. Reunited on a platform of white supremacy, Southerners of all classes made white solidarity an article of faith. Crossroads rang out with tremolo references to white womanhood and "our sacred institutions." Men stood on courthouse steps—a Tillman in South Carolina, a Vardaman in Mississippi, a Hoke Smith in Georgia—and flayed blacks. "The way to control the nigger," W. K. Vardaman told cheering crowds, "is to whip him when he does not obey without it, and another is to never to pay him more wages than is actually necessary to buy food and clothing."

The crowds loved it.

They whooped and hollered and slapped their thighs, and the demagogues laid it on the line. And then what happened? More lynchings—naturally. In the peak years of the Terrible Nineties, which Rayford Logan called the low point of the black odyssey in America, a black was lynched somewhere every day or two. From this time forward, lynching became in Charles S. Johnson's words "a hybrid of sports-vengeance," became in Gunnar Myrdal's words a form of witch-hunting, became in H. L. Mencken's words a diversion which often took "the place of the merry-go-round, the theatre, the symphony orchestra, and other diversions common to larger communities." It was not unusual in these days for newspapers to advertise a lynching and for crowds to come from afar on chartered trains.

As the decades wore on, and as Negro-baiting became more virulent, lynching became more barbarous, and lynchers became more sadistic. Victims, including women, black and white women, were burned at the stake, mutilated, hacked to pieces, and roasted over slow fires. Contrary to the generally accepted view, only a small percentage of the 1217 persons lynched between 1890 and 1900 were accused of rape. Others—the overwhelming majority—were charged with the "crimes" of testifying against whites in court, seeking another job, using offensive language, failing to say "mister" to whites, disputing the price of blackberries, attempting to vote and accepting the job of postmaster.

What were blacks doing all this time?

They were groping in the whiteness that blinded them for a place of safety and black light.

Some—the most courageous, the most desperate—stood alone and defied the marauding crowds and died, having done all that free and outgunned men and women can do.

Others banded together and went forth in small groups to test the white line, as patrols in the night test the main force of the enemy. After months of organizing and testing the line, these freedmen exploded in the hurricane of indignation known to history as the Exodus of 1879. No one knows—and no one will ever know—how many blacks were involved in the Exodus, but there is not the slightest doubt that hundreds of thousands participated at different levels. The movement, which was composed not of leaders and politicians but of ordinary people, of laborers and

maids and cottonpickers, centered in Louisiana but also touched
adjoining states. Approximately fifty thousand of these "Exodus-
ters," as they were called, managed to make it to Kansas and
other Northern areas; but tens of thousands were driven back by
armed men, who patrolled the riverfronts and roads. The leading
personalities of this remarkable movement, which continued for
several years and spread to South Carolina and Alabama, were
Benjamin ("Pap") Singleton, a sixty-nine-year-old agitator who
headed the Tennessee Real Estate and Homestead Association,
and Henry Adams, a thirty-six-year-old former slave and U.S.
Army veteran. In his testimony before a U.S. Senate committee,
Adams said the Exodus was a product of hard planning over a
period of years by "a committee" of blacks. The fundamental
reasons for the Exodus, he said, were white violence, peonage,
the abuse of black women, inadequate educational facilities, and
political intimidation.

After the collapse of this movement and a wave of cotton-
picking strikes, most Southern blacks were forced by circumstances and a cruel history to make some kind of accommodation
with a geographical area that had become a prison. Individual and
unorganized resistance continued and reached, in some states,
impressive proportions, but the great masses of the people were
pushed down, year by year, to a condition that approached slavery. Here and there a black hand reached for a straw and caught
it. But for the average black, life was a shadowy nightmare of dirt
and danger and humiliation. So violent was the assault on his
nervous sytem, so intense and overwhelming was the oppression
to which he was subjected, so forsaken by government and man
did he feel, and so overwhelmed by the shape and size of the
forces that battered him, that he had neither the space nor the
time to formulate alternatives. To work from sunup to sundown
for a whole year and to end up owing "the man" for the privilege
of working; to do this year after year and to sink deeper and
deeper into debt; to be chained to the land by violence and bills at
the plantation store; to be conditioned by dirt and fear and shame
and signs; to become a part of these signs and to feel them in the
deepest recess of the spirit; to be powerless and to curse one's
self for cowardice; to be knocked down in the streets for failing
to call a shiftless hillbilly "mister"; to be a plaything of judges and
courts and policemen; to be black in a white fire and to be-

lieve finally in one's own unworthiness; to be without books and words and pretty pictures; to be without newspapers and radios; to be without understanding, without the rationalizations of psychology and sociology, without Freud and E. Franklin Frazier and *Jet*; to give in finally; to bow, to scrape, to grin; and to hate one's self for one's servility and weakness and blackness—all this was a Kafkaesque nightmare that continued for days and nights and years.

And if a black protested, if he said enough, no more—what then? "And if any black was fantastic enough," W. J. Cash wrote, "to run to the courthouse for redress for a beating or any other wrong, he stood a good chance (provided he was heard at all), not only of seeing his assailant go off scot-free, but of finding the onus somehow shifted to himself, of finding himself in the dock on this or some other count, and of ending by going away for a long time to the county chain gang and the mercies of persons, hand-picked for their skills in adjusting his sense of reality."

The chain gangs were integral parts of the system. Sir George Campbell was told that chain gangs were often used as schools for undisciplined blacks who had grown up since slavery—as schools, in short, for servility. On the slightest pretext unmanageable blacks were arrested, convicted and leased to private individuals and companies, which made large fortunes on their misery. In the turpentine camps and mining camps, on levees and railroad construction projects, manhood was worked and whipped out of them. With chains welded to their bodies, waist deep sometimes in mud and slime, convicts toiled day in and day out. Their quarters were unbelievably filthy. Vermin, investigators reported, crawled over their clothes and bodies. It was not unusual for a female prisoner and a male prisoner to be chained to a bed together at night. After a study of Southern chain gangs, Fletcher Green concluded that they had no parallel except in the persecutions of the Middle Ages and the concentration camps of Nazi Germany.

The Christians, the liberals, the *good* people—what were they doing? They were passing by on the other side with eyes and ears covered. Frederick Douglass and other black leaders made repeated attempts to rally their old abolitionist colleagues ("We need you now, almost as much as ever") but almost all of them—Wendell Phillips was a shining exception—were busy, indifferent or otherwise engaged. Worse, some were hostile, blaming the victims for their oppression.

Imbued with new confidence and contemptuous of Northern liberalism, which they perceived to be timid and ineffective, Southern demagogues and Bourbons moved to the offensive, calling for repeal of the Fourteenth and Fifteenth amendments. The U. S. Congress now became the major forum of racist propaganda. In the 1890s three Southern senators demanded the immediate deportation of all blacks. In the same period Wilkinson Call of Florida proposed that America pay Spain fifty million dollars for Cuba and use it as a dumping ground for blacks.

By the 1890s the Southern view had become the American view. The best indication of this was a black exclusion movement, which rapidly Balkanized most Northern cities. Somewhat to the surprise of Northern blacks, who had lived for decades in all sections of Northern cities, this movement gained new adherents and succeeded in its avowed purpose of creating black and white residential sections. This process can be traced in the birth of Harlem, which was a white community until the twentieth century. In the 1890s the twenty-three thousand blacks in New York City lived in several sections. Many, in fact, lived in close proximity to the rich whites they served as domestics. All this changed markedly in 1903 when a handful of blacks moved into one or two apartment buildings on 134th Street east of Lenox in Harlem. At first, James Weldon Johnson said, the whites paid little or no attention to their new neighbors. But as the black population continued to grow, a panic developed. Whites began fleeing, Johnson said, "as from a plague. The presence of one colored family in a block, no matter how well bred and orderly, was sufficient to precipitate a flight. House after house and block after block was actually deserted."

There was a similar development in Chicago. In the first decades of the century, the black ghetto rolled south and east along State Street with whites fighting to contain the black tide and blacks fighting to break out of the white dams. The first tactic used by whites was violence. Between July, 1917, and March, 1921, fifty-eight bombs were hurled at the homes of black Chicagoans.

Thus, the vicious cycle became national and still more vicious.

If anyone had any doubts on that score, they were swept away by three ominous developments in the 1890s. The first was the elimination of the last pockets of black power in the South. Mississippi, which pioneered in so many anti-black measures, made the first major contribution to that effort by solving a problem that had stumped Southern lawmakers for years. That problem posed itself approximately in these terms: How was it possible to legally disenfranchise poor blacks without at the same time legally disenfranchising poor whites. The answer the South came up with was a wall with holes in it. The wall was made of literacy and property tests and poll taxes. The holes, designed especially for illiterate and propertyless poor whites, were "understanding clauses" and "grandfather clauses." If a man's ancestors voted on or before a selected date in, say, 1866—a date on which unfortunately there were no black voters—then he could escape the other provisions. Or he could slip through the holes of "good" character or the "understanding" clause. If he couldn't read or write and if he was white, surely he could understand and explain an article of the constitution. But if he was black, the "read and write" and "understanding" clauses were unbridgeable walls that no amount of literacy could bridge. The story, possibly apocryphal, is told of a black teacher, a graduate of Harvard and Eton, who presented himself to a Mississippi registrar. The teacher read the state constitution and several books. The registrar produced a passage in Latin, which the teacher read, and a passage in Greek, which the teacher read, and passages in French, German and Spanish, all of which the teacher read. The registrar finally held up a page of Chinese characters and asked: "What does this mean?" The teacher replied: "It means that you don't want me to vote."

This determination was institutionalized by the state of Mississippi at a constitutional convention (August 12–November 1) in 1890. The Mississippi Plan (literacy and "understanding tests") was later adopted with embellishments by other states: South Carolina (1895), Louisiana (1898), North Carolina (1900), Alabama (1901), Virginia (1901), Georgia (1908).

What this meant strategically was spelled out in a revealing statement by Ben Tillman, one of the leaders of the South Carolina Constitutional Convention.

"We have done our level best," he said. "We have scratched our heads to find out how we could eliminate the last one of them [blacks]. We stuffed ballot boxes. We shot them. We are not ashamed."

These methods were extremely effective. In 1896 the 130,344 black voters in Louisiana were in the majority in twenty-six parishes. In 1900, two years after adoption of a new state constitution with a "grandfather clause," the black voters were minuscule minorities in every parish.

Pressing their advantage, Southern Bourbons now launched a coordinated campaign against blacks and whites who could not be dissuaded by legal and economic pressure. Two events in the dying days of the century underscored the growing controversy. The first event, which was designed to eliminate the black federal presence in the South, was the lynching of a black postmaster on February 22, 1898, in Lake City, South Carolina. An appalling report of this lynching was sent to the Cleveland *Gazette*:

> At 1 o'clock Tuesday morning a torch was applied to the post office and house. Back, just within the line of light, were over a hundred white brutes—murderers—armed with pistols and shotguns. By the time the fire aroused the sleeping family, consisting of the postmaster, his wife, four daughters, a son and an infant at the breast, the crowd began firing into the building. A hundred bullet holes were made through the thin boarding and many found lodgement in members of the family within.
>
> The postmaster was the first to reach the door and he fell dead just within the threshold, being shot in several places. The mother had the baby in her arms and reached the door over her husband's body, when a bullet crashed through its skull, and it fell to the floor. She was shot in several places. Two of the girls had their arms broken close to the shoulders and will probably lose them. Another of the girls is fatally wounded. The boy was also shot.
>
> Only two of the seven occupants of the house escaped with slight injuries. The bodies of Mr. Baker and the infant were cremated in the building. All mail matter was destroyed.

The second event, which occurred in November of the same year, was a violent revolution in the state of North Carolina.

Shortly before the election of 1898, some fifty thousand rounds of ammunition and carloads of firearms were shipped to North Carolina by whites in South Carolina and Virginia. Armed with these weapons, the red-shirted Democrats intimidated enough voters to carry the election. The campaign came to a head in Wilmington, where a white mob, including substantial citizens and a former congressman, destroyed a black newspaper office, murdered eleven blacks and wounded scores. When the smoke cleared, the leader of the white forces was elected mayor of Wilmington. All this was witnessed by a number of contemporary witnesses, including Rev. Charles S. Morris, who left a telling account: "Nine Negroes massacred outright; a score wounded and hunted like partridges on the mountain; one man, brave enough to fight against such odds would be hailed as a hero anywhere else, was given the privilege of running the gauntlet up a broad street, where he sank ankle deep in the sand, while crowds of men lined the sidewalks and riddled him with a pint of bullets as he ran bleeding past their doors; another Negro shot twenty times in the back as he scrambled empty handed over a fence; thousands of women and children fleeing in terror from their humble homes in the darkness of the night. . . . All this happened, not in Turkey, nor in Russia, nor in Spain, not in the gardens of Nero, nor in the dungeons of Torquemada, but within three hundred miles of the White House, in the best State in the South, within a year of the twentieth century, while the nation was on its knees thanking God for having enabled it to break the Spanish yoke from the neck of Cuba."

It was by these means, it was by fraud and violence and fire, that the white South was won. It is worth emphasizing that the Wilmington massacre was only one wave in a tide of white violence. From Appomattox on, there were similar massacres in every Southern state. No one knows how many blacks were killed in these years, but Congressman Charles Williams estimated as early as 1880 that 130,000 people had been murdered in the South for political reasons.

In the face of all this, what were blacks to do? There were no simple answers to that question, for the simple reason that there was little, if anything, blacks could do. They were a formless and shapeless mass, outgunned and outmanned, nine to one, by mean and determined adversaries who held all the high ground. To make matters worse, there was no appeal in this age from the syllogism of superior firepower. Africa and Asia didn't exist politically, and world public opinion—and American public opinion—was white, racist, and colonial. Wherever blacks turned in these days, they found their adversaries entrenched and barricaded. But there was more, and worse. For the forces of the age seemed to conspire against black freedom, creating an ambivalent political landscape that condemned blacks to confusion and futility. Nothing in this landscape was what it seemed. To cite a single—and revealing—example, the Republican party, which had earned the undying gratitude of blacks for its support of Emancipation and the Fourteenth and Fifteenth amendments, was also and preeminently the party of predatory business interests and was organized around reactionary labor policies which were objectively anti-black. Even worse, the party was committed to a Southern expansionist policy in collusion with the Southern oppressors of blacks. In significant contrast, the traditional forces of renewal—Northern laborers and Western farmers — were committed to the Democratic party, which was preeminently the party of slavery and which was stridently racist.

What did all this mean? It meant, in plain English, that there was nowhere for blacks to go.

For two generations blacks probed for ways to come to grips with this dilemma. Delegation after delegation waited on the president, and petition after petition was sent to the White House. The most mournful perhaps—certainly the most eloquent—was an open letter the Massachusetts division of the Colored National League addressed to President William McKinley in October, 1899:

> We have suffered, sir—God knows how much we have suffered!—since your accession to office, at the hands of a country professing to be Christian, but which is not Christian; from the hate and violence of a people claiming to be civilized, but who are not civilized, and you have seen our sufferings, witnessed from your high place our awful wrongs and miseries, and yet you have at no time and on no occasion opened your lips in our behalf. Why? we ask. Is it because we are black and weak and despised? Are you silent because without any fault of our own we were enslaved and held for

> more than two centuries in cruel bondage by your fore-
> fathers? Is it because we bear the mark of those sad genera-
> tions of Anglo-Saxon brutality and wickedness, that you do
> not speak?

Since there was no real, that is to say, effective response to the repeated petitions to Republican presidents, various blacks, notably Timothy Thomas Fortune and George Downing, called for independent political action or a "colored Democratic party." Most black leaders—and most black leaders were Republicans in those days—opposed these calls, contending, as Frederick Douglass put it, that there was no way out of the Republican party that did not lead straight into the arms of the enemy.

If, as Douglass and others said or implied, the Republican party was the ship and all else was the sea, it was a sinking ship, full of gaping holes. Worse yet, the white passengers, not to mention the captain and crew, were trying to push black Republicans into the surrounding sea. This was painfully obvious in the "white Southern strategy" pressed by every Republican president from Rutherford B. Hayes to Herbert Hoover and beyond. This strategy was based on the idea that the salvation of the party depended on a breakthrough in the solid white Democratic front. As a tactical means of realizing this goal, Republican presidents and party strategists subordinated black Republican voters and civil rights issues and played up to various white hopes. This meant, on the level of day-to-day politics, that black leaders were relegated to minor positions in the party and civil rights issues were passed over with perfunctory phrases in party platforms. And yet, having said all that, we must at once add that the Republican response, like the black response, was conditioned and contained by the economic and racialist forces of the age. This was, in general, a period of political stalemate, characterized by a series of round-robins in which Republican power in the White House and Senate was countered by Democratic power in the House. Under these conditions, it was relatively easy for white Southerners, seconded by powerful forces in the North and West, to sidetrack or defeat any real attempt to enforce the U.S. Constitution.

A second point to bear in mind is that the Republican party, sinking ship that it was, was the only national white institution to

give even minimal recognition to the human dimensions of
blacks. From the Reconstruction period to the twentieth century,
the party appointed blacks to traditional black posts in national
government (marshal and recorder of deeds of the District of
Columbia, register of the treasury, ministers to Haiti and Liberia)
and a variety of posts in Southern states. This was, as critics
contended, little more than tokenism and it had the general and
no doubt intended effect of silencing or softening the tongue of
black leaders. But here again it was the only recognition available, and it was enthusiastically supported by most blacks, who
apparently received symbolic and practical benefits. At any rate,
there were demonstrations and loud outcries when the Republicans, under white pressure, eliminated traditional black posts.

There were two other indications of the dwindling but continuing Republican concern. The first was the six-year struggle to
enact a federal aid to education bill, introduced in 1884 by
Senator Henry W. Blair of New Hampshire. The bill, which was
designed primarily to eliminate illiteracy among Southern blacks,
passed the Republican-dominated Senate but was blocked in the
House in 1886 and again in 1888. During the protracted public
debate over its features, strong opposition was voiced not only by
white Southerners but also by white liberals, Northern merchants
and sections of the Catholic Church. The tone of the debate was
set by a white liberal named Edward P. Clark, who dubbed the
Blair Bill "A Bill to Promote Mendicancy" and organized a national campaign against it from his editorial position on the New
York *Evening Post*. In phrases that are still current in the Republic, Clark said the bill would damage American self-reliance and
would encourage the "alarming tendency in American character
at the present time . . . to fall back upon the General Government for everything." Partly because of the Clark campaign, and
partly because of the skill of white Southerners, who shrewdly
played upon the fears of merchants and white liberals, the Blair
Bill was defeated in the Senate, 37 to 31, in March, 1890.

The same forces dominated the debate on the Lodge federal
voting rights bill, the second highwater mark of post-Reconstruction Republican concern. When this bill, called by opponents the
"Force Bill," was introduced by Congressman (later Senator)
Henry Cabot Lodge, Republicans controlled the White House
and both houses of Congress. Despite that fact, and despite the

support of President Benjamin Harrison, the bill squeaked by in the House, 155 to 149, and was sidetracked in the Senate by a Democratic filibuster and the defection of free silverite Westerners, who made a last-minute bargain with Democratic senators. The forces responsible for this catastrophic defeat were, in large measures, the same forces that doomed Radical Reconstruction. Who were they? In an interview in the *New York Tribune*, Senator George F. Edmunds of Vermont called them the four D's: "First, the Democrat pure and simple; second, the Dough-face of the North, who always sides with the Southern wing of his party; third, the Demagogue who, in the form of the Mugwump [white liberals and reformers], always seeks to have peace at any price; fourth, Dives, the rich New York grocer, who thinks that if the Election bill were passed he might not be able to sell as much tea and sugar in the South as before." Senator Edmunds might have added a fifth D: the doubting Republican, who never defended the black cause with as much passion as the Democrats who attacked it.

The fate of the Lodge Bill—and the fate of blacks—was sealed one year later with the sweeping presidential victory of Democrat Grover Cleveland, a victory that gave new heart to reactionary forces and shattered the Republican coalition. Curiously but understandably, the most ecstatic celebration of this fact came not from a Southern but from a Northern newspaper, the New York *Sun*:

> "No Force bill! No Negro domination!"
> Every patriot in the land must rejoice that the black cloud which for several months has overhung the free and prosperous South is at last and forever dispelled.
> "No Force bill! No Negro domination!"

With the Cleveland victory, the small band of Republicans pressing for civil rights caved in, and blacks were pushed from the stage of American concerns. Even their former friends, even old abolitionists like Thomas Wentworth Higginson, joined the white chorus, gravely lecturing blacks on their "ignorance" and their unfitness for civil and political rights.

If, as they say, there are impossible historical situations, this was one. For blacks were now enclosed in a situation of maximum peril, and ambush lay on all sides. The Republican party was indifferent. The Democratic party was hostile; so was white labor; so was the white liberal contingent. There was thus, in the aftermath of the Democratic victory and the Republic default, no strategy for blacks except the cruel coming to terms with history, which sometimes leaves an embattled people no option, save the option of falling back little by little, contesting with all the resources at their command every inch of the ground.

This, in essence, was the final program of Frederick Douglass, who remained a persuasive symbol of black assertion until his death on February 20, 1895. During the middle years of this period, Douglass had been unaccountably and uncharacteristically erratic, opposing and then supporting the Black Exodus, opposing and then supporting all-black initiatives and institutions. Douglass's critics said large lecture fees, a series of federal appointments and marriage to a white woman had impaired his vision. A sympathetic historian, Philip S. Foner, entered a general demurrer to these charges but conceded that Douglass lost touch with the masses in the critical years following the Compromise of 1877. But Foner contends—and the record, in general, supports him—that Douglass came storming back in the final years of his life, telling blacks to hold on and hold fast. In speech after speech, he denounced white Americans for betraying the freedmen and the U.S. Constitution. Pointing to the long hot summers of the 1960s, he told white Americans in 1894 and 1895 that they had embarked on a course that would create "an aggrieved class" of black rebels. And he added pointedly: "We want no black Ireland in America."

As for black strategy, Douglass called for a protracted war for position, telling blacks to dig trenches, expose, warn, exhort— and contest every inch of the ground. Blacks, he said, "should keep their grievances before the people and make every organized protest against the wrongs inflicted upon them within their power. They should scorn the counsels of cowards, and hang their banners on the outer wall." Time, he said, would fight the black battle—time and the black birthrate. "Every year adds to the black man's numbers. Every year adds to his wealth and to his intelligence. These will speak for him."

By the thousands and tens of thousands, blacks heeded this and other cries. They created protest groups and filed peti-

tions and suits. In the 1890s conflict spread, intensifying aware-
ness, and blacks broke new ground with the organization of two
pioneer protest organizations. Timothy Thomas Fortune, the editor of the leading black newspaper, the *New York Age*, was the
dominant force behind the first organization, the National Afro-
American League, which was founded at a January, 1890, meeting attended by 147 delegates from 21 states and the District of
Columbia. The first president of the group was J. C. Price, the
thirty-six-year-old president of Livingstone College.

The league organized branches in some forty cities but failed to
attract mass support. It was succeeded in 1898 by the National
Afro-American Council, which was founded in 1898 at a meeting
in Rochester, New York. Fortune, one of the most creative leaders of the day, also played a major role in the founding of this
organization, but the presidency went to the young and dynamic
AME Zion bishop, Alexander Walters. The council, a direct
forerunner of the Niagara movement and the NAACP, pushed a
program of militant protest before it was taken over in 1902
by Booker T. Washington adherents, including, interestingly, a
Booker T. Washington convert, T. Thomas Fortune.

Meanwhile, on a different but allied front, blacks were organizing state and local labor unions and making overtures to the
young labor movement. This was a continuation of currents that
started in the post-Emancipation period with the creation, in
1869, of the National Negro Labor Union. This organization,
which spawned a number of state and local black unions, was
formed to advance the interests of black workers in the labor
market and in white labor unions.

In the 1870s and 1880s black Americans formed several labor
unions, including the Colored Waiters Association of New York,
the caulkers, hod carriers and butchers unions of Baltimore, and
the powerful longshoremen's unions of New Orleans and Charleston.

Of the workers associated with this movement, the most
talented was Isaac Myers, who has been called "the great pioneer
of organized Negro labor." A Baltimore caulker and the leader of
the militant black unionists of Maryland, Myers and seven other
blacks became the first black delegates to a white national labor
assembly when they were seated at the third annual congress of
the National Labor Union. In succeeding years the torch of black

and white labor solidarity was taken up by the Knights of Labor, which adopted an advanced program of industrial unionism and attracted sixty thousand black workers at the height of its influence in the 1880s. After the collapse of this movement, labor leaders continued to organize, especially in cities like St. Louis, Galveston and New Orleans, where blacks dominated the docks. In April, 1892, two thousand black longshoremen staged a successful strike on the St. Louis docks. Six years later, in Galveston, Texas, the state militia was called out to break a four-week strike by black longshoremen.

Although black unions made some gains in this period, they were overwhelmed finally by the major trend of the age, craft unionism dominated by a spirit of black exclusion and subordination. The process was most clearly visible in the initial successes of the American Federation of Labor (AFL), a craft-oriented organization which came down hard on the side of racism after an initial period of rhetorical liberalism. By 1899 the AFL was openly admitting white-only unions. By 1901 the organization was indifferent or hostile to the interests of black workers. Thus, in labor, as in politics, the road to the heights led to a dead-end.

There were other dead-ends, some of them very subtle. One was service in the U.S. Army, with the traditional hope that it would lead to better treatment for blacks in civilian life. Pulled by this theory and pushed by the fact that it was difficult to find employment elsewhere, thousands of blacks found themselves involved in the dirty work of subjugating and policing the American Indians and brown people in the Philippines and the Caribbean. The climax of this chapter, which is perhaps the most ironic and deplorable of black history, came on July 1, 1898, when the black soldiers of the Tenth Cavalry relieved Theodore Roosevelt's Rough Riders. This incident thrilled thousands of blacks who were, like other Americans, infected by the jingoism surrounding the Spanish-American War. But it is well worth noting that other blacks denounced the Spanish-American War and the colonial adventures of the United States. A passionate expression of this opposition came from Attorney Charles G. Baylor of Providence, Rhode Island, who published the following analysis in black newspapers in July, 1898: "Maceo, the great Afro-Cuban military leader was a full-blooded Negro. General

Gomez is an Afro-Cuban—a quadroon. Nearly all the leaders and fighters in the Cuban army of liberation are men who, if in South Carolina, Mississippi or Louisiana, would be made to ride in the "Jim Crow Cars," and would be refused the right to occupy a private residence on Beacon St., in Boston. You see the proposed Afro-Cuban Republic was too close to our own Cuba and Armenia to suit either the northern or southern plutocrats." One year later Lewis H. Douglass, the son of Frederick Douglass, made a similar analysis of American adventures in the Philippines: "It is hypocrisy of the most sickening kind to try to make us believe that the killing of Filipinos is for the purpose of good government and to give protection to life and liberty and the pursuit of happiness. . . . When the United States learns that justice should be blind as to race and color, then may it undertake to, with some show of propriety, expand. Now its expansion means extension of race hate and cruelty, barbarous lynchings and gross injustice to dark people."

As the dead-ends multiplied, at home and abroad, with no sign of an opening, black nationalism revived and gained new adherents and supporters. One of their number, Edwin P. McCabe, a former state auditor of Kansas, organized a campaign for the establishment of an all-black state in Oklahoma Territory. This campaign failed, but other blacks founded more than twenty all-black towns in Oklahoma. There was, on the same plane, repeated attempts to organize African emigration groups, and a small number of blacks managed to organize successful back-to-Africa expeditions. The leading nationalist spokesman was Bishop Henry McNeal Turner, who called for "two or three million" blacks to return "to the land of our ancestors, and establish our own nation, civilization, laws, customs, style of manufacture, and not only give the world, like other race varieties, the benefit of our individuality, but build up social conditions peculiarly our own." The AME bishop added:

"There is no manhood future in the United States for the Negro. He may eke out an existence for generations to come, but he can never be a *man*—full, symmetrical and undwarfed."

A new note in the black dialogue was introduced by Timothy Thomas Fortune, who came out for a vague form of socialism. In his 1884 book, *Black and White*, he called for a new movement based on the class struggle and a condemnation of the evils of capitalism "and the pernicious monopoly in land which limits production and forces population disastrously upon subsistence."

There were some in this age who wanted to fight fire with fire. When blacks in Clarksville, Tennessee, burned part of the town in retaliation for a lynching, the *Chicago Conservator* congratulated them, saying: "We are loath to advocate lawlessness. We deplore the necessity of resort to arson and rapine, but if such things come, let them come." This view was echoed by journalist John E. Bruce, who called for "a resort to force under wise and discreet leaders."

Increasingly, in this age, the voice of collaboration and accommodation was heard. Over the ensuing years, more and more "Uncle Toms," timid, cautious, despairing men, came forward and put themselves at the disposal of the power structure. Sir George Campbell, the distinguished British statesman, met one of these men in Charleston. He was a Democrat who cooperated with the White Democrats — for a price. "His story," the shrewd old Englishman said, "seemed to me a little too much as if it had been rehearsed. He tells very fluently how he was a slave, and how he was educated by his mistress; and how, after emancipation his master and mistress being reduced to poverty, he supported them both, and eventually buried them both—he lays great stress upon the *burying*."

Overcome momentarily by the ferocity of the white attack, many blacks suffered accommodating leadership in silence. But beneath the troubled surface of black life, unseen by social analysts, new seeds, scattered by the plowmen of three great institutions — the black church, the black lodge and the black college—were sending down shoots and breaking up the subsoil for new growths. The focal point of these developments was the black church, which quickly established itself as the dominant institutional force in black American life. Though loosely structured and composed of competing fragments—the major divisions were the independent Baptist churches, the AME and AME Zion denominations and the Negro divisions of white denominations—the black church was an ever-present reality, even to blacks who claimed no formal affiliation.

It has been argued with great force by certain secular and religious historians that most of these churches were conciliatory and accommodating. There is truth in this, but it is not the whole truth or even the most important truth, which is to be found on seven different levels. First of all, these churches were the main and, in many communities, the only windbreak against white power. In many communities, in fact, they were the only institutional structures owned and managed by blacks. Second, they bottomed the black community, linking and annealing the generations, seeding and re-seeding the fields of black being. Third, even the conservative churches taught black power, robing their servants in gowns and titles of authority, teaching them how to speak, how to challenge, how to maneuver, giving them, all the while, the only sense of power available to them. Fourth, they taught political economy, accumulating substantial sums of money and sowing the seeds from which came the first black banks and insurance companies. Fifth, they provided the myths that made it possible for blacks to survive in a situation that could not be changed (because of the balance of power) but which could not be borne without either myth or philosophy or strong drink. Six, they preserved the rhythmic and spiritual treasures of the slave heritage, keeping and enriching the lode of the spirituals, preparing the ground for the gospel songs and maintaining the image of that archetypal black presence—the black preacher. Seventh, they sowed, despite themselves, revolutionary seeds, instilling in their communicants the dangerous idea that there was something higher than the white man at work in history.

This was, all things considered, a lot of sowing, and the seeds planted here found fertile soil in associated institutions, especially fraternal lodges, which were oftentimes managed by the same men who ran the churches. Thus, by 1890, a great deal of black community life revolved around the meetings, socials and political maneuvering of the enormous numbers who belonged to fraternal organizations (Masons, Odd Fellows, Knights of Pythias, True Reformers) and their female auxiliaries. Not only did these lodges organize Black America but they also focused its economic strength, pyramiding the nickels and dimes of dues and assessments into impressive economic empires, which included retail stores, banks, hotels, newspapers, and insurance com-

Bessie Smith, pioneer blues singer, became a nationally known star in the twenties. She was born and reared in poverty in Chattanooga, Tennessee.

George H. White, militant North Carolina politician, was the last of the post-Reconstruction black congressmen. His congressional term ended in 1901.

"Separate but equal" water fountains in a Southern town suggest Jim Crow atmosphere of the Old South. A rash of Jim Crow laws was passed in the first decades of the twentieth century.

panies. We catch a glimpse of what this meant in the estimate of one student who said these organizations collected $168 million from blacks between 1870 and 1920.

Side by side with the churches and lodges, black colleges began to appear. Founded in many cases by far-sighted black men and women, these institutions played a crucial role in redirecting the leadership wave, sending out year after year bands of potential rebels, who were leaven in the lump of black despair. W. E. B. Du Bois said, with only slight exaggeration, that had it not been for black colleges black people would have been driven back into slavery. Du Bois, a graduate of Fisk, was persuasive evidence in favor of his thesis. So also were Timothy Thomas Fortune and George H. White of Howard, J. C. Price of Lincoln (Pa.), and Ida B. Wells of Rust College. The story of Ida B. Wells is, in many ways, the story of the new generation of freedom. Born in Holly Springs, Mississippi, in 1862, orphaned at an early age, she attended Rust College for a year or two and then plowed herself back into the masses, teaching for a spell and then branching out into journalism. After she was driven from the South by whites who resented her antilynching editorials, she settled in Chicago and continued the campaign, publishing in 1895 the *Red Record*, the first statistical record of lynching. The story of her tireless and unrelenting struggle against lynching, of her lecture tours in England and her protests to the White House, is by no means atypical. What she did on the national and international scene was repeated on the local level by thousands of young blacks who grew, like pine trees, on the rocks of the Jim Crow system.

From this great harvest, from the social yield of the church, lodge and college, came social energies that produced two major structural shifts in Black America. The first was the development of a self-conscious bourgeoisie. There were, as we have seen, black merchants and entrepreneurs in the seventeenth and eighteenth centuries. But in the postwar period, as a direct result of the seeds sown in churches, colleges and lodges, the black bourgeoisie increased in size and became a self-conscious stratum. There were, according to the *Negro Yearbook* (1914–1915), two thousand black-owned businesses at the end of the Civil War. By 1903 the number had increased to twenty-five thousand. Among these businesses were the first black banks:

Capital Savings Bank, which opened in Washington, D. C., in
October, 1888, and the Savings Bank of the Grand Fountain
United Order of True Reformers, which was chartered in March,
1888, and opened in Richmond in April, 1889. There was a direct
and reciprocal relationship between these institutions and the
churches and lodges. The True Reformers Bank, for instance,
was an organ of the United Order of True Reformers, which was
founded in 1881 by a former slave, the Reverend William Washington Browne. In the same state, the Independent Order of
St. Luke, under the leadership of a dynamic black woman, Maggie L. Walker, operated a bank, a printing plant, an office building and other business enterprises.

The same forces and figures—ministers, lodge leaders,
teachers and merchants—were the plowmen of the first major
insurance companies. John Merrick, a barber and a former agent
of the True Reformers, was the organizing force in the founding
of North Carolina Mutual in 1898. Another barber, Alonzo F.
Herndon, created the foundations of Atlanta Life Insurance
Company in 1905 by buying two financially pressed church
societies.

The energies flowing through these figures and forces fused
in 1898 at the fourth annual Atlanta University Conference on
"The Negro in Business." In his keynote address John Hope, the
future president of Morehouse College, said the salvation of
Black America depended, to a great extent, on the development
of a business class. "We must," he said, "take in some, if not all,
of the wages, turn it into capital, hold it, increase it," adding: "I
do not believe that the ultimate contribution of the Negro to the
world will be his development of natural forces. It is to be more
than that. There is in him emotional, spiritual elements that
presage gifts from the Negro more ennobling and enduring than
factories and railroads and banks. But without these factories,
railroads and banks, he cannot accomplish his highest aim." The
conferees apparently agreed, for they passed resolutions urging
blacks "to enter into business life in increasing numbers." As for
tactics, the assembled teachers, workers and merchants said:
"The most advisable work for the immediate future would seem
to be: a) Continued agitation in churches, schools and newspapers, and by all other avenues, of the necessity of business
careers for young people. b) Increased effort to encourage saving

and habits of thrift among the young that we may have more capital at our disposal. c) The organization in every town and hamlet where colored people dwell, of Negro Business Men's Leagues, and the gradual federation from these of state and national organizations." Working from this script, and building on this foundation, Booker T. Washington organized the National Business League. At the organizational meeting in Boston, in August, 1900, Washington was elected president and a national program of education and organization was adopted.

The second major shift, flowing with and out of these events and personalities, was the formation of a self-conscious intelligentsia. The first major organizational step on this road occurred in March, 1897, with the founding of the American Negro Academy by a group of ministers and professors, including F. J. Grimké, Kelly Miller, and W. E. B. Du Bois. The first president of the organization was Alexander Crummell, the aging abolitionist theoretician, who articulated, in his keynote address, the theory of "the talented tenth," which was later taken up and embellished by Du Bois. The academy meeting, Crummell told the delegates, was "unlike any other which has ever taken place in the history of the Negro, on the American Continent. There have been . . . numerous conventions of men of our race. There have been religious assemblies, political conferences, suffrage meetings, educational conventions. But *our* meeting is for a purpose which, while inclusive in some respects of these various concerns, is for an object more distinct and positive than any of them." What was this special purpose? The purpose, he answered, was "the civilization of the Negro race in the United States, by the scientific processes of literature, art, and philosophy, through the agency of the cultured men of this same Negro race."

Du Bois echoed these observations in a speech that stressed the unique mission of black Americans:

"We are Americans, not only by birth and by citizenship, but by our political ideals, our language, our religion. Farther than that, our Americanism does not go. At that point, we are Negroes, members of a vast historic race that from the very dawn of creation has slept, but half awakening in the dark forests of its African fatherland. We are the first fruits of this new nation, the harbinger of that black tomorrow which is yet destined to soften the whiteness of the Teutonic today."

Even as Du Bois spoke, there was widening recognition of the "first fruits" of the new synthesis. One sign was the emergence of the first major black poet, Paul Laurence Dunbar, who published his first volume, *Oak and Ivory*, in 1893. Another was the critical success of the first major black novelist, Charles Chesnutt, who published four books, including *The Conjure Woman*, and *The Marrow of Tradition*, between 1899 and 1905. Further evidence of the rising level of group consciousness was the publication in 1883 of the first major work on black history, George Washington Williams's *History of the Negro Race in America from 1619 to 1880*.

Important as these contributions were, they were dwarfed in significance by public recognition of two prodigious contributions by the black masses. In 1870s and 1880s well-mannered and well-scrubbed young men and women went out from Fisk University and sang the old spirituals and the world said that at long last America had created a new thing.

> *Go tell it on the mountain,*
> *Over the hills and everywhere;*
> *Go tell it on the mountain,*
> *That Jesus Christ is born.*

In the same years, but in different places and in different tones, grown men and women strummed guitars on the levees and in mean-looking bars or relieved their despair with cries and hollers in the cotton fields and on the chain gangs.

> *If I'd a had my weight in lime,*
> *I'd a whipped that captain*
> *Till he went stone blind.*

The music went back to the slave cabins and to the polyrhythmic complexity of Africa. It was the same music, and yet, somehow, it was different, a complex fusing of African, European and American elements. It was made up of spirituals and work songs, of devil songs and shouts and stomps, of slow drags, marches, funeral dirges and hymns. It was sad and triumphant, ironic and mocking. It was a new thing, made in America by downtrodden and despised blacks. By the turn of the century Buddy Bolden, the first great shouter, was making the new notes in New Orleans, and W. C. Handy, son and grandson of Methodist ministers, was shaping the new sound with Maharas's Col-

ored Minstrels. In 1900 a boy named Louis Armstrong was born
and he went out into the world and played the music called jazz.
In 1900 or thereabouts a girl named Bessie Smith was born and
she went out into the world and sang the music called the blues.

> *I woke up this mornin', can't even get out of my door,*
> *I woke up this mornin', can't even get out of my door.*
> *That's enough trouble to make a poor girl wonder*
> *   where she wants to go.*

The rhymes and rhythms of the blues-spirituals, the visions
and auguries of the singers and poets and preachers, the shoots
and growths of the academies and colleges and lodges and
churches: these seeds rooted and grew beneath the great white
snow, producing a multifaceted community with different orien-
tations and tendencies. By singular circumstance, representatives of these tendencies converged on Chicago in the last year of
the century for two major conventions, called to assess the damage and chart the future. A contemporary news report said the
conventions were the result of "a wave of intense feeling which
has recently stirred American Negroes." The wave, the newspaper said, was a direct result of "continued lynchings and disturbances, progressive disenfranchisement, the treatment of
Negro soldiers and the hostile attitudes of trade unions."

W. E. B. Du Bois, a brilliant young college professor who would
soon be better known, sent a report on the conventions to the
New York *Independent*. He was impressed by the "air of good-
breeding" surrounding the third biennial session of the National
Association of Colored Women, composed, he said, of women
who were "rather above the average of their race." Among the
striking personalities in attendance were the president, Mary
Church Terrell, "a tall, handsome woman," who was principal of
the Washington Colored High School; and Josephine S. Yates of
Kansas City, who was "perhaps the finest specimen of Negro
womanhood present . . . a dark-brown matron, with a quiet air of
dignity and earnestness." This was a working convention, and the
women listened to a number of papers, including one by Mrs.
Yates on "An Equal Moral Standard for Men and Women," and
another by Miss J. E. Holmes of Atlanta on "The Convict Lease
System."

On the day the National Association of Colored Women adjourned—Thursday, August 17, 1899—the National Afro-Ameri-

can Council convened. This was, Du Bois wrote, "a far different body from the Association; its members were mostly male, its scope and aims far wider, and in its attendance, it was more faithfully representative of the rank and file of the American Negroes." The leading figures in the convention were the president, AME Zion Bishop Alexander Walters, "tall and genial"; AME Bishop Henry McNeal Turner, and secretary Ida B. Wells-Barnett, "who began the anti-lynching crusade."

As might have been expected, this gathering was far from homogenous. "The opposing forces" Du Bois noted, "were easily distinguished; those who desired radical action in regard to lynch law, those who desired to defend the Republican Administration from attack, those who favor some schemes of migration, and those who desired above all to strengthen national organization." In the end the delegates criticized the president and Congress for their inaction in the face of continued lynchings, urged blacks to become artisans and businessmen, and declared "it to be our unalterable purpose to strive by all proper and manly means to vindicate the rights and perform our duties right here in the land of our birth."

With that resolve, Black America, embattled and besieged, crossed the fatal threshold of the twentieth century. At that juncture nine out of every ten blacks lived in the South. Most of them lived at the subsistence level, but internal progress was evident everywhere and was steadily touching the lives of more people. In spite of the fetters imposed by the Jim Crow system, in spite of theft and "grandfather clauses," in spite of lynchings and chain gangs and peonage, in spite of everything, there had been a significant rise in literacy. In 1865, at the end of slavery, about one in every twenty blacks could read and write. In 1900 about six out of every ten blacks ten years of age and older could read and write.

By 1900 black Americans had more than $500,000 invested in funeral homes. There were four black-owned banks and sixty-four drugstores. The professional class had grown to more than 47,000. There were 21,267 teachers, 15,528 ministers, 1,734 doctors, 212 dentists, 310 journalists, 728 lawyers, 2,000 actors and showmen, 236 artists, 247 photographers and 1 black congressman.

George H. White, the last black congressman of the post-Reconstruction era, was a symbol of the shifting fortunes of the four million freedmen, who had multiplied to eight million by 1900. By 1901 almost all of the blacks in Southern legislatures and city councils had been driven from power. Now in 1901 White himself was at the turning of the road. He had been elected to Congress from North Carolina in 1897 and had been reelected in 1899. But it was clear by the middle of his second term that he would not be reelected again. And so when he rose in Congress at the end of the 1901 session, men shifted in their seats to get a better look at him. For better or worse, they would not be seeing his likes again soon.

Making the most of this last opportunity, White reviewed the whole dreary story—the story of the rise of blacks to power political, the undermining of Reconstruction, the gutting of the Fourteenth Amendment and the birth of Jim Crow. Now, he said, the circle had come full cycle, and it was time for goodbyes.

"This, Mr, Chairman, is perhaps the Negroes' temporary farewell to the American Congress; but let me say, Phoenix-like, he will rise up some day and come again. These parting words are in behalf of an outraged, heartbroken, bruised and bleeding, but God-fearing people, faithful, industrious, loyal, rising people—full of potential force."

> *Weel a-bout and turn a-bout*
> *and do just so.*
> *Every time I weel a-about*
> *I jump Jim Crow.*

10

Red, White and Black:
Race and Sex

*In race relations, solicitude about purity of blood
has been a means, not an end. "Pure blood" has
value only when in preserving it a calculable social
advantage can be maintained....*

*Therefore, it is not intermarriage, per se, which is
determining, but rather the cultural advantage
which restriction secures to the white group. Protecting the "honor and sanctity of white womanhood" constitutes a most convincing war cry and an
excellent covering for the basic purpose that colored
people must never be given the opportunity to become the cultural peers of whites.*

OLIVER CROMWELL COX

SIN. Sex. Race.
The three words took deep roots, intertwined and became one in the Puritan
psyche. In the famous sermon delivered at Whitechapel in 1609
for Virginia-bound planters and adventurers, the minister fused
the words in a stern admonition against amalgamation. From

Genesis, he summoned the figure of Abraham, who left his country and his father's house and migrated to a land God had prepared for his seed.

"Abrams posteritie," the preacher said, mixing his races and his metaphors, "[must] keepe to themselves. They may not marry nor give in marriage to the heathen, that are uncircumcised. . . . The breaking of this rule, may breake the necke of all good successe of this voyage, whereas by keeping the feare of God, the planters in shorte time, by the blessing of God, may grow into a nation formidable to all the enemies of Christ."

It was easier said than done. From the beginning, English colonists, following Abraham's example, married and mated with blacks and Indians.* Males and females broke the Whitechapel rule. White women showed such a preference for black men that planters organized a century-long campaign of terror and intimidation. Proscription began early. In 1630, a bare twenty-one years after the Whitechapel sermon, one Hugh Davis was "soundly whipped before an assemblage of Negroes and others for abusing himself to the dishonor of God and the shame of Christians by defiling his body in lying with a Negro." Forty years later colonial males were whipping white women at the post and selling them into slavery to keep them from black males.

There were many reasons for the broad tolerance of the first white Americans. The first, unbelievable as it may seem now, is that the pioneer white women—and the pioneer white men—did not *know* they were white. There was no conception then—and no name—for whiteness.** There was, secondly, no organized system of racism to define and focus the fears and anxieties of whites. Third, and most important, most of the white colonists were indentured servants, who were subjected to the same indignities as black servants and slaves and were held in equal contempt. It is no wonder, then, in this strange climate of equality of

---

*The material in this chapter on amalgamation during the slavery period is based largely on James Hugo Johnston's doctoral dissertation at the University of Chicago, "Race Relations in Virginia and Miscegenation in the South, 1776–1860," Carter G. Woodson's article, "The Beginnings of the Miscegenation of the Whites and Blacks" in the *Journal of Negro History*, and A. W. Calhoun's study, *A Social History of the American Family*.

**See pages 39–40.

oppression, that a strong bond of sympathy developed between black and white indentured servants, who formed the bulk of the population of the first colonies. Black and white servants worked together in the fields, lived in the same huts, and fraternized after hours. "Brought together," as one white historian put it delicately," in intimate and close relationship," black and white servants mated and married. The result was the inevitable result, as eyewitness Peter Fontaine pointed out, saying that colonial Virginia "swarmed" with mulatto children.

This was not, as some historians would have us believe, the results of the casual exploitation of black women. For, as James Hugo Johnston has shown in his excellent study, "Race Relations in Virginia and Miscegenation in the South," the "larger part of such race mixture" was due to the union of black males and white females. Johnston's study and contemporary documents, including court records, newspaper stories and the reports of eyewitnesses, provide most conclusive proof that the white women of this period were free of that "natural race prejudice" attributed to them by historians. Thus, to take only one example, the Chester County, Pennsylvania, court cited "a Negro man . . . and a white woman for having a baster childe. . . . The Negro said she intised him and promised him to marry him; she being examined, confest the same. . . . The court ordered that she shall receive twenty-one lashes on her beare backe . . . and the court ordered the Negroe man never to meddle with any white woman more uppon paine of his life."

This is one example among many, and it illustrates an important tendency which has caused no end of trouble for latter-day white historians. Philip A. Bruce, for instance, as we noted in chapter 2, said that "the class of white women who were required to work in the fields belonged to the lowest rank in point of character; not having been born in Virginia and not having thus acquired from birth a repugnance to association with Africans upon a footing of social equality, they yielded to the temptations of the situations in which they were placed." A contemporary witness, Edward Long, saw things the same way, observing that "the lower class of woman in *England*, are remarkably fond of the blacks, for reasons too brutal to mention."

Whatever the reasons, the practice—contrary to the testimony of Bruce and Long—was not confined to the "lowest rank in point of character." One need only read the will of John Fenwick, the Lord Proprietor of New Jersey, to understand that women of all classes were involved:

"Item, I do except against Elizabeth Adams of having any ye leaste part of my estate, unless the Lord open her eyes to see her abominable transgression against him, me her good father, by giving her true repentance, and forsaking ye Black ye hath been ye ruin of her; and becoming penetent of her sins; upon ye condition only I do will and require my executors to settle five hundred acres of land upon her." The Lord apparently did not open the eyes of Elizabeth Adams, whose granddaughter was one of the founders of a settlement known as Gouldtown, where blacks intermarried with whites and accumulated considerable property.

Some artistocrats, as this example indicates, opposed the free intercourse between black males and white females, but they were not supported by an organized system of racism, and their actions had little or no effect. There were, in fact, other aristocrats who encouraged mingling or looked the other way. Johnston said that in colonies where the numbers of servants and slaves "were comparatively few and when the master's only interest in his indentured servant was in the profits of his labor, many masters must have been little concerned to prevent the intermixture of the two races. Many instances of this lack of interest in race relations could, no doubt, be discovered throughout the entire Colonial period." Thomas Branagan found many instances in Philadelphia as late as the eighteenth century. "Many respectable citizens," he wrote, "who are reduced in temporalities; on their decease their poor orphans are bound out in gentlemen's homes, where the maid servants are generally white, the servants are black, and the employers allow the blacks as many liberties as they think proper to take; and no distinction is made between the white girls and the black men."

As the economic interests of planters changed, their concern and color consciousness changed. With the introduction of black slavery in the last quarter of the seventeenth century, it became a matter of public policy to use every available means to create an unbridgeable chasm between blacks and whites. The central point of this policy was the colonial white woman, who became the primary instrument for organizing the color perceptions of whites and for extending the economic exploitation of blacks. Defending her honor and purity now became a collective imperative. Through her, sex became politics, and bodies became counters in a surrealistic game. This had little or nothing to do with the white woman, who was a mask for a deeper purpose, which was the strengthening of slavery and the permanent subordination of blacks. The problem—from the standpoint of the colonial ruling class—was that neither the white woman nor the white man had been prepared for the roles required by the new script. To teach them their new roles, the colonial ruling class organized a systematic campaign against mixing, which was perceived as a threat not only to Puritan morality but also to Puritan economics. "The increasing number of mulattoes, through intermarriage and illicit relationships," Dr. Lorenzo J. Greene wrote, "soon caused alarm among Puritan advocates of racial purity and white domination. Sensing a deterioration of slavery, if the barriers between master and slaves were dissolved in the equalitarian crucible of sexual intimacy, they sought to stop racial crossing by statute."

Maryland led the way in 1664 with the first antiamalgamation statute. It was an astonishing document, aimed at white women who had resisted every effort to innoculate them with the virus of racial pride. The blunt preamble clearly stated the reasons which drove white men to the extremity of enslaving white women:

> And forasmuch as divers freeborn *English* women, forgetful of their free condition, and to the disgrace of our nation, do intermarry with Negro slaves, by which also divers suits may arise, touching the issue of such women, and a great damage doth befall the master of such Negroes, for preservation whereof for deterring such free-born women from such shameful matches, *be it enacted*: That whatsoever free-born woman shall intermarry with any slave, from and after the last day of the present assembly, shall serve the master of such slave during the life of her husband; and that all the issue of such free-born women, so married, shall be slaves as their fathers were.

Neither hard words nor the threat of slavery deterred the divers freeborn English women. Some of them chose love *and* lifetime slavery; others were reduced to lifetime slavery by planters who forced them to marry black men in order to reap the benefits accruing from the extended service of the mothers and the perpetual slavery of their children. A celebrated case revolved around Irish Nell, an indentured servant who was brought to Maryland by Lord Baltimore. When Baltimore returned to England, he sold Irish Nell to a planter, who forced or encouraged her to marry a black man named Butler. Shocked by the practice of prostituting white women for economic purposes, Lord Baltimore used his influence to get the law repealed. The preamble to the new act of 1681 read:

> Forasmuch as divers free-born *English*, or white women, sometimes by the instigation, procurement or connivance of their masters, mistresses, or dames, and always to the satisfaction of their lascivious and lustful desires, and to the disgrace not only of the *English*, but also of many other Christian nations, do intermarry with Negroes and slaves, by which means, divers inconveniences, controversies, and suits may arise, touching the issue of children of such free-born women aforesaid; for the prevention whereof for the future, *Be it enacted:* That if the marriage of any woman-servant with any slave shall take place by the procurement or permission of the master, such woman and her issue shall be free.

The new law was about as effective as the old one—which is to say, it was not effective at all. E. I. McCormac, the authority on white servitude in Maryland, said: "Mingling of the races in Maryland continued during the eighteenth century, in spite of all laws against it. Preventing marriage of white servants with slaves only led to a greater social evil, which caused a reaction of public sentiment against the servant. Masters and society in general were burdened with the care of illegitimate mulatto children, and it became necessary to frame laws compelling the guilty parties to reimburse the masters for the maintenance of these unfortunate waifs." In 1715, 1717 and 1728, the Maryland Assembly enacted new laws designed to control and stop the rising tide of amalgamation in the colony.

This happened not only in Maryland but also in Virginia and other colonies, not only in the seventeenth century but also in the eighteenth century. Virginia restricted intermarriage in 1691 and was followed by Massachusetts (1705), North Carolina (1715), South Carolina (1717) and Delaware (1717). Although these laws differed in detail, they generally extended the time of white servants who married black men or gave birth to mulatto children. Free white men and women who married blacks were fined, jailed or reduced to servitude; free blacks who stepped across the color line were reduced to slavery or sold out of the colonies. Ministers and other persons who performed interracial marriages were required to pay fines of fifty pounds or so.

Private vigilante associations reinforced the edicts in some communities. The church and other institutions provided additional reinforcement. But nothing worked. Against the law in some communities, against public opinion in others, intermarriage and intermingling continued. There were even some public protests against the new dispensation. On May 11, 1699, "George Ivie and others" sent a petition to the Council of Virginia asking "for the repeal of the Act of the Assembly, Against English peoples marrying with Negroes, Indians or Mulattoes." Of equal or perhaps even more pointed political concern was the action of whites who simply defied the laws. Shortly after the enactment of Virginia's ban on intermarriage, Ann Wall was convicted of "keeping company with a Negro under pretense of marriage." The Elizabeth County court sold Ann Wall for five years and bound out her two mulatto children for thirty-one years. And "it is further ordered," the court said, "that if ye said Ann Wall after she is free from her said master doe at any time presume to come into this county she shall be banished to ye Island of Barbadoes."

Another woman, an indentured servant, was cited in Henrico County, Virginia:

> Henrico County June 1, 1692
> Information
> Maj'r Chamberlaynes woman servant Bridgett by name for bearing a base born child by a Negro.
> Presented to ye grand jury for this County of Hen'co May 16; 1692 & here recorded
>
> Tests: Hen. Randolph, Vo; Cur.

Ye grand jury was busy, too, in Pennsylvania where, as early as 1677, a white servant was indicted for miscegenation in Sussex County. In an unsuccessful attempt to stop intermingling, Pennsylvania banned intermarriage in 1725. Forty-five years later, during the Revolutionary agitation, the state repealed the ban. Thereafter, mixed marriages became common in Pennsylvania. After a visit to Philadelphia in 1805, Thomas Branagan said he had never seen so much intermingling. "There are," he wrote, "many, very many blacks who . . . begin to feel themselves consequential . . . will not be satisfied unless they get white women for wives, and are likewise exceedingly impertinent to white people in low circumstances. . . . I solemnly swear, I have seen more white women married to, and deluded through the arts of seduction by Negroes in one year in Philadelphia, than for eight years I was visiting [West Indies and the Southern states]. . . . There are perhaps hundreds of white women thus fascinated by black men in this city, and there are thousands of black children by them at present."

There is additional evidence of racial mixing in divorce court records. A Westfield, Massachusetts, man won a divorce in 1750 on a complaint that his wife, Agnes, had borne a child for a black man named Primus. In 1751 the Massachusetts legislature dissolved the marriage of Lois Way, who had mothered a child by a slave named Boston. Another slave, also named Boston, won a divorce on a complaint that his wife, Hagar, "not having the fear of God before her eyes and being instigated by a white man has been guilty of the detestable sin of adultery and during the time of intermarriage was delivered of a mulatto bastard child begotten on her body."

To this one may add evidence from colonial newspapers, which were filled with notices of masters seeking black and white runaways. One such notice appeared in the *American Weekly Mercury* of August 11, 1720:

> Runaway in April last from Richard Tilgman, of Queen Anne County in Maryland, a mulatto slave, named Richard Molson, of middle stature, about forty years old and has had the small pox, he is in company with a white woman . . . who is supposed now goes for his wife.

Such notices were common in both Northern and Southern newspapers. Another one appeared in the *Pennsylvania Gazette* of June 1, 1746:

> Runaway from the subscriber the second of last month, at the town of Potomac, Frederick County, Maryland, a mulatto servant named Isaac Cromwell, runaway at the same time, an English servant woman, named Ann Greene.

A number of well-known blacks were products of unions between black men and English women. Lemuel Haynes, who was probably the first black to preach regularly to a white congregation, was the son of a white woman and an African. Haynes, a New Englander, later married a white women, Elizabeth Babbitt. Benjamin Banneker, the astronomer and mathematician, was the grandson of Molly Welsh, a colorful Englishwoman who came to Maryland as an indentured servant.

Not only indentured servants but also aristocrats, not only aristocrats but also aristocratic founding fathers crossed the color line. Benjamin Franklin, it is said, was quite open in his relationship with black women. Carter G. Woodson, a historian not given to exaggeration, said Franklin "seems to have made no secret of his associations with Negro women." Nor, if reliance can be placed on contemporary reports and the hard research of modern scholars, did Thomas Jefferson. It was widely said and believed in the slave period that Jefferson had slave mistresses and slave children. His favorite mistress, the reports said, was Sally Hemings. Light-skinned and attractive, Sally Hemings played an important role in several political campaigns. A favorite slave at Monticello, a mystery woman who was seldom seen and often whispered about, she was the focus of political jibes aimed at Jefferson. Thomas Moore and William Cullen Bryant wrote poems about her and several newspapers, including the *Richmond Examiner*, the *Richmond Recorder*, the *New York Evening Post*, and the *Boston Gazette*, speculated about her relationship with the author of the Declaration of Independence. "By the time he [Jefferson] turned the reins of government over to James Madison in 1809," Pearl M. Graham wrote, "Sally was the busy mother of several younglings who closely resembled Jefferson; poets were writing condemnatory verses; newspapers from Richmond to Boston were expressing disapproval; and in the taverns male voices were singing lustily, to the tune of Yankee Doodle, a popular ditty of the day." The song said:

> Of all the damsels on the green,
> On mountains or in valley,
> A lass so luscious ne'er was seen
> As Monticellian Sally.

Pearl M. Graham and other scholars, including W. Edward

Farrison and Fawn Brodie, subjected the rumors and reports to modern research methods. Farrison, a professor at North Carolina College, was impressed by "the only absolutely authoritative source of truth concerning the paternity of Sally Hemings' children—from Sally Hemings herself." From her, he said, "the quiet stream of family history has flowed on through four generations." In September, 1948, Professor Farrison interviewed three sisters "who were obviously far from being full-blooded Negroes, each of whom was more than sixty-five years of age, and who traced their lineage directly to Sally Hemings through her daughter Harriet, who was born in May, 1801, and whose father those sisters had been told was Thomas Jefferson."

From a study of contemporary and modern sources, Miss Graham proved, to her satisfaction anyway, that Sally Hemings bore Jefferson "at least four children, possibly six." The children, as listed by Jefferson under the name of Sally Hemings in his *Farm Book*, were:

> Hemings, Sally, 1773
> Beverly, 1798
> Harriet, May, 1801
> Madison, Jan, 1805
> Eston, May, 1808

Miss Graham also interviewed the great-granddaughters of Sally Hemings. "These ladies descent," she wrote, "is further substantiated by the Mendelian Law of Heredity. I have been shown a daguerreotype type of Mrs. Kenney—Harriet Hemings' daughter—which so closely resembles some of the portraits of Jefferson himself, painted in his middle years, that it could easily be taken for his own likeness, save for the fact that the daguerreotype process was unknown in his lifetime. All descriptions of Jefferson in his youth agree that his hair was of a sandy red color. Hair of this shade occasionally appears among the descendants of Harriet Hemings. Gertrude Harriet (Kenney) Watson was nicknamed by her mother "Jefferson hair Gertie because her own hair was of precisely this shade."

Jefferson was hardly atypical. Patrick Henry reportedly fathered a black son, Melancthon. According to persistent reports, Alexander Hamilton, who was born in the West Indies, had some "black blood." "If Hamilton was not a Negro," Professor

Maurice R. Davie of Yale University wrote, "he certainly brought two Negro sons into the world. One married a very light-colored wife; the other married into a white family and lived as white."

Kaleidoscopic and disconnected in character, these examples throw a new and revealing light on the racial geography of America. In this light we can better understand the sexual shift that occurred in the nineteenth century after white Americans had been conditioned by two centuries of racist ideas and racist practices. Before the institutionalization of the nineteenth-century system, the major link of the racial-sexual network was the white female. But with the rise of the plantation system and the institutionalization of racism, the focus shifted to the white planter and the black female slave. And it should be said at once —although we shall return to this point in greater detail—that *the gentlemen of the old South did not prefer blondes.* A. W. Calhoun, the authority on the American family, said their nursery training had something to do with it. In his view, the plantation mammy played a central role in the psychological process that led to a fixation on black women and the parallel process of compensatory glorification of white women. There is perhaps some truth in Calhoun's observation, but the problem is clearly at a deeper level. For as Jean-Paul Sartre and Frantz Fanon have shown, the mechanisms that make racists seek mates among their victims are functions not of nursery training but of sadistic impulses created by a system of oppression. Fundamentally, as Sartre said, there is "an aura of rape and massacre" in every sexual encounter between a racist and his victim; and it was this aura that gave "a special sexual signification" to the sustained sexual assault of planters and their allies.

Whether we look at this issue from the standpoint of blacks or whites, the morality of slavery was indefensible. The moral results of slavery, a planter told Frederic Bancroft, "in its most favorable aspects are unprintable." The printable part is revealing. In communities with a large slave population, stories were common, W. J. Cash said, which ran to the tune, "the image, my dear, the living image, of old Colonel Bascombe himself." Plantation amalgamation, as a rule, was the result of what Calhoun called "the master's right of rape." Although mutual attraction played a part in some relationships, force or the threat of force defined all of the relationships. Despite what some commentators say, every sexual contact between a slaveholder and a slave woman was a symbolic or *de facto* rape, for the simple and obvious reason that the *institution* of slavery and the power of slaveholders destroyed the possibility of free choice. Another and related problem here was the indefensible position of a whole class of women whose only weapons were sexual ones. What all this boils down to is that the position of the American slave woman was indefensible. The fact that rape was a real and ever-present possibility was only a metaphor of the extreme vulnerability of her position.

Given these conditions, it is hardly surprising that some slave women used the only weapons they had in veiled but direct struggles with slaveholders and slave mistresses. The court cases of the period indicate that some slave women won these one-sided and dangerous contests. In an 1828 divorce petition, a Virginia white woman complained that her husband "has deserted me, and is now in the city of Richmond or its vicinity with a colored woman in a state of open adultery." Another woman, the mother of four children, complained that her husband had eloped with a comely slave woman named Cynthia, "and to facilitate his purpose, he stole a horse from the said Robert Hoffman to carry the woman and her baggage." The husband was captured and sentenced to three years in jail for stealing the slave woman—he got an additional four years for stealing the horse. Many of these relationships ended in tragedy or heartbreak for the women and children involved. But some planters—a small minority—freed their mistresses and children and sent them to Ohio, Indiana and Pennsylvania. So many black children of white planters were sent to Ohio that black communities developed at Tawawa Springs and other locations.

There were also cases in which planters willed property to their mistresses and children. Such a case was that of Walter Robertson of New Bern, North Carolina, who told his executors that "it is my will that my bosom friend, Ann Rose, for her long and faithful services, be immediately after my death put in possession of all my lands, slaves, household furniture, plate, stocks of horses and cattle, and every kind of real and personal estate which may belong to me."

Attempts to provide for "bosom friends" caused no end of trouble. White relatives often contested the cases and charged that slave women "had the influence over him of a white woman and wife." Another charge was mental derangement. In at least one case, this charge backfired. A Kentucky court ruled in an 1831 case that:

> The fact that the deceased evinced an inclination to marry the slave, Grace, whom he liberated, is not a stronger evidence of insanity than the practice of rearing children by slaves without marriage; a practice but too common, as we all know, from the numbers of our mulatto population. However degrading such things are, and however repugnant to the institutions of society, and the moral law, they prove more against the taste than the intellect. *De gustibus non disputandum*. White men, who may wish to marry Negro women, or who carry on illicit intercourse with them, may, notwithstanding, possess such soundness of mind as to be capable in law, of making a valid will and testament.

Nearing death, some slaveowners, being of sound mind, feared for the future of their black children. A Virginian was "impelled with blushes and confusion to own and acknowledge the cause that brings him forward on this occasion." The cause was a fairly common one. "Your petitioner believes and acknowledges himself to be the father of the said mulatto boy by a woman at that time the property of himself, and as his parent he feels great solicitude for his future welfare and liberty."

In addition to these examples of relatively anonymous beneficiaries, the records also list cases of planters who made it possible for their black children to climb the heights. One such case was that of Robert Purvis, the brilliant black abolitionist. The son of a Charleston merchant and a free black woman, Purvis was sent to Amherst College. After graduation, he lived a life of leisure in Byberry, a Philadelphia suburb, on the legacy bequeathed to him by his father. So fair that he could pass for white, Purvis refused to abandon his mother's people and made an important contribution in the antislavery fight.

James Augustine Healy, the first black Roman Catholic priest in America, and the first black American to become a Catholic bishop, also received aid and encouragement from a white father.

Bishop James A. Healy,
who was the first black American
to become a Roman
Catholic bishop, was the
son of an Irish planter and
a slave. He was
named bishop of Portland,
Maine, in 1875.

James P. Beckwourth, noted
trapper, was one of several
blacks who rose to commanding
positions in Indian tribes.
Beckwourth became
a chief of the Crows.

Born in Georgia in 1830 to an Irish planter and a slave, Healy was carried north in 1837 and enrolled in a Quaker school in Flushing, Long Island. He graduated from Holy Cross College in 1849 and was ordained a priest in 1854 at Notre Dame Cathedral in Paris. Returning to America, Healy worked his way up the hierarchy and was named bishop of Portland, Maine, in February, 1875. The bishop's father, Michael Morris Healy, also aided other members of his slave family. ("His trusty woman Elisa" bore him ten children.) He sent one of the girls and two additional sons to the Long Island school. One of the sons, Patrick Francis Healy, became a Jesuit priest and served as president of Georgetown University from 1873 to 1882. Monsignor Healy is usually called the "second founder" of Georgetown.

Not all planters were as solicitous as Michael Healy.

Frederick Douglass and Booker T. Washington received no help from their white fathers; nor did thousands of other blacks. Many slavemasters sent their children to the cotton fields with other slaves. Worse still was the aura of incest surrounding some relationships between black sisters, white brothers and white fathers. Some planters even sold their own flesh and blood.

Needless to say, some of the best-known men of the South were involved in plantation amalgamation. It was a saying: "The best blood of the South runs in the veins of the slaves." To the names of Jefferson and Henry, we can add the name of Daniel Boone, who was, according to William Wells Brown, the father of his mother. Brown said his father was a man "connected with some of the first families of Kentucky." Another *de facto* integrationist in high place was Colonel Richard Johnson, the Kentuckian who became the ninth vice-president of the United States. Johnson's black mistress was Julia Chinn. The couple had two daughters and Johnson married them off with style—to white men.

Politicians, planters, overseers, bachelors, merchants and ministers participated in what Calhoun called "the wholesale profligacy of the Old South." As an illustration, we might consider the widespread demand for "fancy girls" (prospective concubines and prostitutes), who were sold openly in the major markets of the internal slave trade, especially in New Orleans and Frankfurt, Kentucky. The major buyers in these markets were sports, debauchees, saloonkeepers, wealthy bachelors and planters. Still more unmistakable evidence of the same current was the organized system of concubinage which flourished in cities like New Orleans and Charleston. One could see this principle at work in the *placer* system of New Orleans. In the antebellum period young New Orleans bachelors could shop for *placees*, stunningly attractive black women, well educated and trained in the art of casual domesticity, at the Quadroon Balls, held at the Salle d'Orleans, which later became a convent for black nuns.

How did Southern white women respond to all this?

Many, according to diaries and other documents of the time, seem to have considered their husbands exceptions to the rule. "Any lady," Frances Kemble wrote, "is ready to tell you who is the father of all the mulatto children in everybody's household but her own. These, she seems to think, drop from the clouds. My disgust sometimes is boiling over."

The most startling and significant feature of the sexual dynamics of the Old South was the active involvement of single and married white women. The human passions "which motivated the man," J. H. Johnston wrote, "were also the passions of the women of the South," adding: "There is evidence that the birth of a mulatto to a white woman was not an uncommon affair." Writing later, historian Kenneth Stampp said white women were less involved in antebellum amalgamation than white men but their role "was never negligible." There is an enormous amount of empirical evidence on this point in Southern divorce records. In one petition a Virginia husband said that "about the close of the year 1803, his prospects ... were darkened by an occurrence which he feels himself constrained with infinite regret to recount. His said wife being pregnant was at the time delivered of a child, which was obviously the issue of an illicit intercourse with a black man." Another husband said that "in the month of March, 1801, he intermarried with a certain Elizabeth---, a woman descended from honest and industrious parents, and of unspotted character so far as your petitioner heard, or had any reason to believe. Your petitioner lived with the said Elizabeth, with all the affection and tenderness that could possibly exist between husband and wife, for about four months, when to the great astonishment and inexpressible mortification of your petitioner, the said Elizabeth was delivered of a mulatto child, and is now so bold as to say that it was begotten by a Negro man slave in the neighborhood."

In 1825 the Virginia slave patrol found the wife of a prominent citizen in "one of John Richardson's negro houses, in November last after midnight—she got away." A witness in this case testified that the slave and the planter's wife "lived together, almost as man and wife."

In a North Carolina case, the petition alleged that the "husband and wife had been married and lived together several years, until about three or four months before the husband's death; . . . A witness deposed, that, on the day of separation . . . as he was going to the house, he met the plaintiff coming away in tears. . . . the husband told him, that he had understood that his wife was pregnant by a Negro man, and he had driven the strumpet off, and she should never live with him again. . . . A few months after the separation, he filed a bill against her for a divorce for cause of adultery with a certain Negro . . . by whom she became pregnant of a child. . . . When the copy of the bill was served, it was read to her by the witness, who asked her if it was so, and she held up the child and said, it would show for itself; . . . the witness . . . thought it was a Negro child, and asked her if it were not; and she replied, that she was not the first white woman that Negro had taken in—that, when he first came about her she hated him, but that, after a while, she loved him better than anybody in the world, and she thought he must have given her something."

Unmarried women, some of them poor, some of them rich, were also implicated in the amalgamation of the period. After a detailed analysis of the cases of alleged rape in Virginia between 1789 and 1833, J. H. Johnston concluded that "the student who reads the evidence as submitted to the governor is astonished at the number of cases in which citizens of the communities in which these events transpired testify for the Negro and against the white woman and declare that the case is not a matter of rape, for the woman encouraged and consented to the act of the Negro." In twenty-seven of the sixty cases, judges recommended mercy or citizens sent petitions in favor of the black defendants.

There is some evidence that white women continued to marry blacks during the slave period. In one county, Nansemond, Virginia, there were, according to census data, the following interracial couples in 1830:

> Jacob of Rega, and white wife
> Syphe of Matthews, and white wife
> Jacob Branch, and white wife
> Ely of Copeland, and white wife
> Tom of Copeland, and white wife
> Will of Butler, and white wife
> Davy of Sawyer, and white wife
> Stephen of Newby, and white wife
> Amarian Reed, and white wife

Throughout the slave period, mulattoes were born to black and white mothers in the North. Philadelphia, according to contemporary reports, was a major center of amalgamation. So were New York and other urban centers which received large numbers of poor immigrants from Europe. In neighborhoods like the notorious Five Points of New York City, immigrants and blacks fought each other for bread and living space; but they also mated and married. In the North, as in the South, there was a tendency to wink at backdoor relationships (between black women and white men) and to disparage legal associations. William G. Allen, a black professor at Central College in McGrawsville, New York, kicked up a national storm when he married a white student. In 1853 Allen and his bride fled to England—one step ahead of an enraged posse.

Such, then, was the antebellum system which left a multicolored black and white population—in the North and South—and a legacy of ill will and fear. It is impossible to understand that system if we don't understand first that it was a totalitarian system which imposed itself on its victims. It is also important to remember that most antebellum blacks and whites were not direct participants in the system. Even so, the system and the ideas that crystallized around the system had a sharp impact on all blacks and whites. There is not the slightest question, for instance, that the acts of some white males and the fantasies of others cast a long shadow over white male–white female relationships. Nor can it be doubted that the white female paid an enormous price for her sexual-political role as the fulcrum of the American system of racism.

It is to be observed, too, that the system had repercussions of the gravest sort in Black America, where practically all blacks resented the one-way prerogatives of white males. On occasions, this bitterness flared into open and rather hopeless violence. Nothing shows this more clearly than the case of a Mississippi slave who murdered his overseer in 1859. The slave "introduced as a witness in his own behalf [his wife] who stated that . . . the overseer, had forced her, the witness to submit to sexual intercourse with him; and that she had communicated that fact to the prisoner before the killing took place." The court ruled that "adultery with a slave wife is no defense to a charge of murder."

Standing outside the pale of justice, slaves brought pressure to bear to maintain their own standards. The violation of these standards exposed slave mistresses to the scorn of their peers, who oftentimes shunned them and their children. Candis Goodwin, the daughter of a slave woman and an overseer, recalled that "the children used to laugh at me an' yell, 'Who's yo' pappy? Who's yo pappy?' But my mamma told me how to answer them children. I jus' yell right back at 'em: 'Turkey buzzard laid me, an' the sun hatch me.' " Some black women were marked for life by these relationships. Many years later, various slave women, as Herbert Gutman detailed, could remember random assaults and attacks by overseers and slaveowners. Almost invariably they used barbed words to describe these encounters, words like *mean* and *take away my shame*. One victim, recalled many years later by Ben Horry, was a woman named Susan, a "house woman [who] had three white children, Not WANT 'em HAB 'em. Woman overpower!"

Woman over-power.

In these words we have the whole history and infamy of the sexual exploitation of slavery.

In a system that uses sex to sanctify power, it is impossible to free man or woman or sex without the exercise of power. This became clear in the Reconstruction period when, for a short time, blacks operated at the summit of political power, freeing energies and relationships in the whole society. The first fruit of the new legal order was a deepening of the relationships between black men and black women, who legalized marriage ties at mass registrations and ceremonies. Interestingly enough, most of the regis-

trants—68 per cent of the males and 58 per cent of the females at
three Mississippi centers—identified themselves and their parents as black. A Union officer in Mississippi found this significant, saying that the registrants seemed to be unwilling "to own
any . . . mixture of blood which is not obvious."

In the Reconstruction period, as in the slave period, the
overwhelming majority of blacks continued to marry other
blacks. But with the change in power relationships, there was a
corresponding change in black-white relationships. Nothing
dramatizes this more forcefully than the passage of laws legalizing interracial marriages. Mississippi dropped its ban against
intermarriages in 1870 and was followed by Louisiana (1870),
South Carolina (1872) and Arkansas (1874). This created a new
situation, and various citizens—black and white—took advantage of it, to the dismay of old slaveholders who were scandalized
by the legalization of their secret obsessions and practices.
Especially galling to diehard Southerners was the decided preference some white men of power showed for black women. Governor Franklin J. Moses Jr., the South Carolina-born Republican, was not the only high-ranking official to give public notice of
a preference for blacks over blondes. White papers repeatedly
denounced "Yankees" for walking the streets, arm in arm, with
black women. There were even louder outcries when politicians
and ordinary citizens legalized their preferences.

A. T. Morgan, a planter from Ohio, summed up the new spirit
of the age when he blurted out to his brother: "Look me in the eye,
ole polecat, I am anxious to see how you take it—there, steady
now! . . . God willing, I am going to marry a 'nigger' schoolmarm."

God was willing—and the Reconstruction laws of Mississippi—and Morgan, a state senator who later became sheriff of
Yazoo County, married Carrie Victoria Highgate on August 3,
1870. The bride and groom began housekeeping in Yazoo City
after a hectic wedding trip which included ejection from a bus in
Louisville, Kentucky, and the publication of vulgar stories in
Northern newspapers. Another prominent Mississippian who
took advantage of the liberal laws of the age was Haskins Smith, a
"saddle-colored" member of the legislature who married a young
white woman named Ellen from Port Gibson, Mississippi. How
did Port Gibson take it? There was some grumbling, a white

contemporary said, "but I think the most sensible people in the community concurred in the idea, that if she wanted to marry him it was her business."

The marriage boomlet was not confined to politicians. An Irish contractor in Claiborne County, Mississippi, made the following notation in his diary:

> *Confirmation at Chadenel* I was discusted to see *Joe O Brian* as god father for Boys, he who has a lot of *Niger Bastards* & is now married to a ½ Niger wife What a scandale to me.

"Discusted," many were. But some were in love. After a survey of the evidence, historian A. A. Taylor said that "poor white persons, feeling that the new order was permanent, braved the barriers of caste prejudice and married blacks." He added: "The recognition of the civil rights of the Negroes and their increasing prestige in the economic and political spheres . . . counteracted the proscription of those who intermarried. Poor white women sometimes chose Negro husbands because these men of color were more wealthy and influential than the available mates of their own race."

One could see examples of this all over the reconstructed South. In April, 1969, Bet Hancock, white, married Jim Gour in Timmonsville, South Carolina. A week later C. P. Woods, a white man from Beaufort, married Susan Ulmer. Two months later the *Charleston News* ran, with disapproval, a social item on Paul Harl, a black man who married Josey Brennan in Fairfield County.

Some contemporary observers said that the typical interracial marriage was of a white man and a black woman. But the evidence on that point is not conclusive. The *New York Herald* reported after a North Carolina survey that "the rich white says that his poorer brother has lost all self-respect, that his women take up with Negroes (which is a sadly frequent fact, at least out here)." Sad or not, it was a frequent fact also in South Carolina. In 1879, when Democrats renewed the ban against intermarriage, one of the strongest arguments advanced was that many white women were living in marriage with black men—twenty-five or thirty, the York County representative said, in his township alone. This, in fact, was one of the major reasons for the founding of the Ku Klux Klan and other paramilitary organizations. Explaining the events that led to the founding of the Klan in his state, a North Carolina conservative told a congressional investigating committee: "I do think that the common white people of the country are at times very much enraged against the Negro population. They think that this universal political and civil equality will finally bring about social equality; there are already instances in the county of Cleveland in which poor white girls are having Negro children."

This gave satisfaction to a number of parties, foremost among whom was Bishop Gilbert Haven, a white Methodist leader and a passionate advocate of black-white amalgamation. After a visit to Charleston in 1873, he told Northerners that he had seen the future and that it worked. "If you want to see the coming race in all its virile perfection," he wrote in a public letter, "come to this city. Here is amalgamation made perfect." The bishop was especially impressed by the different hues and tints. "What exquisite tints of delicate brown; what handsome features; what beautiful eyes, what graceful forms. No boorish Hanoverian blood here, but the best Plantagenet . . . It is an improved breed—the best the country has today. It will be so reckoned in the boudoirs of Newport and the court of Washington ere many years."

Bishop Haven was a poor prophet. For when the Democrats returned to power, they immediately enacted laws banning interracial marriages. Mississippi, in a strange choice of language, declared such marriages "incestuous and void." There was a surprising amount of opposition when an intermarriage ban was proposed in the South Carolina legislature in 1879. One white representative said "it was preferable that our people should enter the marriage relation rather than live in concupiscence." The legislature did not agree; the bill was enacted. Sixteen years later, when the intermarriage ban was written into the state constitution, Robert Smalls, black representative from Beaufort, made a counterproposal, introducing an amendment which provided that any white guilty of cohabiting with a black would be barred from public office and that the children of such unions would bear the name of their father and inherit property the same as legitimate children. The amendment caused consternation in the assembly. A white representative found the spectacle enormously amusing. For the first time, he remarked, "The coons [sic] had the dog up a tree." The antiamalgamation provision—without Smalls's amendment—was finally adopted, but not until the legislature had foundered on the delicate question of definition. A legislative committee suggested that an African-American was anyone with one-eighth or more "Negro blood." Some legislators thought one-eighth was too much and suggested a drop or two.

This brought George Tillman to his feet. The record of debate contains the following statement:

> Mr. George Tillman stated, that he was very feeble, but that he felt compelled to say something on this subject. For one, he had felt ashamed when the delegate from Beaufort had clapped his hands, and declared that the coon had a dog up a tree. He was further mortified to see that the gentleman from Newberry . . . and the gentleman from Edgefield . . . goaded and taunted into putting into the constitution, that no person with any trace of Negro blood should intermarry with a white person, and that for such marriage the legislature should provide punishment even beyond that of bastardizing children and adulterizing marriage . . . Mr. Tillman said . . . if the law is made as it now stands, respectable [white] families in Aiken, Barnwell, Colleton, and Orangeburg will be denied the right to intermarry among people with whom they are now associated and identified. At least one hundred [white] families would be affected to his knowledge. They had sent good soldiers to the Confederate army, and are now landowners and taxpayers. He asserted as a scientific fact that there was not a full-blooded Caucasian on the floor of the convention.

Tillman put his finger on a sensitive spot. Passing—crossing the color line by light-skinned blacks—started in the colonial period and was institutionalized during the antebellum period. So many black people crossed over to the white race in that period that white people in Louisiana and other states are nervously sensitive about the subject today. "In Louisiana," Charles S. Mangum, Jr., says, "there has been so much infusion of Negro blood that it has been said that a marriage license would be refused only in cases where the admixture is evident from the appearance or other characteristics of the party making the application." Because of this infusion, courts oftentimes had to decide the delicate question of who was and who wasn't white. In some cases, the courts used professionals who claimed the ability to distinguish between light-skinned blacks and dark-skinned whites. Several cases in courts of almost every Southern state prove that some persons with one-fourth or less "Negro blood" were legally passed into the white race. A typical case, decided in South Carolina in 1843, was reported by Helen T. Catterall in *Judicial Cases Concerning American Slavery And The Negro:*

> Johnson v. Boon . . . Report of Judge O'Neall; tax execution . . . was about to be enforced . . . against the relators, as free mulattoes. They . . . obtained a prohibition nisi, on the ground [that they were] free white men, but were ordered to declare in prohibition. . . . Thomas and John, were in court, and submitted themselves to the inspection of the jury . . . sister . . . was shown . . . I should say, was a quadroon. The father . . . Benjamin Johnson, (a white man) proved that the relators were his children by Sally Johnson. She was the daughter of Lydia Tan, by . . . a Dutchman, . . . her second husband. Lydia Tan's mother was a white woman; her husband, Tan, was a colored man.

Judge O'Neall made his own inspection and reported:

> On inspection, I thought Thomas and John very passable white men. Thomas, particularly, had light or sandy hair, and a sunburnt complexion. . . . The relators . . . had always been regarded *as colored.* . . . They associated with white persons, but never without question. . . . Price proved that the relators *were colored.* . . . From the proof, it seemed in the section where the relators were raised, that little attention, in intercourse, was paid to the question whether the person *were or were not* colored.

In his charge, Judge O'Neall told the jury that

> Color . . . was sometimes a deceptive test, that it ought to be compared with all the circumstances . . . and if the jury were satisfied that the color, blood, and reception in society, would justify them in rating the relators as free white men, they had a right to do so.

What was the verdict of the jury?

> The jury *very properly* found the relators to be free white men.

With or without the help of juries, large numbers of blacks—estimates range from two to thirty thousand a year—have infiltrated the white race. The "white" descendants of these persons have held high positions in American life. In his pioneering sociological study, *The Philadelphia Negro*, W. E. B. Du Bois discovered several cases of "white" Negroes. "Between 1820 and 1860," he wrote, "many natural children were sent from the South and in a few cases their parents followed and were legally married here. Descendants of such children in many cases forsook the mother's race; one became principal of a city school, one a prominent sister in a Catholic church, one a bishop, and one or two officers in the Confederate Army." Other studies have indicated that several "white" bishops, legislators and other highly placed persons were, in part, the descendants of blacks. J. A. Rogers, a black historian who spent several decades studying *Sex and Race*, lists an impressive array of sources in support of his controversial contention that at least one president had a "Negro strain." When the president was asked about the charges, he reportedly replied, according to S. H. Adams's *The Incredible Era*, "How do I know . . . One of my ancestors might have jumped the fence."

Periodically, as in the Rhinelander case of the twenties and the Torregano case of the fifties, Americans are reminded of the large number of "white Negroes." Perhaps the definitive utterance on this subject was made in the thirties by the *Crisis*, which chided whites for a public uproar over a passing case. "Lt. William J. French," the magazine said, "of the United States Army, who committed suicide recently, made an enviable record in the Army. It is now discovered that he had several drops of Negro blood, which seems to disturb some people. We shudder to contemplate the disturbance if all the Negro blood in this country stood revealed."

A complicating factor in the crazy-quilt pattern of American amalgamation is the large-scale intermixture of black and Indian genes. American blacks, Melville J. Herskovits wrote, "have mingled with the American Indians on a scale hitherto unrealized." Johnston said, "The Indian has not disappeared from the land, but is now a part of the Negro population of the United States."

Black-Indian mixtures began in the colonial period when both groups were held as indentured servants and slaves. In the absence of legal prohibitions, squaws took black husbands and braves took black wives. In the decades that followed, whole Indian tribes, Gunnar Myrdal said, "became untraceably lost in the Negro population of the South."

From the colonial period to the end of slavery, Indian reservations in Virginia and other states were vast melting pots. Some tribes held black slaves with whom they intermarried; other tribes welcomed free blacks and fugitive slaves, who adopted breechcloths and moccasins, married Indians and went on the warpath against the white man. In several notable massacres, Indians killed every white and spared every black. J. H. Russell thinks it is extremely significant that the Indians killed no blacks in the Virginia Massacre of 1622. Much later, in Alabama, the Creeks spared blacks in the Fort Mims Massacre. "The Master of Breath," the Creeks said, "has ordered us not to kill any but white people and half-breeds." Such evidence as survives indicates that many Indians believed blacks lived in a primary relationship with the world of spirits and were therefore "good medicine." Peter Kalm, who traveled in America in the middle of the eighteenth century, said Indians called blacks *Manitto*, a word which "in their language signifies not only God but likewise the Devil."

By whatever name, blacks merged pivotally into the lives of American Indians, distinguishing themselves in Indian wars and rising to commanding positions in the tribes.

James P. Beckwourth, the noted black trapper, became a chief of the Crows. One of the leading Creek chiefs, Tustennuggee Emarthla or Jim Boy, was "a colored mixed." John Horse was a famous Seminole black chief. Another distinguished Seminole black was Abraham, a chief counselor who married the widow of a principal chief of the tribe.

A number of black women married Indian braves. Of the two wives of Micanopy, the head chief of the Seminoles, one was a black Indian. The beautiful Che-cho-ter (Morning Dew) was married to Osceola, the fabled Seminole warrior. Morning Dew's capture as a fugitive slave triggered the long and expensive Seminole War.

As these examples and names indicate, blacks were closely identified with the Creeks and Seminoles of Georgia, Alabama and northern Florida. Under the Treaty of Fort Dade, which was hammered out "largely through the negotiations of the Negro, Abraham," most of the Seminoles were transported to Oklahoma. A basic condition of the final settlement was that black Seminoles would be permitted to accompany red Seminoles to the West.

After the Civil War, the Indian Territory was reconstructed, and the U.S. government demanded "the unconditional emancipation of all persons held in bondage, and . . . their incorporation into the tribes on an equal footing with their original members, or suitably provided for." At the same time there were official demands from Radical Republicans for the opening of Indian Territory to black colonization. Speaking in Congress, Senator Jim Lane called for the creation of an African-Indian empire, saying: "The finest specimens of manhood I have ever gazed upon in my life are half-breed Indians crossed with Negroes . . . I should like to see these 80,000 square miles . . . opened up to the Indian and to the black man, and let them amalgamate and build up a race that will be an improvement upon both." Nothing came of Lane's proposal, but some tribes, notably the Seminoles, adopted their black allies and made them equal citizens with equal rights in the land. Certain tribes, the Chickasaws in particular, resisted integration until the federal government intervened and imposed a settlement which gave each freedman forty acres of land. By 1907, to quote Professor Kenneth Wiggins Porter, "it was said that there was then not a Seminole family entirely free from Negro blood and only two or three Creek families." Nineteen years later Professor Herskovits reported that one-third of a sample of 1551 blacks claimed partial Indian ancestry.[*]

Since the turn of the century, the mixing of black, Indian and white genes has followed unpredictable patterns. Most students believe there has been a sharp drop in interracial concubinage in the South, which reached a post-Reconstruction high in some areas, especially the Mississippi Delta, in the first decades of the century. There is also general agreement that there has been an increase in casual relationships since the civil rights revolution of the sixties. This trend is especially noticeable among students, intellectuals, entertainers, athletes, clerks and middle managers of the white-color stratum. The precise extent of these relation-

[*]See "Red and Black" in *The Shaping of Black America*.

ships today is debatable; by their nature they do not lend themselves to statistical analysis. The only thing that can be said with any degree of assurance is that casual relationships are a negligible factor in contemporary amalgamation. Gunnar Myrdal, E. Franklin Frazier and other scholars have pointed out that increasing knowledge of contraception renders most casual relationships sterile.

As for stable relationships, the picture is far from clear. Studies in Boston indicated that interracial marriages there reached a top figure of 13.6 per cent of all black marriages in the 1900-1904 period, dropped to 5.2 per cent in 1914-18 and to 3.7 per cent in 1934-38. Although detailed figures are lacking, there are indications that there was a slight national increase in the forties and fifties. One factor in the increase was the repeal of state antiamalgamation laws. Oregon led the way in 1951 and was followed by Montana (1953), North Dakota (1955), Colorado and South Dakota (1957), Idaho (1959), and Indiana (1965). The final (legal) word on the subject was said in 1967 when the U.S. Supreme Court, in *Loving* v. *the Commonwealth of Virginia*, declared laws banning mixed marriages unconstitutional.

Since that time there has been a dramatic rise in the number of interracial marriages in the North and South. According to U.S. Census Bureau figures, there was a 92.3 per cent increase—a 131 per cent increase for black males-white females and a 25 per cent increase for black females-white males—in the number of black-white interracial marriages between 1970 and 1977. Despite that fact, the number of blacks involved in interracial marriages was still relatively small. Of the 4,024,000 married black males in 1977, 95,000 were married to white women and 20,000 were married to Orientals or members of other races. At that point, only 30,000 black women were married to white men. In 1985 there were 164,000 black-white married couples and 47,000 black women were married to white men.

These figures are worth noting not only because they prove the failure and irrelevancy of the melting-pot solution but also, and more importantly, because they illustrate the assimilative power of black Americans, who are assimilating instead of being assimilated. This is a continuation of a centuries-long process in which black Americans have absorbed genetic influences from a variety of sources and recombined them into a new configuration which is always different and always the same. We can see this clearly if we look for a moment at the impact of three centuries of mixing on the white and black populations. In an article in the *Ohio Journal of Science*, Robert P. Stuckert of the Ohio State University Department of Sociology, estimated that 21 per cent of American whites—one out of every five—have African ancestors. "Over 28 million white persons," he wrote, "are descendants of persons of African origin. Furthermore, the majority of persons with African ancestry are classified as whites."

Even more remarkable is the number of blacks—70 to 80 per cent—with white and Indian ancestors. The most authoritative and scientific study in this area was made in 1930 by Melville J. Herskovits, who used anthropometric measuring devices and genealogical data to determine the ancestry of a sample of 1551 blacks. According to this study, *The Anthropometry of the American Negro*, 71.7 per cent of the sample had white ancestors and 27.2 per cent had some Indian ancestry. Since that time, the number of mixed blacks has increased, not only because of additional black-white marriages but also because of the marriage of blacks (mixed) and blacks (unmixed). In the Herskovits sample, only 22 per cent of black Americans were of unmixed ancestry. Bantu, Mandingo, Yoruba, Akan, Semite, British, Irish, German, French, Spanish, Dutch, Creek, Choctaw, Seminole, Pequot, Marshpee — American blacks are amalgams of different amalgamations. The end product of 300 years of amalgamation, they are genetic metaphors of the impossible possibilities of the peoples of the world, who are not so much equal as complementary, which is, as Teilhard Chardin and Leopold Senghor said, a higher form, perhaps the highest form, of equality.

11

From Booker T. Washington to Martin Luther King Jr.

If there is no struggle there is no progress. Those who profess to favor freedom and yet deprecate agitation, are men who want crops without plowing up the ground, they want rain without thunder and lightning. They want the ocean without the awful roar of its many waters. This struggle may be a moral one, or it may be a physical one, and it may be both moral and physical, but it must be a struggle. Power concedes nothing without a demand. It never did and it never will....Men may not get all they pay for in this world, but they must certainly pay for all they get.

FREDERICK DOUGLASS

WHEN HE was not at the White House with President Theodore Roosevelt or at Skibo Castle with industrialist Andrew Carnegie, when he was not in Julius Rosenwald's office or on H. H. Rogers's yacht, when he was not advising influential whites on "the Negro question" or lecturing blacks on the need for self-help and self-improvement, Booker Taliaferro Washington rose at 6 A.M. and went to his pig pen.

A master psychologist who recognized and dramatized "the power of the pig" in the social life of black Americans, Booker T. Washington made a point of personally tending his prize stock of Berkshires and Poland Chinas. Impeccably turned out in riding gear and fine leather boots, the educator slopped through the mud and checked the girth of his walking bundles of pork. If an idea struck him in the middle of the inspection, he summoned the stenographer who accompanied him almost everywhere and dictated a memorandum on race improvement.

After completing this ritual, he mounted a favorite gray horse and rode over the Tuskegee campus, inspecting the farms and buildings, dictating memorandums as he went. While he rode, his aides were abustle. A research assistant was assembling facts and figures for his next speech; a personal assistant was processing confidential reports from agents in major black communities; and a special aide was sorting incoming letters into four different stacks.

When Washington arrived at his office, every important event in Black America in the preceding twenty-four hours was at his fingertips. Confidential reports from agents had been sorted and analyzed. Important letters—from the president and influential whites and blacks—were ready for his perusal; letters and memorandums were ready for his signature. Deferential aides and assistants stood with pencils poised, awaiting his pleasure. With some impatience, with just a trace of harried haughtiness (he was humble only with influential whites), the former slave from Virginia pulled a chair to him and went to work.

From this office, for some twenty years, Washington practically ruled Black America. Like a reigning monarch, he issued an annual message "To My People." He was the court of last appeal on black political appointments in America and white political appointments in the South. No black institution, his critics said with only slight exaggeration, could get a substantial amount of money without his approval. He made and broke men and institutions with a word or a nod of his head and his silence, in the face of a request for "information," could ruin a career. He corrected messages of presidents and said the word which made Confederates and sons of Confederates postmasters and federal judges. No

other black in American history—not a Powell, not a Dawson—
has ever felt quite so sure of himself as to send a memo like the
following to an American president.

> [A story in the *New York Herald* said] you have inaugurated
> a new policy which means the removal of all colored men from
> office in the South. This same dispatch was sent to several
> Southern papers. The spreading of this falsehood in this man-
> ner has caused a feeling of bitterness among many colored
> people, and I am wondering whether it would not be wise to
> give out a line from the White House denying it. . . . *If you
> cared to make such a statement and wished me to look over it
> before you gave it out, I should be glad to do so* (my emphasis).

Conservative, shrewd, hard-working and, some say, devious,
Washington essayed a program of conciliation and racial submission. He refused to attack Jim Crow directly and urged blacks to
subordinate their political, civil and social strivings to economic
advancement. By implication anyway, he accepted segregation
and concentrated on a program of "industrial education."

Washington admirers say he was not the Thomist (from Uncle
Tom) his critics said he was. That may be true, but it is extremely
difficult to make out exactly what he was. It is true that he
worked hard—behind the scenes—to make separate "equal" and
that he sometimes condemned lynching. But his condemnations
were often couched in extraordinary language. Always careful not
to offend Southern public opinion, he blamed a revolting Mississippi lynching on the lack of education *of the blacks who were
lynched*. His classic condemnation, however, ran in this vein: "It
is unreasonable for any community to expect that it can permit
Negroes to be lynched or burned in the winter, and then have
reliable Negro labor to raise cotton in the summer."

Almost everything Washington said or did was shot through
with paradox. He bowed before the prejudices of the meanest
Southerner but moved in circles in the North which were closed
to all but a few whites. He told black Americans that Jim Crow
was irrelevant, but he violated the law by riding first class in
Pullman cars with Southern white men and women. And, irony of
ironies, he who advised Black America to forget about politics
wielded more political power than any other black American.

A story that Washington liked to tell himself underlines the paradox of his life. In 1901 he kicked up a storm in the South by dining at the White House with President Theodore Roosevelt and his family. Shortly afterwards, he ran into a poor white Southerner. "Say," the white man said, "you are a great man. You know, you're the greatest man in this country." Washington "protested mildly" and said that in his opinion the president was the greatest man in the country. "Huh!" the Southerner shot back. "Roosevelt? I used to think that Roosevelt was a great man until he ate dinner with you. That settled him for me."

Poor whites and rich whites worshipped at the feet of the former slave from Virginia. Industrialist W. H. Baldwin said, "I almost worship this man." Andrew Carnegie gave Tuskegee $600,000 in U.S. Steel bonds but on "one condition only—the revenue of one hundred and fifty thousand of these bonds is to be subject to Booker Washington's order to be used by him first for his wants and those of his family during his life or the life of his widow—if any surplus is left he can use it for Tuskegee." Andrew Carnegie added: "I wish this great and good man to be free from pecuniary cares that he may devote himself wholly to his great Mission."

Although Booker T. Washington commanded enormous financial resources and had the support of the president and the leading white men of his day, although he was supported by major white media and had the support of most black editors, many of whom he was subsidizing or subverting—although he had everything going for him, although he was eloquent and charismatic and devious and shrewd, he was outflanked and driven against the wall by the bad faith of his white supporters and the gathering social forces of the age. To understand Washington's downfall, one must set the stage carefully, and one must focus a big spotlight on two men. The first man was William Monroe Trotter, who was the advance man of a new breed of black activists who fleshed out the renaissance of the black soul. A throwback to the activists of the antislavery era and an anticipation of the rebels of the 1960s, Trotter was a quintessential New England dissident, raised in a Boston suburb saturated with abolitionist memories, and educated at Harvard University.

Raised on the myths of the abolitionist period, he made himself over into an image of the old abolitionists, dedicating himself and all he had to the destruction of the Booker T. Washington image and the Booker T. Washington idea. In 1901, at the height of the reaction, he opened his anti-Washington campaign by founding the Boston *Guardian*. To make sure no one missed the point, he opened the newspaper office in the same building that had housed William Lloyd Garrison's *Liberator*. The message of the *Guardian*, like the message of the *Liberator*, was total equality and total struggle. What that meant, in the context of 1901, as Trotter emphasized week after week, in editorial after editorial, was total opposition to Booker T. Washington and his program.

To forestall this unexpected threat, Washington relied upon a mixed strategy, bargaining with one hand and brandishing a veiled stick with the other. When these methods failed, he fell back to a second line of defense, subsidizing another Boston newspaper and engineering costly and time-consuming suits against the *Guardian*. Undeterred, Trotter went his lonely way, thundering, Cato-like, Booker T. Washington must be destroyed.

If the Trotter campaign illustrated one approach to Booker T. Washington's program, the campaign of his colleague and collaborator, W. E. B. Du Bois, illustrated another. Although the two men had a common background (New England and Harvard) and although they were equally disdainful of Booker T. Washington's ideas and techniques, they differed considerably in temperament and method. Trotter was a bludgeon; Du Bois was a stiletto. Trotter thundered; Du Bois lectured. Trotter was fire; Du Bois was ice—hot ice. More than that, Du Bois was a man of genius who had that undefinable quality called presence. There was in him, even at that early date, something that foretold his later eminence as one of the mountain peaks of the black experience. Three decades later, after the smoke of battle had cleared, the NAACP issued a formal statement which said that Du Bois's ideas "had transformed the Negro world as well as a large portion of the liberal white world, so that the whole problem of the relation of black and white races has ever since had a completely new orientation. He created, what never existed before, a Negro intelligentsia, and many who have never read a word of his writings are his spiritual disciples and descendants. Without him the [NAACP] could never have been what it was and is."

Du Bois, who always spoke the Truth (his capital) as he saw it, agreed, saying:

"I think I may say without boasting that in the period from 1910 to 1930 I was a main factor in revolutionizing the attitude of the American Negro toward caste. My stinging hammer blows made Negroes aware of themselves, confident of their possibilities and determined self-assertion. So much so that today common slogans among the Negro people are taken bodily from the words of my mouth."

This was the man—brilliant, creative, brutally frank—who moved now to the front ranks of the struggle. He was, at that juncture, a proud, brown-skinned man in his middle thirties, a little below medium height, erect, sharp-eyed and sharp-tongued—a reserved figure with chiseled features and a Vandyke beard. He dressed carefully, carried himself well and was never seen without gloves and a cane. He was a descendant of blacks, Frenchmen and Dutchmen, but "thank God," he reportedly said, "no Anglo-Saxon!"

Like Trotter, Du Bois was a New Englander, born in great Barrington, Massachusetts, on February 23, 1868, three years after the ending of the Civil War. With the help of scholarships, he graduated from Fisk and Harvard and went abroad to study at the University of Berlin. Returning to America in 1894 at the age of twenty-six, he taught at Wilberforce University before moving on to the University of Pennsylvania, where he made the pioneer sociological study, *The Philadelphia Negro* (1899), and Atlanta University, where he organized a series of studies on the life and history of black Americans. He believed then that truth, dispassionately presented, would set black people free. But he soon changed his mind. There were, he recalled later, seventeen hundred lynchings between 1885 and 1894—"each death a scar on my soul." The scars created a new Du Bois, a political being wedded to the idea that truth is powerless against force unless it, too, becomes a force. So believing and so saying, Du Bois left his ivory tower and tried, he said later, "with bare hands to lift the earth."

The first fruit of that effort was the publication in 1903 of a book of essays, *The Souls of Black Folks*, which had an impact on its age not unlike the publication fifty-one years earlier of *Uncle Tom's Cabin*. In one of the essays, "On Mr. Booker T.

Washington and Others," he aligned himself with black militants who opposed accommodation, writing: "We have no right to sit silently by while the inevitable seeds are sown for a harvest of disaster to our children, black and white." The black men of America, he said, had a duty to perform, "a duty stern and delicate,—a forward movement to oppose a part of the work of their greatest leader."

What precisely was this duty?

"So far as Mr. Washington preaches thrift, patience, and industrial training for the masses, we must hold up his hands and strive with him, rejoicing in his honors and glorying in the strength of this Joshua called of God and of man to lead the headless host. But so far as Mr. Washington apologizes for injustices, North or South, does not rightly value the privileges and duty of voting, belittles the emasculating effects of caste distinctions, and opposes the higher training and ambition of our brighter minds,—so far as he, the South, or the nation, does this,—we must unceasingly and firmly oppose them."

Like stones dropped into water, these words exploded in the depths of Black America and expanded in ever-widening circles, dividing literate black Americans into Washington and Du Bois parties. Between these two parties, James Weldon Johnson wrote, "there were incessant attacks and counter-attacks; the former [Washington party] declaring that the latter were visionaries, doctrinaires, and incendiaries; the latter charging the former with minifying political and civil rights, with encouraging opposition to higher training and higher opportunities for Negro youth, with giving sanction to certain prejudiced practices and attitudes toward the Negro, thus yielding up in fundamental principles more than could be balanced by any immediate gains. One not familiar with this phase of Negro life in the twelve- or fourteen-year period following 1903 . . . cannot imagine the bitterness of the antagonism between the two wings."

The antagonism between the two wings is generally and inaccurately described as a struggle over industrial education vs. higher education. But the core of the problem lay deeper than this. The whole controversy turned on leadership, not trades; on power, not education. To Washington's program of accommodation, Du Bois opposed a strategy of "ceaseless agitation and insistent demand for equality [involving] the use of force of every sort:

moral suasion, propaganda and where possible even physical resistance." He favored immediate social and political integration and the higher education of a Talented Tenth of the black population. His main interest was in the education of "the group leader, the man who sets the ideals of the community where he lives, directs its thoughts and heads its social movements." He therefore opposed Washington's exclusive stress on education of the hand and heart because without a "knowledge of modern culture" black Americans would have "to accept white leadership, and . . . such leadership could not always be trusted to guide the Negro group into self-realization and to its highest cultural possibilities."

Acting upon the letter and spirit of these words, Du Bois issued, in June, 1905, "a private and confidential" call for selected black men to meet "in the vicinity of Buffalo, New York," to inaugurate "a permanent national forward movement." In July of that year, twenty-nine business and professional men, led by Du Bois and William Monroe Trotter, met secretly at Niagara Falls, Ontario, and organized the germinal Niagara movement. In 1906, the same year that Gandhi began his passive resistance campaign in South Africa, the Niagara militants abandoned caution and held an open meeting at Harpers Ferry, the site of John Brown's martyrdom. The meeting, Du Bois said, was "in significance if not in numbers one of the greatest meetings that American Negroes have ever held . . . and we talked some of the plainest English that has been given voice to by black men in America." Raising demands that are still burning issues in the Republic, they called for "full manhood suffrage," improvement in educational facilities, the integration of public facilities, and "the right of freemen to walk, talk, and be with them that wish to be with us." As for the rest, the Niagara militants said:

"We want the laws enforced against rich as well as poor; against capitalists as well as laborers; against white as well as black. We are not more lawless than the white race, we are more often arrested, convicted and mobbed. We want justice even for criminals and outlaws. We want the Constitution of the country enforced. We want Congress to take charge of the Congressional elections. We want the Fourteenth Amendment carried out to the letter and every state disfranchised in Congress which attempts to disfranchise its rightful voters. We want the Fifteenth

Black women have played important roles in the civil rights fight. Mary McLeod Bethune (left) was a national figure in the thirties and forties. Daisy Bates was a key figure in the Little Rock integration crisis.

Booker T. Washington proposed a program of "industrial education" and temporary political submission.

W. E. B. Du Bois opposed
Washington, demanding
immediate integration.

Thurgood Marshall was
the first black U.S. Supreme
Court justice.

Amendment enforced and no state allowed to base its franchise simply on color. . . . These are some of the chief things we want. How shall we get them? By voting where we may vote; by persistent, unceasing agitation; by hammering at the truth; by sacrifice and work."

If these demands were not heeded, it was not the fault of the Niagara militants, who organized local chapters and filed petitions and suits. They also hammered at the truth in a series of national meetings at abolitionist landmarks, going from Harpers Ferry to Boston to Oberlin. "We may expect a future session at Appomattox," critic Kelly Miller wrote, "so prone is the poetic temperament to avail itself of episodal and dramatic situations."

There was no meeting at Appomattox. Hampered by a lack of resources and the absence of mass support, not to mention the withering fire of Booker T. Washington and a series of internal explosions between Du Bois and Trotter partisans, the Niagara movement stumbled from crisis to crisis and merged, for all practical purposes, with the founding cadres of the NAACP. By this time its historical work was done; for the tide was flowing strongly against accommodation, and Booker T. Washington had been impaled on the pike of white bad faith. If there was any doubt on this score, it was blown away by the wave of violence that crested in the Atlanta Massacre. This event flared up on September 22, 1906, after a political campaign in which white politicians, Hoke Smith in particular, and the white press had used blacks and the issue of black enfranchisement to inflame the political climate. When, on September 24, blacks defended themselves, with women playing an especially vigorous role, the police entered the fray on the side of the white mob. Even the *New York Age*, a Washington ally, was outraged, as its headline indicated:

ATLANTA SLAYS BLACK CITIZENS SCORES KILLED
INFERNAL RESULT OF AGITATIONS BY WHITES
HOKE SMITH IS GUILTY
ABOMINABLE CAMPAIGN OF "THE NEWS" ALSO
RESPONSIBLE
BLACK MEN RETALIATE
BUT ARE DISARMED BY MILITIA—
CLARK UNIVERSITY INVESTED—
DR. BOWEN ARRESTED
TO RETALIATE FATAL—WASHINGTON

If the Atlanta Massacre marked the death knell of accommodation in the South, the Springfield Massacre sounded the same note in the North. For six days in August, 1908, a white mob, made up, the press said, of many of the town's "best citizens," surged through the streets of Springfield, Illinois, killing and wounding scores of blacks and driving hundreds from the city. Shouting, "Lincoln freed you, we'll show you your place," the mob flogged and lynched blacks within sight of Abraham Lincoln's grave. That this should happen in a city intimately identified with Lincoln's life horrified white liberals. William English Walling, a radical white Kentuckian, expressed the growing sense of outrage in a newspaper article, "Race War in the North." It was time, he said, for national action. "Either the spirit of Lincoln and Lovejoy must be revived and we must come to treat the Negro on a plane of absolute political and social equality, or Vardaman and Tillman will soon have transferred the race war to the North. . . . Yet who realizes the seriousness of the situation, and what large and powerful body of citizens is ready to come to their aid."

There was no large and powerful body of citizens ready to come to the aid of blacks, but there were isolated pockets of white concern. Not the least of the concerned whites was Mary White Ovington, a young social worker, who joined with Walling and other liberals, black and white, in a call for a national conference on the race problem. The call for the conference was issued on Lincoln's birthday, February 12, 1909, and was signed by prominent whites and blacks, including Du Bois, Bishop Alexander Walters and Oswald Garrison Villard, the grandson of William Lloyd Garrison. The document contains graphic information on the social conditions that led to the founding of the NAACP and is worth detailed attention:

> If Mr. Lincoln could revisit this country in the flesh [the Call said] . . . he would learn that on January 1, 1909, Georgia had rounded out a new confederacy by disfranchising the Negro, after the manner of all the other Southern States. He would learn that the Supreme Court of the United States, supposedly a bulwark of American liberties, had refused every opportunity to pass squarely upon this disfranchisement of millions. . . .
>
> He would learn that the Supreme Court, according to the official statement of one of its own judges in the Berea College

case, has laid down the principle that if an individual state chooses, it may "make it a crime for white and colored persons to frequent the same market place at the same time, or appear in an assemblage of citizens convened to consider questions of a public or political nature in which all citizens, without regard to race, are equally interested."

In many states Lincoln would find justice enforced, if at all, by judges elected by one element in a community to pass upon the liberties and lives of another. He would see the black men and women, for whose freedom a hundred thousand of soldiers gave their lives, set apart in trains, in which they pay first-class fares for third-class service, and segregated in railway stations and in places of entertainment; he would observe that State after State declines to do its elementary duty in preparing the Negro through education for the best exercise of citizenship.

To correct these wrongs and to call America back to the dream, some three hundred Americans assembled in New York City on May 30, 1909. Some of the old abolitionists, Thomas Wentworth Higginson in particular, and some of the sons of the old abolitionists, William Lloyd Garrison in particular, refused to attend because of the alleged "radical tone" of the conference. Among the prominent blacks in attendance were Du Bois, Trotter, J. Max Barber, Ida B. Wells-Barnett and Mary Church Terrell.

The conference opened in an atmosphere of mutual suspicion. The white liberals, who wanted to avoid an open break with Booker T. Washington, were uneasy in the presence of the Niagara activists. They were especially concerned about Trotter and Ida B. Wells-Barnett, who were considered more militant than Du Bois. During one stormy session a black woman—probably Ida B. Wells-Barnett—leaped up and cried out, Du Bois wrote, "in passionate, almost tearful earnestness—an earnestness born of bitter experience—'They are betraying us again, these white friends of ours." After a long and bitter debate, the breach was papered over and the National Association for the Advancement of Colored People (NAACP) was born. At a second conference in May, 1910, a permanent organization was created and Moorfield Storey, a Boston lawyer, was elected president. The only black officer and the only black incorporator was Du Bois, who resigned from Atlanta University and became director of research and publicity. The new organization opened for business at 20 Vesey Street in lower Manhattan and hired a white woman, Frances Blascoer, as secretary. Within three months, the first NAACP branch office opened in Chicago. In the next seven years, the organization grew slowly. By 1913 there were 1,100 members in a handful of Northern branches. In 1920 the organization hired its first black executive secretary, James Weldon Johnson.

The cast of characters of modern Black America was completed two years after the founding of the NAACP when a group of whites and blacks created the National Urban League, a professional social work agency which concentrated on the socioeconomic problems of urban blacks. Edwin R. A. Seligman was its president, and Eugene Kinckle Jones served for many years as its executive secretary. Ruth Standish Baldwin, wife of industrialist W. H. Baldwin, an ardent Booker T. Washington supporter, was the dominant force in the formative period of the organization, which pursued a strategy of conciliation, using tactics of education, persuasion and negotiation.

By this time it was clear to almost all the players that the tide was running strongly in favor of protest and militancy. Even Booker T. Washington recognized this, for before his death in November, 1915, he moved closer to the position of his early critics. His final magazine article, published after his death, was an attack on segregation. But the last word on this debate was spoken not by Washington or Du Bois. The final word came from the black masses, who demonstrated once again that history is made not by isolated leaders and elites but by the people. In this instance, as in every other instance in black history, the real, that is to say, effective word came not from leaders acting alone but from the dialectical interplay between the leaders and the people and the forces of the ages.

All through this period, as the debate raged in Boston and Atlanta, the black masses were going through a painful process of regeneration, shedding the grave clothes of slavery and replacing them with garments more appropriate to the new age. The Washington-Du Bois debate furthered this process, but it happened onstage and was heard by a small minority. Backstage, behind the walls of thousands of homes, churches and schools, far away from the organizational centers in Tuskegee and Atlanta and Boston, millions of maintaining blacks were making their own analyses and creating the foundations for one of the most important acts in the history of Black America.

These analyses were buttressed and channeled by larger developments in the outside world. Even as Du Bois and Washington debated, money and machines were changing the boundaries and the terms of the debate. To mention only the most obvious but centrally important fact, improved roads were poking inquiring fingers into the Black Belt counties of the South, and improvements in communications were bringing in new light. A major factor in this process, a factor not generally considered a civil rights issue, was the Model T Ford, which freed both blacks and whites from the tyranny of the land. Every throb of the engine, every turn of the wheel, loosened the plantation chains. Degree by imperceptible degree, the circle of black hope widened and deepened, giving rise to concern and hysteria in the white South which recognized vaguely that things were working loose from their old fastenings towards new issues and combinations, as yet undefined. The increasing weight of the black press was partly cause and partly effect of the new currents of change. As the black public increased in literacy, the number of black newspapers increased. As blacks increased in militancy, the number of militant journals increased. In 1870 there were 10 black newspapers; ten years later there were 31; ten years later there were 154.

All currents of this period mingled and reinforced one another, and it was hard to tell where one started and the other ended. It is interesting to note, for example, that Du Bois and Trotter were key influences not only in the revival of the protest movement but also in the renaissance of the black press. Trotter, as we have already noted, played a major role in refocusing the passion of the press with his editorials in the Boston *Guardian*. But Du Bois, who had a passion for journalism, played an equally important role at the NAACP, where he singlehandedly created a new model of journalism in the *Crisis*. As editor of the *Crisis*, Du Bois pushed the black protest in his famous column, "As the Crow Flies." He also used illustrations by black artists and presented stories on black achievement. Though nominally the organ of the NAACP, the magazine, as the NAACP board conceded, was "something of a rival" of the parent organization. Both the *Crisis* and *Opportunity*, the Urban League organ, published creative work by black poets and artists.

Working the other side of the street in the same period, Robert Abbott created a different kind of model in the *Chicago Defender*. Instead of appealing primarily to intellectuals, as Du Bois did, or to militants, as Trotter did, Abbott appealed primarily to the masses. Sensing their new mood, he appealed to it and magnified it, seizing on every instance of bias and shouting it to the world in big red headlines. Given his reach and his goal, which was "to influence the actions of millions of our unseen and unknown fellows," it is not at all surprising that Abbott was a major factor in the Great Migration, which brought millions of blacks to Northern industrial centers. Abbott's philosophy was simple and direct. "I have made an issue," he said, "of every single situation in which our people were denied their rightful share of participation." Following the same philosophy, the *Pittsburgh Courier*, Baltimore *Afro-American* and other black newspapers became, in Arnold Rose's words, "the Negro's weekly shot of racial adrenalin."

Not all shots of racial adrenalin came from the press. The biggest shot of racial pride by far was provided by Jack Johnson, who won the heavyweight championship in 1908 and went on to defeat the Great White Hope, Jim Jeffries, in one of the most widely discussed events of the period. Although Johnson was a prize fighter and although some of his habits distressed some blacks, it was recognized by almost all blacks and almost all whites that his habit of whipping white men in the ring was, in that era, a political act of far-reaching dimensions. This was expressed very clearly on the eve of the Jeffries fight by John Callan O'Laughlin in a story in the *Chicago Tribune*.

"If Johnson gains the victory," he wrote, "it will increase the confidence [blacks] feel in themselves and, some persons fear, cause them to be less respectful of the power of the whites." This fear, he said, was particularly pronounced in the South. "If Johnson wins, the Negroes in the Southern states are likely to regard his victory as evidence of their ability to defeat the white man when fighting on equal terms. They may be encouraged to acts which formerly they would not dare commit." When, after the Johnson victory on July 4, 1910, whites attacked blacks in riots that spread across America, certain men—black and white—suggested that Johnson had done blacks a disservice. A distinguished black intellectual, Professor William Pickens of Talladega, disagreed. He said, in a *Chicago Defender* article, that he was opposed to "pugilism," but believed that Johnson had done "missionary work" in defeating Jeffries. As for the casualties, "It was a good deal better for Johnson to win and a few Negroes to have been killed in body for it, than for Johnson to have lost and all Negroes to have been killed in spirit by the preachments of inferiority from the combined white press. It is better for us to succeed, though some die, than for us to fail, though all live."

Energized by the antics of Jack Johnson, challenged and sustained by a new network of national organizations, and agitated by a vague and yet exciting sense of change in the outer world, black Americans came, in 1913, to a fork in the road of their destiny—the fiftieth anniversary of the Emancipation Proclamation. Giant celebrations were held in that year in Jackson, Mississippi, New Orleans, Louisiana, and Nashville, Tennessee. Three states—New Jersey, New York and Pennsylvania—appropriated money for fiftieth anniversary celebrations.

Although black gains at that point were more apparent than real, they were real enough for all that. In 1913 the 9,828,000 black Americans owned 550,000 homes, operated 937,000 farms and managed some 40,000 businesses. They had accumulated $700 million. More than 70 per cent of the black population was literate, a net gain of 65 per cent in fifty years. There were 40,000 black churches, 35,000 black teachers, 17,495 ministers, 5,606 musicians, 3,553 physicians, surgeons and dentists, 3,433 trained nurses, 798 lawyers, judges and justices, and 1,700,000 black students in public schools. In the same period black ownership of farm land reached a historic high of fifteen million acres.

There was also a significant surge in black-owned businesses. In 1900 there were 40,445 blacks in business or business-related occupations. Twenty years later, in 1920, there were 74,420. During this twenty-year span, the first black old-line legal reserve insurance company, Mississippi Life (1909) was organized in Indianola, Mississippi, by Wayne W. Cox. Also organized in this period were the Afro-American Life Insurance Company (1901) and the Mammoth Life Insurance Company (1915).

The voice of optimism was heard in the land. W. E. B. Du Bois said "the efforts of the Negroes since emancipation have been promising, and beyond what could be reasonably expected." Kelly Miller, the Howard University dean, was moved to write a poem, "I See and Am Satisfied."

Another poem, "Fifty Years," was written by James Weldon Johnson:

> *Just fifty years — a winter's day —*
> *As runs the history of a race;*
> *Yet, as we now look o'er the way,*
> *How distant seems our starting place! ...*
>
> *Courage! Look out, beyond, and see*
> *The far horizon's beckoning span!*
> *Faith in your God-known destiny!*
> *We are a part of some great plan.*

The plan was not immediately perceptible to American racists, who staged a countercelebration, launching a national apartheid movement. Thus, as the black celebrations unfolded, laws requiring segregated residential districts were passed or proposed in Norfolk, Richmond, Roanoke, Greensboro, Atlanta, and Baltimore. While this elaborate tomfoolery was going on, North Carolina was casting about for a way to legally segregate farm land, and Chicago, Philadelphia, Columbus and Atlantic City were considering the advisability of establishing legally separate school systems. These events coincided distressingly with a Jim Crow campaign by the Woodrow Wilson administration, which started segregating government employees in federal bureaus in Washington, D.C. At the same time, terrorists stepped up their attacks in the South, where fifty-one lynchings were reported in the year of Jubilee.

With these events, especially the Wilson assault, something died in Black America. "What happened in Washington in 1913," Henry Blumenthal wrote later, "involved more than the growing toleration of petty prejudices. Worse than that, trust was violated, and hope was lost." Even Booker T. Washington protested, saying: "I have never seen the colored people so discouraged and bitter as they are at the present time." Washington's rival, William Monroe Trotter, played the leading role in a little drama that defined the spirit of the times. On November 12, 1914, Trotter stormed into the White House and had a jaw-to-jaw argument with Wilson. According to reports, he shook his finger at the Virginia-born president, who dismissed him for "insulting" language. The president, Trotter reports, had insulted blacks by saying that segregation was in their best interest.

All this focused the uneasiness of Black America. Out of this uneasiness there came a new feeling, vague at first but always waxing clearer, that there was another way and another and better place. The feeling moved, became a mood, an imperative, a command. Without preamble, without plan, without leadership, the people obeyed that command, going from the plantations to Southern cities, going from there to the big cities of the North. There, they found jobs in wartime industries and sent letters to a cousin or an aunt or a sister or a brother, saying: come. And they came, hundreds and hundreds of thousands, in the biggest migration in American history. The first wave (300,000) came between 1910 and 1920, followed by a second wave (1,300,000) between 1920 and 1930. The third and fourth waves, even larger, came in the thirties (1,500,000) and the forties (2,500,000).

Why did this happen? Why did the people move?

They moved because the sheriff was mean, because planters were mean, because life was mean. They were pushed by drought, boll weevils and tyranny, and they were pulled by the lure of employment in burgeoning wartime industries. Labor agents of Northern industrialists stimulated the movement; so did Robert Abbott and other editors who printed great big headlines of welcome: "GOODBYE DIXIE." New vistas, new hopes, new opportunities: these stimulated the most significant movement in the history of black Americans. Seen thus, as an explosion of hopes and fears, the Great Migration was a revolt, and that revolt continued through the sixties as a permanent element in the black protest. An idea—the idea of freedom—moved the people, sending them in ever-increasing numbers to Chicago, New York, Detroit, Pittsburgh, Gary and Philadelphia. Between 1910 and 1930 three Northern cities, New York (91,709 to 327,796), Chicago (44,103 to 233,903) and Detroit (5,741 to 120,066), more than tripled the percentage of their black populations.

One can scarcely overemphasize the importance of this development which changed black people and America. In the big cities of the North blacks emancipated themselves, casting off the garments of slavery and the feudal South. Under the impact of industrialization and urbanization, the black psyche changed, became more complex, more knowing, more demanding. As blacks worked in different areas on different materials, the things they worked on changed them, giving them new desires and new personalities. In 1910, 656,000 or 12.6 per cent of employed blacks worked in manufacturing and industrial occupations. Twenty years later 1,025,000 or 18.6 per cent of employed blacks were working in manufacturing and industrial jobs.

As black Americans changed, America changed, and the racial front broadened to include the whole nation. On the South Side of Chicago, the North Side of Milwaukee, the East Side of Detroit, on different sides of most major Northern cities, black colonies rooted in and began their march to the city limits, changing the politics and the political perceptions of rich and poor whites. This development created new opportunities for merchants and politicians. Certain of the new merchants were old residents who recognized the marketing possibilities in the new black colonies. Some preceded the main migration in the so-called Migration of the Talented Tenth in the 1890s and the first decade of the twentieth century. Many came on the same trains and buses that brought the migrants. However the merchants came, they were all buoyed up by the new possibilities created by the black cities within the cities of Pittsburgh, Cleveland, New York and Chicago. One sign of this was the founding of the first black insurance companies in the North. In 1915 William Latham, an attorney from Jackson, Mississippi, organized a Chicago mutual health and accident company which was reorganized in 1918 under the name of the Underwriters Insurance Company. This was the first black insurance company north of the Mason-Dixon line, and it was followed by others, notably the Supreme Life and Casualty Company (1919) of Ohio and the Liberty Life Insurance Company (1921) of Chicago. The two companies later merged and became, under the name of Supreme Life Insurance Company, the largest black insurance company in the North.

With the change in economic reality, the political climate changed. Stimulated by the hemorrhage of black people, the black press took on its now-familiar militant tone, and black agitators — nationalists and socialists — came forward to challenge the policies of established black leaders in the NAACP and National Urban League hierarchies. As early as 1922, white men of power in Chicago asked "responsible" black leaders to curb the new agitators.

Another aftereffect of the Great Migration was a renewal of the political struggle. Within a decade after the migration, black Chicagoans had elected two aldermen, a state senator, four state representatives and a county judge. The political renaissance in the North reached a watershed in 1928 with the election of Oscar DePriest, who became the first black congressman in the North and the first black congressman since the departure of George H. White in 1901.

But the migration had repercussions in American on other levels than the economic and political. For the migrants brought their music and their rhymes with them, and this boon changed American secular music and the rhythmic pulsation of American life. This phase of the Great Migration was institutionalized in 1917 when Joe Oliver left New Orleans and settled in Chicago, where he was joined by Louis Armstrong and other pioneer jazz musicians.

The First World War—the one that made the world safe for democracy—followed hard on the heels of the black migrants and changed the meaning of race. There had been a general feeling before this war that the world belonged to Europeans, and that the white West would go from progress to progress, from height to height. But the bloody carnage on the fields of Europe forced an agonizing reappraisal. It became clear in these years and after-wards that machines had loosed terrible forces and that history, a sly and capricious master, had unknown cards up her sleeves. Of at least equal consequence was the fact that the war grew out of and reflected European struggles over colonial empires in Africa and Asia. Flowing with this fact was a new understanding, dimly perceived at first but constantly growing clearer, that the over-whelming majority of the peoples of the world were colored and that a belief in humanity, as Du Bois said, was a belief in colored people. All this—the slaughter of tens of thousands of young men, the death of the idea of white progress, the rising tide of Afro-Asian color, the anarchy of a machine-world that required more machines, more colonial possessions, more weapons and more wars—changed the spiritual and social climate of the West.

All over the world now, men grew anxious. They were not so sure, they would never again be so sure, of the divinity of their mission and the sanctity of their skin.

If all this was not clearly perceived in the first years of the war, it was dimly felt, even in Black America, where there was a new gleam in the eye, a new spring in the walk, a new and defiant tilt to the head. White Americans, perceiving this and feeling that world history was going down another road, responded with hysteria, intensifying repression and giving the war and preparations for the war an overcast of desperation. Despite these signs, which were clear for all to see, black Americans tried to enter the spirit of the occasion. There was patriotism in this, but there was also a clear understanding of the dialectic of blacks and whites and wars, a dialectic based on the fact that the greatest gains of Black America have been gifts not of the Constitution or white goodwill but of wars and catastrophes that forced their fellow citizens to recognize that they were stronger and more secure with black Americans than without them. It was almost certainly that understanding which led Du Bois, at the beginning of the conflict, to write a famous editorial—"Close Ranks"—which urged blacks to forget their special grievances for the remainder of the war. Not a few blacks denounced Du Bois and the war, but many blacks participated on the home front and on the front lines. According to official records, approximately 370,000 black soldiers and 1,400 commissioned officers served in the armed forces. A little more than half of these soldiers served in France. They made an enviable record, fighting at Chateau-Thierry, in Belleau Wood, in the St. Mihiel district, the Champagne sector and at Vosges and Metz. Interestingly and ironically, the first American soldiers cited for valor abroad were two blacks, Henry Johnson and Needham Roberts.

Four of the outstanding American regiments were composed entirely of black enlisted men—the 369th, the 370th, the 371st, and the 372nd. Three of these regiments—the 369th, the 371st and the 372nd—received the Croix de Guerre for valor and the fourth covered itself with distinction in battles in Argonne Forest. The 369th, the old Fifteenth Regiment of New York, was the first allied unit to reach the Rhine. Although the 369th was under fire for 191 days, it never lost a foot of ground, a trench or a soldier through capture. No less courageous was the 370th—the old

Eighth Regiment of Illinois — which was commanded almost entirely by black officers and which fought the last battle of the war.

Despite the valor of black soldiers, it quickly became apparent that the main concern of many American whites was making the world safe for white supremacy. Black officers and soldiers were repeatedly humiliated by white officers, many of whom addressed them as "coons" and "niggers." Many black soliders were forced into labor battalions or assigned to menial duties as orderlies. Especially galling was the attitude of the Wilson administration, which retired Col. Charles Young at the beginning of the war because of "high blood pressure." Young dramatized his fitness by riding horseback from Ohio to Washington, but he was never assigned to combat duty.

Both black and white officers protested American policy. Col. William Hayward, commander of the famous 369th Regiment, said his troops were not permitted to accompany the Rainbow Division to France. He was told, he said, that black was not one of the colors of the rainbow. When Hayward's troops arrived in France, the American high command hurriedly assigned them to a French command.

"Our great American general," Hayward said, "simply put the black orphan in a basket, set it on the doorstep of the French, pulled the bell and went away."

Hayward named his unit: *Les Enfants Perdus* (The Lost Children).

There was little Jim Crow in France, and the Lost Children ate in "white" restaurants, lived in "white" hotels and dated Frenchwomen, some of whom seemed to prefer black skin. This enraged white officers, who spent so much time trying to innoculate Frenchmen with their prejudices that black leaders said white Americans fought more valiantly against blacks than against the Germans.

Among the many manifestations of the Jim Crow war was an order, issued by Brig. Gen. James B. Erwin, that forbade soldiers of the Ninety-second Division to speak to Frenchwomen. American military policemen repeatedly arrested black soldiers for the "crime" of walking down the street with Frenchwomen.

The whole campaign came to a head with an official order "from Pershing's headquarters," dated August 7, 1918. The order was captioned: "[To the] French Military Mission Stationed with the American Army—Secret Information Concerning the

Black American Troops."

Conclusion

1. We must prevent the rise of any pronounced degree of intimacy between French officers and black officers. We may be courteous and amiable with the last, but we cannot deal with them on the same plane as with the white American officer without deeply wounding the latter. *We must not eat with them, must not shake hands or seek to talk or meet with them outside of the requirements of military service.*

2. We must not commend too highly the American troops, particularly in the presence of [white] Americans. . . .

3. Make a point of keeping the native cantonment population from "spoiling" the Negroes. [White] *Americans become greatly incensed at any public expression of intimacy between white women and black men.*

The same fear—the fear that the war was somehow "spoiling the Negroes"—informed the home-front hysteria. Nowhere was this more evident than in East St. Louis, Illinois, which exploded on July 2, 1917, in one of the bloodiest race riots in American history. Led by white workers protesting the employment of blacks, the white citizens of that town killed from forty to two hundred blacks and drove six thousand from their homes.

The NAACP, which had been waging an increasingly effective campaign against lynching, organized a silent parade of protest. On July 28, 1917, some ten thousand New Yorkers marched down Fifth Avenue to protest segregation, discrimination, disenfranchisement, and "the hosts of evils" forced on black Americans. First came little children, dressed in white. Behind them came women, also dressed in white, and men, dressed in clothes of mourning. The children carried signs:

THOU SHALT NOT KILL

MOTHER, DO LYNCHERS GO TO HEAVEN?

MR. PRESIDENT, WHY NOT MAKE AMERICA
SAFE FOR DEMOCRACY

A large streamer preceded the American flag. Sewn on the streamer were the words:

YOUR HANDS ARE FULL OF BLOOD

Marcus Moziah Garvey, black nationalist leader
of the twenties, is led to prison by federal
agents. Garvey, who organized the first mass
movement among black Americans, was
convicted of using the mail to defraud.

Federal troops from 101st Airborne Division escorted nine black children to classes at Little Rock's Central High School on September 25, 1957. Rev. Dunbar H. Ogden, president of the Greater Little Rock Ministerial Association, said: "This may be looked back upon by future historians as the turning point—for good—of race relations in this country."

As a propaganda stroke, the parade was enormously effective. But it had no immediate effect on lynchers and rioters. In fact, lynching increased. There were sixty lynchings in 1918 and seventy-six in 1919. More disturbing than the number was the increasing sadism of the mobs. The Mary Turner lynching of 1918 was unquestionably one of the most barbaric acts ever committed in a civilized country. Though pregnant, the black woman was lynched in Valdosta, Georgia. She was tied to a tree, doused with gasoline and motor oil and burned. As she dangled from the rope, a man stepped forward with a pocketknife and ripped open her abdomen in a crude Caesarean operation. "Out tumbled the prematurely born child," wrote Walter White, "Two feeble cries it gave—and received for the answer the heel of a stalwart man, as life was ground out of the tiny form."

In the wake of these grisly events, Black America began to realize, with horror, that the war had not made America safe for democracy. Lester Granger, one of the angry young men of that day, recalled later that he was disgusted by the "Wilsonian grandiloquence that smacked of sententious hypocrisy." Another angry young man, Asa Philip Randolph, was crisscrossing the country making radical speeches. He had a set piece which never failed to break up a crowd. "I want to congratulate you," he would begin in rich broad "A" tones, "for doing your bit to make the world safe for democracy"—the crowd would snicker and Randolph would hurriedly drop his punch line — "and unsafe for hypocrisy." The Department of Justice didn't think it was funny. After a Cleveland meeting federal agents arrested Randolph.

The white reaction to the rising tide of black militancy was swift and angry. The white press countered with scare headlines ("Negro Trouble Caused by Hun Propaganda") and the Wilson administration considered and rejected a plan to arrest black editors and protest leaders. On one occasion the FBI invaded the New York offices of the NAACP and asked Du Bois what the organization was fighting for. Pulling himself to his full height, his eyes blazing with indignation, Du Bois answered: "We are seeking to have the Constitution of the United States thoroughly and completely enforced." Du Bois elaborated on this theme in the May, 1919, issue of the *Crisis*, which sold 100,000 copies although it was held up for twenty-four hours by postal authorities. In an editorial in that issue, "Returning Soldiers," Du Bois hurled a defiant challenge:

> *We return.*
> *We return from fighting.*
> *We return fighting.*

This, as it happened, was perfectly true. The long-fermenting racial tensions exploded in twenty-six race riots in the Red Summer of 1919. For a whole day blacks and whites struggled in the streets of Washington. For thirteen days blacks and whites hacked, burned and traded shots in Chicago. Troops were called out finally to put down these and similar uprisings in Omaha, Knoxville and Norfolk. There was also a major disturbance in Phillips County, Arkansas, where a white posse killed some fifty blacks and destroyed a black sharecropper organization.

As if things weren't complicated enough, the Ku Klux Klan revived and spread across the North, adding hundreds of thousands of white recruits in Indiana and other Midwestern states. In 1922 the governor of Louisiana conferred with the president on the Ku Klux Klan violence in his state. In 1923 the governor of Oklahoma declared martial law and put down "a state of rebellion and insurrection" caused by Klan activities.

The Klan campaign was partly cause and partly effect of a postwar mood of reaction triggered in part by the rise of Russia and fear of the new currents of freedom released by World War I. The inevitable consequence was a reactionary movement organized around a generalized attack on civil liberties and a national "Red" witch hunt. At the same time, and at first sight somewhat paradoxically, there grew up a national mood of hedonism, linked to the new currents of freedom and erroneously called the Jazz Age. The postwar mood of reaction and giddiness, the Red Summer of 1919, the resurgence of the Klan, the new international climate, the despair, disillusionment and new experiences of the returning black soldiers: this combination of factors and circumstances changed the orientation of Black America and midwifed the Negro Renaissance, which was ushered in by a floodlike surge of racial consciousness based on the affirmation of black values and the celebration of the power and potential of the black masses. This renaissance, which was heralded by the black migrants and militants of the preceding decade, reached its peak in the twenties with a series of cultural and political up-heavals in the black colonies of the North. One of these upheavals occurred on the cultural front in a literary renaissance that dramatized the spiritual and cultural emancipation of Black America. In an extraordinary outburst of intellectual and artistic activity, black writers and artists, such as Countee Cullen, Jean Toomer and Zora Neale Hurston, spoke with unparalleled frank-ness and fervor. The dominant note of the movement was sounded by Langston Hughes: "We younger Negro artists who create now intend to express our individual dark-skinned selves without fear or shame. If white people are pleased, we are glad. If they are not, it doesn't matter. We know we are beautiful. And ugly, too. If colored people are pleased we are glad. If they are not, their displeasure doesn't matter. We build our temple for tomorrow, strong as we know how, and we stand on top of the mountain, free within ourselves."

Another note, from the same mountaintop, a note of defiance, was sounded by Claude McKay:

> *If we must die, let it not be like hogs,*
> *Hunted and penned in an inglorious spot,*
> *While round us bark the mad and hungry dogs,*
> *Making their mock of our accursed lot.*
> *If we must die, O let us nobly die.*

Less defiant, but no less direct, was the work of black scholars like Carter G. Woodson, "the father of black history." With the founding, in 1915, of the Association for the Study of Negro Life and History, Woodson created an ideological base for scholars and activists. In February, 1926, he organized the first Negro History Week, which became an annual institution and was ex-panded in the sixties to Black History Month. In the same period black scholars and activists assumed a universal mission, moving to the forefront of the worldwide struggle for the liberation of peoples of color. Here again the leadership came from Du Bois, who organized a pioneer Pan-African Congress in 1919. By 1925 three Pan-African congresses had been held under the general leadership of African-Americans.

The culmination and quintessence of the nationalist tide came with Marcus Moziah Garvey, who was, with Martin Luther King

Jr. and Asa Philip Randolph, one of the most talented mass leaders in the history of black protest. Shrewdly exploiting the pessimism and despair of the flood of black migrants, Garvey built the first mass movement among American blacks. "Up you mighty race," he shouted, "you can accomplish what you will." Using as a slogan, "Africa for the Africans at home and abroad," Garvey preached a new gospel of a united Africa under the rule of black men. In the process he recruited hundreds of thousands of blacks and stirred Black America as it had never been stirred before.

A master showman, the best one perhaps in the history of Black America, Garvey used pageantry and processions to drive home his ideas. Millions of blacks were thrilled by colorful Garvey parades, led by the African Legion in blue and red uniforms and the Black Star nurses in white. The organization's flag was black (for the race), red (for the blood of the race) and green (for the hope of the race). Always alert to the drama of his cause, Garvey established a chain of cooperative enterprises (grocery stores, laundries, restaurants, hotels and factories). His biggest coup, however, was the establishment of a steamship company called the Black Star Line.

Garvey talked big and dreamed big. James Weldon Johnson said he collected more money (an estimated $10 million in one two-year period) "than any other Negro organization had ever dreamed of." In 1921, at the peak of his power, Garvey announced formation of an African republic. At his investiture as the provisional president of this republic, he was surrounded by a royal black court, made up of Dukes of the Nile and the Niger. Arrested in 1925 on a charge of using the mails to defraud, Garvey was convicted and shipped to the federal penitentiary in Atlanta, where he continued to maintain his innocence. In December, 1927, he was deported to his native Jamaica. In 1940, his dreams shattered, he died in London. Although he failed in his ultimate purpose, he brought the black masses on the stage of history and gave them a new sense of their power and potentialities. Beyond all that, Garvey was, as critic W. E. B. Du Bois later noted, the forerunner of "a mighty coming thing" in Africa and the Americas and the islands of the sea.

While blacks were pressing the Garvey campaign on the political front and the literary crusade on the cultural front, they were at the same time developing new institutions in the economic field. Stimulated by the business hysteria of the age, blacks moved into the mainstream of money, founding import and export houses, chain stores and steamship lines. This boom, which lasted until the 1929 crash, was perhaps the historic high point of black business in America.

"It was during this period," Vishu Oak wrote (*The Negro's Adventure in General Business*), "that Negro businessmen talked about million dollar corporations as if they were playthings and started corporate enterprises for the production of articles of every description, including brooms, dolls, mayonnaise, perfume and toilet goods, hair preparations, hosiery, cotton and woolen goods, mattresses, flour, chemicals, dyes, radios, movies, lumber, burial caskets, tiles, coal, oil and stoves."

Buoyed up by gains directly linked to the expanding black colonies, the horizons of black artists and artisans expanded. The net result was a stream of plays and musical compositions celebrating the black experience. In 1920 *Emperor Jones* opened at the Provincetown Theater with Charles Gilpin in the title role. The next year *Shuffle Along*, the first of a series of popular musicals featuring black talent, opened at the 63rd Street Music Hall in New York. Three years later, *Dixie to Broadway*, "the first real revue by Negroes," opened at the Broadhurst Theater with the celebrated Florence Mills in the starring role. At the same time black musicians expanded their beachhead in the musical field. In 1924 Fletcher Henderson opened at the Roseland Ballroom on Broadway. In 1925 Louis Armstrong recorded the first of the Hot Five and Hot Seven recordings that changed the direction of jazz. Two years later, on December 4, Duke Ellington opened at Harlem's Cotton Club.

At its outer edges, the far-ranging Negro Renassiance merged with the general giddiness of the age. During this period no party was complete without at least one black intellectual. During this period white America searched for the Garden of Eden in the Harlems of America. Langston Hughes was there. Let him tell you about it:

"It was a period when local and visiting royalty were not at all uncommon in Harlem. And when the parties of A'Lelia Walker, the Negro heiress, were filled with guests whose names would turn any Nordic social climber green with envy . . . It was a period when every season there was at least one hit play on Broadway acted by a Negro cast. . . . It was the period (God help us!) when Ethel Barrymore appeared in blackface in Scarlet Sister Mary! It was the period when the Negro was in vogue."

It was the period of the Charleston and the Black Bottom, of bathtub gin and knee-high skirts, of black and tan on the South Side and Jim Crow clubs in Harlem. There was a night in the twenties when Al Capone went to a Baptist church on Chicago's South Side to hear Clarence Darrow lecture on prohibition. There was a night in New York when Nora Holt sang "My Daddy Rocks Me With One Steady Roll" at a bon voyage party for the Prince of Wales. When she finished, a prominent New York matron rushed up to her with tears in her eyes and said:

"My dear! Oh, my dear! How beautifully you sing Negro spirituals."

It was *that* kind of era.

There wasn't a chicken in every pot, but there was pork. Meat was cheap and homebrew was strong, Duke Ellington was at the Cotton Club, Satchmo was at the Sunset, God was in Heaven and Father Divine was in Harlem. It was artificial and unreal, and, in 1929, it seemed that it would go on forever.

The year started all right.

Down in Atlanta, on January 15, Martin Luther King Jr. was born in a big frame house on Auburn Avenue. Three months later, Oscar DePriest, the first black congressman in twenty-eight years, was sworn in as a representative from Chicago. In July, in 1929, the *Crisis* printed a message to American blacks from Mahatma Gandhi:

> Let not the 12 million Negroes be ashamed of the fact that they are the grandchildren of slaves. There is no dishonour in being slaves. There is dishonour in being slave-owners. But let us not think of honour or dishonour in connection with the past. Let us realize that the future is with those who would be truthful, pure and loving. For, as the old wise men have said, truth ever is, untruth never was. Love alone binds and truth and love accrue only to the truly humble.

If the meek were going to inherit the earth, there were no signs of it in 1929. Bill Robinson was dancing up and down stair steps and people were singing "Ain't Misbehavin'." The new black congressman was saying he wasn't going to vote any more money to enforce the Eighteenth Amendment until something was done to enforce the Fourteenth and the Fifteenth. The South was threatening to secede again because Mrs. Hoover had had Mrs. Oscar DePriest in for tea—"a step," said Senator Sheppard, "[which was] fraught with infinite danger to our white civilization." No—there was nothing unusual about 1929; it was an ordinary year. Babies were born and old men died. Funeral services for John Lisle, a Civil War veteran, were held at Charles Jackson's funeral home on the South Side of Chicago. Robert Abbott and his wife returned from a four-month tour of Europe, and Chicago socialites held a glittering round of welcome-home parties. In October there was a new Louis Armstrong record, "When You're Smiling." The Gay Crowd let their hair down at a series of parties celebrating the October 26 football game between Tuskegee and Wilberforce. That same weekend the Harlem night club season went into high gear with the opening of the new revue at Smalls Paradise. Sunday came and Monday and Tuesday—and the bubble burst with the collapse of the stock market.

It took a while for the wound to bleed. On July 31, 1930, state auditors put a seal on Jesse Binga's big bank at 35th and State Street on Chicago's South Side. The word spread fast. Crowds gathered in the streets; some people cursed and some cried. By August 16 three banks on Chicago's South Side had closed. The *Chicago Defender* urged its readers: "Don't Lose Faith." By August 23, however, the *Defender* had abandoned its chins-up attitude. The words were ominous, painful, and true:

GET FIXED

> Times are not what they used to be. There is no use shutting our eyes to this fact. Prosperity has gone into retirement. . . . Our advice is for everyone to get something, and hold onto it. Get it in the city if possible, but, failing this, start toward the farm before the snow flies.

For the overwhelming majority who had no farm to go to and nothing in the world to hold onto, it was a long white winter. For them, and for millions of other Americans, the sun did not shine again until it came up in the wake of defense contracts spawned by the rising sun of Nippon. During the intervening years Black America, in the words of former Urban League director Lester Granger, "almost fell apart." By 1937, 26 per cent of black males and 32 per cent of black females were unemployed. By 1935 about one out of every four blacks was on relief. In Atlanta, Georgia, 65 per cent of the blacks were on welfare rolls. In Norfolk, Virginia, 81 per cent were on relief. In some areas grown men stood on street corners and offered to sell their services for ten cents an hour. In some areas slavery returned.

The black response to this devastating economic blow came on four levels. First of all and most important of all, blacks fell back on the internal resources that had seen them through slavery and the post-Reconstruction plague. They organized rent parties. They sponsored chicken dinners. They sold homebrew. They helped one another—and they survived.

Simultaneous with these measures, blacks began to organize a second level of defense in the political field. By this time black voters in the colonies of the North constituted the balance of power in several Northern states, and black politicians were becoming increasingly effective in pushing the buttons that made politicians move. This began to be visible in 1930 when President Herbert Hoover nominated Judge John H. Parker for a position on the Supreme Court. When a routine check turned up material which indicated that Parker had once opposed black suffrage, the NAACP asked Hoover to withdraw the nomination. Hoover refused, and the NAACP rolled up big guns, organizing mass meetings and inundating Washington leaders with letters. Reacting to this pressure, the Senate, on April 21, 1930, refused to confirm the nomination. It was an excellent campaign, boldly executed. It was also the beginning of a new political era. The *Christian Science Monitor* called the Senate vote "the first national demonstration of the Negro's power since Reconstruction days."

Black political power increased significantly with a major shift in political preferences. For more than one hundred years, black voters, terrified by the Southern wing of the Democratic party, had supported the party of emancipation, agreeing, in principle, with the axiom that "the Republican party is the deck and all outside is the sea." Faced with a choice between the Depression-doomed policies of Hoover and the social programs of Franklin Delano Roosevelt, enormous numbers of blacks leaped from the deck and discovered that the new water of Democracy was fine. It has been estimated that Roosevelt received about one-fourth of the black vote in Northern cities in 1932. Eight years later, he received 52 per cent of the black vote in the bellwether city of Chicago. This made a big difference in local politics in cities like Chicago which sent the first black Democrat—Arthur L. Mitchell—to Congress in 1934.

The reasons for the big shift were simple and obvious. In sharp contrast to the Republicans, the New Deal Democrats offered programs which recognized, if they did not solve, the problems of urban emancipation. But it should be borne in mind, in understanding the thirties, that the New Deal gave least to blacks who needed it most. Of much more pointed political significance is the fact that Franklin Delano Roosevelt never dared to confront the implications of the South's systematic violation of the U.S. Constitution. For all that, the New Deal was a gain for almost all blacks. Despite the fact that the New Deal financed discrimination and segregation in its grants to the South, despite the fact that the New Deal made it easier for blacks to get relief than a job, despite the equivocation and vacillation of New Deal luminaries—despite all that, the New Deal marked a major turning point in black fortunes. There were new housing projects and relief checks and token jobs for token blacks. Under all, undergirding all, was the feeling that blacks were once again citizens, albeit second-class citizens, of the country.

Because they were second-class citizens, even in the New Deal coalition, blacks stepped up their protest activity, creating a third level of offense and defense. The most dramatic expression of the activity on this level was the Buying Power movement, which started in Chicago on the eve of the Depression and spread to other cities. The fundamental objective of this movement was to force white employers, especially white employers receiving substantial income from black buyers and consumers, to hire black workers. Using direct-action tactics (picketing, boycotting and mass pressure), demonstrators concentrated on lunch counters, dime stores, movies, newspapers, bakeries, milk companies and public utilities. By the mid-thirties, groups with similar purposes were springing up all over Black America. The rippling tensions came to a sharp edge in Harlem, where a future congressman, Adam Clayton Powell Jr., made his entree onto the public stage, leading a nonviolent direct-action campaign. In a four-year campaign that touched all bases (the telephone company, the light company, the bus company, the beverage industry, the New York World's Fair, dime stores and department stores), the New York group added some ten thousand jobs to the Harlem work force. Somewhat to the surprise of social commentators, large numbers of middle- and upper-class blacks joined the picket lines. Political scientist Ralph J. Bunche noted this fact at the end of the decade and added: "Never before have Negroes had so much experience with picket lines, and it may be a lesson that will sink in."

At the same time, and on a different level, black Americans began to organize new national structures, including the National Negro Congress, which was founded in Chicago, February 14–16, 1936, at a meeting attended by more than eight hundred delegates respresenting more than five hundred organizations, including the NAACP. With Asa Philip Randolph, the founder-president of the Brotherhood of Sleeping Car Porters, as president, the congress established local councils in cities across the country and pursued a direct-action campaign, using mass appeals, freedom songs, and mass meetings. Randolph later resigned from the organization, which foundered in 1940 amid charges of Communist penetration. A further development of these organizational acts was the founding, in September, 1938, of the Southern Conference on Human Welfare, which brought together leading black and white Southerners under a program of economic, political and cultural democracy. Beyond all these organizational cells there lay the driving pressure of angry black youths who coalesced around the American Youth Congress, the American Student Union, and the Southern Negro Congress.

Important as these organizational gambits were, they had no appreciable effect on the rising level of black unemployment. As a consequence, sizeable numbers of black searched, on the fourth level of response, for new roads and new gods. Some found solace—and food—in the "heavens" and restaurants of Father Divine. Others found material support in the churches of Daddy Grace. Still others—the number is debatable—turned to the party of Lenin. Fishing in troubled waters, Communists made a major effort to convert the black masses and called for a black republic composed of a swath of Black Belt counties across the bottom of the South. This was a serious misreading of black demands, and the Communists made few black converts. According to an authoritative study by Harold F. Gosnell, only five hundred blacks joined the Communist party in Chicago during the vigorous Depression campaign. Although blacks in general shunned the party, they generally accepted the help of left-wing agitators, who organized unemployment councils and led blacks in direct-action thrusts. Time and time again, in this period, "flying squadrons," composed of bold young men of uncertain political persuasions, dashed from apartment house to apartment house, preventing the eviction of black tenants. When all else failed, radicals—black and white—and family members sat on the furniture and sang the spiritual, "I Will Not Be Moved."

As in all other periods of unbearable pressure, as in the 1850s and the 1880s, nationalist pressures grew. After Italy invaded Ethiopia in 1935, Haile Selassie became a national hero and mass meetings were held all over Black America for the oppressed blacks of Africa. In the same decade, there was a dawning sense of identification with the nonwhites of Asia. It is no wonder, then, in this climate of despair, that nationalist organizations grew. There was, for example, the 49th State movement, which was led by Oscar C. Brown, a Chicago leader who asked the government to detach part of Texas and create an-all black state. A second and more important expression of the same mood was the founding of the Nation of Islam by a mystery man named W. D. Fard and Elijah Poole, the son of a Georgia preacher. Taking the name of Elijah Muhammad, Poole established temples in Detroit, Chicago and other Northern centers and proclaimed a program that was reminiscent of the Marcus Garvey crusade. The Muslims called for total separation of black and white Americans and indicated their disdain for white civilization by dropping their "slave" names and substituting the letter "X." Not content with these gestures, other blacks attacked the system directly, using fire and steel. Symptomatic of this approach was the action of New York rioters who attacked the business district of Harlem in 1935 and destroyed some $2 million worth of property.

The new black currents created new problems for established black leaders, as developments at the NAACP indicated. When, in 1934, NAACP founder and officer W. E. B. Du Bois attacked the NAACP program in its own house organ, the *Crisis*, he set off shock waves that reverberated through the upper levels of the leadership directorate in New York City. When Du Bois followed up this gambit by suggesting that blacks organize as blacks and use segregation to kill segregation, he forced an agonizing reappraisal of the dominant trends of black leadership. The NAACP board, horrified, quickly repudiated Du Bois's suggestion, and the sixty-six-year-old leader resigned and returned to his ivory tower at Atlanta University. But the issues he raised were real, and the NAACP, and to a lesser extent the National Urban League, moved to the left and to the black masses, endorsing and organizing youth and workers councils.

Less political in its beginning but of far greater impact in the end was a campaign in the courts. The NAACP had won Supreme Court decisions banning the "grandfather clause," residential segregation, jury trials in an atmosphere of mob pressure, and the Texas Primary law. But its legal campaign had been largely defensive and uncoordinated. A grant from the American Fund for Public Service made it possible for the association to map a long-range legal program under the leadership of Charles Hamilton Houston, the former vice-dean of the Howard University Law School. Houston, who was hired in 1934, mapped a new strategy based on what he called "the soft underbelly" of Jim Crow — graduate schools. By filing a series of suits challenging inequality in graduate school education, he planned to make segregation prohibitively expensive. The first case — filed on March 15, 1933, against the University of North Carolina — was lost on a technicality. In 1935, however, Thurgood Marshall persuaded the Maryland Court of Appeals to order the state university to admit Donald Murray. The next year — on December 8 in Montgomery County, Maryland — the NAACP began its long and generally successful campaign to equalize teachers' salaries.

While Marshall and Houston were pressing these suits, problems were developing in other areas. Lynchings and random attacks on blacks continued, and there was a national furore when the Daughters of the American Revolution barred singer Marian Anderson from Washington's Constitution Hall. (With the support of Eleanor Roosevelt and other New Deal leaders, she sang at the Lincoln Monument.) The most notorious racial case of the decade, however, revolved around the Scottsboro, Alabama, trial of nine blacks who were convicted (on dubious and contradictory testimony) of the alleged rape of two white women of uncertain reputation. The Scottsboro case became an international cause célèbre, triggering marches, demonstrations and protests which continued throughout the thirties.

If civil rights forces failed to prevail in the Scottsboro case, they could point to victories in other fields. Social forces— notably the radio and blacktop roads—contributed to these victories. So did political developments. The emergence of the welfare state, a series of Supreme Court decisions, the New Deal: all these were cracks in the Wall of Degradation. Another and more tangible reason for the increasing weight of blacks was the repeal of the two-thirds rule, an act that stripped the South of veto power over Democratic presidential nominations. Because of these changes, blacks gained new confidence in their collective strength. For the first time since the Reconstruction era, they found themselves part of a victorious national coalition—a coalition composed, to be sure, of an unwieldly combination of Southerners, blacks, and second- and third-generation white ethnic groups.

Another boost to black morale was the emergence of new political leaders, especially the bright young blacks—Robert C. Weaver, William H. Hastie, Ralph J. Bunche, William Trent Jr.—who achieved high visibility as race relations advisors to the Roosevelt administration. The best known of these advisors by far was Mary McLeod Bethune, who played a major role in focusing attention on black problems. Still another contributing cause was the Congress of Industrial Organizations (CIO), which broke taboos (by organizing black workers) and new ground (by staging sit-down strikes). To all this lastly must be added the continuing flow of black genius as expressed in *The Green Pastures* and "The Home of Happy Feet." In this decade and also in the forties, singers Marian Anderson and Paul Robeson received unparalleled critical recognition. But the major boosts to racial pride came from two athletes. In 1936 Jesse Owens stunned Hitler and thrilled the world with a one-man show at the Berlin Olympics. One year later, on June 22, 1937, Joe Louis literally turned Black America out with his defeat of James J. Braddock for the heavyweight boxing championship.

By these measures, by the power of Joe Louis's right hand and the strength of Jesse Owens's legs, by the artistry and witness of Paul Robeson and Marian Anderson and Duke Ellington, by house-rent parties and church suppers, by votes here and demonstrations there, by all these agencies and by others that can only be imagined or hinted at, black Americans survived the great white plague of the thirties and girded themselves for the New World that World War II heralded and announced.

As defense industries geared up in the late thirties and early forties, it became apparent to black Americans that the managers of the American system had learned nothing and forgotten nothing. Although black unemployment was still at a Depression level, defense industries, almost without exception, turned away black workers. Some plants, in fact, welcomed all workers, "except Germans, Italians, and Negroes." There was also segregation and discrimination in the armed forces. Black were barred from the Air Corps, the Marines and other branches of the armed service.

It was World War I all over again, but neither the world nor blacks nor whites were the same, a point black Americans emphasized with a flurry of petitions, demonstrations and protests. The mood of dissatisfaction, of bitterness even, erupted before Pearl Harbor. In an unprecedented show of unity, the NAACP, the National Urban League, churches, sororities and newspapers expressed deep skepticism about a second war to make the world safe for democracy. The skepticism was couched in repeated and angry demands for fair play in defense industries, the armed forces and government apprenticeship programs.

Nor were these demands confined to black leaders. In a letter to the editor of the Raleigh *News and Observer*, a black correspondent said: "This is very likely to be the last war that the white man will be able to lead humanity to wage for plausible platitudes." Another black, according to Gunnar Myrdal, said: "Just carve on my tombstone, 'Here lies a black man killed fighting a yellow man for the protection of a white man.'"

There was a feeling in the air, and no one felt it more than Asa Philip Randolph, who created a March on Washington organization and announced that one hundred thousand blacks would march on Washington to demand jobs in war industries and equality in the armed forces.

The demand and the organization were characteristic of Randolph, who was one of the most remarkable leaders in American history. Born in Crescent City, Florida, in 1889, the son of an African Methodist Episcopal minister, Randolph was a tall, broad-shouldered man who championed nonviolent direct action. As a Socialist agitator, he went to jail in 1918, as we have seen, for shocking the sensibilities of federal agents with radical words about World War I. As a labor organizer, he fought the Pullman Company for twelve years and won recognition for the Brotherhood of Pullman Car Porters, which he headed. Now, as leader of the March on Washington movement, he entered the arena against a shrewd political operator—Franklin Delano Roosevelt.

Roosevelt opposed the March on Washington. So did most white liberals. The march, they said, was impolitic and unwise. Mrs. Roosevelt and Fiorello LaGuardia called Randolph down to New York City Hall and tried to reason with him. Randolph was stubborn; the march, he said, was still on. President Roosevelt sent for Randolph and two of his powerful supporters, Walter White of the NAACP and T. Arnold Hill, acting executive director of the National Urban League.

President Roosevelt sat behind his desk, flanked by the secretary of the navy and the assistant secretary of war. He was cordial but cautious. He challenged the right of the group to put pressure on the White House. He was doing the best he could and he intended to do more, but there must be no pressure, the march must be called off.

Randolph was adamant. Unless something was done and quickly, he said, one hundred thousand blacks would march on the White House.

> The President: We cannot have a march on Washington. We must approach this problem in an analytical way.
> Randolph: Then, Mr. President, something will have to be done and done at once.
> The President: Something will be done, but there must be no public pressure on the White House.
> Randolph: Mr. President, *something must be done now!*

Something was done, almost immediately. Seven days later, on June 25, 1941, President Roosevelt issued Executive Order 8802, which banned discrimination in war industries and apprenticeship programs. This was the first presidential executive order on race relations since the Emancipation Proclamation and it changed the climate of the civil rights struggle. The president later appointed a Fair Employment Practices Committee, which included two blacks, Earl B. Dickerson, a Chicago attorney, and Milton P. Webster, vice-president of the Brotherhood of Sleeping Car Porters.

Although the new committee failed to change employment practices, it was a point of focus that changed the vision of black leadership. During the war and largely as a result of sustained militancy in a tight labor market, black workers made their most dramatic gains since slavery. By 1944 black workers constituted 8.3 per cent of the war production work force. By 1950 blacks had made substantial gains as skilled and unskilled operatives and white-collar workers.

These gains were achieved as a direct result of a struggle that continued unabatedly throughout the war. A major factor in this protest movement was the black press. The *Atlanta Daily World* (the first major black daily published since Reconstruction), the Norfolk *Journal and Guide*, the *Pittsburgh Courier* and the *Chicago Defender* sent war correspondents to the European and Pacific theaters and printed stories on discrimination and segregation. Robert L. Vann's *Courier* and Carl Murphy's *Afro-American* were especially critical of discrimination in war plants and army camps. The *Courier* conducted a "Double V" campaign—for victory at home and victory abroad. So militant was the black press that the federal government considered—and dropped—suggestions that black publishers be prosecuted for impeding the war effort.

In the meantime, a new front opened in the North where blacks began the long process of opening up the downtown sections of major cities. The organized phase of that campaign began in 1942 with the founding of the Congress of Racial Equality (CORE), which staged its first sit-in in a restaurant in Chicago's Loop.

All the while, in army camps in America and abroad, black soldiers were fighting a two-front war against American racism and the forces of Japan and Germany. As in World War I, there were repeated clashes between black and white soldiers, many of whom were confined to menial tasks in labor battalions. According to official records, 1,154,720 blacks were inducted or drafted into the armed services. Black soldiers fought and worked in segregated units, but they fought for the first time in combat units in the Marines and Air Corps. Black women were also inducted into the WACS and WAVES. The first black Air Corps unit, the Ninety-ninth Pursuit Squadron, under the leadership of Col. B. O. Davis Jr., won commendations for its contributions in the European Theater. The first black general in the U.S. Army, Brig. Gen. B. O. Davis Sr., was named on October 16, 1940.

While black and white soldiers were fighting abroad, black and white Americans were struggling in the streets of America. In the summer of 1943, America exploded in the worst series of riots since the summer of 1919. The National Guard was called out to put down a riot that started when blacks were upgraded at a Mobile, Alabama, shipyard. Two persons were killed and martial law was declared in Beaumont, Texas, on June 16. Thirty-four persons died in the Detroit race riot, which started on June 20. In the same year, in August, there was a riot in Harlem.

The events of 1943 marked a major turning point in black history. The hot summer of 1943, like the hot summer of 1963, made Americans realize that they had a serious race problem on their hands. In the wake of this "discovery," there was a flurry of rhetoric and activity. By 1945 more than four hundred human relations and race relations committees, official and unofficial, had been established by American communities. Most of this activity was busy work that barely touched the surface, but underneath a feeling was growing that the race problem was deepening and was becoming dangerous.

This feeling became more marked after V-J Day, which was also the end of an epoch in world history and white and black history. The division of the world into America and Russian spheres of influence and the development of the Cold War were unmistakable signs of the new history. Another and more important sign, from the standpoint of our narrative, was that the end of World War II marked the end of the European (white) expansion that began in the fifteenth century with the slave trade and the appropriation of the land and bodies of Africans and Asians. Now suddenly — after five hundred years, a mere minute in world history — all that was over, and peoples, especially European people, were forced to redefine themselves in a world without divine rights, without colonies, without natives. It took—and is taking — a while for this fact to work itself out, but the new beginning of the world was written in the destruction and re-arrangements of World War II, which changed the world and America forever. That change, expressed tentatively and halting-ly at the founding of the United Nations with African-American participation, gave a new color to relations between lighter and darker peoples all over the world. Nothing indicates this better than the postwar history of America, which began its career as a superpower cloven in conscience and weighed down with the ballast of an undigested past.

This past intruded on the first act of the postwar drama, which was ushered in by riots in Columbia, Tennessee, and Philadel-phia and random attacks on black veterans in the Black Belt counties of the South. There was, at the same time, a wave of reaction and fear, similar to the wave of reaction that followed World War I. The U.S. Congress, in the first years of the peace, was dominated by a loose coalition of Southern Democrats and Northern conservatives, most of them Republicans, who turned down FEPC and anti-poll tax legislation and whittled away steadily at New Deal social and economic policies. Worse yet, a climate of fear moved over the country in the wake of Communist gains in Europe and Asia.

Black Americans, fearing another betrayal, fearing that they had once again wasted their blood, reacted with fury. A chilling barometer of the postwar mood of blacks was an astonishing act by the NAACP, which, on October 23, 1947, filed "An Appeal To The World" with the United Nations, asking that body to inter-vene in the domestic affairs of the United States on behalf of a suffering and persecuted minority. It was this pressure and the increasing militance of black activists that forced President Harry Truman to name a Civil Rights Committee. The committee brought in a long and eloquent report, calling for economic, political and cultural action. The report, like the later Kerner Report, was quoted, filed, and forgotten.

This enraged a number of blacks, foremost among whom was Asa Philip Randolph, who went again to the barricades, threaten-ing in a White House conference and at a session of the Senate Armed Services Committee to lead a civil disobedience move-ment against the proposed peacetime draft. Faced with this threat,

President Truman backtracked, issuing on July 26, 1948, two executive orders which created an FEPC board to eliminate racial discrimination in federal employment and a President's Committee on Equal Treatment and Opportunity in the armed services. The Truman response was apparently a function of conviction, but it also stemmed from material and political considerations. First and perhaps foremost, the war had internationalized the race problem, and the Cold War made some concession to blacks necessary. Secondly, President Truman was besieged by disgruntled Democrats who were organizing a new party, the Progressive party, which rejected the token approach of both the Democratic and Republican parties and called for basic changes in the lives of both white and black Americans. Prominent blacks were given positions of real power in the party, and more than thirty blacks ran for state and federal offices on the party ticket. Propelled by these challenges and no doubt by cogitations of his own, the president urged a "strong" civil rights plank on the Democratic convention. Southern Democrats, offended, bolted the party but did not defeat Truman, who carried the nation and most of the black vote.

Disenchanted by these developments, certain blacks, including Paul Robeson, turned their backs on traditional channels. On April 20, 1949, speaking at a Paris peace conference, Robeson said it was unthinkable to him that blacks would fight against the Soviet Union. Three months later, in an appearance before the House Un-American Activities Committee, Jackie Robinson, the Brooklyn Dodger baseball star, disputed Robeson's statement. One thing led to another and to the Peekskill riots, organized by rightists who used violence to keep Robeson from singing or speaking. Allied with Robeson in the peace and civil rights campaigns was the old Niagara militant W. E. B. Du Bois, who was indicted and acquitted of charges that he participated in a peace movement which received funds from foreign governments. After the acquittal, Du Bois left America and settled in Ghana, where he died on the eve of the March on Washington.

What this all meant—the NAACP petition, the Randolph crusade, the Du Bois and Robeson challenges—was that the pain was becoming unbearable and that somebody had to do something. There were leaders who recognized this, but what they did had no real relevance to the depth of the problem. The traditional reponses, institutionalized in the forties and fifties and carried to new heights in the sixties, revolved around two tactics, which went in different directions but accomplished the same purpose. The first was the creation of higher walls between the masses of blacks and whites. The classic example was the federally subsidized move to federally subsidized — and white — suburban housing on federally subsidized highways.

The second tactic was the creation of wider openings in the higher walls for individual blacks like Jackie Robinson, who became a national folk hero after he integrated baseball in 1947. There was at the same time increasing recognition of black leaders like Ralph J. Bunche, who mediated the Palestine crisis and became in 1950 the first black to receive a Nobel Prize.

More important in terms of its mass impact were generalized gestures like the integration of the armed forces and the opening of new spaces in factories and offices. White strategy apart, this made a big difference in the tone and texture of the black community. By 1953 the sharp increase in the number of black white-collar workers, as E. Franklin Frazier and others pointed out, had created a major shift of power in Black America. By that time blacks owned almost a third of the dwellings they occupied, a two-thirds rise over 1940, and 74,526 blacks were in college, an increase of 56,646 over 1930. An additional fillip to black pride was the continuation of the postwar policy of appointing blacks to highly visible posts. By 1950 there was a bumper crop of black judges and officeholders on the federal and local levels.

The North just then was beginning the open-city leap the South would make ten years later. As a result of direct-action probes by CORE and litigation or the threat of litigation by local NAACP chapters, public facilities (lunch counters, restaurants, hotels) in Northern cities were opening their doors to blacks. In the nation's capital, for example, restaurants were opened to all by court orders. Tangible gains were also evident in the South. By 1953 almost one million blacks were voting in the South, and blacks had been elected to boards, commissions and public offices in Atlanta, Richmond, Nashville, Winston-Salem and other urban areas.

Most of this progress stemmed from impersonal changes, including the industrialization of the South, the artificial expansion

Martin Luther King Jr., and his wife, Coretta, were received by Indian Prime Minister Jawaharlal Nehru during a 1959 visit. King and his wife visited India at the invitation of the Gandhi Peace Foundation.

Escorted by federal marshals, James H. Meredith
registered at the University of Mississippi. Governor
Ross R. Barnett precipitated the gravest constitutional
crisis since the Civil War when he attempted
to prevent Meredith's enrollment.

of the Cold War economy, and changing relations in the world beyond America. Even more important was negative democratization, the wooing of blacks by whites who needed their voices or, at least, their silence in the Cold War struggle.

Another significant, though more diffuse, influence was the increasing power of mass media. The new medium of television changed the nature of race relations, dumping incidents of racial violence into the front rooms of millions of homes and magnifying the appeal of black activists. If television, almost despite itself, played a generally positive role on this level, it played a largely negative role in projecting images of average blacks. Although blacks, with rare exceptions, were absent from regular television programs, they received favorable images in the columns of a new generation of black magazines (*Negro Digest, Our World, Headlines and Pictures*). The first and most successful of the new black publishers was a young Chicagoan, John H. Johnson, who started *Negro Digest* in 1942 and followed his initial success with *Ebony* (1945), a monthly picture magazine, and *Jet* (1951), a weekly news magazine. A cause and effect of the new climate of race relations, these magazines dramatized the achievements of black Americans and made them aware of their power and potential. Filled with colorful advertising displays and feature stories, *Ebony, Jet, Our World* and other black periodicals were major influences in the revolutionary reappraisal Black America made of itself between Pearl Harbor and Montgomery.

Important as the postwar gains were, they must not be taken as all important. For deep in the ghetto, things were going from bad to worse. By the mid-fifties nearly a third of all black homes were dilapidated. Statistics apart, Black America was still an aritificially impoverished colony of white America, and its citizens were sitting ducks for the series of recessions which began in 1952 and became progressively worse during the conservative Eisenhower administration.

It was in this climate of rising hope and rising despair that a group of men, most of them lawyers, made one of the pivotal decisions of black history. The symbol and operative edge of this decision was Thurgood Marshall, director of the NAACP Legal Defense and Educational Fund. Born in Baltimore in 1908, the son of a country club steward and a teacher, Marshall was a graduate of Lincoln

(Pa.) University and the Howard University Law School and a protégé of Charles H. Houston, who died in 1950 just as the legal campaign he designed began to bear fruit. When, in 1938, Houston resigned as special counsel, Marshall succeeded him. In 1939 the legal staff became—for tax purposes—a separate organization and Marshall became the director. In the forties, Marshall and his staff leapfrogged across the country, arguing the subtleties of the Fourteenth Amendment. They won a lot of cases, but they didn't get rid of Jim Crow. For after losing a case, a Southern state would simply set up an inferior law or journalism school at the black state college. Convinced that it was useless to continue on that course, Marshall, a big, loose-joined man with a hooked nose, an easy manner and a fund of funny stories, decided that it was time "to go for the whole hog." At a meeting of NAACP lawyers, it was decided to frame petitions in a manner that would permit a direct attack on segregation if an opportunity presented itself. Opportunity knocked in graduate school cases in Texas and Oklahoma. In the pivotal Texas case, *Sweatt* v. *Painter*, the legislature, assuming that the NAACP was seeking a separate-but-equal law school, changed the name of the black state college to Prairie View State University and adjourned without allocating funds for a law school building. When it became apparent that the door was open for a direct attack on segregation, Marshall exploded with joy, saying: "We got these boys." After preliminary pleadings in the case, the state of Texas realized that the NAACP was attacking segregation. The legislature reconvened and appropriated $2,600,000 for a black law school. But it was too little, too late, too grudgingly given. Using expert testimony from anthropologists, psychologists and sociologists, Marshall and his staff persuaded the Supreme Court to rule on the validity of segregation. The ruling came in three cases decided on June 5, 1950. In the Heman Sweatt case (Texas) the Court held that equality involved more than physical facilities. In the G. W. McLaurin case (Oklahoma) the court said that black students could not be segregated after they were admitted to state universities. In the Elmer W. Henderson case the Court banned dining car segregation.

In 1951 NAACP attorneys and attorneys representing Washington parents began to attack segregation on the elementary and secondary school levels. As expected, the five cases from South

Carolina, Kansas, Virginia, Delaware and Washington, D.C., were lost in lower courts. Twice, in 1952 and 1953, they were argued before the Supreme Court. In a significant development the U.S. government intervened on the side of the black petitioners, stressing the international implications of the cases. On December 2, 1952, Secretary of State Dean Acheson submitted the following statement to the Court: "The continuation of racial discrimination in the United States remains a source of constant embarrassment to this government in the day-to-day conduct of its foreign relations; and it jeopardizes the effective maintenance of our moral leadership of the free and democratic nations of the world."

On Monday, May 17, 1954, the Supreme Court handed down its epochal decision. The decision was read by Chief Justice Earl B. Warren, who posed the fundamental question:

"Does segregation of children in public schools solely on the basis of race, even though the physical facilities and other 'tangible' factors may be equal, deprive the children of the minority group of equal educational opportunities?" Warren paused and said: "We believe that it does." He added:

"We cannot turn the clock back to 1868 when the [Fourteenth] Amendment was adopted, or even to 1896, when Plessy versus Ferguson was written. . . . We conclude that in the field of public education the doctrine of 'separate but equal' has no place." The decision was unanimous. A year later the Court ordered public school desegregation "with all deliberate speed." Although the decision dealt with the narrow issue of segregation in public schools, it destroyed the legal foundations of segregation and redefined the role of blacks in American life.

The reaction in the South was swift and ominous in its implications, as author John Barlow Martin indicated in his book, *The Deep South says "Never"*. Two months after the 1954 decision, a White Citizens Council was formed in Indianola, Mississippi. The councils—one writer called them white-collar Ku Klux Klans—spread across the South. Bankers, merchants and professionals joined the movement and swore resistance to school integration "by every lawful means." The intellectual leader of the resistance was Tom Brady, a Yale-educated circuit judge in Mississippi. In his book, *Black Monday*, Brady said that "when a law transgresses the moral and ethical sanctions and standards of the mores, invariably strife, bloodshed and revolution follow in the wake of its attempted enforcement. The loveliest and purest of God's creatures, the nearest thing to an angelic being that tread this terrestrial ball is a well-bred, cultured Southern white woman or her blue-eyed, golden-haired little girl." Brady did not propose to obey the decision. "We say to the Supreme Court and to the northern world, 'You shall not make us drink from this cup.' . . . We have, through our forefathers, died before for our sacred principles. We can, if necessary, die again."

And so the war—it is not too strong a word—began. There were three lynchings in Mississippi in 1955. Two NAACP leaders, the Reverend George W. Lee and Lamar Smith, were slain on May 13 and August 13, respectively, because they refused to take their names off voter registration lists. On August 28 Emmett Till, a fourteen-year-old Chicagoan, was kidnapped and murdered by white men near Money, Mississippi. In the fall of 1956 skirmishes were fought at Sturgis and Clay, Kentucky, where National Guard units were called out to escort black children through the lines of howling mobs. The Tennessee National Guard was sent to Clinton to put down an uprising by white demonstrators. The next year a dynamite blast destroyed Nashville's new Hattie Cotton Elementary School, which had 388 white students and 1 black student. All the while, week after week, Southern lawyers, brief cases bulging with foolscap, scurried from federal court to federal court, skillfully conducting a rearguard action that the South said would last for at least a century.

At that climactic moment, the black people of Montgomery, led by a black minister, moved the struggle from the courtrooms to the streets, from law libraries to the pews of churches, from the mind to the soul. For twenty years Black America had been inching toward that decision. In the 1930s, as we have seen, Adam Clayton Powell called for a nonviolent direct-action campaign. In the 1940s Asa Philip Randolph organized a national nonviolent movement. In the 1950s CORE opened up downtown Baltimore and St. Louis with nonviolent sit-in campaigns and sent the first Freedom Riders into the South. Now, in 1955, Martin Luther King Jr. fused these elements and added the missing link, that which has sustained and bottomed Black America since slavery—the black church. By superimposing the image of the black preacher on the image of Gandhi, by adding songs and symbols with concrete significance in Black America, King transformed a spontaneous local protest into a national passive resistance movement with a method and an ideology. "Love your enemies," he said, and tens of thousands of blacks straightened their backs and sustained a year-long bus boycott which was, as King pointed out, "one of the greatest [movements] in the history of the nation." The movement brought together laborers, professionals and students. More importantly perhaps, it fired the imagination of blacks all over America. Ironically, and significantly, all this happened in the state of Alabama, thirty-seven miles from Tuskegee, forty years after the death of Booker T. Washington.

The minister who led the protest was a product of the post-Washington renaissance. The son and grandson of ministers, born on January 15, 1929, King inherited a tradition of protest. His grandfather, A. D. Williams, was one of the leaders of a protest group which pressured into existence Atlanta's first black high school, named for Booker Taliaferro Washington. King attended Booker T. Washington High School and went on to Atlanta's Morehouse College, where he was tutored by Benjamin E. Mays, who has been called "the last of the great schoolmasters." From Morehouse King went to Crozier Seminary and to Boston University, where he received the Ph.D. degree in systematic theology. After marrying Coretta Scott, a concert singer from Marion, Alabama, King went to Montgomery and started preaching the social gospel to the members of the Dexter Avenue Baptist Church which sits, like a nagging conscience, at the foot of the Alabama state capitol on Goat Hill.

Near this spot, at the old Exchange Hotel, William Yancey introduced Jefferson Davis, the new president of the Confederacy, saying, "The man and the hour have met." Near this site, on December 1, 1955, Rosa Parks played midwife for a new man and a new hour, refusing on an impulse to obey an ancient custom which required blacks to yield their seats on Montgomery buses to white customers. Mrs. Parks, a seamstress and a member of the local NAACP branch, was arrested, and black Montgomery staged, on December 5, a one-day boycott in protest. The one-day boycott grew into a movement; the movement spread across the South.

Elected president of the Montgomery Improvement Association, which coordinated the movement, King embarked on the task of translating theory into practice. A car pool was organized, and regular mass meetings, organized around sermons and spirituals, were held. Skillfully utilizing the resources of television and mass journalism, King made Montgomery an international way station. For twelve months black Montgomery walked. Finally, on December 21, 1956, after a Supreme Court decision, the buses were integrated. King later moved to Atlanta, where he established a general headquarters for the Southern Christian Leadership Conference, a nonviolent direct-action group organized in 1957. On May 17, 1957, the rising young leader made his national debut at the Prayer Pilgrimage, which brought some fifty thousand blacks to Washington in the largest civil rights demonstration to that date.

After Montgomery the tempo of events picked up and the arena of action changed from the courts to the streets. The idea of Montgomery, the idea of direct nonviolent action, swept from community to community, gathering to itself new color and strength as it moved. A succession of bus boycotts in Atlanta, Tallahassee, Florida, and other Southern communities signalled the new departure. Another development of the period was the Tuskegee movement, which organized a boycott of white merchants to protest political exclusion.

Out of this confluence of moods and militant men, women and children came a Second Reconstruction which ranged over the North and South.

The Second Reconstruction assumed form and focus on September 25, 1957, when soldiers of the 101st Airborne Division escorted nine black children into Little Rock's Central High School. It was the first time in eighty-one years that a president had dispatched American troops to the South to protect the constitutional rights of black people, and perceptive observers predicted that future historians would call it a major turning point in black-white relations in the South.

As the struggle widened and deepened in the South, the black colonies of the North came awake. Enraged by televised images of white mobs attacking black schoolchildren and stimulated by the heroism of Southern demonstrators, Northern blacks began to

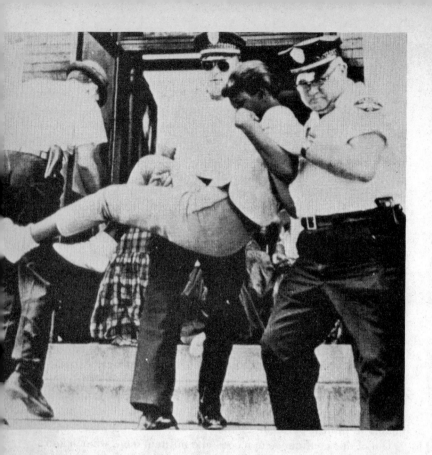

Police in Albany, Georgia, removed black teenagers from the steps of the Carnegie Library on July 31, 1962. Fifteen teenagers were arrested after they knelt and prayed on the steps of the "white" library.

Roy Wilkins, executive secretary of the NAACP, Martin Luther King Jr., and A. Philip Randolph, veteran labor and protest leader, clasped hands before the Lincoln Monument in Washington, D.C. after the 1963 March on Washington and vowed to continue the civil rights struggle.

look at their situation with new eyes. There were, to be sure, obvious differences between the South and the North, but the differences were more apparent than real. For although there were no Jim Crow signs in the North, there were invisible signs and an interlocking network of barriers that confined black children to schools which were in fact (*de facto*) segregated. The same barriers confined black adults to subordinate positions in the economy and the political structure. The situation in Northern colonies was bad, and it was getting worse in the wake of the recessions of the Eisenhower years. In 1957 the black unemployment rate was 7.9 per cent. In 1958 black unemployment was 12.6 per cent. The fundamental problem here was racism compounded by technological changes. By the end of the fifties, technological forces—automation, the electronic revolution, the shift of factories and market shares to the suburbs and Germany and Japan—were changing the profile of the work force; and white workers, aided by powerful unions, were appropriating black preserves in the service industries (waiters, bellhops, etc.). As a consequence, the black share of the labor market was growing smaller and the number of permanently employed blacks was growing larger.

Agitated by this growing threat and urged on by larger currents in the world, including the emergence of Ghana (1957) and other African states, Northern blacks created their own freedom movement, which was harder and, in some respects, more militant than the Southern movement it reflected and echoed. An important aspect of this movement was the revolt of black intellectuals, who embarked in this decade on a perilous journey of self-naming and self-legitimization. The grand outcome was a literary efflorescence which reached higher peaks than the Negro Renaissance of the twenties. Among the major names in this new renaissance were James Baldwin, Lorraine Hansberry, Gwendolyn Brooks, John Killens, Ossie Davis, Ruby Dee and LeRoi Jones (Imamu Baraka). The new mood of black writers and artists was sharpened and focused in the pages of magazines like *Black World*, edited by Hoyt Fuller.

A less visible internal tension was reflected in the migration of modern jazz, which has always reflected the internal stresses of black life. In the early forties, with the Be-Bop movement, jazz became opaque, discordant and menacing, reflecting the new anguish of the black spirit. In the early fifties, jazz became cool, uninvolved and withdrawn. Now, in the wake of Montgomery and Ghana and Emmett Till, jazz became hard, hot and hostile, cresting in the late fifties with the Soul movement, which was a return, literally and figuratively, to roots.

Almost parallel with the revolt of black intellectuals was an enormous expansion of black nationalism, which overflowed its traditional boundaries and became a major theme of literature, music and politics. A major spokesman for one phase of the nationalist resurgence was Malcolm X, a Nation of Islam leader who later formed his own organization. Although Malcolm X was assassinated before he could organize his ideas into a movement, he was an enormously talented theorist who influenced millions with his articulate expositions on television programs and his lectures on public platforms. During the same period traditional nationalist groups, such as the Nation of Islam, reached the peak of their influence.

Propelled by these different currents, Northern demonstrators and activists escalated the struggle to unprecedented heights of contention and controversy. By the eve of the Emancipation Proclamation Centennial, nationalists like Elijah Muhammed were calling for creation of a black state in America, while other activists, with different perceptions, were pressing an increasingly volatile campaign in the streets. By that time suits challenging *de facto* segregation had been filed in more than a dozen Northern cities and sit-ins had been staged in Chicago (schools and beaches), Cairo, Illinois (restaurants and recreational facilities) and Englewood, New Jersey (schools).

As this critical juncture three events united the Southern and Northern movements and changed their character and direction. The first event occurred in Greensboro, North Carolina, where, on February 1, 1960, four students from North Carolina A&T College sat down at a "white" lunch counter in a Woolworth store and demanded service. This was the opening salvo of an unexampled student protest movement which shook the South to its foundation and set the stage for the student rebellions of the sixties. Within three months thousands of black—and some white—students were taking seats at "white" lunch counters and demanding service. If, as generally happened, the students were refused service, they refused to move until arrested.

The movement, patterned on the passive resistance techniques of Gandhi, raced across the South, hitting chain stores, department stores, libraries, supermarkets and movies. By February 10 the movement had spread to fifteen Southern cities in five states. With the organization of the Student Nonviolent Coordinating Committee (SNCC) on April 15, 1960, the youth revolution became an organized force. By September, 1961, seventy thousand students had participated in sit-in movements in twenty Southern states. According to a report of the Southern Regional Council, 3600 students had been arrested by September, 1961, and one or more establishments in more than one hundred Southern and Border States had been desegregated.

The meaning of all this was as plain as daylight, as the Southern Regional Council pointed out, saying that "the South is in a time of change, the terms of which cannot be dictated by white Southerners." Carl Blair, president of the Montgomery (Ala.) Chamber of Commerce was moved to strong words. "There's a revolution," he said, "of the Negro youths in this nation."

The sit-in struggle spilled over into the political arena and influenced the 1960 presidential race between John F. Kennedy and Richard M. Nixon. When King was arrested in an Atlanta sit-in, Senator Kennedy called Mrs. King to express concern. Some political observers said the call added immeasurably to the huge black vote that gave him an onion-skin margin over Nixon.

Scarcely had the South recovered from the sit-ins when it was struck by a second blow, which came in the form of thirteen CORE members who set out from Washington, D.C., on May 4, 1961, for an integrated Freedom Ride through the South. Testing compliance with integration orders of the Interstate Commerce Commission and federal courts, the black and white riders demanded equal and integrated service on buses and in terminals and lunch counters. At several stops, including Birmingham, Alabama, they were beaten and manhandled while policemen looked the other way. After a group of Freedom Riders were attacked in Montgomery, Alabama, on May 20, 1961, Attorney General Robert F. Kennedy dispatched some six hundred U.S. marshals to the city. The Alabama governor later declared martial law and called out the National Guard. The whole campaign converged on Jackson, Mississippi, where scores of riders were arrested. On December 12, 1961, the Freedom Rider movement merged into a city-by-city assault, which established the pattern for the struggles of 1962 and 1963. The arrest of twelve Freedom Riders in Georgia triggered the militant Albany movement, the coordinating umbrella for a citywide assault on segregation by Martin Luther King Jr., SNCC and elements of CORE and the NAACP.

The sounds of this struggles were still filling the air waves when the South and America were convulsed by the third event, the abortive attempt to prevent the enrollment of James H. Meredith, an Air Force veteran, at the University of Mississippi. Resurrecting John C. Calhoun's doctrine of interposition, Mississippi Governor Ross R. Barnett attempted in September, 1962—the 100th anniversary of Lincoln's preliminary Emancipation Proclamation—to place state power between the university and the orders of a federal court. The "Mississippi insurrection" failed, but it precipitated the gravest federal-state crisis since the Civil War. Two whites were killed in rioting on the university campus. More than twelve thousand federal troops, marshals and National Guardsmen were mobilized to preserve order and implement the court decisions.

With the Mississippi insurrection, the wounds of the Civil War were reopened anew and for the next ten years America resounded to the clash of black and white actors reenacting the roles of a century-old struggle. Of all those who witnessed the event perhaps Paul Guihard understood it best. The French reporter, who was killed during rioting on the university campus, wrote in his last dispatch:

"The Civil War has never ended."

12

The Time of the Whale

> *We want greater venturesomeness. We have sat on the river bank and caught catfish with pin hooks. The time has come to harpoon a whale.*
>
> JOHN HOPE

IT WAS A year of funerals and births, a year of endings and a year of beginnings, a year of hate, a year of love. It was a year of water hoses and high-powered rifles, of struggles in the streets and screams in the night, of homemade bombs and gasoline torches, of snarling dogs and widows in black. It was a year of passion, a year of despair, a year of desperate hope. It was 1963, the 100th year of black emancipation and the first year of the Black Revolution.

In this year, which marked a fundamental forking point in American race relations, blacks hurled themselves in larger and larger numbers against the unyielding bars of the cage of caste.

They surged through the streets in waves of indignation.

They faced police dogs and armored police tanks.

They were clubbed, bombed, stoned, murdered.

In scores of cities, North and South, there were riots and near-riots, and small wars were fought in Cambridge (Md.), Danville (Va.), Savannah and Birmingham. There were, all told, more than ten thousand racial demonstrations (sit-ins, lie-ins, sleep-ins, pray-ins, stall-ins) in this year, and more than five thousand black Americans were arrested for political activities.

In a paradoxical act of political poetry, this bubbling cauldron came to a boil on the one hundredth anniversary of the Emancipation Proclamation. As the curtain rose on the drama, there were disquieting omens that this celebration was not going to go by the book. Black unemployment was at a 1930 depression level; and black schools, Lincoln and the Supreme Court to the contrary notwithstanding, were separate and transparently unequal. In the North there was widening panic over the increasing power of the descendants of the freedmen, who constituted 60 per cent of the population of Washington, D.C., 23 per cent of the population of Chicago and 29 per cent of the population of Detroit. In the South, where the power of black numbers was equally real, and where blacks constituted 38 per cent of the population of Birmingham, there was rising hysteria and open defiance of the orders of federal courts. When the year of decision opened, federal troops were maintaining an uneasy vigil at the University of Mississippi; and police and rebels of the Student Nonviolent Coordinating Committee (SNCC) were fighting a guerilla war in the wilds of the Black Belt counties of southwest Georgia and central Mississippi.

There were, to be sure, signs of progress: glittering middle-class oases in Chicago, New Orleans and Los Angeles; black bureaucrats near the top levels of the Kennedy administration, and mushrooms of black Babbits with new cars, new appliances and new hopes. But all this was overshadowed by the creeping misery of the masses and the open defiance of reactionaries. President Kennedy put his finger on the raw materials of revolt in a special message to Congress on the Emancipation Centennial:

"The Negro baby born in America today—regardless of the section or state in which he is born—has about one-half as much chance of completing high school as a white baby born in the same place on the same day—one-third as much chance of completing college—one-third as much chance of becoming a professional man—twice as much chance of becoming unemployed—about one-seventh as much chance of earning $10,000 a year—a life expectancy which is seven years less—and the prospects of earning only half as much."

These facts—clear, undisputed, ominous—defined the Centennial and America. What was worse was the dawning realization that this was the bitter fruit of one hundred years of patience. More and more people, as the weeks wore on, cast cold and disapproving eyes on sentimental celebrations of an emancipation that had not yet been achieved. More and more people, as Lincolnmania spread, cast about for a dramatic expression of the death of black hope and the death of black patience.

Wyatt Tee Walker, the assistant to Martin Luther King Jr., spoke for thousands of black activists: "We've got to have a crisis to bargain with. To take a moderate approach hoping to get white help, doesn't work. . . . You've got to have a crisis."

And a crisis was what America got.

Centennial orators were declaiming and officials were reading congratulatory proclamations when the first shots of the campaign of 1963 were fired. When, on February 28, white terrorists tried to assassinate a Mississippi activist, enraged SNCC workers converged on Greenwood, Mississippi, and organized a voter registration campaign. Hundreds of native Mississippians marched on the registrar's office and were repulsed by heavily armed officers and K-9 police dogs. The campaign attracted national attention when comedian Dick Gregory joined the demonstrations.

The sounds of Greenwood — the whining of police dogs, the screams of demonstrators and the curses and countercurses of policemen and adult onlookers — were still echoing in the air when a second and larger front opened in Birmingham, Alabama. The opening salvo in this campaign was fired on Wednesday, April 3, when Martin Luther King Jr., stepped from an airliner and announced that he would lead racial demonstrations in the streets of the Alabama city until "Pharaoh lets God's people go."

The Pharaohs of Birmingham had been on King's mind for a long time. For seven years, ever since Montgomery, King had been moving from city to city, from tactic to tactic, trying to find the key to the American soul. As the Emancipation Proclamation

Centennial approached, King and his aides decided that they needed an American Bastille, i.e., a key point that could yield more than a local or symbolic victory. With characteristic boldness, King selected Birmingham, which was widely regarded as an impregnable fortress of bigotry. He felt, he said later, that "if Birmingham could be cracked, the direction of the entire nonviolent movement in the South could take a significant turn. It was our faith that 'as Birmingham goes, so goes the South.' "

King and his aides drew up a battle plan for the proposed series of demonstrations. In a moment of prophetic genius, they designated the campaign "Project C." What precisely did the "C" mean? It was a shorthand symbol for a new concept: confrontation.

"Project C" was scheduled for the fall of 1962, but negotiations with Birmingham officials led to several postponements. By January, however, King was convinced that a showdown was necessary for racial progress in Birmingham and America. He therefore dispatched aides to Birmingham to secretly recruit workers and lay the groundwork for the confrontation.

The project began as scheduled on April 3, the day after Birmingham's municipal election. And it unfolded according to a brilliantly conceived plan tied to the major events of the betrayal, crucifixion and triumph of Jesus. First, there were probes and scouting expeditions (sit-ins and picketing at downtown stores) by little bands of demonstrators, who fanned out over the city, testing the strength of the police. Then, on Saturday, April 6, the campaign entered its second phase with a token street demonstration led by the Reverend Fred Shuttlesworth, president of the Alabama Christian Conference, an SCLC affiliate. On the next day, Palm Sunday, there was the first reconnaissance in force and the first direct conflict between the main antagonists, *demonstrators* representing the black community and *policemen* representing the white community. To no one's surprise, the first contest was won hands down by the police, who routed more than six hundred demonstrators.

With the shadowboxing over, both sides dug in for trench warfare. Martin King directed his nonviolent army from a suite in the A. G. Gaston Motel in the heart of the black community. From this center aides fanned out over the city, organizing nonviolent workshops and nightly mass meetings. Opposing King and his demonstrators was a force of police and firemen commanded by Police Commissioner Eugene ("Bull") Connor, a tough, chunky segregationist who had become a national symbol of Southern intransigence.

The main battleground of this improbable but nonetheless grim war was the Kelly Ingram Park, a square block of tall elms, concrete walkways and dirty green grass in the middle of the black business district. On one side of this park was the yellow brick structure of the Sixteenth Street Baptist Church. From this church, day after day, swarmed hundreds of demonstrators who tried to penetrate the defenses of police deployed in depth around barricades two blocks away. The strategic objectives of the demonstrators were downtown stores and city hall. Between the church and the downtown section were policemen and firemen who used high-pressure hoses and K-9 police dogs to drive demonstrators back through the park to Sixteenth Street. Legal reinforcements were provided by a local judge who issued a sweeping injunction barring protest marches.

On Good Friday, April 12, Martin Luther King Jr. openly defied this order by leading a mass march of fifty or more disciples and some one thousand onlookers. Far from being intimidated by the symbolism of the day, "Bull" Connor dispersed the marchers and arrested King and about fifty demonstrators.

So far, so good: all this—King's arrest and the increasing truculence of "Bull" Connor—was in the script; so apparently was the uproar that followed. From his Easter vacation headquarters in Palm Beach, President Kennedy phoned the Justice Department for "information." Kennedy later placed a personal call to Coretta King to assure her of the safety of her imprisoned husband. The president's brother, Attorney General Robert F. Kennedy, bestirred himself, placing his crisis-weary civil rights staff on standby alert.

There then occurred an incident that was not in the script. Eight leading white churchmen of Birmingham—Roman Catholic, Protestant, Jewish—denounced King as an interloper and urged "our own black community to withdraw support" from these "unwise and untimely" demonstrations.

This development, totally unexpected, proved to be a boon to the campaign. King, with the instinct for drama and the inventiveness of a great general, counterattacked with devastating effect. From his cell, he answered his detractors in a memorable "Letter from a Birmingham Jail" that became a civil rights classic. In this letter King dealt first with the charge that he was an "outsider," saying that he was in Birmingham because he was invited there and because he had organizational ties there. He added:

> Beyond this, I am in Birmingham because injustice is here. Just as the eighth century prophets left their little villages and carried their "thus saith the Lord" far beyond the boundaries of their hometowns: and just as the Apostle Paul left his little village of Tarsus and carried the gospel of Jesus Christ to practically every hamlet and city of the Greco-Roman world, I, too, am compelled to carry the gospel of freedom beyond my particular hometown. Like Paul, I must constantly respond to the Macedonian call for aid.

As for the criticism of his timing, King said:

> We know through painful experience that freedom is never voluntarily given by the oppressor; it must be demanded by the oppressed. Frankly, I have never yet engaged in a direct action movement that was "well-timed" according to the timetable of those who have not suffered unduly from the disease of segregation. For years now I have heard the word "Wait." It rings in the ear of every Negro with a piercing familiarity. This "Wait" has always meant "Never." It has been a tranquilizing thalidomide, relieving the emotional stress for a moment only to give birth to an ill-formed infant of frustration. We must come to see with the distinguished jurist of yesterday that "justice too long delayed is justice denied." We have waited for more than three hundred and forty years for our constitutional and God-given rights.

Continuing in the same vein, King said he was not afraid of tension or a crisis. Indeed, he said, the campaign was designed to create a crisis:

> Nonviolent direct action seeks to create such a crisis and establish such creative tension that a community that has consistently refused to negotiate is forced to confront the issue. It seeks to dramatize the issue so that it can no longer be ignored. . . . This may sound rather shocking. But I must confess that I am not afraid of the word tension. I have earnestly worked and preached against violent tension, but there

is a type of constructive nonviolent tension that is necessary for growth. Just as Socrates felt that it was necessary to create a tension in the mind so that individuals could rise from the bondage of myths and half-truths to the unfettered realm of creative analysis and objective appraisal, we must see the need of having nonviolent gadflies to create the kind of tension in society that will help men to rise from the dark depths of prejudice and racism to the majestic heights of understanding and brotherhood. So the purpose of direct action is to create a situation so crisis-packed that it will inevitably open the door to negotiation.

What King was saying, in plain English, was that he was in Birmingham to stay and that Birmingham leaders had to fish or cut bait. Even as he wrote, events on the Birmingham streets added exclamation points to his eloquence. Day after night after day, Birmingham rang with the cries of demonstrators, the eerie whines of wolfish K-9 dogs, and the epithets of white policemen. Beyond all this there lay the driving pressure of black onlookers—unemployed adults and restless youth—who stood on the sidelines, waiting, watching. On April 20, the day King posted bond and resumed direct command of the demonstrations, it was as clear as the statue of Vulcan on Birmingham's Red Mountain that the contest would go on until someone was either knocked down or knocked out.

All this was as clear to "Bull" Connor as anything needed to be. His strategy was simple: he intended to wear the demonstrators down. The strategy almost worked, for by May 1 the enthusiasm of the demonstrators was waning and Connor was as close as he ever would be to a decision on points. Almost a thousand blacks were either in jail or out on bond, and men were saying that "Bull" was unbeatable. Studying the situation, feeling the pulse of the wavering black community, King and his lieutenants decided that a truly audacious act was necessary. But how do you define audacity?

In the rooms of the Gaston Motel, King and his aides wrestled with that question and came up with a classic solution. It is easy, in retrospect, to say that the decision they made was brilliant. But the sun was hooded by clouds then, and few men were willing to take responsibility for the death of a child. Many people would say later that they had a hand in the decision. But back there, in the early hours of the morning, it was all in one man's hand. And history records that some time before May 1, 1963, Martin Luther King Jr. decided to take the calculated risk of committing thousands of children to the front lines of an explosive conflict involving nightsticks, police dogs, and high-powered water hoses that could strip bark off an oak tree.

Events moved rapidly now. Mimeograph machines clanked and within hours leaflets were on the streets:

> FIGHT FOR FREEDOM FIRST THEN GO TO SCHOOL. . . . Join thousands in jail who are making their witness for freedom. Come to the 16th Street Baptist Church now . . . and we'll soon be free. It's up to you to free our teachers, our parents, yourself and our country.

The black youths of Birmingham were waiting for the call; many, in fact, had demanded assignment to the front lines. Now they flocked to the yellow brick church on the edge of the battlefield, leaving public schools virtually empty. The day the tide turned, the day schoolchildren were committed to the struggle, was Thursday, May 2. It was a hot muggy day with tempers and temperatures near the fever level. A little before noon, black people began to gather on the sidewalks along Sixteenth Street and Sixth Avenue.

"Bull" Connor stood wide-legged, a straw hat pulled down over one eye, watching the gathering crowd and listening to the freedom songs coming from the Sixteenth Street Baptist Church, where the students had assembled. Connor barked; firemen brought up three red pumpers, and blue-coated police shifted into position. All the while, firemen in dun-colored uniforms and knee-length slickers tinkered with the gadgets on the hoses, like violinists tuning up before a concert.

Then suddenly it happened: hundreds of singing, shouting, dancing youths burst through the door of the church and marched on the barricades. Some of them wiggled through and reached city hall and downtown street corners. The next day the same drama was repeated, and "Bull" Connor abandoned the amenities. Hundreds of teenagers were bowled over by high-powered hoses and washed under cars like garbage. Policemen then waded in with clubs and dogs, arresting hundreds and herding them into detention cells at the jail and the state fairground.

Demonstrators protesting segregation in Birmingham, Alabama, were dispersed by police. The demonstrations marked a new phase of the protest movement.

Some 250,000 Americans participated in the mammoth March on Washington demonstration on August 28, 1963. Asa Philip Randolph was one of the leaders of the March.

President Lyndon Baines Johnson distributes pens he used in signing the Civil Rights Bill of 1964. Among those receiving pens was Roy Wilkins of the NAACP.

The Selma-to-Montgomery March was climaxed by a major rally at the Alabama state capitol in March, 1960. Alabama National Guardsmen and a contingent of federal troops protected marchers.

"Turn Left or Get Shot" sign greeted motorists approaching a roadblock manned by National Guardsmen in riot-torn Watts section of Los Angeles in August, 1965. The Watts rebellion marked a major turning point in race relations in America.

The summer of 1966 was marked by rebellions and riots in Omaha, Chicago, Cleveland and other major cities. Ohio National Guardsmen patrolled the Hough area of Cleveland.

The use of hoses, billy clubs and dogs on boys and girls, some of them five and six years old, turned Birmingham into a volcano of swirling emotions. Pictures of snarling dogs sinking fangs into the flesh of black children produced a similar ferment in the world beyond Birmingham. Equally revolting, though oddly symbolic, was the picture of a white policeman with his knee on the neck of a black woman. Sen. Wayne Morse told the Senate that the Birmingham spectacle "would disgrace a Union of South Africa or a Portuguese Angola." The *New York Times* commented editorially that the Birmingham "barbarities" were "revoltingly reminiscent of totalitarian excesses."

With pressure mounting for federal intervention, the Kennedy brothers acted, sending Burke Marshall to Birmingham to negotiate a settlement. Marshall initiated what he called a "dialogue," but Birmingham's white leaders balked at demands for desegregation of facilities in downtown stores and the upgrading of black workers. What changed their minds was the intensity of the demonstrations. On Monday, May 6, wave after wave of youthful demonstrators poured out of the church and "Bull" Connor shouted to a police captain, "I told you these sons of bitches ought to be watered down." At a mass meeting that night, a King aide shouted: "War has been declared in Birmingham. War has been declared on segregation."

So it had; the next day the demonstrations reached scorching intensity, and Birmingham tottered on the edge of social disorder. More than two thousand youths participated in the demonstrations and thousands penetrated police lines and surged through the downtown area, singing freedom songs and wandering through stores. When police tried to disperse crowds in black districts, sullen onlookers pelted them with rocks and bottles in a riot that lasted more than an hour.

That same day, Tuesday, May 7, Sheriff Melvin Bailey told an emergency meeting of the Senior Citizens Committee, a group of about seventy of the city's top industrial, commercial and professional leaders, that unless the demonstrations were ended it would be necessary to impose martial law. The committee immediately empowered a subcommittee to come to terms with black leaders. After a nightlong meeting in the home of a black insurance executive, a tentative agreement was reached. Three days later on Wednesday, May 10, Fred Shuttlesworth told a press conference, "The city of Birmingham has reached an accord with its conscience." He announced agreement on a four-point program which called for the desegregation of lunch counters, restrooms, fitting rooms and drinking fountains "in planned stages within the next ninety days," the upgrading and hiring of black workers on a nondiscriminatory basis in Birmingham businesses, the release of demonstrators (some 2,400 had been arrested) on nominal bond and the creation of a biracial committee.

Not surprisingly, Eugene Connor and other segregationists denounced the agreement and called for a white boycott of merchants. On Saturday, May 11, the Ku Klux Klan held a rally and cross burning in the suburbs to dramatize opposition to "Martin Luther King, atheists or so-called ministers of the nigger race." The grand dragons of Georgia, South Carolina, Tennessee and Mississippi offered condolences to the good white people of Birmingham. "It is regrettable," one speaker said, "that you are having these troubles. . . . King should be met with force. King and Kennedy are worse than Castro. We need to go back to the old-time religion time and the old-time Klan time. . . . In Atlanta, they're putting on a show about Cleopatra, and Cleopatra is a black girl and she kisses a white boy. . . . You have just as much civil rights as any Communist. There will be bloodshed in every state."

The meeting ended with a blessing from a minister:

"Heavenly Father we are grateful. . . . We know that these things cannot prevail, for they are of the devil. The terrible tide of black tyranny."

The crowd dispersed then, and a voice on the microphone cautioned the Klan members to "drive carefully." A second voice said, "Run over any niggers you see." The first voice objected: "No, no. Wait till next year."

Someone, whether a Klansman or not, didn't wait. At 10:45 on the same night, the home of the Reverend A. D. King, brother of Martin Luther King Jr., and a leader of the Birmingham movement, was rocked by two dynamite explosions. Less than an hour later the A. G. Gaston Motel, headquarters of the campaign, was heavily damaged by another bombing attack.

What happened next was rage—a blind, choking, mind-numbing rage. Thousands of blacks rushed through the streets, hurling rocks and bottles. Striking out blindly, the rioters burned a block of houses and stores, smashed police vehicles and attacked police. For more than three hours, rioters—silhouetted by flames that leaped one hundred and fifty feet into the air—commanded the streets. Some fifty persons, including a policeman and a white taxi driver, were injured. By dawn on Mother's Day, a nine-block area was virtually devastated. President Kennedy ordered federal troops into ready positions near Birmingham, but the disturbance ended without further violence.

But this was one of those endings which make a thousand beginnings. For with Birmingham, a new epoch began. The flames from that event leaped across the country, igniting inflammable material and welding blacks of all ranks and creeds into a mass of indignation. With a desperation born of a century of denial, with a hope born of the concrete experience of seeing walls come tumbling down, blacks poured into the streets, screaming: "Freedom! Freedom! Freedom NOW!" In June and July Birmingham-type demonstrations pushed scores of cities to the edge of civil war. In Danville, Virginia, police, armed with submachine guns and armored cars, broke up a protest demonstration and waded in with billy clubs. After the march some fifty demonstrators were taken to hospitals with broken heads and lacerations. A month-long series of demonstrations in Savannah, Georgia, culminated in pitched battles in the downtown section. When demonstrators lay down in the streets to stop traffic, officers, equipped with shotguns and bayonets, counterattacked with barrages of tear gas and concussion grenades.

The worst encounter occurred in Cambridge, Maryland, where a campaign for desegregation of public facilities led to altercations which continued for several days. In the course of this struggle, bands of armed and angry men stalked each other in the shadows of the streets. On June 11, Cambridge abandoned the formalities and went to war. All through that night there were sounds of warfare—careening cars, screaming men, shattering glass, sirens, yells and the short angry barks of rifles and pistols. At one point two carloads of whites drove through the black section exchanging gunfire in what one eyewitness said was "virtually a Wild West gun duel." Major George E. Davidson of the state police reported "shooting all over the city—almost on the

scale of warfare." Cambridge's petite war ended with the arrival
of the National Guard and the declaration of modified martial law.
Attorney General Kennedy later called Gloria Richardson, the
tough-minded leader of the Cambridge black community, and
Mayor Calvin W. Mowbray, the leader of the white community, to
the Justice Department, where, like representatives of foreign
powers, they signed a truce. The agreement later broke down,
and Cambridge remained under limited martial law for more than
a year.

Meanwhile, another crisis, the assassination of Medgar Evers,
heightened the tensions between black and white Americans.
Evers, symbol and portent of the crisis, was a metaphor of an age
of dying hope. Tall, heavy-set and stout-hearted, he was a native
Mississippian who had served in the army in World War II. After
the defeat of Nazi racists, he returned to America to fight native
exponents of the *Herrenvolk* creed. As it turned out, the Battle of
Mississippi was more protracted and more dangerous. Threats,
floggings, bombings, blood, terror: all this was part of his daily
life as field secretary of the Mississippi NAACP. Evers was in the
forefront of every effort to crack the cotton curtain in Mississippi,
and he played an important role in the successful penetration of
the defenses of the University of Mississippi. As the revolution
reached new dimensions of strife in the spring of 1963, he went
into the streets to lead a massive effort to desegregate public
facilities in Jackson. More than seven hundred persons, including
NAACP secretary Roy Wilkins, went to jail before the mass demonstration ended. As a local man, Evers bore the brunt of white
reaction to the street demonstrations and the voter registration
campaign that followed. And toward the end it seems that Evers
knew that death was near. He had always known that death was
possible, but now he turned around within himself and looked the
thing full in the face, telling a reporter: "If I die, it will be in a
good cause. I've been fighting for America just as much as soldiers in Vietnam."

In the next few days, Evers moved about the beleaguered
streets of Jackson, so his friends remembered later, with the air
of a man who *knows*. "I'm looking to be shot," he told a friend,
"any time I step out of my car." To Gloster Current, an NAACP
colleague, he was more explicit, saying: "Everywhere I go, somebody has been following me." It was Tuesday, June 11, just be-

fore midnight, when Evers dropped Current off after a mass meeting. "I'm tired," Medgar Evers said, "I'm tired." So saying, as Current remembered later, "he just held my hand and held it and held it."

Fifteen minutes later Evers stepped out of his car in the driveway of his home. A white man, crouching in a honeysuckle thicket one hundred and fifty feet away, steadied himself, peered through the telescopic sight on a high-powered rifle, fired one bullet and ran. The bullet plowed through Evers's body, slammed through a window and wall and came to rest in the kitchen of the house. Myrlie Evers ran outside, screaming. "Medgar," she said, "was lying there on the doorstep in a pool of blood. I tried to get the children away, but they saw it all."

The inevitable happened. On the day of the funeral, which was attended by UN Undersecretary Ralph J. Bunche, Martin Luther King Jr., and other notables, a group of youths gathered near the funeral home. They stood silent for a moment, and then they began to sing a spiritual:

> Before I'd be a slave
> I'd be buried in my grave
> And go home to my Lord and be free.

The volume swelled, pulling others to the little knot of defiant mourners. In the sweltering heat the crowd swayed, sobbed, shouted:

> No more killin' here!
> No more killin' here!

Suddenly the people began to move, oozing like an overflowing river toward the main business district. Somebody started to run and the crowd lurched forward, breaking through a blockade of police and storming to the edge of Capitol Street, which was filled now with rural whites. A wall of blue-helmeted police halted the forward movement of the youths and slowly pushed them back towards the black district. For several minutes the police and the black crowd dueled with epithets, nightsticks and lobbed bottles. Then John Doar, the No. 2 man in the civil rights section of the Justice Department, stepped into the no-man's land between the contending groups and succeeded in quenching the fire. But a white policeman had the last word, saying:

"He didn't stop it, he just postponed it."

This was the mood of both white and black Americans as Medgar Evers was lowered to his final resting place in Arlington Cemetery. Now, in May and June, President Kennedy altered his civil rights strategy. Until that moment Kennedy had pursued a sophisticated form of tokenism, appointing blacks to highly visible and unprecedented posts and damping down discontent with highly publicized feints in the halls of Congress. Kennedy's record at that juncture, compared with the record of his predecessors, was impressive; but judged by the demands of the time it was inordinately timid. The president and his brother, the attorney general, apparently had deep convictions. But they wanted to solve the problem without hurting anyone and without alienating Southern senators, who controlled key parts of the Kennedy domestic and foreign programs.

The failure of this policy was written in the blood of Jackson and the bombs of Birmingham; and Kennedy, who had a superb sense of history, shifted gears and proposed one of the most aggressive civil rights programs ever sponsored by an American president. His first step came on the eve of the Evers assassination. After outmaneuvering the Alabama governor and forcing the registration of two black students at the University of Alabama, the president made a fourteen-and-a-half minute speech, which was probably one of the most momentous acts of his career. For in this speech an American president said for the first time that segregation was morally wrong. "One hundred years of delay have passed," the president said, "since President Lincoln freed the slaves, yet their heirs, their grandsons, are not fully free. They are not yet freed from the bonds of injustice; they are not yet freed from social and economic oppression. And this nation, for all its hopes and all its boasts, will not be fully free until all its citizens are free." The president added:

> We preach freedom around the world, and we mean it. And we cherish our freedom here at home. But are we to say to the world—and much more importantly to each other—that this is the land of the free, except for the Negroes; that we have no second-class citizens, except for Negroes; that we have no

class or caste system, no ghettos, no master race, except with respect to Negroes?

Now the time has come for this nation to fulfill its promise. The events in Birmingham and elsewhere have so increased the cries for equality that no city or state or legislative body can prudently choose to ignore them.

He concluded with a call for action:

The fires of frustration and discord are burning in every city, North and South. . . . We face, therefore, a moral crisis as a country and a people. It cannot be met by repressive police action. It cannot be left to increased demonstrations in the streets. It cannot be quieted by token moves or talk. It is a time to act in the Congress, in your state and local legislative body, and, above all, in all of our daily lives. . . . Those who do nothing are inviting shame as well as violence. Those who act boldly are recognizing right as well as reality.

The president acted boldly, beginning a series of frank discussions with labor leaders, businessmen, religious leaders and civil rights leaders. On the day Medgar Evers was buried, he sent to Congress a civil rights bill which guaranteed equal rights in public accommodations and gave the attorney general power to file suits to force compliance with the Fourteenth and Fifteenth amendments.

While the bill worked its way through Congress, the fires of frustration and discord leaped higher and higher, taking new shape and creating ominous shadows in the black colonies of the North. In city after city, blacks used their bodies to protest racism. They staged marathon sit-ins in the offices of the New York City mayor and the New York governor in a month-long crisis that led to the arrest of more than seven hundred demonstrators. Hundreds more were arrested in Chicago, St. Louis and other cities. There was also trouble in Philadelphia, where more than fifty persons, half of them police, were injured in three days of demonstrations at a construction site. The main objectives in the Northern campaign were increased employment of black workers in skilled trades and the ending of *de facto* segregation in public schools. The months of July and August saw the completion of an antisegregation consensus in the black community that became even deeper and broader. The movement generated its own intensity and reached new heights in a Detroit march of more than two hundred thousand persons.

The swirling currents of rebellion forced established civil rights organizations to change their tactics. With CORE, SNCC and SCLC preempting headlines and hearts with bold, even flamboyant, action, the NAACP and the National Urban League hurried to get into step. Meeting in an uproarious convention in Chicago, the NAACP called for a stepped-up campaign of direct action.

As various voices swelled the fast-rising chorus of the Freedom Now movement, white liberals and moderates began, belatedly, to face racial reality. The governors of Kentucky, Indiana, Illinois, Minnesota and California issued executive orders barring racial discrimination in certain limited areas. Roman Catholic, Protestant and Jewish church leaders issued strong statements urging racial justice. In Rome, Pope Paul VI expressed concern over the escalating struggle in the streets and churches of America. In America, thousands of priests, rabbis, preachers and nuns joined picket lines and participated in demonstrations. Eugene Carson Blake of the Presbyterian Church underlined the central challenge of the age, saying: "Some time or other we are all going to have to stand and be on the receiving end of a fire hose." Blake and other Protestant, Roman Catholic and Jewish clergymen helped organize the powerful civil rights coalition which linked religious, labor and civil rights forces.

The mammoth March on Washington was a visible sign of the potential of this coalition. More than two hundred and fifty thousand Americans—about sixty thousand of them white—participated in the August 28, 1963, demonstration in Washington, D.C. They came from points all over America and from several overseas. They assembled in Washington on the grassy slopes of the Washington Monument and walked about a mile to the Lincoln Monument, where they said with their bodies that blacks had been waiting 100 years and 240 days and that they were still not free and that 100 years and 241 days were too long to wait.

For almost three hours the multitude listened to speakers who demanded immediate passage of a civil rights bill and immediate implementation of the basic guarantees of the Declaration of Independence and the Thirteenth, Fourteenth, and Fifteenth amendments.

In a memorable speech Martin Luther King Jr. etched the mood of the crowd. He came to the lectern late in the afternoon, when the shadows were long on the grass; he read for a time from a prepared text and then he began to improvise, speaking of a dream big enough to include all men, all women and all children, black and white.

"I have a dream," he said, over and over again, and each elaboration evoked hysterical cheers.

> I have a dream that one day this nation will rise up and live out the true meaning of its creed: "We hold these truths to be self-evident; that all men are created equal."
>
> I have a dream that one day on the red hills of Georgia the sons of former slaves and the sons of former slaveowners will be able to sit down together at the table of brotherhood. . . .
>
> This is our hope. This is the faith with which I return to the South. . . . With this faith, we will be able to work together, to pray together, to struggle together, to go to jail together, to stand up for freedom together, knowing that we will be free one day.
>
> This will be the day when all of God's children will be able to sing with new meaning, "My country 'tis of thee, sweet land of liberty, of thee I sing. Land where my fathers died, land of the Pilgrims' pride, from every mountain side, let freedom ring."

King ended with a ringing peroration:

> And if America is to be a great nation this must become true. So let freedom ring from the prodigious hilltops of New Hampshire. Let freedom ring from the mighty mountains of New York. Let freedom ring from the heightening Alleghenies of Pennsylvania! Let freedom ring from the snowcapped Rockies of Colorado!
>
> Let freedom ring from the curvaceous peaks of California!
>
> But not only that; let freedom ring from Stone Mountain of Georgia!
>
> Let freedom ring from every hill and mole hill of Mississippi. From every mountainside, let freedom ring.

> When we let freedom ring, when we let it ring from every village and hamlet, from every state and every city, we will be able to speed up that day when all of God's children, black men and white men, Jews and Gentiles, Protestants and Catholics, will be able to join hands and sing in the words of that old Negro spiritual: "Free at last! Free at last! Thank God Almighty, we are free at last."

It was a magnificent evocation which called back all the old men and women who had that same dream and died dishonored. But, unfortunately, freedom didn't ring. There was a stillness on the hilltops of New Hampshire and in Birmingham there was hate. Eighteen days after the march a car careened past the Sixteenth Street Baptist Church and a hand tossed a bomb. Inside the church, black children were completing the Sunday School lesson: "Love thy neighbor." For an eerie second there was complete silence and then, with a rush of air and a deafening explosion, hate spoke. The church crumbled in smoke and fire and a man stood screaming in the debris: "Love 'em? Love 'em? *I hate 'em!*" Four children died in the blast and twenty-one persons were injured. Later that day, two additional black youths were killed, one by a policeman.

The tempo of the Black Revolution changed now—nobody was playing. A rent strike began in Harlem and spread to other cities, and an integration campaign got underway in Chester, a Philadelphia suburb. The cracks were still further widened by a massive school boycott in Chicago. Two hundred and twenty thousand children, about half of the enrollment, boycotted Chicago schools on October 22, 1963, as a protest against *de facto* segregation and the policies of Benjamin C. Willis, the superintendent of schools.

During this time of rising hope and determination, the forces of reaction were not idle. So long as civil rights battles were fought on distant battlefields in faraway Birmingham and Mississippi, Northerners gave their assent. But when the fight came home, when blacks poured into Northern streets demanding an end to segregation in schools and the housing market, the Northern white community began to stiffen. There was, in fact, something akin to a white panic which was reflected in a precipitous drop in the popularity of President Kennedy.

To add to the confusion, a white resistance movement developed and spread across the country. In Chicago, Detroit, New York and Cleveland, in cities and towns all over America, whites began to organize in support of "neighborhood schools" and "community residential sections." Property owners associations in Chicago and Parents and Taxpayers (PAT) in New York held mass meetings and staged mass marches on city hall. In California and Illinois real estate interests financed campaigns to force referendums on the issue of open occupancy. By January millions of whites were organized in parents, taxpayers and real estate associations that black leaders called Northern counterparts of the White Citizens Councils of the South.

With white resistance spreading in the North, white supremacists moved to the offensive in the South. Virginia revived an old "John Brown statute" which made it a felony to incite blacks "to acts of violence and war against the white population" and vice versa. Georgia followed suit, excavating a slave era law which made insurrection a felony punishable by death. In Alabama officers crushed demonstrations with electric cattle prods and a liberal use of peace bonds. In Orangeburg, South Carolina, black demonstrators were summarily arrested and confined in barbed-wire compounds that resembled concentration camps. The height of this campaign came in Plaquemine, Louisiana, where officers bombarded a black church with tear gas grenades and fire hoses. Black demonstrators said a state policeman with an electric cattle prod rode a horse down the aisle of the church at the height of the counterattack.

The ultimate consequence was a hardening of attitudes on both sides and a polarization of blacks and whites into mutually hostile groups. By November, in the North and South, people were quietly choosing sides for a confrontation many believed inevitable. Then, for the second time in this explosive year, a high-powered rifle spoke, claiming the life of President Kennedy. The Kennedy assassination shattered the gathering battle lines and temporarily restored the broken ranks of the American community. That this should happen in the United States of America on the 100th anniversary of the Emancipation Proclamation of a president who died in a similar manner horrified black Americans, who wandered, wailing, through the angry streets. The young president, by a series of audacious acts, had captured the hearts of black Americans; and when he went to his grave, under circumstances and in a ceremony not unlike the Lincoln ceremony, black Americans played leading roles as honor guards and functionaries. Among the international who's who of mourners were Emperor Haile Selassie, resplendent in a uniform garnished with decorations and a chartreuse sash, and Martin Luther King Jr., somber and thoughtful in a dark suit. Finally, on November 25, John Fitzgerald Kennedy was laid to rest in an Arlington Cemetery grave not too far from the grave of Medgar Evers.

The new president, Lyndon Baines Johnson, the first Southern-based president since Lincoln's successor, Andrew Johnson, moved swiftly to reknit the broken bonds of community. Immediately after the funeral he placed long-distance calls to civil rights leaders and asked their support. Then he went before Congress and asked for immediate passage of the Kennedy civil rights programs, saying that "no memorial or eulogy could more eloquently honor President Kennedy's memory than the earliest possible passage of the Civil Rights Bill for which he fought. We have talked for 100 years or more. Yes, it is time now to write the next chapter—and to write it in books of law."

The president later conferred with James Farmer, executive director of CORE: Whitney Young, executive director of the National Urban League; and Roy Wilkins and Martin Luther King Jr. King said he told the president that the civil rights demonstrations would resume after the period of national mourning.

Two days after the end of the period of mourning, the demonstrations began again in Atlanta, Georgia, with SNCC leading the way. The momentum picked up in January and February with demonstrations in Princess Anne, Maryland, which became the first community in 1964 to deploy K-9 police dogs. There then followed a series of school boycotts in Harlem (464,000 absent in February and 267,000 absent in March), Cleveland (68,000 absent in April), Cincinnati (26,455 absent in February) and Chicago (172,350 absent in February). The continuing conflict over *de facto* school segregation led to riots in Cleveland and Chester, Pennsylvania.

If black folk were growing more set in their anger, the wrath of white folk was also rising. The voices of opposition in the North swelled and crystallized in "a white backlash," a euphemism for the surfacing of latent bigotry. In letters to the editor, in mass marches and rallies, white Americans struck back at black activities. Perhaps the best indication of the depth of white hysteria was the success of George Wallace, the Alabama segregationist, who won a surprisingly large number of votes in the Wisconsin, Indiana and Maryland presidential primaries. Sen. Barry Goldwater, a leading opponent of the civil rights bill, became the rallying point of the "backlash" after his nomination as the Republican candidate for president. Goldwater denied that he was a racist, but there was an undeniable undertone of racial hysteria in his unsuccessful presidential campaign against President Lyndon B. Johnson.

A deeper, because less conscious, source of friction was the activity of federal agents, who undermined the movement with an underground campaign of spying, bugging and break-ins. Throughout this period, as later evidence proved, agents from the FBI, CIA and army intelligence infiltrated civil rights groups, bugged telephones and disseminated false and defamatory information to media. In the course of these activities, coordinated by FBI Director J. Edgar Hoover, who personally loathed Martin Luther King Jr., federal officials compiled a list of activists for possible detention. The principal target of the counterintelligence thrust was Martin Luther King Jr., whose home, offices and hotel rooms were bugged. The FBI also tried to change the direction of the movement by promoting FBI-approved black leadership. This approach was explored at a preliminary conference in FBI headquarters on December 3, 1963. The results of the conference were summarized the next day in a memorandum by Assistant Director William C. Sullivan:

> Recognizing the delicacy of this entire situation because of the prominence of King, the primary purpose of the conference was to explore how best to carry on one investigation to produce the desired results without embarrassment to the Bureau. Included in the discussion was a complete analysis of the avenues of approach aimed at neutralizing King as an effective Negro leader and developing evidence concerning King's continued dependence on Communists, for guidance and direction.

Although the FBI failed to develop evidence of Communist links, Sullivan, less than two weeks later, approved a proposal designed to promote a new leader for Black America. This pleased FBI Director J. Edgar Hoover, who attached a note to Sullivan's memorandum:

"I am glad to see that light has finally, though dismally delayed, come to the DID [Domestic Intelligence Division]. . . ."

Failing in this effort, the FBI tried to make King commit suicide, threatening release of alleged damaging information. In November, 1964, bureau agents sent the following letter to King:

> King, there is only one thing left for you to do. You know what it is. You have just 34 days in which to do. . . . You are done. There is but one way out for you. You better take it before your filthy fraudulent self is bared to the Nation.

This had little or no effect on King's status as a leader, although it caused great personal anguish and helped create the climate of intolerance that led to his death. The House Select Committee on Assassinations said later that the FBI "in the Domestic Intelligence Division's COINTELPRO campaign against Dr. King, grossly abused and exceeded its legal authority and failed to consider the possibility that actions threatening bodily harm to Dr. King might be encouraged by the program."

The COINTELPRO operation happened underground. Aboveground, there was continuing friction in the South, where black and white college students mounted a large-scale assault on the closed society of Mississippi. The Mississippi Summer Project, sponsored by SNCC and other civil rights organizations, was marred by numerous incidents (church burnings, arrests, Klan assaults) and the murder of two whites—Andrew Goodman and Michael H. Schwerner—and one black—James E. Chaney—by Ku Klux Klan terrorists.

In the midst of this furore, on July 2, 1964, Congress passed the Civil Rights Act of 1964, which guaranteed access to public accommodations, such as restaurants, hotels and amusement areas, and authorized the federal government to sue to desegregate facilities, including schools. The act also mandated nondiscrimination in federal programs and required equal employment.

By the time this act was signed, the character of the movement had undergone critical alterations. Before the summer of 1964, movement dialogue had been dominated by professional rebels, trained in nonviolent techniques, who operated primarily in the South. Now the center of gravity shifted to the North and new groups — the angry young men of the Korean War and the so-called underclass, the permanently depressed stratum of the black working class—pushed to the fore, bringing with them the sharp steel of a deeper discontent. With this development, the stage was set for the worst season of racial violence in twenty-one years. Beginning with a riot in Harlem on July 18, 1964, the Black Fury rolled across the land, engulfing Brooklyn, Philadelphia, Rochester and the Chicago suburb of Dixmoor. There was a new dimension to these rebellions, which generally began with a minor police incident and expanded into assaults on white symbols of authority (police and firemen) and control (white-owned stores). In Harlem, where one person was killed, 140 injured and 500 arrested, the triggering incident was the slaying of a fifteen-year-old youth by an off-duty policeman. A protest march on a Harlem police station quickly became a generalized rebellion with the smashing and looting of white-owned stores and guerrilla attacks on officers. For the first time in black America, there was a widespread use of Molotov cocktails (bottles filled with gasoline and improvised wicks). Though spontaneous and unorganized, the Harlem rebellion and the rebellions that followed revealed a dawning sense of revolutionary discontent. A Harlem woman spoke for millions of black Americans when she told a *Time* magazine reporter:

"I clean the white man's dirt all the time, I work for four families and some I don't care for, and some I like. And Saturday I worked for some I like. And when I got home and later when the trouble began, something happened to me. I went on the roof to see what was going on. I don't know what it was, but hearing the guns I felt like something was crawling on me, like the whole damn world was no good, and the little kids and the big ones and all of us was going to get killed because we don't know what to do. And I see the cops are white and I was crying. Dear God, I am crying! And I took this pop bottle and it was empty and I threw it down on the cops, and I was crying and laughing."

In the weeks that followed, federal and state officials moved to contain the rebellion. President Johnson, who had already outlined plans for a "War on Poverty," redoubled his efforts, announcing several new programs and appointing Sargent Shriver head of the Office of Economic Opportunity. By year's end Shriver had fashioned a bureaucracy to carry out the president's announced goal of "conquering poverty" and striking away "the barriers to full participation in our society." From the beginning the "War on Poverty" was mired in political and economic complications. Big-city mayors, largely Democratic, feared the impact of the new programs and moved to keep them within the bounds of the status quo. Another and more tangible reason for the limited impact of the War on Poverty was that it was funded at a level that guaranteed a sham war.

A further response to the Red Summer of 1964 came from black radicals who called for a new program of radical political action. The major symbol of this emerging mood phase was Malcolm X, who left the Nation of Islam and formed the Organization for Afro-American Unity. Malcolm X called for a socioeconomic program of self-defense and self-assertion in concert with the emerging nations of Africa. He also projected a vision of black control of black communities. While organizing this new vision, he was assassinated by black gunmen in full view of hundreds of his followers at the Audubon Ballroom in New York.

Onto this stage, already crowded with social villains, came an onrush of new problems. Martin Luther King Jr., fresh from Oslo, where he had received a Nobel Price for Peace, was engaged at that moment in a voter registration campaign in Selma, Alabama. On Sunday, March 7, 1965, King's aides and John Lewis of SNCC began a Selma-to-Montgomery march to protest the slaying of Jimmie Lee Jackson and the arrest of almost a thousand demonstrators. As the five hundred marchers crossed Selma's Edmund Pettus Bridge, two hundred state troopers and sheriff's deputies lobbed canisters of tear gas and attacked with billy clubs and whips. The brutal scene, witnessed later that day by millions of television-viewers, shocked the nation and sent thousands of blacks and whites to Selma to join the struggle, which continued for two weeks. During the struggle, three white Unitarian ministers, including the Reverend James J. Reeb, were attacked and beaten. Reeb died later in a Birmingham hospital.

After a nationwide flurry of demonstrations and an unheard-of sit-in at the White House, President Johnson told a televised press conference that "what happened in Selma was an American tragedy." Later, on March 15, President Johnson went before a joint session of Congress and called for immediate passage of legislation to eliminate barriers to the right to vote.

Robert C. Weaver, secretary of the Department of Housing and Urban Development, became the first black cabinet member in 1966.

Malcom X (top, right), charismatic black nationalist leader, was assassinated in New York City in 1965.

Edward Brooke (right), first black U.S. senator since Reconstruction, was elected in 1966.

Black students seized Howard
University administration building
in 1968 and demanded black-oriented
curriculum. Student protest spread
to predominantly white campuses.

Speaking with emotion, the president told Congress that the problem before the nation was neither black nor white. The problem, he said, was history:

"At times history and fate meet at a single time in a single place to shape a turning point in man's unending search for freedom. So it was at Lexington and Concord. So it was a century ago at Appomattox. So it was last week in Selma, Alabama."

Appropriating the words of the Freedom movement anthem, Johnson called for a maximum effort:

"[The effort] of American Negroes to secure for themselves the full blessings of American life . . . must be our cause too. Because it's not just Negroes, but really it's all of us who must overcome the crippling legacy of bigotry and injustice. And *we shall overcome*."

Two days later, U.S. District Judge Frank M. Johnson Jr. upheld the right of demonstrators to stage a fifty-mile march from Selma to Montgomery. Judge Johnson enjoined Governor Wallace and other Alabama officials from "harassing or threatening" the marchers. When the Alabama governor informed the president that he could not be responsible for the safety of the marchers, Johnson federalized the Alabama National Guard and dispatched a contingent of U.S. Army troops. Protected thus by the armed might of America, the second Montgomery march began on Sunday, March 21, and ended four days later with a rally of some forty thousand at the Alabama state capitol. The real climax of the march came five months later with the passage of a Voting Rights Bill which authorized the president to suspend literacy tests and send federal examiners into Black Belt counties to register voters. The net effect of this bill was to return the South, in a limited sense, to the first Reconstruction period. Shortly thereafter black voters became a major force in Black Belt counties and a balance of power in some Southern states, electing scores of legislators and other public officials.

The Voting Rights Act was admirable in many respects, but it did not begin to address itself to the structural problems of the color-caste system. In an eloquent commencement address at Howard University, President Johnson conceded this fact, saying:

> You do not wipe away the scars of centuries by saying:
> Now you are free to go where you want, do as you desire, and
> choose the leaders you please.

> You do not take a person who, for years, has been hobbled by chains and liberate him, bring him up to the starting line of a race and then say, "You are free to compete . . ." and still justly believe that you have been completely fair.

President Johnson went on to hail the real gains of the black middle class:

> The number of Negroes in schools of higher learning has almost doubled in fifteen years. The number of nonwhite professional workers has more than doubled in ten years. The median income of Negro college women now exceeds that of white college women. And there are also the enormous accomplishments of distinguished individual Negroes. . . .
>
> These are proud and impressive achievements. But they tell only the story of a growing middle-class minority, steadily narrowing the gap between them and their white counterparts.
>
> But for the great majority of Negro Americans—the poor, the unemployed, the uprooted and the dispossessed—there is a much grimmer story. They still are another nation. Despite the court orders and laws, despite the legislative victories and the speeches, for them the walls are rising and the gulf is widening.

Looking beyond his immediate audience to the holders of political and economic power, the president listed "the facts of this American failure:"

> Thirty-five years ago the rate of unemployment for Negroes and whites was about the same. Today the Negro rate is twice as high.
>
> In 1948 the 8 per cent unemployment rate for Negro teenage boys was actually less than that of whites. By last year the rate had grown to 23 per cent, as against 13 per cent for whites.
>
> Between 1949 and 1959, the income of Negro men relative to white men declined in every section of this country. From 1952 to 1963 the median income of Negro families compared to white actually dropped from 57 per cent to 53 per cent.
>
> In the years 1955 through 1957, 22 per cent of experienced Negro workers were out of work at some time during the year. In 1961 through 1963 that proportion had soared to 29 per cent.

Since 1947 the number of white families living in poverty has decreased 27 per cent, while the number of poor nonwhite families decreased only 3 per cent.

The infant mortality of nonwhites in 1940 was 70 per cent greater than whites. Twenty-two years later it was 90 per cent greater.

Moreover, the isolation of Negroes from the white communities is increasing, rather than decreasing, as Negroes crowd into the central cities and become a city within a city.

To correct these inequities and "To Fulfill These Rights," President Johnson announced that he would soon summon a White House Conference on Civil Rights. As for the Voting Rights Act, the president said it was a step, but only a step, in the right direction, adding:

"But this victory—as Winston Churchill said of another triumph for freedom—is not the end. It is not even the beginning of the end. But it is, perhaps, the end of the beginning."

For Marquette Frye, a twenty-one-year-old unemployed worker, it was not even the beginning of the beginning.

Frye was a citizen of that other nation the president invoked, and it was his arrest on a charge of suspicion of drunken driving that detonated the Watts explosion which made the other nation visible and real. Frye was arrested about 7 P.M. on Wednesday, August 11, near 116th Street and Avalon Boulevard in the south central ghetto of Los Angeles. The arrest gave rise to charges of police brutality in a community that had long regarded white policemen as the occupation troops of an alien and hostile government. Within an hour thousands of blacks were eddying in the hot night (it had climbed to 94 degrees on Wednesday), bombarding police and passing motorists with bricks, bottles, and slabs of concrete. Helmeted police tried to seal off the area, but they soon withdrew in disorder, pursued by young men who hurled stones and shouted: "This is the end for you, Whitey." As the police retreated, the youths of Watts exploded, attacking whites, pillaging stores and screaming defiance. The human explosion reached a peak in Los Angeles shortly after midnight and burned out towards dawn.

The sun of Thursday, August 12, came up in a smog of uncertainty, and Watts was soon astir with the sounds of the coming confrontation. In the midmorning sun young men clustered on street corners and taunted the police: "Wait until night, Whitey. We gonna get you." By late afternoon the streets were jammed with the advance guards of the opposing camps—young black men and apprehensive police. When the sun went down the lid came off Watts. Old people poured out of the houses and apartment buildings and joined young people, who were determined to settle old accounts with the police. Pawnshops, hardware stores and war surplus houses were raided, stripped of guns and set on fire. The streets were barricaded with bus benches, and pitched battles were fought with policemen. Some policemen were mobbed and had to club their way to safety. Taunting rebels tried to pull other police out of their squad cars; still others were lured into traps with false reports and ambushed. Surging through the streets, clashing with police, setting fires, stoning firemen, attacking, scattering, regrouping, passing the word, clutching at rumors, shouting, screaming, crying, the insurgents were transformed by the fire of battle into an awesome power. Eyewitnesses reported a "carnival gaiety" among participants, who exchanged two- and three-finger salutes and shouted a slogan: "Burn, Baby, Burn." Before dawn the balance of forces in Watts had changed. Robert Richardson, a black reporter for the *Los Angeles Times*, wrote: "They [the insurgents] knew they had the upper hand. They seemed to sense that neither the police nor anyone else could stop them."

Now in the night, as the color of power changed, the crowd turned mean, lashing out indiscriminately at everything white that moved. The demonstrators smashed car windows and attacked the occupants, shouting: "This is for Bogalusa! This is for Selma!" Eyewitnesses reported that blacks detached themselves from the crowd and saved the lives of some menaced whites. As the hurricane in the streets grew in intensity, black leaders tried to calm the crowd. Dick Gregory, the comedian and civil rights leader, was shot in the leg while trying to disperse demonstrators on Central Avenue.

On the next day, Friday the thirteenth, the insurgents streamed into the streets again. Milling wildly, people smashed into stores and took what they wanted. Whole blocks of stores were picked clean and burned. The looting, according to witnesses, was leisurely and orderly. Some looters went through the stock to find

the right size; others hired rental trailers to haul away re-
frigerators, stoves and air-conditioners. As the McCone Report
later noted, the rebels were very selective, focusing on stores
notorious for high prices, high financing and bad manners. Particularly hard hit were food markets, liquor stores, clothing stores,
department stores and pawn shops. The McCone Report noted
"with interest that no residences were deliberately burned, that
damage to schools, libraries, public buildings were minimal and
that certain types of business establishments, notably service
stations and automobile dealers, were for the most part unharmed."
Also unharmed, for the most part, were black-owned establishments with hand-lettered signs in the window: "Blood Brother,"
"Negro-owned," "We Own This One." After "liberating" (the
insurgents' word) the merchandise, the insurgents torched the
buildings, and by midday towering billows of smoke crisscrossed
the Los Angeles sky. By this time also mobile bands of rebels were
staging what Police Chief William H. Parker called "Viet Cong-
type raids" on firemen, policemen and merchants.

Events hurried on now at an ever-dizzier pace. Everywhere
there was whirling movement, confused cries, burglar alarms,
screaming sirens, shouting teenagers, the crunch of billy clubs,
the whang of rifles, a thunderous, thousand-tongued tumult of
blood and fire and steel. At first blush it seemed that all was
confusion and disorder. But underneath there was a wild kind of
order that made Watts a major insurrection comparable in its day
and time to Nat Turner's historic attack 134 years before. Beneath
the surface disorder, shielded from the eyes of reporters and history, there were even nameless leaders—bold young men and
even bolder women who left their imprint on a rebellion staged
for the purpose of asserting that black people would no longer submit to the degradations forced on them. A black witness reported
that one band of rebels went from store to store smashing windows and taking what they wanted. All of the men, he said, were
armed with pistols and rifles, and the group was led by a black
woman armed with two bricks. Another witness, Sgt. John S.
McElhinney, helicopter pilot for the Los Angeles Police Department, reported: "On the ground you might be at an intersection
and nothing at all would be going on there. But two blocks away
all hell's breaking loose. We're riding along [in the helicopter]
and don't see a thing. Then, all of a sudden, they're there. There

might be fifty of them, there might be a hundred. Where in the hell they came from I don't know." The war of fire and disruption continued throughout the day with the police rapidly losing any semblance of control. Police Inspector John Kinsling announced that the rebels had "completely captured Watts," and Governor Pat Brown interrupted a European vacation and flew back to California, saying: "From here it is awfully hard to direct a war. That's what this is."

White Los Angeles, which lives on dreams, which has no reality apart from the unreality it purveys as the film capital of the world, was shocked by the reality that forced its way through the flames. The first reaction in Hollywood, Beverly Hills and other elegant enclaves was shock, followed by panic and a run on gun stores. But even here unreality reigned, for well-to-do-blacks, who were also seeking reassurance, discovered that some gun stores were selling to white people only. In many parts of the divided city, civic life came to a halt, and public and social events were postponed or cancelled. The University of Southern California postponed classes, and the Los Angeles County Museum was closed on an emergency basis for the first time in fifty-two years.

By this time, Friday afternoon, the rebellion was spreading to other California cities, and echoes were returning to Watts from Chicago, where blacks were also in open revolt. In Los Angeles itself the insurgents smashed out of the police perimeter and moved towards downtown Los Angeles. Before this thrust was blunted, the rebels moved as far north as Central and Washington, less than three miles from the center of the city.

Outmanned and outgunned, city and state officials declared Watts in a state of insurrection and called out the National Guard. The first of more than thirteen thousand National Guardsmen moved into the forty-five-square-mile area that night and started establishing a military perimeter. Machine-gun emplacements were set up at intersections, road blocks were established, and all cars entering or leaving the area were stopped and the occupants searched. Guardsmen later began a street-by-street sweep in an attempt to enforce an 8 P.M. to dawn curfew. When the columns of heavily armed troops advanced, the rebels melted away in front of them and reformed behind or leapfrogged ahead. At many points skirmishes thickened into full-scale battles. One detachment of guardsmen ran into a volley of bullets and answered with a salvo of machine-gun fire. Guardsmen also fought off an armed attack on a police station and killed one sniper.

Throughout that day and the next day, Saturday, looting and burning of stores continued. Gen. Roderic L. Hill, the California adjutant general, commented: "Every indication is that the situation is as bad or worse at this time today as it was at this time yesterday. We have in my opinion armed insurrection, and I would add complete disregard for law and order on the part of a significant number of the population of Los Angeles." Although sniping continued, the troops gradually contained the disorder and Police Chief Parker, the main target of the rebellion, announced on Sunday: "We're on top and they're on the bottom." In the opinion of many blacks and whites, Parker's statement on the end of the insurrection contained the real reason for the beginning of the insurrection.

On the sixth day, Monday, August 17, Watts was numb and relatively quiet. The area itself looked like a war zone. Whole blocks lay in rubble and ashes. Walter Fischer, correspondent of *Der Stern*, said, "It looks like Germany during the last months of World War II." By actual count two hundred businesses had been totally destroyed and more than seven hundred had been heavily damaged. The toll for the six-day insurrection: 34 persons killed, 1,032 injured, 4,000 arrested. Total property damage was estimated at $35 million.

Governor Brown appointed an eight-member commission, headed by John A. McCone, former director of the Central Intelligence Agency, to investigate "the immediate and underlying causes of the Los Angeles riots and to recommend means to prevent their occurrence." Five months later the McCone Commission submitted a controversial 101-page report. Most black leaders criticized the substance of the report, though all agreed with its grim conclusion:

"As a commission, we are seriously concerned that the existing breach, if allowed to persist, could in time split our society irretrievably. So serious and explosive is the situation that, unless it is checked, the August riots may seem by comparison to be only a curtain-raiser for what could blow up one day in the future."

The words were relevant but they were not translated into deeds, and the problem grew worse, compounded by America's deepening involvement in the Vietnam War. President Johnson tried to maintain a consensus with a White House Conference on Civil Rights in the spring of 1966. But the conference was boycotted by the Student Nonviolent Coordinating Committee and attacked by the Congress of Racial Equality. The cracks were still further widened on June 6 by the attempted assassination of James Meredith, an event that triggered a march on the Mississippi capitol. During the march latent conflicts in the Civil Rights movement surfaced with Stokely Carmichael of SNCC and Floyd McKissick of CORE championing a more radical Black Power posture oriented toward the black masses.

With the call for Black Power, the movement entered a decisively new phase. Most Black Power advocates denounced the integration orientation of the old civil rights coalition and called for a new strategy based on black control of the organizations, institutions and resources of the black community. Some black-oriented leaders urged creation of parallel or independent power blocs (black political parties and black unions) outside existing structures. At the other end of the spectrum were nationalists who called for the creation of an independent black state on American soil. Despite different emphases and different strategies, most members of the new movement stressed black pride, black dignity and black self-determination. Many whites and some blacks denounced Black Power as a retrograde movement which masked what they called racism in reverse. But the leaders of the new movement said a new strategy based on the massed power of the black community was essential for the liberation of black Americans. After the Mississippi march, new powers, adapted to new times and destinies, crystallized in the black community. Militant black students organized black student unions on college campuses and used tactics of disruption to press demands for black faculty members and black-oriented courses.

Meanwhile, alarming reports were coming in from all over. In 1966 National Guardsmen were mobilized to put down uprisings in Omaha, Chicago, Dayton and Cleveland. In the same summer police fought pitched battles with rebels in Brooklyn, Jacksonville, Philadelphia, Atlanta and scores of other cities. Eleven persons were killed and over four hundred were injured in the forty-three riots of that year. The urban warfare assumed a new and more threatening dimension in the summer of 1967 with major rebellions in Newark (23 killed, 1,500 wounded) and Detroit (43 killed, 2,000 wounded). The Detroit Rebellion, which lasted for seven days, cost $45 million and led to the first use of federal troops in an American riot since the Detroit riot of 1943. Eighty-three persons were killed in riots in more than one hundred cities in 1967.

The response to this unparalleled domestic crisis was vague and uncertain. Committees of inquiry were appointed, and there were demands for "law and order" and repression. But two investigating committees, the Select Commission on Civil Disorders in New Jersey and the National Advisory Commission on Civil Disorders, told Americans that the issue could not be resolved without a new level of commitment and concern. In a report issued on February 10, 1968, the Select Commission on Civil Disorders in New Jersey said:

> Although violence has marked the path of many ethnic and social groups, the major issues that were in contention in those conflicts have long since been resolved. But one great issue remains unresolved: It is the place of the Negro in American society. It is this issue that almost tore the nation apart 100 years ago. It is this question that led to the Chicago riot of 1919, the Harlem riots of 1935 and 1943, and the mounting disorders . . . since World War II. In the wake of the major racial conflicts of this century, commissions like this were established. They investigated . . . and made recommendations. Many chapters in these earlier volumes read much like some in this report. Poor housing, unemployment and inferior education of Negroes figure prominently in the report on the 1919 Chicago riot, just as they do in our analysis of the conditions in Newark in 1967. The mood in our cities clearly indicates that commissions like ours will have outlived their usefulness unless action is forthcoming from their recommendations.

Who was responsible for this situation?

> The burden of responsibility weighs most heavily on those in positions of leadership power and with control over the resources that will be needed to produce tangible results.

> . . . The fate of the city today is in the hands of the police-
> man on the beat, the landlord of the tenement building, the
> shop steward in the factory, the employer, the storekeeper,
> the social worker, the public employer behind his desk or the
> neighbor who will not be a neighbor.

As for solutions, the commission said:

> We need fewer press releases from police commissioners
> on community relations and more respect by patrolmen for
> the dignity of each citizen. We need fewer speeches from
> employers and union leaders on equal opportunity in the fu-
> ture, and more flexible hiring standards now. We need more
> principals, teachers and guidance counselors who want their
> students to succeed instead of expecting them to fail. We
> need more social workers who respect and foster a client's
> pride instead of treating him as an irritant or a child. Subur-
> ban residents must understand that the future of their com-
> munities is inextricably linked to the fate of the city, instead
> of harboring the illusions that they can maintain invisible
> walls or continue to run away.

And so, in summation:

> If the events of last July had one effect, it was to show that
> we can no longer escape the issue. The question is whether
> we shall resort to illusion, or . . . come to grips with reality.

An equally forthright report came from the National Advisory
Commission on Civil Disorders, which included two blacks, Roy
Wilkins of the NAACP and Senator Edward Brooke. After a
seven-month study the commission reported, on February 29,
1968, that America was "moving toward two societies, one black,
one white—separate and unequal." The commission added:

"This deepening racial division is not inevitable. The movement apart can be reversed. Choice is still possible. Our principal
task is to define that choice and press for a national resolution.

"To pursue our present course will involve the continuing
polarization of the American community and, ultimately, the destruction of basic democratic values."

The eleven-member commission, headed by Governor Otto
Kerner of Illinois, said "white racism" was chiefly responsible for

Detroit Rebellion marked a new phase in the revolt of the urban masses. Federal troops were mobilized to quell the 1967 rebellion.

Smoke from fires set by rebels settled over the U.S. Capitol during the rebellion which followed the assassination of Martin Luther King Jr.

the "explosive mixture" of poverty, discrimination and resentment in the black community. The Kerner Commission report called for a "massive and sustained" national commitment to action and concluded:

"What white Americans have never fully understood—but what the Negro can never forget—is that white society is deeply implicated in the ghetto. White institutions created it, white institutions maintain it, and white society condones it.

"It is time now to turn with all the purpose at our command to the major unfinished business of this nation. It is time to adopt strategies for action that will produce quick and visible progress. It is time to make good the promises of American democracy to all citizens—urban and rural, white and black, Spanish-surname, American Indian and every minority group."

Since these words were not heeded—then or later—the fury increased, propelled not only by civil rights grievances but also by mounting concern over the Vietnam War. In the spring of 1968 black and white students linked forces and staged demonstrations for "Peace and Freedom." To the dismay of government officials and some civil rights leaders, certain activists, most notably Martin Luther King Jr., Stokely Carmichael and Floyd McKissick, moved beyond traditional civil rights boundaries and assumed leadership in the antiwar movement.

Realizing that the situation was rapidly worsening, Martin Luther King tried to change the movement—and history—by bringing together poor whites and poor blacks in a Poor People's Campaign. The objective of the campaign was an economic bill of rights, including a guaranteed annual income, full employment, decent housing and quality education. Under King's plan, poor people, black and white, would converge on Washington, D.C., and would demonstrate, beginning on April 20, 1968, until the government responded to their demands. King said:

"We will place the problems of the poor at the seat of the government of the wealthiest nation in the history of mankind. If that power refuses to acknowledge its debt to the poor, it will have failed to live up to its promise to insure life, liberty, and the pursuit of happiness to its citizens."

While King was mobilizing forces for the campaign, he made an unscheduled detour to help striking sanitation workers in Memphis, Tennessee. The detour became an ordeal and a farewell.

For a riot, triggered by the frustrations of angry youths, forced a larger commitment. And it was there, near the end of that campaign, that he was seized by the same premonition that came, in a similar situation, to Medgar Evers. Nothing shows this more clearly than his last public speech. There had been a bomb scare that morning and other threats against his life, and when he rose, on the night of Wednesday, April 3, to address the two thousand people jammed into Mason Temple Church, he alluded to the incidents in a manner that seemed to aide Andrew Young "almost morbid." He concluded the speech, one of the greatest of his career, with a direct reference to his own death:

"Well, I don't know what will happen now. We've got some difficult days ahead. But it really doesn't matter to me now, because I've been to the mountaintop. I won't mind.

"Like anybody, I'd like to live a long life. Longevity has its place but I'm not concerned about that now. I just want to do God's will and He's allowed me to go up to the mountain. And I've looked over. And I've seen the Promised Land.

"So I'm happy tonight. I'm not worried about anything. I'm not fearing any man. 'Mine eyes have seen the glory of the coming of the Lord.' "

The next day, Thursday, April 4, King walked out of room 306 at the Lorraine Motel shortly before 6 P.M. At 6:01 P.M., the official report said, as King stood behind the iron balcony railing in front of room 306, the report of a high-powered rifle cracked the air. A slug tore into the right side of his face, violently throwing him backward. The thirty-nine-year-old leader, called by Ralph D. Abernathy "the most peaceful warrior of the twentieth century," was pronounced dead at 7:05 P.M. in the emergency room of St. Joseph Hospital. Two months later, on June 8, a man identified as his assassin—James Earl Ray—was captured at a London airport. Although Ray later pleaded guilty to charges of killing King and was sentenced to ninety-nine years in prison, there were persistent reports that he was a cog in a larger conspiracy. The House Select Committee on Assassinations, headed by Congressman Louis Stokes, investigated these reports and concluded that "there is a likelihood" that Ray assassinated King "as a result of a conspiracy" with unindicted conspirators.

Future investigations and sentences apart, the assassination had immediate and sensational consequences in America, where

Widow and children of the assassinated
leader are pictured at funeral service
in Atlanta's Ebenezer Baptist Church.
Among the mourners were Vice-President Hubert
Humphrey and Supreme Court Justice
Thurgood Marshall.

Aides and followers of Martin
Luther King Jr. accompanied his
coffin on the final trip through
the streets of Atlanta, Georgia.

black communities exploded, one after another, like firecrackers on a string. According to press reports and other documents, forty-six persons were killed in black rebellions in 126 cities. Federal troops were mobilized to put down rebellions in Chicago, Baltimore and Washington, D.C.

To counteract this fury, and to express their sorrow, Americans of all races and creeds joined forces in an unprecedented tribute to a black American. President Johnson declared a national day of mourning and ordered U.S. flags to fly at half mast on U.S. installations at home and abroad. In cities across the country schools and public facilities closed to honor the man eulogized as one of the greatest spiritual leaders of the century. On the day of the funeral—Tuesday, April 9—more than two hundred thousand Americans followed King's coffin, which was carried through the streets of Atlanta on a wagon, borne by two Georgia mules. Among the mourners were scores of dignitaries, including Sen. Robert F. Kennedy, who was assassinated two months later in the midst of his presidential campaign.

If there were casualties in the King-led struggle, there were also gains. For in the sixties, and as a direct result of the direct action of the sixties, black Americans made their biggest gains since slavery, eliminating legal barriers and scoring so many firsts that the phrase "the first Negro" lost its meaning. It was during this period, for example, that President Johnson appointed the first black cabinet member—Secretary of Housing and Urban Development Robert C. Weaver—and the first black Supreme Court justice—Thurgood Marshall. There was also rare recognition of black genius in other fields. To cite only two examples, Sidney Poitier received the Academy Award in 1963 for his role in *Lilies of the Field*, and James Baldwin was honored for his novels and essays, including *The Fire Next Time*.

While individual blacks were breaking through racial barriers on these levels, the masses of blacks were making their greatest gains since slavery in income, health, education, employment and voter participation, as a few facts and figures will indicate. From 1965 to 1969 the proportion of blacks at the lower end of the income spectrum (below $3,000) was markedly reduced while the proportion at the upper end ($10,000 and above) rose dramatically. By 1970 some 28 percent of black families were in the

$10,000 and over category, compared to 11 per cent in 1960. By this time the number of blacks employed in better-paying white collar and craftsmen occupations had increased from about three million in 1960 to about five million in 1971. Nor were these gains confined to the economic field. In 1971, 18 per cent of young blacks were in college, compared to about 10 per cent in 1965. In 1972 there were 2,264 black elected officials, 206 of them in state legislatures, more than double the 1964 figures.

By the end of this period, the 23,000,000 black Americans had an annual income of more than $100 billion dollars a year and constituted the second largest African community in the world.

Not the least of the paradoxes of the Black Revolution is that it also extended the boundaries of freedom for white women, white students, and poor people of all races and creeds.

The years immediately following were downhill years, strangely and ominously redolent of another time, precisely one hundred years before, when America came to a fork in the road and veered sharply to the right, back towards slavery. And as the sixties receded into history, the memory of that other time, the downhill time marking the end of the first Reconstruction, dominated public discourse. For there were unmistakable trends in the descending years of the early seventies, that the furies were gathering for the burial of the hopes spawned by the Second Reconstruction.

Three massive facts dominated this situation.

The first and certainly most important fact was the death of that feverish, kaleidoscopic maelstrom of acts, energies and hopes called the Black Revolution. For seventeen years, ever since the festival of Montgomery, that phenomenon had absorbed all energies and hopes. Now suddenly the great wave of passion and hope subsided. The demonstrations died down, and the long hot summers cooled. The summer of 1970 was relatively quiet; so were the summers of 1971 and 1972. Not that militant energies disappeared. There were rearguard actions in the prisons and on black and white college campuses. But these explosions, important as they were, were distant echoes of the many-tongued, many-layered actions of the masses, who disappeared now from the stage of history, as they disappeared in the twenties and thirties and forties, presumably to gather new strength for a new charge under more favorable conditions. Thus, in the aftermath

Congressional Black Caucus
(top) was organized by black
representatives in 1971.
Black leaders, including Vernon E. Jordan, Benjamin L.
Hooks and Coretta Scott
King, discussed civil rights
issues with President Jimmy
Carter. Andrew Young
(center, left) helped influence
American foreign policy during his tenure as UN Ambassador.

New NAACP leader, Benjamin L. Hooks (right above) received congratulations from Roy Wilkins, who retired in 1977, Mrs. Aminda Wilkins (l.) and Mrs. Frances Hooks. Leaders of the post-King generation (left) included Jesse Jackson (l.), president of People United to Save Humanity (PUSH), and Joseph E. Lowery, president of the Southern Christian Leadership Conference (SCLC).

William T. Coleman was secretary of transportation in the Ford administration. Patricia R. Harris held two cabinet posts, secretary of housing and urban development and secretary of health, education and welfare, in the Carter administration.

of Watts and Selma, Black America entered the postrevolutionary phase of a revolution that never really happened, the postrevolutionary phase of a revolution that turned in on itself because it could not be accomplished historically at that particular time under the particular ratio of forces. By 1972 blacks had been struggling in the streets of America for seventeen years. They had tried everything or almost everything. They had marched, demonstrated, boycotted, protested, petitioned, dreamed, prayed, rioted — and they had not overcome. So inevitably there was a turning within and a turning away and a groping for new avenues of escape and assertion.

The second fact, linked to and defined by the first, was the deterioration of the base of black life. By the beginning of the seventies, blacks had suffered through a forty-year run—with the exception of World War II — of disastrously high levels of unemployment; and large sectors of Black America were locked into a state of almost permanent Depression. The 1971 annual report of the NAACP said that the employment situation of "urban blacks in 1971 was worse than at any time since the Great Depression of the thirties." The situation then, and later, was particularly distressing for young black males, who had unemployment rates of 40 and 50 per cent. Under the impact of this situation, and a national epidemic of hard drugs, the social structures of Black America were pushed into strange and disturbing shapes. The most significant and mournful reflection of these external pressures was the rising level of unmarried mothers and broken homes.

The third and final fact was a new white consensus based on the idea that America had done enough for blacks and that it was time to go back to the old "morality" and the old verities of free enterprise and rugged individualism. This was, more than anything else, a flanking maneuver designed to repeal the sixties and to dam up energies released by the Black Revolution, which had stirred companion revolts among white women and white youths.

The political expression of this consensus was Richard Milhous Nixon, who defeated Vice-President Hubert Humphrey in the 1968 presidential contest and proclaimed a Nixon doctrine based on five points:

1. A get-tough policy on welfare and a sweeping attack on the social legislation of the Roosevelt, Truman, Kennedy and Johnson administrations.

2. A hard-money policy which penalized the poor and intensified the depression in the black community;

3. A campaign of pressure on First Amendment guarantees of free speech. In 1971 and 1972 there was widespread electronic surveillance of activists and civil rights leaders.

4. A policy of appeasement of racist interests. Ignoring the appeals of civil rights leaders, the president used his office to give aid to forces opposing integration and compensatory efforts to redress the racial imbalances in American society. Time and time again, in 1971 and 1972, the president attacked "forced busing," "forced integration," quotas and welfare recipients.

5. A policy of appeasement of colonial forces and benign neglect of Africans.

The net effect of all this, whatever the intention—and the intention was not too far removed from the effect—was to put a parenthesis around the black gains of the sixties. Significantly, and ominously, the social and economic indicators began to turn downward in the Nixon years. The overall income position of black families, for example, declined, with the ratio of median family income of blacks to whites dropping from 61 per cent in 1970 to 58 per cent in 1973. Even more alarming was the rise in black unemployment. After declining for several years in the sixties, the unemployment rate for blacks began to rise in 1970 and reached 13.7 per cent for blacks (7.6 per cent for whites) in 1975. At the same time the percentage of black children living with both parents dropped from 64 per cent in 1970 to 56 per cent in 1974.

If all this sounds depressing, it must be added that blacks managed to hold onto and extend some of their gains. There were, for instance, 3503 blacks holding elective offices in forty-five states and the District of Columbia at the end of May, 1975, an increase of 1643 or 88 per cent since 1970. The largest number of black elected officials were in Louisiana and Illinois. In the same period the number of black mayors spiralled from 8 in 1971 to 135 in 1975. By that time blacks held the mayor's office in Atlanta, Detroit, Los Angeles, Washington, Gary and Newark. Meanwhile, in the wholly different sphere of education, blacks were pressing forward with new enthusiasm. Between 1970 and 1974 there was a 56 per cent growth in black college enrollment.

Building on these bases, blacks deepened their group life and organized new forms and institutions. In 1971 the Reverend Jesse Jackson, a former aide of Martin Luther King Jr., broke away from the Southern Christian Leadership Conference and founded People United To Serve Humanity (PUSH). Jackson later attracted millions of black and white voters in two unprecedented campaigns for the Democratic nomination for president.

This initiative was foreshadowed by the first national black political convention in Gary, Indiana. Three thousand delegates and five thousand observers attended the convention (March 10-12, 1972), which disintegrated amid internecine squabbles between nationalists and black elected officials. In the presidential campaign of that year, almost all black voters rallied behind Sen. George S. McGovern, who was soundly trounced by Richard Nixon. To the surprise of blacks and liberals, Nixon carried forty-nine of the fifty states. Even more disquieting was the evidence of the depth of the mood of reaction. Nowhere was this more clearly visible than in the disintegration of the New Deal coalition (blacks, big-city ethnic groups, labor unions, intellectuals), which had been largely responsible for the social gains of the post-World War II period. For the first time since the thirties, a majority of voters in labor union families, according to political surveys, supported the Republican candidate. There were also defections by white urban ethnic groups. Political analysts said increasing pressure from blacks for jobs and living space and the exploitation of white fears were largely responsible for these defections.

The Watergate controversy, triggered by Frank Willis — a black night watchman who thwarted a Republican-inspired break-in at Democratic headquarters in Washington's Watergate complex — temporarily halted the rising tide of reaction and paved the way for the triumph of Jimmy Carter, the first president elected from the Deep South since the Zachary Taylor campaign in 1848. The election of the former Georgia governor was made possible by the Freedom movement of the sixties, which changed Southern voting patterns and created the black voting pools that ensured his victory. In recognition of this fact, the new president gave unexampled recognition to individual blacks, naming two cabinet members (Secretary of Housing and Urban Development Patricia Harris and UN Ambassador Andrew Young) and more federal judges than all other presidents combined.

Although President Carter broke new ground in recognizing individual blacks, he was less than successful in dealing with rising levels of inflation and unemployment. The failure of federal policy in these areas was reflected in the Miami riots of May, 1980—the first major riots since the sixties—and a succession of racial disturbances in Chattanooga, Tennessee, Wichita, Kansas, and other cities.

Another factor having deep disintegrative effects was a resurgence of the Ku Klux Klan and other right-wing groups. This was followed by a sharp increase in random attacks on blacks and the bombing and firing of the homes of blacks.

The rightward movement reached a turning point in November, 1980, with the presidential victory of Ronald Reagan, who inaugurated a crusade based on a repudiation of the New Deal and, his critics said, the repeal of the twentieth century. Although Reagan denied that he was biased against blacks, he sponsored programs that intensified the economic woes of Black America and accentuated the widening racial chasms, and a number of critics, including Supreme Court Justice Thurgood Marshall, said he was the worst civil rights president in this century. By the end of his second term, black unemployment and poverty rates were up and black college enrollment was down. Black college enrollment, according to the American Council on Education, reached a peak in 1976, when 1,032,000 blacks made up 9.4 per cent of the college population. By 1984 there were 1,070,000 black college students, 8.8 per cent of the total.

Although blacks and their allies managed to blunt some of the president's more extreme gestures, such as the nomination of Judge Robert H. Bork, the Supreme Court and other institutions moved to the right. To make things even more vexing, significant sectors of White America returned or tried to return to the "good old days" before the Freedom movement. One could see examples of this all over America in the eighties. A chilling reminder of the continuing hold of racism was the attack on a group of blacks in the Howard Beach section of New York City. When racists attacked demonstrators in all-white Forsyth County, Ga., thousands of blacks and whites descended on the area in a mini-revival of the Freedom movement of the sixties. Despite this activity, there was forward movement in the middle sectors and at the highest levels of the cultural world. Bill Cosby, to cite a single spectacular instance, was repeatedly named the most popular figure on American television. This was, in fact, an era of unprecedented recognition of black cultural genius. So many black men and women won so many major cultural honors in the seventies and eighties that the announcements ceased to astonish.

At the same time blacks continued their march through the political marshes of America, picking up new positions at almost every election. Between January, 1986 and January, 1987, the number of black elected officials rose from 6,424 to 6,681. But these gains were challenged and mortgaged by a resurgence of racism and the steady erosion of the economic foundations of Black America.

If there was any doubt on this score, it was burned away by the worst urban riot since the Civil War—the four-day insurrection in the South Central section of Los Angeles. The immediate cause of the insurrection was police repression, but the root cause was an explosive mixture of despair and defiance growing out of depression-level unemployment aggravated by an epidemic of hard drugs and a national policy of evasion and urban neglect. All the evasions and divisive policies of the 1980s came to a head on March 3, 1991, when a group of Los Angeles police officers beat motorist Rodney King, who had been stopped for an alleged speeding violation. A witness videotaped the beating, which triggered a hurricane of emotion when it was aired on national television. When, on April 29, 1992, an all-white jury in the Los Angeles suburb of Simi Valley acquitted the white policemen, South Central Los Angeles erupted in rioting that spread to other areas of the city. Federal troops were mobilized to put down the insurrection which cost the lives of fifty-eight persons. The unrest spread to other American cities and forced a belated reappraisal of urban policy.

Thus, as black and white Americans approached the twenty-first century, and as the struggle widened and deepened, more and more blacks were forced to deal with the fundamental paradox of the post-sixties world: the fact that everything had changed in American race relations, although, fundamentally, nothing had changed.

The reactionary period inaugurated by Ronald Reagan continued under his successor, former Vice President George Bush, who openly campaigned against "quotas" and civil rights legislation, and who stacked the federal courts with white conservatives opposed to the civil rights gains of the sixties and seventies. (Only twenty blacks were appointed to the federal courts in the twelve years of the Reagan and Bush administrations.) To make things even more interesting, Bush and white conservatives recruited and promoted a small but noisy group of black conservatives who opposed affirmative action plans and the philosophy and policies of the Civil Rights Movement. When Bush named Clarence Thomas, a leader of the black conservative movement, to succeed ailing Supreme Court Justice Thurgood Marshall, the stage was set for one of the defining moments of the Reagan-Bush Movement, a bruising confirmation confrontation took place between civil rights forces and conservatives and wavering moderates. The confirmation hearing took an unexpected turn when Anita Hill, a University of Oklahoma law professor, said that Thomas had sexually harassed her when she worked for him in Reagan's Equal Employment Opportunity Commission. Thomas denied the charges and was narrowly confirmed by the Senate, but the close vote— 52 to 48—enraged millions of women, who started mobilizing for what was called The Year of the Woman.

The main beneficiary of this ferment was Arkansas Governor Bill Clinton, who ran for president on a progressive platform that appealed to women, blacks, and the millions of Americans threatened by the economic policies of the Reagan and Bush years. Propelled by record-breaking levels of black support, the Arkansas governor was elected president in a pivotal campaign that marked, in the view of some observers, a fundamental turning point in the fortunes of both blacks and women.

Independent studies indicated that black voters, who represented 9 per cent of the total vote, provided the margins of victory in key states, giving Clinton 82 per cent of their vote, compared to 11 per cent for George Bush and 7 per cent for Ross Perot. The Joint Center for Political and Economic Studies said newly registered black voters alone provided the Clinton margin of victory in states like Georgia and New Jersey.

Responding to the black mandate, Clinton began a season of precedent-breaking by naming Vernon Jordan, an influential Washington lawyer and a former head of the National Urban League, chairman of his transition team. He also named four blacks—a new record—to his cabinet: Secretary of Commerce Ronald H. Brown, Secretary of Agriculture Mike Espy, Secretary of Energy Helen O'Leary, and Secretary of Veterans Affairs Jesse

Brown. The new president's inauguration was characterized by diversity and the highest level of black participation in history.

If the new Clinton era did not immediately inaugurate what President Clinton called "a new season of American renewal," it did call forth a new sense of hope and energy. And across the months that followed, African-Americans reversed some of the policies of the Reagan-Bush years and occupied new ground. Forced back on themselves by external pressures, buffeted by new technologies and new modes of pacification and oppression, they nevertheless found within themselves new resources and reorganized themselves around new axes. Regardless of racism, regardless of unemployment, regardless of everything, they worked and prayed and danced and endured. Having come so far with so little against so many, they honored the human spirit by refusing to give up the long march that Ralph Ellison called "one of the great human experiences and one of the great triumphs of the human spirit in modern times, in fact, in the history of the world."

Landmarks and Milestones

1619

July

30 Virginia House of Burgesses met at Jamestown. First colonial legislature in America passed a measure which legalized white servitude. Similar measures were passed later by other colonies. White indentured servitude lasted for more than two centuries and involved most of the first white immigrants.

August

-- History of Black America began with landing of twenty blacks at Jamestown, Virginia. John Rolfe said the ship arrived "about the latter end of August" and that it "brought not anything but 20 and odd Negroes." Surviving evidence suggests that the twenty blacks were accorded the status of indentured servants.

1624

--- First black child born in English America christened William in the Church of England at Jamestown.

1641

December

-- Massachusetts became the first colony to give statutory recognition to slavery. Other colonies followed: Connecticut, 1650; Virginia, 1661; Maryland, 1663; New

1641

York and New Jersey, 1664; South Carolina, 1682; Rhode Island and Pennsylvania, 1700; North Carolina, 1715; Georgia, 1750.

1644

February

-- First black legal protest in America pressed by eleven blacks who petitioned for freedom in New Netherlands (New York). Council of New Netherlands freed the eleven petitioners because they had "served the Company seventeen or eighteen years" and had been "long since promised their freedom on the same footing as other free people in New Netherlands."

1649

--- Colonial officials reported that "there are in *Virginia* about fifteene thousand *English,* and of *Negroes* brought thither, three hundred good servants."

1651

July

24 Anthony Johnson, a free black who was probably one of the first twenty settlers, received a grant of 250 acres of land in Northampton County, Va., for importing five persons. Johnson established a settlement on the banks of the Pungoteague River.

1652

May

10 John Johnson, a free black, granted 550 acres in Northampton County, Va., for importing eleven persons.

1654

November

21 Richard Johnson, a free black, granted 100 acres of land in Northampton County for importing two persons.

1663

September

13 First serious slave conspiracy in colonial America. Plot of white servants and slaves in Gloucester County, Va., was betrayed by an indentured servant.

1664

September

20 Maryland enacted first antiamalgamation law to prevent widespread intermarriage of English women and
black men. Other colonies passed similar laws: Virginia, 1691; Massachusetts, 1705; North Carolina,
1715; South Carolina, 1717; Delaware, 1721; Pennsylvania, 1725.

1688

February

18 First formal protest against slavery by organized white
body in English America made by Germantown (Pa.)
Quakers at monthly meeting. The historic "Germantown Protest" denounced slavery and the slave trade.

1704

- - - Elias Neau, a Frenchman, opened school for blacks in
New York City.

1708

- - - Slave revolt, Newton, Long Island (N.Y.). Seven whites
killed. Two black male slaves and an Indian slave were
hanged, and a black woman was burned alive.

1712

April

7 Slave revolt, New York City. Nine whites were killed
and twenty-one slaves were executed.

1723

April

13 Massachusetts governor issued proclamation on the
"fires which have been designedly and industriously
kindled by some villainous and desperate Negroes or
other dissolute people as appears by the confession of
some of them."

1731

November

9 Benjamin Banneker, black inventor and scientist, born
in Ellicott's Mills, Maryland.

1739

September

9   Slave revolt, Stono, South Carolina, led by rebel named
        Jemmy. Twenty-five whites were killed before the in-
        surrection was put down.

1741

March

-- Succession of suspicious fires and reports of slave con-
        spiracies created hysteria in New York in March and
        April. Thirty-one slaves and five whites were executed.

1746

November

6   Absalom Jones, major leader of Black Pioneer period,
        born in slavery in Sussex, Delaware.

1750

September

30 Crispus Attucks escaped from his slaveholder in Fram-
        ingham, Massachusetts.

1753

July

18 Lemuel Haynes, pioneer black minister, born in West
        Hartford, Connecticut.

1759

January

17 Paul Cuffe born near Dartmouth, Massachusetts.

1760

February

14 Richard Allen born in slavery in Philadelphia.

December

25 Jupiter Hammon, New York slave who was probably
        the first black poet, published *An Evening Thought:
        Salvation by Christ, with Penentential Cries.*

1770

March

5   Crispus Attucks was the first of five persons killed in
        Boston Massacre. Some historians have called him the
        first martyr of the American Revolution.

1770

June

   28 Quakers, led by Anthony Benezet, opened a school for blacks in Philadelphia.

1773

January

   6 Massachusetts slaves petitioned the legislature for freedom. There is a record of eight freedom petitions during the Revolutionary War period.

   --- Phillis Wheatley's book, *Poems on Various Subjects, Religious and Moral*, published, the second book by an American woman and the first book by a black.

   --- Pioneer black church established between 1773 and 1775 at Silver Bluff, S.C., across the Savannah River from Augusta. Other black Baptist churches were organized in the 1773–76 period in Virginia and Georgia.

1775

March

   6 Prince Hall and fourteen other blacks were initiated into British Military Lodge No. 441 of the Masons at Fort Independence, Massachusetts. Hall was a leather dresser and caterer. On July 3, 1775, African Lodge No. 1 was organized in Boston by a group of black Masons.

April

   14 First abolitionist society in United States organized in Philadelphia.

   19 Black and white Minutemen fought British soldiers at Lexington and Concord.

May

   10 Black patriots participated in the first aggressive action of American forces, the capture of Fort Ticonderoga by Ethan Allen and "the Green Mountain Boys."

June

   17 Black soldiers fought at Battle of Bunker Hill and Breed's Hill. Among the heroes of the battle were Peter Salem and Salem Poor.

1775

July

10 Horatio Gates, George Washington's adjutant general, issued order excluding blacks from Continental Army.

October

8 Council of general officers decided to bar slaves and free blacks from Continental Army.

23 Continental Congress approved resolution barring blacks from the army.

November

7 Lord Dunmore, deposed royal governor of Virginia, issued proclamation which promised freedom to male slaves who joined the British army.

12 General Washington issued order which forbade recruiting officers to enlist blacks.

December

31 Alarmed by impact of the Dunmore proclamation, Washington reversed himself and authorized the enlistment of free blacks.

1776

January

16 Continental Congress approved Washington's order on the enlistment of free blacks.

July

4 Declaration of Independence adopted. A section denouncing the slave trade was deleted.

1777

July

2 Vermont became the first American colony to abolish slavery. By 1783 slavery was prohibited in Massachusetts and New Hampshire. Pennsylvania passed a gradual emancipation law in 1780. Connecticut and Rhode Island barred slavery in 1784 and were followed by New York (gradual emancipation) and New Jersey in 1799 and 1804, respectively. Slavery died in the North as a direct result of forces set in motion by the Rights of Man movement.

1778

February

-- Rhode Island General Assembly in precedent-breaking act authorized the enlistment of slaves.

1780

November

29 Lemuel Haynes, Revolutionary War veteran, licensed to preach in the Congregational Church.

After the winter of Valley Forge, blacks—slaves and free men—were welcomed into the American army. There were black soldiers in the Revolutionary army from all of the original thirteen colonies. Most of the estimated five thousand black soldiers fought in integrated units. Black soldiers were in the front lines in most of the big battles of the war. They were at White Plains, Stillwater, Bennington, Bemis Heights, Saratoga, Stony Points, Trenton, Princeton, Eutaw, S.C., and Yorktown. Blacks were critical factors in the battles of Rhode Island, Long Island, Red Bank, Savannah, Monmouth and Fort Griswold. There were black fifers and drummers in some units.

1781

September

4 Los Angeles, California, founded by forty-four settlers of whom at least twenty-six were descendants of Africans. Among the black settlers, according to H. H. Bancroft's authoritative *History of California,* were "Joseph Moreno, Mulatto, 22 years old, wife a Mulattress, five children; Manuel Cameron, Mulatto, 30 years old, wife Mulattress; Antonio Mesa, Negro, 38 years old, wife Mulattress, six children; Jose Antonio Navarro, Mestizo, 42 years old, wife, Mulattress, three children; Basil Rosas, Indian, 68 years old, wife, Mulattress, six children."

1784

December

5 Death of poet Phillis Wheatley, in Boston.

1785

September

28 David Walker born free in Wilmington, North Carolina.

1787

April

12 Richard Allen and Absalom Jones organized Philadelphia's Free African Society which Du Bois called "the first wavering step of a people toward a more organized social life."

May

6 African Lodge No. 459 organized in Boston with Prince Hall as Master.

July

13 Continental Congress excluded slavery from Northwest Territory.

September

17 U.S. Constitution approved at Philadelphia convention with three clauses protecting slavery.

October

17 Boston blacks, led by Prince Hall, petitioned legislature for equal school facilities.

November

1 First free school in New York City, the African Free School, opened.

1788

January

20 Pioneer African Baptist church organized in Savannah, Ga., with Andrew Bryan as pastor.

1790

United States population: 3,929,214. Black population: 757,208 (19.3 per cent).

1791

August

22 Haitian Revolution began with revolt of slaves in northern province.

- - - Mathematician Benjamin Banneker served on commission which surveyed the District of Columbia.

1792

\---   Benjamin Banneker issued his first annual almanac.

1793

February

  12 First fugitive slave law enacted by Congress. The measure made it a criminal offense to harbor a fugitive slave or prevent his arrest.

1794

March

  14 Eli Whitney patented cotton gin which made cotton king and increased demand for slave labor.

July

  17 Absalom Jones and his followers dedicated African Church of St. Thomas in Philadelphia. On August 12, 1794, the St. Thomas parishioners affiliated with the Protestant Episcopal Church.

  -- Richard Allen organized Philadelphia's Bethel African Methodist Episcopal Church.

1795

August

  6 Absalom Jones ordained a deacon in the Protestant Episcopal Church.

1796

\---   Boston African Society was established with forty-four members.

1797

January

  30 Congress refused to accept the first recorded petition from American blacks.

\---   Sojourner Truth born a slave in Hurley, New York.

\---   Boston Masons, led by Prince Hall, established first black interstate organization, creating lodges in Philadelphia and Providence, Rhode Island.

1800

United States population: 5,308,483. Black population: 1,002,037 (18.9 per cent).

January

2   Antislavery petition from free blacks of Philadelphia presented to Congress.

August

30   Storm forced suspension of attack on Richmond, Va., by Gabriel Prosser and some one thousand slaves. Conspiracy was betrayed by two slaves. Prosser and fifteen of his followers were hanged on October 7.

September

7   Zion AME Church dedicated in New York City.

October

2   Nat Turner, leader of major slave rebellion, born in Southampton County, Virginia.

1804

January

1   Jean Jacques Dessalines proclaimed independence of Haiti, the second republic in the Western Hemisphere.

5   Ohio legislature passed the first of a succession of Northern Black Laws which restricted the rights and movement of free blacks in the North. Most Northern states passed Black Laws. Constitutions of three states —Illinois, Indiana, Oregon—barred black settlers.

September

--   Absalom Jones ordained a priest in the Protestant Episcopal Church.

1806

October

9   Death of mathematician Benjamin Banneker (74), in Ellicott's Mills, Maryland.

1807

March

2   Congress banned the slave trade, prohibiting "the importation of slaves into the United States or the territories thereof" after January 1, 1808.

1807

December

4   Death of Prince Hall, activist and Masonic leader, in Boston.

1810

United States population: 7,239,881. Black population: 1,377,808 (19 per cent).

February

1   Charles Lenox Remond born in Salem, Massachusetts.

---   First insurance company managed by blacks, the American Insurance Company of Philadelphia, established.

1811

January

8–10   Louisiana slaves rebelled in two parishes about thirty-five miles from New Orleans. Revolt was suppressed by U.S. troops.

1812

May

6   Martin R. Delany, pioneer black nationalist, born free in Charles Town, Virginia.

1814

September

21   Andrew Jackson issued proclamation at Mobile, Ala., urging free blacks "to rally around the standard of the eagle" in the War of 1812.

Blacks fought in the land and water battles of the War of 1812. A large number of black sailors fought with Matthew Perry and Isaac Chauncey in the battles on the upper lakes and were particularly effective at the Battle of Lake Erie. Two battalions of black soldiers were with Andrew Jackson when he defeated the British at the Battle of New Orleans. Jackson issued his famous proclamation to black troops at New Orleans on

1814

December 18, 1814: "TO THE MEN OF COLOR.—
Soldiers! From the shores of Mobile I collected you to
arms; I invited you to share in the perils and to divide
the glory of your white countrymen. I expected much
from you, for I was not uninformed of those qualities
which must render you so formidable to an invading
foe. I knew that you could endure hunger and thirst and
all the hardships of war. I knew that you loved the land
of your nativity, and that like ourselves, you had to
defend all that is most dear to you. But you surpass my
hopes. I have found in you, united to these qualities,
that noble enthusiasm which impels to great deeds."

1815

December

23 Henry Highland Garnet, minister, abolitionist and diplomat, born a slave in Kent County, Maryland.

1816

April

9 African Methodist Episcopal Church organized at general convention in Philadelphia. On April 10, Richard
Allen was elected bishop.

July

27 Fort Blount on Apalachicola Bay, Fla., attacked by
U.S. troops. Fort, which was held by fugitive slaves and
Indians, was taken after siege of several days.

December

28 American Colonization Society organized in hall of the
House of Representatives.

1817

January

-- Philadelphia blacks held meeting at Bethel Church to
protest colonization society's campaign "to exile us
from the land of our nativity."

February

-- Frederick Douglass, the most celebrated black of the
nineteenth century, was born in Tuckahoe, Talbot
County, Maryland.

1817

September

9   Death of Captain Paul Cuffe (58), entrepreneur and activist, in Westport, Massachusetts.

October

17   Samuel Ringgold Ward, minister, abolitionist, author, born on the Eastern Shore of Maryland.

1818

February

13   Death of Absalom Jones (71), Philadelphia.

April

18   Andrew Jackson defeated force of Indians and blacks at Battle of Suwanee, ending First Seminole War.

1820

United States population, 9,638,453. Black population: 1,771,656 (18.4 per cent).

February

6   "Mayflower of Liberia" sailed from New York City with eighty-six blacks. Ship arrived in Sierra Leone, March 9.

March

3   Missouri Compromise enacted. The measure prohibited slavery to the north of southern boundary of Missouri.

1821

June

21   African Methodist Episcopal Zion (AMEZ) Church formally organized at meeting in New York City.

1822

May

30   House slave betrayed Denmark Vesey conspiracy. Vesey conspiracy, one of the most elaborate slave plots on record, involved thousands of blacks in Charleston, S.C., and vicinity. Thirty-seven blacks were hanged.

July

2   Denmark Vesey and five of his aides hanged at Blake's Landing, Charleston, South Carolina.

30   James Varick consecrated as the first bishop of the African Methodist Episcopal Zion Church.

1822

September

27   Hiram R. Revels, first black U.S. senator, born free, Fayetteville, North Carolina.

1823

- - -   Alexander Lucius Twilight, who was probably the first black to graduate from an American college, received A.B. degree at Middlebury College.

1826

August

23   Edward A. Jones received B.A. degree from Amherst College.

September

6   John B. Russwurm received A.B. degree from Bowdoin College.

1827

March

16   First black newspaper, *Freedom's Journal*, published in New York City.

July

4   Slavery abolished in New York State.

1829

August

10   Race riot, Cincinnati. More than one thousand blacks left the city for Canada.

September

28   *Walker's Appeal*, radical antislavery pamphlet, published in Boston by David Walker. *Appeal* denounced slavery and called for slave revolt.

1830

United States population: 12,866,020. Black population: 2,328,642 (18.1 per cent).

January

21   Portsmouth (Ohio) blacks forcibly deported by order of city officials.

April

6   James Augustine Healy, first black Roman Catholic bishop in America, born to Irish planter and slave on plantation near Macon, Georgia.

1830

September

20 First national black convention met at Philadelphia's
Bethel AME Church and elected Richard Allen president. Thirty-eight delegates from eight states attended
the first national meeting of blacks.

1831

January

1 William Lloyd Garrison published first issue of abolitionist journal, the *Liberator*.

March

26 Death of Richard Allen (71), who was nominated by
author Vernon Loggins for the title "Father of the
Negro."

June

6–11 Second national black convention met in Philadelphia.
There were fifteen delegates from five states.

August

21–23 Nat Turner rebellion, Southampton County, Virginia.
Some sixty whites were killed. Nat Turner was not captured until October 30.

November

11 Nat Turner hanged, Jerusalem, Virginia.

1832

January

6 New England Anti-Slavery Society organized at African
Baptist Church on Boston's Beacon Hill.

June

4–13 Third national black convention met in Philadelphia
with twenty-nine delegates from eight states. Henry
Sipkins of New York was elected president.

1833

June

3–13 Fourth national black convention met in Philadelphia
with sixty-two delegates from eight states. Abraham D.
Shadd of Pennsylvania was elected president.

27 Prudence Crandall, a liberal white woman, arrested for
conducting an academy for black females at Canterbury, Connecticut. Academy was later closed.

1833

September

28   Death of Rev. Lemuel Haynes (88), Revolutionary War
veteran and pioneer black preacher, in Granville, New
York.

December

4   American Anti-Slavery Society organized.

1834

June

2–13   Fifth national black convention met in New York with
fifty delegates from eight states.

August

Slavery abolished in the British Empire.

1835

June

1–5   Sixth national black convention met in Philadelphia
with thirty-five delegates from six states and the District of Columbia.

August

10   Mob of white citizens and a hundred yoke of oxen
pulled a black school to a swamp outside the town of
Canaan, New Hampshire.

1836

- - -

Alexander Lucius Twilight, minister and educator,
elected to the Vermont legislature.

1837

March

4   *Weekly Advocate* changed its name to the *Colored
American*, the second major black newspaper. Some
forty black newspapers were published before the Civil
War.

November

7   Elijah P. Lovejoy murdered by proslavery mob while
defending his press in Alton, Illinois.

December

25   Seminole Indian force defeated by American troops at
Battle of Okeechobee. Black chief John Horse shared
command with Alligator Sam Jones and Wild Cat.

1837

--- The Cheyney State Training School was established in Pennsylvania.

1838

--- Charles Lenox Remond began his career as an antislavery agent. Remond was one of the first blacks employed as a lecturer by the antislavery movement.

--- *Mirror of Liberty*, pioneer black magazine, published in New York City by abolitionist David Ruggles.

1839

February

25 Seminoles and their black allies shipped from Tampa Bay, Fla., to the West.

April

5 Robert Smalls, Civil War hero and Reconstruction congressman, born in Beaufort, South Carolina.

July

-- Slave rebels, led by Joseph Cinquez, killed captain and took over slaver *Amistad* in most celebrated of American slave mutinies. Rebels were captured off Long Island on August 26.

November

13 Liberty party, the first antislavery political party, organized at Warsaw, New York. Samuel Ringgold Ward and Henry Highland Garnet were among the earliest supporters of the new political departure.

1841

March

1 Blanche Kelso Bruce, first black to serve a full term in the United States Senate, was born a slave in Prince Edward County, Virginia.

9 U.S. Supreme Court freed Joseph Cinquez and *Amistad* rebels, ruling that they were free persons.

September

-- Pioneer black magazine, a short-lived quarterly called the *African Methodist Episcopal Church Magazine*, published in Brooklyn.

1841

November

7   Slave revolt on the *Creole,* which was en route to New
       Orleans, from Hampton, Virginia. Rebels overpowered
       crew and sailed ship to the Bahamas, where they were
       granted asylum and freedom.

25 Thirty-five *Amistad* survivors returned to Africa.

1842

November

17 Capture of George Latimer in Boston led to first of the
       fugitive slave cases which embittered North and South.
       Boston abolitionists raised money to purchase Latimer
       from his slaveholder.

1843

June

1   Sojourner Truth left New York and began her career as
       an antislavery activist.

August

15 National black convention met at Buffalo, N.Y., with
       approximately seventy delegates from twelve states.
       The highlight of the convention was a stirring address
       by Henry Highland Garnet, a twenty-seven-year-old
       Presbyterian pastor who called for a slave revolt and a
       general slave strike. Amos G. Beman of New Haven
       Conn., was elected president of the convention.

30 Blacks participated in a national political convention
       for the first time at Liberty party convention in Buffalo.
       Samuel R. Ward led the convention in prayer; Henry
       Highland Garnet was a member of the nominating
       committee; and Charles R. Ray was one of the conven-
       tion secretaries.

1845

May

3   Macon B. Allen, first black lawyer admitted to the bar,
       passed examination at Worcester, Massachusetts.

1845

October

--   William A. Leidesdorf named sub-consul to Mexican territory of Yerba Buena (San Francisco) and became first black diplomat.

---   Frederick Douglass published the first of three autobiographies, *Narrative of Frederick Douglass.*

1847

July

26   President Joseph Jenkins Roberts, a native of Virginia, declared Liberia an independent republic.

September

--   William A. Leidesdorf elected to San Francisco town council, receiving the third highest vote. Leidesdorf, who was one of the first black elected officials, became the town treasurer in 1848.

October

6–9   National black convention met in Troy, N.Y., with more than sixty delegates from nine states. Nathan Johnson of Massachusetts was elected president.

December

3   Frederick Douglass published the first issue of his newspaper, the *North Star.*

1848

February

15   Sarah Roberts barred from white school in Boston. Her father, Benjamin Roberts, filed the first school integration suit on her behalf.

May

18   Death of William A. Leidesdorf (38), in San Francisco.

July

19–20   Frederick Douglass was the only male to play a prominent role at the first Women's Rights Convention at Senecca Falls, New York. He seconded the women's suffrage motion introduced by Elizabeth Cady Stanton.

August

9–10   Free Soil party organized at Buffalo, N.Y., convention attended by black abolitionists.

1848

September

6   National black convention met in Cleveland with some seventy delegates. Frederick Douglass was elected president of the convention.

December

26   William and Ellen Craft escaped from slavery in Georgia. Mrs. Craft impersonated a slaveholder and her husband, William, assumed the role of her servant in one of the most dramatic of the slave escapes.

1849

---   Harriet Tubman escaped from slavery in Maryland, summer. She returned to the South nineteen times and brought out more than three hundred slaves.

October

16   George Washington Williams, the first major black historian, born in Bedford Springs, Pennsylvania.

---   Charles L. Reason named professor of belles lettres and French at Central College, McGrawville, New York. William G. Allen and George B. Vashon also taught at the predominantly white college.

---   Avery College established in Allegheny, Pennsylvania.

1850

United States population: 23,191,876. Black population: 3,638,808 (15.7 per cent).

March

--   Massachusetts Supreme Court rejected the argument of Charles Sumner in the Boston school integration suit and established the "separate but equal" precedent.

September

18   Fugitive Slave Act passed by Congress as one component of the Compromise of 1850.

1851

February

15   Black abolitionists invaded Boston courtroom and rescued a fugitive slave.

1851

September

11   In Christiana, Pa., confrontation, blacks dispersed slave catchers. One white was killed and another was wounded.

October

1   Black and white abolitionists smashed into a courtroom at Syracuse, N.Y., and rescued a fugitive slave.

---   Abolitionist William C. Nell published *Services of Colored Americans in the Wars of 1776 and 1812*, the first extended work on the history of American blacks. Revised edition of the book was published in 1855 with new title, *The Colored Patriots of the American Revolution*.

1852

March

20   *Uncle Tom's Cabin*, a novel by Harriet Beecher Stowe, published in Boston.

---   Martin R. Delany published *The Condition, Elevation, Emigration and Destiny of the Colored People of the United States*, the first major statement of the black nationalist position. Delany said, "The claims of no people, according to established policy and usage, are respected by any nation, until they are presented in a national capacity." He added: "We are a nation within a nation;—as the Poles in Russia, the Hungarians in Austria; the Welsh, Irish, and Scotch in the British dominions."

1853

July

6–8   National black convention met in Rochester, N.Y., with 140 delegates from nine states. James W. C. Pennington of New York was elected president of this meeting which is generally considered the largest and most representative of the early black conventions.

---   William Wells Brown published *Clotel*, the first novel by a black American.

1854

January

1   Lincoln University, one of the first black colleges, chartered as Ashmun Institute in Oxford, Pennsylvania.

May

24   Anthony Burns, celebrated fugitive slave, arrested by United States deputy marshals in Boston. Two thousand United States troops escorted him through the streets of Boston when he was returned to the South on June 3.

30   Kansas–Nebraska Act repealed Missouri Compromise and opened Northern territory to slavery.

June

10   James Augustine Healy, first black American Roman Catholic bishop, ordained a priest in Notre Dame Cathedral, Paris.

August

24   John V. DeGrasse, prominent physician, admitted to Massachusetts Medical Society.

24–26   National emigration convention met in Cleveland with some one hundred delegates. William C. Munroe of Michigan was elected president.

1855

October

16–19   More than one hundred delegates from six states held a black convention in Philadelphia.

---   John Mercer Langston, one of the first blacks to win public office, elected clerk of Brownhelm Township, Lorain County, Ohio. In 1856 he was elected clerk of the township of Russia, near Oberlin. In 1857 he was elected to the council of the incorporated village of Oberlin. From 1871 to 1878 Langston was president of the board of health of Washington, D.C. In 1889 he was elected to the U.S. Congress from Virginia. The pioneer black lawyer also served as minister to Haiti and vice-president of Howard University.

1856

April

5   Booker Taliaferro Washington born a slave in Franklin County, Virginia.

August

30   Wilberforce University founded by the Methodist Episcopal Church. On March 30, 1863, the university was transferred to the African Methodist Episcopal Church.

1857

March

6   Dred Scott decision by U.S. Supreme Court opened Northern territory to slavery and denied citizenship to American blacks.

1858

May

8   John Brown held antislavery convention, which was attended by twelve whites and thirty-four blacks, at Chatham, Canada.

---   *The Escape*, first play by an American black, published by William Wells Brown.

1859

February

--   Arkansas legislature required free blacks to choose between exile and enslavement.

October

16–17   John Brown attacked Harpers Ferry, Va., with thirteen white men and five blacks. Two of the five blacks were killed, two were captured and one escaped.

December

2   John Brown hanged at Charlestown, Virginia.

16   John Copeland and Shields Green, two black members of John Brown's band, hanged at Charlestown.

---   The last slave ship, the *Clothilde*, landed shipment of slaves at Mobile Bay, Alabama.

1860

United States population: 31,443,790. Black population: 4,441,830 (14.1 per cent).

November

6   Abraham Lincoln elected president.

December

18   South Carolina was declared an "independent commonwealth."

BLACKS IN CONFEDERACY: Confederacy was the first to recognize that blacks were major factors in the war. South impressed slaves to work in mines, repair railroads and build fortifications, thereby releasing a disproportionately large percentage of able-bodied whites for direct war service. A handful of blacks enlisted in rebel army, but few, if any, fired guns in anger. Regiment of fourteen hundred free blacks received official recognition in New Orleans but was not called into service. It later became, by a strange mutation of history, the first black regiment officially recognized by the Union army.

BLACKS IN UNION ARMY: The 185,000 black soldiers in the Union army were organized into 166 all-black regiments (145 infantry, 7 cavalry, 12 heavy artillery, 1 light artillery, 1 engineer). Largest number of black soldiers came from Louisiana (24,052), followed by Kentucky (23,703) and Tennessee (20,133). Pennsylvania contributed more black soldiers than any other Northern state (8,612). Black soldiers participated in 449 battles, 39 of them major engagements. Sixteen black soldiers received Congressional Medals of Honor for gallantry in action. Some 37,638 black soldiers lost their lives during the war. Black soldiers generally received poor equipment and were forced to do a large amount of fatigue duty. Until 1864, black soldiers (from private to chaplain) received seven dollars a month whereas white soldiers received from thirteen to one hundred dollars a month. In 1863 black units, with four exceptions (Fifth Masschusetts Cavalry, Fifty-fourth

1860

and Fifty-fifth Massachusetts Volunteers and Twenty-ninth Connecticut Volunteers), were officially designated United States Colored Troops (USCT). Since the War Department discouraged applications from blacks, there were few commissioned officers. The highest-ranking of the seventy-five to one hundred black officers was Lt. Col. Alexander T. Augustana, a surgeon. Some 200,000 black civilians were employed by Union army as laborers, cooks, teamsters and servants.

BLACKS IN UNION NAVY: One out of every four Union sailors was a black. Of the 118,044 sailors in the Union navy, 29,511 were blacks. At least four black sailors won Congressional Medals of Honor.

1861

March

11 Confederate Congress, meeting in Montgomery, Ala., adopted constitution which declared that the passage of any "law denying or impairing the right of property in Negro slaves" was prohibited.

April

12 Confederate soldiers attacked Fort Sumter, in the Charleston, S.C., harbor.

15 President Lincoln called for 75,000 troops to put down the rebellion. Lincoln administration rejected black volunteers. For almost two years black Americans fought for the right, as one humorist put it, "to be kilt."

May

24 Maj. Gen. Benjamin F. Butler declared slaves "contraband of war."

August

6 Congress passed Confiscation Act, authorizing the appropriation of the property, including slaves, of rebel slaveholders.

30 John C. Frémont issued proclamation freeing slaves of Missouri rebels. Lincoln revoked the proclamation.

1861

September

17   First day school for freedmen founded at Fortress Monroe, Va., with a black teacher, Mary Peake.

25   Secretary of U.S. Navy authorized enlistment of slaves.

1862

March

6   President Lincoln sent message to Congress recommending gradual and compensated emancipation.

13   Congress forbade Union officers and soldiers to aid in the capture and return of fugitive slaves, ending what one historian called the "military slave hunt."

April

16   Congress abolished slavery in Washington.

May

9   Three generals organized black regiments without official approval. David ("Black David") Hunter began organizing First South Carolina Volunteers, the first black regiment, on May 9; Jim Lane began organizing First Kansas Colored Volunteers in August and Ben Butler issued call to the free blacks of New Orleans on August 22.

—Gen. David Hunter issued proclamation freeing slaves of Georgia, Florida and South Carolina rebels. Lincoln revoked the proclamation.

13   Robert Smalls, a black pilot and future congressman, sailed armed Confederate steamer, the *Planter*, out of Charleston, S.C., harbor and presented it to the U.S. Navy.

July

17   Congress authorized president to accept blacks for military service.

—Congress passed the Second Confiscation Act, which freed the slaves of all rebels.

1862

July

22 President Lincoln submitted draft of Emancipation Proclamation to his cabinet.

August

14 President Lincoln received first group of blacks to confer with a U.S. president on a matter of public policy. He urged blacks to emigrate to Africa or Central America and was bitterly criticized by Northern blacks.

25 Secretary of war authorized Gen. Rufus Saxton to arm up to five thousand slaves.

September

17 Gen. George B. McClellan checked Robert E. Lee's Northern advance at Battle of Antietam.

22 President Lincoln, in preliminary Emancipation Proclamation, warned South that he would free slaves in all states in rebellion on 1 January 1863.

27 First Louisiana Native Guards, the first black regiment to receive official recognition, mustered into army. Regiment was composed of free blacks of New Orleans.

October

28 First Kansas Colored Volunteers repulsed and drove off superior force of rebels at Island Mound, Missouri. This was the first engagement for black troops.

December

1 President Lincoln, in message to Congress, recommended the use of federal bonds to provide compensation for states that abolished slavery before 1900.

1863

January

1 President Lincoln signed Emancipation Proclamation which freed slaves in rebel states with exception of thirteen parishes (including New Orleans) in Louisiana, forty-eight counties in West Virginia, seven counties (including Norfolk) in eastern Virginia. Proclamation did not apply to slaves in Border States.

1863

January

26 War Department authorized Massachusetts governor to recruit black troops. The Fifty-fourth Massachusetts Volunteers was first black regiment recruited in North.

March

10 Two infantry regiments, First and Second South Carolina Volunteers, captured and occupied Jacksonville, Fla., causing panic along Southern seaboard.

May

1 Confederate congress passed resolution which branded black troops and their officers criminals. Resolution, in effect, doomed captured black soldiers to death or slavery.

22 War Department established Bureau of Colored Troops and launched aggressive campaign for recruitment of black soldiers.

27 In ill-conceived assault on Port Hudson, La., two Louisiana regiments (First and Third Native Guards) made six gallant but unsuccessful charges on rebel fortification. A black captain, André Cailloux, was hero of the day.

June

7 Three regiments and small detachment of white troops repulsed division of Texans in hand-to-hand battle at Milliken's Bend, Louisiana.

July

9 Union troops entered Port Hudson. With the fall of Vicksburg (on July 4) and Port Hudson, Union controlled Mississippi River and Confederacy was cut into two sections. Eight black regiments played important roles in siege of Port Hudson.

13-17 Hostility to draft and fear of blacks, "the cause" of the war and potential competitors in the labor market, led to "New York Draft Riots," one of the bloodiest race riots in American history. Mobs swept through streets, murdered blacks and hanged them on lamp posts.

1863

July

17   Union troops, with First Kansas volunteers playing leading role, routed rebels at Honey Springs, Indian Territory. Black troops captured colors of a Texas regiment.

18   Fifty-fourth Massachusetts Volunteers, regiment composed of free blacks of North, made famous charge on
Fort Wagner in the Charleston, S.C., harbor. Sgt.
William H. Carney won Congressional Medal of Honor
for his bravery in the charge and became the first black
soldier to receive the coveted award.

30   President Lincoln issued "eye-for-an-eye" order, warning Confederacy that the Union would shoot a rebel
prisoner for every black prisoner shot, and would con-
demn a rebel prisoner to a life of hard labor for every
black prisoner sold into slavery. Order had restraining
influence on Confederate government, though individual commanders and soldiers continued to murder
captured black soldiers.

1864

February

19   Knights of Pythias established.

20   Confederate troops defeated three black and six white
regiments at Battle of Olustee, about fifty miles from
Jacksonville, Florida.

April

12   Confederate General Nathan Bedford Forrest captured
Fort Pillow, Tenn., and massacred the inhabitants,
sparing, the official report said, neither soldier nor civilian, black nor white, male nor female. Fort was held by
a predominantly black force.

18   Surrounded by a superior rebel force, First Kansas
Colored Volunteers smashed through rebel lines and
sustained heavy casualties in an engagement at Poison
Spring, Arkansas. Captured black soldiers were murdered by the Confederate troops.

1864

April

30 Fighting rearguard action, six infantry regiments checked rebel troops at Jenkins' Ferry, Saline River, Arkansas. Enraged by atrocities committed at Poison Spring (above), Second Kansas Colored Volunteers went into battle shouting, "Remember Poison Spring!" Regiment captured rebel battery.

May

4 Ulysses S. Grant crossed the Rapidan and began his duel with Robert E. Lee. At the same time Ben Butler's Army of the James moved on Lee's forces. Black division in Grant's army did not play a prominent role in Wilderness Campaign, but Ben Butler gave his black infantrymen and his eighteen hundred black cavalrymen important assignments. Black troops of the Army of the James were the first Union soldiers to take possession of James River (at Wilson's Wharf Landing, Fort Powhatan and City Point).

24 Two regiments, First and Tenth U.S.C.T., repulsed attack by rebel General Fitzhugh Lee. Also participating in battle at Wilson's Wharf Landing, on bank of James River, were a small detachment of white Union troops and a battery of light artillery.

June

15 Grant outwitted Lee by shifting campaign from Cold Harbor to Petersburg. Surprise attack by Gen. W. F. ("Baldy") Smith succeeded but Smith hesitated and permitted rebels to reinforce their lines. Gen. Charles J. Paine's division spearheaded the attack, knocking mile-wide hole in Petersburg defenses and capturing 200 of 300 rebels captured that day.

—Congress passed bill equalizing pay, arms, equipment and medical services of black troops.

16 Siege of Petersburg and Richmond began. Thirty-two black infantry regiments and black cavalry regiments were involved in siege. Black troops were especially

1864

prominent in following engagements: Deep Bottom, August 14–16; Darbytown Road, October 13; Fair Oaks, October 27–28; Hatcher's Run, October 27–28.

June

19 In famous duel between the USS *Kearsage* and the CSS *Alabama* off Cherbourg, France, a brave black sailor, Joachim Pease, displayed "marked coolness" and won a Congressional Medal of Honor.

July

15 Gen. A. J. Smith with fourteen thousand men, including a brigade of black troops, defeated Nathan B. Forrest at Harrisburg, near Tupelo, Mississippi.

30 Union exploded mine under rebel lines near Petersburg, committed three white and one black divisions and was soundly defeated. Black division of Ninth Corps sustained heaviest casualties in ill-planned attack. Only Union success of day was scored by Forty-third U.S.C.T. which captured two hundred rebels and two stands of colors. Decatur Dorsey of Thirty-ninth U.S.C.T. won a Congressional Medal of Honor.

August

5 John Lawson, a black gunner on flagship of Admiral David Farragut, exhibited marked courage in Battle of Mobile Bay and won a Congressional Medal of Honor.

September

2 William Tecumseh Sherman occupied Atlanta.

19–30 In series of battles around Chaffin's Farm in suburb of Richmond, black troops captured entrenchments at New Market Heights, made gallant but unsuccessful assault on Fort Gilmer and helped repulse Confederate counterattack on Fort Harrison. Thirteen blacks won Congressional Medals of Honor in the engagements.

October

4 *New Orleans Tribune*, first black daily newspaper, founded by Dr. Louis C. Roudanez. The newspaper, published in both English and French, started as a tri-weekly but soon became an influential daily.

1864

October

4–7   National black convention met in Syracuse, New York.

December

3   Twenty-fifth Corps, largest all-black unit in history of U.S. Army, established in Army of the James.

10–29   Mixed cavalry force, including Fifth and Sixth Colored Cavalry regiments, invaded southwest Virginia and destroyed salt mines at Saltville. Sixth Cavalry was especially brilliant in an engagement near Marion, Virginia.

15–16   In one of the decisive battles of the war, two brigades of black troops helped crush one of the South's finest armies at the Battle of Nashville. Black troops opened the battle on the first day and successfully engaged the right of the rebel line. On the second day Col. Charles R. Thompson's black brigade made brilliant charge up Overton Hill. Thirteenth U.S.C.T. sustained more casualties than any other regiment involved in the battle.

1865

January

15   Black division, under command of Maj. Gen. Charles Paine, participated in Fort Fisher (N.C.) expedition that closed Confederate's last major port.

16   Gen. William T. Sherman issued his Field Order No. 15 setting aside "the islands from Charleston, south, the abandoned rice fields along the river for thirty miles back from the sea, and the country bordering the St. John's River, Florida," for exclusive settlement by blacks. The order provided that "each family should have a plot of not more than forty (40) acres of tillable ground . . . in the possession of which land the military authorities will afford them protection until such time as they can protect themselves. . . . " Gen. Rufus Saxton, South Carolina Freedmen's Bureau director, later settled some 40,000 blacks on forty-acre tracts in the area. In South Carolina and other states black settlers were given possessory titles pending final action on the confiscated and abandoned lands of Confederate rebels (see August below).

1865

January

31 Congress passed the Thirteenth Amendment which, on ratification, abolished slavery in America. The vote in the House was 121 to 24.

February

1 John S. Rock became the first black admitted to practice before the U.S. Supreme Court.

12 Henry Highland Garnet, first black to speak in the Capitol, delivered memorial sermon on the abolition of slavery at services in the House of Representatives.

18 Rebels abandoned Charleston. First Union troops to enter the city included Twenty-first U.S.C.T., followed by two companies of the Fifty-fourth Massachusetts Volunteers.

March

3 Congress established Bureau of Refugees, Freedmen, and Abandoned Lands (Freedmen's Bureau) to aid white refugees and former slaves.

—Congress chartered Freedmen's Savings and Trust Bank with business confined to blacks.

13 Jefferson Davis signed bill authorizing use of slaves as soldiers in the Confederate army.

April

2 Black soldiers of the Twenty-fifth Corps were among the first Union soldiers to enter Petersburg.

3 Fifth Massachusetts Colored Cavalry and units of the Twenty-fifth Corps were in the vanguard of Union troops entering Richmond.

—Second Division of Twenty-fifth Corps helped chase Robert E. Lee's army from Petersburg to Appomattox Courthouse, April 3–10. The black division and white Union soldiers were advancing on General Lee's trapped army with fixed bayonets when the Confederate troops surrendered.

1865

April

9 Nine black regiments of Gen. John Hawkins's division
helped smash Confederate defenses at Fort Blakely,
Alabama. Capture of the fort led to fall of Mobile.
Sixty-eighth U.S.C.T. had the highest number of
casualties in the engagement.

11 President Lincoln recommended suffrage for black
veterans and blacks who were "very intelligent."

14 President Lincoln was shot and critically wounded at
Ford's Theatre in Washington.

15 Death of Abraham Lincoln, Washington.

May

11 Blacks held mass meeting in Norfolk (Va.) and demanded equal rights and ballots. Other equal rights
meetings and conventions were held in Petersburg,
Va., June 6; Vicksburg, Miss., June 19; Alexandria,
Va., August 3; Nashville, Tenn., August 7–11; Raleigh,
N.C., September 29–October 3; Richmond, September
18; Jackson, Miss., October 7.

13 Two white regiments and a black regiment, the Sixty-
second U.S.C.T., fought last action of war at White's
Ranch, Texas.

July

26 Patrick Francis Healy, first black awarded Ph.D. degree, passed final examinations at Louvain in Belgium.

August

-- President Andrew Johnson moved to reverse policy of
distributing abandoned land to freedmen.

September

3 U.S. Army commander in South Carolina ordered
Freedmen's Bureau to stop seizing abandoned land.

6 Thaddeus Stevens, powerful U.S. congressman, urged
confiscation of estates of Confederate leaders and the
distribution of land to adult freedmen in forty-acre lots.

1865

October

19 Gen. O. O. Howard, head of the Freedmen's Bureau, told a freedmen's mass meeting at Edisto, S.C., that the government had decided to return their land to the planters. In South Carolina, Virginia and other Southern states, freedmen organized militarily and resisted attempts to repossess the land.

November

20–25 Blacks held protest convention in Zion Church in Charleston and demanded equal rights and repeal of the Black Codes.

22–25 Mississippi legislature enacted Black Codes which restricted the rights and freedom of movement of freedmen. The Black Codes enacted in Mississippi and other Southern states virtually reenslaved the freedmen. In some states any white could arrest any black. In other states minor officials could arrest black "vagrants" and "refractory and rebellious Negroes" and force them to work on roads and levees without pay. "Servants" in South Carolina were required to work from sunrise to sunset, to be quiet and orderly and go to bed at "reasonable hours." It was a crime in Mississippi for blacks to own farm land; in South Carolina blacks had to get a special license to work outside the domestic and farm laborer categories.

December

18 Thirteenth Amendment ratified.

25 Reports from all over the South said freedmen had abandoned plantations in expectation of a general distribution of land. General Rufus Saxton, Freedmen's Bureau commander in South Carolina, said "the impression is universal among the freedmen that they are to have the abandoned and confiscated lands, in homesteads of forty acres, in January next."

-- Atlanta University, Shaw University and Virginia Union University founded.

1866

January

9 Fisk University established. Rust College(Miss.) and Lincoln(Mo.) were also founded in 1866.

February

5 Congressman Thaddeus Stevens offered amendment to Freedmen's Bureau bill authorizing the distribution of public land and confiscated land to freedmen and loyal refugees in forty-acre lots. The measure was defeated in the House by a vote of 126 to 37.

7 Black delegation, led by Frederick Douglass, called on President Johnson and urged ballots for former slaves. Meeting ended in disagreement and controversy after Johnson reiterated his opposition to black suffrage.

April

9 Civil Rights Bill passed over the president's veto. The bill conferred citizenship on blacks and gave them "the same right, in every State and territory . . . as is enjoyed by white citizens."

May

1–3 White Democrats and police attacked freedmen and their white allies in Memphis, Tennessee. Forty-six blacks and two white liberals were killed. More than seventy were wounded. Ninety homes, twelve schools and four churches were burned.

June

13 House passed the Fourteenth Amendment which was sent to the states for ratification on June 16.

July

24 Congress passed resolution readmitting the state of Tennessee.

30 White Democrats, led by police, attacked a convention of black and white Republicans in New Orleans. More than 40 persons were killed, and at least 150 were wounded. Gen. Philip H. Sheridan, military commander of the state, said, "It was no riot; it was an absolute massacre . . . which the mayor and the police of the city perpetrated without the shadow of a necessity."

1866

--- Edward G. Walker, son of abolitionist David Walker, and Charles L. Mitchell elected to Massachusetts assembly from Boston and became the first blacks to sit in the legislature of an American state in the post-Civil War perod.

1867

January

8 Legislation giving the suffrage to blacks in the District of Columbia was passed over President Andrew Johnson's veto.

February

14–25 Morehouse College organized in Augusta, Georgia. The institution was later moved to Atlanta.

25 New registration law in Tennessee abolished racial distinctions in voting.

March

2 First of a succession of Reconstruction acts passed by Congress. The acts divided the former Confederate states into five military districts under the command of army generals. Elections were ordered for constitutional conventions and freedmen were enfranchised. Commanders in some states changed the status of blacks by military orders. In March Maj. Gen. E.R.S. Canby opened the jury box to blacks in South and North Carolina. In April thirty blacks were named policemen in Mobile, Alabama.

—Blacks voted in municipal election in Alexandria, Va., for perhaps the first time in the South. The election commissioners refused to count the fourteen hundred votes and military officials suspended local elections pending clarification of the status of the freedmen.

—Howard University established. Also founded or chartered in 1867 were Talladege College, Morgan State University, Johnson C. Smith College, and St. Augustine's College.

1867

March

19   Congressman Thaddeus Stevens called up resolution
providing for the enforcement of the Second Confiscation Act of July, 1962. Measure, which provided for the
distribution of public and confiscated land to the
freedmen, was defeated.

27   Black demonstrators in Charleston staged ride-ins on
streetcars. On May 1, the Charleston City Railway
Company adopted a resolution guaranteeing the right of
all persons to ride in streetcars.

April

1   Blacks voted in municipal election in Tuscumbia,
Alabama. Military officials set aside the election pending clarification on electoral procedures.

24   Black demonstrators staged ride-ins on Richmond, Va.,
streetcars. Troops were mobilized to restore order.

--   First national meeting of the Ku Klux Klan held at the
Maxwell House, Nashville.

May

1   Reconstruction of the South began with the regis-
tering of black and white voters in the South. Gen.
Philip H. Sheridan ordered registration to begin in Louisiana on May 1 and to continue until June 30. Registration began in Arkansas in May. Other states followed
in June and July. By the end of October, 1,363,000
citizens had registered in the South, including 700,000
blacks. Black voters constituted a majority in five
states: Alabama, Florida, Louisiana, Mississippi and
South Carolina.

7   Black demonstrators staged ride-in to protest segregation on New Orleans streetcars. Similar demonstrations
occurred in Mobile, Ala., and other cities.

14   Riot, Mobile, Ala., after a black mass meeting. One
black and one white were killed.

1867

May

-- Knights of White Camelia, a paramilitary white supremacist organization, founded in Louisiana.

August

1 Blacks voted for the first time in a state election in the South, contributing to Republican sweep in Tennessee.

—Gen. Philip H. Sheridan dismissed the board of aldermen in New Orleans and named new appointees, including several blacks.

7 Death of actor Ira Aldridge (63), Lodes, Poland.

September

13 Gen. E. R. S. Canby ordered South Carolina courts to impanel black jurors.

27–28 Louisiana voters endorsed constitutional convention and elected delegates in first election under Reconstruction acts. The vote was 75,000 for the convention and 4,000 against. Elections for delegates to the conventions were held in other Southern states in October and November.

October

-- Monroe Baker, a well-to-do black businessman, named mayor of St. Martin, Louisiana. He was probably the first black to serve as mayor of a town.

November

5 First Reconstruction constitutional convention (eighteen blacks, ninety whites) opened in Montgomery, Alabama.

23 Louisiana constitutional convention (forty-nine white delegates and forty-nine black delegates) met in Mechanics Institute, New Orleans.

19–20 South Carolina citizens endorsed constitutional convention and selected delegates. Records indicated that 66,418 blacks and 2350 whites voted for the convention and 2278 whites voted against holding a convention.

1867

The total vote cast was 71,046. *Not a single black voted against the convention.*

December

3 Virginia constitutional convention (twenty-five blacks, eighty whites) met in Richmond. Because of political and legal complications, the Virginia constitution was not adopted until July 6, 1869.

9 Georgia constitutional convention (33 blacks, 137 whites) opened in Atlanta.

1868

January

7 Mississippi constitutional convention (seventeen blacks, eighty-three whites) met in Jackson.

—Arkansas constitutional convention (eight blacks, forty-three whites) met in Little Rock.

14 South Carolina constitutional convention, the first official assembly in the West with a black majority, met in the Charleston Clubhouse with seventy-six black delegates and forty-eight white delegates. Two-thirds of the black delegates were former slaves. A *New York Herald* reporter wrote: "Here in Charleston is being enacted the most incredible, hopeful, and yet unbelievable experiment in all the history of mankind."

—North Carolina constitutional convention (15 blacks, 118 whites) met in Raleigh.

20 Florida constitutional convention (eighteen blacks, twenty-seven whites) met in Tallahassee.

February

10 Conservatives, aided by military forces, seized convention hall and established effective control over Reconstruction process in Florida. Republican conservatives drafted new constitution which concentrated political power in hands of governor and limited the impact of the black vote.

1868

February

23   W. E. B. Du Bois born in Great Barrington, Massachusetts.

24   House of Representatives voted, 126 to 47, to impeach President Andrew Johnson.

April

1   Hampton Institute opened.

14-16   South Carolina voters approved constitution, 70,758 to 27,228, and elected state officers, including the first black cabinet officer, Francis L. Cardozo, secretary of state. New constitution required integrated education and contained a strong bill of rights section: "Distinctions on account of race or color, in any case whatever, shall be prohibited, and all classes of citizens shall enjoy equally all common, public, legal and political privileges."

16-17   Louisiana voters approved new constitution and elected state officers, including the first black lieutenant governor, Oscar J. Dunn, and the first black state treasurer, Antoine Dubuclet. Article Thirteen of the new constitution banned segregation in public accommodation: "All the persons shall enjoy equal rights and privileges upon any conveyances of a public character; and all places of business, or of public resort, or for which a license is required by either State, parish or municipal authority, shall be deemed places of a public character and shall be opened to the accommodation and patronage of all persons, without distinction or discrimination on account of race or color."

May

16   Senate failed by a margin of 34 to 16 to cast the two-thirds vote necessary to oust President Johnson.

20-21   Republican National Convention, meeting in Chicago, nominated U. S. Grant for the presidency. Convention marked the national debut of black politicians. P. B. S.

1868

Pinchback of Louisiana and James J. Harris were delegates to the convention. Harris was named to the committee that informed Grant of his nomination. Blacks also served for the first time as presidential electors. Robert Meacham was a presidential elector in Florida. The South Carolina electoral ticket included three black Republican leaders, B. F. Randolph, Stephen A. Swails, and Alonzo J. Ransier.

June

1   Texas constitutional convention (nine blacks, eighty-one whites) met in Austin.

—Florida General Assembly (nineteen blacks, fifty-seven whites) met in Tallahassee.

—Solomon George Washington Dill, poor white ally of black Republicans, assassinated in his home by white terrorists. Dill had allegedly made "incendiary speeches" to South Carolina blacks.

19   Maj. Gen. E. R. S. Canby removed the mayor and aldermen of Columbia, S.C., and made new appointments, including three blacks: C. M. Wilder, Joseph Taylor and William Simonds.

22   Congress readmitted state of Arkansas on condition that it would never change its constitution to disenfranchise blacks.

25   Congress readmitted North Carolina, South Carolina, Louisiana, Georgia, Alabama and Florida on condition "that the constitutions of said states shall never be amended or changed as to deprive any citizen or class of citizens of the United States of the right to vote in said states who are entitled to vote by the constitutions thereof herein recognized."

29   Louisiana legislature met in New Orleans. The temporary chairman of the house was a black representative,

1868

R. H. Isabelle. Oscar J. Dunn presided over the senate. Seven of the thirty-six senators were black. Thirty-five of the 101 representatives were black.

July

1 North Carolina legislature (21 blacks, 149 whites) met in Raleigh.

4 Georgia legislature (34 blacks, 186 whites) met in Atlanta.

6 South Carolina General Assembly met in Janney's Hall, Columbia, with eighty-five black representatives and seventy whites. There were ten blacks and twenty-one whites in the senate and seventy-five blacks and forty-nine whites in the house. This was the first—and last—American legislature with a black majority. Robert Somers said later that the South Carolina Assembly was "a proletariat parliament the likes of which could not be produced under the widest suffrage in any part of the world save in some of these Southern states."

9 Francis L. Cardozo installed as secretary of the state of South Carolina and became the first black cabinet officer on the state level.

13 Oscar J. Dunn, a former slave, formally installed as lieutenant governor of Louisiana, the highest elective office held to date by an American black. Antoine Dubuclet was installed as state treasurer.

—Alabama legislature (26 blacks, 106 whites) met in Montgomery.

21 Fourteenth Amendment ratified.

August

1 Gov. Henry C. Warmoth endorsed a joint resolution of the legislature calling for federal military aid. Warmoth said there had been 150 political assassinations in Louisiana in June and July.

1868

August

11 Death of Thaddeus Stevens (76), architect of the Radical Reconstruction program, in Washington.

September

3 Lower house of Georgia legislature, ruling that blacks were ineligible to hold office, expelled twenty-eight representatives. Ten days later the senate expelled three blacks. Congress refused to admit the state until the legislature seated the black representatives.

19 White Democrats attacked demonstrators, who were marching from Albany to Camilla, Ga., and killed nine blacks. Several whites were wounded.

22 Race riot, New Orleans.

28 Opelousas Massacre, St. Landry Parish, Louisiana. Republicans said Democratic terrorists killed two or three hundred blacks.

October

6 Black state convention at Macon, Ga., protested expulsion of black politicians from Georgia legislature.

26 White terrorists killed several blacks in St. Bernard Parish, near New Orleans.

-- B. F. Randolph, state senator and chairman of the state Republican party, assassinated in daylight at Hodges Depot in Abbeville, South Carolina.

November

3 First black elected to Congress, John W. Menard, defeated a white candidate, 5,107 to 2,833, in an election in Louisiana's Second Congressional District to fill an unexpired term in the Fortieth Congress.

—U. S. Grant elected president with black voters in the South providing the decisive margin. Grant received a minority of the white votes in defeating Democrat Horatio Seymour, 3,015,071 votes to 2,709,613.

1868

November

6 Jonathan Gibbs, minister and educator, appointed secretary of state by the Florida governor.

9 Arkansas Governor Powell Clayton declared martial law in ten counties and mobilized the state militia in Ku Klux Klan crisis.

1869

January

13 National convention of black leaders met in Washington, D.C. Frederick Douglass was elected president.

February

20 Tennessee Governor W. C. Brownlow declared martial law in nine counties in Ku Klux Klan crisis.

23 Louisiana governor signed public accommodations law.

26 Fifteenth Amendment guaranteeing the right to vote sent to the states for ratification.

27 John W. Menard spoke in Congress in defense of his claim to a contested seat in Louisiana's Second Congressional District. Congress decided against both claimants. Congressman James A. Garfield of the examining committee said "it was too early to admit a Negro to the U.S. Congress." Menard was the first black to make a speech in Congress.

March

3 University of South Carolina opened to all races. Two blacks—B. A. Boseman and Francis L. Cardozo—were elected to the seven-man board of trustees.

13 Arkansas legislature passed anti-Klan law.

April

6 Ebenezer Don Carlos Bassett, principal of the Institute for Colored Youth, Philadelphia, named minister to

1869

Haiti and became the first major black diplomat and the first American black to receive a major appointment from the United States government.

April

12   North Carolina legislature passed anti-Klan law.

July

6   Black candidate for lieutenant governor, Dr. J. H. Harris, defeated by a vote of 120,068 to 99,600 in Virginia election.

15   A. J. Hayne, black captain of the Arkansas militia, assassinated in Marion, Arkansas.

August

6   White conservatives suppressed black vote and captured Tennessee legislature in election marred by assassinations and widespread violence.

October

5   First Reconstruction legislature (27 blacks, 150 whites) met in Richmond, Virginia.

November

30   James Lynch elected secretary of state in Mississippi contest.

December

6   National black labor convention met in Washington. James M. Harris of North Carolina elected president.

---   Among the colleges and universities founded in 1869 were Clark, Claflin, Dillard and Tougaloo.

1870

United States population: 39,818,449. Black population: 4,880,009 (12.7 per cent).

January

10   Georgia legislature reconvened and admitted black representatives and senators.

11   First reconstruction legislature met in Jackson, Mississippi. Thirty-one of the 106 representatives were black. Five of the thirty-three senators were black.

1870

January

20 Hiram R. Revels elected to the U.S. Senate by the Mississippi legislature. He was elected to fill the unexpired term of Jefferson Davis. The term ended on March 3, 1871.

26 Congress admitted Virginia to the Union on condition that it would never change its constitution to disenfranchise blacks.

February

1 Jonathan Jasper Wright, the first black to hold a major judicial position, elected to the South Carolina Supreme Court.

17 Congress passed resolution readmitting Mississippi on condition that it would never change its constitution to disenfranchise blacks.

25 Hiram R. Revels of Mississippi sworn in as first black U.S. senator and first black representative in Congress.

26 Wyatt Outlaw, black leader of the Union League in Almanance County, N.C., lynched.

March

7 Gov. William W. Holden of North Carolina denounced Klan violence and issued proclamation declaring Almanance County in a state of insurrection.

16 Hiram R. Revels made his first speech in the Senate, opposing the readmission of Georgia without adequate safeguards for black citizens. This was the first official speech by a black in Congress.

30 Fifteenth Amendment ratified.

April

9 American Anti-Slavery Society dissolved.

May

31 Congress passed the first Enforcement Act which provided stiff penalties for public officials and private citi-

1870

zens who deprived citizens of the suffrage and civil rights. The measure authorized the use of the U.S. Army to protect the rights of blacks.

July

1   James W. Smith of South Carolina entered West Point. Smith, the first black student, did not graduate.

8   Governor W. W. Holden of North Carolina declared Casswell County in a state of insurrection.

August

4   White conservatives suppressed black vote and carried North Carolina election in a campaign marred by political assassinations and violence. Campaign effectively ended Radical Reconstruction in North Carolina. The conservative legislature impeached Governor Holden on December 14.

October

19   First blacks elected to the House of Representatives. Black Republicans won three of the four congressional seats in South Carolina: Joseph H. Rainey, Robert C. DeLarge and Robert B. Elliott. Rainey was elected to an unexpired term in the Forty-first Congress and was the first black seated in the House.

—Republicans swept South Carolina elections with a ticket of six whites and two blacks: Alonzo Ransier, lieutenant governor; Francis L. Cardozo, secretary of state.

November

8   Democratic governor elected in Tennessee.

December

12   Joseph H. Rainey, first black in the House of Representatives, sworn in as congressman from South Carolina.

16   Colored Methodist Episcopal Church organized in Jackson, Tennessee.

20   Jefferson F. Long of Macon, Ga., elected to an unexpired term in the Forty-first Congress.

1870

December

20 Georgia Democrats carried state election with a campaign of violence and political intimidation.

-- Robert H. Wood, Mississippi political leader, elected mayor of Natchez.

--- Allen University, Benedict College and LeMoyne-Owen College established.

1871

January

16 Jefferson F. Long of Georgia sworn in as the second black congressman.

February

1 Jefferson Long of Georgia became the first black to make an official speech in the House of Representatives. He opposed leniency to former Confederates.

28 Second Enforcement Act gave federal officers and courts control of registration and voting in congressional elections.

March

1 J. Milton Turner named minister to Liberia and became the first black diplomat accredited to an African country. James W. Mason was named minister in March, 1870, but never traveled to his post.

4 Forty-second Congress convened (1871–73) with five black congressmen: Joseph H. Rainey, Robert Carlos DeLarge and Robert Brown Elliott, South Carolina; Benjamin S. Turner, Alabama; Josiah T. Walls, Florida. Walls was elected in an at-large election and was the first black congressman to represent an entire state.

April

20 Third Enforcement Act defined Klan conspiracy as a rebellion against the United States and empowered the

1871

president to suspend the writ of habeas corpus and declare martial law in rebellious areas.

June

-- Ku Klux Klan trials began in federal court in Oxford, Mississippi. Many whites, including doctors, lawyers, ministers and college professors, were arrested and jailed in the anti-Klan campaign. Of the 930 indicted in Mississippi, 243 were tried and found guilty. Some 1180 were indicted in South Carolina and 1849 were indicted in North Carolina.

October

6 Fisk Jubilee Singers began first national tour.

17 President Grant suspended the writ of habeas corpus and declared martial law in nine South Carolina counties affected by Klan disturbances.

November

22 Lt. Gov. Oscar J. Dunn died suddenly in the midst of a bitter struggle for control of the Louisiana state government. Dunn aides charged that he was poisoned.

28 Ku Klux Klan trials began in Federal District Court in Columbia, South Carolina.

December

6 P. B. S. Pinchback elected president pro tem of the Louisiana senate and acting lieutenant governor.

19 Democratic governor elected in Georgia in campaign marked by violence and political intimidation.

1872

January

2 Mississippi legislature met. John R. Lynch was elected Speaker of the house at the age of twenty-four.

February

7 Alcorn A&M College opened.

27 Charlotte E. Ray, first black woman lawyer, graduated from Howard University. She was admitted to practice on April 23.

1872

April

10-14   National black convention met in New Orleans. Frederick Douglass was elected president.

June

5-6   Republican National Convention met in Philadelphia with substantial black representation from Southern states. For the first time in American history, three blacks addressed a major national political convention: Robert B. Elliott, chairman of the South Carolina delegation; Joseph H. Rainey, South Carolina delegate; John R. Lynch, Mississippi delegate.

27   Poet Paul Laurence Dunbar born in Dayton, Ohio.

September

21   John Henry Conyers of South Carolina became the first black student at Annapolis Naval Academy. He later resigned.

October

16   South Carolina Republicans carried election with a ticket of four whites and four blacks: Richard H. Gleaves, lieutenant governor; Henry E. Hayne, secretary of state; Francis L. Cardozo, treasurer; Henry W. Purvis, adjutant general. Blacks won 97 of the 158 seats in the General Assembly and four of the five congressional districts.

November

4   Three blacks elected to major offices in Louisiana elections: C. C. Antoine, lieutenant governor; P. G. Deslonde, secretary of state; W. B. Brown, superintendent of public education. P. B. S. Pinchback was elected congressman at large. Fourth black official, Treasurer Antoine Dubuclet, won elections in 1870 and 1874.

26   South Carolina General Assembly met in Columbia. Stephen A. Swails was elected president pro tem of the senate, and Samuel J. Lee was elected Speaker of the house. The Assembly named four blacks to the seven-man governing board of the University of South

1872

Carolina: Samuel J. Lee, J. A. Bowley, Stephen A. Swails and W. R. Jervay. Macon B. Allen was elected judge of the Inferior Court of Charleston. Allen, the first black lawyer, thus became the second black to hold a major judicial position and the first black with a major judicial position on the municipal level.

December

9 P. B. S. Pinchback was sworn in as governor of Louisiana after H. C. Warmoth was impeached "for high crimes and misdeameanors."

12 Attorney General George Williams sent a telegram to "Acting Governor Pinchback," saying that the black politician "was recognized by the President as the lawful executive of Louisiana."

1873

January

13 P. B. S. Pinchback relinquished the office of governor, saying at the inauguration of the new Louisiana governor: "I now have the honor to formally surrender the office of governor, with the hope that you will administer the government in the interests of all the people [and that] your administration will be as fair toward the class that I represent, as mine has been toward the class represented by you."

14 P. B. S. Pinchback elected to the U.S. Senate. Since he had previously been elected to Congress, he went to Washington with the unique distinction of being both a senator-elect and a congressman-elect.

April

13 Colfax Massacre, Easter Sunday morning, Grant Parish, Louisiana. More than sixty blacks were killed.

14 U.S. Supreme Court decision in Slaughterhouse cases began process of diluting the Fourteenth Amendment. The Court said the Fourteenth Amendment protected *federal* civil rights, not "civil rights heretofore belonging exclusively to the states."

1873

July

1   Henry O. Flipper of Georgia entered West Point Military Academy.

October

7   Henry E. Hayne, secretary of state, accepted as a student at the University of South Carolina. Scores of blacks attended the university in 1874 and 1875.

November

16   W. C. Handy born in Florence, Alabama.

--   Blacks won three state offices in Mississippi election: Alexander K. Davis, lieutenant governor; James Hill, secretary of state; T. W. Cardozo, superintendent of education. Blacks won 55 of the 115 seats in the house and 9 out of 37 seats in the senate—42 per cent of the total number.

--   Richard T. Greener, first black graduate of Harvard University, named professor of metaphysics at the University of South Carolina.

December

1   Forty-third Congress (1873–75) convened with seven black congressmen: Richard H. Cain, Robert Brown Elliott, Joseph H. Rainey and Alonzo J. Ransier, South Carolina; James T. Rapier, Alabama; Josiah T. Walls, Florida; John R. Lynch, Mississippi.

---   Mifflin Wister Gibb elected city judge in Little Rock and became the first black to hold such a position.

---   Bennett College, Wiley College, and Alabama State College founded.

1874

January

--   I. D. Shadd elected Speaker of the lower house of the Mississippi legislature.

17   Armed Democrats seized Texas government and ended Radical Reconstruction in Texas.

1874

February

3 Blanche Kelso Bruce elected to a full six-year term in the U.S. Senate by the Mississippi legislature.

March

11 Death of Charles Sumner (63), militant white advocate of equal rights.

—Frederick Douglass named president of the failing Freedmen's Bank.

April

27 White League, paramilitary white supremacist organization, founded at Opelousas, Louisiana.

June

28 Freedmen's Bank closed. Black depositors had some $3 million in the bank, which had an imposing headquarters in Washington and branches in various cities. President Frederick Douglass said later that the Freedmen's Bank had been "the black man's cow and the white man's milk."

July

31 Patrick Francis Healy, S. J., inaugurated as president of Georgetown University, the oldest Catholic university in America, and became the first black to head a predominantly white university.

August

26 Sixteen blacks lynched in Tennessee.

30 White Democrats killed more than sixty black and whites in Coushatta Massacre in Louisiana.

September

14 White Democrats seized statehouse in Louisiana coup d'etat. President Grant ordered the revolutionaries to disperse, and the rebellion collapsed. Twenty-seven persons (sixteen whites and eleven blacks) were killed in battles between Democrats and Republicans.

October

-- South Carolina Republicans carried election with reduced margin. Republican ticket was composed of four

1874

whites and four blacks: R. H. Gleaves, lieutenant governor; Francis L. Cardozo, treasurer; Henry E. Hayne, secretary of state; H. W. Purvis, adjutant general.

November

3 James Theodore Holly, a black American who emigrated to Haiti in 1861, elected bishop of Haiti. He was consecrated in a ceremony at New York's Grace Church on November 8.

4 Democrats swept off-years elections, winning a majority in the House of Representatives.

24 Robert B. Elliott elected Speaker of the lower house of the South Carolina legislature. Stephen A. Swails was reelected president pro tem of the senate.

December

7 White Democrats killed seventy-five Republicans in massacre at Vicksburg, Mississippi.

21 President Grant issued proclamation on violence in Mississippi.

1875

January

5 President Grant sent federal troops to Vicksburg, Mississippi.

March

1 Civil Rights Bill enacted by Congress. Bill gave blacks the right to equal treatment in inns, public conveyances, theaters and other places of public amusement.

5 Blanche Kelso Bruce sworn in as a U.S. senator. Mississippi politician was the first black to serve a full term in the Senate. His term ended on March 3, 1881.

June

2 James A. Healy, first black Roman Catholic bishop, consecrated in cathedral at Portland, Maine.

July

4 White Democrats killed several blacks in terrorist attacks in Vicksburg, Mississippi.

1875

July

10   Mary McLeod Bethune, educator and civil rights leader, born in Mayesville, South Carolina.

September

1   White Democrats attacked Republicans at Yazoo City, Mississippi. One white and three blacks were killed.

4–6   Clinton Massacre, Clinton, Mississippi. Twenty to thirty blacks killed.

8   Mississippi governor requested federal troops to protect black voters. Attorney General Edward Pierrepont refused the request and said "the whole public are tired of these annual autumnal outbreaks in the South. . . ."

November

2   Democrats suppressed black vote by fraud and violence and carried Mississippi election. "The Mississippi Plan"—staged riots, political assassinations, massacres and social and economic intimidation—was used later to overthrow Reconstruction governments in South Carolina and Louisiana.

December

6   Forty-fourth Congress (1875–77) convened with historic high of eight blacks. One U.S. senator, Blanche K. Bruce, Mississippi. Seven black congressmen: Jeremiah Haralson, Alabama; Josiah T. Walls, Florida; John R. Lynch, Mississippi; John A. Hyman, North Carolina; Charles E. Nash, Louisiana; Joseph H. Rainey, Robert Smalls, South Carolina.

16   William J. Whipper elected judge of the circuit court of Charleston by South Carolina General Assembly. Governor Daniel H. Chamberlain, acting in concert with white Democrats and conservatives, refused to sign his commission.

19   Carter G. Woodson born in New Canton, Buckingham County, Virginia.

1875

December

25 Charles Caldwell, militant black militia officer, assassinated in Clinton, Mississippi.

--- Alabama A&M College, Knoxville College and Lane College established.

1876

March

8 Senate refused to seat P.B.S. Pinchback.

July

8 White terrorists attacked Black Republicans in Hamburg, S.C., killing five.

August

14 Prairie View State University founded.

September

6 Race riot, Charleston, South Carolina.

15–20 White terrorists attacked Republicans in Ellenton, South Carolina. Two whites and thirty-nine blacks were killed.

October

16 Race riot, Cainhoy, South Carolina. Five whites and one black killed.

26 President sent federal troops to South Carolina.

November

7 President Rutherford B. Hayes and Samuel J. Tilden claimed the presidential election. Republicans and Democrats claimed elections in Louisiana, South Carolina and Florida.

--- Edward A. Bouchet received the Ph.D. degree in physics at Yale University and became the first black to receive a doctorate at an American university.

--- Edward Bannister, the first black artist to win wide critical acclaim, awarded prize at Philadelphia Centennial Exposition for his work *Under the Oak*.

1876

--- Meharry Medical College established at Central Tennessee College.

1877

February

26 At a conference in the Wormley Hotel in Washington, representatives of Rutherford B. Hayes and representatives of the South negotiated agreement which paved the way for the election of Hayes as president and the withdrawal of federal troops from the South.

March

18 President Hayes appointed Frederick Douglass marshal of District of Columbia.

April

10 Federal troops withdrawn from Columbia, South Carolina. Democrats took over state government.

20 Federal troops withdrawn from public buildings in New Orleans. Democrats took over state government.

June

15 Henry O. Flipper received degree at West Point and became the first black graduate.

September

27 John Mercer Langston named minister to Haiti.

October

15 Forty-fifth Congress (1877–79) convened. One U.S. senator, Blanche K. Bruce, Mississippi. Three U.S. congressmen: Richard H. Cain, Joseph H. Rainey, Robert Smalls, South Carolina.

--- Jackson College (Miss.) established.

1878

April

21 The ship *Azor* left Charleston with 206 black emigrants bound for Liberia.

May

23 Atty. John Henry Smyth named minister to Liberia.

1879

February

-- Southern blacks fled political and economic exploitation in "Exodus of 1879." Exodus continued for several years. One of the major leaders of the Exodus movement was a former slave, Benjamin ("Pap") Singleton.

March

18 Forty-sixth Congress (1879–1881) convened. One U.S. senator: Blanche K. Bruce, Mississippi.

May

-- White terrorists, led by Gen. James R. Chalmers, one of the Confederate heroes of the Fort Pillow Massacre, closed Mississippi River to black migrants, blockading landings and threatening to sink all boats.

--- Livingstone College founded.

1880

United States population: 50,155,783. Black population: 6,580,793 (13.1 per cent).

November

2 Republican James A. Garfield elected president.

24 More than 150 delegates from Baptist churches in eleven states organized the Baptist Foreign Mission Convention of the United States at a meeting in Montgomery, Alabama. Rev. William H. McAlpine was elected president.

--- Southern University established.

1881

May

17 Frederick Douglass appointed recorder of deeds for District of Columbia.

19 Blanche Kelso Bruce appointed register of treasury by President Garfield.

1881

June

30   Henry Highland Garnet, former abolitionist leader and Presbyterian minister, named minister to Liberia. He died in Monrovia shortly after his arrival.

July

2   President Garfield shot in Washington, D.C. He died on September 19 and was succeeded by Vice-President Chester A. Arthur.

4   Booker T. Washington established Tuskegee Institute. Also founded in 1881 were Spelman College, Morris Brown College, and Bishop College.

December

5   Forty-seventh Congress (1881–83) convened. Two black congressmen, Robert Smalls, South Carolina; John R. Lynch, Mississippi.

24–31   Exodus of five thousand blacks from Edgefield County, South Carolina. Migrants, protesting exploitation and violence, settled in Arkansas.

---   Tennessee started modern segregation movement with Jim Crow railroad car and was followed by Florida (1887), Mississippi (1888), Texas (1889), Louisiana (1890), Alabama, Kentucky, Arkansas and Georgia (1891), South Carolina (1898), North Carolina (1899), Virginia (1900), Maryland (1904), Oklahoma (1907).

---   United Order of True Reformer established.

1882

February

13   Death of Henry Highland Garnet (66), diplomat and protest leader, in Monrovia, Liberia.

April

12   John Henry Smyth named to second tour of duty as minister to Haiti.

---   Forty-nine blacks were reported lynched in 1882.

1882

---   Virginia State College established.

1883

September

24   National black convention met in Louisville, Kentucky.

October

15   U.S. Supreme Court declared Civil Rights Act of 1875 unconstitutional.

November

3   Race riot, Danville, Virginia. Four blacks killed.

26   Death of Sojourner Truth, Battle Creek, Michigan.

December

3   Forty-eighth Congress (1883–85) convened. Two black representatives, James E. O'Hara, North Carolina; Robert Smalls, South Carolina.

---   George L. Ruffin appointed city judge in Boston.

---   Fifty-three blacks reported lynched in 1883.

1884

June

--   John R. Lynch, former congressman from Mississippi, elected temporary chairman of Republican convention and became first black to preside over deliberations of a national political party.

November

4   Grover Cleveland won election and became the first Democratic president of the United States since the Civil War.

15   Colonization of Africa organized at international conference in Berlin, November 15–February 26.

22   T. Thomas Fortune started *New York Freeman*, which later became the *New York Age*.

--   The *Philadelphia Tribune* founded by Christopher J. Perry.

1884

---   Fifty-one blacks reported lynched in 1884.

1885

January

24   Death of Martin R. Delany (72), politician and black nationalist, in Wilberforce, Ohio.

March

2   George W. Williams, minister, lawyer and historian, named minister to Haiti. The appointment was vacated by the new administration.

May

7   Dr. John E. W. Thompson, graduate of the Yale University Medical School, named minister to Haiti.

June

24   Samuel David Ferguson consecrated bishop of the Protestant Episcopal Church and named bishop of Liberia. He was the first black American with full membership in the House of Bishops.

September

11   Moses A. Hopkins, minister and educator, named minister to Liberia.

December

7   Forty-ninth Congress (1885–87) convened. Two black congressmen: James E. O'Hara, North Carolina; Robert Smalls, South Carolina.

---   Seventy-four blacks reported lynched in 1885.

1886

March

17   Carrollton Massacre, Carrollton, Mississippi. Twenty blacks killed.

April

24   Augustus Tolton ordained a Roman Catholic priest in Rome and assigned to America.

August

25   Some six hundred delegates organized the American National Baptist Convention at a St. Louis meeting. Rev. William J. Simmons was elected president.

1886

--- Seventy-four blacks reported lynched in 1886.

--- Kentucky State College founded.

1887

March

11 Charles H. J. Taylor of Kansas named minister to Liberia. He resigned November 11, 1887.

28 James M. Trotter of Boston named recorder of deeds by Democratic President Grover Cleveland.

--- Seventy blacks reported lynched in 1887.

--- Florida A&M University and Central State College were established.

1888

April

24 Ezekiel Ezra Smith, North Carolina minister and educator, named minister to Liberia.

October

17 Capital Savings Bank of Washington, D.C., the first black bank, opened in Washington, D.C. The Savings Bank of the Order of True Reformers (Richmond, Va.) was chartered on March 2, 1888.

November

6 Republican Benjamin Harrison elected president.

--- Sixty-nine blacks reported lynched in 1888.

1889

March

4 Fifty-first Congress convened. Three black congressmen: Henry P. Cheatham, North Carolina; Thomas E. Miller, South Carolina; John M. Langston, Virginia.

April

3 Savings Bank of the Order of True Reformers opened in Richmond, Virginia.

1889

April

15   Asa Philip Randolph born in Crescent City, Florida.

July

1   Frederick Douglass named minister to Haiti.

---   Ninety-four blacks reported lynched in 1889.

1890

United States population: 62,947,714. Black population: 7,488,676 (11.9 per cent)

January

25   National Afro-American League, pioneer black protest organization, founded at Chicago meeting. Joseph C. Price, president of Livingstone College, was elected president.

March

20   Blair Bill which provided federal support for education and allocated funds to reduce illiteracy among the freedmen was defeated in the Senate, 37–31.

August

12   Mississippi Constitutional Convention began systematic exclusion of blacks from political life of South, August 12–November 1. The Mississippi Plan (literacy and "understanding tests") was later adopted with embellishments by other states: South Carolina (1895), Louisiana (1898), North Carolina (1900), Alabama (1901), Virginia (1901), Georgia (1908), Oklahoma (1910). Southern states later used "white primaries" and other devices to exclude black voters.

16   Alexander Clark, journalist and lawyer, named minister to Liberia.

October

15   Alabama Penny Savings Bank organized in Birmingham.

---   Eighty-five blacks reported lynched in 1890.

---   Savannah State College established.

1891

January

22 Lodge Bill, which called for federal supervision of U.S. elections, abandoned in the Senate after a Southern filibuster.

23 Chicago's Provident Hospital incorporated with first training school for black nurses.

August

4 Death of George Washington Williams (41), Blackpool, England.

September

3 John Stephens Durham, assistant editor of the Philadelphia *Evening Bulletin*, named minister to Haiti.

Cottonpickers organized union and staged strike for higher wages in Texas.

December

2 Fifty-second Congress convened. One black congressman: Henry P. Cheatham, North Carolina.

--- One hundred and thirteen blacks were reported lynched in 1891.

--- North Carolina A&T College, Delaware State College and West Virginia State College established.

1892

January

11 William D. McCoy of Indiana was appointed minister to Liberia.

April

-- Black longshoremen struck for higher wages in St. Louis, Missouri.

August

13 Baltimore *Afro-American* founded.

November

8 Democrat Grover Cleveland elected president.

--- One hundred and sixty one blacks reported lynched.

1893

July

1   Walter Francis White born in Atlanta, Georgia.

9   Daniel Hale Williams performed "world's first successful heart operation" at Chicago's Provident Hospital.

August

7   Fifty-third Congress (1893–95) convened. One black congressman, George W. Murray, South Carolina.

---   One hundred and eighteen blacks were reported lynched in 1893.

1895

February

20   Death of Frederick Douglass (78), Anacostia Heights, District of Columbia. Douglass was the leading black spokesman for almost fifty years. He was a major abolitionist and a lecturer and editor.

21   North Carolina legislature, dominated by black Republicans and white Populists, adjourned for the day to mark the death of Frederick Douglass.

23   William H. Heard, AME minister and educator, named minister to Liberia.

March

11–12   New Orleans laborers attacked by whites. Six blacks were killed.

18   Two hundred blacks left Savannah, Ga., for Liberia.

September

18   Booker T. Washington delivered "Atlanta Compromise" address at Cotton States Exposition in Atlanta.

28   Three Baptist groups—the Foreign Mission Convention of the United States, the American National Baptist Convention, the Baptist National Education Convention — merged and established the National Baptist Convention at an Atlanta meeting.

1895

October

-- National Medical Association founded in Atlanta.

December

2 Fifty-fourth Congress (1895–97) convened. One black congressman: George W. Murray, South Carolina.

4 South Carolina Constitutional Convention adopted new constitution with "understanding clause" designed to eliminate black voters.

--- One hundred and thirteen blacks were reported lynched in 1895.

--- Fort Valley State College established.

1896

May

18 U.S. Supreme Court decision (*Plessy* v. *Ferguson*) upheld doctrine of "separate but equal" and began age of Jim Crow.

July

21 National Federation of Afro-American Women and the Colored Women's League merged and created the National Association of Colored Women. Mary Church Terrell was elected president at meeting at Washington's Nineteenth Street Baptist Church.

November

3 Republican William McKinley defeated Democratic candidate William J. Bryan in presidential race.

--- Seventy-eight blacks reported lynched in 1896.

--- South Carolina State College established.

1897

March

5 American Negro Academy founded.

15 Fifty-fifth Congress (1897–99) convened. One black congressman: George H. White, North Carolina.

1897

June

17   William Frank Powell, New Jersey educator, named minister to Haiti.

November

15   Death of John Mercer Langston (67), Washington, D.C.

---   One hundred and twenty-three blacks reported lynched in 1897.

---   Langston University and Voorhees College founded.

1898

February

11   Owen L. W. Smith of North Carolina, AME Zion minister and educator, named minister to Liberia.

22   Black postmaster lynched and his wife and three daughters shot and maimed for life in Lake City, S. C.

March

17   Death of Blanche Kelso Bruce (57), in Washington.

April

21   Spanish-American War began.

May

12   Louisiana adopted new constitution with "grandfather clause" designed to eliminate black voters.

June

24   American troops, including Tenth Cavalry, drove Spanish forces from entrenched positions at La Guasimas, Cuba.

July

1   Tenth Cavalry made charge at El Caney and relieved Theodore Roosevelt's Rough Riders. Four black regiments in regular army were conspicuous in fighting around Santiago in Spanish–American War. Sixteen regiments of black volunteers were recruited during the war.

August

--   Black longshoremen struck for higher wages and better working conditions in Galveston, Texas.

1898

September

15 National Afro-American Council founded in Rochester, New York. Bishop Alexander Walters of the AME Zion Church was elected president. The organization proposed a program of assertion and protest.

October

20 North Carolina Mutual and Provident Insurance Company founded by John Merrick and associates in Durham, North Carolina.

November

10 Race riot, Wilmington, North Carolina. Eight blacks were killed.

--- National Benefit Life Insurance Company organized in Washington, D.C., by Samuel W. Rutherford. National Benefit was the largest black insurance company for several years.

--- One hundred and one blacks reported lynched in 1898.

1899

April

4 Musician Edward Kennedy ("Duke") Ellington born in Washington, D.C.

11 White and black workers rioted over jobs at Pana, Ill., mines. Six persons killed.

June

2 Black Americans observed day of fasting called by National Afro-American Council to protest lynchings and racial massacres.

10 Improved Benevolent and Protective Order of Elks founded in Cincinnati.

December

4 Fifty-sixth Congress convened. One black congressman: George H. White, North Carolina.

--- Eighty-five blacks reported lynched in 1899.

1900

United States population: 75,994,575. Black population: 8,833,994 (11.6 per cent).

July

4   Daniel Louis ("Satchmo") Armstrong born in New Orleans, Louisiana.

23–25   Pan-African Congress met in London. Among the leaders of the Congress were H. Sylvester Williams, a West Indian lawyer with a London practice, W. E. B. Du Bois, and Bishop Alexander Walters.

24–27   Race riot, New Orleans. Two white policemen killed.

August

5   Death of James Augustine Healy (70), black Roman Catholic bishop, Portland, Maine.

23–24   National Negro Business League organized at Boston meeting. Booker T. Washington was elected president.

November

6   Republican William McKinley defeated William Bryan in presidential election.

- - -   One hundred and six blacks reported lynched in 1900.

- - -   James Weldon Johnson and J. Rosamond Johnson composed "Lift Ev'ry Voice and Sing."

1901

January

16   Death of Hiram Revels (73), Aberdeen, Mississippi.

March

4   Term of George H. White, last of post-Reconstruction congressmen, ended at noon.

6   President McKinley assassinated in Buffalo, New York. He was succeeded by Theodore Roosevelt.

October

16   Booker T. Washington dined at the White House with President Roosevelt and was criticized in the South.

1901

November

9 Boston *Guardian* founded by William Monroe Trotter.

11 Alabama adopted new constitution with "grandfather clause" designed to eliminate black voters.

--- One hundred and five blacks reported lynched in 1901.

--- Grambling College established.

1903

March

16 Ernest Lyon, Methodist minister and educator from Maryland, named minister to Liberia.

April

27 U.S. Supreme Court upheld clauses in Alabama constitution which disfranchised blacks.

--- Publication of W. E. B. Du Bois's *The Souls of Black Folk* crystallized opposition to Booker T. Washington's program of social and political subordination.

--- Maggie L. Walker named president of Richmond's St. Luke Bank and Trust Company and became the first black woman to head a bank.

--- Eighty-four blacks reported lynched in 1903.

1904

October

3 Mary McLeod Bethune opened Daytona Normal and Industrial School in Daytona Beach, Florida. In 1923 the school merged with Cookman Institute and became Bethune-Cookman College.

--- Seventy-six blacks reported lynched in 1904.

1905

May

5 First issue of *Chicago Defender* published.

1905

July

11-13 Black intellectuals and activists organized Niagara movement at meeting near Niagara Falls. Delegates from fourteen states, led by W. E. B. Du Bois and William Monroe Trotter, demanded abolition of all distinctions based on race.

September

6 Atlanta Life Insurance Company established by A. F. Herndon.

November

23 Henry Watson Furness, an Indiana physician, named minister to Haiti. He was the last black minister to Haiti in this period. Woodrow Wilson appointed a white minister in 1913.

--- Fifty-seven blacks reported lynched in 1905.

1906

February

9 Death of Paul Laurence Dunbar (33), Dayton, Ohio.

June

-- John Hope became the first black president of Morehouse College

August

13 Black soldiers raided Brownsville, Texas, in retaliation for racial insults. One white man killed, two wounded.

September

22-24 Race riot, Atlanta. Ten blacks and two whites killed. Martial law proclaimed.

October

22 Three thousand blacks demonstrated and rioted in Philadelphia to protest a theatrical presentation of Thomas Dixon's *The Clansman*.

November

6 President Roosevelt ordered discharge of three companies of Twenty-fifth Regiment for alleged involvement in the Brownsville Raid.

--- Sixty-two blacks reported lynched in 1906.

1908

January

29   Alpha Phi Alpha Fraternity, founded at Cornell University in 1906, incorporated.

July

2   Thurgood Marshall born in Baltimore.

August

14–19   Race riot, Springfield, Illinois. Troops called out. Riot led to the founding of NAACP.

November

3   Republican W. H. Taft elected president.

December

26   Jack Johnson defeated Tommy Burns at Sydney, Australia, for heavyweight championship.

---   Eighty-nine blacks reported lynched in 1908.

1909

February

12   NAACP founded. Call for organizational meeting was issued on 100th anniversary of Abraham Lincoln's birth by forty-seven whites and six blacks.

March

18   President Roosevelt appointed a committee, including Emmet J. Scott, to investigate disturbances in Liberia.

April

6   Commander Robert E. Peary reached North Pole. The only American with Peary was the man he identified as "my Negro assistant," Matthew Henson.

May

17   White firemen on Georgia Railroad struck to protest employment of blacks.

31   Some three hundred blacks and whites met at the United Charities Building in New York City at the first NAACP conference, May 31 and June 1.

November

7   Knights and Ladies of St. Peter Claver organized in Mobile, Ala., by four Josephite priests and three Catholic laymen.

1909

December

4   *New York Amsterdam News* founded by James H. Anderson.

---   Tennessee State A&I University established.

---   Sixty-nine blacks reported lynched in 1909.

1910

United States population: 93,402,151. Black population: 9,827,763 (10.7 per cent).

March

25   Liberian Commission recommended financial aid to Liberia and the establishment of a U.S. Navy coaling station in the African country.

May

12–14 Second NAACP conference, held in New York City, created a permanent national structure.

June

13   William D. Crum, a South Carolina physician, appointed minister to Liberia.

November

1   First issue of the *Crisis* published by editor W. E. B. Du Bois.

December

19   First city ordinance requiring white and black residential areas passed by Baltimore City Council. Similar laws were passed in Norfolk, Richmond, Roanoke, Greensboro, St. Louis, Oklahoma City, Dallas and Louisville.

---   Norfolk *Journal and Guide* established under the leadership of P. B. Young Sr.

---   Pittsburgh *Courier* founded.

---   North Carolina College founded.

---   Sixty-seven blacks reported lynched in 1910.

1911

March

9   White firemen of the Cincinnati, New Orleans and Texas Pacific Railroad struck to protest the hiring of black firemen.

26   William H. Lewis appointed assistant attorney general of the United States.

May

15   Kappa Alpha Psi Fraternity, founded at Indiana University, incorporated.

June

20   NAACP incorporated in New York.

October

--   Three organizations—the Committee for Improving the Industrial Conditions of Negroes in New York, the Committee on Urban Conditions and the National League for the Protection of Colored Women— merged, under the leadership of Dr. George E. Hayne and Eugene Kinckle Jones, to form the National Urban League. Eugene Kinckle Jones was named executive secretary.

---   Sixty blacks reported lynched in 1911.

1912

January

1   Second annual report of the NAACP listed total receipts from May through December, 1911, of $10,317.43. Organization had local chapters in Chicago, Boston and New York.

September

27   First published blues composition, W. C. Handy's *Memphis Blues*, went on sale in Memphis.

November

5   Woodrow Wilson elected president.

---   Sixty-one blacks reported lynched.

---   *St. Louis Argus* established.

1913

January

29 Alpha Kappa Alpha Sorority, founded at Howard University in 1908, incorporated.

-- Black Americans celebrated the fiftieth anniversary of Emancipation Proclamation. Major celebrations were held at Jackson, Mississippi, New Orleans and Nashville. Three states—Pennsylvania, New York and New Jersey—appropriated money for official celebrations of the event.

March

10 Death of Harriet Tubman, Auburn, New York.

April

11 Woodrow Wilson and his cabinet discussed relations between blacks and whites in government departments. Shortly thereafter the Wilson administration began segregating blacks and whites in government departments. By the end of the year there were separate working areas and separate lavatories and lunchrooms in many government departments in the capital.

September

10 George W. Buckner, a physician from Indiana, named minister to Liberia.

--- *Cleveland Call & Post* established.

--- Fifty-one blacks reported lynched in 1913.

1914

June

27 U.S. signed treaty of commerce with Ethiopia.

October

28 Omega Psi Phi Fraternity, founded at Howard University, incorporated.

1915

February

23 Death of Robert Smalls (75), Reconstruction congressman, in Beaufort, South Carolina.

1915

May

8   Death of Henry McNeal Turner (82), first black chaplain in the U.S. Army and AME bishop.

17   National Baptist Convention chartered.

June

21   U.S. Supreme Court (*Guinn* v. *United States*) said "grandfather clauses" in the Oklahoma and Maryland constitutions violated the Fifteenth Amendment.

July

28   U.S. Marines landed in Haiti and the country became a *de facto* protectorate of the United States.

September

9   Association for the Study of Negro Life and History organized at Chicago meeting. The name of the organization, the major organizing center for the dissemination of information on black history, was changed in the sixties to the Association for the Study of Afro-American Life and History.

October

25   Atty. James L. Curtis named minister to Liberia.

November

14   Death of Booker T. Washington (59) educator and organizer, in Tuskegee, Alabama.

December

4   Ku Klux Klan received charter from Fulton County, Ga., Superior Court. Modern Klan spread to Alabama and other Southern states and reached height of its influence in the twenties. By 1924 the organization was strong in Oklahoma, Indiana, California, Oregon, Indiana, and Ohio. At the height of its influence, the organization had an estimated four million members.

---   Great Migration began. Approximately two million Southern blacks moved to Northern industrial centers in the following decades.

---   NAACP led protest demonstrations against showing of movie *Birth of a Nation*.

1915

---   Fifty-six blacks reported lynched in 1915.

---   First Spingarn Medal presented to Ernest E. Just for his achievements as a scientist.

1916

January

1   First issue of *Journal of Negro History* published.

November

7   Woodrow Wilson reelected president.

---   Spingarn Medal awarded to Col. Charles Young, U.S. Army, for organizing the Liberian constabulary and establishing order on the frontiers of Liberia.

---   Fifty blacks were reported lynched in 1916.

1917

January

17   U.S. succeeded Denmark as the sovereign authority in the Virgin Islands.

April

6   America entered World War I. President Wilson, who had just inaugurated a policy of segregation in government agencies, told Congress that "the world must be made safe for democracy."

May

27–30   Race riot, East St. Louis, Illinois. One black killed.

July

1–3   Race riot, East St. Louis, Illinois. Estimates of number killed ranged from forty to two hundred. Martial law was declared. A congressional investigating committee said, "It is not possible to give accurately the number of dead. At least thirty-nine Negroes and eight white people were killed outright, and hundreds of Negroes were wounded and maimed. 'The bodies of the dead Negroes,' testified an eye witness, 'were thrown into a morgue like so many dead hogs.' There were three hundred and twelve buildings and forty-four railroad freight cars and their contents destroyed by fire."

1917

July

28   Ten thousand blacks marched down Fifth Avenue, New York City, in silent parade protesting lynchings and racial indignities.

August

23   Race riot, Houston, between soldiers of Twenty-fourth Infantry Regiment and white citizens. Two blacks and eleven whites killed. Martial law declared.

November

5   U.S. Supreme Court decision (*Buchanan* v. *Warley*) struck down Louisville, Ky., ordinance which required blacks and whites to live in separate residential areas.

December

11   Thirteen black soldiers hanged for alleged participation in Houston riot.

---   Jazz migration began. Joe Oliver left New Orleans and settled in Chicago and was joined by other stars.

---   Thirty-six blacks reported lynched in 1917.

---   Spingarn Medal presented to Harry T. Burleigh, composer and singer, for excellence in the field of music.

1918

July

25–28   Race riot, Chester, Pennsylvania. Three blacks and two whites were killed.

26–29   Race riot, Philadelphia. Three whites and one black were killed.

August

27   Dr. Joseph L. Johnson named minister to Liberia.

September

3   Five soldiers hanged for alleged participation in Houston riot of 1917.

29   Edward Thomas Demby elected suffragan bishop of the Protestant Episcopal diocese of Arkansas.

1918

November

11   Armistice signed, ending World War I. Official records listed 370,000 black soldiers and 1400 black commissioned officers. A little more than half of these soldiers served in the European Theater. Three black regiments—the 369th, 371st and 372nd—received the Croix de Guerre for valor. The 369th was the first American unit to reach the Rhine. Various individual blacks were decorated for bravery. The first soldiers in the American army to be decorated for bravery in France were Henry Johnson and Needham Roberts of the 369th Infantry Regiment. Blacks were angered by a series of racial incidents.

21   Henry B. Delany elected suffragan bishop of the Protestant Episcopal diocese of North Carolina.

December

28   Death of George H. White (66), last of the post-Reconstruction congressmen, Philadelphia.

---   Sixty blacks were reported lynched in 1918.

---   Spingarn Medal awarded to William Stanley Braithwaite, poet, literary critic and editor, for distinguished achievement in literature.

1919

February

19–21   Pan-African Congress, organized by W. E. B. Du Bois, met at Grand Hotel, Paris. There were fifty-seven delegates—sixteen from the United States and fourteen from Africa—from sixteen countries and colonies. Blaise Diagne of Senegal was elected president and Du Bois was named secretary.

May

10   Race riot in Charleston, South Carolina. Two blacks were killed.

25   Death of Madame C. J. Walker (52), wealthy cosmetics manufacturer, at Irvington-on-the-Hudson, New York.

1919

June

3 Liberty Life Insurance Company (Chicago), the first old-line legal reserve company organized by blacks in the North, incorporated.

July

13 Race riots, Longview and Gregg counties, Texas. Martial law declared. There were twenty-six riots during the "Red Summer" of 1919.

19–23 Race riot, Washington, D.C., triggered by raids on black residential areas by white soldiers. Six persons killed and more than one hundred wounded.

27 Troops were mobilized to put down Chicago riot which erupted on July 27 and continued for several days. Fifteen whites and twenty-three blacks were killed and more than five hundred were injured.

October

1–3 Race riot, Elaine, Phillips County, Arkansas. Five whites and twenty-five to fifty blacks reported killed.

--- Seventy-six blacks were reported lynched in 1919.

--- *Kansas City Call* founded by Chester Arthur Franklin.

--- Spingarn Medal presented to Archibald Grimké, president of the American Negro Academy and former U.S. consul to Santo Domingo.

1920

United States population: 105,710,620. Black population: 10,463,131 (9.9 per cent).

January

31 Phi Beta Sigma Fraternity, founded at Howard University in 1914, incorporated.

May

23 Methodist Episcopal Church conference, meeting in Des Moines, Iowa, elected two black bishops—

1920

Matthew W. Clair of Washington, D.C., and Robert E. Jones of New Orleans.

August

1 National convention of Marcus Garvey's Universal Improvement Association opened in Liberty Hall in Harlem. The next night Garvey addressed twenty-five thousand blacks in Madison Square Garden. Garvey's nationalist movement reached its height in 1920–21.

November

2 Warren G. Harding elected president.

3 *Emperor Jones* opened at the Provincetown Theater with Charles Gilpin in the title role.

6 James Weldon Johnson became the first black executive secretary of the NAACP.

--- Fifty-three blacks reported lynched in 1920.

--- Spingarn Medal awarded to W. E. B. Du Bois for "the founding and calling of the Pan African Congress."

1921

May

23 *Shuffle Along,* first of a succession of popular musicals featuring black talent, opened at the 63rd Street Music Hall, New York City.

June

1 Race riot, Tulas, Oklahoma. Twenty-one whites and sixty blacks were killed.

August

28 Second Pan-African Congress met in London, Brussels and Paris, August 28 to September 6. Of the 113 delegates, 39 were from Africa and 36 were from America.

October

26 Solomon Porter Hood named minister to Liberia.

December

21 Death of P.B.S. Pinchback (84), major Reconstruction politician, Washington, D.C.

1921

The Negro Renaissance, a period of extraordinary activity on the part of black artists and extraordinary receptivity on the part of the white public, reached a peak in the twenties. Among the writers who contributed to the movement were Claude McKay, *Harlem Shadows*, 1922; Jean Toomer, *Cane*, 1923; Alain Locke, *The New Negro*, 1925; Langston Hughes, *The Weary Blues*, 1926; Countee Cullen, *Color*, 1925.

---   Doctor of Philosophy degrees awarded for first time to black women—Eva B. Dykes, English, Radcliffe; Sadie T. Mossell, Economics, University of Pennsylvania; Georgiana R. Simpson, German, University of Chicago.

---   Fifty-nine blacks were reported lynched in 1921.

---   Spingarn Medal awarded to actor Charles S. Gilpin for his performance in the title role of *Emperor Jones*.

1922

January

8   Death of Col. Charles R. Young (58), Lagos, Nigeria.

26   Dyer antilynching bill passed in the House by a vote of 230 to 119. Bill was killed in the Senate by a filibuster.

March

4   Death of Bert Williams (46), New York City.

November

20   Louisiana governor conferred with president on KKK violence in his state.

---   Fifty-one blacks were reported lynched in 1922.

---   Spingarn Medal awarded to Mary B. Talbert, former president of the National Association of Colored Women, for service to black women and for restoration of the Frederick Douglass home.

1923

March

30 Zeta Phi Beta Sorority, founded at Howard University in 1920, incorporated.

June

21 Marcus Garvey sentenced to five years in prison after his conviction on charges of using the mail to defraud. Garvey said the charges were political.

August

3 Calvin Coolidge became president on the death of President Harding.

September

15 Governor said Oklahoma was in a "state of virtual rebellion and insurrection" because of KKK activities. Martial law was declared.

October

24 Department of Labor said some 500,000 blacks had left the South in the preceding twelve months.

29 *Runnin' Wild* opened at Colonial Theater, Broadway. Miller and Lyles production introduced Charleston to New York and the world.

November

7–8 First session of Third Pan-African Congress convened in London. Second session was held in Lisbon.

--- Twenty-nine blacks were reported lynched in 1923.

--- Spingarn Medal awarded to George Washington Carver, head of the department of research, Tuskegee Institute, for his pioneering work in agricultural chemistry.

1924

October

29 *Dixie to Broadway*, "the first real revue by Negroes," opened at Broadhurst Theater, New York City, with Florence Mills in starring role.

November

4 Calvin Coolidge elected president.

1924

--- Fletcher Henderson, the first musician to make a name with big band jazz, opened at the Roseland Ballroom on Broadway.

--- Spingarn Medal awarded to singer Roland Hayes for the "reputation he has gained as a singer in England, Germany and France and especially in America where he was last year soloist for the Boston Symphony Orchestra . . . and because [he has] so finely interpreted the beauty and charm of the Negro folk song."

1925

February

8   Marcus Garvey entered federal prison in Atlanta.

--   Students staged strike at Fisk University to protest policies of white administration.

May

19   Malcolm X born in Omaha, Nebraska.

August

25   Brotherhood of Sleeping Car Porters organized at a mass meeting in Elks Hall in Harlem. A. Philip Randolph was elected president.

September

8   Ossian Sweet, prominent Detroit doctor, arrested on murder charges after shots were fired into a mob in front of the Sweet home in a previously all-white area. Sweet was defended by Clarence Darrow, who won an acquittal in the second trial.

November

11   Louis Armstrong recorded the first of Hot Five and Hot Seven recordings that influenced the direction of jazz.

--- Xavier University established.

--- Spingarn Medal awarded to James Weldon Johnson, former U.S. consul in Venezuela and Nicaragua and NAACP executive secretary, for his work as an author, diplomat and leader.

1926

February

-- Carter G. Woodson organized the first Negro History Week celebration in the second week of February "to include the birthday of [Abraham] Lincoln and the generally accepted birthday of [Frederick] Douglass." The week was later expanded into Black History Month.

June

20 Mordecai W. Johnson became the first black president of Howard University.

July

26 National Bar Association incorporated.

--- Spingarn Medal awarded to Carter G. Woodson for "ten years devoted service in collecting and publishing the records of the Negro in America."

1927

March

7 Supreme Court decision (*Nixon* v. *Herndon*) struck down Texas law which barred blacks from voting in "white primary."

July

9 Atty. William T. Francis named minister to Liberia.

August

21–24 Fourth Pan-African Congress met in New York City.

November

1 Death of Florence Mills (32), dancer and singer, New York City.

December

4 Duke Ellington opened at the Cotton Club in Harlem.

-- President Coolidge commuted Marcus Garvey's sentence. Garvey was taken to New Orleans and deported to his native Jamaica.

--- Spingarn Medal awarded to Anthony Overton, publisher, insurance executive and cosmetics manufacturer, for his achievements as a businessman.

1928

November

6   Oscar DePriest elected to Seventy-first Congress from Illinois' First Congressional District (Chicago). He was the first black congressman from the North and the first black in Congress since the departure of George H. White in 1901.

---   *Atlanta Daily World* founded by W. A. Scott Jr. The newspaper became a daily in 1933.

---   Spingarn Medal presented to Charles W. Chesnutt, the first black to receive widespread critical recognition as a novelist. He was cited for his "pioneer work as a literary artist depicting the life and struggle of Americans of Negro descent."

1929

January

15   Martin Luther King Jr. born in Atlanta. He was first given the name of Michael Luther King Jr. The name was formally changed to Martin at a later date.

April

1   Morehouse College, Spelman College and Atlanta University affiliated, creating a new Atlanta University. John Hope, president of Morehouse College, was named president.

15   Oscar DePriest sworn in as a congressman.

October

29   Collapse of stock market and the beginning of the Great Depression. By 1937, 26 per cent of black males were unemployed.

December

30   Sigma Gamma Rho Sorority incorporated.

---   "Don't Buy Where You Can't Work" campaign began in Chicago with picketing of chain stores on South Side, fall. The campaign spread to New York, Cleveland, Los Angeles and other cities and continued throughout the Depression.

1929

--- Mordecai W. Johnson received Spingarn Medal for his work as the first black president of Howard University.

1930

United States population: 122,775,046. Black population: 11,891,143 (9.7 per cent).

February

26 *The Green Pastures* opened at Mansfield Theater.

March

31 President Hoover nominated Judge John J. Parker of North Carolina for a seat on the U.S. Supreme Court. The NAACP launched a national campaign against the appointment. Parker was not confirmed by the Senate.

September

10 Charles E. Mitchell, certified public accountant and banker from West Virgina, named minister to Liberia.

December

19 James Weldon Johnson resigned as executive secretary of the NAACP, citing health reasons.

--- Spingarn Medal awarded to Henry A. Hunt, principal, Fort Valley High and Industrial School, Fort Valley, Ga., for his pioneering work as an educator.

--- Delta Sigma Theta Sorority, founded at Howard University in 1913, incorporated.

1931

March

9 Walter F. White named NAACP executive secretary.

25 Death of Ida B. Wells–Barnett (78), Chicago.

April

6 First Scottsboro trial began in Scottsboro, Alabama. Trial of nine black youths accused of raping two white women on a freight train became a cause célèbre.

August

15 Roy Wilkins joined NAACP as assistant secretary.

1931

--- Spingarn Medal awarded to Richard B. Harrison for his portrayal of the "Lawd" in *The Green Pastures*.

1932

November

8 Franklin Delano Roosevelt elected president.

--- Spingarn Medal awarded to Robert R. Moton, president of Tuskegee Institute, for his "thoughtful leadership in conservative opinion and action."

1933

March

15 NAACP began coordinated attack on segregation and discrimination, filing a suit against the University of North Carolina on behalf of Thomas Hocutt. Case was lost on a technicality after the president of a black college refused to certify the records of the plaintiff.

--- *Los Angeles Sentinel* founded by Leon H. Washington.

--- Spingarn Medal presented to YMCA secretary Max Yergan for his achievements as a missionary in South Africa, "representing the gift of cooperation . . . American Negroes may send back to their Motherland."

1934

April

7 Death of William Monroe Trotter in Boston, sixty-two years after his birth on April 7, 1872.

June

26 W. E. B. Du Bois resigned from his position at the NAACP in a disagreement over policy and racial strategy.

October

26 At a New York City conference, representatives of the NAACP and the American Fund for Public Service planned a coordinated legal campaign against segregation and discrimination. Charles H. Houston, vice-dean of the Howard University Law School, was named director of the NAACP legal campaign.

1934

November

7   Arthur L. Mitchell defeated Oscar DePriest in a Chicago election and became the first black Democratic congressman.

December

15   Death of Maggie Lena Walker (69), first black woman to head a bank, in Richmond.

---   Spingarn Medal awarded to William Taylor Burwell Williams, Tuskegee dean and agent of the Jeanes and Slater funds, for his achievements as an educator.

1935

June

25   Joe Louis defeated Primo Carnera at Yankee Stadium.

July

22   Lester Walton appointed minister to Liberia.

October

2–4   Italy invaded Ethiopia. American blacks held mass meetings of protest and raised funds for the Ethiopian defenders.

November

5   Maryland Court of Appeals ordered the University of Maryland to admit Donald Murray.

December

5   National Council of Negro Women founded in New York City with Mary McLeod Bethune as president.

---   Langston Hughes's play, *The Mulatto*, began a long run on Broadway.

---   Swing Age began with the commercial success of big bands. The decade of the thirties was the heyday for big bands of Chick Webb, Andy Kirk, Cab Calloway, Count Basie, Jimmie Lunceford and Duke Ellington.

---   Mary McLeod Bethune awarded Spingarn Medal for her work as founder-president of Bethune-Cookman College and her national leadership.

1936

January

11   Charles W. Anderson entered lower house of the Kentucky legislature.

February

14–16   National Negro Congress organized at Chicago meeting attended by 817 delegates representing more than 500 organizations. Asa Philip Randolph of the Brotherhood of Sleeping Car Porters was elected president of the new organization.

20   Death of John Hope (67), president, Atlanta University.

June

24   Mary McLeod Bethune, founder-president of Bethune-Cookman College, named director of Negro Affairs of the National Youth Administration. She was the first black woman to receive a major appointment from the federal government. The educator held the post until January 1, 1944.

August

9   Jesse Owens won four gold medals at Olympics, Berlin.

December

8   NAACP filed first suit in campaign to equalize the salaries of black and white teachers. *Gibbs* v. *Board of Education* in Montgomery County, Md., was the first of a succession of suits that eliminated wage differentials between black and white teachers.

---   *Michigan Chronicle* founded by Louis E. Martin.

---   Spingarn Medal presented to John Hope posthumously for his achievement as president of Morehouse College and for his creative leadership in the founding of the Atlanta University Center.

1937

March

26   William H. Hastie confirmed as judge of Federal District Court in Virgin Islands and became the first black federal judge.

1937

June

22   Joe Louis defeated James J. Braddock for heavyweight boxing championship.

September

26   Singer Bessie Smith died of injuries sustained in an automobile accident near Clarksdale, Mississippi.

October

1   Pullman Company formally recognized the Brotherhood of Sleeping Car Porters.

---   Spingarn Medal awarded to Walter White, NAACP secretary, for his leadership and work in the antilynching movement.

1938

April

10   Death of Joe ("King") Oliver, pioneer jazz star, Savannah, Georgia.

June

26   James Weldon Johnson died of injuries received in an automobile accident near his summer home in Wiscosset, Maine.

November

8   First black woman legislator, Crystal Bird Fauset of Philadelphia, elected to Pennsylvania legislature.

December

12   U.S. Supreme Court rules in *Missouri ex rel Gaines* that a state must provide equal educational facilities for blacks within its boundaries. Lloyd Gaines, the plaintiff in the case, disappeared after the decision and was never located.

1939

April

9   Seventy-five thousand blacks and whites attended a Marian Anderson concert on Easter Sunday at the Lincoln Monument in Washington. Outdoor concert was scheduled after the Daughters of the American Revolution refused, for racial reasons, to permit Miss Anderson to sing in Constitution Hall.

1939

July

22   Jane Matilda Bolin appointed judge of court of domestic
       relations, New York City, by Mayor Fiorello LaGuardia
       and became the first black woman judge.

October

11   NAACP Legal Defense and Educational Fund incorpo-
       rated as a separate organization with Thurgood Mar-
       shall as director.

---   Spingarn Medal presented to Marian Anderson, "one of
       the greatest singers of our time," for her "special
       achievement in the field of music."

1940

United States population: 131,669,275. Black population: 12,865,518 (9.8 per cent).

February

--   Richard Wright's *Native Son* published.

June

5   The American Negro Theatre was organized by Fred-
       erick O'Neal and Abram Hill.

10   Death of Marcus Garvey (52), London, England.

August

1   Benjamin E. Mays, who has been called "the greatest
       schoolmaster of his generation," named president of
       Morehouse College.

September

27   Black leaders protested discrimination in the armed
       forces and war industries at a White House meeting
       with President Roosevelt.

October

9   The White House released a statement which said that
       government "policy . . . is not to intermingle colored
       and white enlisted personnel in the same regimental
       organizations."

16   Benjamin Oliver Davis Sr. named the first black gen-
       eral in the regular army.

1940

October

25   Committee on the Participation of Negroes in the National Defense Program met with President Roosevelt.

---   National Newspaper Publishers Association founded.

---   Spingarn Medal presented to Dr. Louis T. Wright for his civil rights leadership and his contributions as a surgeon.

1941

January

15   Yancey Williams, a Howard University student, asked a federal court to order the secretary of war and other government officials to consider his application for enlistment in the Army Air Corps as a flying cadet.

16   The War Department announced formation of first Army Air Corps squadron for black cadets.

A black scientist helped save thousands of lives during World War II. Dr. Charles Richard Drew set up and ran the pioneer blood plasma bank in Presbyterian Hospital in New York City. This bank served as one of the models for the system of banks operated later by the American Red Cross. On October 1, 1940, in response to a British appeal, Dr. Drew was appointed medical director of the plasma project of Great Britain. As director of the first great experiment in the gross production of human plasma, Dr. Drew created models for later developments in the United States and Europe. When the project ended in 1941, Dr. Drew became the first director of a new project charged with the responsibility of setting up donor stations to collect blood plasma for the American armed services. He resigned three months later and became professor of surgery at Howard University. Under an American Red Cross ruling in World War II, Dr. Drew's blood, ironically enough, would have been segregated from the blood of white donors.

1941

March

30   National Urban League presented one-hour program over a national radio network and urged equal participation for blacks in national defense program.

April

18   Dr. Robert Weaver named director of Office of Production Management section charged with integrating blacks into the national defense program.

—Bus companies of New York City agreed to hire black drivers and mechanics. Agreement ended a four-week boycott.

28   Supreme Court ruled in railroad Jim Crow case brought by Congressman Arthur Mitchell that separate facilities must be substantially equal.

May

1   Asa Philip Randolph issued a call for 100,000 blacks to march on Washington, D.C., to protest discrimination in the armed forces and war industries.

June

18   President Roosevelt conferred with A. Philip Randolph and other leaders of the March on Washington movement and urged them to call off a scheduled demonstration. Randolph refused.

25   President Roosevelt issued Executive Order 8802 which forbade racial and religious discrimination in war industries, government training programs and government industries. Randolph called off scheduled march.

July

10   Death of Ferdinand ("Jelly Roll") Morton (56), pioneer jazz pianist, in Los Angeles.

19   President Roosevelt appointed FEP Committee.

—First U.S. Army flying school for black cadets dedicated at Tuskegee, Alabama.

1941

August

6   Black private and white military policeman shot to death on bus in North Carolina during fight between black and white soldiers. This was the first of a series of serious racial incidents (between black and white soldiers and black soldiers and white civilians) which continued throughout the war.

December

7   Dorie Miller of Waco, Texas, messman on USS *Arizona*, manned machine gun during Pearl Harbor attack and downed four planes. He was awarded the Navy Cross.

---   Lester Granger named executive director of the National Urban League.

---   Spingarn Medal presented to novelist Richard Wright, "one of the most powerful of contemporary writers," for "his powerful depiction in his books, 'Uncle Tom's Children,' and 'Native Son,' of the effect of proscription, segregation and denial of opportunities to the American Negro."

1942

February

28   Race riot, Sojourner Truth Homes, Detroit.

March

7   First cadets graduated from flying school at Tuskegee.

June

18   Bernard W. Robinson, Harvard medical student, made ensign in U.S. Naval Reserve and became first black to win a commission in the U.S. Navy.

September

29   *Booker T. Washington*, the first U.S. merchant ship commanded by a black captain (Hugh Mulzac), launched at Wilmington, Delaware.

October

20   Sixty leading Southern blacks issued "Durham Manifesto" calling for fundamental changes in race relations after a Durham, North Carolina, meeting.

1942

November

1   John H. Johnson published first issue of *Negro Digest*.

3   William L. Dawson elected to Congress from Chicago.

- - -   Black and white advocates of direct, nonviolent action organized Congress of Race Equality in Chicago. Three CORE members staged sit-in at Stoner's Restaurant in Chicago's Loop.

- - -   Spingarn Medal presented to Asa Philip Randolph "for organizing the Sleeping Car Porters under the Brotherhood of Sleeping Car Porters and securing recognition for them; and because of his fearless, determined mobilization of mass opinion that resulted in . . . Executive Order No. 8802, which banned racial discrimination in defense industries and government work."

1943

January

5   William H. Hastie, civilian aide to secretary of war, resigned to protest segregation and discrimination in armed forces.

—Death of George Washington Carver (78), Tuskegee.

Feburary

28   *Porgy and Bess* opened on Broadway with Anne Brown and Todd Duncan in starring roles.

May

25   Riot at Mobile, Ala., shipyard over the upgrading of twelve black workers.

26   President Edwin Barclay of Liberia, first African president to pay an official visit to an American president, arrived at White House.

June

2   Ninety-ninth Pursuit Squadron flew first combat mission, strafing enemy positions on the heavily fortified Italian island of Pantelleria.

1943

June

16   Race riot, Beaumont, Texas. Two killed.

20   Race riot, Detroit. Thirty-four killed. Federal troops called out.

--   National Congress of Racial Equality organized.

July

2   Lt. Charles Hall, Brazil, Ind., became first black pilot to shoot down Nazi plane.

August

1-2   Race riot, Harlem.

October

19   Theater Guild presentation of *Othello* opened at Shubert Theater with Paul Robeson in title role. Production ran for 296 performances and set record for Shakespearean drama on Broadway.

December

15   Death of Thomas W. ("Fats") Waller (39), in Kansas City, Missouri.

---   San Francisco *Sun-Reporter* established.

---   Spingarn Medal presented to William H. Hastie "for his distinguished career as a jurist and as an uncompromising champion of equal justice."

1944

April

3   Supreme Court (*Smith* v. *Allwright*) said "white primaries" that excluded blacks were unconstitutional.

24   United Negro College Fund incorporated.

August

1   Adam Clayton Powell Jr. elected first black congressman from East.

20   *Anna Lucasta*, starring Hilda Simms and Frederick O'Neal, opened on Broadway.

1944

--- Spingarn Medal presented to Charles R. Drew "who set up and ran the blood plasma bank in the Presbyterian Hospital in New York City which served as one of the models for the widespread system of blood banks now in operation for the American Red Cross."

1945

March

12 First state fair employment practices law signed by the New York governor.

April

12 Death of President Franklin Delano Roosevelt, White Springs, Georgia. Vice-President Harry S. Truman assumed the office of president.

25 United Nations founded at San Francisco meeting attended by black American consultants, most notably W. E. B. Du Bois, Mary McLeod Bethune, Ralph J. Bunche and Walter White.

May

8 Germany surrendered on V-E Day.

June

21 Col. B. O. Davis Jr. named commander of Godman Field (Ky.) and became the first black to head an Army Air Force base in the United States.

September

2 Japanese surrendered on V-J Day, ending World War II. A total of 1,154,720 blacks were inducted or drafted into the armed services. Official records listed 7,768 black commissioned officers on August 31, 1945. At the height of the conflict 3,902 black women (115 officers) were enrolled in the Women's Army Auxiliary Corps (WACS) and 68 were in the Navy auxiliary, the WAVES. The highet ranking black women were Major Harriet M. West and Major Charity E. Adams. Distinguished Unit Citations were awarded the 969th Field Artillery Battalion, the 614th Tank Destroyer Battalion and the 332nd Fighter Group.

1945

September

18 One thousand white students walked out of three Gary, Ind., schools to protest integration. There were similar disturbances in Chicago and other Northern and Western metropolitan areas.

October

12 Jesse James Payne was lynched in Madison County, Florida.

15–21 Fifth Pan-African Congress met in Manchester, England. W. E. B. Du Bois was elected president.

23 Brooklyn Dodgers signed Jackie Robinson and sent him to their leading farm club, the Montreal Royals in the International League.

November

1 First issue of *Ebony* magazine published by John H. Johnson. The first issue sold 25,000 copies.

3 Irving C. Mollison, a Chicago Republican, sworn in as U.S. Customs Court judge in New York City.

--- Spingarn Medal presented to Paul Robeson "for his outstanding achievement in the theatre, on the concert stage, and in the general field of racial welfare."

1946

January

9 Death of poet Countee Cullen (42), New York City.

February

7 Filibuster in U.S. Senate killed FEPC bill.

26 Race riot, Columbia, Tennessee. Two killed and ten wounded.

March

13 Col. B. O. Davis Jr. assumed command of Lockbourne Air Force Base, Ohio.

May

1 Mrs. Emma Clarissa Clement named "American Mother of the Year" by the Golden Rule Foundation.

1946

May

7   William H. Hastie inaugurated as the first black governor of the Virgin Islands.

June

3   U.S. Supreme Court (*Irene Morgan* v. *Commonwealth of Virginia*) banned segregation in interstate bus travel.

10   Death of Jack Johnson, first black heavyweight champion, after an automobile accident near Raleigh.

July

2   Death of Anthony Overton (81), publisher, cosmetics manufacturer and banker, Chicago.

August

10   Race riot, Athens, Alabama.

November

1   Dr. Charles S. Johnson became the first black president of Fisk University.

December

5   President Truman created Committee on Civil Rights by Executive Order No. 9808. Two blacks—Atty. Sadie M. Alexander and Channing H. Tobias—were members of the committee.

---   Spingarn Medal presented to Thurgood Marshall, director of the NAACP Legal Defense and Educational Fund, "for his distinguished service as a lawyer before the Supreme Court."

1947

January

3   NAACP report said 1946 was "one of the grimmest years in the history of the National Association for the Advancement of Colored People." The report deplored "reports of blowtorch killing and eye-gouging of Negro veterans freshly returned from a war to end torture and racial extermination" and said "Negroes in America have been disillusioned over the wave of lynchings, brutality and official recession from all of the flamboyant promises of post war democracy and decency."

1947

April

9 CORE and the Fellowship of Reconciliation sent twenty-three black and white Freedom Riders through the South to test compliance with court decisions.

10 Jackie Robinson joined the Brooklyn Dodgers and became the first black in the major leagues in modern times. Larry Doby joined the Cleveland Indians on July 6 and became the first black in the American League. Three other blacks played in the major leagues in 1947: Dan Bankhead, pitcher, Brooklyn Dodgers; Willard Brown, outfielder, St. Louis Browns; Henry Thompson, infielder, St. Louis Browns.

September

21 Archbishop Joseph E. Ritter said he would excommunicate St. Louis Catholics who continued to protest integration of parochial schools.

October

23 NAACP petition on racism, "An Appeal to the World," presented to United Nations at Lake Success.

29 President's Committee on Civil Rights condemned racial injustices in America in formal report, "To Secure These Rights."

- - - Texas Southern University established.

- - - Spingarn Medal awarded to Dr. Percy L. Julian for his achievements as a scientist.

1948

January

12 U.S. Supreme Court decision (*Sipuel* v. *Oklahoma State Board of Regents*) said a state must afford blacks "an opportunity to commence the study of law at a state institution at the same time as [other] citizens."

February

2 President Truman sent Congress a special message urging adoption of a civil rights program, including a

1948

fair employment practices commission and anti-lynching and anti-poll tax measures.

February

3 Rosa Ingram and her fourteen- and sixteen-year-old sons condemned to death for the alleged murder of a white Georgian. Mrs. Ingram said she acted in self-defense.

12 First Lt. Nancy C. Leftenant became the first black accepted in the regular army nursing corps.

March

31 A. Philip Randolph told Senate Armed Services Committee that unless segregation and discrimination were banned in draft programs he would urge black youths to resist induction by civil disobedience.

April

6 Death sentence of Rosa Ingram and sons commuted to life imprisonment.

May

1 Glenn H. Taylor, U.S. senator from Idaho and vice-presidential candidate of Progressive party, arrested in Birmingham for trying to enter a meeting through a door marked "for Negroes."

3 Supreme Court ruled in *Shelley* v. *Kraemer* that federal and state courts could not enforce restrictive covenants which barred persons from owning or occupying property because of their race.

22 Death of poet Claude McKay (58), Chicago.

June

9 Oliver W. Hill elected to Richmond, Va., City Council.

July

14 Alabama and Mississippi Democrats bolted the Democratic convention after adoption of a "strong" civil rights plank.

23–25 Progressive party convention, meeting in Philadelphia, nominated Henry Wallace for president. New party made major effort to attract blacks. Approximately 150

1948

black delegates and alternates attended the convention. The keynote speaker was Charles P. Howard, an attorney, publisher and former Republican from Des Moines, Iowa. Thirty-seven blacks ran for state and local offices on the party ticket. Ten blacks ran for Congress. The party attracted few black voters but forced the Democratic party to make serious gestures to hold the black vote.

July

26   President Truman issued Executive Order No. 9981 directing "equality of treatment and opportunity" in the armed forces.

September

18   Ralph J. Bunche confirmed by United Nations Security Council as acting UN mediator in Palestine.

October

1   California Supreme Court voided state statute banning interracial marriages.

---   Edward Dudley named ambassador to Liberia.

---   Spingarn Medal presented to Channing H. Tobias for his "consistent role as a defender of fundamental American liberties."

1949

January

18   Congressman William L. Dawson elected chairman of House Expenditures Committee. He was the first black to head a standing committee of Congress.

March

1   Joe Louis retired as heavyweight boxing champion after holding the title for a record eleven years and eight months.

June

3   Wesley A. Brown became the first black graduate of Annapolis Naval Academy.

22   Ezzard Charles defeated Jersey Joe Walcott for the world heavyweight championship.

1949

August

8   Peter Murray Marshall of New York appointed to American Medical Association's House of Delegates.

28   Riot prevented Paul Robeson from singing at the Lakeland picnic grounds near Peekskill, Westchester County, New York.

September

4   Riot prevented Paul Robeson concert at Peekskill.

October

3   WERD, first black-owned radio station, opened in Atlanta.

15   William Hastie nominated for the U.S. Circuit Court of Appeals. He was the first black to sit on the court.

November

25   Death of dancer Luther ("Bill") Robinson (71).

---   Ralph J. Bunche received the Spingarn Medal for his contributions to the Myrdal study and his achievements as UN mediator of the Palestine conflict.

---   CORE chapter pressed sit-in campaign designed to end segregation in downtown facilities in St. Louis.

1950

United States population: 150,697,361. Black population: 15,042,286 (10 per cent).

January

15–17   More than 4,000 delegates from one hundred national organizatons attended National Emergency Civil Rights Conference in Washington.

April

1   Death of Charles R. Drew (45), surgeon and developer of the blood bank concept, after an automobile accident near Burlington, North Carolina.

3   Death of Carter G. Woodson (74), "father of black history," Washington, D.C.

1950

April

22   Death of Charles Hamilton Houston (54), architect of the NAACP legal campaign, Washington, D.C.

June

5   U.S. Supreme Court undermined the legal foundations of segregation in three landmark cases, *Sweatt* v. *Painter*, *McLaurin* v. *Oklahoma State Regents* and *Henderson* v. *United States*.

July

21   Black troops of Twenty-fourth Infantry Regiment recaptured Yechon after sixteen-hour battle, scoring first U.S. victory in Korean War.

August

24   Chicago Atty. Edith Sampson was named the first black representative (alternate delegate) in the U.S. delegation to the United Nations.

September

27   Ezzard Charles defeated Joe Louis in heavyweight championship fight in New York City.

---   Gwendolyn Brooks awarded Pulitzer Prize (May 1) for her book of poetry, *Annie Allen*. She was the first black cited by the Pulitzer committee.

---   Ralph J. Bunche, director of the UN Trusteeship division and former professor of political science at Howard University, awarded the Nobel Peace Prize (September 22) for successful mediation of the Palestine conflict. He was the first black to receive a Nobel citation.

---   Charles H. Houston awarded the Spingarn Medal posthumously for his pioneering work in developing the NAACP legal campaign.

1951

February

16   New York City Council passed bill prohibiting racial discrimination in city-assisted housing developments.

1951

May

10 Z. Alexander Looby elected to Nashville City Council.

12 Death of former congressman Oscar DePriest (80), Chicago.

24 Racial segregation in Washington, D.C., restaurants ruled illegal by Municipal Court of Appeals.

June

-- NAACP began frontal attack on segregation and discrimination at elementary and high school levels, arguing that segregation was discrimination in cases before three-judge federal courts in South Carolina and Kansas. The South Carolina court, with a strong dissent from Judge E. Waites Waring, held that segregation was not discrimination, June 23. Kansas Court ruled that the separate facilities at issue were equal but said that segregation had an adverse effect on black children.

21 Pfc. William Thompson of Brooklyn, N.Y., awarded Congressional Medal of Honor posthumously for heroism in Korea. This was the first grant of a Congressional Medal of Honor to a black American since the Spanish-American War.

July

12 Governor Adlai Stevenson called out National Guard to stop rioting in Cicero, Illinois. Mob of 3,500 tried to keep black family from moving into all-white city.

October

1 Twenty-fourth Infantry Regiment, last of all-black units military units authorized by Congress in 1866, deactivated in Korea.

November

1 *Jet* magazine founded by John H. Johnson, publisher of *Ebony* magazine.

December

3 President Truman named committee to monitor compliance with antidiscrimination provisions in U.S. government contracts and sub-contracts.

1951

December

25   Harry T. Moore, Florida NAACP official, killed and his wife seriously injured by bomb blast which wrecked their home in Mims, Florida.

---   Spingarn Medal presented to Mabel K. Staupers for her leadership in the field of nursing.

1952

January

12   University of Tennessee admitted first black student.

February

12   Congressional Medal of Honor awarded posthumously to Sgt. Cornelius H. Charlton for heroism in Korea.

May

9   Death of actor Canada Lee (45), New York City.

December

29   Death of Fletcher Henderson (55), arranger and bandleader, New York City.

30   Tuskegee Institute reported that 1952 was the first year in seventy-one years of tabulation that there were no lynchings in America.

---   Spingarn Medal presented posthumously to Harry T. Moore, who was Florida state director of the NAACP, for his civil rights leadership.

1953

June

8   U.S. Supreme Court banned segregation in Washington, D.C., restaurants.

19   Albert W. Dent, president of Dillard University, elected president of National Health Council.

—Bus boycott began Baton Rouge, Louisiana.

August

4   Movement of black families into Trumbull Park housing project in Chicago triggered virtually continuous

1953

riot which lasted more than three years and required assignment of more than one thousand policemen to keep order.

August

13 President Eisenhower established Government Contract Compliance Committee to supervise antidiscrimination regulations in government contracts.

September

11 J. H. Jackson, pastor of Olivet Baptist Church, Chicago, elected president of the National Baptist Convention at Miami meeting.

24 *Take a Giant Step*, drama by playwright Louis Peterson, opened on Broadway.

December

2 Dr. Rufus Clement, president of Atlanta University, elected to Atlanta Board of Education.

31 Hulan Jack sworn in as Manhattan Borough president.

--- Spingarn Medal presented to Paul R. Williams for his achievements as an architect.

1954

March

4 President Eisenhower named J. Ernest Wilkins of Chicago assistant secretary of labor.

May

17 U.S. Supreme Court in landmark *Brown* v. *Board of Education* decision declared segregation in public schools unconstitutional. The unanimous decision was read by Chief Justice Earl B. Warren.

24 Dr. Peter Murray Marshall installed as president of New York County Medical Society and became the first black to head an American Medical Association unit.

July

11 First White Citizens Council organized in Indianola, Mississippi.

1954

July

24 Death of Mary Church Terrell (90), educator and civil rights leader, Annapolis, Maryland.

August

7 Charles H. Mahoney was confirmed by the Senate and became the first black to serve as a full delegate to the United Nations.

19 Ralph J. Bunche named undersecretary of the United Nations.

September

7–8 School integration began in Washington, D.C., and Baltimore, Md., public schools.

October

27 B. O. Davis Jr. became the first black general in the U.S. Air Force.

30 Defense Department announced elimination of all segregated regiments in the armed forces.

November

2 Charles C. Diggs Jr. of Detroit elected Michigan's first black congressman.

- - - Spingarn Medal presented to Dr. Theodore K. Lawless for his research on skin-related diseases.

1955

January

7 Marian Anderson made debut at Metropolitan Opera House as Ulrica in Verdi's *Masked Ball*. She was the first black singer in the company's history.

March

12 Death of Charlie Parker (34), one of the founders of the modern jazz movement, in New York City.

21 Death of Walter White (61), New York City. Roy Wilkins succeeded him as NAACP executive, April 11.

April

18 Bandung Conference of leaders of colored nations of Africa and Asia opened in Indonesia.

1955

May

18 Death of Mary McLeod Bethune (79), educator and civil rights leader, Daytona Beach, Florida.

31 Supreme Court ordered school integration "with all deliberate speed."

July

9 E. Frederic Morrow appointed administrative aide to President Eisenhower and became the first black to hold an executive position on the White House staff.

August

28 Emmett Till (14) kidnapped and lynched in Money, Mississippi.

November

7 Supreme Court in Baltimore case banned segregation in public recreational facilities.

25 Interstate Commerce Commission banned segregation in buses and waiting rooms involved in interstate travel.

December

1 Rosa Parks, a seamstress and activist, arrested after she refused to give her seat to a white man on a Montgomery (Ala.) bus.

5 Historic bus boycott began in Montgomery. At a mass meeting at the Holt Street Baptist Church Martin Luther King Jr. was elected president of the boycott organization.

—Asa Philip Randolph and Willard S. Townsend elected vice-presidents of the AFL-CIO.

--- Carl Murphy, publisher of the Baltimore *Afro-American*, awarded Spingarn Medal for his contributions as a publisher and civil rights leader.

1956

January

1 Sudan proclaimed independent.

1956

January

30 Home of Martin Luther King Jr., Montgomery bus boycott leader, bombed.

February

3 Autherine J. Lucy admitted to University of Alabama. She was suspended February 7 after a riot at the university and expelled February 29.

March

11–12 Manifesto denouncing Supreme Court ruling on segregation in public schools issued by one hundred Southern senators and representatives.

April

11 Singer Nat Cole attacked on stage of Birmingham theater by white supremacists.

23 U.S. Supreme Court refused to review lower court decision which banned segregation in intrastate bus travel.

May

30 Bus boycott began in Tallahassee, Florida.

June

5 Federal court ruled that racial segregation on Montgomery city buses violated Constitution.

August

30 White mob prevented enrollment of students at Mansfield High School, Mansfield, Texas.

September

2 Tennessee National Guard sent to Clinton, Tenn., to quell mobs demonstrating against school integration.

10 Louisville, Ky., public schools integrated.

12 Black students entered Clay, Ky., elementary school under National Guard protection. They were barred from the school on September 17.

19–22 First international conference of black writers and artists met at the Sorbonne in Paris.

1956

November

5   Death of pianist Art Tatum (46), Los Angeles.

13   Supreme Court upheld lower court decision which banned segregation on city buses in Mongomery, Alabama. Federal injunctions prohibiting segregation on the buses were served on city, state and bus company officials, December 20. At two mass meetings Montgomery blacks called off year-long bus boycott. Buses were integrated on December 21.

December

25   Home of Rev. F. L. Shuttlesworth, Birmingham protest leader, destroyed by dynamite bomb.

26   Birmingham blacks began mass defiance of Jim Crow bus laws.

27   Federal Judge Dozier Devane granted temporary injunction restraining city officials from interfering with integration of Tallahassee, Fla., city buses and said "every segregation act of every state or city is as dead as a doornail."

---   Spingarn Medal awarded Jack Roosevelt ("Jackie") Robinson, first black in the major leagues, for his conduct on and off the baseball field.

1957

February

13–14   Southern Christian Leadership Conference organized at New Orleans meeting with Martin Luther King Jr. as president.

March

6   Ghana became an independent state.

April

28   W. Robert Ming, Chicago lawyer, elected chairman of American Veterans Committee. He was the first black to head a major national veterans organization.

1957

May

17 Prayer Pilgrimage, biggest civil rights demonstration to date, held in Washington.

June

-- Tuskegee boycott began. Blacks boycotted city stores in protest against act of state legislature which deprived them of municipal votes by placing their homes outside city limits.

July

6 Althea Gibson won women's single championship at Wimbledon, England.

August

3 Archibald J. Carey, Chicago minister and attorney, appointed first black chairman of President's Committee on Government Employment Policy.

29 Congress passed the Civil Rights Act of 1957, the first federal civil rights legislation since 1875. The bill established a civil rights commission and a civil rights division in the Justice Department. It also gave the Justice Department authority to seek injunctions against voting rights infractions.

September

9 Nashville's new Hattie Cotton Elementary School with enrollment of 1 black and 388 whites virtually destroyed by dynamite blast.

—Rev. F. L. Shuttlesworth mobbed when he attempted to enroll his daughters in "white" Birmingham school.

24 President Eisenhower ordered federal troops to Little Rock, Ark., to prevent interference with school integration at Central High School.

—President made nationwide TV and radio address to explain why troops were sent to Little Rock.

25 Soldiers of 101st Airborne Division escorted nine black students to Central High School.

1957

September

26   Order alerting regular army units for possible riot duty in other Southern cities cancelled by Army Secretary Wilbur M. Brucker.

November

27   Federal troops left Little Rock.

--   Dorothy Height, YMCA official, elected president of the National Council of Negro Women.

December

5   New York became the first city to legislate against racial or religious discrimination in housing market with adoption of Fair Housing Practices Law.

---   Martin Luther King Jr. awarded Spingarn Medal for his leadership of the Montgomery Bus Boycott.

1958

February

5   Clifton R. Wharton Sr. confirmed as minister to Rumania. Career diplomat was the first black to head a U.S. embassy in Europe.

April

10   Death of W. C. Handy (84), composer and musician, in New York City.

May

8   President Eisenhower ordered federalized National Guard removed from Central High School, Little Rock.

12–13   Summit Meeting of National Negro Leaders called for stepped-up campaign against discrimination and desegregation. President Eisenhower was sharply criticized for a speech which, in effect, urged the leaders to "be patient" in seeking full citizenship rights.

May

20   Robert N. C. Nix elected to Congress.

27   Ernest Green graduated from Little Rock's Central High School with six hundred white classmates.

1958

June

30   Supreme Court reversed decision of lower court which had confirmed $100,000 contempt fine imposed by Alabama on NAACP for refusing to divulge membership.

August

19   Members of NAACP Youth Council began series of sit-ins at Oklahoma City lunch counters.

September

20   Martin Luther King Jr. stabbed in chest by a mentally disturbed black woman while he was autographing books in a Harlem department store. Woman was placed under mental observation.

October

25   Ten thousand students, led by Jackie Robinson, Harry Belafonte and A. Philip Randolph, participated in the Youth March for Integrated Schools in Washington.

---   Daisy Bates, head of the Arkansas chapter of the NAACP, and the nine students who integrated Little Rock's Central High School were awarded the Spingarn Medal for their courage and leadership in the civil rights struggle.

1959

March

11   *Raisin in the Sun*, first Broadway play by a black woman, opened at Barrymore Theater with Sidney Poitier and Claudia McNeil in the starring roles. Lorraine Hansberry's drama was the first Broadway play with a black director—Lloyd Richards—in the modern era.

15   Death of Lester Young (49), New York City.

April

25   Mack Parker lynched, Poplarville, Mississippi.

May

22   Brig. Gen. B. O. Davis Jr. promoted to major general.

June

26   Prince Edward County, Va., Board of Supervisors abandoned school system to prevent integration.

1959

July

17 Death of singer Billie Holiday (44), New York City.

December

21 Citizens of Deerfield, Ill., authorized a plan which blocked building of interracial housing development.

--- Spingarn Medal was presented to Edward Kennedy ("Duke") Ellington, composer, pianist and jazz pioneer, for his contributions to the arts.

--- Motown Records established by Berry Gordy Jr.

1960

United States population: 179,323,175. Black population: 18,871,831 (10.5 per cent).

February

1 Four students from North Carolina A&T College started Sit-in movement at Greensboro, N.C., five-and-dime store. By February 10, the movement had spread to fifteen Southern cities in five states.

23 Race riot, Chattanooga, Tenn., at sit-in demonstration.

25 Alabama State College students staged first sit-in in Deep South at Montgomery, Ala., courthouse.

27 Police arrested some one hundred students in Nashville sit-in demonstrations.

March

1 One thousand Alabama State students marched on state capitol and held protest meeting.

2 Alabama State Board of Education expelled nine Alabama State students for participating in sit-in demonstrations.

3 Pope John elevated Bishop Laurian Rugambwa of Tanganyika to College of Cardinals, the first black cardinal in the modern era.

1960

March

8   Montgomery, Ala., police broke up protest demonstration on Alabama State campus and arrested thirty-five
students, a teacher and her husband.

12   Police used tear gas to break up student protest demonstration at Tallahassee, Florida.

16   San Antonio, Texas, became first major Southern city
to integrate lunch counters. Four national chain stores
announced on October 17 that counters in about 150
stores in 112 cities in North Carolina, Virginia, West
Virginia, Kentucky, Texas, Tennessee, Missouri, Maryland, Florida and Oklahoma had been integrated.

22   Associated Press reported that more than one thousand
blacks had been arrested in sit-in demonstrations.

30   Eighteen students suspended by Southern University.
Southern University students rebelled March 31, boycotted classes and requested withdrawal slips. Rebellion collapsed after death of professor from heart
attack.

April

15–17 Student Nonviolent Coordinating Committee organized
by young activists at a meeting on the Shaw University
campus.

—Eighty-three demonstrators indicted in Atlanta, Ga.,
on charges stemming from sit-in demonstrations at Atlanta restaurants.

19   Home of Z. Alexander Looby, counsel for 153 students
arrested in sit-in demonstrations, destroyed by dynamite bomb. More than two thousand students marched
on the Nashville City Hall in protest.

25   Consent judgement in Memphis federal court ended
restrictions barring black voters in Fayette County,

1960

Tennessee. This was the first voting rights case under the Civil Rights Act.

May

6   President Eisenhower signed Civil Rights Act of 1960.

June

30   Zaire proclaimed independent.

July

1   Somali proclaimed independent.

31   Elijah Muhammad, leader of the Nation of Islam, called for creation of a black state in America at a New York meeting.

August

1   Dahomey proclaimed independent. Independence was also celebrated in Niger (August 3), Upper Volta (August 5), Ivory Coast (August 8), Chad (August 11), Congo Brazzaville (August 15), Gabon (August 17), and Senegal (August 20).

7   Black and white students staged kneel-in demonstrations in Atlanta churches.

27   Race riot, Jacksonville, Fla., after ten days of sit-in demonstrations. Fifty reported injured.

September

22   Mali proclaimed independent.

October

1   Nigeria proclaimed independent.

19   Martin Luther King Jr. arrested in Atlanta sit-in and ordered to serve four months in the Georgia State Prison for violating a probated traffic sentence.

26   John F. Kennedy, Democratic presidential candidate, called Mrs. Martin Luther King Jr. and expressed his concern about the imprisonment of Dr. King.

27   Martin Luther King Jr. released on bond from the Georgia State Prison in Reidsville. Political observers

1960

said the Kennedy call increased the number of black voters who insured his election.

November

8 John F. Kennedy defeated Richard Nixon in the presidential election.

—Otis M. Smith elected auditor general of Michigan and became the first black chosen in a statewide election since the Reconstruction period.

10 Andrew Hatcher named associate press secretary to President Kennedy.

14 U.S. marshals and parents escorted four black girls to two New Orleans schools.

28 Death of Richard Wright (52), Paris, France.

December

30 Two U.S. courts issued temporary injunctions to prevent eviction of about seven hundred black sharecroppers in Haywood and Fayette counties, Tennessee.

- - - Poet Langston Hughes presented Spingarn Medal and cited as "the poet laureate of the Negro race."

1961

January

3 Adam Clayton Powell elected chairman of the House Education and Labor Committee.

11 Riot, University of Georgia. Two black students—Charlayne Hunter and Hamilton Holmes—were suspended but a federal court ordered them reinstated. They returned to classes on January 16.

February

6 Jail-in movement started in Rock Hill, S.C., when students refused to pay fines and requested jail sentences. Student Nonviolent Coordinating Committee urged southwide "Jail, No Bail" campaign.

1961

11 Robert Weaver sworn in as administrator of the Housing and Home Finance Agency, highest federal post to date by a black American.

15 Nationalists disrupted UN session on Congo with demonstration for slain Congo Premier Patrice Lumumba.

March

2 Some 180 black students and a white minister arrested in Columbia, S.C., after antisegregation march.

7 Atlanta Chamber of Commerce announced that black and white leaders had agreed on a plan for desegregation of lunchrooms and other facilities.

9 Clifton R. Wharton sworn in as ambassador to Norway.

25 Meeting place of National Civil War Centennial Commission shifted from Charleston to Charleston Naval Station after a national controversy over segregated hotels in Charleston.

April

27 Sierra Leone proclaimed independent.

May

4 Thirteen Freedom Riders began bus trip through South.

14 Bus with first group of Freedom Riders bombed and burned by segregationists outside Anniston, Alabama. Group was attacked in Anniston and Birmingham.

20 Mob attacked Freedom Riders in Montgomery.

—Attorney General Robert F. Kennedy dispatched four hundred U.S. marshals to Montgomery to keep order in Freedom Rider controversy.

21 Governor Patterson declared martial law in Montgomery and called out National Guard.

1961

May

22 Attorney general ordered two hundred additional U.S. marshals to Montgomery.

24 Twenty-seven Freedom Riders arrested in Jackson, Mississippi. On June 12, Hinds County Board of Supervisors announced that more than one hundred "Freedom Riders" had been arrested.

26 Freedom Ride Coordinating Committee established in Atlanta.

31 Judge Irving Kaufman ordered Board of Education of New Rochelle, N.Y., to integrate schools.

August

1 Whitney Young Jr. named executive director of the National Urban League.

9 James B. Parsons became first black appointed to Federal District Court in continental United States.

September

21 Southern Regional Council announced that Sit-in movement had affected twenty states and more than one hundred cities in Southern and Border States in period from February, 1960, to September, 1961. At least seventy thousand blacks and whites had participated in the movement, the report said. The council estimated that 3,600 had been arrested and that at least 141 students and 58 faculty members had been expelled by college authorities. SRC said one or more establishments in 108 Southern and Border State cities had been desegregated as a result of sit-ins.

22 Interstate Commerce Commission issued regulation prohibiting segregation on interstate buses and in terminal facilities.

23 President Kennedy named Thurgood Marshall to U.S. Circuit Court of Appeals.

1961

September

28   *Purlie Victorious*, a farce by playwright Ossie Davis, opened on Broadway.

October

10   Otis M. Smith appointed to Michigan Supreme Court.

November

29   Freedom Riders attacked by white mob at bus station in McComb, Miss., November 29–December 2.

December

9   Tanzania proclaimed independent.

11   U.S. Supreme Court reversed conviction of sixteen sit-in students who had been arrested in Baton Rouge.

12   More than seven hundred demonstrators, including Martin Luther King Jr., arrested in Albany, Ga., in five mass marches on city hall to protest segregation. Arrests triggered militant Albany movement.

15   Police used tear gas and leashed dogs to stop mass demonstration by fifteen hundred blacks in Baton Rouge, Louisiana.

---   Kenneth B. Clark, psychologist and educator, awarded Spingarn Medal for pioneering studies that influenced the Supreme Court decision on school desegregation.

1962

January

16   Suit accusing New York City Board of Education of using "racial quotas" filed in U.S. District Court on behalf of black and Puerto Rican children.

18–28   Southern University closed because of demonstrations protesting expulsion of sit-in activists.

23   Demonstrations against discrimination in off-campus housing staged by students at University of Chicago,

1962

January 23–February 5. CORE charged that the university operated segregated apartment houses.

January

31 Lt. Comdr. Samuel L. Gravely assumed command of destroyer escort, USS *Falgout*. Navy said he was the first black to command a U.S. warship.

February

2 Seven whites and four blacks arrested after all-night sit-in at Englewood, N.J., city hall.

—Four black mothers arrested after sit-in at Chicago elementary school. Mothers later received suspended $50 fines. Protests, picketing and demonstrations continued for several weeks against *de facto* segregation, double shifts and mobile classrooms.

5 Suit seeking to bar Englewood, N.J., from maintaining "racially segregated" elementary schools filed in U.S. District Court.

12 Bus boycott started in Macon, Georgia.

April

16 Three Louisiana segregationists were excommunicated by Archbishop Joseph Rummel for continuing their opposition to his order for integration of New Orleans parochial schools.

May

10 *Southern School News* reported that 246,988 or 7.6 per cent of the black pupils in public schools in seventeen Southern and Border States and the District of Columbia attended integrated classes in 1962.

28 Suit alleging *de facto* school segregation filed in Rochester, N.Y., by NAACP.

June

26 Sit-in demonstrations and passive resistance movement began in Cairo, Illinois. Demonstrations against segregation in swimming pool, skating rink and other facilities continued for several months.

1962

July

10 Martin Luther King Jr. arrested during demonstration in Albany, Georgia.

21 More than 160 activists jailed after demonstration in Albany. By August 1 almost one thousand demonstrators had been arrested in the Georgia city.

27 Martin Luther King Jr. jailed in Albany, Georgia.

August

6 Jamaica proclaimed independent.

15 Shady Grove Baptist Church was burned in Leesburg, Georgia.

28 Seventy-five ministers and laymen—blacks and whites—from North arrested after prayer demonstration in downtown Albany.

31 Trinidad-Tobago proclaimed independent.

September

9 Two churches burned near Sasser, Georgia. Black leaders asked the president to stop the "Nazi-like reign of terror in southwest Georgia."

10 Supreme Court Justice Hugo Black vacated an order of a lower court, ruling that the University of Mississippi had to admit James H. Meredith, a black Air Force veteran whose application for admission had been on file and in the courts for fourteen months.

11 Two youths involved in voter registration drive in Mississippi were wounded by shotgun blasts fired through the window of a home in Ruleville. James Forman, of the Student Nonviolent Coordinating Committee (SNCC), asked the president to "convene a special White House Conference to discuss means of stopping the wave of terror sweeping through the South, especially where SNCC is working on voter registration."

1962

13 Mississippi Governor Ross R. Barnett defied the federal government in impassioned speech on statewide radio-television hookup, saying he would "interpose" the authority of the state between the University of Mississippi and federal judges who had ordered the admission of James H. Meredith. Barnett said, "There is no case in history where the Caucasian race has survived social integration." He promised to go to jail, if necessary, to prevent integration at the state university. His defiance set the stage for the gravest federal-state crisis since the Civil War.

—President Kennedy denounced the burning of churches in Georgia and supported voter registration drive in the South.

17 Fourth black church burned near Dawson, Georgia. Three white men later admitted burning the church. They were sentenced to seven-year prison terms.

20 Governor Barnett personally denied James H. Meredith admission to the University of Mississippi.

24 U.S. Circuit Court of Appeals ordered Board of Higher Education of Mississippi to admit Meredith to the university or be held in contempt.

25 Governor Barnett again defied court orders and personally denied Meredith admission to the university.

—A black church was destroyed by fire in Macon, Georgia. This was the eighth church burned in Georgia since August 15.

26 Mississippi barred Meredith for the third time. Lt. Gov. Paul Johnson and a blockade of state patrolmen turned back Meredith and federal marshals about four hundred yards from the gate of the school.

1962

September

28 Governor Barnett found guilty of civil contempt of the federal court. United States Court of Appeals for the Fifth Circuit ordered Barnett to purge himself of contempt or face arrest and a fine of $10,000 a day.

29 Lt. Gov. Paul Johnson found guilty of civil contempt.

30 Large force of federal marshals escorted James H. Meredith to the campus of the University of Mississippi. President Kennedy federalized the Mississippi National Guard and urged Mississippians to accept the orders of the court in a radio-TV address.

—University of Mississippi students and adults from Oxford, Miss., and other Southern communities rioted on the university campus. Two persons were killed and one hundred or more were wounded.

October

1 Some twelve thousand federal soldiers restored order on the University of Mississippi campus.

—James H. Meredith, escorted by federal marshals, registered at the University of Mississippi.

—Edwin A. Walker, former major general in the U.S. Army, was arrested and charged with inciting insurrection and seditious conspiracy. Walker, who led federal troops during the Little Rock integration crisis, had called for "volunteers" to oppose federal forces in Mississippi. Witnesses said he led students in charges against federal marshals during the campus riot.

9 Uganda proclaimed independent.

November

6 Edward W. Brooke elected attorney general of Massachusetts.

—Gerald Lamb elected treasurer of Connecticut.

1962

November

—Otis M. Smith elected to a full term on the Michigan Supreme Court.

—Five blacks, including one newcomer, were elected to the House of Representatives. The newcomer, Augustus F. Hawkins, was elected from Los Angeles and became the first black congressman from the West.

20   President Kennedy issued executive order barring racial discrimination in federally financed housing.

---   Robert C. Weaver, economist and government official, awarded Spingarn Medal for his leadership in the movement for open housing.

1963

March

1   Emancipation Centennial protests began with voter registration campaign in Greenwood, Mississippi.

9   Carl T. Rowan named ambassador to Finland.

30   Air Force Captain Edward J. Dwight Jr. named to fourth class of aerospace research pilots at Edwards Air Base and became the first black astronaut candidate. He was dropped from the program in 1965.

April

3   Martin Luther King Jr. opened antisegregation campaign in Birmingham. More than two thousand demonstrators, including King, were arrested before the campaign ended.

May

10   Rev. Fred L. Shuttlesworth announced agreement on limited integration plan which ended the Birmingham demonstrations.

11–12   Bombing of motel and home of integration leader triggered three-hour riot in Birmingham.

1963

June

11 Two black students, escorted by federalized National Guard troops, enrolled at University of Alabama despite the opposition of Gov. George C. Wallace.

—President Kennedy told nation in radio-TV address that segregation was morally wrong and that it was "time to act in the Congress, in your state and local legislative body, and . . . in all of our daily lives."

12 Medgar W. Evers (37), NAACP field secretary in Mississippi, assassinated in front of his Jackson home by a segregationist.

12-13 Civil rights group demonstrated at Harlem construction sites to protest discrimination in building trades unions. Demonstrations and marches were held in metropolitan areas in June, July and August to dramatize discontent over housing, school and job discrimination.

18 Three thousand black students boycotted Boston public schools as protest against *de facto* segregation.

July

12 National Guard troops imposed limited martial law in Cambridge, Md., after open confrontations between demonstrators and white segregationists.

August

27 W. E. B. Du Bois (95), scholar, protest leader and a founder of the NAACP, died in Accra, Ghana.

28 More than 250,000 persons participated in March on Washington demonstration, the largest civil rights demonstration in history.

September

15 Four black girls killed in bombing of Sixteenth Street Baptist Church in Birmingham.

October

22 Some 225,000 students boycotted Chicago schools in Freedom Day protest of *de facto* segregation.

1963

November

22 John Fitzgerald Kennedy (46), thirty-fifth president of the United States, assassinated in Dallas, Texas.

December

12 Kenya proclaimed independent.

--- Medgar Wiley Evers awarded Spingarn Medal posthumously for his civil rights leadership.

1964

January

21 Carl T. Rowan named director of the United States Information Agency.

23 Twenty-fourth Amendment to the U.S. Constitution eliminated poll tax requirements in federal elections.

February

3 School officials reported that 464,000 black and Puerto Rican students boycotted New York City public schools. More than 267,000 were absent during second boycott, March 16.

25 Muhammad Ali defeated Sonny Liston for world heavyweight boxing championship.

—Some 172,000 students boycotted Chicago public schools.

March

12 Malcolm X resigned from the Nation of Islam.

April

20 School officials said 86 per cent of the black students in Cleveland schools participated in one-day boycott.

22 New York police arrested 294 demonstrators at opening of World Fair.

June

10 U.S. Senate imposed cloture for first time on a civil rights measure, ending Southern filibuster by a vote of

71–29. Civil rights bill, with public accommodation and fair employment sections, was signed by President Johnson on July 2.

June

28 Organization for Afro-American Unity founded in New York by Malcolm X.

July

6 Malawi proclaimed independent.

18–22 Race riot, Harlem. Rioting spread to the Bedford-Stuyvesant section of Brooklyn.

25 Race riot, Rochester, New York. Governor Nelson Rockefeller mobilized the National Guard.

August

2 Race riot, Jersey City, New Jersey.

4 Bodies of three civil rights workers discovered on farm near Philadelphia, Mississippi. Three young men, two white and one black, had been missing since June 21. FBI said they were murdered on night of their disappearance by segregationists. Eighteen whites, including several police officers, were charged with conspiracy to deprive the victims of their civil rights.

11–12 Race riot, Paterson, N. J.; 12–13, Elizabeth, N. J.; 15–16, Dixmoor, a Chicago suburb.

20 President Johnson signed Economic Opportunity Act.

25 Credentials Committee of Democratic party seated all-white Mississippi delegation and two members of integrated Freedom Democratic party as "delegates at-large." Both factions rejected the "peace" formula.

28–30 Race riot, Philadelphia.

September

15 Rev. K. L. Buford and Dr. Stanley Smith were elected to Tuskegee City Council and became first black elected officials in Alabama in twentieth century.

1964

October

24   Zambia proclaimed independent.

November

3   John Conyers Jr. elected to House of Representatives from Detroit.

December

3   J. Raymond Jones elected leader of New York Democratic organization (Tammany Hall).

---   Nobel Peace Prize awarded (December 10) to Dr. Martin Luther King Jr. at ceremonies in Oslo, Norway. He was the third black and the youngest person to receive the award.

---   Academy Award for best actor of the year presented (April 13) to Sidney Poitier for his performance in *Lilies of the Field*.

---   Spingarn Medal presented to NAACP executive secretary Roy Wilkins for his contribution to "the advancement of the American people and the national purpose."

---   Independence Bank of Chicago organized.

1965

January

2   Voter registration drive, led by Martin Luther King Jr., started in Selma, Alabama.

12   Lorraine Hanbsberry (34) died in New York City.

February

1   More than seven hundred demonstrators, including Martin Luther King Jr., arrested in Selma.

15   Nat King Cole (45), singer and pianist, died in Santa Monica, California.

1965

February

21 Malcolm X (39) assassinated in Audubon Ballroom at a rally of his organization. Three blacks were later convicted of the crime and sentenced to life imprisonment.

23 Constance Baker Motley elected Manhattan Borough president, the highest elective office held by a black woman in a major American city.

26 Jimmie Lee Jackson, civil rights activist, died of injuries reportedly inflicted by officers in Marion, Alabama.

March

7 Alabama state troopers and sheriff's deputies dispersed Selma-to-Montgomery civil rights march with tear gas and billy clubs.

9 Three white Unitarian ministers, including the Rev. James J. Reeb, attacked on streets of Selma, Alabama. Reeb, who was participating in civil rights demonstrations, died later in Birmingham hospital.

21 Thousands of marchers, led by Martin Luther King Jr. completed first leg of five-day Selma-to-Montgomery march. Marchers were protected by federalized Alabama National Guardsmen and U.S. Army troops.

25 Selma-to-Montgomery march ended with rally of some fifty thousand at Alabama capitol. One of the marchers, a white civil rights worker named Viola Liuzzo, was shot to death on U.S. Highway 80 after the rally by white terrorists. Three Klansmen were convicted of violating her civil rights and sentenced to ten years in prison.

April

16 Maj. Gen. B. O. Davis Jr., assistant deputy chief of staff of the U.S. Air Force, named lieutenant general, the highest rank attained by a black to date in the armed services.

1965

May

19 Patricia R. Harris named ambassador to Luxembourg. She was the first black woman ambassador.

30 First black student, Vivian Malone, graduated from the University of Alabama.

August

6 President signed Voting Rights Bill which authorized the suspension of literacy tests and the sending of federal examiners into South.

11 Six-day insurrection started in Watts section of Los Angeles. National Guard was mobilized on August 13. Rebellion toll: 34 killed, 1,032 injured, 4,000 arrested, $35 million in property damage.

—U.S. Senate confirmed nomination of Thurgood Marshall as U.S. solicitor general.

12 Jonathan M. Daniels, white Episcopal seminary student from Massachusetts, killed and Richard F. Morrisroe, white Roman Catholic priest from Chicago, seriously wounded by shotgun blasts fired by white special deputy sheriff in Hayneville, Alabama. They were participating in civil rights demonstrations in Lowndes County.

12-14 Race riot, West Side of Chicago. National Guard was placed on stand-by alert, August 14.

25 James M. Nabrit Jr. named ambassador and assigned to the UN delegation.

September

8 Actress Dorothy Dandridge (41) died in Hollywood.

December

25 Congress of Racial Equality announced that its national director, James Farmer, would resign on March 1.

--- Seaway National Bank of Chicago established.

1965

--- Spingarn Medal presented to Leontyne Price, "the outstanding soprano of our era."

1966

January

3 Floyd B. McKissick, North Carolina attorney, named
national director of Congress of Racial Equality.

6 Harold R. Perry became second black Roman Catholic
bishop in U.S. history.

7 Martin Luther King Jr. opened campaign in Chicago.

10 Julian Bond, communications director of the Student
Nonviolent Coordinating Committee, denied seat in
lower house of Georgia legislature because of his opposition to Vietnam War.

18 Robert C. Weaver was sworn in as secretary of housing
and urban development and became the first black
cabinet member.

March

9 Andrew F. Brimmer became the first black governor of
the Federal Reserve Board.

April

1-24 First world festival of black art held in Dakar, Senegal. One of the largest delegations came from Black
America.

11 Emmett Ashford became the first black major league
umpire.

13 Martin Luther King Jr. denounced Vietnam War, which,
he said, was "rapidly degenerating into a sordid military adventure."

18 Bill Russell named coach of the Boston Celtics basketball team and became the first black to coach a major,
predominantly white team in professional athletics.

1966

April

21 Milton Olive Jr. awarded Congressional Medal of Honor for bravery in Vietnam.

May

16 Stokely Carmichael named chairman of the Student Nonviolent Coordinating Committee.

-- National Welfare Rights Organization organized.

June

1–2 Approximately 2,400 persons attended White House Conference on Civil Rights.

6 James Meredith wounded by white sniper as he walked along U.S. Highway 51 near Hernando, Miss., on second day of 220-mile voter registration march from Memphis to Jackson. March was continued on June 7 by Martin Luther King Jr., Floyd McKissick, Stokely Carmichael and other civil rights workers. It ended on June 26 with rally of some thirty thousand at Mississippi state capitol. During the three-week march, Carmichael launched the Black Power movement.

July

5 National Guard mobilized in Omaha after third night of rioting.

12–15 Race riot, Chicago. National Guard mobilized.

19 Governor James A. Rhodes declared state of emergency in Cleveland and dispatched National Guard troops to riot-torn Hough district.

August

5 Martin Luther King Jr. stoned during Chicago march.

7 Race riot, Lansing, Michigan.

27 Race riot, Waukegan, Illinois.

28 National Guard mobilized to protect Milwaukee marchers protesting judge's membership in lily-white club.

1966

August

30   Constance Baker Motley confirmed as U.S. district judge and became the first black woman on the federal bench.

    —Race riot, Benton Harbor, Michigan. National Guard mobilized.

September

1–2   National Guard mobilized to stop rioting in Dayton, Ohio.

6   Race riot, Atlanta.

27–29   National Guard mobilized in San Francisco.

October

--   Black Panther party founded in Oakland (Calif.) by Huey Newton and Bobby Seale.

November

8   Edward W. Brooke (Republican, Mass.) elected to U.S. Senate and became the first black senator since the Reconstruction era and the first black senator elected by popular vote.

---   Racial violence was reported in forty-three cities in 1966, with eleven killed, more than four hundred injured and three thousand arrested.

---   John H. Johnson, publisher of *Ebony* and *Jet* magazines, awarded Spingarn Medal "for his productive imagination . . . in the perilous field of publishing" and "for his contributions to the enhancement of the Negro's self-image through his publications."

1967

January

9   Rep. Adam Clayton Powell Jr. ousted as chairman of the House Education and Welfare Committee on a charge of wrongfully appropriating congressional funds. Powell accused his critics of racism.

1967

January

9   Georgia legislature, bowing to legal decisions and national pressure, seated Rep. Julian Bond, a critic of the Vietnam War.

16   Lucius D. Amerson, first black sheriff in the South in the twentieth century, sworn in at Tuskegee (Macon County), Alabama.

    —First black government installed in the Bahamas.

March

1   U.S. House of Representatives expelled Rep. Adam Clayton Powell Jr. by a vote of 307 to 116. Civil rights leaders said Powell was ousted because of his race.

April

11   Harlem voters defied Congress and reelected Congressman Adam Clayton Powell Jr.

28   World Boxing Association and New York State Athletic Commission withdrew recognition of Muhammad Ali as world heavyweight boxing champion because of his refusal to serve in the U.S. armed forces.

29   Mrs. Robert W. Claytor elected president of the YWCA, the first black president of the organization.

May

12   H. Rap Brown replaced Stokely Carmichael as chairman of Student Nonviolent Coordinating Committee.

June

2–5   Race riot, Roxbury section of Boston.

11–13   Race riot, Tampa, Florida. National Guard mobilized.

12   U.S. Supreme Court ruled that a Virginia law banning racial intermarriage was unconstitutional.

12–15   Race riot, Cincinnati, Ohio. Three hundred persons were arrested, and the National Guard was mobilized.

1967

June

13 Thurgood Marshall, U.S. solicitor general, named to the Supreme Court by President Johnson. He was confirmed by the Senate on August 30 and became the first black Supreme Court justice.

20 Muhammad Ali convicted in Houston, Texas, federal court of violating Selective Service Act by refusing induction into the armed services. He was fined $10,000 and sentenced to five years in prison. Ali, an opponent of the Vietnam War, had refused to report for service on grounds that he was a Muslim minister.

27–30 Race riot, Buffalo, New York. Two hundred arrested.

30 Maj. Robert H. Lawrence Jr. named first black astronaut. He was killed during a training flight on December 8, 1967.

July

12–17 Twenty-three killed in Newark rebellion. The racial uprising spread to ten of the city's twenty-three square miles. More than 1,500 persons were injured and 1,300 were arrested. Police reported 300 fires. The Newark rebellion, the worst outbreak of racial violence since Watts, spread to other New Jersey communities, including New Brunswick, Englewood, Paterson, Elizabeth, Palmyra, Passaic, and Plainfield. The National Guard was mobilized.

17–19 Race riot, Cairo, Illinois. National Guard mobilized.

19–20 Riot, Durham. National Guard mobilized.

20 Riot, Memphis. National Guard mobilized.

20–23 More than one thousand persons attended the first Black Power Conference in Newark, New Jersey.

1967

July

23–30   Forty-three persons killed in rebellion in Detroit. Fed-
              eral troops were called out for the first time since the
              Detroit riot of 1943 to quell the largest racial rebellion
              in a U.S. city in the twentieth century. More than two
              thousand persons were injured and some five thousand
              were arrested. Police reported 1,442 fires. Rioting
              spread to other Michigan cities.

24–26   Riot, Cambridge, Maryland. National Guard mobilized.

30   Riot, Milwaukee, July 30–August 3. National Guard
              mobilized. Four persons killed.

September

6   President Lyndon B. Johnson named Walter E. Wash-
              ington commissioner and "unofficial" mayor of Wash-
              ington, D.C.

November

7   Carl B. Stokes elected mayor of Cleveland, Ohio, and
              Richard G. Hatcher elected mayor of Gary, Indiana.
              Stokes was sworn in on November 13 and became the
              first black to serve as mayor of a major American city.

--   A report of the Senate Permanent Investigating Com-
              mittee said there were seventy-five major riots in 1967,
              compared with twenty-one major riots in 1966. The
              committee reported that eighty-three persons were
              killed in 1967 riots, compared with eleven in 1966 and
              thirty-six in 1965.

---   Spingarn Medal presented to Edward W. Brooke for his
              public service as the first black U.S. senator since Re-
              construction.

1968

February

8   Officers killed three students during demonstrations on
              the campus of South Carolina State in Orangeburg,

1968

South Carolina. Students were protesting segregation at an Orangeburg bowling alley.

February

20 State troopers used tear gas to stop demonstrations at Alcorn A&M College.

29 National Advisory Commission on Civil Disorders (the Kerner Commission) said white racism was the fundamental cause of the riots in American cities. The commission said America was "moving toward two societies, one black, one white—separate and unequal."

March

4 Martin Luther King Jr. announced plans for Poor People's Campaign in Washington. He said he would lead a massive civil disobedience campaign in the capital to pressure the government to provide jobs and income for all Americans. He told a press conference that an army of poor whites, poor blacks and Hispanics would converge on Washington on April 20 and demonstrate until their demands were met.

19–21 Howard University students seized administration building. Students were demanding campus reform and black-oriented curriculum.

22–24

State troopers mobilized to put down student rebellion on campus of Cheyney State College.

28 Race riot in Memphis, Tenn., interrupted protest march led by Martin Luther King Jr. in support of striking sanitation workers. National Guard called up.

29 Students seized building at Bowie State College.

April

4 Martin Luther King Jr. assassinated by white sniper in Memphis, Tennessee. Assassination precipitated national crisis and rioting in more than one hundred cities. Forty-six persons were killed in major rebellions

1968

in Washington, Chicago and other cities. Twenty thousand federal troops and thirty-four thousand National Guardsmen were mobilized to quell disturbances. Memorial marches and rallies were held throughout the country. Many public school systems closed and the opening of the baseball season was postponed. President Lyndon B. Johnson declared Sunday, April 6, a national day of mourning and ordered all U.S. flags on government buildings in all U.S. territories and possessions to fly at half-mast.

April

7   Some three hundred Tuskegee students held twelve of the school trustees captive for twelve hours and demanded campus reforms.

9   Martin Luther King Jr. buried after funeral services at Ebenezer Baptist Church and memorial services at Morehouse College, Atlanta. More than 300,000 persons marched behind coffin of slain leader which was carried through streets of Atlanta on farm wagon pulled by two Georgia mules. Scores of national dignitaries, including Vice-President Humphrey, attended funeral.

—Ralph David Abernathy elected to succeed King as head of Southern Christian Leadership Conference.

10 U.S. Congress passed Civil Rights Bill banning (in three stages) racial discrimination in the sale or rental of approximately 80 per cent of the nation's housing. President Johnson signed bill on April 11. Bill also made it a crime to interfere with civil rights workers and to cross state lines to incite a riot.

12 Black students occupied administration building at Boston University in demand for Afro-American history courses and additional black students.

22 Trinity College students occupied school administration building to protest campus bias.

1968

April

23–24 Columbia University operations virtually ended for the year by black and white students who seized five buildings on campus.

26 Students seized administration building at Ohio State.

29–30 Poor People's Campaign began with Ralph Abernathy, SCLC president, leading delegation of leaders representing poor whites, blacks, Indians, and Spanish-Americans to Capitol Hill for conferences with cabinet members and congressional leaders.

May

3 Black students seized finance building at Northwestern University and demanded black-oriented curriculum and campus reforms.

6–8 Four hundred students seized administration building at Cheyney State College.

11 Nine caravans of poor people arrived in Washington for first phase of Poor People's Campaign. Caravans started from different sections of country on May 2 and picked up demonstrators along the way. In Washington, demonstrators erected camp called Resurrection City on sixteen-acre site near Lincoln Monument.

June

8 James Earl Ray, alleged assassin of Martin Luther King Jr., captured at London airport.

18 Supreme Court banned racial discrimination in sale and rental of housing.

19 Fifty thousand demonstrators participated in Solidarity Day March of Poor People's Campaign. Marchers walked from Washington Monument to Lincoln Monument, where they were addressed by Vice-President Humphrey, presidential candidate Eugene McCarthy, Mrs. Martin Luther King Jr. and Ralph Abernathy.

1968

June

24   Resurrection City closed. More than one hundred residents were arrested when they refused to leave site. Other residents, including Ralph Abernathy, were arrested during demonstration at Capitol. National Guard was mobilized later in the day to stop disturbances.

July

23–24   Race riot, Cleveland. Eleven persons, including three policemen, were killed and National Guard was mobilized. Riot was sparked by alleged ambush of police detail by black radicals.

27–28   Riot, Gary, Indiana.

August

5   Senator Edward Brooke named temporary chairman of Republican National Convention, Miami, Florida.

8   Riot, Miami, Florida. National Guard mobilized to put down rioting which erupted while Republicans were holding national convention in Miami Beach.

28   The Rev. Channing E. Phillips of Washington, D.C., became first black nominated for president by a major party. Phillips was nominated as favorite son candidate by District of Columbia delegation at Democratic convention in Chicago and received 67½ votes.

September

9   Arthur Ashe became the first winner of the U.S. Open Tennis championship, defeating Tom Okker of the Netherlands at Forest Hills Stadium, New York.

October

16   John Carlos and Tommie Smith staged Black Power demonstration on victory stand after winning 200-meter event at Olympics in Mexico City. Carlos and Smith said they were protesting racism in America.

November

5   A record number of black congressmen and the first black woman representative were elected to Congress. The nine black congressmen and Sen. Edward W.

1968

Brooke topped the previous high of eight in the Forty-fourth Congress of 1875–77. The first black woman representative, Shirley Chisholm of the Bedford-Stuyvesant section of Brooklyn, defeated former CORE director James Farmer, in New York's Twelfth Congressional District. On the same day Harlem voters defied congressional critics and reelected Adam Clayton Powell Jr. In addition to Powell, the following incumbents were reelected: William L. Dawson (Ill.), Charles C. Diggs (Mich.), Augustus Hawkins (Calif.), Robert N. C. Nix (Pa.) and John Conyers (Mich.). Elected to Congress for the first time were Mrs. Chisholm, Louis Stokes (Ohio) and William L. Clay (Mo.).

December

14   Classes at San Francisco State suspended after demonstrations by Black Student Union and Third World Liberation Front.

---   Sammy Davis Jr. awarded Spingarn Medal for his "superb and many-faceted talent," and his contributions to the civil rights movement.

1969

January

3   Rep. Adam Clayton Powell Jr. seated by Congress.

March

10   James Earl Ray pleaded guilty in a Memphis court to charges of killing Martin Luther King Jr. He was sentenced to ninety-nine years in prison. The House Select Committee on Assassinations said later that Ray fired the shot that killed King but that he was probably one element in a larger conspiracy.

20   Civil rights forces mobilized in support of striking hospital workers in Charleston, South Carolina.

27   Black Academy of Arts and Letters founded at Boston meeting. Dr. C. Eric Lincoln, professor of religion and

1969

sociology at Union Theological Seminary, was elected president of the organization.

April

14   Student Afro-American Society seized the Columbia College admissions office and demanded a special admissions board and staff.

19   One hundred black students, carrying rifles and shotguns, seized the Student Union Building at Cornell University to protest university "racism."

May

17   The Rev. Thomas Kilgore, a Los Angeles pastor, was elected president of the predominantly white American Baptist Convention.

21–23   Police and National Guardsmen fired on demonstrators at North Carolina A&T College. One student was killed and five policemen were injured.

26   National Black Economic Development Conference adopted manifesto in Detroit meeting calling for $500 million in reparations from white churches.

June

5   Race riot, Hartford, Connecticut.

16   U.S. Supreme Court ruled that the suspension of Adam Clayton Powell Jr. from the House of Representatives was unconstitutional.

19   State troopers ordered to Cairo, Ill., to quell racial disturbances.

July

31   National Guard mobilized in racial disturbances in Baton Rouge, Louisiana.

August

23   U.S. Justice Department reported that rioting in urban areas in 1969 was down at least 50 per cent from 1968. U.S. officials expressed a belief that the period of large-scale racial rebellions was over.

1969

August

30 National Guard mobilized to put down racial disturbances in Fort Lauderdale, Florida.

September

1-5 Large-scale racial disorders were reported in Hartford, Connecticut. Five hundred were arrested and scores were injured.

October

8 Police officers and blacks exchanged sniper fire on Chicago's West Side. One youth was killed and nine policemen were injured.

14-18 Race riot, Springfield, Massachusetts.

17 Dr. Clifton R. Wharton Jr. elected president of Michigan State University and became the first black to head a major, predominantly white university in the twentieth century.

29 U.S. Supreme Court said school systems must end segregation "at once" and "operate now and hereafter only unitary schools." In Mississippi case, *Alexander* v. *Holmes*, the Court abandoned the principle of "all deliberate speed."

31 Race riot, Jacksonville, Florida.

December

4 Two Black Panther leaders—Fred Hampton and Mark Clark—killed in Chicago police raid. Civil rights leaders said the two men were murdered in their beds.

- - - Pulitzer Prize for photography awarded to Moneta Sleet Jr. of *Ebony* magazine. He was the first black male cited by the Pulitzer committee.

- - - Clarence Mitchell Jr., director of the Washington Bureau of the NAACP, awarded the Spingarn Medal "for the pivotal role he . . . played in enactment of civil rights legislation."

1970

United States population: 203,200,000. Black population: 22,600,000 (11.1 per cent).

January

-- Dr. Benjamin E. Mays, president-emeritus, Morehouse College, named president of Atlanta Board of Education.

17 John M. Burgess installed as bishop of the Protestant Episcopal diocese of Massachusetts.

February

16 Joe Frazier knocked out Jimmy Ellis in the second round of their New York fight and became the world heavyweight boxing champion.

March

20 Students struck at the University of Michigan and demanded increased black enrollment. The strike ended April 2 after the administration agreed to meet their demands.

April

8 Senate rejected Supreme Court nominee G. Harold Carswell, who was opposed by liberals and civil rights groups because of his racial views.

May

12 Race riot, Augusta, Georgia. Six blacks were killed. Authorities said five of the victims were shot by police.

14 Two students killed by officers in major racial disturbance at Jackson State University (Miss.).

21 National Guard mobilized to quell disturbances at Ohio State University. Black and white students were demanding an end to ROTC programs and the admission of additional black students.

June

16 Kenneth A. Gibson elected mayor of Newark.

-- Race riot, Miami, Florida.

22 Richard Nixon signed bill extending Voting Rights Act of 1965 to 1975.

1970

June

23 Charles Rangel defeated Adam Clayton Powell in Democratic primary in Harlem, ending the political career of one of the major political symbols of the post-World War II period.

29 NAACP chairman Stephen Gill Spottswood told the NAACP convention that the Nixon administration was "anti-Negro" and was pressing "a calculated policy" inimical to "the needs and aspirations of the large majority" of citizens.

July

4-8 More than one hundred persons were injured in rioting in Asbury Park, New Jersey.

29 One person was killed in six days of rioting in Hartford, Connecticut.

August

3-7 Two thousand delegates and observers attended Congress of African Peoples convention in Atlanta.

7 Four persons, including the presiding judge, killed in courthouse shootout in San Rafael, Marin County, California. Police charged that activist Angela Davis helped provide the weapons used by the convicts and issued a nationwide warrant for her arrest.

14 City University of New York inaugurated open admissions policy designed to increase the number of poor and minority students.

29-31 One policeman killed and six wounded in racial confrontation between police and Black Panther activists in Philadelphia.

31 Lonnie McLucas, a Black Panther activist, convicted in New Haven, Conn., court of conspiracy to murder Alex Rackley, an alleged FBI informant. Charges against other defendants in the case were later dismissed.

1970

September

14–15   One black killed and two whites injured in shootout between activists and police officers in a New Orleans housing project.

October

13   Angela Davis arrested in New York City and charged with unlawful flight to avoid persecution for her alleged role in California courthouse shootout.

November

3   Twelve blacks elected to the Ninety-second Congress, including five new congressmen: Ralph H. Metcalfe (Ill.), George Collins (Ill.), Charles Rangel (N.Y.), Ronald Dellums (Calif.), and Parren Mitchell (Md.).

—Wilson Riles elected superintendent of public instruction in California.

—Richard Austin elected secretary of state in Michigan.

5   National Guard mobilized in Henderson, N. C., riots.

7–9   Race riots, Daytona Beach, Florida.

9   Death of William L. Dawson (84), Democratic congressman and party leader, in Chicago.

26   Death of B. O. Davis Sr. (93), first black general, in Chicago.

- - -   Charles Gordone awarded Pulitzer Prize for his play, *No Place To Go*.

- - -   Painter Jacob Lawrence awarded Spingarn Medal "in tribute to the compelling power of his work which has opened to the world . . . a window on the Negro's condition in the United States" and "in salute to his unswerving commitment" to the black struggle.

1971

January

4 Dr. Melvin H. Evans inaugurated as the first elected governor of the Virgin Islands.

-- Congressional Black Caucus organized.

6 Cecil A. Partee elected president pro tem of the Illinois state senate.

21 Twelve black congressmen boycotted Richard Nixon's State of the Union message because of his "consistent refusal" to respond to the petitions of black Americans.

February

4–9 National Guard mobilized to quell rioting in Wilmington, North Carolina. Two persons killed.

11 Whitney Young Jr., National Urban League director, drowned during recreational swim at international conference in Lagos, Nigeria.

25 President Nixon met with members of the Congressional Black Caucus and appointed a White House panel to study a list of recommendations made by the group.

March

1 Defense Department limited electronic surveilance after disclosure of "civil disturbance information collection plan" which directed the gathering of information on civil rights groups.

23 The Rev. Walter Fauntroy, a former aide of Martin Luther King Jr., became the first nonvoting congressional delegate from the District of Columbia since the Reconstruction period.

April

20 U.S. Supreme Court ruled unanimously that busing was a constitutionally acceptable method of integrating public schools.

1971

April

28 Samuel Lee Gravely Jr. became the first black admiral in the U.S. Navy.

May

5 Riot, Brownsville section of New York City.

18 President Nixon rejected the sixty demands of the Congressional Black Caucus, saying his administration would continue to support "jobs, income and tangible benefits, the pledges that this society has made to the disadvantaged in the past decade." The caucus expressed deep disappointment with the reply and said the Nixon administration "lacked a sense of understanding, urgency and commitment in dealing with the critical problems facing black Americans."

20 Pentagon report said blacks constituted 11 per cent of U.S. soldiers in Southeast Asia. The report said 12.5 per cent of all soldiers killed in Vietnam since 1961 were black.

21–26 National Guard mobilized to quell riot in Chattanooga, Tennessee. One person was killed and four hundred were arrested.

25 Young black woman, Jo Etha Collier, killed in Drew, Miss., by bullet fired from passing car. Three whites were arrested on May 26 and charged with the unprovoked attack.

June

14 Justice Department filed suit against the St. Louis suburb of Black Jack, charging the community with illegally using municipal procedures to block an integrated housing development.

15 Vernon E. Jordan Jr., former executive director of the United Negro College Fund, appointed executive director of the National Urban League.

1971

June

16–20 Racial disturbance, Jacksonville, Florida.

19–23 Mayor declared a state of emergency in Columbus, Ga., racial disturbance.

28 U.S. Supreme Court unanimously overturned the draft evasion conviction of Muhammad Ali.

July

6 Death of Louis ("Satchmo") Armstrong (71) in Corona, Queens, New York.

August

18 White policemen killed during raid on headquarters of the Republic of New Africa in Jackson, Mississippi. R. Obadele (R. Henry), president of the organization, and ten of his followers were arrested.

21 George Jackson, one of three convicts known as the Soledad Brothers, killed in an alleged escape attempt from the California prison at San Quentin. An autopsy report revealed that he was shot in the back.

September

9 Inmates seized Attica State Correctional Facility (N.Y.) and held several guards hostage. They issued a list of demands which included coverage by the state minimum wage law, better food and no reprisals.

9 Six Klansmen arrested in connection with the bombing of ten school buses in Pontiac, Michigan.

13 Fifteen hundred troopers and officers stormed the Attica Prison. Thirty-two convicts and ten guards were killed. Investigation showed that nine of the ten guards were killed by the storming party.

October

14–23 Two killed in Memphis racial disturbances.

November

24 Prison rebellion, Rahway State Prison, New Jersey.

1971

December

6   Lewis Franklin Powell confirmed as Supreme Court justice despite opposition by civil rights organizations.

9   Death of Ralph J. Bunche (67), Nobel Peace Prize winner and undersecretary of the UN from 1955 to his retirement in October, 1971, in New York City.

10   William H. Rehnquist confirmed as Supreme Court justice despite opposition by civil rights organizations.

18   People United To Serve Humanity (PUSH) founded at Chicago meeting by the Rev. Jesse Jackson.

---   Spingarn Medal presented to the Rev. Leon H. Sullivan, founder of Opportunities Industrialization Centers of America (OIC) for his leadership.

1972

January

10–12   Two black youths and two deputy sheriffs killed during racial disturbance in Baton Rouge, Louisiana.

27   Death of gospel singer Mahalia Jackson (60), Evergreen Park, Illinois.

25   Rep. Shirley Chisholm opened her unsuccessful campaign for president.

March

10–12   Three thousand delegates and five thousand observers attended the first black political convention in Gary, Indiana. The NAACP and other groups withdrew from the convention after the adoption of resolutions critical of busing and the state of Israel.

27   Two surviving Soledad Brothers, Fleeta Dumgo and John Cluchette, acquitted by an all-white jury of charges that they killed a white guard at Soledad Prison in 1970. Third Soledad Brother, George Jackson, was killed in August, 1971, in alleged escape attempt.

1972

April

4   Death of Adam Clayton Powell Jr. (63), former congressman and civil rights leader, in Miami.

11   Benjamin L. Hooks, a Memphis lawyer-minister, named to the Federal Communications Commission.

19   Maj. Gen. Frederic E. Davidson assumed command of the Eighth Infantry Division in Germany and became the first black to lead an army division.

—National Education Association study revealed that blacks had lost thirty thousand teaching jobs since 1954 in seventeen Southern and Border states because of discrimination and desegregation.

27   Death of Kwame Nkrumah (62), African statesman and first president of Ghana, in exile, in Conarky, Guinea.

June

4   Angela Davis acquitted by white jury in San Jose, Calif., of charges stemming from a 1970 courtroom shootout.

17   Frank Wills, Washington security guard, foiled break-in at offices of Democratic National Committee in first event of the Watergate conspiracy.

24   The rules committee of the Democratic National Convention approved the nomination of Yvonne Brathwaite Burke as cochairperson of the convention.

29   U.S. Supreme Court ruled in 5–4 decision that the death penalty was cruel and unusual punishment that violated the Eighth Amendment. At the time of the ruling, blacks and members of other minority groups constituted 483 of the 600 persons awaiting execution.

—NAACP annual report said the unemployment of "urban blacks in 1971 was worse than at any time since the great depression of the thirties." The report also said

1972

that more school desegregation occurred in 1971 than in
any other year since the 1954 school decision.

July

4 NAACP convention adopted emergency resolution
charging that President Nixon was "leading the mob in
its assault upon the Fourteenth Amendment's Equal
Protection clause."

10 Democratic convention opened in Miami Beach,
Florida. Blacks constituted 15 per cent of the delegates.
The convention nominated Sen. George S. McGovern
for president. Rep. Shirley Chisholm received 151.95 of
the 2,000-plus ballots on the first roll call.

13 Bureau of Census report said black unemployment av-
eraged 9.9 per cent in 1971, compared with a 5.4 per
cent rate for whites. The report also said that 31.8 per
cent of all black families were headed by a woman, an
increase from the 28 per cent reported in 1970.

25 U.S. health officials conceded that blacks had been
used as guinea pigs in forty-year syphilis experiment.

August

16 Rev. Philip A. Potter, a black Methodist minister from
Dominica, named general secretary of the World Council of Churches.

21 Republican convention opened in Miami Beach,
Florida, with fifty-six black delegates—4.2 per cent of
the total.

September

13 Two blacks—Johnny Ford of Tuskegee and A.J.
Cooper of Prichard—elected mayors in Alabama.

28 Secretary of the army cleared the military records of
167 soldiers who were dishonorably discharged in 1906
because they refused to identify alleged participants in
the Brownsville Raid (see page 512).

1972

October

11   Prison uprising, Washington, D.C., jail.

12–13   Forty-six black and white sailors injured in race riot on the aircraft carrier *Kitty Hawk* off North Vietnam.

24   Death of Jack Roosevelt ("Jackie") Robinson (53), first black in major leagues in twentieth century, in Stamford, Connecticut.

November

17   President Nixon reelected, carrying forty-nine of the fifty states, despite massive black vote for Sen. McGovern. Sixteen blacks were elected to Congress. Andrew Young of Atlanta was the first black elected to Congress from the Deep South since the Reconstruction era. Also elected for the first time were Barbara Jordan (Tex.) and Yvonne Brathwaite Burke (Calif.). Republican Senator Edward W. Brooke of Massachusetts was overwhelmingly endorsed for a second term.

16   National Guard mobilized after officers killed two students during Southern University demonstrations.

December

7   W. Sterling Cary elected president of the National Council of Churches.

8   Death of Rep. George Collins (47), in airplane crash, near Midway Airport, Chicago.

—Atty. Jewel Lafontant named deputy solicitor general.

21   Death of Horace Mann Bond (70), former president of Lincoln University (Pa.), in Atlanta.

---   Spingarn Medal awarded to Gordon B. Parks "in recognition of his unique creativity, as exemplified by his outstanding achievements as photographer, writer, film-maker and composer."

1973

May

29 Thomas Bradley elected mayor of Los Angeles.

June

5 Cardiss R. Collins of Chicago elected to Congress. She succeeded her late husband.

4 Death of Arna Bontemps (72), writer and educator, in Nashville, Tennessee.

October

16 Maynard Jackson elected mayor of Atlanta.

November

6 Coleman Young elected mayor of Detroit.

—Marcus A. Foster, superintendent of schools in Oakland, Calif., killed in ambush after Board of Education meeting. Two members of the Symbionese Liberation Army, a West Coast terrorist group, were convicted of the slaying, but the conviction of one of the men was overturned on a legal technicality.

- - -   Spingarn Medal presented to Wilson C. Riles, superintendent of public instruction, California, "in recognition of the stature he has attained as a national leader in the field of education."

1974

April

8 Henry ("Hank") Aaron broke Babe Ruth's major league baseball record by hitting his 715th home run in a game at Atlanta Stadium.

22 Joint Center for Political Studies reported that 2991 blacks held elective offices in 45 states and the District of Columbia, compared with 2621 in April, 1973, and 1185 in 1969. The Center reported 108 black mayors. Michigan had the largest number of black elected officials (194), followed by Mississippi (191).

May

9 House Judiciary Committee opened hearings to decide whether to recommend the impeachment of President

1974

Nixon in the Watergate controversy. Two blacks—Rep. John Conyers of Michigan and Rep. Barbara Jordan of Texas—were members of the committee.

May

19–27 Approximately five hundred delegates and observers, almost half of them from America, attended the Sixth Pan-African Congress in Dar es Salaam, Tanzania.

24 Death of Edward Kennedy ("Duke") Ellington (75), composer and bandleader, in New York City.

June

30 A black man shot and killed Mrs. Martin Luther King Sr. and deacon Edward Boykin during church services at Ebenezer Baptist Church, Atlanta. The assailant, Marcus Chennault of Dayton, Ohio, was later convicted and sentenced to death.

August

9 President Nixon resigned and was succeeded by Vice-President Gerald Ford.

September

12 Haile Selassie deposed by military leaders after fifty-eight years as the ruling monarch of Ethiopia.

October

3 Frank Robinson named manager of the Cleveland Indians and became the first black manager in the major leagues.

15 National Guard mobilized to restore order in Boston school busing crisis.

30 Muhammad Ali defeated George Foreman for heavyweight boxing title in Zaire.

November

5 State Sen. Mervyn M. Dymally elected lieutenant governor of California.

—State Sen. George L. Brown elected lieutenant governor of Colorado.

1974

November

5   Walter E. Washington, became the first elected mayor
of Washington, D.C., in the twentieth century.

—Harold Ford of Memphis elected to House of Representatives.

- - -   Spingarn Medal awarded Damon J. Keith "in tribute to
his steadfast defense of constitutional principles as revealed in a series of memorable decisions he handed
down as a United States District Court judge."

1975

January

1   Samuel Du Bois Cook became president of Dillard University.

14   William T. Coleman named secretary of transportation
by President Ford. He was the second black to hold a
cabinet position.

February

25   Death of Elijah Muhammad (77), leader of the Nation of
Islam, in Chicago. He was succeeded by his son, Wallace D. Muhammad.

April

10   Death of Josephine Baker (68), singer and entertainer,
in Paris.

11   Lee Elder, first black to compete in the Masters tournament, failed to qualify for the final two rounds.

18   James B. Parsons named chief judge of the Federal
District Court in Chicago and became the first black to
hold that position.

—Death of Percy Julian (76), holder of more than 138
chemical patents, and a pioneer synthesizer of cor-
tisone drugs.

1975

May

21 Lowell W. Perry confirmed as chairman of the Equal Opportunity Commission (EEOC).

27 Death of Ezzard Charles (53), former heavyweight boxing champion, in Chicago.

June

25 Mozambique proclaimed independent.

July

5 Arthur Ashe won the men's single championship at Wimbledon, defeating Jimmy Connors.

August

9 Death of Julian ("Cannonball") Adderly (46), saxophonist and bandleader, in Gary, Indiana.

15 Joanne Little acquitted of murder charges in the August 27, 1974, killing of a white jailer. The defense said she stabbed the jailer with an ice pick after he made sexual advances.

27 Death of Haile Selassie (83), deposed emperor of Ethiopia, in Addis Ababa.

September

1 Gen. Daniel ("Chappie") James Jr. promoted to rank of four-star general and named commander-in-chief of the North American Air Defense Command.

2 Joseph W. Hatchett of Florida sworn in as first black supreme court justice in the South in the twentieth century.

November

11 Angola proclaimed indepdepent.

December

17 Death of Noble Sissle (86), pioneer jazz figure.

--- Spingarn Medal presented to Henry ("Hank") Aaron "for his memorable home-run record which stands as a landmark" and for his sportsmanship.

1976

January

7   Dr. Mary Frances Berry named chancellor of the University of Colorado.

9   Death of Lester B. Granger (79), former director of the National Urban League, in Alexandria, Louisiana.

23   Death of Paul Robeson (77), singer, actor, activist, in Philadelphia.

April

5   FBI documents, released in response to a freedom of information suit, revealed that the government mounted an intensive campaign against civil rights organizations in the sixties. In a letter dated August 25, 1967, the FBI said the government operation, called COINTELPRO, was designed "to expose, disrupt, misdirect, discredit or otherwise neutralize the activities of black nationalists, hate-type groups, their leadership, spokesmen, membership and supporters, and to counter their propensity for violence and civil disorders." A later telegram specifically named the Student Nonviolent Coordinating Committee and the Southern Christian Leadership Conference as organizations having "radical and violence prone leaders, members and followers."

July

1   Kenneth Gibson, mayor of Newark, became the first black president of the U.S. Conference of Mayors.

August

18   Vice Admiral Samuel L. Gravely Jr. assumed command of the U.S. Third Fleet.

September

10   Death of Mordecai Johnson (86), first black president of Howard University, in Washington.

October

25   Gov. George Wallace granted a full pardon to Clarence ("Willie") Norris, the last known survivor of the nine Scottsboro Boys who were convicted in 1931 of the alleged rape of two white women on a freight train.

1976

October

30 The Rev. Joseph H. Evans elected president of the United Church of Christ.

November

2 Jimmy Carter, former governor of Georgia, elected president with strong support from black voters.

—Seventeen black congressmen reelected.

6 Benjamin Hooks, Federal Communications Commission member, named to succeed Roy Wilkins as executive director of the NAACP.

December

16 Rep. Andrew Young of Georgia named ambassador and chief delegate to the United Nations.

21 Patricia R. Harris named secretary of housing and urban development by President-elect Carter.

- - - Spingarn Medal presented to Alvin Ailey "in recognition of his international pre-eminence in the field of dance."

1977

January

2 Death of Erroll Garner (53), jazz pianist, in Los Angeles.

15 Second World Festival of Black and African Art (FESTAC) opened in Lagos, Nigeria. Largest delegation outside Nigeria came from United States of America. The festival continued until February 12.

23–30 Televised production of *Roots*, novel by Alex Haley, established records. Some 130 million viewers watched the episodes during the eight-night presentation.

February

11 Clifford Alexander Jr. confirmed as the first black secretary of the army.

1977

February

28 Death of comedian Eddie ("Rochester") Anderson (71).

March

8 Henry L. Marsh III elected mayor of Richmond.

27 Death of Shirley Graham Du Bois (69), author and widow of W. E. B. Du Bois, in Peking, China.

May

9 Mabel Murphy Smythe confirmed as ambassador to the republic of Cameroon.

June

6 Joseph Lawson Howze installed as bishop of the Roman Catholic diocese of Biloxi, Mississippi.

September

1 Death of Ethel Waters (80), singer and actress, in Chatsworth, California.

24 John T. Walker installed as the first black bishop of the Episcopal diocese of Washington.

October

26 Dr. Clifford R. Wharton Jr. named chancellor of the State University of New York.

November

12 Ernest N. Morial elected mayor of New Orleans.

--- Spingarn Medal awarded to Alexander P. Haley "for his unsurpassed effectiveness in portraying the legendary story of an American of African descent."

1978

January

16 Three black astronauts—Maj. Frederick D. Gregory, Maj. Guion S. Bluford and Dr. Ronald E. McNair—named.

February

15 Leon Spinks defeated Muhammad Ali for heavyweight boxing championship. Ali regained the title on September 15 and became the first person to win the title three times.

1978

February

25 Death of Daniel ("Chappie") James Jr. (58), retired Air Force general and the first black promoted to four-star rank, at the Air Force Academy, Colorado.

June

28 U.S. Supreme Court ordered the University of California Medical School at Davis to admit Allan P. Bakke in so-called reverse discrimination suit.

30 Larry Doby became manager of the Chicago White Sox baseball team. He was fired on October 19.

August

22 Death of Jomo Kenyatta (83), president of Kenya.

October

10 Death of Congressman Ralph H. Metcalfe (68), in Chicago.

27 President Carter signed Hawkins-Humphrey full employment bill.

November

4 William Howard Jr., 32, elected president of the National Council of Churches.

7 Five newcomers elected to Congress: William Gray III (Pa.), Bennett Stewart (Ill.), Melvin Evans (R., Virgin Islands), Julian Dixon (Calif.) and George Leland (Tex.).

—Lt. Gov. Mervyn Dymally defeated in California election.

—Senator Edward W. Brooke defeated in Massachusetts election.

18 More than nine hundred persons, most of them black Americans, died in mass murder and suicide pact in Jonestown, Guyana.

--- Spingarn Medal presented to Ambassador Andrew J. Young "in recognition of the deftness with which he has

1978

handled relations between this nation and other countries" and "for his major role in raising the consciousness of American citizens to the significance in world affairs of the massive African continent."

1979

January

30 Franklin A. Thomas named president of the Ford Foundation. He was the first black to head a major American foundation.

February

23 Frank E. Petersen Jr. named the first black general in the Marine Corps.

May

16 Death of Asa Philip Randolph (90), labor leader and civil rights pioneer, in New York.

31 Zimbabwe proclaimed independent.

June

27 U.S. Supreme Court ruled in *Weber* v. *Kaiser Aluminum and Chemical Corporation* that employers and unions can establish voluntary programs, including the use of quotas, to aid minorities in employment.

July

9 Dr. Walter Massey named director of the Argonne National Laboratory.

19 Patricia R. Harris, secretary of housing and urban development, named secretary of health, education and welfare.

August

1 James Patterson Lyke installed as auxiliary bishop of the Cleveland diocese of the Roman Catholic Church.

15 Andrew Young resigned under pressure as UN ambassador after unauthorized meeting with representatives of the Palestine Liberation Organization. Resignation created a storm of controversy and divided the black and Jewish communities.

1979

August

22 Two hundred black leaders, meeting in New York, expressed support for Andrew Young and demanded that blacks be given a voice in shaping American foreign policy.

31 Donald McHenry named to succeed Andrew Young as UN ambassador.

September

23 Lou Brock stole a record 935th base and became the all-time major league record holder.

October

3 Death of artist Charles White (61), in Los Angeles.

30 Richard Arrington elected mayor of Birmingham.

November

3 Klansmen fired on an anti-Klan rally in Greensboro, N.C., and killed five persons.

15 Study compiled by the Anti-Defamation League of B'nai B'rith indicated a sharp rise in Ku Klux Klan activity. Study said Klan membership in 22 states increased from 8,000 to 10,000 in the twenty-month period ending in November, 1979, and that the number of sympathizers grew from 30,000 to 100,000.

--- Spingarn Medal awarded to Rosa L. Parks, who was the catalyst in the Montgomery Bus Boycott of 1955–56.

--- Nobel Prize in economics awarded to Professor Arthur Lewis of Princeton. He was the first black cited in a category other than peace.

1980

United States population: 226,500,000. Black population: 26,500,000 (11.7 per cent).

January

20 Two persons killed in a night of racial violence in Idabell, Oklahoma.

1980

March

15   Scores injured in Klan-related incidents in Georgia, Tennessee, California, Indiana and North Carolina, in March and April.

31   Death of Jesse Owens (66), who won four gold medals at the Berlin Olympics, 1936, in Tuscon, Arizona.

April

8   State troopers mobilized to stop disturbances in Wrightsville, Georgia. Racial incidents were also reported in 1980 in Chattanooga, Tenn., Oceanside, Calif., Kokomo, Ind., Wichita, Kan., and Johnston County, North Carolina.

12   Liberian President William R. Tolbert Jr. and twenty-seven others were killed in coup d'etat by army enlisted men led by Master Sergeant Samuel K. Doe.

May

17–19   Major race riot, Miami, Florida. Sixteen persons were killed and more than three hundred were injured.

29   Vernon E. Jordan Jr., president of the National Urban League, critically injured in attempted assassination in Fort Wayne, Indiana.

July

12   Death of John W. Davis (92), civil rights activist and former president of West Virginia State College, in Englewood, New Jersey.

5–17   Forty injured in racial disturbances in Miami, Florida.

October

13   Unprovoked slayings of six blacks in Buffalo, N.Y., triggered demands for national investigation.

---   Spingarn Medal awarded to Rayford W. Logan, historian and author, "in tribute to his lifetime of service as an educator and historian."

November

4   Ronald Reagan elected president of the United States despite widespread opposition from civil rights groups and black voters.

1981

January

9   Labor Department announced that black unemployment rate in December, 1980, was 14 per cent.

14 James Frank, president of Lincoln University (Mo.), installed as first black president of the National Collegiate Athletic Association (NCAA).

22 Samuel Pierce named secretary of housing and urban development by Ronald Reagan.

March

5   U.S. government granted Atlanta some $1 million to finance mental health and social programs in the wake of a mysterious series of abductions and slayings involving at least twenty-two black youths.

6   Dr. Bernard Harleston, former dean of arts and sciences at Tufts University, appointed president of New York's City College.

29 Death of Eric Williams (69), prime minister of Trinidad and Tobago, in Port of Spain. Dr. Williams was also a historian and the author of the classic work, *Capitalism and Slavery*.

April

10 Death of Howard Thurman (81), theologian and director of the Howard Thurman Trust, in San Francisco. He was eulogized as one of the greatest preachers and spiritual influences of the century.

12 Death of Joe Louis (66), regarded by many as the greatest heavyweight champion of all times, in Las Vegas, Nevada. He won the title in 1937 and held it until his retirement in 1949, the longest reign of any heavyweight champion.

20 Death of Archibald J. Carey (73), former chairman of the President's Committee on Government Employment Policy, in Chicago.

1981

April

22 Death of Brailsford Reese Brazeal (76), economist and former dean of Morehouse College, in Atlanta.

29 Buffalo, N.Y., grand jury indicted Pvt. Joseph G. Christopher of the U.S. Army on murder charges stemming from the racially motivated slayings of three blacks in September, 1980.

May

1 Death of Dr. Clarence A. Bacote (75), historian and political scientist, in Atlanta.

11 Death of Hoyt J. Fuller (57), literary critic and editor of *First World* magazine and former editor of *Black World*, in Atlanta.

28 Death of musician Mary Lou Williams (71), in Durham, North Carolina.

July

17 Fulton County (Atlanta) grand jury indicted Wayne B. Williams, a twenty-three-year-old photographer, for the murder of two of the twenty-eight black youths killed in a series of slayings and disappearances in Atlanta. Williams denied the charges but was convicted in February, 1982.

31 Attorney Arnette R. Hubbard installed as the first woman president of the National Bar Association.

August

10 The Coca-Cola Bottling Company agreed to pump $34 million into black businesses and the black community, ending a national boycott called by PUSH.

September

8 Death of Roy Wilkins (80), longtime executive director of the NAACP, in New York.

9 Vernon E. Jordan resigned as president of the National Urban League and announced plans to join a Washing-

1981

ton law firm. He was succeeded by John E. Jacob, executive vice president of the league.

19 More than 300,000 demonstrators from labor and civil rights organizations protested the social policies of the Reagan administration in Solidarity Day march in Washington, D.C.

28 Joseph Paul Franklin, an avowed racist, sentenced to life imprisonment for killing two black joggers in Salt Lake City, Utah.

October

27 Andrew Young, former UN Ambassador, elected mayor of Atlanta.

28 Edward M. McIntrye elected first black mayor of Augusta, Georgia.

29 Death of William O. Walker (85), publisher of the Cleveland *Call Post*, in Cleveland.

November

3 Coleman Young reelected mayor of Detroit.

—Thurman L. Milner elected mayor of Hartford, Connecticut.

—James Chase elected mayor of Spokane, Washington.

30 —Four newcomers elected to Congress: Mervyn Dymally (Calif.), Augustus Savage (Ill.), Harold Washington (Ill.) and George W. Crockett Jr. (Mich.).

--- Spingarn Medal awarded to Coleman A. Young "in recognition of his singular accomplishments as Mayor of the City of Detroit."

1982

February

5   Unemployment rate for blacks fell to 16.8 per cent from 17.3 per cent, according to U.S. Labor Department report.

27 Wayne B. Williams convicted of murdering two of twenty-eight young blacks slain in a two-year period in Atlanta. After he was sentenced to two life terms in prison, he appealed to the Georgia Supreme Court. The two murder convictions were upheld on December 5, 1983.

June

8   Death of Leroy ("Satchel") Paige (75), in Kansas City, Missouri.

29 President Reagan signed bill that extended for 25 years provisions of the Voting Rights Act of 1965.

August

11 U.S. Army Lt. Gen. Roscoe Robinson Jr. promoted to four-star general and became the second black in U.S. military history to hold that rank.

October

4   Death of Heman Marion Sweatt (69), plaintiff in famous separate-but-equal case of *Sweatt* v. *Painter*, in Atlanta.

November

2   Los Angeles Mayor Tom Bradley narrowly defeated by Republican George Deukmejian in his bid to become the first black elected governor. In other elections, four blacks were elected to Congress for the first time: Katie Hall of Gary, Ind., Alan Wheat of Kansas City, Mo., and Major Owens and Edolphus Towns of New York City. Owens succeeded Shirley Chisholm, who retired.

December

28–31 Shooting of black by Miami police triggered race riot in Miami.

1983

February

4   U.S. Labor Department reported that the unemployment rate for Blacks remained at a "record high" of 20.8 per cent.

1983

February

12 Death of Eubie Blake (100), pianist and composer, New York City.

April

11 Charles Thomas became the first black on the Virginia Supreme Court.

29 Harold Washington sworn in as the first black mayor of Chicago.

May

15 Death of photographer James Van Der Zee (96), who gained fame for his work in Harlem, in Washington, D. C.

August

23 Labor leader Charles A. Hayes won special election in Chicago's First Congressional District to replace Harold Washington.

30 Lt. Col. Guion S. Bluford Jr., one of the crew members of the space shuttle *Challenger*, became the first American black to fly into outer space.

September

17 Vanessa Williams, a 20-year-old Syracuse University student from Millwood, N.Y., became the first black woman to win the Miss America title. On July 23, 1984, Williams resigned after nude photos were published in a national magazine. Another black woman, Suzette Charles, the first runner-up, was then crowned Miss America.

October

25 U.S. Marines and Rangers invaded the tiny Caribbean island of Grenada in the first large-scale U.S. military invasion in the area since the invasion of the Dominican Republic in 1965.

November

2 President Reagan signed into law a bill designating the third Monday of January each year as a federal holiday in honor of Martin Luther King Jr.

3 Jesse Jackson, president of Operation PUSH, declared his candidacy for president of the United States. His

1983

November

campaign generated unprecedented fervor. He won several contests, including the South Carolina and Louisiana primaries.

8 W. Wilson Goode became the first black mayor of Philadelphia.

1984

March

13 Republican James L. Usry elected first black mayor of Atlantic City, New Jersey.

18 Death of Clarence Mitchell (73), former Washington lobbyist for the NAACP, in Baltimore, Maryland.

28 Death of Benjamin E. Mays (89), minister, educator and civil rights leader who served as president of Morehouse College for 27 years, in Atlanta.

April

1 Death of Marvin Gaye (44), in Los Angeles. Singer was shot by his father, Marvin Gay Sr.

2 Georgetown University's basketball team won the NCAA championship and John Thompson became the first black coach to lead a team to a Division 1 NCAA national title.

26 Death of William (Count) Basie (77), in Hollywood, Florida.

July

17 Jesse Jackson formally withdrew from presidential race in speech at Democratic convention in San Francisco.

August

4-11 Carl Lewis became the first person to win four gold medals in track and field at an Olympics since Jesse Owens' 1936 triumph. Lewis won gold medals in the 100- and 200-meter dashes, long jump and 4 x 100 meter relay.

October

7 Walter Payton of the Chicago Bears broke Jim Brown's career rushing record of 12,312 yards.

1984

October

10   Anglican Bishop Desmond Tutu was awarded the 1984 Nobel Peace Prize for his opposition to South Africa's apartheid policy.

November

11   Death of the Rev. Martin Luther King Sr. (84), longtime civil rights leader and father of Martin Luther King Jr., in Atlanta.

21   Prominent Black Americans launched series of protests against the policy of apartheid and the policies of the Reagan administration. By December 5, nearly 40 had been arrested for picketing South African embassies in Washington and other cities.

1985

January

4   Leontyne Price made her farewell appearance at New York's Metropolitan Opera in the title role of *Aida*.

4   Rep. William H. Gray elected chairman of the House Budget Committee, the highest congressional post held by a black.

13   Death of Jerome Holland (69), educator and former ambassador to Sweden, in New York City. He was the first black on the New York Stock Exchange board of directors.

25   Bernhard H. Goetz, a white man accused of shooting four youths on New York subway, indicted on a minor charge of illegal possession of a weapon. The case triggered a national controversy.

March

23   Death of Patricia Roberts Harris (60), the first black woman ambassador, and the first black woman cabinet member, in Washington, D. C.

May

13   Fire killed 11 people, including five children, and destroyed sixty-one homes after police and firemen bombed home of militant group in Philadelphia. Mayor W. Wilson Goode later apologized for attack on MOVE headquarters.

1985

July

1 Death of Pauli Murray (74), author, lawyer and first black woman Episcopal priest in the United States, in Pittsburgh.

31 Dr. Laval S. Wilson, 49, named first black school superintendent in Boston.

November

5 State Senator L. Douglas Wilder elected lieutenant governor of Virginia and became the first black to hold this position in a Southern state since Reconstruction. In other elections, Detroit Mayor Coleman Young was reelected.

1986

January

16 Martin Luther King Jr.'s bust unveiled in the Great Rotunda of the United States Capitol.

20 Millions of Americans celebrated first Martin Luther King Jr. national holiday.

28 Space shuttle *Challenger* exploded shortly after liftoff and Ronald McNair, a black physicist, and six other astronauts were killed.

February

7 U.S. Labor Department reported that the black unemployment rate fell from 14.9 per cent to 14.4 per cent.

8 Debi Thomas became the first black to win the senior U.S. singles figure-skating championship.

March

1 Sidney Barthelemy elected mayor of New Orleans.

6 Blue-ribbon commission appointed by Mayor W. Wilson Goode said the mayor and other public officials were "grossly negligent" during the May 1985 bombing of the headquarters of the MOVE organization.

May

11 Death of Frederick Douglas ("Fritz") Pollard (92), football player and coach, and the first black named to an

1986

May

All-American football team (Brown University), in Silver Springs, Maryland.

13 Sharpe James defeated Kenneth Gibson in Newark, N. J., mayoral race.

July

2 U.S. Supreme Court upheld affirmative action as a remedy for past discrimination by a 6–3 vote.

August

31 Death of Earl B. Dickerson (95), lawyer, insurance executive and civil rights activist, in Chicago.

October

15 Edward Perkins confirmed as the country's first black ambassador to South Africa.

23 The Center for Disease Control reported that blacks accounted for 25 per cent of the U.S. victims of AIDS.

29 National Academy of Sciences report said that acquired immune deficiency syndrome (AIDS) had taken the lives of approximately 25,000 Americans.

November

5 Arizona Governor-elect Evan Mecham created a political furore by announcing plans to rescind a state holiday in honor of Martin Luther King Jr. In other elections, four blacks were elected to Congress for the first time: Mike Espy, Mississippi's first black congressman since Reconstruction; the Rev. Floyd Flake, Queens, New York; John Lewis, Atlanta; and Kweisi Mfume, Baltimore.

December

20 Michael Griffith killed while fleeing white mob in Howard Beach section of New York City.

1987

January

14 In "State of Black America" report, the National Urban League presented its harshest criticism of President Reagan. The group said "Black Americans enter 1987 beseiged by the resurgence of raw racism, persistent

1987

January

economic depression and the continued erosion of past gains."

17 Marchers celebrating Martin Luther King's birthday attacked in all-white Forsyth County, Georgia.

24 Twenty thousand black and white marchers staged massive protest march in Forsyth County, Georgia.

February

25 Death of E. D. Nixon (87), labor and civil rights leader and one of the catalysts of the Montgomery Bus Boycott, in Montgomery, Alabama.

April

6 Jackie Robinson, the first black in major league baseball in modern times, honored on fortieth anniversary of his historic breakthrough.

7 Chicago Mayor Harold Washington reelected.

8 Al Campanis, Los Angeles Dodger executive, fired for alleged racist slur on national television program celebrating Jackie Robinson's achievements. Campanis questioned the managerial potential of black baseball players.

16 August Wilson received Pulitzer Prize for his play *Fences*.

May

5 Thomas V. Barnes defeated Mayor Richard G. Hatcher in Gary primary.

6 Thurgood Marshall, the first black Supreme Court justice, criticized plans for national celebration of bicentennial of the U.S. Constitution. He reminded Americans that the original document excluded blacks, native Americans, and women.

June

5 Dr. Mae C. Jemison, a Los Angeles-based physician, named the first black woman astronaut.

1987

June

16 Bernhard H. Goetz was found innocent of the attempted murder of four black youths he shot on a New York City subway.

22 Death of Robert N.C. Nix Sr. (81), Pennsylvania's first black congressman, in Philadelphia.

August

16 Death of historian Charles H. Wesley (95), former president of Wilberforce and Central State universities, in Washington, D.C.

24 Death of activist Bayard Rustin (75 or 77), in New York City.

30 Death of Wade Hampton McCree Jr. (67), law school professor and former federal judge, in Detroit.

October

10 Jesse Jackson announced that he would make a second race for the presidency.

23 U.S. Senate rejected the nomination of Judge Robert Bork to the Supreme Court.

27 Death of novelist John O. Killens (71), in Brooklyn.

November

3 Kurt L. Schmoke elected the first black mayor of Baltimore.

—Carrie Saxon Perry elected mayor of Hartford, Connecticut, and became the first black woman mayor of a major city in the northeast.

5 Lt. Gen. Colin L. Powell named White House national security adviser.

25 Chicago Mayor Harold Washington died after a heart attack. The first big-city black mayor to die in office, he was buried on November 20 after five days of mourn-

1987

ing. On December 2, after turbulent demonstrations, the city council named a black alderman, Eugene Sawyer, to succeed him.

December

1 Death of novelist James Baldwin (63), in St. Paul de Vence, France.

15 Death of civil rights leader Septima Poinsette Clark (89), who played a role in the founding of the Southern Christian Leadership Conference and the Student Nonviolent Coordinating Committee, on St. John's Island, South Carolina.

1988

January

16 Sports commentator Jimmy (The Greek) Snyder was fired by CBS Sports for making remarks called racist. Snyder told a Washington TV reporter that if more blacks moved into coaching "there's not going to be anything left for white people."

31 Doug Williams, the first black to quarterback a Super Bowl team, passed for a record 340 yards and tied a record with four touchdown passes in leading the Washington Redskins to a 42–10 victory over the Denver Broncos. Williams was named most valuable player of Super Bowl XXII, which was played in San Diego, California.

February

5 The U.S. Labor Department said the unemployment rate for blacks was 12.2 per cent, compared to a national rate of 5.7 per cent and a Hispanic rate of 7.2 per cent.

12 More than 200 students occupied the African-American studies building at the University of Massachusetts to protest the beating of two black students by six white men. The occupation ended on February 17 after the university administration accepted a list of racial grievances.

1988

March

24 Death of blues singer Memphis Slim (72), in Paris.

2 Death of author J. Saunders Redding (81), in Ithaca, New York.

3 Juanita Kidd Stout was sworn in as justice of the Pennsylvania Supreme Court and became the first black woman to sit on a state supreme court.

8 Presidential candidate Jesse Jackson won five state primaries on "Super Tuesday."

March

10 The Dartmouth College administration disciplined four white students accused of harassing a black professor.

12 Death of painter Romare Bearden (75), in New York City.

15 Eugene Antonio Marino, auxiliary bishop of Washington, D.C., named archbishop of Atlanta and became the first black Catholic archbishop in America.

31 Toni Morrison won the Pulitzer Prize for her novel, *Beloved*.

April

12 Frank Robinson named manager of the Baltimore Orioles and became the first black baseball manager since he was fired by the San Francisco Giants in 1984.

26 Death of Frederick D. Patterson (86), founder of the United Negro College Fund and president-emeritus of Tuskegee University, in New Rochelle, New York.

May

1 The Rev. Sherman G. Hicks installed as the first black bishop of the Evangelical Lutheran Church.

3 A Philadelphia grand jury cleared Mayor W. Wilson Goode and his top aides of criminal responsibility in the 1985 fire-bombing that led to the death of eleven

1988

persons and the destruction of 60 homes. After a two-year investigation of "this city's greatest tragedy," the jury criticized the mayor and his aides for their actions in the attack on the house of the militant black group, MOVE.

10   Robert Brown elected the first black mayor of Orange, New Jersey.

June

18   Death of Sallie Martin (92), sometimes called "The Mother of Gospel Music," in Chicago.

24   Atlanta University and Clark College merged, becoming Clark Atlanta University.

29   Motown Records sold to MCA/Boston Ventures partnership for $61 million.

July

14   NAACP posthumously presented the 73rd Spingarn Medal to Dr. Frederick D. Patterson, founder of the United Negro College Fund.

August

2   Congressional Black Caucus sent a letter to Japanese Premier Noboru Takeshita protesting anti-black remarks and anti-black practices in Japan.

4   A fire destroyed the first black fraternity house at the University of Mississippi. Investigators said they "strongly" suspected arson as the cause of the fire at the Phi Beta Sigma fraternity house.

9   Death of M. Carl Holman (69), poet, civil rights leader and former president of the National Urban Coalition, in Washington, D.C.

15   Bishop College (Dallas, Texas) closed.

27   More than sixty thousand marched in Washington, D.C., to commemorate the 25th anniversary of the 1963 March on Washington.

1988

31   The Census Bureau reported that the median income among black families was $18,098 in 1987, compared to the $32,274 median income among whites. The bureau said the poverty rate in 1987 among whites was 10.5 per cent, but that the poverty rate among blacks was 33.1 per cent. The poverty rate for all children was 10.5 per cent, compared to 45.8 per cent for black children.

September

13   President Reagan signed bipartisan fair housing bill, which expanded protection against housing discrimination.

24   The Most Rev. Barbara C. Harris of Massachusetts elected the first woman bishop of the Episcopal Church.

---   Jackie Joyner-Kersee broke her own world record in winning the heptathlon at the Seoul Olympics. She also won the gold medal in the long jump. Among other major winners were Carl Lewis, who won the long jump and the men's 100 meter; Florence Griffith Joyner, who set a world record in the 200 meter and won gold medals in the 100 meter and 4-by-100 meter relay. Her three gold medals and one silver medal was the second best effort for a woman in Olympic history. Kenny Monday won the 163-pound wrestling event and became the first black to win a wrestling gold medal.

October

7   Death of singer Billy Daniels (73), in Los Angeles.

23   Jesse Jackson met with presidential candidate Michael Dukakis and later criticized George Bush and the Republicans for using photographs of convict Willie Horton to spread "horrible" racial fears.

24   Death of businessman S. B. Fuller (83), founder and president of Chicago's Fuller Products Co., in the Chicago suburb of Blue Island.

1988

November

4 TV star Bill Cosby and his wife, Camille, donated $20 million to Atlanta's Spelman College, the largest single gift to a black college by black Americans.

8 Republican George Bush received a small number of black votes but was elected president of the United States. Donald M. Payne elected New Jersey's first black congressman and became the 24th member of the congressional black.

December

3 Barry Sanders of Oklahoma State University won the Heisman Trophy.

5 Rep. William H. Gray (D-Pa.) won a three-way race for chairman of the House Democratic caucus, and became the first black admitted to the top ranks of congressional leadership.

15 Death of Wiley A. Branton (65), who represented the black students in the Little Rock integration crisis and who served as dean of the Howard University Law School, in Washington, D.C.

20 Death of Max Robinson (49), the first black anchor of a network (ABC) newscast, in Washington, D.C.

21 The Rev. Jesse Jackson and a group of black leaders called for the abandonment of the term "black" and the use of the term "African-Americans" to designate African descendants in America.

22 Morehouse Medical School President Louis W. Sullivan named secretary of health and human services.

1989

January

3 Rep. John Conyers (D-Mich.) elected chairman of the Government Operations Committee of House of Representatives.

1989

—Dennis Green named head football coach at Stanford University.

6 Death of Elizabeth D. Koontz (69), former head of the National Education Association, in Salisbury, North Carolina.

11 The National Collegiate Athletic Association approved a new rule—Proposition 42—that eliminated athletic scholarships for freshmen who do not meet minimum academic standards. Critics said the proposition and the standard tests used to qualify students were racially biased.

13 Death of poet Sterling A. Brown (87), in Tacoma Park, Maryland.

16–18 Three days of rioting erupted in Overtown section of Miami after a policeman shot and killed a black motorcyclist.

20 Anna Perez named press secretary to Barbara Bush.

22 Jerry Rice named most valuable player as San Francisco 49ers defeat Cincinnati in Super Bowl XXIII.

23 The U.S. Supreme Court banned a Richmond, Va., program that set aside 30 per cent of the city's public works funds for minority-owned construction companies. The 6–3 ruling, written by Justice Sandra Day O'Connor, said the program constituted "reverse" discrimination. In dissent, Justice Thurgood Marshall criticized the ruling, saying that it constituted "a full-scale retreat from the court's long-standing solicitude to race-conscious remedial efforts directed toward deliverance of the century-old promise of equality of economic opportunity."

1989

February

2   Lt. Comdr. Evelyn Fields named first woman to command a Navy ship.

3   Bill White, a former baseball star and a radio announcer for the New York Yankees, named president of the National League. He assumed the position on April 1.

10 Ronald H. (Ron) Brown elected chairman of the Democratic Party and became the first black to head a major national political party.

11 The Most Rev. Barbara Harris confirmed as the first woman bishop of the Episcopal Church.

26 Death of trumpet player Roy Eldridge (78), in Valley Stream, New York.

March

1   Dr. Louis W. Sullivan, former president of the Morehouse Medical School, confirmed as secretary of health and human services by a vote of 98–1. Republican Sen. Jesse Helms voted no.

7   Republican National Committee Chairman Lee Atwater resigned from the board of trustees of Howard University after students demonstrated to protest his appointments. The students deplored Atwater's stand on civil rights and what they called the racist strategy of the 1988 presidential campaign of Republican George Bush.

10 The Labor Department said that black unemployment was 11.9 per cent in February, compared to white unemployment of 4.3 per cent.

April

13 The Centers for Disease Control said that 27 per cent of all reported cases of AIDS occurred among blacks, although blacks made up only 12 per cent of the total population.

1989

May

10 Death of Richard R. Green (52), first black chancellor of the New York City public school system, after a severe asthma attack, in New York City.

31 Cito Gaston named manager of the Toronto Blue Jays of baseball's American League.

June

4 Singer Ruth Brown won a Tony Award for her role in the Broadway play, *Black and Blue*. Henry LeTang, Frankie Manning, and Fayard Nichols shared a Tony Award for the choreography of the same musical.

12 The U.S. Supreme Court continued its assault on civil rights legislation, ruling that white workers claiming reverse discrimination could seek redress under civil rights legislation passed to protect black workers. In a separate ruling on the same day, the court ruled out a belated challenge to a discriminatory seniority system.

15 The U.S. Supreme Court limited a landmark 1866 civil rights decision to forbid claims of racial harassment in the workplace.

14 Rep. William Gray (D-Pa.) elected majority whip of the House of Representatives and became the first black to hold the position.

August

1 Gwendolyn S. King named the first black commissioner of the Social Security Administration.

6 National Urban League President John E. Jacob told the organization's annual conference that recent Supreme Court decisions were threats to the vital interests of American blacks.

7 Death of Rep. Mickey Leland (44) (D-Tex.), in an airplane crash in western Ethiopia near the Sudanese border. Leland, who was chairman of the House Select

1989

Committee on Hunger, was flying in a small plane to a refugee camp.

22 Huey P. Newton, co-founder of the Black Panther Party, shot to death in an Oakland neighborhood. Three days later, police arrested a suspect identified as a drug dealer.

September

2 The National Guard was called out to quell disturbances growing out of clashes between police and black students during a weekend outing in Virginia Beach, Virginia. Authorities said 43 people were injured and 260 were arrested.

16 Debbye Turner of Missouri crowned Miss America. She was the third black woman to wear the crown.

20 *A Dry White Season* opened and Euzhan Palcy became the first black woman director of a full-length feature film for a major U.S. studio.

21 Gen. Colin Powell confirmed as chairman of the Joint Chiefs of Staff, the highest military position held by an African-American.

29 Yusuf K. Hawkins, a 16-year-old black youth, killed in the Bensonhurst section of Brooklyn by a gang of white youths. The event inflamed racial tensions in New York City. Police arrested and charged six white youths.

October

3 Maynard Jackson, the first black mayor of Atlanta, returned to that office with a landslide victory. He succeeded Mayor Andrew Young, who was barred by law from running for a third consecutive term. Jackson served as mayor of the city from 1974 through 1982.

—Art Shell, former offensive lineman with the old Oakand Raiders, was named head coach of the Los Angeles

1989

Raiders and became the first black head coach since 1925.

18 The U.S. Census Bureau said the poverty rate for blacks in 1988 was 31.6 per cent, compared to 10.1 per cent for whites and 26.8 per cent for Hispanics.

21 Businessmen Peter Bynoe and Bertram Lee of the Denver Nuggets of the NBA became the first blacks with a substantial minority ownership interest of a major league sports franchise.

November

1 Frank Robinson named American League manager of the year.

5 Civil Rights Memorial dedicated in Montgomery, Alabama.

7 L. Douglas Wilder elected governor of Virginia and became the first black elected governor of an American state in a statewide canvass. Other notable victories included the election of the first black mayor of New York City (David Dinkins), Seattle (Norman Rice), New Haven, Connecticut (John C. Daniels), and Durham (Chester L. Jenkins). Mike White was elected mayor of Cleveland. Coleman Young, Richard Dixon, and Carrie Saxon Perry were reelected mayor of Detroit, Dayton, Ohio, and Hartford, Connecticut, respectively.

22–27 Air Force Col. Frederick D. Gregory commanded the space shuttle mission *Discovery* and became the first black to lead a space mission.

December

1 Death of Alvin Ailey (58), dancer, choreographer, and director of the Alvin Ailey American Dance Theater, in New York City.

24 Death of Ernest Nathan (Dutch) Morial (60), the first black mayor of New Orleans, in New Orleans.

1990

United States population: 248,709,873. Black population: 29,987,060 (12.1 per cent).

January

1 Death of fashion designer Patrick Kelly (40), in Paris.

8 The National Collegiate Athletic Association revised the controversial Proposition 42, permitting first year student-athletes to receive financial aid based on need and retaining a provision barring first-year sports participation by students failing to meet minimum educational requirements.

13 L. Douglas Wilder of Virginia sworn in as first elected black governor in the United States.

18 Washington, D.C. Mayor Marion S. Barry Jr. arrested by city police and FBI agents who videotaped him smoking crack cocaine in a sting operation. He was later convicted and sentenced to federal prison.

February

2 The Labor Department said the unemployment rate among whites in January was 4.6 per cent, compared to the 11.3 per cent rate among blacks.

3 New Orleans Mayor Sidney Barthelemy reelected to a second term.

23 Bishop College in Dallas, Texas, sold at a bankruptcy auction to businessman Comer J. Cottrell, who said he would try to keep it open as a predominantly black institution.

March

22 A Department of Health and Human Services study said the health gaps between blacks and whites was widening, with an average life expectancy of 69.4 for blacks in 1987, compared with 75.6 for whites. The infant mortality rate for blacks was 17.9 per 1,000 in 1987, compared with 8.6 for whites.

1990

29   The Education Department said enrollment of black students at private colleges and universities rose by 7.1 per cent between 1986 and 1988. In the same time period, black enrollment at public universities and colleges rose by only 0.2 per cent.

April

1   Franklyn G. Jenifer became the fourth black president of Howard University.

17   Death of Rev. Ralph D. Abernathy (64), in Atlanta.

23   Derrick A. Bell Jr., the first black law professor at Howard University, started an unpaid leave of absence to protest the school's failure to appoint a black woman to its tenured faculty. When, in 1992, Bell did not return to the school at the end of the sabbatical, the school fired him.

—Death of Clifton R. Wharton (90), the first black career foreign service officer to reach the ranks of minister and ambassador, of a heart attack in Phoenix, Arizona. He joined the foreign service in 1924 and was appointed ambassador to Norway in 1961.

25   Death of Dexter Gordon (67), tenor saxophone great who won an Academy Award nomination for his role in the jazz film, 'Round Midnight, in Philadelphia.

May

16   Death of entertainer Sammy Davis Jr. (64), in Beverly Hills, California.

June

20–28   U.S. visit of Nelson Mandela, freed South African activist and a leader of the African National Congress, triggers huge turnouts in New York, Boston, Atlanta, Los Angeles, and other cities and raised the level of pride and hope in Black America. The South African leader addressed a joint session of Congress on June 27.

1990

August

7   Former Atlanta Mayor Andrew Young was defeated (62 per cent to 38 per cent) by Lt. Gov. Zell Miller in a runoff for the Georgia Democratic gubernatorial nomination.

27 Death of actor-director Raymond St. Jacques (60), in Los Angeles.

September

8   Marjorie Judith Vincent, a law student from Illinois, crowned Miss America at annual beauty pageant. She succeeded Debbye Turner, the third black named Miss America.

November

6   Two blacks—Gary Franks of Connecticut and William Jefferson of Louisiana—were elected to the House of Representatives and increased the number of blacks in Congress to 25. Franks was the first black Republican elected to Congress since 1932.

—Harvey Gantt, former mayor of Charlotte, North Carolina defeated by incumbent Jesse A. Helms in race for U.S. Senate seat. Helms received 53 per cent of the vote, compared to Gantt's 47 per cent. Observers said Republican Helms ran a racist campaign.

—Arizona voters defeated two propositions that would have established Martin Luther King Jr. Day as a paid holiday for state workers. A number of national groups announced that they would not hold conventions in the state until Arizona established an official holiday honoring the slain civil rights leader.

9   New York City's Freedom National Bank, one of the country's largest black-owned Banks, declared insolvent by federal regulators. The bank, founded in 1965, had 22,000 depositors and $91 million in deposits. The Federal Deposit Insurance Corp. issued refunds to depositors.

1990

15   The U.S. Golf Association followed the lead of the Professional Golfers Association and announced that it would require clubs hosting golf tournaments to ban discrimination against minorities and women.

December

7   North Carolina Democrats elected Daniel T. Blue the first black speaker of a Southern legislature since Reconstruction.

1991

January

16   The Persian Gulf War started with the U.S. attack on Iraq. A disproportionately large number of the U.S. forces engaged were black. Some black leaders criticized the war and the number of black personnel deployed in the Persian Gulf.

March

3   Motorist Rodney G. King beaten by Los Angeles policemen after he was stopped for an alleged speeding violation.

4–5   Airing of videotape of Rodney King beating on national TV sparked national outrage.

8   Detailed breakdown of 1990 census data indicated 30,000,000 blacks, an increase of 13.2 per cent since 1980. The Census Bureau said 77 per cent of the white children and 37 per cent of black children lived in two-parent families. Blacks and other minorities charged that they were undercounted and pressed legal challenges in coordination with some cities and states. On April 18, the bureau reported that four to six million people had been overlooked and that blacks were undercounted 6 per cent more than non-blacks.

21   U.S. Defense Department report said that blacks made up 24.5 per cent of the force in Operation Desert Storm and were 15 per cent of the fatalities.

1991

25   Whoopi Goldberg won Oscar for best supporting actress for her role in *Ghost*. She was the second black woman to win an acting Oscar.

April

15   A posthumous Medal of Honor was awarded to Cpl. Freddie Stowers for heroism in World War I. From the Spanish-American War to the Korean War, black servicemen were denied the highest U.S. military award for racial reasons. In announcing the award, the Army said failure to recognize Stowers and other black servicemen was due to error, not racism.

17–19   African-American and African leaders met in Abidjan, Ivory Coast, in the first Summit Meeting of Africans and African-Americans. The summit, organized by the Rev. Leon H. Sullivan, called for closer ties between Africans and African-Americans and urged Western governments to cancel Africa's foreign debt. "Hold on, Africa!" the Rev. Sullivan said in his keynote speech. "We are coming! Home of our heritage, land of our past, we can help. We have 2 million college graduates in America. We earn $300 billion a year. Three centuries ago they took us away in a boat, but today we have come back in an airplane."

28   Death of civil rights leader Floyd B. McKissick (69), a former director of the Congress of Racial Equality, in Soul City, North Carolina.

May

22   Hal McRae named managed of the Kansas City Royals baseball team and became the fifth black manager in major league history.

28   Death of journalist Ethel L. Payne (79), in Washington, D.C.

June

3   U.S. Supreme Court extended the ban on race-based juror exclusion, ruling in *Edmonson* v. *Leesville Concrete Co.* that potential jurors in civil cases could not be peremptorily challenged on the basis of race alone.

1991

18 Wellington Webb elected the first black mayor of Denver, Colorado.

20 Rep. William H. Gray, the third-ranking Democrat in the House of Representatives and the highest ranking black in Congress, announced that he would resign his position and succeed Christopher Edley as president of the United Negro College Fund.

24 James P. Lyke installed as Roman Catholic archbishop of Atlanta, succeeding Eugene Marino.

27 Justice Thurgood Marshall, 82, the first black on the Supreme Court, announced his retirement after 24 years service, citing "advancing age and medical condition." As chief counsel for the NAACP, Marshall played a major role in the legal fight that led to the *Brown* v. *Board of Education* decision, overturning legal segregation. On June 27, in his final dissent on the Court, Marshall said the court's conservative majority was recklessly overturning decisions protecting the rights of blacks and minorities.

28 Shooting of black suspect by police provoked widespread unrest in black neighborhoods in Miami.

July

1 President Bush nominated black conservative Judge Clarence Thomas of the U.S. District of Columbia Court of Appeals to fill the vacated seat of Thurgood Marshall on the Supreme Court.

10 President Bush unilaterally lifted U.S. trade and investment sanctions against South Africa. The sanctions had been imposed by Congress to pressure the South African government to abandon apartheid. In lifting the sanctions, President Bush said the government had made encouraging moves in that direction. Top Democratic leaders in Congress and black leaders criticized

1991

the move, citing the large number of black political prisoners and the denial of the vote to black South Africans.

17   Death of Roman Catholic Bishop Harold R. Perry (74), the first black Catholic bishop in the 20th century and the first black minister to deliver the opening prayer in Congress, in New Orleans.

August

2   Rep. John Lewis (D-Ga.) named deputy whip of the Democratic majority of the House of Representatives.

19   A Hasidic Jewish driver struck and killed a 7-year-old black, setting off four days of rioting in the Crown Heights section of New York City.

October

3   Willie Herenton, a former superintendent of schools, elected first black mayor of Memphis, Tennessee.

4   The Harold Washington Library Center, the world's largest public circulating library, dedicated in Chicago in memory of the city's first black mayor.

11   Death of comedian Redd Foxx (68), who created the role of Fred Sanford in the TV hit, *Sanford and Son*, of a heart attack on the set of TV series, *The Royal Family*, in Los Angeles.

21   A Federal Reserve Board report said black Americans were twice as likely to be turned down for a mortgage as whites in the same income group.

November

2   Civil rights leader Jesse Jackson announced that he would not seek the 1992 Democratic presidential nomination.

5   Lucien Blackwell won election to fill congressional seat vacated by William H. Gray III.

1991

21 President Bush reversed himself and signed the Compromise Civil Rights Act of 1991, making it easier for workers to sue in job discrimination cases.

1992

January

10 Dennis Green, Stanford University football coach, named coach of the Minnesota Vikings and became the second black coach in the NFL in the modern era.

27 U.S. Supreme Court limited the reach of the 1965 Voting Rights Act.

29 Death of blues singer Willie Dixon (76), composer of "Hoochie Koochie Man," "My Babe," and other numbers, in Burbank, California.

February

1 U.S. officials started forcibly repatriating Haitian refugees picked up at sea while fleeing their homeland. Black leaders and high-ranking white Democrats said the policy was racist.

7 The Labor Department announced that the unemployment rate of black workers increased to 13.7 per cent from 12.7 per cent.

10 Death of Alex Haley (70), Pulitzer Prize-winning author of *Roots*, of a heart attack, in Seattle. Television mini-series based on the book set TV record. Haley also authored with Malcolm X *The Autobiography of Malcolm X*. He played a major role in creating national passion for genealogy.

—Former heavyweight boxing champion Mike Tyson convicted of raping an 18-year-old Miss Black America beauty contestant in Indianapolis. He was later sentenced to six years in prison. Tyson and his defense attorney said he was innocent and that the potential

1992

jury pool didn't reflect the racial composition of the
county. The verdict was appealed.

15 NAACP Director Benjamin L. Hooks announced that
he would retire in 1993. He had headed the organization since 1977.

17 Gov. Zell Miller named Fulton County Superior Court
Judge Leah Sears-Collins to the state supreme court.
She was the first woman to sit on the court.

26 Death of Marguerite R. Barnett (49), the first black
woman to head a major white university, in Wailuku,
Hawaii. She became president of the University of
Houston in 1990.

April

16 Philadelphia Police Chief Willie L. Williams named
chief of the Los Angeles Police Department.

23 Former Washington, D.C. Mayor Marion S. Barry Jr.
released from federal prison in Loretto, Pa., after serving six-month sentence for cocaine possession.

29 A superior court jury in the Los Angeles suburb of Simi
Valley acquitted four white policemen who were videotaped beating motorist Rodney King. Within hours, rioting broke out in the South Central section of Los
Angeles and spread to other areas of the city. The National Guard and federal troops were mobilized to deal
with the rebellion, which lasted several days and cost
the lives of 58 persons. Authorities said it was the
largest urban riot since the Civil War. There were also
demonstrations and riots in other American cities.

30 The last episode of *The Cosby Show*, one of the most
influential shows in TV history, ran on NBC-TV.

May

13 Death of singer Mary Wells (49), who helped popularize
Motown songs, in Los Angeles.

1992

June

18   U.S. Supreme Court ruled in *Georgia* v. *McCollum* that defendants in criminal cases could not bar potential jurors solely on the basis of race.

22   U.S. Supreme Court ruled 5–4 that a St. Paul, Minn., law that made it a crime to engage in inflammatory racist or sexist speech was unconstitutional.

26   Willie L. Williams, former Philadelphia police chief, became chief of the Los Angeles Police Department.

26   U.S. Supreme Court ruled, 8–1, that so-called race neutral policies did not relieve the state of Mississippi of its obligation to eliminate segregation in the public university system. Some educators said that the decision threatened the existence of historically black public colleges.

July

6   *Waiting To Exhale*, Terry McMillan's blockbuster novel, listed on *Publishers Weekly* bestsellers list. Three black women novelists—Toni Morrison, Alice Walker, and Terry McMillan—created a sensation by moving onto *The New York Times* bestseller list and jointly holding sway for three weeks.

23   The Census Bureau announced that the gap between the median income of white households and black households narrowed slightly in the 1980s. The median income for blacks in 1989, the bureau said, was $19,758 or 63 per cent of the $31,435 median income of whites. In 1979, blacks had earned 62 per cent of the white median income. The study also showed measurable gains in the proportion of blacks over age 25 who had graduated from high school. The proportion increased from 31.4 per cent in 1970, to 51.2 per cent in 1980, to 63.1 per cent in 1990. The proportion of blacks with college degrees increased from 8.4 per cent in 1980 to 11.4 per cent in 1990.

1992

August

5 The U.S. Attorney's office in Los Angeles announced that a federal grand jury had indicted the four white police officers acquitted in Simi Valley on federal charges of violating the civil rights of Rodney King.

25 Death of actor Frederick O'Neal (86), the first black president of Actors' Equity Association, in New York.

September

24 Tom Bradley announced that he would not seek a sixth term as mayor of Los Angeles.

October

5 Death of singer Eddie Kendricks (52), tenor with the Temptations, in Birmingham.

8 Nobel Prize for literature awarded to Derek Walcott, a West Indian-born poet and playwright living in America.

22 Death of actor Cleavon Little (53), who starred in the movie *Blazing Saddles* and received a Tony for the title role in the musical *Purlie*, in Sherman Oaks, California.

November

3 The conservative Reagan-Bush years ended with the election of Arkansas Gov. Bill Clinton as the 42nd president of the United States. Black voters, who represented 8 per cent of the total vote, were the margins of victory in key states, giving Clinton 82 per cent of their votes, compared to 11 percent for George Bush and 7 per cent for Ross Perot. The Joint Center for Political and Economic Studies said black voters alone provided the Clinton margin of victory in states like Georgia and New Jersey.

Other electoral news:

Carol Moseley-Braun of Illinois defeated a white male opponent and became the first black woman and the first black Democrat in the U.S. Senate.

Sixteen new House members—eleven men and five

1992

women—brought the total number of blacks in Congress to a historic high of 40. Among the new House members were the first post-Reconstruction representatives from Alabama (Earl Hilliard), Florida (Corrine Brown, Alcee Hastings, and Carrie Meek), North Carolina (Eva Clayton and Melvin Watt), South Carolina (Jim Clyburn), and Virginia (Bobby Scott).

Pamela Carter elected attorney general of Indiana.

Jackie Barret of Fulton County (Atlanta), Georgia became the first black woman sheriff.

6 President-elect Bill Clinton named Vernon E. Jordan Jr. chairman of his transition team, making him the first black American to head the transition team of a U.S. president. The president-elect also named a black woman, Alexis Herman, deputy director of the transition team.

18 Spike Lee's epic movie *Malcolm X* opened to generally favorable reviews.

December

2 President-elect Bill Clinton asked poet Maya Angelou to compose and read a poem at his January Inauguration.

12 President-elect Clinton named National Democratic Chairman Ronald H. (Ron) Brown, 51, secretary of commerce. He was later confirmed by the Senate and became the first black to hold that position.

17 President-elect Clinton named Jesse Brown, 48, a Vietnam War veteran and the director of the Disabled Veterans of America, secretary of veterans affairs. He was later confirmed and became the first black to hold that position.

21 President-elect Clinton named Hazel R. O'Leary, 55, a Minnesota Power Company executive, secretary of energy. She was later confirmed and became the first black and the first woman to hold that position.

1992

22 President-elect Clinton named educator/businessman Clifton R. Wharton Jr., 67, undersecretary of state, the highest position held by a black in that department.

24 President-elect Clinton named Rep. Mike Espy, 39, (D-Miss.), secretary of agriculture. He was later confirmed and became the first black to hold that position.

Black Firsts

Beginnings

The first black Americans were the twenty blacks who arrived at Jamestown, Virginia, "about the latter end of August" in 1619. Surviving evidence indicates that the first black settlers were not slaves. It appears from the record that they were assigned the same status—indentured servitude—as most of the first white immigrants. At the time of the first detailed census in 1624–25, the twenty-three blacks in Virginia—eleven males, ten females, and two children—constituted some 2 per cent of the total population of 1227. Among the blacks identified by name were Angelo, Edward, Antonio, Mary and John Pedro.

The first black born in America, a boy named William, was delivered in 1623 or 1624. In an early edition of J. C. Hotten's *Lists of Emigrants to America* the first black family is identified as "ANTONEY Negro; ISABELL Negro; and WILLIAM theire Child Baptised."

The first general institution organized and managed by blacks was probably the Free African Society of Philadelphia, founded on April 12, 1787, by Richard Allen and Absalom Jones and their followers. W.E.B. Du Bois called the organization "the first wavering step of a people toward organized social life."

The first settler in Chicago was Jean Baptiste Pointe DuSable, a black trader and trapper, who built the first house on the banks of the Chicago River in the 1770s.

At least twenty-six of the forty-four founding fathers and mothers of Los Angeles were descendants of Africans. Among the black founders, according to H. H. Bancroft's *History of California*, were "Joseph Moreno, Mulatto, 22 years old, wife a Mulattress, five children; Manuel Cameron, Mulatto, 30 years old, wife Mulattress: Antonio Mesa, Negro, 38 years old, wife, Mulattress, six children; Jose Antonio Navarro, Mestizo, 42 years old, wife, Mulattress, three children; Basil Rosas, Indian, 68 years old, wife, Mulattress, six children."

The first black Masonic lodge was African Lodge No. 459, which was organized in Boston on May 6, 1787, with Prince Hall as Master.

The first national black convention met at Philadelphia's Bethel African Methodist Episcopal Church on September 20, 1830. There were thirty-eight delegates from eight states. Richard Allen was elected president.

The first Negro History Week was celebrated in the second week of February, 1926. Dr. Carter G. Woodson organized the celebration "to include the birthday of [Abraham] Lincoln and the generally accepted birthday of [Frederick] Douglass."

The first performance of *Lift Ev'ry Voice and Sing*, widely regarded as the Black National Anthem, occurred on February 12, 1900, at a celebration of Abraham Lincoln's birthday. The song was written especially for the occasion by James Weldon Johnson and his brother, J. Rosamond Johnson. Johnson said later that he did not use pen and paper in composing the last two stanzas. "While my brother worked at his musical setting I paced back and forth on the front porch, repeating the lines over and over to myself, going through all the agony and ecstasy of creating. As I worked through the opening and middle lines of the last stanza:

> God of our weary years,
> God of our silent tears,
> Thou who hast brought us thus far on our way,
> Thou who hast by Thy might
> Led us into the light,
> Keep us forever in the path, we pray;
> Lest our feet stray from the places, our God,
>   where we met Thee,
> Lest, our hearts drunk with the wine of the world,
>   we forget Thee. . . .

I could not keep back the tears, and made no effort to do so." The anthem was sung for the first time by a chorus of five hundred schoolchildren.

The first black secretary of the National Association for the Advancement of Colored People was James Weldon Johnson, who was appointed to the position on November 6, 1920. He was preceded by three white women (Mary White Ovington, Frances Blascoer and Mary Childs Nerney) and two white men (Royal Nash and John R. Shillady).

The first black president of a major American foundation was Franklin Thomas, who was named president of the Ford Foundation on January 30, 1979.

Politics

The first black elected to public office was Alexander Lucius Twilight, who was sent to the Vermont legislature in 1836 by the voters of Orleans County. The second known black official was William A. Leidesdorf, who was named sub-consul to the Mexican territory of Yerba Buena (San Francisco) in October, 1845. In September, 1847, Leidesdorf was elected to the San Francisco town council, receiving the third highest vote. He became the town treasurer in 1848 and served on the three-man committee that established San Francisco's first school. Another pioneer public official was John Mercer Langston, who was elected clerk of Brownhelm township, Lorain County, Ohio, in the spring of 1855. In 1856 he was elected clerk of the township of Russia, near Oberlin. In 1857 he was elected to the council of the incorporated village of Oberlin. From 1871 to 1878 Langston was president of the Board of Health of Washington, D.C. In 1889 he was elected to the U.S. Congress from Virginia.

The first black diplomat and the first black to receive a major government appointment was Ebenezer Don Carlos Bassett, principal of the Institute for Colored Youth, Philadelphia, who was named minister to Haiti on April 6, 1869, by President Grant.

The first black to receive a major government appointment in the United States was Frederick Douglass, who was named U.S. marshal of the District of Columbia on March 18, 1877. After a bitter fight he was confirmed by the Senate, 30-12.

The first black to head a major agency of the U.S. government was Robert C. Weaver, who was sworn in as administrator of the Housing and Home Finance Agency on February 11, 1961.

The first black cabinet member was Robert C. Weaver, who was named secretary of the Department of Housing and Urban Development by President Johnson. He was sworn in on January 18, 1966. The second black cabinet member was William T. Coleman, who was named secretary of transportation on January 14, 1975, by President Ford. Patricia Roberts Harris, the first black woman cabinet member, was the first black to hold two cabinet posts. She was secretary of housing and urban development and secretary of health, education and welfare in the Carter administration.

The first black named to an executive position in the White House was E. Frederic Morrow, who was appointed administrative aide to President Eisenhower on July 9, 1955.

The first black governor of the Federal Reserve Board was Andrew F. Brimmer, who was named to the position on February 26, 1966, by President Johnson.

The first blacks to confer with an American president on a matter of public policy met with Abraham Lincoln on August 14, 1862. The meeting ended in controversy after the president urged black Americans to emigrate to Africa or Central America.

The first black accredited to an African country was J. Milton Turner of Missouri, who was named minister to Liberia on March 1, 1871.

The first black to head a U.S. embassy in Europe was Clifton R. Wharton Sr., who was confirmed as minister to Rumania on February 5, 1958. He was later (March 9, 1961) named ambassador to Norway.

The first black United Nations Ambassador was Andrew Young, who was named to the post by President Carter. Ambassador Young was confirmed on January 26, 1977.

The first black named to the U.S. delegation to the United Nations was Chicago Atty. Edith S. Sampson, who became an alternate delegate on August 24, 1950. She was appointed by President Truman.

The first black named a permanent delegate to the United Nations was Charles Mahoney, a Detroit insurance executive, who was appointed by President Eisenhower and confirmed by the Senate on August 7, 1954.

The first black ambassador in the U.S. delegation to the UN was Franklin H. Williams, who was appointed to the Economic and Social Council on June 26, 1964, by President Johnson.

The first black U.S. senator was Hiram Rhodes Revels, who was elected to the Forty-first Congress to fill the unexpired term of Jefferson Davis. Senator Revels was elected by the Mississippi legislature on January 20, 1870, and was seated on February 25, 1870. He was the first black in Congress.

The first black to serve a full term as a U.S. senator was Blanche Kelso Bruce of Mississippi, who entered Congress on March 5, 1875.

The first black elected to the U.S. Senate by popular vote was Edward W. Brooke (Republican, Mass.), who won the general election on Nov. 8, 1966.

The first black elected to Congress was John Willis Menard, who defeated a white candidate, 5,107 to 2,833, on November 3, 1868, in a contest to fill an unexpired term in the Second Congressional District of Louisiana. Menard's victory was contested and he was not seated, primarily because of the general belief "that it was too early to admit a Negro to the U.S. Congress." Menard pleaded his own case on February 27, 1869, and became the first black to speak on the floor of the House.

The first black in the House of Representatives was Joseph H. Rainey of South Carolina, who was seated on December 12, 1870.

The first black congressman from the North was Oscar DePriest, who was elected to the Seventy-first Congress from Illinois's First Congressional District (Chicago) on November 6, 1928. He was sworn in on April 15, 1929.

The first black Democrat elected to Congress was Arthur Mitchell, who defeated DePriest on November 7, 1934.

The first black congressman from the East was Adam Clayton Powell Jr., who was elected to the Seventy-ninth Congress from Harlem on August 1, 1944.

The first black congressman from the West was Augustus F. Hawkins, who was elected to the Eighty-eighth Congress from Los Angeles on November 6, 1962.

The first black congressman from the Deep South in the twentieth century was Andrew Young, who was elected to the Ninety-third Congress from Georgia on November 7, 1972.

The youngest black congressman was John R. Lynch of Mississippi, who entered the House of Representatives in 1873 at the age of twenty-six.

The first black to preside over the U.S. Senate was Blanche K. Bruce, who was called to the chair on February 14, 1879, and on May 4, 1880.

The first black to preside over the House of Representatives was Rep. Joseph H. Rainey of South Carolina, who was called to the Speaker's chair in May, 1874, during debate on legislation dealing with American Indians. The next day the headline in the *New York Herald* said: "A Liberated Slave in the Speaker's Chair."

The first black to head a congressional committee was Blanche K. Bruce, who was made chairman of a select committee on Mississippi River levees in the Forty-fifth Congress (1877–79).

The first black to head a standing committee of Congress was Rep. William L. Dawson of Chicago, who was named chairman of the House Expenditures Committee on January 18, 1949. Rep. Adam Clayton Powell Jr. was named chairman of the powerful House Education and Labor Committee in 1961.

The first black to preside over a national political convention was John R. Lynch, who was elected temporary chairman of the Republican convention in June, 1884.

The first black cochairperson of a national political convention was California Assemblywoman Yvonne Brathwaite Burke, who was named (June 24) cochairman of the Democratic convention of 1972.

The first black keynoter of a national political convention was Rep. Barbara Jordan of Texas, who made the main address on July 12 at the Democratic convention of 1976.

The first black nominated for president at a major national convention was Rev. Channing E. Phillips of Washington, D.C., who was a favorite-son candidate of the District of Columbia and received 67½ votes on the first ballot at the Democratic convention on August 28, 1968.

The first black chairman of a major Democratic organization was J. Raymond Jones, who was elected leader of the New York Democratic organization (Tammany Hall) on December 3, 1964.

The first black governor was P. B. S. Pinchback, who became governor of Louisiana on December 9, 1872, on the impeachment of Governor H. C. Warmoth. A contemporary newspaper report said Justice J. C. Taliaferro of the state supreme court administered the oath of office in an "impressive voice, while the by-standers stood with uncovered heads, and P. B. S. Pinchback was then governor in place of H. C. Warmoth." Pinchback relinquished the office on January 13, 1873, saying at the inauguration of the new governor: "I now have the honor to formally surrender the office of governor, with the hope that you will administer the government in the interests of all the people [and that] your administration will be as fair toward the class that I represent, as mine has been toward the class represented by you."

The first black governor of the Virgin Islands was William H. Hastie, who was inaugurated on May 7, 1946.

The first black lieutenant governor was Oscar J. Dunn, a former slave, who was formally installed in Louisiana on July 13, 1868.

The first black lieutenant governors in the twentieth century were Mervyn M. Dymally of California and George L. Brown of Colorado, who were elected on November 5, 1974.

The first black state legislators in the post-Civil War period were Edward G. Walker and Charles L. Mitchell, who were elected to the lower house of the Massachusetts legislature from Boston in 1866.

The first black named president pro tem of a state senate was P. B. S. Pinchback, who was elected by the Louisiana senate in 1871.

The first black named president pro tem of a state senate in the twentieth century was Cecil Partee, who was elected by the Illinois senate on January 6, 1971.

The first black named Speaker of a state legislature was John R. Lynch of Mississippi, who was elected in January, 1872, at the age of twenty-four.

The first black named Speaker of a state legislature in the twentieth century was the Rev. S. Howard Woodson, who was elected by the New Jersey Assembly on December 10, 1973. K. Leroy Irvis was named Speaker of the Pennsylvania Assembly on May 23, 1977. Willie L. Brown was elected Speaker of the California Assembly on December 1, 1980.

The first American legislature with a black majority was the South Carolina General Assembly that met in Janney's Hall, Columbia, on July 6, 1868, with eighty-five black legislators and seventy white legislators.

The first black elected to a state cabinet office was Francis L. Cardozo, who was installed as secretary of state in Columbia, S.C., on July 9, 1868.

The first black elected to a state cabinet post in the twentieth century was Otis M. Smith, who won a statewide contest for auditor in Michigan on November 8, 1960. Edward W. Brooke won the general election for attorney general of Massachusetts and Gerald Lamb was elected treasurer of Connecticut on November 6, 1962. Five other blacks won statewide elective offices in the 1970s: Richard H. Austin, secretary of state, Michigan, 1970; Wilson C. Riles, superintendent of public instruction, California, 1970; Henry E. Parker, treasurer, Connecticut, 1974; Roland W. Burris, comptroller, Illinois, 1978; Vel R. Phillips, secretary of state, Wisconsin, 1978.

The first black mayor is an unknown soldier. There were several sheriffs and mayors in the South during the Reconstruction period. One of the first black mayors was Robert H. Wood, who was elected mayor of Natchez, Miss., in December, 1870.

The first black mayors of major cities in the twentieth century were Carl B. Stokes of Cleveland, Ohio, and Richard G. Hatcher of Gary, Indiana. They were elected on November 7, 1967. Mayor Stokes was inaugurated on November 13 and became the first black mayor of a major American city.

The first black to hold a major elective position in a major American City was Hulan Jack, who was sworn in as Manhattan Borough president on December 31, 1953.

The first black mayor of a major Southern city was Maynard Jackson, who was elected in Atlanta on October 16, 1973. Henry L. Marsh was elected mayor of Richmond on March 8, 1977, and Ernest W. Morial was elected mayor of New Orleans on November 12, 1977. Richard Arrington was elected mayor of Birmingham on October 30, 1979.

Entertainment

The first black drama group, the African Company, produced plays at the African Grove in New York City in the 1820s.

The first black *Othello* was probably James Hewlett, who played the role in productions of the African Company in 1821. The first black to win international renown as *Othello* was Ira Aldridge who opened at Covent Garden in the title role on April 10, 1833. The 1945 New York production of *Othello*, starring Paul Robeson, ran for 296 performances and set a record for Shakespearean drama on Broadway.

The first Broadway production with an all-black company was John W. Isham's 1896 production of *Oriental America*.

The first black musical comedy produced, directed and managed by blacks was Bob Cole's *A Trip to Coontown*, which opened in New York in 1898 and ran for three seasons.

The first black superstar was Bert Williams, who was also the first black star of an otherwise all-white Broadway production, the Ziegfeld *Follies* of 1910.

The first black female superstar with an international following was Florence Mills, who starred in the 1924 production of *Dixie to Broadway*, which has been called "the first real revue by Negroes." She died at the height of her fame on November 1, 1927.

The first black actor to achieve stardom in America in serious roles was Charles Gilpin, who played the title role in the 1921 production of *Emperor Jones*.

The first Broadway play by a black writer was the 1923 production of Willis Richardson's *The Chipwoman's Fortune*. Garland Anderson's *Appearances* was produced in 1925.

The first Broadway play by a black writer to win the New York Drama Critics Award as the best play of the year was Lorraine Hansberry's *Raisin in the Sun* (1960).

The first black recording artists were probably Bert Williams and George Walker, who cut several numbers for the Victor Talking Machine Company on October 11, 1901.

The first published blues number was W. C. Handy's *Memphis Blues*, which went on sale in Memphis, Tenn., on September 27, 1912.

The first black film was *The Railroad Porter*, a 1912 comedy directed by Bill Foster, a pioneer black filmmaker.

The first black movie production company was the Lincoln Motion Picture Company, which was founded in Los Angeles in 1915 by two black actors, Clarence Brooks and Noble Johnson, black druggist James T. Smith and a white camerman, Harry Grant.

The first full-length black film was *Birthright,* produced and directed in 1918 by pioneer filmmaker Oscar Micheaux.

The first feature-length black Hollywood films were *Hearts in Dixie,* a 1929 production which has been called "the first real talking picture," and *Hallelujah,* a 1929 movie which starred Daniel Haynes and Nina Mae McKinney.

The first black actor in a full-length Hollywood film was Sam Lucas, who played the role of Tom in the 1914 film *Uncle Tom's Cabin.*

The first modern film produced by a black was Harry Belafonte's *Odds Against Tomorrow* (1959).

The first film with a script by black writers (Langston Hughes and Clarence Muse) was *Way Down South* (1939).

The first modern film directed by a black was Gordon Parks's *The Learning Tree* (1969).

The first black honored by the Motion Picture Academy was Hattie McDaniel, who received an Oscar in 1940 for her supporting role in *Gone with the Wind,* which was criticized by blacks for its distortion of history and the black personality.

The first black to receive an Academy Award for best actor of the year was Sidney Poitier, who was cited in 1963 for his performance in *Lilies of the Field.*

The first black to perform with an American opera company was Caterina Jarboro, who was featured in a Chicago Opera Company production of *Aida* at the New York Hippodrome on July 22, 1933. She also sang the title role of the opera in Milan, Italy, in May, 1930. La Julia Rhea sang the role of *Aida* in a major production of the Chicago Opera on December 26, 1937. Also featured in that production was William Franklin.

The first black signed by the Metropolitan Opera was Marian Anderson, who appeared as Ulrica in Verdi's *Masked Ball* on January 7, 1955.

The first black musicial director of an American orchestra was Henry Lewis, who was named director of the New Jersey Symphony on February 15, 1968.

The first black with his own network radio show was Nat King Cole. The show ran for seventy-eight weeks in 1945–46 on NBC radio and was sponsored by a hair tonic manufacturer.

The first black with his own network TV show was Nat King Cole. *The Nat King Cole Show* ran for sixty-four weeks in 1956-57 on NBC-TV.

Sports

The first black in major league baseball was Moses Fleetwood Walker, who was a catcher on the Toledo team of the American Association in 1884.

The first black in the major leagues in the modern era was Jackie Robinson, who joined the Brooklyn Dodgers on April 10, 1947. Robinson played his first major league game against the Boston Braves at Brooklyn's Ebbets field on April 15, 1947. Larry Doby joined the Cleveland Indians on July 6 and became the first black player in the American League. Three other blacks were signed by major league teams in 1947; Dan Bankhead, the first pitcher in the major leagues, Brooklyn Dodgers; Willard Brown, outfielder, St. Louis Browns; Henry Thompson, infielder, St. Louis Browns.

The first black players in a World Series were Jackie Robinson and Dan Bankhead, who played with the Brooklyn Dodgers in the 1947 play-offs against the New York Yankees.

The first black enshrined in the Baseball Hall of Fame was Jackie Robinson (1962).

The first black college basketball teams, according to Edwin B. Henderson's *The Negro In Sports*, were fielded in 1909 and 1910 by Lincoln (Pa.), Virginia Union, Hampton and Wilberforce.

The first black selected for All-American basketball honors was Don Barksdale of UCLA (1947).

The first black signed by a National Basketball Association team was Charles ("Chuck") Cooper, who signed a contract with the Boston Celtics in April, 1950. The New York Knickerbockers signed Nat ("Sweetwater") Clifton later in the same year.

The first black world champion in boxing was George Dixon, who won the bantamweight title on June 27, 1890, defeating Nunc Wallace in the eighteenth round.

The first black heavyweight boxing champion was Jack Johnson, who won the title on December 26, 1908, defeating Tommy Burns in the fourteenth round in Sydney, Australia.

The first black middleweight champion was Tiger Flowers, who won the title in New York on February 26, 1926, defeating Harry Greb in fifteen rounds.

The first black welterweight champion was Joe Walcott, who won the title at Fort Erie, Ontario, on December 18, 1901, defeating Rube Ferns in five rounds.

The first black lightweight champion was Joe Gans, who won the title at Fort Erie on May 12, 1902, by knocking out Frank Erne in the first round.

The first black college football game was played on Thanksgiving Day, 1892, by Biddle University (now Johnson C. Smith University) and Livingstone College. Biddle won by a score of 4–0. At least four black colleges fielded football teams in 1894: Howard, Lincoln (Pa.), Tuskegee and Atlanta University.

The first black player in professional football was Fritz Pollard, who played for the Akron Indians of the American Professional Football League in 1919. Blacks played on professional teams until the 1930s.

The first black player in professional football in the modern era was Kenny Washington, who was signed by the Los Angeles Rams on March 21, 1946. On May 7, 1946, the Rams signed a second star, Woody Strode. Two other blacks were signed in the same year by the Cleveland Browns: Ben Willis (August 6, 1946) and Marion Motley (August 9, 1946).

The first black All-American from a major college was William H. Lewis of Harvard, who was selected as the center on Walter Camp's 1892 and 1893 teams. Paul Robeson of Rutgers was selected as the end on Camp's 1917 and 1918 teams.

The first black to win the Heisman Trophy as the football player of the year was Ernest Davis of Syracuse, who was cited in 1961.

The first black elected to the Football Hall of Fame was Emlen Tunnell, defensive back, New York Giants (1967).

The first black to win a major professional golf tournament was Charles Sifford, who won the Long Beach (Calif.) Open on November 10, 1957.

The first black to play in the Masters Tournament at Augusta, Ga., was Lee Elder, who was invited in April, 1975.

The first players to win the American Tennis Association championship were Tally Holmes of Washington and Lucy Stone of Baltimore, who won the men's and women's titles, respectively, at Druid Hill Park in Baltimore on August, 1917.

The first black to win a nationally recognized tennis title was Lorraine Williams, who won the junior girls' championship in 1953.

The first black to win a major tennis title was Althea Gibson, who won the (women's singles title) French Open on May 26, 1956. On September 8, 1957, she became the first black to win a major U.S. national championship, defeating Louise Brough at Forest Hills for the women's singles title. Arthur Ashe won the

U.S. amateur men's singles championship on August 25, 1968.
Ashe was also the first player to win the U.S. Open champion-
ship, defeating Tom Okker on September 9, 1968, at Forest Hills
Stadium in New York.

The first black to win a Wimbledon championship was Althea
Gibson, who captured the women's singles title on July 6, 1957.
Arthur Ashe won the men's singles championship on July 5, 1975,
defeating Jimmy Connors.

The first black jockey—and the first jockey—to win the Kentucky Derby was Oliver Lewis, who won the first race in 1875.
Thirteen of the fourteen jockeys in the first race were black.

The first jockey to win the Kentucky Derby three times was
Isaac Murphy, who was victorious in 1884, 1890 and 1891.

The first black to compete in the Olympics was George Poage
of the Milwaukee Athletic Club, who ran in the 400-meter race
and the 400-meter hurdles in the 1904 games in St. Louis.

The first black to win an Olympic gold medal was DeHart
Hubbard of the University of Michigan, who won the broad jump
with a leap of 24 feet 5½ inches on July 8, 1924, in Paris.

The first black coach of a major professional team was Fritz
Pollard, who was player-coach of the Akron Indians in 1919. He
coached the team to the world professional championship in 1920.

The first black coach of a predominantly white professional
team in the modern era was John McLendon, who coached the
Cleveland Pipers in the American Basketball League in the
1961–62 season.

The first black coach of a major, predominantly white professional team was Bill Russell, who was signed by the Boston Celtics basketball team on April 18, 1966.

The first black manager of a major league baseball team was
Frank Robinson, who was named manager of the Cleveland In-
dians in 1975. In 1978 Larry Doby was named manager of the
Chicago White Sox.

The first black coach of a major league baseball team was John ("Buck") O'Neil, who was signed by the Chicago Cubs in 1962.

The first black (assistant) coach in the National Football League was Emlen Tunnell, who was signed by the New York Giants on May 1, 1963.

The first black coach to win more than two hundred games was the legendary A. J. ("Jake") Gaither of Florida A&M, who had a career record of 203 victories.

Religion

The first black churches were established in the Revolutionary War period in South Carolina, Georgia and Virginia. Some authorities believe the first black church was a Baptist church established between 1773 and 1775 at Silver Bluff, S.C., across the Savannah River from Augusta, Georgia.

The first black churches in the North were the African Church of St. Thomas and Bethel AME Church. The African Church of St. Thomas was dedicated on July 17, 1794. On August 12, 1794, the St. Thomas parishioners joined the Protestant Episcopal Church. Bethel AME Church of Philadelphia was dedicated, according to Richard Allen, in July, 1794. There are indications in the *Journal and Letters of Francis Asbury* that the Bethel dedication occurred in June, 1794.

The first black minister certified by a predominantly white denomination was Lemuel Haynes, who was licensed to preach in the Congregational Church on November 29, 1780. Haynes was also the first black pastor of a white church. In 1785 he was ordained and named pastor of a white church in Torrington, Connecticut. In 1787 he was called to a white church in Rutland, Vermont. Another pioneer minister, Absalom Jones, was ordained as a priest in the Episcopal Church in September, 1804.

The first black bishop was Richard Allen, who was elected at a general convention of the African Methodist Episcopal Church in Philadelphia on April 10, 1816. James Varick was elected bishop of the African Methodist Episcopal Zion Church on July 30, 1822.

The first black bishop of a predominantly white denomination was James A. Healy, who was consecrated bishop of the Roman Catholic diocese of Maine on June 2, 1875. The first black Roman Catholic bishop in the twentieth century was Harold R. Perry, who was consecrated in New Orleans on January 6, 1966. On January 28, 1973, Joseph L. Howze was named auxiliary bishop of Mississippi.

The first black president of the United Church of Christ was Dr. Joseph H. Evans, who was elected leader of the predominantly white church group on October 30, 1976.

The first black bishop to head an Episcopal diocese in America was John M. Burgess, who was installed as bishop of Massachusetts on January 17, 1970. On September 24, 1977, John T. Walker was installed as the sixth bishop of the Episcopal diocese of Washington, D.C.

The first black Methodist bishops to head predominantly white districts were Prince A. Taylor, who was elected bishop of New Jersey on June 25, 1964, and James Thomas, who was elected bishop of Iowa on July 10, 1964. In 1973 Bishop Charles Franklin Golden was elected president of the Council of Bishops of the Methodist Episcopal Church.

The first black moderator of the United Presbyterian Church was Dr. Edler Garnet Hawkins, who was elected on May 21, 1964.

The first black president of the predominantly white American Baptist convention was Thomas Kilgore Jr., who was elected at the annual convention in Boston on May 17, 1969.

The first black president of the National Council of Churches was the Reverend W. Sterling Cary, who was elected on December 7, 1972.

Judiciary

The first black judge was Jonathan Jasper Wright, who was elected by the General Assembly to the South Carolina Supreme Court on February 1, 1870, to fill an unexpired term. He was elected on December 9, 1870, to a full six-year term.

The first black judge on the municipal level was Macon B. Allen—the first black lawyer—who was elected judge of the Inferior Court of Charleston by the South Carolina General Assembly on November 26, 1872. Mifflin W. Gibbs was elected city judge of Little Rock, Ark., in 1873.

The first black Supreme Court justice was Thurgood Marshall, who was nominated by President Johnson and confirmed by the Senate on August 30, 1967.

The first black federal judge was William H. Hastie, who was confirmed as judge of the Federal District Court of the Virgin Islands on March 26, 1937.

The first black federal judge in the continental United States was James B. Parsons, who was named to the Federal District Court of Northern Illinois on August 9, 1961, by President Kennedy. On April 18, 1975, Judge Parsons was named chief judge of the court. Wade H. McCree Jr. was sworn in as a federal district judge in Michigan on October 9, 1961.

The first black on the U.S. Circuit Court of Appeals was William H. Hastie, who was nominated by President Truman on October 15, 1949.

The first black justice of a state supreme court in the twentieth century was Otis Milton Smith, who was named to the Michigan court on October 10, 1961. He was elected to a full term on November 6, 1962.

Professions

The first black physician was James Derham, who was born in slavery in 1767. Derham mastered the profession while assisting his physician master. In 1783 he bought his freedom and established a large practice among blacks and whites. By 1788 he was one of the leading physicians in New Orleans. Dr. Benjamin Rush, a nationally known physician, said: "I have conversed with him upon most of the acute and epidemic diseases of the country where he lives. I expected to have suggested some new medicines to him, but he suggested many more to me."

The first black to graduate from an American medical college was probably James Hall, who received a degree from the Medical College of Maine in 1822.

The first black admitted to a medical society was John V. De Grasse, who was inducted into the Massachusetts Medical Society in 1854.

The first black lawyer was Macon B. Allen, who practiced in Maine in 1843 and 1844 and was formally admitted to the bar after he passed the examination at Worcester, Massachusetts, on May 3, 1845.

The first black lawyer admitted to practice before the U.S. Supreme Court was John S. Rock of Massachusetts, who was certified by the court on February 1, 1865.

The first successful operation on the human heart was performed at Chicago's Provident Hospital on July 9, 1893, by Dr. Daniel Hale Williams.

The first black to graduate from an American school of dentistry was Robert Tanner Freeman, who received a degree from Harvard University in 1867. Several blacks practiced the profession in the eighteenth and nineteenth centuries without formal certification.

Education

The first black to receive a degree from an American college was Lemuel Haynes, who was awarded an honorary M.A. at the second commencement of Middlebury College in 1804.

The first black college graduate was probably Alexander Lucius Twilight, who received a bachelor's degree from Middlebury College in 1823. Twilight, who was not prominently identified with black causes, was an educator and politician. Edward A. Jones received a B.A. degree at Amherst College on August 23, 1826. John B. Russwurm graduated from Bowdoin College on September 6, 1826.

The first black to receive a Ph.D. degree was Patrick Francis Healy, who passed the final examinations at Louvain in Belgium on July 26, 1865.

The first black to receive a Ph.D. degree from an American university was Edward A. Bouchet, who was awarded a degree in physics at Yale University in 1876. Bouchet, the principal of a high school in Galliopolis, Ohio, died in 1918.

The first black inducted into Phi Beta Kappa was Edward A. Bouchet, who was inducted at Yale University in 1874.

The first black colleges were the Cheyney State Training School (Pa.), established in 1837; Avery College (Pa.), established in 1849; Lincoln University (Pa.), established in 1854; Wilberforce University, established in 1856.

The first black president of the major denominational schools established after the Civil War was John Hope, who was elected president of Morehouse College in June, 1906. The first black president of Howard University was Mordecai Johnson, who was elected on June 20, 1926. Dr. Charles S. Johnson became the first black president of Fisk on November 1, 1946.

The first black president of a predominantly white university was Patrick Francis Healy, S.J., who was inaugurated at Georgetown University, the oldest Catholic university in America, on July 31, 1874.

The first black president of a major, predominantly white university in the twentieth century was Clifton R. Wharton Jr., who was named president of Michigan State University on October 17, 1969. In 1978 Wharton became chancellor of the State University of New York.

The first black professor at a predominantly white university was Charles L. Reason, who was named professor of belles lettres and French at Central College, McGrawville, N.Y., in 1849. In 1873 Richard T. Greener, the first black graduate of Harvard University, was named professor of metaphysics at the University of South Carolina.

The first black to head a predominantly white academic association was E. Franklin Frazier, who was elected president of the American Sociological Society in 1948.

The first black Rhodes scholar was Alain L. Locke, who was selected in 1907. The second black Rhodes scholar, Joseph Stanley Sanders, was not selected until 1960.

Military

The first black general in the regular army was B. O. Davis Sr., who was appointed by President Franklin Delano Roosevelt on October 16, 1940.

The first black general was Maj. Gen. Robert B. Elliott, commanding general, National Guard, South Carolina (1870).

The first black general in the U.S. Air Force—and the second black general—was B. O. Davis Jr., who was appointed on October 27, 1954. The West Point graduate retired in 1970 with the rank of lieutentant general.

The first black four-star general was Daniel ("Chappie") James, who was promoted to that rank and named commander-in-chief of the North American Air Defense Command on September 1, 1975.

The first black admiral in the U.S. Navy was Samuel Lee Gravely Jr., who was appointed on April 28, 1971.

The first black to head an armed forces base in the United States was B. O. Davis Jr., who was named commander of Godman Field (Ky.) on June 21, 1945.

The first black to command an army division was Maj. Gen. Frederic E. Davidson, who assumed command of the Eighth Infantry Division in Germany on April 19, 1972.

The first black general in the Marine Corps was Frank E. Peterson Jr., who achieved the rank on February 23, 1979.

The first black to earn the Congressional Medal of Honor was Sgt. William H. Carney, who was cited for gallantry in the charge of the Fifty-fourth Massachusetts Volunteers on Fort Wagner in the Charleston, South Carolina, harbor on July 18, 1963. From the Spanish-American War to the Korean War, blacks were denied Congressional Medals of Honor because of their race. The first black awarded a Medal of Honor after the Spanish-American War was Pfc. William Thompson of Brooklyn, N.Y., who was cited posthumously on June 21, 1951, for heroism in Korea.

The first black graduate of the West Point Military Academy was Henry O. Flipper of Georgia, who was admitted on July 1, 1873, and graduated on June 15, 1877. The first black student at West Point was James W. Smith of South Carolina, who was admitted on July 1, 1870. He left the Academy on June 26, 1874, without receiving a degree.

The first black graduate of the Annapolis Naval Academy was Wesley A. Brown, who graduated on June 3, 1949. The first black student at Annapolis, John Henry Conyers of South Carolina, did not graduate. He was admitted on September 21, 1872.

Women

The first black woman to graduate from an American college was Mary Jane Patterson, who graduated from Oberlin College in 1862.

The first black woman awarded a Ph.D. degree was Sadie M. Alexander, who received a degree in economics in 1921 from the University of Pennsylvania. Two other black women received Ph.D. degrees in the same year: Eva B. Dykes, English, Radcliffe; Georgianna R. Simpson, German, the University of Chicago.

The first black woman lawyer was Charlotte E. Ray, who graduated from Howard University Law School on February 27, 1872. She was admitted to practice in April, 1872. In 1910 there were 777 black male lawyers and 2 black women lawyers.

The first black woman physicians were Rebecca Cole, who practiced in New York from 1872 to 1881; Susan McKinney, who graduated from the New York Medical College in 1870; and Rebecca Lee, who graduated from the New England Female Medical College on March 1, 1864.

The first black woman to receive a dental degree in the United States was Ida Gray Nelson Rollins, who graduated from the University of Michigan Dental School in 1887. The first black woman to practice dentistry professionally was probably Emeline Roberts Jones of Connecticut, who assisted her dentist husband and developed a large practice after his death in 1864.

The first black woman to receive a major appointment from the U.S. government was Mary McLeod Bethune, who was named Director of Negro Affairs of the National Youth Administration on June 24, 1936.

The first black woman named to the cabinet of a U.S. president was Patricia R. Harris, who was named secretary of the Department of Housing and Urban Development by President Jimmy Carter on December 21, 1976.

The first black woman ambassador was Patricia R. Harris, who was named ambassador to Luxembourg on May 19, 1965, by President Johnson.

The first black woman in Congress was Rep. Shirley Chisholm, who was elected to the Ninety-first Congress from Brooklyn on November 5, 1968.

The first black woman general was Hazel Johnson, who was appointed on September 1, 1979.

The first black woman judge was Jane Matilda Bolin, who was appointed judge of the court of domestic relations of New York City by Mayor Fiorello LaGuardia on July 22, 1939.

The first black woman named to the federal bench was Constance Baker Motley, who was confirmed as U.S. District Judge in southern New York on August 30, 1966.

The first black woman elected to a state legislature was Crystal Bird Fauset, who was elected to the Pennsylvania House of Representatives on November 8, 1938.

The first black woman elected to a major position in a major city was Constance Baker Motley, who was victorious in the election for Manhattan Borough president on February 23, 1965.

The first black woman to write a Broadway play was Lorraine Hansberry, who created *Raisin In The Sun*, which opened at the Barrymore Theater on March 11, 1959, with Sidney Poitier and Claudia McNeil in starring roles. *Raisin* was also the first Broadway drama in more than a half century with a black director, Lloyd Richards.

The first black woman nominated for an Academy Award for best actress of the year was Dorothy Dandridge, who was cited in 1955 for her role in *Carmen Jones*.

The first black woman millionaire and one of the first major black entrepreneurs was Madame C. J. Walker, who made a fortune with a line of beauty products in the first decades of the twentieth century. She died on May 25, 1919.

The first black woman to head a bank was Maggie Lena Walker who was named president of Richmond's St. Luke Bank and Trust Company in 1903.

The first black woman nominated for president of the U.S. was Rep. Shirley Chisholm, who received 151.95 votes on the first ballot at the 1972 Democratic convention.

The first black voted female athlete of the year was Althea Gibson, who was cited on January 23, 1958.

The first black woman to win a gold medal in the Olympics was Alice Coachman of Albany State Teachers College, who won the running high jump in the 1948 games in London.

Communications

The first black newspaper, *Freedom's Journal*, was published in New York City on March 16, 1827.

The first black magazines were founded in the 1830s and 1840s: *Mirror of Liberty*, published in New York, August, 1838; the *African Methodist Episcopal Church Magazine*, published in September, 1841, Brooklyn.

The first black daily newspaper, the *New Orleans Tribune*, was founded in New Orleans by Dr. Louis C. Roudanez in July, 1864. The paper started as a triweekly and became a daily in October.

The first major black daily newspaper in the twentieth century was the *Atlanta Daily World*. The paper, founded as a weekly by W. S. Scott Jr. in 1928, became a daily in 1933.

The first commercially successful general magazine was *Negro Digest*, published November 1, 1942, by John H. Johnson. In November, 1945, Johnson founded *Ebony* magazine, which is the largest black magazine in the world.

The first black-owned radio station was WERD which went on the air in Atlanta on October 3, 1949. The first black-owned TV station, Detroit's WGPR-TV, went on the air on September 29, 1975.

The Arts

The first black poet was Jupiter Hammon, a New York slave who wrote *An Evening Thought: Salvation by Christ with Pentential Cries*, published December 25, 1760.

The first author and the first major black poet was Phillis Wheatley, whose book, *Poems on Various Subjects, Religious and Moral*, was published in 1773. This was the second book published by an American woman.

The first black novelist was William Wells Brown, who wrote *Clotel: or, The President's Daughter*, published in 1853.

The first black playwright was William Wells Brown, whose play, *The Escape*, was published in 1858.

Awards and Prizes

The first Springarn Medal, presented annually by the NAACP for outstanding achievement by a black American, was awarded on February 12, 1915, to biologist Ernest E. Just, head of the department of physiology, Howard University, for pioneering research on fertilization and cell division.

The Spingarn committee of the NAACP also cited Dr. George Washington Carver, the agricultural chemist, and Dr. Percy Julian, the industrial chemist. Carver, who was born of slave parents on a farm near Diamond Grove, Mo., about 1864, made one hundred products from the sweet potato, almost one hundred from the pecan and fifty from the peanut. He also developed several products from the clay of the South and was the first to use soybeans in paint making. In 1935 Dr. Percy Julian made a successful synthesis of the drug physostigmine, which is used in the treatment of glaucoma. Dr. Julian's research work on the soybean led to the development of a male sex hormone, a weatherproof covering for battleships and a product which became the base of the aero-foam fire extinguishers in World War II. Other black scientists who have made basic contributions are Lloyd Hall, an industrial chemist who received over eighty patents on the preparation and curing of salts, spices and food products, and Dr. William A. Hinton, who developed the famous Hinton test for detection of syphilis.

The first black awarded the Nobel Peace Prize was Ralph J. Bunche, who was honored on September 22, 1950, for his successful mediation of the Palestine conflict.

The youngest person awarded the Nobel Peace Prize was Martin Luther King Jr., who was honored on December 10, 1964, in his thirty-fifth year.

The first black to receive a Pulitzer Prize was Gwendolyn Brooks, who was cited on May 1, 1950, for her book of poetry, *Annie Allen*.

The first black male to receive a Pulitzer Prize was Moneta J. Sleet Jr. of *Ebony* magazine who was honored in 1969 for photographs of Coretta Scott King and her daughter at the funeral of Martin Luther King Jr.

The first black admitted to the National Institute of Arts and Letters was W. E. B. Du Bois, who was inducted in 1943.

Business and Inventions

The first black inventor to receive official recognition was Henry Blair of Maryland, who received a patent for a corn harvester on October 14, 1834.

Since the colonial period, Afro-Americans have been hewers of the human spirit. Benjamin Banneker, the astronomer and mathematician, produced the first scientific writing by a black American in his almanac, which was issued annually after 1792. Banneker also wrote a dissertation on bees and constructed what was probably the first clock made in America. It is said that a Georgia slave was partly responsible for the invention of the cotton gin. Jo Anderson, another slave, was a trusted helper of Cyrus McCormick while he was developing his reaping machine in Rockbridge, Va., in the 1830s. Equally inventive was Norbert Rillieux, a New Orleans machinist and engineer, who was granted a patent on a vacuum cup which revolutionized sugar refining methods of his day. Between 1872 and 1920 Elijah McCoy of Detroit received over fifty-seven patents for inventions on automatic lubricating appliances and other devices pertaining to telegraphy and electricity. Many of his inventions were used on locomotives on the Canadian and Northwestern railroads and on steamships on the Great Lakes. Perhaps the greatest of the early inventors was Jan E. Matzeliger who created the first machine for attaching soles to shoes, "the first appliance of its kind capable of performing all the steps required to hold a shoe on its last, grip and pull the leather down around the heel, guide and drive the nails into place, and then discharge the complete shoe from the machine." Matzeliger's patent was bought by the United Shoe Machinery Company of Boston, which became a multimillion-dollar corporation. Matzeliger died in 1889 in obscurity. Another major inventor was Garrett A. Morgan, who invented the "gas inhalator," the prototype of the gas mask. He also invented the three-way automatic stopsign. In 1923 he sold the patent to General Electric Corporation for $40,000. Other leading black inventors and creators include Philadelphia confectioner Augustus Jackson, who was known in the nineteenth century as "the man who invented ice cream"; Saratoga (N.Y.) chef Hyram S. Thomas, who reportedly created the potato chip; and George F. Grant, who contributed (1899) the golf tee.

The first black insurance company was the American Insurance Company of Philadelphia, established in 1810.

The first black bank, the Capital Savings Bank of Washington, D.C., opened on October 17, 1888. The Savings Bank of the Order of True Reformers was chartered on March 2, 1888, and opened in Richmond on April 3, 1889.

The first black on the New York Stock Exchange was Joseph L. Searles III, who began floor training on February 13, 1970, as a floor partner in the firm of Newburger, Loeb and Company.

The first black named to the board of directors of the New York Stock Exchange was Jerome H. Holland, who was elected on March 2, 1972.

Select Bibliography

Adams, Samuel. *The Writings of Samuel Adams.* Edited by Henry Alonzo Cushing. 4 vols. New York, 1904–08.

Alexis, Stephen. *Black Liberator: The Life of Toussaint Louverture.* New York, 1949.

Aptheker, Herbert. *The Negro in the Civil War.* New York, 1938.

———. *American Negro Slave Revolts.* New York, 1943.

———, ed. *A Documentary History of the Negro People in the United States,* 4 vols. New York, 1951, 1973, 1974.

Armstrong, Louis. *Satchmo: My Life in New Orleans.* New York, 1954.

Ballagh, James C. *White Servitude in the Colony of Virginia.* Baltimore, 1895.

———. *A History of Slavery in Virginia.* Baltimore, 1902.

Bancroft, Frederic. *Slave-Trading in the Old South.* Baltimore, 1931.

Bardolph, Richard. *The Negro Vanguard.* New York, 1959.

Barnes, Gilbert H. *The Antislavery Impulse, 1830–1844.* New York, 1933.

Barry, Williams. *A History of Framingham, Massachusetts*. Boston, 1847.

Barth, Heinrich. *Travels and Discoveries in North and Central Africa, 1849–1855*. 3 vols. New York, 1857–59.

Beard, Charles A., and Mary R. *The Rise of American Civilization*. 2 vols. New York, 1927.

Bennett, Lerone, Jr. *The Negro Mood*. Chicago, 1964.

———. "The March," in *The Day They Marched*, edited by Doris E. Saunders. Chicago, 1963.

———. *What Manner of Man: A Biography of Martin Luther King, Jr.* Chicago, 1964.

———. *Confrontation: Black and White*. Chicago, 1965.

———. *Black Power U.S.A., The Human Side of Reconstruction, 1867–1877*. Chicago, 1967.

———. *Pioneers in Protest*. Chicago, 1968.

———. *The Shaping of Black America*. Chicago, 1975.

———. *Wade in the Water*. Chicago, 1979.

Bentley, George R. *A History of the Freedmen's Bureau*. Philadelphia, 1955.

Billingsley, Andrew. *Black Families in White America*. Englewood Cliffs, 1968.

Blassingame, John W. *The Slave Community*. New York, 1979.

Bond, Horace Mann. *The Education of the Negro in the American Social Order*. New York, 1934.

Bontemps, Arna, and Conroy, Jack. *They Seek a City*. New York, 1945.

Botkin, B. A, ed. *Lay My Burden Down*. Chicago, 1945.

Bovill, E. W. *Caravans of the Old Sahara*. London, 1933.

———. *The Golden Trade of the Moors*. London, 1958.

Bradford, Sarah H. *Harriet, The Moses of Her People*. Auburn, 1897.

Bragg, George F., Jr. *Men of Maryland*. Baltimore, 1925.

Brawley, Benjamin G. *The Negro Genius*. New York, 1937.

———. *Negro Builders and Heroes*. Chapel Hill, 1937.

Brazeal, B. R. *The Brotherhood of Sleeping Car Porters*. New York, 1946.

Bremer, Fredrika. *The Homes of the New World*. 2 vols. New York, 1853.

Brisbane, Robert H. *The Black Vanguard*. Valley Forge, 1970.

Broderick, Francis L. *W. E. B. Du Bois, Negro Leader in a Time of Crisis*. Stanford, 1959.

————, and Meier, August, eds. *Negro Thought in the Twentieth Century*, Indianapolis, 1965.

Brodie, Fawn M. *Thaddeus Stevens, Scourge of the South*. New York, 1959.

————. *Thomas Jefferson*. New York, 1974.

Brown, Sterling A. *Negro Poetry and Drama*. Washington, 1937.

————, *et al*, eds. *The Negro Caravan*. New York, 1941.

Brown, William Wells. *Narrative of William Wells Brown*. Boston, 1848.

————. *The Black Man*. New York, 1963.

————. *The Negro in the American Rebellion*. Boston, 1867.

Buck, Paul H. *The Road to Reunion*. Boston, 1937.

Buckler, Helen. *Doctor Dan, Pioneer in American Surgery*. Boston, 1954.

Buckmaster, Henrietta. *Let My People Go*. New York, 1941.

Budge, E. A. W. *The Egyptian Sudan*. 2 vols. London, 1907.

————. *A History of Ethiopia, Nubia and Abyssinia*. 2 vols. London, 1928.

Butcher, Margaret Just. *The Negro in American Culture*. New York, 1956.

Butler, Benjamin F. *Butler's Book*. Boston, 1892.

Calhoun, A. W. *A Social History of the American Family*. 3 vols. New York, 1917.

Campbell, George. *White and Black*. New York, 1889.

Carmichael, Stokely, and Hamilton, Charles V. *Black Power*. New York, 1967.

Carroll, Joseph C. *Slave Insurrections in the United States, 1800–1865*. Boston, 1938.

Cash, Wilbur J. *The Mind of the South*. New York, 1941.

Catterall, Helen T. *Judicial Cases Concerning American Slavery and the Negro*. 5 vols. Washington, 1926–37.

Chicago Commission on Race Relations. *The Negro in Chicago*. Chicago, 1922.

Clark, Kenneth B. *Dark Ghetto*. New York, 1965.

Clarke, John Henrik, ed. *Marcus Garvey and the Vision of Africa*. New York, 1963.

Cornish, Dudley Taylor. *The Sable Army: Negro Troops in the Union Army, 1861–65*. New York, 1956.

Courlander, Harold. *Negro Folk Music, U.S.A.* New York, 1963.

Cronon, Edmund David. *Black Moses: The Story of Marcus Garvey.* Madison, 1955.

Daniels, John. *In Freedom's Birthplace.* Boston, 1914.

Davidson, Basil. *The Lost Cities of Africa.* Boston, 1959.

———. *Black Mother.* Boston, 1961.

Davis, David. B. *The Problem of Slavery in the Age of Revolution, 1770–1823.* Ithaca, 1975.

DeForest, John William. *A Volunteer's Adventures.* New Haven, 1946.

Delafosse, Maurice. *The Negroes of Africa.* Washington, 1931.

Delany, Martin R. *The Condition, Elevation, Emigration, and Destiny of the Colored People of the United States.* Philadelphia, 1852.

Detweiler, Frederick G. *The Negro Press in the United States.* Chicago, 1922.

Donald, David. *Lincoln Reconsidered.* New York, 1956.

Donnan, Elizabeth. *Documents Illustrative of the History of the Slave Trade to America.* Washington, 1930–35.

Douglass, Frederick. *The Life and Times of Frederick Douglass.* Hartford, 1881.

———. *My Bondage and My Freedom.* New York, 1855.

Drake, St. Clair, and Cayton, Horace R. *Black Metropolis.* New York, 1945.

Du Bois, W. E. B. *The Suppression of the African Slave Trade to the United States of America.* New York, 1896.

———. *The Philadelphia Negro.* Philadelphia, 1899.

———. *The Souls of Black Folk.* Chicago, 1903.

———, ed. *The Negro Church.* Atlanta, 1903.

———. *Black Reconstruction.* New York, 1935.

———. *Black Folk: Then and Now.* New York, 1939.

———. *Dusk of Dawn.* New York, 1940.

———. *The Autobiography of W. E. B. Du Bois.* New York, 1968.

Dumond, Dwight L. *Antislavery.* Ann Arbor, 1961.

Dyer, Frederick H. *A Compendium of the War of the Rebellion.* Des Moines, 1908.

Eaton, John. *Grant, Lincoln and the Freedmen.* New York, 1907.

Edmonds, Helen G. *The Negro and Fusion Politics in North Carolina, 1894–1901.* Chapel Hill, 1951.

Ellison, Ralph. *The Invisible Man*. New York, 1952.

Embree, Edwin. *Brown America*. New York, 1931.

———. *13 Against the Odds*. New York, 1944.

Emilio, Luis F. *History of the Fifty-fourth Regiment of Massachusetts Volunteer Infantry*. Boston, 1894.

Fage, J. D. *An Introduction to the History of West Africa*. Cambridge, England, 1959.

Fairservis, Walter A., Jr. *The Ancient Kingdoms of the Nile*. New York, 1962.

Fauset, Arthur Huff. *Sojourner Truth*. Chapel Hill, 1938.

Ficklen, John R. *History of Reconstruction in Louisiana Through 1868*. Baltimore, 1910.

Filler, Louis. *The Crusade Against Slavery*. New York, 1960.

Fleming, Walter, ed. *Documentary History of Reconstruction*. 2 vols. Cleveland, 1906–07.

Foley, Albert S. *Bishop Healy: Beloved Outcaste*. New York, 1954.

Foner, Phillip S. *The Life and Writings of Frederick Douglass*. 4 vols. New York, 1950.

Forten, Charlotte. *The Journal of Charlotte Forten*. Edited by Ray Allen Billington. New York, 1953.

Fox, Stephen R. *The Guardian of Boston: William Monroe Trotter*. New York, 1970.

Fox, William F. *Regimental Losses in the American Civil War*. Albany, 1889.

Franklin, John Hope. *From Slavery to Freedom*. New York, 1980.

———. *The Free Negro in North Carolina*. Chapel Hill, 1943.

———. *Reconstruction*. Chicago, 1961.

Frazier, E. Franklin. *The Negro Family in the United States*. Chicago, 1939.

———. *The Negro in the United States*. New York, 1957.

———. *Black Bourgeoisie*. Glencoe, 1957.

Freyre, Gilberto. *The Masters and the Slaves*. Translated by Samuel Putnam. New York, 1946.

Frobenius, Leo. *The Voice of Africa*. Translated by Rudolf Blind. 2 vols. London, 1913.

Gage, Thomas. *The Correspondence of General Thomas Gage*. Edited by Clarence E. Carter. 2 vols. New Haven, 1931–33.

Gara, Larry. *The Liberty Line: The Legend of the Underground Railroad*. Lexington, 1961.

Gardiner, Alan. *Egypt of the Pharaohs*. London, 1961.

Garfinkel, Herbert. *When Negroes March*. Glencoe, 1959.

Garrison, W. P., and Garrison, F. L. *William Lloyd Garrison*. 4 vols. Boston, 1894.

Gosnell, Harold F. *Negro Politicians, The Rise of Negro Politics in Chicago*. Chicago, 1935.

Greenberg, Jack. *Race Relations and American Law*. New York, 1959.

Greene, Evarts B., and Harrington, Virginia D. *American Population before the Federal Census of 1790*. New York, 1932.

Greene, Lorenzo J. *The Negro in Colonial New England*. New York, 1942.

Greene, Lorenzo J., and Woodson, Carter G. *The Negro Wage Earner*. Washington, 1930.

Greene, Robert E. *Black Defenders of America, 1775–1973*. Chicago, 1974.

Gutman, Herbert G. *The Black Family in Slavery and Freedom*. New York, 1976.

Guzman, Jessie P., ed. *Negro Year Book*. Tuskegee, 1947, 1952.

Hamilton, Charles V. *The Bench and the Ballot*. New York, 1973.

Handy, W. C. *Father of the Blues*. Edited by Arna Bontemps. New York, 1941.

Harding, Vincent. *There Is a River*. New York, 1981.

Hare, Maud (Cuney). *Negro Musicians and Their Music*. Washington, 1936.

Harlan, Louis R. *Booker T. Washington*. New York, 1972.

Harris, Abram L. *The Negro Capitalist*. Philadelphia, 1936.

Hayes, Lawrence J. W. *The Negro Federal Government Worker, 1883–1938*. Washington, 1941.

Henderson, Edwin B. *The Negro in Sports*. Washington, 1949.

Herodotus. *The History of Herodotus*. Translated by George Rowlinson. Chicago, 1952.

Herskovits, Melville J. *The American Negro: A Study in Racial Crossing*. New York, 1928.

———. *The Myth of the Negro's Past*. New York, 1941.

———. *Cultural Anthropology*. New York, 1955.

Higginbotham, A. Leon. *In the Matter of Color: Race and the American Legal Process, The Colonial Period*. New York, 1978.

Higginson, Thomas W. *Army Life in a Black Regiment*. Boston, 1870.

———. *Travellers and Outlaws*. Boston, 1889.

Hirshon, Stanley P. *Farewell to the Bloody Shirt*. Bloomington, 1962.

Holland, Frederic M. *Frederick Douglass*. New York, 1895.

Holt, Thomas. *Black Over White: Negro Political Leadership in South Carolina During Reconstruction*. Urbana, 1977.

Hoskins, G. A. *Travels in Ethiopia*. 2 vols. London, 1835.

Hoskins, James. *Pinckney Benton Stewart Pinchback*. New York, 1973.

Hotten, John C. *The Original Lists of Persons of Quality*. New York, 1881.

Hughes, Langston. *The Big Sea*. New York, 1940.

Humphreys, A. A. *The Virginia Campaign of 1864 and 1865*. New York, 1883.

Hurd, John C. *The Law of Freedom and Bondage in the United States*. 2 vols. Boston, 1858–62.

Jahn, Janheinz. *Muntu*. Translated by Marjorie Greene. New York, 1961.

Jensen, Merrill, ed. *American Colonial Documents to 1776*, in *English Historical Documents*, edited by David C. Douglass. London, 1955.

Jernegan, Marcus W. *Laboring and Dependent Classes in Colonial America, 1607–1783*. Chicago, 1931.

Johnson, Allen, and Malone, Dumas, eds. *Dictionary of American Biography*. 22 vols. New York, 1928–1936.

Johnson, Charles S. *The Negro in American Civilization*. New York, 1930.

———. *Shadow of the Plantation*. Chicago, 1934.

———. *The Negro College Graduate*. Chapel Hill, 1938.

———. *Patterns of Negro Segregation*. New York, 1943.

Johnson, James Weldon. *Black Manhattan*. New York, 1930.

———. *Along This Way*. New York, 1933.

———, and J. Rosamond Johnson. *The Books of American Negro Spirituals*. New York, 1940.

Johnson, Robert U., and Buel, Clarence C., eds. *Battles and Leaders of the Civil War*. 4 vols. New York, 1887–88.

Jones, Hugh. *The Present State of Virginia*. New York, 1865.

Kardiner, Abram, and Ovesey, Lionel. *The Mark of Oppression*. New York, 1951.

Kemble, Frances A. *Journal of a Residence on a Georgian Plantation in 1838–39*. New York, 1963.

Kesselman, Louis C. *The Social Politics of FEPC*. Chapel Hill, 1948.

Key, V. O., Jr. *Southern Politics in State and Nation*. New York, 1949.

Kidder, Frederic. *History of the Boston Massacre*. Albany, 1870.

King, Coretta Scott. *My Life with Martin Luther King Jr*. New York, 1969.

King, Martin Luther, Jr. *Stride Toward Freedom*. New York, 1958.

———. *Why We Can't Wait*. New York, 1964.

———. *Where Do We Go From Here: Chaos or Community?* Boston, 1968.

Kluger, Richard. *Simple Justice*. New York, 1975.

Konvitz, Milton R. *The Constitution and Civil Rights*. New York, 1947.

Korngold, Ralph. *Citizen Toussaint*. Boston, 1945.

———. *Thaddeus Stevens*. New York, 1955.

Lacy, Dan. *The White Use of Blacks in America*. New York, 1972.

Ladner, Joyce A. *The Death of White Sociology*. New York, 1973.

Lamson, Peggy. *The Glorious Failure: Black Congressman Robert Brown Elliott and the Reconstruction in South Carolina*. New York, 1973.

Leakey, L. S. B. *The Progress and Evolution of Man in Africa*. London, 1961.

Lester, John C. *The Ku Klux Klan*. New York, 1905.

Levine, Lawrence W. *Black Culture and Black Consciousness*. New York, 1977.

Lewinson, Paul. *Race, Class and Party*. New York, 1932.

Lincoln, C. Eric. *The Black Muslims in America*. Boston, 1961.

Litwack, Leon F. *North of Slavery*. Chicago, 1961.

Locke, Alain. *The New Negro*. New York, 1925.

———. *Negro Art: Past and Present*. Washington, 1936.

Loewen, James W., and Sallis, Charles. *Mississippi: Conflict and Change*. New York, 1974.

Logan, Rayford. *The Negro in American Life and Thought: The Nadir, 1877–1901*. New York, 1954.

————, ed. *What the Negro Wants*. Chapel Hill, 1944.

————, ed. *Memoirs of a Monticello Slave*. Charlottesville, 1951.

Loggins, Vernon. *The Negro Author*. New York, 1931.

Lonn, Ella. *Reconstruction in Louisiana after 1868*. New York, 1918.

Lugard, Flora Louisa. *A Tropical Dependency*. London, 1911.

Lynch, John Roy. *The Facts of Reconstruction*. New York, 1913.

Lynd, Staughton. *Class Conflict, Slavery, and the U.S. Constitution*. Indianapolis, 1967.

Lynn, Annella. *Interracial Marriages in Washington, D.C., 1940–47*. Washington, 1953.

McCormac, E. I. *White Servitude in Maryland*. Baltimore, 1904.

McKay, Claude. *Harlem: Negro Metropolis*. New York, 1940.

McPherson, James. *The Struggle for Equality: Abolitionists and the Negro in the Civil War and Reconstruction*. Princeton, 1964.

McWilliams, Carey. *Brothers Under the Skin*. Boston, 1943.

Malcolm X. *The Autobiography of Malcolm X*. Edited by Alex Haley. New York, 1964.

Mangum, Charles S. *The Legal Status of the Negro*. Chapel Hill, 1940.

Mannix, Daniel P. *Black Cargoes: A History of the Atlantic Slave Trade*. New York, 1962.

Martin, John Bartlow. *The Deep South Says "Never."* New York, 1957.

Martineau, Harriet. *Society in America*. 2 vols. New York, 1837.

May, Samuel J. *Some Recollections of Our Antislavery Conflict*. Boston, 1869.

Mays, Benjamin E., and Nicholson, J. W. *The Negro's Church*. New York, 1932.

Mays, Benjamin E. *Born to Rebel*. New York, 1971.

Mazyck, Walter H. *George Washington and the Negro*. Washington, 1932.

Miller, John C. *Sam Adams: Pioneer in Propaganda*. Boston, 1936.

Miller, Kelly. *Race Adjustment*. New York, 1908.

Miller, Loren. *The Petitioners: The Story of the Supreme Court of the United States and the Negro*. New York, 1966.

Montagu, M. F. Ashley. *Man's Most Dangerous Myth: The Fallacy of Race*. New York, 1945.

Moon, Henry L. *Balance of Power*. Garden City, 1949.

Moore, George H. *Historical Notes on the Employment of Negroes in the American Army of the Revolution*. New York, 1862.

Moran, Charles. *Black Triumvirate*. New York, 1957.

Morgan, A. T. *Yazoo*. Washington, 1884.

Morgan, Edmund S. *American Slavery, American Freedom: The Ordeal of Colonial Virginia*. New York, 1975.

Murray, Florence, ed. *The Negro Handbook*. New York, 1942, 1944, 1946–47, 1949.

Murray, Pauli. *States' Laws on Race and Color*. Cincinnati, 1951.

Myrdal, Gunnar. *An American Dilemma*. New York, 1943.

Nell, William C. *The Colored Patriots of the American Revolution*. Boston, 1855.

Nichols, Lee. *Breakthrough on the Color Front*. New York, 1954.

Noel, Donald L, ed. *The Origins of American Slavery and Racism*. Columbus, 1970.

Nordhoff, Charles. *The Cotton States in the Spring and Summer of 1875*. New York, 1876.

Northup, Solomon. *Narrative of Solomon Northup*. Auburn, 1853.

Nowlin, William F. *The Negro in American Politics*. Boston, 1931.

Nugent, Nell M. *Cavaliers and Pioneers, A Calendar of Virginia Land Grants, 1623–1800*. Richmond, 1929.

Oak, Vishnu. V. *The Negro's Adventure in General Business*. Yellow Springs, 1949.

Olmsted, Frederick Law. *The Cotton Kingdom*. Edited by Arthur Schlesinger. New York, 1953.

Ottley, Roi. *Black Odyssey*. New York, 1948.

———. *The Lonely Warrior: The Life and Times of Robert S. Abbott*. Chicago, 1955.

Ovington, Mary White. *Portraits in Color*. New York, 1927.

———. *The Walls Came Tumbling Down*. New York, 1947.

Owens, William A. *Black Mutiny*. Boston, 1953.

Payne, Daniel A. *History of the African Methodist Episcopal Church*. Nashville, 1891.

Peck, James. *Freedom Ride*. New York, 1962.

Penn, I. Garland. *The Afro-American Press*. Springfield, 1891.

Pierson, Donald. *Negroes in Brazil*. Chicago, 1942.

Porter, Dorothy. *Early Negro Writing, 1760–1837*. Boston, 1971.

Powell, Adam Clayton. *Marching Blacks*. New York, 1945.

Quaife, Milo M. *Checagou*. Chicago, 1933.

Quarles, Benjamin. *Frederick Douglass*. Washington, 1948.

——. *The Negro in the Civil War*. Boston, 1953.

——. *The Negro in the American Revolution*. Chapel Hill, 1961.

——. *Lincoln and the Negro*. New York, 1962.

——. *The Negro in the Making of America*. New York, 1964.

——. *Black Abolitionists*. New York, 1969.

Record, Wilson. *The Negro and the Communist Party*. Chapel Hill, 1951.

Reddick, L. D. *Crusader Without Violence*. New York, 1959.

Richardson, Joe M. *The Negro in the Reconstruction of Florida*. Tallahassee, 1965.

Rogers, J. A. *Sex and Race*. 3 vols. New York, 1940–44.

Rose, Arnold M. *The Negro's Morale*. Minneapolis, 1949.

Rose, Willie Lee. *Rehearsal for Reconstruction: The Port Royal Experiment*. Indianapolis, 1964.

Rowan, Carl T. *Go South to Sorrow*. New York, 1957.

Ruchames, Louis. *Race, Jobs and Politics: The Story of FEPC*. New York, 1953.

Russell, John H. *The Free Negro in Virginia*. Baltimore, 1913.

Sandburg, Carl. *Abraham Lincoln: The Prairie Years*. New York, 1926.

——. *Abraham Lincoln: The War Years*. 4 vols. New York, 1939.

Saunders, Doris E., ed. *The Ebony Handbook*. Chicago, 1974.

Schor, Joel. *Henry Highland Garnet*. Westport, 1977.

Scott, Emmett J., and Stowe, Lyman Beecher. *Booker T. Washington, Builder of a Civilization*. Garden City, 1916.

Sertima, Ivan Van. *They Came Before Columbus*. New York, 1976.

Shoemaker, Don, ed. *With All Deliberate Speed*. New York, 1957.

Siebert, Wilbur H. *The Underground Railway from Slavery to Freedom*. New York, 1898.

Simmons, William J. *Men of Mark*. Cleveland, 1887.

Smith, Abbott E. *Colonists in Bondage: White Servitude and Convict Labor in America*. Chapel Hill, 1947.

Smith, S. D. *The Negro in Congress*. Chapel Hill, 1940.

Spencer, Samuel R. *Booker T. Washington and the Negro's Place in American Life*. Boston, 1955.

Spero, Sterling D., and Harris, Abram L. *The Black Worker*. New York, 1931.

Stampp, Kenneth M. *The Peculiar Institution*. New York, 1956.

Stearns, Marshall W. *The Story of Jazz*. New York, 1956.

Sterling, Dorothy. *Freedom Train: The Story of Harriet Tubman*. Garden City, 1954.

Steward, Austin. *Twenty-Two Years a Slave*. Rochester, 1857.

Still, William. *The Underground Railroad*. Philadelphia, 1879.

Sydnor, Charles S. *Slavery in Mississippi*. New York, 1933.

Tabb, William K. *The Political Economy of the Black Ghetto*. New York, 1970.

Tally, Thomas W. *Negro Folk Rhymes*. New York, 1922.

Taylor, A. A. *The Negro in South Carolina During Reconstruction*. Washington, 1924.

Temple, J. H. *History of Framingham, Massachusetts*. Framingham, 1887.

Thurman, Howard. *Deep River*. Richmond, Ind., 1975
———. *With Head and Heart*. New York, 1980.

Tindall, George B. *South Carolina Negroes, 1877–1900*. Columbia, 1952.

Toppin, Edgar A. *A Biographical History of Blacks in America*. New York, 1969.

Torrence, Ridgely. *The Story of John Hope*. New York, 1948.

Tragle, Henry Irving. *The Southampton Revolt*. Amherst, 1971.

Truth, Sojourner. *Narrative of Sojourner Truth*. Boston, 1850.

Ullman, Victor. *Martin R. Delany*. Boston, 1971.

Villard, Oswald Garrison. *John Brown*. Boston, 1910.

Vincent, Charles. *Black Legislators in Louisiana During Reconstruction*. Baton Rouge, 1976.

Wade, Richard C. *Slavery in the Cities*. New York, 1964.

Walls, William J. *The African Methodist Episcopal Zion Church*. Charlotte, 1974.

The War of the Rebellion: A Compilation of Official Records of the Union and Confederate Armies. 128 vols. Washington, 1880–1901.

Warmoth, Henry C. *War, Politics and Reconstruction*. New York, 1930.

Washington, Booker T. *Up from Slavery*. New York, 1901.

Washington, Booker T., Du Bois, W. E. B., *et al.* *The Negro Problem*. New York, 1903.

Weatherford, Willis Duke. *The Negro from Africa to America*. New York, 1924.

Weaver, Robert C. *The Negro Ghetto*. New York, 1948.

Wells, Ida B. *Crusader For Justice: The Autobiography of Ida B. Wells*. Edited by Alfreda M. Duster. Chicago, 1970.

Wesley, Charles H. *Negro Labor in the United States, 1850–1925*. New York, 1927.

———. *Richard Allen*. Washington, 1935.

———. *Prince Hall*. Washington, 1977.

Wharton, Vernon Lane. *The Negro in Mississippi, 1865–1890*. Chapel Hill, 1947.

Wheatley, Phillis. *Phillis Wheatley: Poems and Letters*. Edited by Charles F. Heartman. New York, 1915.

White, Walter. *Rope and Faggott*. New York, 1929.

———. *A Man Called White*. New York, 1948.

———. *How Far the Promised Land*. New York, 1955.

Wiley, Bell Irwin. *Southern Negroes, 1861–1865*. New Haven, 1938.

Williams, Eric. *The Negro in the Caribbean*. Washington, 1942.

———. *Capitalism and Slavery*. Chapel Hill, 1938.

Williams, George W. *History of the Negro Race in America, 1619–1880*. 2 vols. New York, 1883.

———. *A History of the Negro Troops in the War of the Rebellion*. New York, 1888.

Williamson, Joel. *After Slavery: The Negro in South Carolina During Reconstruction, 1861–1877*. Chapel Hill, 1965.

Wilmore, Gayraud S. *Black Religion and Black Radicalism*. Garden City, 1972.

Wilson, Joseph T. *The Black Phalanx*. Hartford, 1888.

Wolseley, Roland E. *The Black Press, U.S.A.* Ames, 1971.

Wood, Peter H. *Black Majority: Negroes in Colonial South Carolina from 1670 through The Stono Rebellion*. New York, 1974.

Woodson, Carter G. *A Century of Negro Migration*. Washington, 1918.

———. *Free Negro Heads of Families in the United States in 1830*. Washington, 1925.

————. *The Negro Professional Man and the Community.* Washington, 1934.

————. *The History of the Negro Church.* Washington, 1945.

————. *The Negro in Our History.* Washington, 1947.

————, ed. *Negro Orators and Their Orations.* Washington, 1925.

————, ed. *The Mind of the Negro as Reflected in Letters Written During the Crisis, 1800–1860.* Washington, 1926.

Woodward, C. Vann. *Origins of the New South, 1877–1913.* Baton Rouge, 1951.

————. *The Strange Career of Jim Crow.* New York, 1957.

Work, Monroe N., ed. *Negro Year Book.* Tuskegee, 1914–15, 1918–19, 1925–26.

Writers Program, WPA. *The Negro in Virginia.* New York, 1940.

Young, A. S. *Negro Firsts in Sports*, Chicago, 1963.

Zinn, Howard. *SNCC: The New Abolitionists.* Boston, 1964.

UNPUBLISHED STUDIES

Johnston, James Hugo. "Race Relations in Virginia and Miscegenation in the South, 1776–1860." Ph.D. dissertation, University of Chicago, 1937.

Risinger, Robert G. "Routine Slave Life in the Ante-Bellum South, 1830–1860." Master's thesis, University of Chicago, 1947.

PAMPHLETS AND SPECIAL SOURCES

American Anti-Slavery Society. *Annual Reports.* New York, 1834–39.

The Annals, American Academy of Political and Social Science, November, 1928. Entire volume devoted to "The American Negro." Edited by Donald Young.

The Annals, American Academy of Political and Social Science, March, 1956. Entire volume devoted to "Race Desegregation and Integration." Edited by Ira De A. Reid.

Civil War Papers read before the Commandery of the State of Massachusetts, Military Order of the Loyal Legion of the United States. Boston 1900.

  Carter, S. A. "Fourteen Months Service with Colored Troops."

  Prescott, R. B. "The Capture of Richmond."

Congress of Racial Equality. *Cracking the Color Line*. New York, n.d.

Journal of Negro History. "Documents: Thomas Jefferson's Thoughts on the Negro," 3 (1918).

————. "Documents: Letters of George Washington Bearing on the Negro," 2 (1917).

Military Essays and Recollections: Papers read before Commandery of the State of Illinois, Military Order of the Loyal Legion of the United States. Chicago, 1894.

  Freeman, Henry V. "A Colored Brigade in the Campaign and Battle of Nashville."

  Furness, William Elliott. "The Negro as a Soldier."

National Advisory Commission on Civil Disorders. *Report*. Washington, D.C., 1968.

National Association for the Advancement of Colored People. *Annual Reports*. New York, 1911–1981.

Ovington, Mary White. *How the National Association for the Advancement of Colored People Began*. New York, 1914.

Peabody, Andrew Preston. *Street Mobs in Boston Before the Revolution*. Pamphlet reprinted from *Atlantic Monthly* article. Boston, 1888.

Personal Narratives of Events in the War of the Rebellion, Soldiers and Sailors Historical Society of Rhode Island.

  Addeman, J. M. "Reminiscences of Two Years with Colored Troops." (Providence, 1880).

  Califf, Joseph M. "Record of Services of Seventh Regiment, United States Colored Troops." (Providence, 1878).

  Morgan, Thomas J. "Reminiscences of Services with Colored Troops in the Army of the Cumberland, 1863–65." (Providence, 1885).

  Rickard, James H. "Services with Colored Troops in Burnside's Corps" (Providence, 1894).

Sherman, George R. "The Negro As A Soldier." (Providence, 1913).

Turner, Nat. *The Confessions of Nat Turner*. Edited by T. R. Gray. Richmond, 1832.

U.S. Commission on Civil Rights. *1961 Commission on Civil Rights Report*. 5 vols. Washington, 1970.

———. *Racism in America*. Washington, 1970.

U.S. Department of Commerce, Bureau of the Census. *Negro Population 1790–1915*. Washington, 1918.

———. *Negroes in the United States, 1920–32*. Washington, 1935.

———. *The Social and Economic Status of Negroes in the United States, 1970*. Washington, 1971.

———. *Minority-owned Businesses: 1969*. Washington, 1971.

———. *The Social and Economic Status of the Black Population in the United States, 1971*. Washington, 1972.

———. *The Social and Economic Status of the Black Population in the United States, 1972*. Washington, 1973.

———. *The Social and Economic Status of the Black Population in the United States: An Historical View, 1790–1978*. Washington, 1979.

U.S. Department of Labor. *The Economic Situation of Negroes in the United States*. Washington, 1962.

———. *Negro Migration in 1916–17*. Washington, 1919.

ARTICLES

Adams, Randolph G. "New Light on the Boston Massacre," American Antiquarian Society, *Proceedings* 26 (1937).

Aptheker, Herbert. "Militant Abolitionism," *Journal of Negro History* 5 (1941).

———. "Negro Casualties in the Civil War," *ibid.* 32 (1947).

———. "The Negro in the Union Navy," *ibid.* 32 (1947).

Baker, Henry E. "Benjamin Banneker, the Negro Mathematician and Astronomer," *Journal of Negro History* 3 (1918).

———. "The Negro in the Field of Invention," *ibid.* 2 (1917).

Bauer, Raymond, and Bauer, Alice. "Day to Day Resistance to Slavery," *Journal of Negro History* 27 (1942).

Bell, Howard H. "Expressions of Negro Militancy in the North, 1840–60," *Journal of Negro History* 65 (1960).

———. "National Negro Conventions of the Middle 1840s: Moral Suasion vs. Political Action," *ibid.* 52 (1957).

Bennett, Lerone, Jr. "The King Plan for Freedom," *Ebony* (July, 1956).

———. "The South and the Negro: Martin Luther King, Jr.," *ibid*. (April, 1957).

———. "Daisy Bates: First Lady of Little Rock," *ibid*. (September, 1958).

———. "The Revolt of Negro Youth," *ibid*. (May, 1960).

———. "Was Abraham Lincoln A White Supremacist?" *ibid*. (February, 1968)

Bigelow, Martha M. "The Significance of Milliken's Bend in the Civil War," *Journal of Negro History* 65 (1960).

Binder, Frederick M. "Pennsylvania Negro Regiments in the Civil War," *Journal of Negro History* 37 (1952).

Bond, Horace Mann. "Social and Economic Forces in Alabama Reconstruction," *Journal of Negro History* 23 (1938).

Brisbane, Robert H. "New Light on the Garvey Movement," *Journal of Negro History* 36 (1951).

Brooks, Walter H. "The Priority of the Silver Bluff Church and Its Promoters," *Journal of Negro History* 7 (1922).

Brown, Sterling A. "Negro Folk Expression," *Phylon* 14 (1953).

Davis, John W. "George Liele and Andrew Bryan, Pioneer Negro Baptist Preachers," *Journal of Negro History* 3 (1918).

Davis, T. R. "Negro Servitude in the United States," *Journal of Negro History* 8 (1923).

Dufty, William. "A. Philip Randolph," *New York Post* (December 28, 1959–January 3, 1960).

Eliofson, Eliot. "African Sculpture," *Atlantic* (April, 1959).

Farrison, W. Edward. "Origin of Brown's *Clotel*," *Phylon* 15 (1954).

Garrett, Romeo B. "African Survivals in American Culture," *Journal of Negro History* 51 (1966)

Graham, Pearl M. "Thomas Jefferson and Sally Hemings," *Journal of Negro History* 54 (1961).

Granger, Lester. "End of an Era," *Ebony* (December, 1960).

Greene, Lorenzo J. "Some Observations on the Black Regiment of Rhode Island in the American Revolution," *Journal of Negro History* 27 (1952).

Greene, Samuel A. "The Boston Massacre," American Antiquarian Society, *Proceedings* 5 (1900).

Gross, Bella. "The First National Negro Convention," *Journal of Negro History* 31 (1946).

Handlin, Oscar, and Handlin, Mary F. "Origins of the Southern Labor System," *William and Mary Quarterly* 7 (1950).

Hansberry, William Leo. "Indigenous African Religions," in *Africa Seen by American Negroes*. Paris, 1958.

Hartgrove, W. B. "The Negro Soldier in the American Revolution," *Journal of Negro History* 1 (1916).

Jackson, Luther P. "Virginia Negro Soldiers and Seamen in the American Revolution," *Journal of Negro History* 27 (1942).

Lindsay, Arnett G. "The Negro In Banking," *Journal of Negro History* 14 (1929).

Lofton, James M., Jr. "Denmark Vesey's Call to Arms," *Journal of Negro History* 33 (1948).

Logan, Rayford. "Estevanico, Negro Discoverer of the Southwest," *Phylon* 1 (1940).

Mandel, Bernard. "Samuel Gompers and the Negro Workers," *Journal of Negro History* 60 (1955).

Marshall, Thurgood. "An Evaluation of Recent Efforts to Achieve Racial Integration Through Resort to the Courts," *Journal of Negro Education* 21 (1952).

Morrison, Allan. "A. Philip Randolph: Dean of Negro Leaders," *Ebony* (November, 1958).

Morse, W. H. "Lemuel Haynes," *Journal of Negro History* 4 (1919).

Pei, Mario. "Swahili," *Holiday* (April, 1959).

Perkins, A. E. "Oscar James Dunn," *Phylon* 4 (1943).

Porter, Dorothy B. "The Organized Educational Activities of Negro Literary Societies, 1828–1846," *Journal of Negro Education* 5 (1936).

Porter, Kenneth Wiggins. "Negroes and the Seminole War, 1817–1818," *Journal of Negro History* 36 (1951).

———. "Relations Between Negroes and Indians Within the Present Limits of the United States," *ibid.* 17 (1932).

———. "Florida Slaves and Free Negroes in the Seminole War, 1835–1842," *ibid.* 28 (1943).

Puttkammer, Charles W., and Worthy, Ruth. "William Monroe Trotter, 1872–1934," *Journal of Negro History* 63 (1958).

Reddick, L. D. "The Great Decision," *Phylon* 15 (1954).

————. "The Negro Policy of the United States Army, 1775–1945," *Journal of Negro History* 34 (1949).

Rudwick, Elliott M. "The Niagara Movement," *Journal of Negro History* 62 (1957).

Savage, W. S. "The Influence of Alexander Leidesdorf on The History of California," *Journal of Negro History* 38 (1953).

Seeber, Edward D. "Phillis Wheatley," *Journal of Negro History* 24 (1939).

Sherwood, Henry N. "Paul Cuffee," *Journal of Negro History* 8 (1923).

Stafford, A. O. "Antar, the Arabian Negro Warrior, Poet and Hero," *Journal of Negro History* 11 (1916).

Taylor, A. A. "The Negro In The Reconstruction of Virginia," *Journal of Negro History* 11 (1926)

Towner, Lawrence W. " 'A Fondness for Freedom': Servant Protest in Puritan Society," *William and Mary Quarterly* 19 (1962).

Turner, Lorenzo D. "African Survivals in the New World with Special Emphasis on the Arts," in *Africa Seen by American Negroes*. Paris, 1958.

Walden, Daniel. "The Contemporary Opposition to the Political Ideals of Booker T. Washington," *Journal of Negro History* 65 (1960).

Weisberger, Bernard. "The Dark and Bloody Ground of Reconstruction Historiography," *Journal of Southern History* 25 (1959).

Wesley, Charles H. "The Negroes of New York in the Emancipation Movement," *Journal of Negro History* 24 (1939).

Whitelaw, W. Menzies. "Africa," *Collier's Encyclopedia*. New York, 1953.

Wish, Harvey. "Slave Disloyalty under the Confederacy," *Journal of Negro History* 23 (1938).

Wood, L. Hollingsworth. "The Urban League Movement," *Journal of Negro History* 3 (1924).

Woodson, Carter G. "The Beginnings of the Miscegenation of the Whites and Blacks," *Journal of Negro History* 3 (1918).

NEWSPAPERS AND MAGAZINES

Afro-American (Baltimore)
Black World

Chicago Defender
Crisis
Ebony
Harper's Weekly
Jet
Negro Digest
New Orleans Tribune
New York Post
New York Times
Pittsburgh Courier
Southern School News

Index

FOR THE BEST IN PAPERBACKS, LOOK FOR THE

In every corner of the world, on every subject under the sun, Penguin represents quality and variety—the very best in publishing today.

For complete information about books available from Penguin—including Pelicans, Puffins, Peregrines, and Penguin Classics—and how to order them, write to us at the appropriate address below. Please note that for copyright reasons the selection of books varies from country to country.

In the United Kingdom: For a complete list of books available from Penguin in the U.K., please write to *Dept E.P., Penguin Books Ltd, Harmondsworth, Middlesex, UB7 0DA*.

In the United States: For a complete list of books available from Penguin in the U.S., please write to *Consumer Sales, Penguin USA, P.O. Box 999— Dept. 17109, Bergenfield, New Jersey 07621-0120*. VISA and MasterCard holders call 1-800-253-6476 to order all Penguin titles.

In Canada: For a complete list of books available from Penguin in Canada, please write to *Penguin Books Canada Ltd, 10 Alcorn Avenue, Suite 300, Toronto, Ontario, Canada M4V 3B2*.

In Australia: For a complete list of books available from Penguin in Australia, please write to the *Marketing Department, Penguin Books Ltd, P.O. Box 257, Ringwood, Victoria 3134*.

In New Zealand: For a complete list of books available from Penguin in New Zealand, please write to the *Marketing Department, Penguin Books (NZ) Ltd, Private Bag, Takapuna, Auckland 9*.

In India: For a complete list of books available from Penguin, please write to *Penguin Overseas Ltd, 706 Eros Apartments, 56 Nehru Place, New Delhi, 110019*.

In Holland: For a complete list of books available from Penguin in Holland, please write to *Penguin Books Nederland B.V., Postbus 195, NL-1380AD Weesp, Netherlands*.

In Germany: For a complete list of books available from Penguin, please write to *Penguin Books Ltd, Friedrichstrasse 10-12, D-6000 Frankfurt Main 1, Federal Republic of Germany*.

In Spain: For a complete list of books available from Penguin in Spain, please write to *Longman, Penguin España, Calle San Nicolas 15, E-28013 Madrid, Spain*.

In Japan: For a complete list of books available from Penguin in Japan, please write to *Longman Penguin Japan Co Ltd, Yamaguchi Building, 2-12-9 Kanda Jimbocho, Chiyoda-Ku, Tokyo 101, Japan*.

FOR THE BEST IN HISTORY, LOOK FOR THE

☐ **ON WAR**
Carl Von Clausewitz
Edited by Anatol Rapoport

In his famous treatise of 1832, Clausewitz examines the nature and theory of war, military strategy, and the combat itself.

462 pages   ISBN: 0-14-044427-0

☐ **SIX ARMIES IN NORMANDY**
From D-Day to the Liberation of Paris
John Keegan

Keegan's account of the summer of 1944's momentous events on the battlefields of Normandy is superb; he "writes about war better than almost anyone in our century."—*Washington Post Book World*

366 pages   ISBN: 0-14-005293-3

☐ **WOMEN IN WAR**
Shelley Saywell

Shelley Saywell tells the previously untold stories of the forgotten veterans of our time—the millions of women who faced combat in some of the most important military struggles of this century.

324 pages   ISBN: 0-14-007623-9

☐ **THE FACE OF BATTLE**
John Keegan

In this study of three battles from three different centuries, John Keegan examines war from the fronts—conveying its reality for the participants at the "point of maximum danger."

366 pages   ISBN: 0-14-004897-9

☐ **VIETNAM: A HISTORY**
Stanley Karnow

Stanley Karnow's monumental narrative—the first complete account of the Vietnam War—puts events and decisions of the day into sharp, clear focus. "This is history writing at its best."—*Chicago Sun-Times*

752 pages   ISBN: 0-14-007324-8

☐ **MIRACLE AT MIDWAY**
Gordon W. Prange
with Donald M. Goldstein and Katherine V. Dillon

The best-selling sequel to *At Dawn We Slept* recounts the battles at Midway Island—events which marked the beginning of the end of the war in the Pacific.

470 pages   ISBN: 0-14-006814-7

☐ **THE MASK OF COMMAND**
John Keegan

This provocative view of leadership examines the meaning of military heroism through four prototypes from history—Alexander the Great, Wellington, Grant, and Hitler—and proposes a fifth type of "post-heroic" leader for the nuclear age.

368 pages   ISBN: 0-14-011406-8

☐ **THE SECOND OLDEST PROFESSION**
Spies and Spying in the Twentieth Century
Phillip Knightley

In this fascinating history and critique of espionage, Phillip Knightley explores the actions and missions of such noted spies as Mata Hari and Kim Philby, and organizations such as the CIA and the KGB.

436 pages   ISBN: 0-14-010655-3

☐ **THE STORY OF ENGLISH**
Robert McCrum, William Cran, and Robert MacNeil

"Rarely has the English language been scanned so brightly and broadly in a single volume," writes the *San Francisco Chronicle* about this journey across time and space that explores the evolution of English from Anglo-Saxon Britain to Reagan's America.   *384 pages   ISBN: 0-14-009435-0*